# THE
# DICTIONARY
## OF MULTIMEDIA

### TERMS & ACRONYMS

### FOURTH EDITION

# BRAD HANSEN

FRANKLIN, BEEDLE & ASSOCIATES, INC.
8536 SW ST. HELENS DRIVE, SUITE D
WILSONVILLE, OREGON  97070
503/682–7668
WWW.FBEEDLE.COM

## *Dedication*

*For my daughter, Claire.*
*—B.H.*

| | |
|---|---|
| President and Publisher | Jim Leisy (jimleisy@fbeedle.com) |
| Manuscript Editor | Eve Kushner |
| | Jeni Lee |
| | Forrest Spencer |
| | Stephanie Welch |
| Production | Tom Sumner |
| | Stephanie Welch |
| Proofreading | Senta Gorrie |
| | Susan Skarzynski |
| Illustration | Jeff Ong |
| | Bill DeRouchey |
| | Ian Shadburne |
| Cover Design | Ian Shadburne |
| Marketing Group | Christine Collier |
| Order Processing | Krista Brown |

Library of Congress Cataloging-in-Publication Data is available from the publisher.

ISBN (hardback): 1-887902-35-X
ISBN (paperback): 1-887902-73-2

# Contents

# Contents: Tables

# Contents:
# Expanded Definitions

# Numbers

**3/4-inch** (adj.) Describes a videotape used in Sony U-matic video recorders. This format is used by some video professionals and in many television studios.

**2.21:1 aspect ratio** (n.) See *Cinemascope.*

**2.5G** (n.) Wireless technology in a stage of development between second and third generation (2G and 3G). It most often is used in reference to General Packet Radio Service (GPRS) or the Enhanced Data GSM Environment (EDGE), both of which enable wireless data services over mobile phone networks. Data transfer rates from 56 Kbps to 384 Kbps over mobile devices are expected with these technologies.

**2B+D** (n.) The basic ISDN access formula, with two bearer (B) channels and one data (D) channel. Also known as BRI (basic rate interface).

**2B1Q** (n.) Two binary one quaternary; an ISDN digital subscriber loop encoding method used in the U.S. It encodes a two-bit (dibit) group using a four state digital line code, with two amplitude levels in both polarities. This operation cuts in half the actual transmission rate of the digital loop. The 2B1Q process also substitutes digital echo cancellation for time compression multiplexing.

**2-D graphics** (n.) Artwork and designs that exist in a single plane, or in two dimensions. Basic drawing applications are two-dimensional, and information is defined on an x-y plane.

**2X** See *double-speed.*

**3:2 pulldown** (n.) A method of converting film at 24 frames per second (fps) to interlaced video at 30 fps, with two fields per frame. The first two fields of video are derived from the first field of film. The next three fields of video are derived from the next frame of film. This process is repeated, alternating two video fields, then three video fields from each subsequent frame of film. This can cause noticeable flicker when the two fields in a single frame of interlaced video come from two different frames in the original film. See figure under *interfield frames.*

**3-D sound** (n.) A three-dimensional sound field. A true 3-D sound field is capable of positioning sound anywhere in a semi-spherical shell surrounding the listener, above as well as behind.

**3-dB down point** (n.) The frequency point where the amplitude response is attenuated 3 decibels (dB) relative to the level of the main passband. See *passband.*

**3-D Geometry File** (3-DGF) (n.) A cross-platform format developed by Macromedia for exchanging three-dimensional geometric data.

**3-DGF** See *3-D Geometry File.*

**3DO** (n.) A manufacturer and marketer of an interactive multimedia player capable of high-resolution graphics and fast animation. The player reads specially formatted CDs and is designed to deliver games, movies, and educational applications. Pronounced "THREE-dee-OH."

**3G** (n.) Short for "third generation"; a telecommunications industry term for the next generation of wireless applications. It represents a move from "dial-in" circuit-switched communications to broadband "always on" packet-based wireless networks moving data at higher speeds. The first generation of wireless communications employed analog technology, which was gradually replaced by digital wireless communications and hybrids. Third generation (3G) technologies offer expectations for data transfer between 384 Kbps and 2 Mbps, and greater reliability.

**4:2:2** (n.) In A:B:C notation, the ratio of the sampling rates used to translate three components of an analog video signal into a digital signal. These ratios are used to define CCIR-601, the standard used for professional video production equipment and D-1 format digital videotape. See also *video color sampling.*

**4:3** (n.) The standard aspect ratio for a computer screeen. See also *aspect ratio.*

**5.1 surround sound** (Pronounced "five-point-one") (n.) The digital audio multichannel format used to encode digital soundtracks for film, DVD, and HDTV. It refers to five discrete, full bandwidth (20-20 kHz) channels. These five are left front, right front, center front, left surround, and right surround. The ".1" usually refers to a

limited bandwidth (20–120 Hz) *subwoofer* channel, but it may also refer to a special effects channel. The term is used by Dolby Digital and also by DTS Zeta Digital to describe the home version of their Coherent Acoustics system for theaters.

**8-bit audio** (n.) A sound file that is digitized or played back using an 8-bit sample size. The quality is inferior to that of a 16-bit sample. It is adequate for spoken words and some sound effects but too noisy and limited in frequency range for high-quality music. Two factors significantly affect the quality of digital audio. These are the bit depth and the sample rate, or the frequency at which a sound is sampled. Common bit depths are 8-bit, 16-bit, and 24-bit. Common sample rates are 11,025; 22,050; 44,100; and 48,000 samples per second.

**8-bit color** (n.) A monitor setting or graphic file format that allocates eight bits of memory to each pixel and yields up to 256 different colors simultaneously.

**8 mm videotape** (n.) An eight-millimeter-wide videotape format used in camcorders. Hi-8, which employs S-video separation of color and luminance, is a higher quality version.

**8-to-14 modulation** (EFM) (n.) The process that turns each eight-bit byte of data into 14 "channel" bits during the mastering of a compact disc.

**10BASE2** (Pronounced "ten-base-TWO") (n.) Local area network (LAN) wiring that employs thin coaxial cable with BNC-style connectors. It supports the IEEE 802.3 Ethernet standard running at up to 10 Mbps over a maximum distance of 200 meters. Devices on a 10BASE2 network are typically connected to a router, a switch, or a hub.

**10BASE5** (Pronounced "ten-base-FIVE") (n.) Local area network (LAN) wiring that employs standard 50-ohm coaxial cable with BNC-style connectors. It supports the IEEE 802.3 Ethernet standard running at up to 10 Mbps over a maximum distance of 500 meters. Devices on a 10BASE5 network are typically connected to a router, a switch, or a hub.

**10BASE-T** (Pronounced "ten-base-TEE") (n.) Local area network (LAN) wiring that employs copper twisted-pair cable. It supports the IEEE 802.3 Ethernet standard running at up to 10 Mbps. Devices on a 10BASE-T network are typically connected to a router, a switch, or a hub.

**16:9** (n.) An aspect ratio of the horizontal size of an image to the vertical size. The 16:9 ratio has been adopted for the high-definition television (HDTV) video format.

**16-bit bus** (n.) A type of data bus that can exchange 16 bits of data at a time with a microcomputer's processor or memory.

**16-bit color** (n.) A video monitor setting that allocates five bits of memory apiece to the red and the blue components of each pixel and six bits to the green component, providing up to 65 536 different colors at once.

**23B+D** (n.) The Primary ISDN access in North America with 23 bearer (B) channels and one data (D) channel. It is based on the 1.544 megabit per second (Mbps) 24-channel DS-1 standard. Also known as PRI (primary rate interface).

**30B+2D** (n.) The Primary ISDN access in nations using the Conference of European Postal and Telecommunications (CEPT) digital carrier system. It consists of 30 bearer channels and two data channels.

**802.11** (n.) A series of wireless specifications developed by a working group of the Institute of Electrical and Electronics Engineers (IEEE). These standards are used to manage packet traffic over wireless networks.

**802.X** (n.) Refers to any of the local area network (LAN) and metropolitan area network (MAN) standards developed by IEEE.

# A

A3D (n.) A proprietary 3-D sound technology first developed by Crystal River Engineering, which is now an advanced technology subsidiary of Aureal Semiconductor.

AAL See *ATM Adaptation Layer*.

AAP See *Association of American Publishers*.

A:B:C notation See *video color sampling*.

abend (n.) Abnormal end; an error message indicating the unexpected termination of a program or signal that may be either recoverable or unrecoverable.

ABI See *Application Binary Interface*.

ABIOS See *Advanced Basic Input/Output System*.

ablation (n.) The use of a laser beam to burn pits into thin metal film for optical data storage. The process is used to create CDs.

abort (v.) To cancel a computing procedure while in progress.

ABR See *automatic baud rate detection*.

A-B roll (n.) An editing process in which videotape is played from two tape machines, A and B. As the tapes are rolled, portions of each are dubbed onto a third tape, the composite master. Video editors use this technique to import footage from multiple source tapes. The resulting product is often enhanced by placing transitions between segments from different sources and by using special effects.

ABS See *Alternative Billing Service*.

abscissa (n.) The x-coordinate, plotted on a graph in response to the input of a function. The y-coordinate is referred to as the *ordinate*. Pronounced "ab-SISS-a."

absolute time (n.) The time that elapses from the exact beginning of an audio CD or a digital audio tape (DAT) to any given point in the program material that follows. This information is used to determine the precise start and stop times of a recorded program.

absorption (n.) Receiving an impulse without a corresponding reflection or echo. Absorption is the act or process of absorbing. Sound energy is absorbed when it passes through a medium or when it strikes a surface. Sound molecules lose energy upon striking atoms on the surface of a material, which become agitated and warmer. Absorption, then, is literally the conversion of sound energy into heat. The ability of a material to absorb sound is quantified

**A**

by a value ranging from 0 (total reflection) to 1 (total absorption), and it varies with sound frequency and the angle of incidence.

**abstract class** (n.) In object-oriented programming, a class without instances. Instead, it has concrete classes as subclasses. Example: *mammal* is an abstract class, and *cow* is a concrete class.

**abstraction** (n.) 1. A process in which something is made into a function of something else, or is "parameterized." Bracket abstractions make a term into a function of a variable. 2. A process of hiding details or generalizing. Example: in abstract syntax, the details of the syntax are ignored.

**abstract machine** (n.) Software that executes an intermediate language used in a compiler or interpreter. This processor is not intended to be implemented in hardware. It has an instruction set, a register set, and a model of memory. It may be used to make a language implementation easier to port to various platforms. A virtual machine is an abstract machine for which an interpreter exists.

**abstract syntax** (n.) A form of data structure independent of machine-oriented encoding or language.

**Abstract Syntax Notation One** (ASN/1) (n.) Language used to encode Simple Network Management Protocol (SNMP) packets. It is also used by Open Systems Interconnection (OSI) protocols for describing abstract syntax, and it is defined in the ISO standard documents 8824.2 and 8825.2.

**Abstract Windowing Toolkit** (AWT) (n.) The independent windowing, graphics, and user interface toolkit in the Java programming environment.

**AC** See *alternating current.*

**AC-3** See *audio coding-3.*

**Academy curve** (n.) An equalization method applied to the standard monaural track used for sound in film, also known as the N (normal) curve. It has changed little since becoming a standard in 1938. The response is flat between 100 Hz and 1.6 kHz. Response is reduced 7 dB at 40 Hz, 10 dB at 5 kHz and 18 dB at 8 kHz. The severe reduction of the high end of the spectrum conceals the high-frequency crackling noise inherent in early film sound production.

**Accelerated Graphics Port** (AGP) (n.) An interface specification developed in 1997 by Intel Corporation. It is based on the peripheral component interconnect (PCI) bus and was designed to facilitate three-dimensional graphics. AGP creates its own dedicated channel, so the graphics controller can directly access main memory, rather than use the PCI bus. This point-to-point channel is 32 bits wide. It runs at 66 MHz but supports data transmission at both the rising and falling ends of the clock cycle for increased speed. The total effective bandwidth is 533 Mbps at double speed (2X) throughput. Three-dimensional textures are stored in main memory, rather than in video memory. Among the requirements for implementing AGP are the OSR 2.1 version of Windows 95 or Windows 98 and a Pentium hardware system with an AGP bus slot. Optional features of AGP include the following:

- Direct Memory Execute mode, which allows textures to be stored in main memory.

- multiple throughput rates: 1X (266 Mbps), 2X (533 Mbps), 4X (1.07 Gbps).

- pipelining, which allows the graphics card to send multiple instructions at once, rather than one at a time.

- sideband addressing, which hastens data transfer by sending command instructions over a separate parallel channel.

**accelerator card** (n.) A circuit board inserted into a slot on the motherboard that increases the processing speed and performance of the CPU. Production artists use graphics accelerators to increase productivity because these artists must wait for the screen to redraw every time they edit an image.

**Acceptable Use Policy** (AUP) (n.) An Internet Service Provider's statement of permissible uses.

**acceptance testing** (n.) Formal testing conducted to determine whether a system satisfies the stated criteria for a customer.

**access** (v.) To seek and retrieve information from a hard disk, floppy disk, CD-ROM, or any other digital or analog storage medium.

**Access** (n.) 1. A relational database application integrated into the Microsoft Office Pro suite. 2. A query language similar to English used in Pick, an operating system developed by VMark Computer, Inc.

**ACCESS.bus** (n.) Developed by Digital Equipment Corporation, this bus format is based on the Inter-Integrated Circuit serial bus invented by Philips Semiconductors and Signetics. The ACCESS.bus Industry Group supports it as an alternative to the Universal Serial Bus (USB) from Intel Corporation. Software drivers are required to provide the interface between ACCESS.bus hardware and application programs. Physically, ACCESS.bus runs at a relatively low speed over limited distances. It replaces the limited number of specialized ports in a PC with one general-purpose port that supports multiple peripherals in a daisy chain. Pointing devices, modems, printers, a keyboard, and a monitor using the Video Electronics Standards Association (VESA) Display Data Channel (DDC) standard may all be connected on the same bus. It supports up to 125 devices, and each device may operate at a different data rate, up to 100 kilobits per second (Kbps). The maximum cable length is eight meters. *Hot plugging,* which allows a device to be connected or disconnected without turning off power to a computer, and *auto-addressing,* which automatically identifies a unit attached to the bus and shakes hands without user intervention, are features of the standard.

**Access Control List** (ACL) (n.) List of the services available on a server. Each item on the list also has a list of the hosts permitted to use that particular service.

**access line** (n.) The connecting line between a customer's premises and the central office of a local telephone company.

**access method** (n.) The way in which network devices access a network. This method is determined by the Systems Network Architecture (SNA), which controls the flow of network information.

**access node** (n.) The connection point in a local telephone network at which numerous access lines are consolidated into fewer feeder lines. Access lines are normally multiplexed onto digital loop carrier (DLC) systems supporting T1 transmission. A private branch exchange (PBX) is another type of access node, as are cellular antenna sites and optical network units (ONUs).

**access point** (n.) A base station in a wireless LAN, usually connected to an Ethernet hub or server. Users who roam with mobile devices are handed off from one access point to another.

**access time** (n.) The time required to locate and load data from storage after the *seek* command is issued. Typically, this measurement includes the time it takes the reading head to move between the most distant segments of the medium and to position itself radially. To begin reading or writing, the head must be positioned over the proper sector. This radial motion is called *seeking*, and the collection of sectors available under multiple heads is called a *cylinder*. The time it takes for a disk to rotate until the proper sector is located under the heads is *rotational latency*, which combines with seek time to yield the total access time.

**accounting management** (n.) The control of individual and group access to network resources to ensure proper bandwidth and security or to assess charges to clients. It is one of five categories of network management defined by the ISO for management of Open Systems Interconnection (OSI) networks.

**accumulator** (n.) A register in the central processing unit (CPU) where intermediate results are stored. Access to main memory is not as fast as access to the accumulator, which typically has a direct path to and from the arithmetic and logic unit (ALU). Late-model CPUs generally have many registers that may be used as accumulators.

**ACD** See *Automatic Call Distribution* or *Automatic Call Distributor*.

**ACI** See *adjacent channel interference*.

**ACID test** (n.) A test of the atomicity, consistency, isolation, and durability of transaction processing. Passing the ACID test means having a high degree of resilience and recoverability. The term is derived from the process of testing metals with strong acid to determine gold content.

**ACIS** (n.) A geometric engine owned by Spatial Technologies that is named for its inventors (Andy, Charles, and Ian's System). It employs a sophisticated object-oriented approach to modeling and is used in several computer-aided design (CAD) programs.

**ACK** (n.) An acknowledgment character that is returned to a sending device by a receiving device to indicate that the data has been received correctly.

**ACL** See *Access Control List* or *Association for Computational Linguistics*.

**ACM** See *addressed call mode* or *Association for Computing Machinery*.

**acoustic coupler** (n.) Device that connects a modem to a telephone line with the use of a handset. It converts electrical signals from the modem into sound with a loudspeaker, against which the mouthpiece of the handset is placed. The earpiece is placed against a microphone. The sound from the connected circuit is converted into electrical signals. The signals are then returned to the modem. Although this device was popular in the 1970s, it is rarely used because modems now connect directly to telephone lines.

**acoustic echo canceller** (n.) See *echo cancellation*.

**acoustic feedback** (n.)A phenomenon that occurs when the sound from a loudspeaker is picked up by the microphone feeding it, reamplified by the same loudspeaker into the same microphone, and reamplified in a loop. Each time the signal becomes stronger until the system is overloaded and *rings* or *feeds back* on itself, producing a loud howling or squealing sound. These buildups occur at particular frequencies called *feedback frequencies*.

**acoustic treatment** (n.) The materials used to change the temporal, spectral, and spatial qualities of the sound in a room. The physical tools used by an acoustician to treat a room are absorbers, reflectors, and diffusers. Absorbers attenuate sound, reflectors redirect sound, and diffusers uniformly distribute sound. Some virtual acoustic treatments can be applied to a sound by a digital signal processor after the recording.

**acquisition** (n.) 1. The process of capturing assets or transferring information from an analog to a digital format. 2. In telecommunications, the process of locking tracking equipment onto a signal from a communications satellite and synchronizing with it.

**acquisition time** (n.) The time required for a sample-and-hold (S/H) circuit to capture an analog value that it receives and output that signal digitally.

**Acrobat** (n.) A program developed by Adobe for cross-platform document exchange in which files are created in the Portable Document Format (.pdf) from PostScript. The full complement of Acrobat tools consists of the Distiller, the Exchange package, the Catalog package, and the Reader. The Reader is freely distributed so that it may be installed and used on any computer to decipher an Acrobat document.

**acronym** (n.) An identifier derived from the letters or initials of a phrase and used as an abbreviation.

**ACT** See *annual change traffic*.

**ActionMedia II** (n.) One of the first video capture cards developed by Intel that employs their Digital Video Interactive (DVI) compression technology. It has been replaced by the Intel Smart Video Recorder.

**active attack** (n.) In network security, an attempt at intrusion that results in an unauthorized change of state, which may involve the manipulation or addition of files.

**active crossover** (n.) The process of employing individual power amplifiers for each output frequency band and sending a signal containing the restricted frequency band to the appropriate loudspeakers. A stereo two-way crossover is a two-channel unit that divides the incoming signal into low and high outputs. A mono three-way crossover is a single channel device with low, midrange, and high outputs. The user can often select the low-to-mid and the mid-to-high crossover points. See *passive crossover*.

**active DBMS** (n.) Active database management system; a conventional database management system combined with a means of event detection and condition monitoring. Event handling may be rule based, as it is in an expert system.

**active equalizer** (n.) A variable equalizer (EQ)

8

that requires power to operate, available in many different configurations and designs. They are popular because they are inexpensive, small in size, lightweight, indifferent to loads, have good isolation (high input and low output impedances), and can boost a signal as needed. Disadvantages are increased noise in the signal, limited dynamic range, and RFI susceptibility. They are used in almost every audio production environment.

**active matrix display** (n.) A liquid crystal display (LCD) panel that has three transistors (red, green, and blue) for each pixel and that yields better color and resolution than a *passive matrix display*. Thin film transistor (TFT) technology makes this possible.

**active monitor** (n.) The process in an IBM token ring network that detects the presence of a token, removes circulating frames with invalid destinations, and performs introductions between nodes on the ring.

**active object** (n.) An object in programming that encompasses its own thread of control.

**Active Streaming Format** (n.) See *Advanced Streaming Format*.

**active video lines** (n.) Video traces that are scanned on the screen between the horizontal and vertical blanking intervals. The lines are generated by the electron gun in a cathode-ray tube (CRT). About 483 lines are visible or active in the NTSC 525-line system used in the United States.

**active window** (n.) The portion of the screen that is prepared to accept input from an input device.

**ActiveX** (n.) A Microsoft software technology released in 1996. ActiveX, originally referred

to as Object Linking and Embedding (OLE), is loosely based on the Component Object Model (COM), but it provides substantially different services to developers. An ActiveX *component* is a unit of executable code (an *.exe* file) that follows the ActiveX specification for providing *objects*. This technology allows programmers to assemble reusable software components into applications and services. An ActiveX component or control should be able to interact with other programs over the Internet, regardless of the language in which they were written.

**actor** (n.) Any object that exists as a concurrent process in object-oriented programming (OOP).

**actuator** (n.) The mechanism that moves the read and write heads of a disk drive across the platter surfaces.

**Ada** (n.) Named after Ada Lovelace, a programming language similar to Pascal that was designed at Honeywell in 1979. The Pentagon mandated its use for Department of Defense software projects. Ada is a complex, block-structured language intended for embedded applications.

**Adaptable User Interface** (AUI) (n.) A toolkit from Oracle used to write applications that are portable between different windowing systems. A single call-level interface is provided with a resource manager and editor for several graphical user interfaces (GUIs), including the Mac OS, Microsoft Windows, and X Window System.

**adapter** 1. (n.) In audio and video applications, an object that allows a different type of connector to be plugged into each end, making a connection despite incompatible termination. An example is a gender changer, which is used to connect two cables both having male termination. 2. (adj.) Describes a type of interface card that connects to peripherals or to a network.

**adaptive answering** (n.) A feature commonly found on a Class 1 faxmodem that allows it to answer an incoming call and to determine whether the signal is a fax or data call.

**Adaptive Data Compression** (ADC) (n.) A Hayes modem protocol.

**adaptive delta modulation** (ADM) (n.) A variation of delta modulation in which the step size may vary from sample to sample.

**adaptive differential pulse code modulation** (ADPCM) (n.) A standard method endorsed by the Interactive Multimedia Association (IMA) for storing digital audio on a multiple-session CD-ROM XA or a CD-i. The procedure reduces the amount of data needed by examining previously encoded data and adaptively predicting future encoding, eliminating some redundancy, and storing the differences between successive digital samples rather than full values. It is an extension of the pulse code modulation (PCM) audio encoding format. Another version of this audio encoding process standardized by the CCITT for telecommunications applications can transmit a voice over a 32-kilobit-per-second (Kbps) digital channel. Each sample is defined by three or four bits that represent the difference between adjacent samples.

**adaptive noise reduction filter** (n.) An intelligent video noise filtering system that analyzes each pixel and applies an appropriate filter to remove the noise. Edge detail is maintained and compression is improved.

**adaptive spectral perceptual entropy coding** (ASPEC) (n.) A high-quality digital audio standard for compressing sound at low bit rates for network transmission. It was collaboratively developed by AT&T Bell Laboratories, Thomson Consumer Electronics, the Fraunhofer Society, and CNET.

**ADAT** See *Alesis Digital Audio Tape.*

**ADAT Optical Data Interface** (n.) The proprietary multichannel optical (fiber optic) digital interface specification for the Alesis family of ADAT modular digital multitrack recorders. This standard describes transmission of eight channels of digital audio data through a single fiber optic cable.

**ADB** See *Apple Desktop Bus.*

**ADC** See *Adaptive Data Compression* or *analog-to-digital converter.*

**ADCCP** See *Advanced Data Communications Control Procedures.*

**A/D converter** (n.) See *analog-to-digital converter.*

**additive color mixing** (n.) The process of creating hues by mixing colored light rather than pigments. Mixing the additive primary colors in equal proportions results in white. See figure.

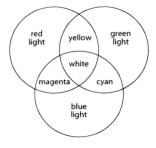

*additive color mixing*

**additive synthesis** (n.) In audio production, creating a composite waveform by summing multiple individual waveforms.

**address** 1. (n.) Any label that identifies the location of data in either static or dynamic memory, such as a frame number on coded videotape. 2. (n.) An unsigned integer used to select one fundamental element of storage, usually a word from a computer's main memory or another storage device. The central processing unit (CPU) outputs addresses on its address bus, which may be connected to an address decoder, a cache controller, a memory management unit, or some other device. 3. (n.) In computer networking, an email address, Internet address, or media access control (MAC) address on a network. 4. (n.) In telecommunications, a telephone number. 5. (v.) To send a message to a particular location.

**addressability** (n.) The existence of a method to control delivery of services to certain, select subscribers on a system. In the cable industry, this allows an operator to activate, disconnect, or scramble the signal received by a subscriber remotely from the headend. After a subscriber signals the service provider, the provider's computer addresses the subscriber's set-top box, temporarily allowing it to descramble the program so that it may be viewed. Any addressable set-top box may be controlled by this method.

**addressable converter** (n.) A device connected to a cable television receiver to give the program provider the capacity to transmit or to block services to an individual subscriber.

**address bus** (n.) The system of connections carrying a binary-coded address from the microprocessor through a computing system. The address bus is a subset of the processor and memory buses, which consist of the data lines, the address lines, and the control lines. The address bus indicates which particular addresses in the memory and system buses are to be used in a data transfer operation. It identifies the precise location where the next bus transfer or memory transfer will occur. The size of the memory bus controls the amount of memory that the central processing unit (CPU) can address directly.

**address code** (n.) 1. Time code stamped on a tape to identify each frame of video. The hour, minute, second, and frame numbers are expressed by eight digits in the format hh:mm:ss:ff. 2. The cue code placed in the vertical blanking interval (VBI) of a videodisc frame as a point of reference.

**addressed call mode** (ACM) (n.) In telecommunications, a mode that allows control signals to initiate and terminate calls under the V.25bis specification.

**address mask** (n.) In electronic messaging, a subnet ID that uses some of the most significant bits of the host address portion of an Internet Protocol (IP) address to divide the single network into smaller addressable portions. See also *subnet*.

**address resolution** (n.) The translation of an Internet address into the corresponding Ethernet address, or physical address, usually done with Address Resolution Protocol (ARP). It consists of a library routine and processes that convert hostnames into Internet addresses. See also *domain name system*.

**Address Resolution Protocol** (ARP) (n.) The method by which a host Ethernet address is determined from its Internet address. A server sends an ARP packet with the Internet address of another host and waits for it to send back an Ethernet address. Every host typically maintains a cache of address translations to expedite the process. ARP, defined in RFC 826, allows the Internet address to be independent of the Ethernet address. Hosts not compatible with ARP must perform constant mapping.

**address space** (n.) 1. The range of addresses (either physical or virtual) that a processor can access. It depends on the width of the processor's address bus and address registers. 2. The range of physical addresses or virtual addresses allocated to a process.

**address track time code** (ATTC) (n.) Longitudinal time code (LTC) recorded on a designated track of an analog videotape or in the center of an analog audio tape.

**adjacent** (adj.) In network technology, simple network access (SNA) nodes are adjacent if they are connected to a given node with no intervening nodes. In the Open Systems Interconnection (OSI) model, adjacent nodes are those that share a common segment, whether in Ethernet, Fiber Distributed Data Interface (FDDI), or token ring networks.

**adjacent channel interference** (ACI) (n.) Noise caused when two or more channels are present at frequencies that are too near one another in the spectrum.

**ADM** See *adaptive delta modulation.*

**ADN** See *advanced digital network* or *Advanced Digital Network.*

**Adobe Type Manager** (ATM) (n.) A utility that extrapolates a screen resolution character at 72 dots per inch (dpi) from a PostScript character in order to display it cleanly on a monitor.

**ADPCM** See *adaptive differential pulse code modulation.*

**ADR** See *Automatic Dialog Replacement.*

**ADSL** See *Asymmetric Digital Subscriber Line.*

**ADSP** See *AppleTalk Data Stream Protocol.*

**ADSR** (n.) Attack, decay, sustain, release; a circuit that defines the shape of a synthesized sound over time. ADSR settings specify amplitude levels that change at various stages as a note sounds. These settings determine the package, or envelope of a sound, which is not related to the pitch. See figure.

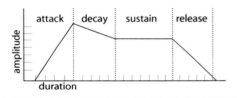

*ADSR curve*

**Advanced Basic Input/Output System** (ABIOS) (n.) Service routines built into IBM-compatible computers that support multitasking.

**Advanced Data Communications Control Procedures** (ADCCP) (n.) A standard, bit-oriented, data link control protocol that the U.S. government uses for communications.

**advanced digital network** (ADN) (n.) In general, a group of computers, peripherals, or other equipment connected to one another for the purpose of passing information and sharing resources. Networks can be either local or remote. The topology of a network is the geographic arrangement of links and nodes, which may be arranged in the shape of a star, tree, or ring.

**Advanced Digital Network** (ADN) (n.) The brand name used by Pacific Telesis for its inexpensive, leased 56-kilobit-per-second digital network service.

**advanced intelligent network** (AIN) (n.) Telephone network architecture implemented by major telephone companies worldwide. These networks direct telephone calls according to criteria specified by the telephone company. The three core components of an AIN are listed below. These components communicate through out-of-band signaling or over a signaling network using Signaling System 7 (SS7) protocol.

1. Signal Control Points (SCPs): Computer databases that store customer-specific information used by the network to route calls.
2. Signal Switching Points (SSPs): Digital telephone switches that can talk to SCPs and ask them for customer-specific instructions about how the call should be completed.
3. Signal Transfer Points (STPs): Packet switches that shuttle messages between SSPs and SCPs.

**Advanced Interactive Executive** (AIX) (n.) The IBM version of Unix.

**Advanced Mobile Phone Service** (AMPS) (n.) Commonly referred to as analog cellular, this technology was the first generation of wireless communications. The technology uses frequency-modulated transmission and frequency spacing to distinguish between concurrent users. It operates in the 800 MHz spectrum, and has been available in Canada, the U. S., Mexico, Australia, and a few other countries since the early 1980s. The voice channels (30 kHz) are transmitted analog, but modem setup and control operations are digital.

The disadvantages are short battery life, poor sound quality, and a much higher power output rate than newer digital phones. This outdated format does not compete favorably with TDMA, CDMA, GSM, or iDEN.

**Advanced National Radio Data Service** (ARDIS) (n.) A nationwide packet data communications system provided by American Mobile Satellite Corporation. It offers connectivity at speeds up to 19.2 Kbps.

**Advanced Power Management** (APM) (n.) System that conservatively allocates power for essential functions in battery-operated notebook computers.

**Advanced Research Projects Agency** (ARPA) (n.) U.S. government organization that developed packet-switching techniques and created the network called ARPANET, which was the precursor to the Internet.

**Advanced RISC Machine** (ARM) (n.) Advanced reduced instruction set computing machine; an inexpensive, power-efficient, 32-bit RISC microprocessor that has embedded control, computing, digital signal processing (DSP), consumer multimedia, and other applications. It is licensed for production by Cirrus Logic, Sharp, Texas Instruments, VLSI Technology, and others. It has a small orthogonal instruction set in which every instruction includes a four-bit code.

**Advanced SCSI Programming Interface** (ASPI) (n.) Advanced Small Computer System Interface Programming Interface; developed by Adaptec, a protocol used to configure devices and media on a Small Computer System Interface (SCSI) chain.

**Advanced Streaming Format** (ASF) (n.) Multimedia file format for data that must flow at a

13

constant bit rate and must be decoded or realized in real time. It was designed by Microsoft and is the standard file format for Windows media files. ASF files can deliver audio, video, or scripting commands to a client computer. Formerly called *Active Streaming Format*.

**Advanced Technology Attachment** (ATA) (n.) The name give to Western Digital's IDE disk interface by ANSI when it was standardized. *ATA-2* and *Fast-ATA* are names used for the EIDE interface.

**Advanced WavEffect** (AWE) (n.) A sound synthesis process employed by the EMU8000 music synthesizer integrated circuit (IC) located on the Sound Blaster AWE32 card.

**AE** See *automatic exposure*.

**AECT** See *Association for Educational Communications and Technology*.

**aerial cable** (n.) A wire suspended overhead from poles or buildings, as opposed to an underground cable. Cable television companies rent space on poles from the telephone companies and electric companies that own the poles.

**AES24** (n.) The Audio Engineering Society (AES) standard under development for sound systems that use computer networks to control audio equipment. The title of the first published section is "Application Protocol for Controlling and Monitoring Audio Devices via Digital Data Networks—Part 1: Principles, Formats, and Basic Procedures." The complete standard will be divided into several parts and issued separately. The second part is "Part 2: Data Types, Constants, and Class Structure." The remaining two parts are under development by working group SC-10, the Subcommittee for Sound System Control.

**AES3 interface** (n.) Formerly known as the AES/EBU interface, the AES3 designation clarifies that isolation is a feature of the interface, which the EBU specification did not provide. It is the serial transmission format standardized for professional digital audio signals in the 1992 publication: "AES Recommended Practice for Digital Audio Engineering—Serial Transmission Format for Two-Channel Linearly Represented Digital Audio Data." It specifies time division multiplex for data, and balanced line drivers to transmit two channels of digital audio data on a single twisted-pair cable using three-pin XLR connectors. The American National Standards Institute originally issued it as ANSI S4.40-1985. The consumer version of this format is referred to as s/pdif.

**AES/EBU** See *Audio Engineering Society/European Broadcast Union*.

**AES/EBU interface** (n.) See *AES3 interface*.

**AF** See *audio frequency*.

**AFC** See *automatic frequency control*.

**affordance** (n.) A tangible aspect of an object that allows action or manipulation. Examples: handles, buttons, and scroll bars.

**AFK** (adj.) Shorthand for "away from keyboard." See *shorthand*.

**AFL** See *After Fade Listen*.

**AFSK** See *audio frequency shift keying*.

**After-Fade Listen** (AFL) (n.) Used on recording consoles and mixers, AFL refers to a signal monitored after the main channel fader; thus, it reflects the position of the main fader level. This point of access to the signal is also referred

**A**

to as *post fade*. The acronym PFL means Pre-Fade Listen.

**AGC** See *automatic gain control.*

**agent** (n.) The portion of a system that prepares and exchanges information on behalf of a client or server. *Intelligent agent* refers to some automatic process capable of communicating with other agents.

**AGP** See *Accelerated Graphics Port.*

**AH** See *Authentication Header.*

**AI** See *artificial intelligence.*

**AIFF** See *Audio Interchange File Format.*

**AIIM** See *Association for Information and Image Management.*

**AIN** See *advanced intelligent network.*

**AIX** See *Advanced Interactive Executive.*

**a-law** (Pronounced "AY-law") (n.) Standardized in the ITU G.711 specification, a method of coding eight-bit companded audio with pulse code modulation (PCM) to yield a 64 dB dynamic range. It is used to transmit digital voice channels over telephone lines worldwide, except in North America, Japan, and South Korea, where $\mu$-*law* coding is used. It is not interchangeable with $\mu$-law coding. A converter must be used to translate between these two differently coded PCM voice messages. See also $\mu$-*law* under *mu-law.*

**Alesis Digital Audio Tape** (ADAT, pronounced "AY-dat") (n.) Developed by Alesis Corporation, an eight-track audio recording format that uses S-VHS cassettes for recording media. This was the first practical, inexpensive, digital

multitracking machine, and it became popular in project studios. The TASCAM DA-88 is another popular eight-track digital recorder that uses Hi-8 cassettes rather than S-VHS. The DA-88 format was adopted by Sony and is commonly used in feature film production. Pronounced "a-LEE-sis."

**ALGOL 60** (n.) See *Algorithmic Language 1960.*

**algorithm** (n.) A type of formula that defines a sequence of steps necessary to perform a process.

**algorithmic** (adj.) Describes a program structured like a mathematical procedure that solves a problem with a limited number of steps.

**Algorithmic Language 1960** (ALGOL 60) (n.) A compact, portable programming language developed in 1960 and designed for scientific computations.

**alias** (n.) 1. In the Mac OS 7.0 and higher, an icon that represents or points to the original file. Multiple aliases can be created and placed where they may provide convenient access to the original file. It is analogous to a "shortcut" in the Windows OS. 2. A short name that is translated into a longer name or string to save space. Many command interpreters allow a user to define aliases for commands. The computer loads the aliases into memory when the interpreter starts and expands them without needing to refer to any file. 3. Another name for a host with the same Internet address as the original host. A hostname alias can indicate that the host provides a particular network service, such as Archie, FTP, or the web. With this provision, services to hosts can be changed by moving an alias from one Internet address to another without bothering the clients.

**aliasing** (n.) 1. The appearance of unwanted visual effects, known as *jaggies,* in digitized

15

images. An example is the stairstep effect on raster display systems that do not have a high enough resolution to reproduce smooth diagonal lines or circles. 2. In audio sampling, a distortion-producing reflection caused by the fact that all frequency components higher than half the sampling frequency are reflected in the lower range. Aliasing creates artifacts. It can be avoided by processing the waveform to be sampled with a low-pass filter at half the sample rate before digitizing.

**alignment** (n.) 1. In a tape recorder, the positioning of the head in relation to the tape path. 2. In a word-processed or graphic document, the horizontal and vertical relationships of elements.

**all-pass filter** (n.) An audio filter that provides only phase shift or phase delay without noticeably changing the magnitude characteristics of a waveform.

**alpha blending** (n.) A technique used to produce atmospheric effects in three-dimensional graphics. Alpha values determine how transparent a pixel will be.

**alpha channel** (n.) 1. In video production, a separate signal used to control visual effects such as overlay and transparency. 2. In a digital graphics environment, the bits that control the percentage of visibility between upper and lower layers, or foreground and background elements.

**alphanumeric** (adj.) Describes a combination of letters, numerals, and other symbols used for codes and computational expressions.

**alpha test** (n.) The initial testing on software to evaluate general functionality. It occurs before a beta test, in which software is field-tested by users.

**alt** (n.) 1. One of the Usenet newsgroup hierarchies founded by John Gilmore and Brian Reid in which anyone can create a new group without going through normal voting procedures. 2. Refers to the many free newsgroups available through Usenet. It is something of an icon for topics related to alternative culture.

**Alt** (n.) A modifier key on many computer keyboards, including the IBM PC and the Macintosh.

**Altair 8800** (n.) The first microcomputer kit.

**AltaVista** (n.) A web site maintained by Digital Equipment Corporationm (DEC) with a very efficient web and Usenet search engine. It once held the distinction of being the largest web index, referencing millions of pages and articles.

**ALTEL** See *Association of Long Distance Telephone Companies.*

**Alternate Mark Inversion** (AMI) (n.) In telecommunications, a marking process used in the DS-1 digital signal, where the first mark "1" is a positive voltage and the next mark "1" is a negative voltage. Often used to refer to a DS-1 with robbed bit signaling and without B8ZS coding.

**alternate routing** (n.) A feature of network switches—DACs and PBXs—where a call is completed over secondary circuit routes when primary circuit routes are not available.

**alternating current** (AC) (n.) In the United States, 120-volt electricity delivered by utility companies. It changes polarity from positive to negative 60 times per second. In other countries, the rate of alternation is often 50 cycles per second (cps). Direct current (DC), by contrast, is a continuous stream of current in one direction with constant polarity. The regular pulse of AC can be picked up by audio systems that are not well grounded, introducing an undesirable 60-cycle hum. Compare *direct current*.

**Alternative Billing Service** (ABS) (n.) Intelligent network service enabling subscribers to charge a call to a telephone number other than the one they are using with a credit card or ID number.

**ALU** See *arithmetic and logic unit*.

**AM** See *amplitude modulation*.

**ambient** (adj.) Describes a natural state, such as room temperature. Ambient sounds are referred to as *environmental* because they exist in a natural environment.

**American National Standards Institute** (ANSI) (n.) A U.S. government body that approves standards in many areas, including computers and communications. ANSI is a member of the ISO. ANSI and ISO standards may be purchased from ANSI Sales, 1430 Broadway, New York, NY 10018. Telephone: (212) 642–4900.

**American Society of Composers, Authors, and Publishers** (ASCAP) (n.) A licensing agency that controls the rights for the broadcast and performance of musical compositions.

**American Society of Mechanical Engineers** (ASME) (n.) An international body that has established hundreds of codes and standards for mechanical and electromechanical devices.

**American Standard Code for Information Interchange** (ASCII, pronounced "ASK-ee") (n.) The standard seven-bit code developed in 1965 by Robert W. Bemer to define text characters in a compatible format across different types of data processors. The original ASCII

character set consisted of 128 numbers, ranging from 0 through 127, assigned to letters, numbers, punctuation marks, and a few very common special characters. IBM introduced the extended ASCII character set in 1981, an eight-bit code for its personal computers. This increased the number of characters represented to 256, allowing for special mathematical and graphical characters. The characters are referred to by names, such as ampersand, asterisk, backslash, caret, colon, comma, commercial at, Ctrl-C, dollar, dot, double quote, equals, exclamation mark, greater than, hash, opening brace, opening bracket, left parenthesis, less than, minus, percent, plus, question mark, closing brace, closing bracket, right parenthesis, semicolon, single quote, slash, space, tilde, underscore, vertical bar, and zero. The code works relatively well for English language text, but ASCII text is unable to represent many characters correctly in foreign languages. Software is described as "eight-bit clean" if it correctly handles character sets that use all eight bits. See table.

**American wire gauge** (AWG) (n.) A standard method used in the U. S. for classifying wire diameter according to the Brown & Sharpe (B&S) Wire Gauge.

**America Online** (AOL) (n.) A large online Internet service provider based in Vienna, Virginia. It offers millions of subscribers electronic mail, conferencing, software libraries, and computing support. In 1994, AOL Internet FTP was made available to subscribers, and in May 1995 full Internet access included the WWW. Web access must be filtered through the AOL servers.

**AMI** See *Alternate Mark Inversion*.

**Amiga** (n.) A line of microcomputers developed by Commodore Business Machines and

## ASCII Character Codes

| Decimal | Hex | Symbol | Function | Decimal | Hex | Symbol | Function |
|---|---|---|---|---|---|---|---|
| 0 | 0 | ^@ | (NUL) Fill Character | 52 | 34 | 4 | Four |
| 1 | 1 | ^A | (SOH) Start of Heading | 53 | 35 | 5 | Five |
| 2 | 2 | ^B | (STX) Start of Text | 54 | 36 | 6 | Six |
| 3 | 3 | ^C | (ETX) End of Text | 55 | 37 | 7 | Seven |
| 4 | 4 | ^D | (EOT) End of Transmission | 56 | 38 | 8 | Eight |
| 5 | 5 | ^E | (ENQ) Enquire (request response) | 57 | 39 | 9 | Nine |
| 6 | 6 | ^F | (ACK) Acknowledge | 58 | 3A | : | Colon |
| 7 | 7 | ^G | (BEL) Bell (sound a tone) | 59 | 3B | ; | Semicolon |
| 8 | 8 | ^H | (BS) Backspace | 60 | 3C | < | Less-than Sign |
| 9 | 9 | ^I | (HT) Horizontal Tab | 61 | 3D | = | Equals Sign |
| 10 | A | ^J | (LF) Line Feed | 62 | 3E | > | Greater-than Sign |
| 11 | B | ^K | (VT) Vertical Tab | 63 | 3F | ? | Question Mark |
| 12 | C | ^L | (FF) Form Feed | 64 | 40 | @ | At Sign |
| 13 | D | ^M | (CR) Carriage Return | 65 | 41 | A | |
| 14 | E | ^N | (SO) Shift Out (change character set) | 66 | 42 | B | |
| 15 | F | ^O | (SI) Shift In (change character set) | 67 | 43 | C | |
| 16 | 10 | ^P | (DLE) Data Link Escape | 68 | 44 | D | |
| 17 | 11 | ^Q | (DC1) Data Control 1 (XON) | 69 | 45 | E | |
| 18 | 12 | ^R | (DC2) Data Control 2 | 70 | 46 | F | |
| 19 | 13 | ^S | (DC3) Data Control 3 (XOFF) | 71 | 47 | G | |
| 20 | 14 | ^T | (DC4) Data Control 4 | 72 | 48 | H | |
| 21 | 15 | ^U | (NAK) Negative Acknowledge | 73 | 49 | I | |
| 22 | 16 | ^V | (SYN) Synchronous Idle | 74 | 4A | J | |
| 23 | 17 | ^W | (ETB) End of Transmission Block | 75 | 4B | K | |
| 24 | 18 | ^X | (CAN) Cancel (end a command) | 76 | 4C | L | |
| 25 | 19 | ^Y | (EM) End of Medium | 77 | 4D | M | |
| 26 | 1A | ^Z | (SUB) Substitute (also end of file) | 78 | 4E | N | |
| 27 | 1B | ^[ | (ESC) Escape | 79 | 4F | O | |
| 28 | 1C | ^\ | (FS) File Separator | 80 | 50 | P | |
| 29 | 1D | ^] | (GS) Group Separator | 81 | 51 | Q | |
| 30 | 1E | ^^ | (RS) Record Separator | 82 | 52 | R | |
| 31 | 1F | ^_ | (US) Unit Separator | 83 | 53 | S | |
| 32 | 20 | | (SP) Space Character | 84 | 54 | T | |
| 33 | 21 | ! | Exclamation Mark | 85 | 55 | U | |
| 34 | 22 | " | Double Quotes | 86 | 56 | V | |
| 35 | 23 | # | Pound Sign | 87 | 57 | W | |
| 36 | 24 | $ | Dollar Sign | 88 | 58 | X | |
| 37 | 25 | % | Percent Sign | 89 | 59 | Y | |
| 38 | 26 | & | Ampersand | 90 | 5A | Z | |
| 39 | 27 | ' | Single Quote | 91 | 5B | [ | Opening Bracket |
| 40 | 28 | ( | Open Parenthesis | 92 | 5C | \ | Backslash |
| 41 | 29 | ) | Close Parenthesis | 93 | 5D | ] | Closing Bracket |
| 42 | 2A | * | Asterisk | 94 | 5E | ^ | Caret |
| 43 | 2B | + | Plus Sign | 95 | 5F | _ | Underscore |
| 44 | 2C | , | Comma | 96 | 60 | ' | |
| 45 | 2D | – | Minus Sign, Hyphen | 97 | 61 | a | |
| 46 | 2E | . | Period | 98 | 62 | b | |
| 47 | 2F | / | Slash | 99 | 63 | c | |
| 48 | 30 | 0 | Zero | 100 | 64 | d | |
| 49 | 31 | 1 | One | 101 | 65 | e | |
| 50 | 32 | 2 | Two | 102 | 66 | f | |
| 51 | 33 | 3 | Three | 103 | 67 | g | |

**A**

---

**ASCII Character Codes** (continued)

| Decimal | Hex | Symbol | Function | Decimal | Hex | Symbol | Function |
|---------|-----|--------|----------|---------|-----|--------|----------|
| 104 | 68 | h | | 116 | 74 | t | |
| 105 | 69 | i | | 117 | 75 | u | |
| 106 | 6A | j | | 118 | 76 | v | |
| 107 | 6B | k | | 119 | 77 | w | |
| 108 | 6C | l | | 120 | 78 | x | |
| 109 | 6D | m | | 121 | 79 | y | |
| 110 | 6E | n | | 122 | 7A | z | |
| 111 | 6F | o | | 123 | 7B | { | Opening Brace |
| 112 | 70 | p | | 124 | 7C | \| | Bar |
| 113 | 71 | q | | 125 | 7D | } | Closing Brace |
| 114 | 72 | r | | 126 | 7E | ~ | Tilde |
| 115 | 73 | s | | 127 | 7F | | |

---

used by consumers for games, video processing, and multimedia. Amigas are known for advanced graphics capabilities. Commodore Business Machines went bankrupt in April 1994, and the German company Escom AG bought it in April 1995.

**A-mode** (n.) The mode a video editing system is in while it assembles segments in the order specified on the edit decision list (EDL). This process usually involves multiple changes of source reels.

**ampere** (n.) 1. A unit of electrical current. One ampere of steady current when flowing in straight parallel wires of infinite length and negligible cross section, separated by a distance of one meter in free space, produces a force between the wires of 2E-7 newtons per meter of length 2. A unit in the International System specified as one International coulomb per second and equal to 0.999835 ampere. It is named for André Marie Ampère.

**Ampère, André Marie** (1775-1836) French physicist and mathematician who formulated Ampère's law, a mathematical description of the magnetic field produced by a current-carrying conductor.

**ampersand** (n.) ASCII character 38, "&."

**amplifier** (n.) An electronic device that boosts signal strength. Amplifiers, or amps, are required to drive speakers for audio output. They are also required at regular intervals in a cable television system between the headend and the subscriber, approximately every 1500 feet.

**amplifier classes** (n.) A system of classification based on the relationship between the output voltage and the input voltage of audio power amplifiers. Each class is defined by the design of the output stage. The classification system is based on the amount of time the output devices operate during one complete cycle of signal swing. This is also defined in terms of output bias current, which is the amount of current flowing in the output devices with no applied signal. With the exception of class A, it is assumed that a simple output stage consists of two complementary devices, one with positive polarity and the other with negative polarity, using tubes or any type of transistor.

· **class A** In this design, both output devices conduct continuously for the entire cycle of signal swing, or the bias current flows in the output devices at all times. The identifying factor in class A operation is that both devices are always on. There is no condition where one or the other is turned off. For this reason, class A amplifiers are not complementary designs. They are single-ended designs with a single type of polarity output. Class A is the most inefficient of all power amplifier designs, averaging about 20% efficiency, which means that it draws five times as much power from the source as it delivers to the load. Class A amplifiers are heavy and run hot because they are constantly operating at full power. The benefit is that class A designs are the most linear, with the least amount of distortion.

- class B This design is the opposite of class A. The two output devices are never allowed to be on at the same time, or the bias is set so that current flow in an output device is zero when not stimulated with an input signal. Each output device operates for exactly one half of a complete sinusoidal signal cycle. Class B designs have high efficiency but poor linearity. The extra time it takes to turn the output devices on and off results in high crossover distortion. These designs are restricted to power-consumption critical applications such as battery-operated equipment and communications audio.

- class AB This design is a blending of class A and class B. Both output devices are allowed to be on at the same time, as in class A, but only slightly overlap. Only a small amount of current is allowed to flow through both devices simultaneously, unlike the full load current in class A designs. However, enough current is allowed to keep each device operating so they respond instantly to the input demand. This

eliminates the non-linearity of class B design, without the inefficiency of class A design. With 50% efficiency and excellent linearity, class AB is the most popular audio amplifier design.

- class AB plus B In this design, two pairs of output devices are used. One pair operates class AB, while the other pair operates class B.

- class C This design is used exclusively in the broadcast industry for radio frequency (RF) transmission. The output devices take turns operating. Each is pulsed on for a percentage of the half cycle, instead of operating continuously for the entire half cycle. It is a very efficient design capable of massive output power. Radio frequency–tuned circuits overcome the distortion created by the pulsed operation of Class C designs.

- class D This design is referred to as a *switching power amplifier*. The output devices are rapidly switched on and off several times for each cycle. Theoretically, since the output devices are either on or off, they do not dissipate any power. Class D operation approaches 90% efficiency. This design is similar to the original "class S" designs.

- class E This class is designed for rectangular input pulses, not sinusoidal audio waveforms. The output load is a tuned circuit, with the output voltage resembling a damped single pulse. Normally, class E employs a single transistor driven to act as a switch.

The following amplifier classifications are generally agreed upon, but they do not have any official status:

- **class F** This is a class of tuned power amplifiers, and the load is a tuned resonant circuit. The circuit may be tuned for one or more harmonic frequencies, as well as the carrier frequency. Designs in this group are also known as "biharmonic," "polyharmonic," "Class DC," "single-ended Class D," "High-efficiency Class C," and "multiresonator."

- **class G** In this design, the power supply voltage is changed from a lower level to a higher level when larger output swings are required. Typically, a switch connects a single class AB output stage to two power supply rails. The output stage is generally connected to the lower supply voltage, but automatically switches to the higher rails for large signal peaks (rail-switching). Using two power supplies improves efficiency enough to allow significantly more power at a given size and weight. Class G is common in pro audio applications.

- **class H** This design improves on class G by modulating the higher power supply voltage by the input signal. This allows the power supply to track the audio input and provide just enough voltage for optimum operation of the output devices. It is sometimes called a *tracking power amplifier*. The efficiency is comparable to class G designs.

- **class S** First invented in 1932, this design is used for both amplification and amplitude modulation. It is similar to class D; however, the pulse width modulation (PWM) voltage waveform is applied to a low-pass filter that allows only the slowly varying average voltage component to

appear across the load. Class D amplifiers also operate in this fashion.

**amplify** (v.) To increase the amplitude or power of a given signal. In relation to audio, to increase the sound pressure level (SPL). Amplitude is the height of a waveform, or the measurement of a signal from trough to peak.

**amplitude** (n.) A degree of magnitude, size, or power. In physics, it is the maximum absolute value of a periodically varying quantity. In mathematics, it is either the maximum absolute value of a periodic curve measured along its vertical axis, or the angle made with the positive horizontal axis by the vector representation of a complex number. In electronics, it is the maximum absolute value reached by a voltage or current waveform.

**amplitude modulation** (AM) (n.) The process of adding information to a constant carrier signal by modulating or changing its amplitude in direct correlation with another signal. See figure.

**amplitude shift keying** (ASK) (n.) A form of digital modulation in which discrete changes in the carrier signal's amplitude convey a digital signal.

**AMPS** See *Advanced Mobile Phone Service*.

**analog** (n.) A method of representing physical variables that flow and change continuously, such as voltage, pressure, or motion. Their values are expressed as the quantitative magnitude of the variables. Analog devices are often controlled by knobs and sliders, and their output is shown by dials, gauges, and meters. The output of an analog system is analogous to changes that it tracks or measures on a scale of infinite variety.

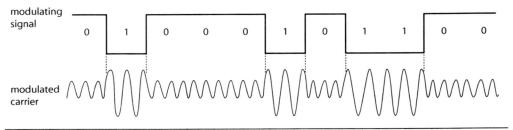

modulating signal

0 1 0 0 0 1 0 1 1 0 0

modulated carrier

*amplitude modulation*

**analog loopback** (n.) A self-test process for modems in which keyboard data is sent to the transmitter, modulated into analog form, sent back to the receiver, demodulated into digital form, and returned to the screen to complete a verification loop.

**analog RGB** (n.) Analog red-green-blue; a video signal that sends separate signal lines for red, green, and blue picture information. Each of the signals is encoded as a proportional voltage rather than as digital bits. Video systems for most microcomputers employ this method of displaying images.

**analog-to-digital converter** (ADC, A/D converter) (n.) A circuit that converts changes in voltage, pressure, or motion over time into a stream of digits to define an event with time-based binary data.

**analog video** (n.) A continuous electronic signal generated by a camera or a videotape source that represents an infinite number of smooth gradations between video levels. By contrast, a digital video signal assigns a finite series of steps in the gradations and is stored as data.

**anchor** (n.) An area (span, region, or button) in the content of a hypertext node that can serve as either the source or the destination of a hypertext link. The source anchor could be a word, phrase, image, or possibly the entire node.

The destination anchor could be a node or a location within the node. Activating a source anchor by clicking on it causes the link to be followed and the anchor at the opposite end of the link to be displayed. Anchors are typically colored or highlighted in some way to make them stand out from the text around them. In HTML, anchors are created with the <A (anchor destination)> construct. The opening "A" tag of a source anchor has a hypertext reference (HREF) attribute giving the destination in the form of a URL or page. It is followed by the text that serves as the hypertext link in the referring document. Example: <A HREF="http://www.hansenmedia.com/content"> The Knowledge Base Online</A>. See the section on linking in the appendix on HTML.

**anchor point** (n.) In a drawing program, the beginning or ending point of a Bezier curve.

**AND** (n.) Logic operator in an "if-then" proposition. If a series of statements is all true, the AND of those statements is true. If any statement in the series is false, the AND of those statements is false.

**AND gate** (n.) A logic gate whose output is 1 under the condition that all inputs are 1.

**anechoic** (adj.) Meaning without echo, the term is used to describe specially designed rooms, anechoic chambers, that are built to emulate a free field by absorbing virtually the entire sound field.

**angle bracket** (n.) One of two characters: < (less than), which is ASCII 60, or > (greater than), which is ASCII 62.

**angry fruit salad** (n.) Jargon for a graphic image with too many colors.

ANI See *automatic number identification.*

**animatic** (n.) A compilation of key scenes used to plan and lay out video spots and motion pictures.

**animation** (n.) The rapid display of a series of still images or objects that are repositioned in each frame to simulate movement on a still background.

**annual change traffic** (ACT) (n.) A small portion of the code in an application that a software developer modifies during a calendar year.

**anonymous FTP** (n.) Anonymous file transfer protocol; Internet hosts often provide this interactive service, which allows a user to transfer documents, files, programs, and other archived data using FTP. Users log in under the user name *ftp* or *anonymous* with their email address as the password. This grants access to a directory hierarchy containing publicly accessible files, normally in the *pub* subdirectory. A reference to a file available by FTP may also take the form of a URL beginning with the letters *ftp* and followed by a colon.

**anonymous remailer** (n.) System that disguises the identity of the sender of email over the Internet. It can be used to post to Usenet newsgroups anonymously.

**ANSI** See *American National Standards Institute.*

**antenna** (n.) Hardware that sends and receives signals, part of all wireless communication devices. Service operators typically mount antennas on a building, tower or rooftop. A miniature antenna may be embedded in a PC card for connecting a laptop to a wireless LAN.

**antenna gain** (n.) The capacity to receive or transmit signals, measured in reference to a standard antenna model. The isotropic antenna is often used for the reference model. An ideal isotropic antenna is one that radiates equally well in all directions. An antenna gain equal to the isotropic antenna reference is expressed as 0 dBi in gain. If the antenna gain were two times that of the isotropic antenna reference, the difference would be expressed as 3 dBi.

**anti-aliasing** (n.) Software alterations in the representation of data to help diagonal or curved lines appear smooth and continuous when displayed from computer-generated sources. In audio applications, the smoothing of steps between discrete samples to reduce the undesirable effects of low bit-rate capture. See figure.

*anti-aliased letters on left; aliased letters on right*

**anti-aliasing filter** (n.) A low-pass filter applied at the input of digital audio converters to attenuate frequencies above the half-sampling frequency to prevent aliasing.

**anti-imaging filter** (n.) A low-pass filter applied at the output of digital audio converters to attenuate frequencies above the half-sampling frequency to eliminate image spectra present at multiples of the sampling frequency.

AOL See *America Online.*

**Apache** (n.) A popular HTTP server for Unix that anyone can use for free. Developed in 1995, it is based on Hypertext Transfer Protocol daemon (HTTPd), a program written at the National Center for Supercomputing Applications (NCSA). Apache is currently the most widely used HTTP server on the Internet, running on more than half of all web servers. Among its features are authentication databases, content negotiation, and configurable error messages, all based on a database management system (DBMS). It is available at *http://www.apache.org.*

APD See *avalanche photodiode.*

APDA See *Apple Programmers and Developers Association.*

APDU See *application protocol data unit.*

**aperture** (n.) The opening in a camera lens that regulates the amount of light that can enter. The size of the aperture is measured in f-stops. See also *f-stop* or *iris.*

API See *Application Programming Interface.*

APM See *Advanced Power Management.*

**apogee** (n.) Point in a satellite's orbit that is farthest from Earth's center.

**apparent power** (n.) The result of multiplying the root mean square (rms) value of the voltage by the rms value of the current in an electronic circuit. It is expressed in watts (W) for resistive loads and in voltamperes (VA) for reactive loads. It is the amount of power that appears to be available, but because of *power factor,* the real power is actually less. Also called *average power.*

**Apple Desktop Bus** (ADB) (n.) The original input/output (I/O) port and protocol used on a Macintosh to connect the keyboard, mouse, and other devices. It has been replaced by USB.

**Apple Programmers and Developers Association** (APDA) (n.) The source for all the tools needed to conduct high-level multimedia development using the Macintosh platform. APDA can be contacted at (800) 282–2732 in the United States or (800) 637–0029 in Canada.

**Apple Remote Access** (ARA) (n.) A communications protocol through which a user can dial up a host Macintosh from a remote modem and share the host's desktop on the remote computer. Files can be downloaded or uploaded between the two connected computers.

**AppleScript** (n.) An object-oriented shell language for the Macintosh, comparable to an extended version of HyperTalk, the scripting language developed for HyperCard.

**applet** (n.) A small Java program that can be attached to an HTML document for the WWW and executed by a Java-enabled browser running on any platform with a virtual machine that handles Java bytecode. A full Java application runs outside the browser. Before Java, the term referred to any small application that performed a specific task.

**AppleTalk** (n.) A local area network (LAN) protocol developed by Apple Computer for connecting peripherals and computers. It is a part of the system software that Apple Computer provides, and it operates over a variety of wiring types. Technically, it is a carrier sense multiple access with collision detection (CSMA/CD) network running at 230 kilobits per second (Kbps) that can connect up to 32 devices using shielded twisted-pair cable for a distance of approximately 1000 feet.

**AppleTalk Data Stream Protocol** (ADSP) (n.) A protocol that provides a simple transport method for networked data.

**Apple Unix** (A/UX) (n.) A version of Unix that runs on networked Apple computers.

**Apple Video Compressor** (n.) Developed by Apple Computer, the original compression and decompression CODEC used for QuickTime. Early versions of the CODEC have been updated.

**application** (n.) 1. A software program that creates or reads a data file. 2. The set of data and program software contained on a CD.

**Application Binary Interface** (ABI) (n.) The emulation in software of a hardware-software platform other than the native one, allowing foreign applications to run. An example would be running a Windows application under the Unix operating system.

**application layer** (n.) In the OSI model, this top layer provides the functionality that allows software programs to run and files to be accessed.

**application-level gateway** (n.) A firewall system in which service is provided by processes that maintain complete TCP connection state and sequencing. Application level firewalls typically re-address traffic and give outgoing messages an address that appears to have originated from the firewall itself, rather than from the internal host.

**application program** (n.) A complete stand-alone program that performs a specific function directly for the user, as opposed to system software such as the operating system kernel, server processes, and libraries, which support applications. Word processors and spreadsheets are common examples of applications. A client or browser is a networking application. Applications run in *user mode,* whereas operating systems and utilities run in *supervisor mode.* The short form is *app.*

**Application Programming Interface** (API) (n.) The interface or conventions by which an application program accesses the operating system and other services. It is defined at the source code level and provides a level of abstraction between the application and the kernel to ensure the portability of the code.

**application protocol data unit** (APDU) (n.) The highest-level view of communication in the OSI seven-layer model, this packet of data is exchanged between two application programs across a network. An individual packet exchanged at this level could be transmitted as several packets at a lower layer, in addition to containing headers for routing.

**Application-Specific Integrated Circuit** (ASIC) (n.) An integrated circuit that performs a particular function. The basic circuit building blocks provided by the circuit manufacturer are configured and interconnected for a specific use. They are used in automobiles and microwave ovens.

**ARA** See *Apple Remote Access.*

25

**arbitration** (n.) The bidding of multiple devices attached to a single bus to control the bus.

**Archie** (n.) Available as a Unix command via Telnet, a tool that allows users to search a database of anonymous FTP sites.

**architecture** (n.) The general design of a computer hardware and software system. A system with *open architecture* allows the addition of internal cards and external peripherals.

**archival** (adj.) Describes a storage medium that preserves data for an extended period. Archival media must remain stable without degrading over time.

**archive** (v.) To record information in long-term storage.

**archive site** (n.) An Internet host where program source, documents, email, or news messages are stored for public access via anonymous FTP, gopher, a Web browser, or some other document distribution system. It is also referred to as an *FTP archive*.

**archiving** (n.) The process of moving data from online storage to nearline (optical disc) or offline (tape) storage. A directory is stored along with the data.

**ARCnet** See *Attached Resource Computer Network*.

**ARDIS** See *Advanced National Radio Data Service*.

**area code** (n.) A three-digit number designating a toll center in the United States, Canada, or Mexico. Area codes are distributed according to the North American Numbering Plan (NANP).

**areal density** (n.) *Bits per inch (bpi)* x *tracks per inch (tpi).* This calculation indicates how many bits per square inch exist on the surface of a disk. *Bit density* x *track density = areal density.*

**argument** (n.) In programming, a value or reference assigned to a function, command, or procedure. In the function square(a) = a * a, *a* is the formal argument. Normally, arguments to a program are given after the command and are separated by spaces. In the example "run thisfile," *run* is the command and *thisfile* is the argument.

**arithmetic and logic unit** (ALU) (n.) The portion of a central processing unit (CPU) that performs mathematical functions, including multiplication, addition, subtraction, and Boolean operations. Most often, floating-point operations are done by a separate unit.

**ARJ** (n.) Archive program used by IBM-compatible computers to compress data and to store or transfer smaller files. See also *tape archive* or *ZIP*.

**ARM** See *Advanced RISC Machine* or *asynchronous response mode*.

**ARP** See *Address Resolution Protocol*.

**ARPA** See *Advanced Research Projects Agency*.

**ARQ** See *automatic request for retransmission*.

**ARS** See *Automatic Route Selection*.

**array** (n.) 1. A set of coordinates that define rows and columns. A two-dimensional array is described with x- and y-coordinates, whereas a three-dimensional array requires x-, y-, and z-coordinates. 2. A group of identically typed data items distinguished by their subscripts. An array typically has any number of dimensions. A single variable, or *scalar*, might be considered an array. An array with one dimension might be considered a *vector*. An array might be represented as X[a,b,c,d], where *X* is the array name and *a, b, c,* and *d* are the subscripts, or *indexes*. Each index is written in separate brackets in the C language. Arrays are more useful for storing data to be accessed later in an unpredictable order than they are for storing items that will be sequentially called.

**artifact** (n.) Evidence of undesirable distortion that appears in digitized audio or video files as a result of inaccurate information introduced during capture or compression. Artifacts may take the form of new, unwanted data or the degradation of existing content.

**artificial intelligence** (AI) (n.) Software that makes decisions based on accumulated experience and information. The software features functions normally associated with human intelligence, such as learning, adapting, reasoning, and self-correcting.

**artificial light** (n.) In a video production or camera shoot, this is indoor or outdoor illumination from a man-made source, such as fluorescent bulbs, quartz lamps, or the headlights of an automobile.

**artwork** (n.) Any type of graphics prepared for computer display, printing, or video. This may include drawings, paintings, photographs, maps, graphs, charts, captions, titles, and all elements in which artistic design considerations are of primary concern.

**AS** See *autonomous system.*

**ASCAP** See *American Society of Composers, Authors, and Publishers.*

**ASCII** See *American Standard Code for Information Interchange.*

**ASF** See *Advanced Streaming Format.*

**AS/400** (n.) An IBM minicomputer originally released in 1988. It provides multiuser support and is used by many small businesses. Programming for the system may be done in assembly language, C, Cobol, SQL, BASIC, and RPG.

**ASIC** See *Application-Specific Integrated Circuit.*

**ASIO** See *audio stream input/output.*

**ASK** See *amplitude shift keying.*

**ASME** See *American Society of Mechanical Engineers.*

**ASN/1** See *Abstract Syntax Notation One.*

**ASPEC** See *adaptive spectral perceptual entropy coding.*

**aspect ratio** (n.) Resolution expressed in relative height and width values. The standard ratio for computer screens is 4:3. This is the basis for the standard resolutions of 240:180, 320:240, 640:480, 800:600, 1024:768, and 1600:1200, all of which are used in digital video. The aspect ratio for television monitors is wider, and the problem of *overscan* introduces variables related to the safe viewing area around the edges. The ratio of modern motion pictures varies from 5:3 to 7:3, creating a problem when a wide-format motion picture is transferred to a 4:3 ratio screen. A 35 mm photograph has dimensions of 36 mm x 24 mm, resulting in a 3:2 ratio. A letterbox ef-

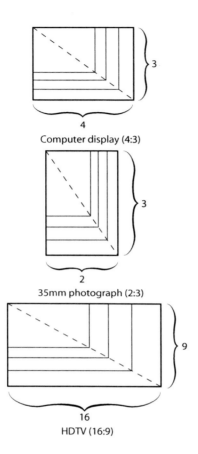

Computer display (4:3)

35mm photograph (2:3)

HDTV (16:9)

*aspect ratios*

fect occurs when photos are ported to the computer screen. See figure.

**ASPI** See *Advanced SCSI Programming Interface.*

**assemble editing** (n.) Placing video sequences back-to-back on a videotape without providing a constant reference signal or uninterrupted time code. This process is prone to minor timing errors. *Insert editing,* or placing sequences on top of an existing reference track, is more stable.

**assembly** (n.) The conversion of instructions and data written in a computer programming language into lower-level machine code.

**assembly language** (n.) A lower-level programming language that consists of words and phrases used to control a microprocessor. An assembler converts the subroutines of assembly language into machine code that a computer can read.

**asset** (n.) Any piece of data (such as an audio, graphic, text, or video file) used in a multimedia program.

**assigned numbers** (n.) The RFC standard (STD) 2, which identifies the currently assigned values from several series of numbers used in network protocol implementations. STD 2 is periodically updated, and the latest values may be secured from the Internet Assigned Numbers Authority (IANA). Anyone developing a protocol or application that requires the use of a link, socket, or port should contact the IANA for a number assignment.

**Association for Computational Linguistics** (ACL) (n.) International professional society for people addressing issues that involve language and computing. The ACL publishes a quarterly journal, *Computational Linguistics,* and sponsors special interest groups (SIGs). The ACL has more than 2000 members.

**Association for Computing Machinery** (ACM) (n.) The established international scientific and educational computer society. ACM was established in 1947 by mathematicians and electrical engineers, and it offers computer scientists a forum for sharing knowledge.

**Association for Educational Communications and Technology** (AECT) (n.) Professional group that promotes the study of how current technologies are applied in education, particularly at the institutional level.

**Association for Information and Image Management** (AIIM) (n.) A global organization of users and providers of information and document management technologies. Their expanded definition of the term *document* includes content in a variety of formats, such as print, email, voice messages, film, and video. The focus is on helping users apply technology to improve critical business processes. There are more than 650 corporations and 9000 individuals among its members. AIIM originated as the National Microfilm Association in 1945 and changed its name in 1983. AIIM provides a forum for information exchange and works to advance worldwide standards of interoperability in cooperation with the American National Standards Institute (ANSI).

**Association of American Publishers** (AAP) (n.) Industry group whose members represent major publishers of print materials, as well as associated professionals. The organization has worked to define standards for document preparation and other issues that affect digital content developers.

**Association of Long Distance Telephone Companies** (ALTEL) (n.) Trade association whose members are alternative long distance carriers and service resellers.

**Association of Visual Communicators** (AVC) (n.) Group of graphics professionals dedicated to communicating effectively by using images.

**assurance** (n.) In network security, the measure of confidence that security features will adequately enforce established security goals for an information and data communications system.

**ASX** (n.) The designated extension for a Windows Media reference file that is placed on an HTTP server, providing the Windows Media Player with the location of an ASF file on a Microsoft NT or NetShow server. ASX files may contain references to multiple movies, different content locations, temporal aspects, and other information.

**asymmetrical compression** (n.) Any video or audio compression process in which more time and resources are required to encode than to decode.

**asymmetrical modulation** (n.) Duplex data transmission technique that divides a link into two channels, one fast and one slow. During transmission between two modems, the one transmitting the most data uses the faster channel. The modem transmitting less data is given the slower "back" channel (450 bps). The channels may be dynamically reversed during a connection if the volume of data changes in either direction.

**asymmetric codec** (n.) A codec that takes longer to encode than to decode. Most video encoders that perform the operation in software are considered asymmetric, because it takes more time for the computer to encode a video frame than it does to play that frame.

**Asymmetric Digital Subscriber Line** (ADSL) (n.) Method of transmitting data at a high rate over existing twisted-pair wiring from a telephone company's central office to a business or residence. In this method, the downstream rate is faster than the upstream rate—hence, the "asymmetric" qualifier. The ADSL standards are defined in the ANSI T-1.413 specification. The standards define two categories of digital transmission. Category I specifies a basic feature set for ADSL systems with various options. Category II is designed for higher data rates over longer distances and allows for greater noise immunity than Category I. Category II requires the use of Trellis-coded modulation, echo cancellation, and forward error correction, all of which enable simultaneous transmission upstream and downstream sharing a frequency spectrum. A line-encoding scheme using carrier amplitude and carrier phase modulation provides a one-way data channel to the subscriber at up to 6.4 megabits per second (Mbps), which is adequate for full-motion, full-screen video in the MPEG-2 format. That scheme also provides for an upstream flow of 640 kilobits per second (Kbps), divisible into channels to offer several services simultaneously. The maximum length of the copper single twisted pair used for transmission is 18 000 feet and varies widely depending on line conditions. With this technology, a standard telephone drop to a home can deliver compressed video that exceeds cable in quality, voice service, and fast modem connections to the Internet. The Universal ADSL Working Group (UAWG) Consortium is a group of network operators, computer companies, and telecommunications providers that developed a standard for splitterless ADSL, or ADSL Lite, referred to as G.lite by the International Telecommunications Union–Telecommunications Standardization Sector (ITU-T). Splitterless ADSL lowers the speed of service from a maximum of 8 Mbps to 1.5 Mbps, greatly reducing the risk of interference between voice and data signals. The ADSL Forum has a web server at *http://www.sbexpos.com/sbexpos/associations/ adsl/home.html.*

Terms related to ADSL:

- **Access Node** (n.) Concentration point for broadband and narrowband data that may be located at a central office or remote site.

- **ATU-C** (n.) ADSL transmission unit–central; located at the central office end of a network, this unit can be integrated with an access node.

- **ATU-R** (n.) ADSL transmission unit–receiver; located at the customer premises end, this unit can be integrated with a Service Module (SM).

- **loop** (n.) Twisted-pair copper telephone line with a wide range of transmission characteristics based on diameter, distance, age, and connections.

- **Premises Distribution Network** (PDN) (n.) System for connecting the ATU-R to SMs. It may be passive or active, point-to-point, or multipoint.

- **Service Module** (SM) (n.) Unit that performs terminal adaptation functions, taking the form of a local area network (LAN) router, PC interface, or set-top box.

- **Single-Line Digital Subscriber Line** (SDSL) (n.) High-Data-Rate DSL over a single telephone line. A nonstandard implementation using plain old telephone service (POTS) for symmetric services to individual users.

- **splitter** (n.) Filter that separates high-frequency (ADSL) and low-frequency (POTS) signals at the network end and at the premises end.

- **Synchronous Transfer Mode** (STM) (n.) Transmission of data at a constant rate.

- **T-SM** (n.) Interface between the ATU-R and the Premises Distribution Network.

- **U-C** (n.) Interface between the loop and the POTS splitter on the network side. The asymmetry of the signals on the line requires that both ends of the loop be interfaced separately.

- **U-C2** (n.) Interface between the POTS splitter and the ATU-C.

- **U-R2** (n.) Interface between the POTS splitter and the ATU-R.

- **VA** (n.) Logical interface between the ATU-C and the Access Node.

- **VC** (n.) Logical interface between the Access Node and the network.

**asynchronous** (adj.) 1. Describes the performance of computer operations in sequential stages, rather than in a continuous variable stream. 2. The opposite of realtime conferencing in email applications. In realtime conferencing, more than one person can participate in a conversation at the same time from different locations; in asynchronous communication, they must take turns. 3. In telecommunications, a mode in which two devices are free to send data in a continuous stream at any time. Each byte begins with a start bit and ends with a stop bit. This is the most common mode of communication between computer modem users.

**asynchronous response mode** (ARM) (n.) In an unbalanced data connection, a mode in which the secondary station may begin transmitting to the primary station without obtaining permission.

**Asynchronous Transfer Mode** (ATM) (n.) A means of transmitting data. This mode combines different data types (audio, video, or text) with a sophisticated formula for allocating bandwidth and shuttling packets, or cells, of a fixed length (53 bytes). It provides a common means of transporting all types of data, some

of which exist as streams that are reassembled on reception.

**asynchronous transmission** (n.) Method of transferring data in which each packet of information is individually synchronized by means of start and stop elements in the header.

**ATA** See *Advanced Technology Attachment.*

**Atari** (n.) A company that manufactured 16- and 32-bit microcomputers with built-in MIDI in the 1970s and 1980s. They currently manufacture stand-alone video game hardware and software for use with television sets.

**ATDT** See *Attention Dial Tone.*

**ATM** See *Adobe Type Manager* or *Asynchronous Transfer Mode.*

**ATM Adaptation Layer** (AAL) (n.) Protocol used on top of Asynchronous Transfer Mode (ATM) to support high-level service requirements, converting non-ATM bit streams into ATM cells. The five adaptation layer levels provide both connection-oriented and connectionless services for data transfer. Layer 5 for computer networking provides error recovery and retransmission of undelivered or corrupted packets.

**Attached Resource Computer Network** (ARCnet) (n.) A local area network (LAN) configuration that operates at 2.5 megabits per second (Mbps) over coaxial cable using a token-passing protocol. It features a distributed star topology and is reliable and easily expanded.

**attachment** (n.) Any file linked to an email message that can be opened and viewed with an application on the recipient's computer.

**attachment unit interface** (AUI) (n.) A 15-pin

31

connector used to couple computers on an Ethernet network.

**attack** (n.) An attempt to bypass security controls on a computer. The attack may be intended to alter, release, or deny data. The success of an attack depends on the vulnerability of the computer system and the effectiveness of countermeasures.

**ATTC** See *address track time code.*

**Attention Dial Tone** (ATDT) (n.) A modem command required to make an initial connection with another modem.

**attenuate** (v.) To reduce the strength of a signal. In audio applications, attenuators often appear as faders or sliding potentiometers that control the decibel levels of individual channels on mixing boards.

**attenuator pad** (n.) In electronics, a passive network that reduces the voltage or power level of a signal with negligible distortion, but with insertion loss. It is typically a simple resistive network, although any combination of inductors, resistors, and capacitors may be used. A pad may also provide impedance matching. Pads are named according to the topology of the network they form, with the two most common being an *L-pad* and a *T-pad.* An L-pad is a two-legged network shaped like a backward letter "L." It usually consists of two resistors that are fixed or adjustable. A variable L-pad consists of two variable potentiometers that are ganged together. The ganged sections work to provide either constant input or constant output impedance regardless of the attenuation setting. The term is used generally to include all L-shaped networks. Volume and level controls are examples. A T-pad is a three-legged network shaped like a letter "T." It consists of three resistors that are fixed or adjustable. A variable T-pad consists of two or three variable potentiometers that are ganged together.

**audio** (n., adj.) Refers to all the sounds that are audible to humans, as well as the broadcast and reception of sounds. Audio travels through the air as a series of vibrations, or cycles of alternating pressure zones. Each cycle of compression is followed by rarefaction, or relaxation, producing a wave.

**audio bridge** (n.) Any communications link that allows multiple duplex connections over four-wire telephone connections. To avoid feedback, audio bridges do not connect inputs to their own outputs.

**audio cable** (n.) An appropriate cable for audio signals with a single copper conductor surrounded with a heavy layer of insulation. This is covered by a thick surrounding copper shield and jacket. It is used most often as a constant-impedance unbalanced transmission line.

**audio coding-3** (AC-3) (n.) A digital audio data compression algorithm developed by Dolby Labs and used in HDTV transmission and for DVD audio. It provides 5.1-channel surround sound. A competing algorithm is the DTS Zeta Digital sound format. AC-1 and AC-2 are other versions developed by Dolby for different applications.

**audioconference** (n.) A meeting over telephone lines with participants in different geographic locations who speak with one another simultaneously. Full-duplex systems allow users to hear other voices while they speak into their headsets. Half-duplex systems allow either reception or transmission of a signal at any given moment but not synchronous two-way communication.

**audio dub** (n., v.) Replacing all or part of a videotape's sound track without affecting prerecorded images.

**Audio Engineering Society/European Broadcast Union** (AES/EBU) (n.) Two groups that developed similar digital audio transmission standards, specifying transmission of data in a stream with encoded stereo audio signals, along with optional information. The signals are in the high-frequency range, and 110-ohm balanced cables should be used to connect devices.

**audio frequency** (AF) (n.) Sounds within the normal range of human hearing, approximately 20 Hz to 20 kHz.

**audio frequency shift keying** (AFSK) (n.) In telecommunications, a method of modulating a carrier wave with audio frequencies (AFs) to send digital signals.

**audiographics** (n.) A hardware and software system that permits computer users in different locations to connect over telephone lines and to share data, graphics, and voice signals in real time. With an audiographic connection, users can work on the same application or document simultaneously, see the data on their computer screens, and discuss their progress over a voice channel. In the most basic application, the term refers to any single-frame transmission of graphics with audio signals.

**audiographic teleconferencing** (n.) A realtime conference over telephone lines, typically ISDN, using both an audio and a data connection. A computer screen may be shared at multiple sites and used as an electronic whiteboard. One powerful feature of this type of teleconferencing is that it allows users to share an application. In this way, users at remote sites can dynamically update a shared document.

**Audio Interchange File Format** (AIFF) (n.) A sound file format defined by Apple Computer and others that can include both sampled sound and MIDI data. The AIFF-C variation stores the data in compressed form. AIFF files can be imported by most multimedia authoring programs for the Macintosh and by some programs running on IBM-compatible computers. The raw sample data in an AIFF file is identical to that in a .wav file, but it is packaged differently.

**Audio Publishers Association** (n.) A resource center for audiobook listeners and industry professionals, accessible on the Internet.

**audio stream input/output** (ASIO) (n.) A multichannel audio transfer protocol developed by Steinberg in 1997 for audio and MIDI sequencing applications, allowing access to the multichannel capabilities of sound cards.

**audiotex** (n.) Interactive voice response (IVR) equipment and services. Audio information services include many 900-number services.

**audio track** (n.) The section or layer of an audio tape, videotape, or videodisc containing the sound signal that accompanies the video signal. Systems with two separate audio tracks can produce stereo sound or two independent monophonic tracks.

**Audio-Video Interleaved** (AVI) (n.) A digital video architecture that can be used in Microsoft Windows. Known as *Video for Windows,* it is a common standard for synchronized audio/video delivery on IBM-compatible computers. In this file format, blocks of audio data are woven into a stream of video frames.

**audit** (n.) The independent examination of records and activities conducted to ensure compliance with established policies and procedures. An audit may result in recommended procedural changes.

**audit trail** (n.) A chronological record of system resource usage in a computer security system. The record includes user login, file access, any business conducted, and whether any attempted security violations occurred—legitimate and unauthorized.

**AUI** See *Adaptable User Interface* or *attachment unit interface*.

**AUP** See *Acceptable Use Policy*.

**Aurora** (n.) The code name for the component that helps manage different types of information in version 4.0 and later of the Netscape browser. Aurora allows the combination of different types of local and remote files in the same environment, using Extensible Markup Language (XML) and the resource description framework (RDF) standard.

**authenticate** (v.) To establish the validity of a claimed user or object.

**authentication** (n.) The act of positively identifying a user, a device, or some other entity in a computing system. This is a prerequisite to allowing the entity access to resources in a system or on a network.

**Authentication Header** (AH) (n.) A field that immediately follows the IP header in an IP datagram. It provides authentication and integrity checking for the datagram.

**author** 1. (v.) To create an interactive computer program with the use of an authoring language or system. Developers without formal programming skills can use scripting commands to prepare applications for computer systems or CD-ROMs. Authoring requires a disciplined

approach to preparing the elements of a multimedia program with careful planning and design. 2. (n.) A person who participates in the creation of a multimedia program or an interactive CD-ROM.

**authoring software** (n.) A program that facilitates the development of interactive multimedia. Systems vary widely in their capabilities, and factors such as the platform, audience, and desired results should be taken into consideration when selecting the appropriate tool. It requires less time to develop interactive multimedia with the aid of an authoring system than it does to program it in compiled code. The methods used to develop graphics, text, video, audio, animation, and other media objects generally are not affected by the choice of an authoring system. Software designed for creating and editing specific media types is used to refine objects to be imported into the authoring environment, although an authoring tool may have some rudimentary editing features. Here are descriptions of the primary types of authoring paradigms:

- **flow control with icons** (n.) An approach characterized by rapid prototyping and short development time. A palette of icons presents the tools for interaction, and a flowline connects the icons. Runtime speed may be slower than that of other development tools.

- **frame-based system** (n.) An approach that uses screens, frames, or cards as the workplace and that brings media types onto each frame. This system generally provides a way to control the timing of a presentation and the layering of assets. An icon palette is available, and conceptual links are made between objects that represent media types, such as graphics, audio, and video files. A scripting language is provided to set up interaction. With this type of tool, it is difficult to see the connections while building a program. Some frame-based systems provide a matrix, or a *score,* that shows the progression of frames on the horizontal axis and the media channels, or *tracks,* on the vertical axis.

- **hierarchical object** (n.) A system that defines relationships with metaphors represented by embedded objects (media types or events) and iconic properties (controls or conditional statements), similar to an object-oriented programming language.

- **hypermedia linking** (n.) A tool that allows conditional relationships to be built between elements and that gives the author a means to direct traffic. Most programs show the relationship between elements but do not offer a visual map of the connections.

- **scripting language** (n.) An approach similar to traditional programming. File names identify multimedia elements, sequencing, and hot spots. An object-oriented version of the scripting language is usually implemented.

The table on the following page lists widely used authoring programs, identifies the publisher, indicates the platforms on which programs may be developed or run, and describes the authoring paradigm and prominent features. Programs that offer a cross-platform player require that the authoring be done in the original environment. After development, the program can be ported to the player platform as a self-contained module.

**auto-answering** (n.) The capability of a terminal, modem, computer, or similar device to respond to an incoming call on a dial-up telephone line and to establish a data connection with a remote device without operator intervention.

**auto-assembly** (n.) In video postproduction, the use of an edit decision list (EDL) as well as a computerized edit controller to automate the process of making a final edited master tape.

**autobaud** See *automatic baud rate detection.*

**autochanger** (n.) An optical media system that can store and retrieve data from multiple CDs, similar to a jukebox that plays phonograph records.

**Autodesk Animator** (n.) Developed by Autodesk, a collection of PC animation tools that create files in the Autodesk proprietary FLC and FLI formats.

**autodial** (n.) The capability of a terminal, modem, computer, or similar device to place a call over the switched telephone network and establish a connection without operator intervention. Also known as *autocall.*

**autoexec.bat** (n.) A batch file, or command set, that is automatically executed by a PC running MS-DOS whenever the system is turned on or booted.

**autofeed** (n., adj.) A mode in which a scanner can operate continuously. A new page is loaded automatically when the previous page has been scanned.

**autoformer** (n.) Abbreviation for *autotransformer* or *self-transformer.* A type of transformer that self-magnetizes to produce the transformer voltage. This type of transformer has a single winding with one part acting as the primary winding and the other part acting as the secondary winding, as opposed to the separate pri-

## Authoring Software

| Tool | Platform | Features |
| --- | --- | --- |
| Apple Media Tool, Apple Computer | Macintosh, Windows player | Frame-based; powerful and extensible. |
| Authorware, Macromedia | Macintosh, Windows | Flow control with icons; broad external media support; optimal for CBT and rapid prototyping; ports to Shockwave for the WWW. |
| CourseBuilder, Discovery Systems Int'l. | Macintosh, Windows player | Flow control with icons; creates interactive courseware without scripting. |
| cT, Carnegie Mellon University & WorldWired | Macintosh, Windows, Unix | Scripting system with web player; handles video, hot-text, and response tracking. |
| Director, Flash, Macromedia | Macintosh, Windows | Frame-based with scripting; animation; object-based scripting language; creates Shockwave/Flash files for the WWW. |
| Grasp, Paul Mace Software | DOS | Scripting language. |
| HyperCard, Apple Computer | Macintosh | Frame-based with scripting; the original card metaphor; HyperTalk language. |
| HyperWriter, Ntergard | DOS, Windows | Frame-based, document metaphor; CBT uses. |
| IconAuthor, AimTech | Windows, OS/2, NT, Unix, Macintosh player | Flow control with icons; data-handling features are a plus for CBT tracking; portable to the WWW. |
| MediaForge, Strata | Windows | Iconic; extensible with Visual Basic adaptation; flexible and powerful. |
| Oracle Media Objects, Oracle | Macintosh, Windows | Frame-based with scripting. |
| Quest, Allen Communications | Windows | Frame-based with scripting; language is ANSI C. |
| Scala MM100, Scala, Inc. | DOS, Windows | Interface is event list with timing controls. |
| ScriptX, Kaleida Labs | Macintosh, Windows player | Scripting language; powerful, but out of production. |
| SuperCard, Allegiant | Macintosh, Windows player | Frame-based with scripting; hypertext; external media handling. |
| Toolbook, Asymetrix Corporation | Windows | Frame-based with scripting; database linking; MCI compliant; macros perform interactive functions; ports to the WWW, outputs Java; optimized for CBT. |

mary and a secondary windings found in most transformers. With no secondary winding, there is no air gap and no true isolation between primary and secondary windings. One winding is common to both the primary and the secondary circuits associated with that winding. The transformed voltage is usually 70.7V in the U.S. and 100V elsewhere. Autoformers are commonly used and relatively inexpensive.

**Automated Information System** (AIS) (n.) Refers to any equipment that is part of an interconnected system or subsystem used in the automatic acquisition, storage, manipulation, control, display, transmission, or reception of data, including hardware and software. The term is commonly used in U.S. government documents.

**automatic baud rate detection** (ABR, autobaud) (n.) Performed by a receiving device, this process determines the code level, speed, and stop bits of incoming data by reading a predetermined initial character. ABR permits a receiving device to accept data flexibly from a variety of transmitting devices operating at different speeds.

**Automatic Call Distribution** (ACD) (n.) A method of routing and tracking telephone signals.

**Automatic Call Distributor** (ACD) (n.) Telephone system that handles a high volume of incoming and outgoing calls. This technology is used increasingly by telemarketers. An ACD can answer an incoming call, search a database for handling instructions, and send the call to a recorded message or to the appropriate person. These systems can automatically dial a series of numbers and transfer the call to an operator if a human voice answers the call.

**Automatic Dialog Replacement** (ADR) (n.) An automated process for substituting a new voice track for the original, often to eliminate unwanted sounds from production audio tracks. ADR systems play short segments of actors' dialog repeatedly in a constant rhythm so that they can hear it through headphones and recreate their original performance, improving synchronization with the picture. This process is also referred to as *looping*.

**automatic exposure** (AE) (n.) Circuitry in a video recorder or still camera that monitors light levels and adjusts the iris or shutter speed to compensate for changing light conditions.

**automatic frequency control** (AFC) (n.) The process of locking a receiver to a television station's or FM radio station's frequency.

**automatic gain control** (AGC) (n.) A limiting circuit used in audio playback systems to prevent damaging high-volume levels. It is also used

in consumer-level recording devices to boost the recording level during quiet passages or to reduce the level when loud sounds occur.

**automatic number identification** (ANI) (n.) Caller ID service provided by local exchange carriers in which the caller's number is sent to the receiving number before the second ring. It is one of several Custom Local Area Signaling Services (CLASS), all of which require Signaling System 7 (SS7) interoffice signaling.

**automatic request for retransmission** (ARQ) (n.) In data communications, a situation in which the receiver asks the transmitter to resend a frame or a block of information, generally as a result of error correction.

**Automatic Route Selection** (ARS) (n.) In telephony, the capability of a switch (PBX) to automatically determine an optimal route and establish a circuit. It is also known as Least Cost Routing (LCR).

**autonomous system** (AS) (n.) Collection of routers operating under a single administrative authority using a common Interior Gateway Protocol (IGP) for packet routing.

**AutoPlay** (n.) A CD-ROM standard developed by Microsoft. AutoPlay lets Windows systems detect a disc and load its program automatically.

**auto repeat** (n.) A feature of many media playback devices, this mode allows program material to be continuously replayed until it is interrupted.

**A/UX** See *Apple Unix*.

**auxiliary data field** (n.) A 288-byte field that precedes the data field in a CD-ROM sector. It contains error correction codes on a mode 1 disc, but it may contain data on a mode 2 disc.

**avalanche photodiode** (APD) (n.) Device that detects light and converts it to electrical signals.

**avatar** (n.) 1. The name of the superuser account on numerous Unix systems. Some people prefer this name to the conventional name, which is *root*. 2. An object on the screen that graphically represents the user in an interactive multiuser dimension (MUD). The user can move around and control this object.

**AVC** See *Association of Visual Communicators.*

**average power** See *apparent power.*

**AVI** See *Audio-Video Interleaved.*

**AWE** See *Advanced WavEffect.*

**A-weighting** See *weighting filters.*

**AWG** See *American wire gauge.*

**awk** (n.) Developed in 1978, an interpreted language for manipulating text. It has been included with many versions of Unix. The name comes from the initials of its authors, Alfred Aho, Peter Weinberger, and Brian Kernighan. The GNU version is called *gawk.* The computing language Perl was inspired in part by awk.

**AWT** See *Abstract Windowing Toolkit.*

# B

**B8ZS** (binary 8 zero substitution *or* bipolar 8 zero substitution) (n.) A process used with DS-1 signals to maintain ones density, in which a special code is substituted for eight consecutive zeros and marked by two bipolar violations. B8ZS allows the use of a full 64kb/s DS-0 for data transmission. This technique is not compatible with older Alternate Mark Inversion (AMI) equipment.

**babbling tributary** (n.) In LAN technology jargon, a workstation that constantly sends meaningless messages.

**backbone** (n., adj.) In relation to networks, the primary trunk or high-speed connection within a network that connects shorter, often slower, stub and transit networks. It carries the heaviest traffic and is the top level in a hierarchical network. Stub and transit networks that connect to the same backbone are guaranteed to be interconnected.

**backbone site** (n.) A major Internet, Usenet, or mail site that processes a great deal of third-party traffic. Important backbone sites since early 1993 include UUNet, the mail machines at the University of California at Berkeley, and the Western Research Laboratories of Digital Equipment Corporation (DEC).

**back channel** (n.) Return connection in a two-way data circuit, such as a coaxial cable or satellite circuit. This upstream channel usually has lower bandwidth than the forward channel.

**backdoor** (n.) A breach that designers or maintainers purposely leave in the security of a system. Some operating systems are shipped with privileged accounts, or backdoors, intended for use by field service technicians or the maintenance programmers. Also referred to as a *trapdoor* or *wormhole*.

**back-electromotive force** (back-emf) (n.) Also known as *back-voltage*, this is a phenomenon found in all moving-coil electromagnetic systems, like loudspeakers. After a signal stops, the speaker cone continues moving, causing the voice coil to move through the magnetic field, creating a new voltage moving in the opposite direction. If the loudspeaker is allowed to do this, the cone vacillates in an undesirable way. To prevent back-emf, the loudspeaker must receive zero ohms from the source. See *damping factor*.

**back-emf** See *back-electromotive force*.

**back end** (n.) Software that performs the last stage of a process, executing a task that is transparent to the user. The term refers to network applications that run on a server without making the client aware of their operations.

**background** (n.) 1. The area of a screen or frame over which images or objects are placed; the most distant element in composite layering. 2. The place where less critical events or operations are conducted during shared processing in a multitasking environment. Print spooling while a document is being edited is an example, as is the ability to receive a facsimile while performing other computing functions.

**background music** (n.) Music without lyrics and typically not performed by the original artist, used to replace silence.

**back light** (v.) To illuminate a subject from behind in a video production or camera shoot, creating a sense of depth by separating the foreground from the background. This process can result in silhouetting if done improperly.

**backplane** (n.) High-speed communications bus to which individual components are connected, such as expansion cards on a PC.

**back up** (v.) To record an archival copy of data on a storage medium.

**backup** (n., adj.) The copy of data that is recorded and stored for archival purposes, typically offline.

**Backus-Naur form** (BNF) (n.) High-level syntax that can be used to express context-free grammars formally. This type of notation is rarely documented but is commonly used to specify the syntax of programming languages. The BNF for a city, state, and zip code would appear as follows:

<address> ::= <city-name> "," <state-code>

<zip-code> <end-of-line-character>

In translation, this would yield the name of a city followed by a comma, a state code, and a zip code followed by an end-of-line (EOL) character.

**bad sector** (n.) Area on the surface of a disk that is unable to hold data reliably due to damaged formatting or a flaw in the medium itself.

**bad track table** (n.) Label attached to a hard disk drive case identifying flawed tracks. The low-level formatting program initially used to define tracks and sectors on the disk contains this information.

**balance control** (n.) Found on professional and consumer stereo preamplifiers, a balance control is used to change the relative power between the left and right channels. One channel is apparently strengthened by attenuating the opposite channel. In analog designs, this is accomplished by the use of a dual potentiometer with an "M-N taper." An M-N taper consists of a "shorted" output for the first 50% of travel and then a linear taper for the last 50% of travel, operating in reverse for each channel. With the control in the center detent position, there is no attenuation of either channel. Rotating it causes one channel to be attenuated, while having no effect on the other channel. Contrast with *crossfader*.

**balanced circuit** (n.) Any circuit in which two branches are electrically alike and symmetrical with respect to a common ground. The two lines in the circuit are driven equally and oppositely with respect to ground. The receiving circuits have matching impedances, which provides common mode rejection. Balanced lines are used to connect speakers and to connect data signals, as in the RS-422 specification. The signal is transmitted over one wire and received back on another wire. The shield does not carry any information, and it must be earth grounded at each end to be successful. The ground is not needed to transmit the signal, only for shielding and safety purposes. In an unbalanced circuit, the signal is transmitted between one wire and the shield cable. The circuit flows through the wire and back through the shield cable connected to ground. The ground serves as the return path, and the circuit does not work without it. A balanced circuit has great common-mode rejection, or noise canceling properties. Induced noise appears equally (commonly) on each wire. A good balanced circuit has exactly equal impedance between each line relative to the ground, with equal noise susceptibility. The balanced input stage amplifies only the difference between the lines and rejects all noise that is common to the lines.

**balanced line** (n.) A grounded line with two conductors that carry equal voltages that are opposite in polarity. In a balanced-to-ground line, the impedance-to-ground levels in both conductors are equal in strength. Audio connections made with this type of line are less susceptible to interference and radio frequency (RF) noise.

**balanced-to-ground** (n.) An implied three-wire circuit, where the impedance-to-ground on one wire equals the impedance-to-ground on the other wire. This is the preferred method of transmitting data, according to the Electronic Industries Association (EIA) RS-422 standard.

**balun** (n.) Abbreviation of balanced-unbalanced, jargon used by radio engineers that refers to the *bal*anced to *un*balanced transformer used to interface with a radio antenna. It also applies to any interface (usually a transformer) between balanced and unbalanced circuits. A balun may also transform impedance, as in a common 300 ohm balanced to 75 ohm unbalanced line converter used to connect balanced twisted-pair cabling with unbalanced coaxial cable.

**band** (n.) Frequency range between two defined limits. The audio band of frequencies that can be detected by the human ear lies between approximately 20 Hz and 20 kHz.

**band-limiting filter** (n.) A low-pass filter and a high-pass filter in series, which act together to restrict the overall frequency range of a system.

**bandpass filter** (n.) 1. A filter that allows a finite number of frequencies to pass through, with neither of the high or low cutoff frequencies set to zero or infinity. The cutoff frequencies in an audio filter are often set to define the half power points, such as plus or minus 3 dB. 2. In an asymmetric digital subscriber line (ADSL), the voice frequency band of 300 Hz is blocked and redirected to a telephone set by a bandpass filter. All other frequencies are passed through to the modem or transceiver. A plain old telephone service (POTS) splitter is essentially a combination low-pass and high-pass filter, in which frequencies below 10 kHz go to the phone service, and frequencies between 15 kHz and 1 MHz go to ADSL.

**bandwidth** (n.) 1. The transmission capacity of an electronic medium, such as network wiring, fiber-optic cable, or microwave links. 2. The range of signal frequencies in which a piece of audio or video gear can operate. 3. The difference between high and low limiting frequencies. See the accompanying table for commonly accepted definitions of bandwidths in telecommunications and broadcasting. The public telephone system has a bandwidth of about 3 kHz. 4. In audio, the numerical difference between the upper and lower cutoff points of a band of frequencies. This number is used to calculate the quality factor, or "Q," of a filter. See figure and table.

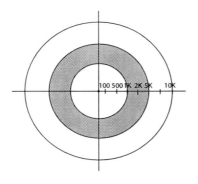

*bandwidth between 1K and 5K is shaded*

**bang path** (n.) A specified series of machine names through which a mail message from one user to another will pass. It is possible to identify an explicit Unix-to-Unix CoPy (UUCP) path through which email is to be routed. See also *mail path* or *Unix-to-Unix CoPy.*

**banner** (n.) 1. Any title page automatically added to a print job by a print spooler. 2. In relation to the Internet, this is a rectangular box that appears on a web page and which is linked to a site. It typically contains a logo and a marketing blurb intended to attract visitors to the site.

**bar** (n.) A unit of atmospheric pressure equal to ten newtons per square centimeter.

**bar code** (n.) A pattern of parallel lines whose variable thickness and separation encode a message that an optical scanner or wand can read and that a computer can then decode. Many businesses use a bar code as a universal product code (UPC) on retail items, and libraries use it to catalog books. It can be used to control videodisc playback as well. See figure.

*bar code*

### Definitions of Bandwidths in Broadcasting and Telecommunications

| Acronym | Definition | Frequency Range |
|---|---|---|
| ELF | Extremely Low Frequency | under 300 Hz |
| ILF | Infra Low Frequency | 300 Hz–3 kHz |
| VLF | Very Low Frequency | 3 kHz–30 kHz |
| LF | Low Frequency | 30 kHz–300 kHz |
| MF | Medium Frequency | 300 kHz–3 MHz |
| HF | High Frequency | 3 MHz–30 MHz |
| VHF | Very High Frequency | 30 MHz–300 MHz |
| UHF | Ultra-High Frequency | 300 MHz–3 GHz |
| SHF | Super High Frequency | 3 GHz–30 GHz |
| EHF | Extremely High Frequency | 30 GHz–300 GHz |

**B**

**barker channel** (n.) Cable TV channel dedicated to promoting pay-per-view events, most often by displaying crawling text.

**barn doors** (n.) A set of folding flaps that cover the front of a video light and are adjusted to control dispersion.

**barrel distortion** (n.) The situation in which the vertical sides of a video display area curve outward. Compare *pincushion distortion.* See figure.

*barrel distortion*

**barrier strip** (n.) Another term for a terminal strip connector.

**baseband** (n.) A transmission medium with capacity for a single channel, often found in a local area network (LAN). In a baseband LAN, the entire capacity of the cable is used to transmit a single digital signal. All data transmitted or received on the cable shares one channel and travels at a very high speed, which allows each device to use the channel for a brief period. All attached devices, such as computers and peripherals, take turns using the same cable. In videoconferencing applications, baseband refers to audio and video signals that are transmitted over separate cables. Compare with *broadband.*

**baseband signaling** (n.) The transmission of a digital or analog signal at its original frequencies in its original form, not altered by modulation.

**base multitimbral specification** (n.) A synthesizer subsystem standard that Multimedia Personal Computer (MPC) audio board manufacturers follow in implementing MIDI playback. According to this specification, three pitched tones are available at once to play up to six notes, and two percussive timbres can play two percussive notes.

**base station** (n.) In telephony, a transmission and reception station for handling cellular traffic, typically with an antenna, a microwave dish, and electronic circuitry. It is also referred to as a cell site, because it holds one or more transmitting (TX) or receiving (RX) cells. Base stations are constructed and placed on structures that are elevated over the coverage area. A group of base stations within an area form a wireless network. Most 800 MHz sites are spaced 6–8 miles apart, and 1900 MHz sites are spaced about 2 miles apart. In wireless LAN applications, a base station is the access point to the LAN.

**BASIC** See *Beginners' All-Purpose Symbolic Instruction Code.*

**Basic Encoding Rules** (BER) (n.) Standard method of encoding data units. This method is described in Abstract Syntax Notation One (ASN/1), which refers to the abstract syntax description language used to encode data, not a specific encoding technique.

**Basic Input/Output System** (BIOS) (n.) A file that contains system control instructions for a microcomputer. Instructions in the ROM of the BIOS help start up a system and define the existing input and output connections.

**Basic Rate Interface** (BRI) (n.) One of the com-

43

mon interfaces used in an Integrated Services Digital Network (ISDN). It consists of two full-duplex bearer B-channels at 64 kilobits per second (Kbps), along with a data D-channel at 16 Kbps. The B-channels can accommodate videoconferencing, voice, or facsimile data, whereas the D-channel handles private data. The BRI "U" interface uses two wires, whereas the BRI "T" interface uses four wires.

**batch compression** (n.) Grouping two or more files together to be compressed sequentially, avoiding the need to start each compression job manually.

**batch file** (n.) In MS-DOS, a text-based file with the file name extension .bat that carries out commands when executed. Batch files can be used to avoid retyping commands, to load other programs, or to change a computer's parameters. Batch processing consists of the continuous execution of a series, or batch, of commands.

**baud** (n.) A communication channel's capacity, as measured in symbols or transitions per second. This measurement is equivalent to bits per second (bps) only for two-level modulation with no framing or stop bits. A symbol is a unique state of the communication channel, distinguishable by the receiver from all other possible states. The term *baud* was originally a unit of telegraph signaling speed, set at one Morse code dot per second. It was proposed at the International Telegraph Conference of 1927 and named after J.M.E. Baudot (1845–1903), the French engineer who constructed the first successful teleprinter. The term *baud* causes much confusion and is usually best avoided. The use of bits per second (bps), bytes per second (Bps), or—more accurately—characters per second (cps) is recommended.

**Baudot code** (n.) Data transfer code used for teletype (TTY), radio teletype (RTTY), and telecommunications devices for the deaf (TDD). This 5-bit code has undergone numerous revisions.

**Baxandall tone control** (n.) A commonly used type of active bass and treble tone control circuit based on research by British engineer P.J. Baxandall in 1952. The Baxandall design exhibits very low harmonic distortion, which is accomplished by using negative feedback.

**bay** (n.) In the physical frame of a microcomputer case, a space for installing an internal drive or a peripheral.

**Bayonet-Neill-Concelman** (BNC) (n.) A round connector attached to the end of a coaxial cable and used in video applications. It is pushed onto the receptacle and then locked with clockwise twisting. See figure.

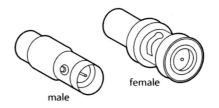

*BNC connectors*

**BBS** See *bulletin board system.*

**BCC** See *blind carbon copy* or *block check character.*

**BCD notation** See *binary-coded decimal notation.*

**B-channel** (n.) An ISDN user channel that carries digital data at 64 kilobits per second (Kbps). It can carry a mixture of data types, including voice data that is encoded with pulse code modulation (PCM).

**B**

**Because It's Time Network** (BITNET) (n.) Network that was widely used by educational institutions in the 1980s and that had nodes on hundreds of college campuses. It was officially discontinued in 1996.

**Beginners' All-Purpose Symbolic Instruction Code** (BASIC) (n.) An algebraic computer programming language that was designed by John G. Kemeny and Thomas E. Kurtz at Dartmouth College in 1963. The language employs "if-then" logic statements and other English commands as well as mathematical formulas. BASIC interpreters became standard features in mainframes and minicomputers.

**bel** (n.) A unit of pressure equal to ten decibels. The term originally was used in telephony to define the amount lost in a signal level over a one-mile distance of telephone wire.

**Bellcore** (n.) Bell Communications Research; a company owned by the seven Regional Bell Operating Companies (RBOCs) that was formed in 1984 with the divestiture of AT&T. Its mission was to provide centralized research and development services for the RBOCs. It has also coordinated communications for the federal government. Bellcore was purchased in 1996 by Science Applications International Corporation (SAIC).

**Bell 43401** (n.) A publication from Bell that defines the requirements for data transmission over DC-continuous, private metallic circuits provided by the telephone company, primarily for limited-distance applications.

**Bell Operating Company** (BOC) (n.) The name of any of the 22 regulated telephone companies formed by the divestiture of the former AT&T Bell System. They were created in December 1983 by a consent decree between AT&T and the U.S. government. As part of this

agreement, they were permitted to carry local (intraLATA) traffic exclusively and forced to hand off long-distance (interLATA) traffic to competitive exchanges (interexchange carriers, or IXCs). The seven Regional Bell Operating Companies (RBOCs) are known as *Baby Bells.* These holding companies are made up of some, but not all, of the 22 BOCs. The RBOCs are Ameritech, Bell Atlantic, BellSouth, NYNEX, Pacific Telesis, SBC Communications, and US West. RBOCs are generally known as *local exchange carriers* (LECs).

**Bell standards** (n.) A set of standards defined by AT&T for modem communications, numbered as follows:

- Bell 103: Any AT&T 300-bps modem that provides asynchronous transmission with both originate and answer capabilities. Frequency shift keying (FSK) type.

- Bell 113: Any AT&T 300-bps modem that provides asynchronous transmission with either originate or answer capabilities, not both. FSK type.

- Bell 201, 201B, and 201C: Any AT&T 2400-bps modem that provides synchronous transmission. 201B applies to full-duplex public telephone line operation; 201C applies to half-duplex public telephone line operation. Differential phase shift keying (DPSK) type.

- Bell 202: Any AT&T 1800-bps modem that provides asynchronous transmission and uses a four-wire circuit for full-duplex operation. Also describes an AT&T 1200-bps modem that provides asynchronous transmission and that uses a two-wire circuit for half-duplex operation. FSK type.

- Bell 208, 208A, and 208B: Any AT&T

4800-bps modem that provides synchronous transmission. Bell 208A refers to leased-line applications, whereas 208B was designed for public telephone line operation. Phase shift keying (PSK) type.

- Bell 209: Any AT&T 9600-bps modem that provides synchronous transmission and that uses a four-wire leased-line circuit for full-duplex operation. Combined PSK and amplitude shift keying (ASK) type or quadrature amplitude modulation (QAM) type.

- Bell 212 and 212A: Any AT&T 1200-bps modem that provides synchronous transmission and that uses a public telephone line for full-duplex operation. PSK type.

**benchmark** (n.) A task or series of tasks used to test the capabilities of a processor or system for speed and performance.

**bending radius** (n.) The least amount of curvature that can be put into a cable under a specified degree of tension. It affects the size of bends in conduits and the size of openings at pull boxes where loops can form. It is a critical aspect of cable deployment, particularly in hybrid fiber networks and fiber-optic cable systems.

**BeOS** (n.) An operating system for desktop computers created by Be, Inc. It is optimized for streaming media, both audio and video. The 64-bit multithreaded system is compatible with multiprocessors and has built-in Internet services in an efficient design.

**BER** See *Basic Encoding Rules* or *bit error rate*.

**Berkeley Internet Name Domain** (BIND) (n.) Domain name system (DNS) developed and distributed by the University of California at Berkeley. It is commonly used by Internet hosts.

**Berkeley Software Distribution** (BSD) (n.) Implementation of the Unix operating system and utilities developed by the University of California at Berkeley. The version number of the distribution is typically used to identify it; 4.3 BSD is version 4.3 of the Berkeley Unix distribution. It is commonly used on machines that serve as an Internet host.

**Bernoulli principle** (n.) The airfoil principle named for the Swiss mathematician Daniel Bernoulli (1700–1782). This principle states that pressure in a fluid decreases with the rate of flow. It has been applied to the design of removable media and disk drives.

**bespoke** (adj.) Describes custom-made computer-based training software or courseware.

**Bessel crossover** (n.) An audio speaker crossover circuit design with flat phase response and decreasing amplitude response. Linear phase response reduces ringing from sudden transitions between signal levels, but it exhibits a sluggish roll-off rate.

**best-effort** (adj.) A phrase used to identify low-priority network traffic on the Internet. Real-time communication, such as video and audio streams that require a minimum bandwidth and latency, is given a higher priority. Email can tolerate an arbitrary delay, so it is classified as a best-effort service.

**betacam** (n.) A professional-quality 0.5-inch video recording and playback format developed by Sony. Betacam is portable and provides video quality comparable to 1-inch videotape. Betacam SP is a higher-quality ver-

**B**

sion that uses true component video signals.

**Betamax** (n., adj.) A consumer videotape format developed by Sony, sometimes referred to as *Beta*. The format calls for 0.5-inch (12.65 mm) tape in a 6-inch x 3.75-inch (155 mm x 95 mm) cassette. Although the format offers superior resolution, it was eclipsed in popularity by the VHS system developed by Matsushita and JVC.

**beta test** (n.) A second and final test for a software product, usually done by actual users in real-world situations with the *beta release*.

**bezel** (n.) The housing that encases the front of a video monitor. Touch screens usually have a large bezel for their controlling electronics. Pronounced "BEHZ-ul."

**Bézier curve** (n.) A graphic element defined by a formula consisting of two anchor points and two vector values, as opposed to a bitmap. See also *vector data*. Pronounced "behz-ee-yay." See figure.

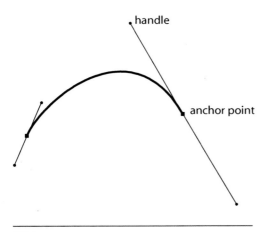

*Bézier curve*

**B-frame** (n.) (Bi-directional frame) An MPEG frame that is defined in part by the difference between both the previous and the following frames. B-frames do not contain enough data to make up an entire picture, and therefore cannot be edited independently.

**BGP** See *Border Gateway Protocol.*

**BGs** (n.) Background sounds that are mixed in an audio production. Typically, they are environmental sounds, such as crowds or outdoor noises, edited to fit the length of a scene or spot. Pronounced "BEE-gees."

**bias** (n.) In audio engineering, a high-frequency signal in the 100 kHz range, recorded on magnetic tape along with the audio signal to compensate for the tape characteristics. The characteristic frequency response would be very narrow if just the audio signal were recorded on tape, and low-frequency distortion would be high. With the bias adjusted properly, the frequency response is relatively flat across the audible range. With bias set too low, bass distortion will be audible, and with too much bias, the high frequency response will drop off. Engineers usually set the bias so that the reproduction of a 10 kHz tone (at 15 ips) is as high as possible, then to increase the bias until the reproduced level drops a small amount. This is called *overbias*. The amount of optimal overbias differs from one tape to another. Bias is necessary because of the phenomenon of inertia. A tape contains many small magnetic particles called domains. These domains are exposed to a magnetic field from the record head and oscillate in polarity as the AC signal voltage changes. These small domains have their own inertia. Each time the analog signal moves from positive to negative and back again, the voltage passes the zero point for an instant. At this moment, the domain is at rest, and there is a short period of inertia before it starts moving again. The high frequency of a bias signal ensures that the domains are always kept in motion, negating the effect of inertia at audio frequencies.

**bid** (v.) To vie for connectivity or access among other competing lines that address the same bus.

**bidirectional** (adj.) 1. Describes the capability to transmit data in two directions, both sending and receiving, but not necessarily the capability to do so simultaneously. 2. Describes a microphone pattern that picks up sounds equally well on the two opposing sides. See *microphone pattern*.

**bifilar windings** (n.) In professional audio, this describes a pair of adjacent wires used to wind a transformer. The technique provides unity coupling and reduces leakage inductance.

**big-endian** (adj.) Describes the method of storing and transmitting binary data so that the most significant bit (or byte) is at the head, or beginning of a packet. The term is adapted from the Lilliputians in *Gulliver's Travels* by Jonathan Swift; they debated whether soft-boiled eggs should be opened at the big end or the little end. Compare *little-endian*.

**big iron** (n.) Fast, powerful computers. The term originally described Cray supercomputers and some IBM mainframes.

**bilinear filtering** (n.) A means of predicting the most appropriate pixel value in a three-dimensional texture on the screen, based on interpolation from the four adjacent pixels in the texture.

**bilinear transform** (n.) A mathematical method used in the transformation of an analog function into an equivalent digital function. In audio applications, a bilinear trans-form ensures that a stable analog filter results in a stable digital filter, preserving the frequency-domain characteristics.

**binary 8 zero substitution** See *B8ZS*.

**binary code** (n.) A code in which each element has one of two possible values, a 1 or a 0, expressed by the presence or absence of a pulse or a high- or low- voltage level in the circuitry.

**binary-coded decimal notation** (BCD notation) (n.) A binary number system in which each digit in decimal notation is represented by adding four digits in binary notation. Multiple sets of four-digit groupings are used to represent larger decimal numbers. The weighting of binary digits in each column is 8, 4, 2, 1. The number five, 0101, is the result of adding 4 plus 1. Here are more examples:

| | | | |
|---|---|---|---|
| 0 = 0000 | 9 = 1001 | | |
| 1 = 0001 | 10 = 0001 | 0000 | |
| 2 = 0010 | 11 = 0001 | 0001 | |
| 3 = 0011 | 23 = 0010 | 0011 | |
| 4 = 0100 | 48 = 0100 | 1000 | |
| 5 = 0101 | 76 = 0111 | 0110 | |
| 6 = 0110 | 99 = 1001 | 1001 | |
| 7 = 0111 | 213 = 0010 | 0001 | 0011 |
| 8 = 1000 | 952 = 1001 | 0101 | 0010 |

**binary digit** (bit) (n.) A numeral in the base-two binary notation system; a 1 or a 0.

**binary file** (n.) A file that contains nontextual data, such as an image or an application.

**binary notation** (n.) The base-two numbering system that uses the digits 1 and 0. This system can be used to represent any type of data. Logic circuits can define these two digits as different states in many ways. Binary notation is not divided into discrete groups of four digits like binary-coded decimal notation. The value of each column increases by a power of two, from right to left (1, 2, 4, 8, 16, 32, 64). Here are examples:

| | |
|---|---|
| 0 = 0000 | 10 = 1010 |
| 1 = 0001 | 11 = 1011 |
| 2 = 0010 | 12 = 1100 |
| 3 = 0011 | 13 = 1101 |
| 4 = 0100 | 14 = 1110 |
| 5 = 0101 | 16 = 10000 |
| 6 = 0110 | 32 = 100000 |
| 7 = 0111 | 37 = 100101 |
| 8 = 1000 | 64 = 1000000 |
| 9 = 1001 | 74 = 1001010 |

**binary phase shift keying** (BPSK) (n.) Digital modulation scheme used for upstream signaling on hybrid fiber-coax (HFC) networks.

**binary synchronous communication** (BSC; bisync, pronounced "BYE-sink") (n.) An industry-standard IBM communications protocol that is character- or byte-oriented. A defined set of control characters is used to synchronize the transmission of binary-coded data between two stations, both of which must be synchronized prior to data transmission.

**binary transfer** (n.) A method of transferring information between computers that involves the use of error correction protocol, such as XModem or Systems Network Architecture (SNA). This method is useful if the data is not purely text-based ASCII characters.

**binaural audio** (n.) Two audio tracks that are recorded with special microphone placement for each track to give the listener a perception of depth, or three-dimensional sound, when the tracks are played back together. This is different from simple stereo audio.

**BIND** See *Berkeley Internet Name Domain.*

**BinHex** (n.) Process that converts an eight-bit file into a seven-bit ASCII code with the file name extension .hqx. A file is converted to lines of letters, numbers, and punctuation. BinHex files can be sent through email systems and stored on any type of computer, because they consist exclusively of text and do not require that a system be "eight-bit clean." Converting a file to text makes it larger, so it takes longer to transmit a BinHex type of file.

**BIOS** See *Basic Input/Output System.*

**bipolar** (b) (adj.) In semiconductors, a design based on the flow of current across a PN junction. See *PNP.*

**bipolar 8 zero substitution** See *B8ZS.*

**bipolar transmission** (n.) A signaling method used in digital transmission in which a signal carrying a binary value alternates between positive and negative polarities. The signal amplitude can represent a 0 or 1 at either polarity, and the spaces with no value are represented by zero amplitude.

**bis** (n.) The second version of an original CCITT standard. In common usage, the term appears after the "V.x" designation, as in "V.42bis," which refers to a modem specification. The third version in a succession is referred to as "V.xter," as in "V.27ter."

**B-ISDN** See *Broadband Integrated Services Digital Network.*

**bisync** See *binary synchronous communication.*

**bit** (n.) Binary digit; representing a single unit (either 0 or 1) of data, it is the smallest unit in computer information handling. Computer processing capability is evaluated by the number of bits handled at once. PCs use 8-, 16-, 32-, or 64-bit microprocessors.

**bit-block transfer** (n.) A technique for moving pixel blocks in memory onto a monitor. More efficient than moving individual bits or bytes, this method is referred to as *blitting*.

**bit clock** (n.) A synchronizing signal that serves as a reference for the rate of individual data bits moving through an interface.

**bit depth** (n.) On computer monitors, each pixel can be represented by a variable number of bits used to describe the pixel's color. Bit depth is the number of bits used in this capacity. A bit depth of two means that only black or white pixels can be shown, a bit depth of four allows the display of 16 colors, a bit depth of eight allows 256 colors, a bit depth of 16 represents 65 536 colors, and 24-bit color yields 16.7 million colors.

**bit error** (n.) A case in which the value of an encoded bit is altered in transmission, and it is interpreted incorrectly by the receiver.

**bit error rate** (BER) (n.) A unit of measurement defining the number of bit writing errors compared with the total number of bits received during a transmission, or the percentage of bits in error found in a given volume or area of storage medium.

**bitmap** (n.) 1. An image defined by discrete values that are assigned to each pixel. 2. A common PC graphics file format in which the image is stored as a pattern of dots with the file name extension .bmp.

**BITNET** See *Because It's Time Network*.

**bit-oriented** (adj.) Describes a communications protocol or transmission procedure in which control information is encoded in fields of one or more bits. It is intended for full-duplex link operation. Bit orientation requires less overhead and is more efficient than byte oriented protocols.

**bit rate** (n.) The speed at which data is moved, expressed in bits per second (bps). If a file size is known and the data transfer rate at which it streams is known, it is possible to determine the duration of time that an audio or video file will play, based on its size. To calculate the duration of playback for an existing MPEG file of known size and bit rate, divide the file size by the data transfer rate. A 5-MB (megabyte) file equals 5000 KB (kilobytes). If the data transfer rate is 150 KBps, the 5000-KB file contains 33 seconds of running video (5000 divided by 150). A bit rate expressed in megabits per second (Mbps) is a factor of 8.192 times the same rate expressed in kilobytes per second (KBps), because a kilobyte is equal to 1024 bits times 8.

**bits per inch** (bpi) (n.) The number of units of binary data that can be written within the area of a square inch on the surface of a disk or other type of storage medium.

**bits per second** (bps) (n.) A rate of data transfer, not to be confused with Bps, which refers to bytes per second.

**bitstream transmission** (n.) The transmission of characters at a fixed rate of speed. No stop and start elements are used, and there are no pauses between bits of data in the stream.

**bit stuffing** (n.) The process of adding bits, or marks, to a data stream. It is used in bit-oriented data link protocols to prevent the "flag" sequence (01111110) from entering the data block. It is also used to balance the input/output (I/O) flow in asynchronous data communications buffers for DS-2 and DS-3 applications.

**BlackBerry** (n.) A two-way wireless device developed by Research in Motion in Ontario, Canada. The device allows users to receive email and voice mail (translated into text) and page other users over a wireless network service. Also known as a RIM device, it has a miniature QWERTY keyboard for typing messages. It uses the Short Messaging Service protocol (SMS). To transmit data, BlackBerry users must subscribe to a wireless service.

**black box** (n.) An electronic circuit or assembly that can be isolated from a system in order to perform a special function, such as controlling an external peripheral.

**blackburst** (n.) Also known as *house sync,* a timing signal or clock reference consisting of a video signal without a picture or any positional information.

**blanking interval** (n.) 1. In a video display, the short duration at the end of a scan line when the signal is suppressed and when the beam repositions itself. 2. The time it takes a video player to locate the next frame to display. See figure.

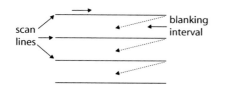

*blanking interval between scan lines*

**bleed** (n.) The blurring of color borders in a video image or in printed graphics. The result is color that overruns its defined boundary.

**blending** (n.) The combination of two pixels in the context of a graphic.

**blind carbon copy** (BCC) (n.) Part of an email header that lists addresses to which a message should be sent but that will not be seen by all recipients. It is defined in RFC 822 and supported by many mail systems.

**blinkenlights** (n.) Humorous jargon for front-panel lights found on electronic equipment.

**block** (n.) 1. In a CD-ROM or CD-i, the user data portion of a logical sector. 2. Any group of bits transmitted as a unit or packet. It contains control delimiters at the beginning and end, a header, a data stream, and check characters used for error correction.

**block check character** (BCC) (n.) A control character appended to each packet of data that is transmitted in blocks. The BCC allows the receiver to check for errors and request retransmission if necessary.

**block diagram** (n.) Rough graphical layout of a system's logical structure.

**block error correct** (v.) To add 276 bytes of error correction code to the end of each block of data while premastering a CD-ROM, allowing errors in the user data block to be corrected.

**blocking** (n.) The inability of a network, switch, or access node to grant service to a requesting user due to the unavailability of a transmission channel.

**Blue Book standard** (n.) 1. The format used by CDs that are designed for laser disc players. 2. One of the four standard references from Adobe Systems on the page-layout and graphics-control language PostScript. The other guides are known as the Green Book, the Red Book, and the White Book.

**blue screen** (n.) A solid blue background used

when shooting video with special lighting so that the background can be "keyed" out, leaving only the subject, which may be placed over any background of the compositor's choice. This is the technique used by television weather forecasters, who appear with a map juxtaposed behind them.

**blue screen of death** (n.) Jargon for the condition of a monitor after a Windows NT system suffers an error from which it cannot recover.

**Bluetooth** (n.) In 1998, Intel and Microsoft established an industry consortium that included IBM, Toshiba, Ericsson, and Nokia with the goal of standardizing data transfer and synchronization between various mobile devices over short distances. The consortium named their technology after BlueTooth, the 10th century Danish king who unified Denmark. The technology itself is intended to provide a single protocol through which digital devices may communicate. The Bluetooth consortium listed over 1800 members in 2001.

Bluetooth is a standard for wireless communications between devices in a personal area network (PAN) using radio frequency for a range of approximately 10 meters. The technology uses radio waves in the 2.4 GHz band. No line of sight is required. It operates in a confined area, but supports multipoint connections, not just point-to-point. Bluetooth can support data transfer rates of 1 to 2 Mbps, with higher speeds expected as the technology evolves. Any two devices that follow the standard can communicate and exchange data without a connecting cable. A group of devices, such as a mobile phone, a digital camera, and a handheld computer could network with each other simultaneously if they were all compatible with the standard.

Several manufacturers, including Intel, have designed the sending and receiving radio frequency chip sets for installation in Bluetooth appliances. In 2002 it is expected that products deploying the technology will be available to consumers. Component products that can be integrated into finished products are available now. Version 1.1 of the specification was released in April 2001.

**Blumlein, Alan Dower** (1903–1942) An English engineer who over 15 years participated in writing 128 patents. He developed stereophonic sound, designed new uses for microphones, and designed a lateral disc-cutting system that made vinyl records possible. He also helped develop the 405-line TV system broadcast used in Great Britain and improved radar system designs.

**blur filter** (n.) A type of image filter that averages pixels together to soften the picture. It is used to minimize subtle differences between frames of compressed video.

**BMP** (n.) A three-character MS-DOS extension at the end of a file name that identifies the file as containing a bitmapped pattern (for example, filename.bmp).

**BNC** See *Bayonet-Neill-Concelman.*

**BNF** See *Backus-Naur form.*

**board** (n.) Short for printed circuit board; an internal plug-in unit with printed circuit wiring and components. It can control some essential function of the computer's central processor or provide a special feature, such as telecommunications, audio, or video control and display. Also known as a *card.*

**boat anchor** (n.) Jargon for obsolete hardware.

**BOC** See *Bell Operating Company.*

**bomb** (n., v.) Synonym for crash, referring to the failure of software or the operating system.

**bonding** (n.) Also referred to as "dial-in channel aggregation," this takes place at the customer premises through inverse multiplexing. The process splits a high-bandwidth signal for transport through the network over multiple lower-bandwidth channels. At the receiving end, the lower-bandwidth signals are recombined into the original high-bandwidth signal. The industry standards for inverse multiplexing ISDN connections are defined by the Bandwidth On Demand Interoperability Group (BONDING) Consortium and are listed in ISO 13871.

**bookmark** (n.) A pointer or reference to an HTML document. In Netscape Navigator, a user can archive a bookmark. In MS Internet Explorer, a bookmark is stored in the *Favorites* directory.

**Boolean algebra** (n.) Named for the logician George Boole (1815–1864), this term means two-valued logic in computer science. Boole's work, which inspired the descriptive term in mathematics, concerned the algebra of sets, involving the operations of intersection, union, and complement of sets.

**Boolean operator** (n.) A qualifying term that refines a definition. Examples include "AND" (items that include both terms that appear in a query), "NOT" (items that contain one term but not another), and "OR" (items that are derived from either class defined). In general, a Boolean operator is a variable that can accept only true or false values.

**Boolean search** (n.) A type of search for information in which qualifiers such as "AND," "OR," and "NOT" are used.

**boost/cut equalizer** (n.) A common type of graphic EQ with 10 to 31 bands on 1-octave to 1/3-octave spacing. The output is flat with all sliders in the center détente position. Each frequency range has bandpass filters that boost signals when the sliders are raised and attenuate signals when sliders are lowered.

**boot** (v.) To start a computer and prepare it to process commands by loading the operating system.

**boot record** (n.) Under the ISO 9660 standard, the record that identifies the location of a boot file on a CD-ROM. This file contains an operating system that can be loaded.

**boot sequence** (n.) The sequence in which a microprocessor receives instructions from ROM to check its circuits and then tries to load files from a disk drive. It initially tries the A: (floppy) drive, and if the necessary files are not found, it tries to read from the C: (first hard disk) drive.

**boot virus** (n.) An MS-DOS virus that infects the boot record program on hard disks and floppy disks or that infects the master boot record on hard disks and that is loaded into memory before MS-DOS. The virus takes control of the computer, infecting any floppy disks subsequently inserted.

**Border Gateway Protocol** (BGP) (n.) Exterior gateway protocol defined in RFCs 1267 and 1268 by the Internet Engineering Task Force (IETF).

**bot** (n.) Truncation of *robot;* a term most often found in multiuser dimensions (MUDs) and Internet Relay Chats (IRCs). It refers to a character that is not a person but rather a collection of responses from a computer program.

**bottleneck** (n.) Refers to any point in a system that responds more slowly than the rest of the system, causing overall delays.

**Boucherot cell** See *Zobel network.*

**bounce** (v.) 1. To mix two or more audio tracks into one. Also called *ping-ponging.* 2. To return a piece of email because of a delivery error.

**bound variable** (n.) In programming logic, a quantified variable. It is a formal argument in a function that is replaced by the actual argument when the function is applied.

**boundary node** (n.) In the IBM Simple Network Architecture (SNA), this is a subarea node that can provide certain protocol support for adjacent subarea nodes. This node can transform network addresses to local addresses, and vise versa. It can also perform session-level sequencing and flow control for other incapable peripheral nodes.

**Bourne shell** (n.) The first command line interpreter shell and script language for Unix, written by S. R. Bourne of Bell Laboratories in 1978. The Berkeley C shell is more widely used today.

**bpi** See *bits per inch.*

**bps** See *bits per second.*

**Bps** See *bytes per second.*

**BPSK** See *binary phase shift keying.*

**branch** (v.) To leap from one location in a program to another, based on programmed responses to user input.

**branching point** (n.) A path that a user can choose, given two or more directions or destinations.

**branch prediction** (n.) A function that a microprocessor with "instruction pre-fetch" performs by guessing whether or not a branch will be taken and by fetching the anticipated code in advance from its location. A branch instruction and the instruction that immediately follows it are stored in the *branch target buffer.* Based on this pattern, the microprocessor predicts which way the instruction will branch the next time it is executed. A pipeline break is avoided when a branching prediction is correct.

**breach** (n.) In network security, a violation of the controls of an information system. It may expose and compromise information or system components. In general, a breach is any successful defeat of security controls resulting in penetration of the system.

**break** (v.) 1. To stop a program in progress temporarily to debug. The point at which it stops is the *breakpoint.* 2. To send an RS-232 break of two character widths over a serial line.

**BRender** (n.) A three-dimensional Application Programming Interface (API) provided by Argonaut, a British game developer. Pronounced "BE-render."

**BRI** See *Basic Rate Interface.*

**bridge** (n.) 1. A connecting device between two or more subnetworks, or local area networks (LANs), that run similar cabling and protocols. It uses the bottom two layers of the Open Systems Interconnection (OSI) model to create an extended network on which workstations on different subnetworks can share data. 2. A balanced electrical network, such as the

Wheatstone bridge.

**bridge disc**(n.) A technique for storing data on a CD-ROM XA disc that allows the data to be played back on several platforms. A Photo-CD is a type of bridge disc that can be played on a CD-i or Photo-CD player, as well as on a multiple-session CD-ROM drive.

**bridge/router** (n.) A sophisticated networking device that performs the functions of a bridge, a router, or both simultaneously. It can route multiple protocols, such as TCP/IP and XNS, while bridging other traffic.

**bridge tap** (n.) In telecommunications, a segment of cable not on a direct path between a central office (CO) and a subscriber.

**broadband** (adj.) Describes any transmission medium that supports a wide frequency range, including audio and video frequencies. It can be multiplexed to carry several independent channels, each in its own bandwidth. Broadband transmission is often in the range of 1 MHz or more. At the minimum, the term refers to bandwidth greater than that required for voice, which telecommunications standards have set at 4 kHz. ISDN is considered a broadband medium. Cable television employs broadband techniques to send multiple channels over a single cable. Compare *baseband*.

**Broadband Integrated Services Digital Network** (B-ISDN) (n.) ISDN services offered at rates higher than the Primary access rate (23B+D) of 1.544 Mbps or 2.048 Mbps. Proposed broadband ISDN service is defined by CCITT as switched services from 150–600 Mbps) using cell-relay technology or ATM.

**broadband LAN** (n.) A local area network

(LAN) that is distributed via broadband coaxial cable, often using CATV technology and broadband modems. It is most commonly used with Ethernet (CSMA/CD) and token bus.

**broadband PCS** (BPCS) (n.) Services that transmit voice, data, and multimedia information. Messaging, caller ID, and voice-mail are typically supported by broadband PCS services over frequency bands in the 1850–2200 MHz range.

**broadband wireless** (n.) A generic term for high-speed wireless transmission at rates above 250 kbps. Broadband for wired connections is generally considered above 1.5 Gbps.

**broadcast** (v.) 1. To transmit television and radio programs through the air. 2. In network applications, to forward a message to numerous destinations.

**broadcast quality** (n.) Loosely defined, the level of quality at which television stations will transmit, adhering to the NTSC format in the United States. This format calls for 525 lines of video at a rate of 60 fields per second, with the appropriate levels of brightness and color (luma and chroma).

**browse** (v.) To scan networked information with no particular target in mind.

**browser** (n.) 1. Software that allows a user to search through information on a server. The term usually refers to a universal client application, such as Netscape Navigator or MS Internet Explorer, that interprets HTML documents. 2. The name Eastman Kodak uses on Photo-CDs for the database program that lets users search for images by keyword or title.

**brute force** (n.) A way of programming that

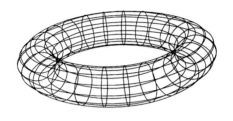

*torus formed by a bicubic B-spline surface*

relies on a computer's processing power instead of elegant technique or useful abstraction.

**BSC** See *binary synchronous communication*.

**BSD** See *Berkeley Software Distribution*.

**B-spline** (n.) A basic spline from which an approximated curve is derived, typically used in the creation of wire-frame models for a dimensional figure. See figure.

**bubble memory** (n.) A filmlike storage device made of materials that are easily magnetized in just one direction, either upward or downward. When a magnetic field is imposed on the film, the areas in opposite alignment to the field shrink to bubbles. Bubble memory is nonvolatile and requires very low power levels but is not as fast as electrically erasable programmable read-only memory (EEPROM).

**buffer** (n.) 1. Memory space that temporarily stores a small amount of data to help compensate for differences in the rate at which one device transfers data to another. A buffer can also be used to store small bits of data that are used repeatedly (such as a digitized beep or some other sound). Most CD-ROM drives have buffers. 2. A storage space in which data is held temporarily until it is passed to or from a host computer or peripheral device.

**buffer amplifier** (n.) Any amplifier in which the reaction of output-load-impedance variation on the input circuit is reduced to a minimum for isolation purposes. It isolates the loading effects of the output stage on the input stage, separating the two. Both analog and digital circuits use buffers to minimize similar loading effects.

**buffer overflow** (n.) A condition that occurs when an attempt is made to store more data in a buffer than it can handle. This results from using a buffer too small to hold all the data that must accumulate before a piece of it can be processed. The overflow may be caused by a mismatch in the processing rates of the producing and consuming processes.

**bug** (n.) An undesirable aspect of a software or hardware system that may cause it to malfunction.

**build** (n.) An interim version of software in which bugs are resolved and features are refined prior to release.

**bulletin board system** (BBS) (n.) An accessible computing system that provides an electronic database. Users can log into the BBS and leave messages for a group, or they can download files. Topic groups are usually established, allowing any user to submit or read a message. A BBS often offers users archives of files, personal email, and other services, depending on the preferences of the system operator, or *sysop*. There are thousands of local bulletin board systems run by hackers from their homes.

**bulletproof** (adj.) Describes an extremely robust, crash-resistant software development with great powers of recovery. Synonymous with *armor-plated.*

**bump** (v.) To adjust the timing between audio and video tracks in precise framing units while both are running. Frequently used to fine-tune lip sync and to position sound effects.

**bump map** (n.) A texture map that can be applied to the surface of a three-dimensional image to simulate natural surfaces, patterns, or imperfections.

**bundled title** (n.) A CD-ROM that is packaged with hardware components, peripherals, or entire systems and that is not priced separately from the other items.

**burn-in** (n.) An initial period of operation in which a manufacturer or reseller screens equipment and circuits for problems and establishes that components are stable.

**burst** (n.) In color television reception, a signal that provides a reference for the 3.58-MHz oscillator. The signal is sent during the vertical blanking interval (VBI).

**burst EDO DRAM** (n.) Burst Extended Data Out Dynamic Random Access Memory; a type of EDO DRAM in which read or write cycles are batched in bursts of four. Burst EDO bus speeds range from 40 MHz to 66 MHz, much faster than the 33 MHz that is available with the use of fast page-mode RAM or EDO DRAM.

**burst error** (n.) An error that contains a group of consecutive bits, often because of scratches on the surface of a CD-ROM.

**bus** (n.) 1. The connection or path between the CPU and the input/output (I/O) devices or the connection between two processors. Types of buses that have traditionally been used in IBM-compatibles include ISA, VESA, and PCI. The NuBus system was used on older Macintosh computers. In 1995, Apple Computer replaced the NuBus with the 64-bit PCI bus in selected Power Macintosh models. Today, USB is the most widely used bus in computer applications, with Firewire (IEEE 1394) gaining popularity. 2. A signal- or power-transmitting conduit that allows two or more lines to be connected and their signals to be mixed.

**bus architecture** (n.) A set of connections between functional units in a computer. Buses exist within the central processing unit (CPU), connecting it to external memory and peripheral devices. The width of the bus determines the size in bits of the largest data unit it can carry. The bus width and the number of data units transmitted per second determine a computer's performance. Most microprocessors have 32-bit buses both internally and externally. The internal bus in most microcomputers is wider than the external bus.

**bus master** (n.) In a microcomputer, this device drives both the address bus and bus control signals at some point in time. In a simple architecture, only the central processing unit (CPU) can be the bus master, so all communications between input/output (I/O) devices (slaves) must involve the CPU. Advanced architectures allow other capable devices or processors to control the bus. Direct memory access (DMA) is a basic form of bus mastering, in which the CPU sets up the I/O device to read from contiguous blocks of memory and to signal the CPU when it has done so. Full bus mastering indicates that an I/O device is capable of performing complex sequences without CPU intervention.

**Butterworth crossover** (n.) An audio crossover circuit that uses low-pass filters to achieve flat magnitude response. It is based on Butterworth polynomials, named after the British engineer S. Butterworth, who first described these equations in 1930.

**button** (n.) A graphic component of an interface that represents some embedded function. When clicked, a button can branch the user to another location in the program.

**buyout music** (n.) Audio tracks sold with a license that allows the purchaser to duplicate and use them in productions without paying royalties.

**by hand** (adv.) Describes a way of performing a repetitive or tedious operation that could be done automatically by a computer but that a programmer performs step by step. For example, HTML can either be created by an editing program or coded by hand.

**bypass mode** (n.) An operating mode on ring networks, such as Fiber Distributed Data Interface (FDDI), and on token ring networks. In this mode, an interface is removed, or bypassed, from the ring.

**byte** (n.) A measurable number of consecutive bits that are usually treated as a unit. Bytes of eight bits usually represent either one character or two digits. A computer's storage capacity or memory is figured in kilobytes (KB). One KB equals 1024 bits, or 2 to the 10th power.

**byte aligned** (adj.) Describes information in memory that is located an exact multiple of eight bits from the starting point.

**bytecode** (n.) A portable file format into which Java programs are compiled. The bytecode is distributed to a computer that interprets it into native processor instructions on the fly as the Java program is executed.

**bytecode compiler** (n.) A translator that outputs a Java program in bytecode intended for interpretation by a bytecode interpreter. The same bytecode can be executed on any processor on which the bytecode interpreter runs, which is an advantage over outputting machine code for each particular processor on which the code will run. The Java engine compiles bytecode for the Java Virtual Machine (JVM).

**bytes per second** (Bps) (n.) A rate of data transfer, not to be confused with bps, which refers to bits per second.

# C

c See *centi-*.

C See *Celsius*.

C (n.) Programming language created by Dennis Ritchie at AT&T Bell Labs in 1972. It was intended for systems programming on the PDP-11 computer and was used to reimplement Unix. C is a terse, low-level, permissive language. It is the dominant language in systems and microcomputer applications programming because it is transportable and easily adapted to new environments. The original C has been standardized and modified to become ANSI C.

C++ (n.) A superset of the C language developed by Bjarne Stroustrup at AT&T Bell Laboratories in 1986. C++ is one of the most popular object-oriented languages. In C++, a *class* is a user-defined type. Constructors and destructors are member functions called to create or destroy instances. C++ allows implicit type conversion and default function arguments. It permits the overloading of both operators and function names. In May 1989, version 2.0 added such features as multiple inheritance, type-safe linkage, pointers to members, and abstract classes.

cable 1. (n.) Any kind of wire or cord used to transmit signals or connect equipment. Cables can contain single or multiple wires and are shielded to reduce interference. Most cables allocate at least one wire as a ground. Coaxial cable is used for video applications. 2. (adj.) Describes local television service delivered over cable rather than broadcast through the air.

cable loss (n.) Attenuation of a signal's strength as it travels through a cable. Higher frequencies suffer from greater loss than lower frequencies in coaxial cables.

cable modem (n.) A device that enables a user to connect a computer to the coaxial cable provided by a cable television (CATV) network. A special type of modem must be installed at the cable provider's site, or headend, which turns the cable system into a local area network (LAN) that can serve digital programming as well as access to digital services, such as a web server. Cable modems are capable of multimegabit data transfer and do not require connection and disconnection to the network for each session, since they are always online. The service is asymmetric, with a downstream rate of transfer to the user that is faster than the upstream rate. A different modulation scheme is used for traffic in each direction. Available bandwidth from the cable provider is shared by all users on a circuit, and data throughput is reduced as the number of users increases.

A group of cable television providers has formed

a working group, Data Over Cable Service Interface Specifications (DOCSIS), to formalize standards in this emerging technology.

**cable tap** (n.) In an Ethernet network, a device that connects a transceiver to the main cable.

**cable television** (CATV) (n.) Local television service delivered over cable rather than broadcast through the airwaves. It was called *Community Antenna Television* before the installation of cable.

**cache** (n.) A portion of processor memory that holds recently accessed data, designed to speed up subsequent access to the same data. When data is read from or written to main memory, a copy is saved in the cache, along with its address in main memory. The cache monitors the address of subsequent reads to determine whether the data requested is already in the cache. If it is, the situation is referred to as a *cache hit,* and the instruction to read the data from main memory is aborted. If a *cache miss* occurs, the data is fetched from main memory and saved in the cache. Typically, a cache is constructed with faster memory chips than those in the main memory, so a cache hit returns data much more quickly than normal memory access does. When a processor writes to main memory, the data is first written to the cache on the assumption that it will be read again soon. In a *write-through cache,* data is written to main memory at the same time as it is cached. In a *write-back cache,* data is written to main memory only when it is forced out of the cache. Pronounced "CASH."

**cache line** (n.) The smallest unit of memory that can be transferred between main memory and a cache. A whole line is read and cached at once from main memory, rather than just a single word or byte. This takes advantage of page-mode Dynamic RAM (DRAM), permit-

ting faster access to consecutive locations.

**caching** (n.) The use of memory or disk storage to speed data processing. Frequently used data is temporarily stored where it can be quickly accessed later.

**CAD/CAM** See *computer-aided design/computer-aided manufacturing.*

**caddy** (n.) The case or cartridge used to enclose the medium in early CD-ROM drives. Late model drives are caddiless, so the CD rests in an open tray.

**CAI** See *computer-aided instruction.*

**CAL** See *computer-aided learning.*

**call** (n., v.) In computer programming, to invoke a procedure or subroutine and to transfer control to it. Ordinarily, control is returned to the program at the instruction immediately after the point from which the call was made.

**callback modem** (n.) A modem that returns a call and opens a connection if the security code input during a dialup session is authorized for access. A callback modem is often used to verify a caller's identity before granting access to secure information.

**call setup** (n.) The process of establishing a connection between two devices. In the voice network, call setup is achieved by interpreting the dialed number and establishing a connection between the caller and the destination. The process for a data call is similar, but it requires negotiation of other parameters.

**CAM** See *computer-aided manufacturing.*

**camcorder** (n.) Contraction of *camera* and *recorder;* portable videotaping gear. The usual formats are VHS and 8 mm, along with their higher-resolution versions, S-VHS and Hi-8. VHS-Compact (VHS-C) is a smaller version of VHS. Sony refers to its professional digital video camera as DVCAM.

**cameo lighting** (n.) Illumination of foreground subjects with a directional light on a stark black background.

**Cannon plug** (n.) See *XLR connector.*

**CAP** See *competitive access provider* or *carrierless amplitude/phase.*

**capacitance** (n.) 1. The degree to which a substance or device conducts or passes electricity. 2. The ability to store an electric charge, measured in farads.

**capacitor** (n.) One of the components in a circuit that stores voltage, acting like a holding tank. The charge is released when it is triggered.

**capacity** (n.) In telecommunications, the quantity of traffic a facility can carry. The measurement depends on the type of facility. Data lines are measured in bits per second (bps). Switch capacity is measured by the maximum number of calls a facility can switch in an hour or the number it can maintain simultaneously. Coaxial cable and wireless communications systems are measured in bandwidth.

**capstan** (n.) A roller or spindle that controls the speed and movement of magnetic tape through a recorder or player. See figure.

**carbon-based life form** (n.) Jargon for human being. Compare *silicon-based life form.*

**card** (n.) Short for printed circuit board; an

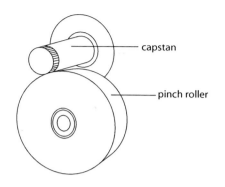

*capstan*

internal plug-in unit with connections between components traced on the surface of the board. A card can control some essential function of the computer's central processor or provide a special feature, such as telecommunications, audio, or video control and display. Also known as a *board.*

**cardinality** (n.) According to set theory, the number of elements in a set. Two sets with the same number of elements have the same cardinality, which is known as *bijection.*

**carpal tunnel syndrome** (n.) The swelling of tendons in the wrist, compressing the median nerve and causing pain and numbness in the hand. Poor posture at a computer terminal may result in strain and could contribute to this ailment.

**carriage return** (CR) (n.) A control character in EBCDIC or ASCII code that positions the cursor at the left margin.

**carrier band** (n.) Frequency range that can be modulated to carry information on a given transmission system.

**carrier detect signal** (n.) Signal that tells attached data terminal equipment (DTE) that a modem is receiving a signal from another modem. Also called a *received line-signal*.

**carrierless amplitude/phase** (CAP) (n.) A variant of quadrature amplitude modulation (QAM), this form of modulation is used for telecommunications line coding. CAP was the industry standard for early deployment of ADSL, and is used in voice-band modems. Some telecommunications providers use CAP modulation for signal transmission.

**carrier sense multiple access with collision detection** (CSMA/CD) (n.) A Media Access Control (MAC) technology in which all devices attached to a local network listen for transmissions in progress before attempting to transmit. If two or more devices begin transmitting at the same time, each defers for a random period of time before attempting to transmit again. CSMA/CD is used in Ethernet and packet radio applications.

**carrier signal** (n.) A constant sine wave that can be modulated with a second signal that contains data. The high-pitched tone that a modem emits is an audible carrier signal. Changes, or modulation, in the carrier's amplitude, frequency, or phase can convey information.

**carrier wave** (n.) Generated at a transmitting station, a radio frequency wave on which signal information is modulated.

**cascade** (v.) With reference to hardware, to connect numerous multiple-port devices in order to expand the number of ports or available input/output (I/O) lines.

**Cascading Style Sheets** (CSS) (n.) A World Wide Web Consortium (W3C) recommendation that provides a method of defining the layout and presentation features of an HTML document. Specifications about how a page should look in terms of headings, indents, margins, fonts, and all matters related to appearance may be placed in a single location and are referenced by the page. Alternatively, a style feature, such as colored text, may be designated before each tag it affects in an *inline style sheet*. In the example below, the heading "Welcome to our site" would appear in blue letters:

```
<H1 style="color:blue">Welcome to our site</H1>
```

It is more efficient to embed all style definitions at the head of a document, defining what color each level of headings should be. This is called an *embedded style sheet*. A style class can be invented and applied to any tag. Class names begin with a period, and their function is enclosed in braces. Here is a simple example of an embedded style sheet:

```
<STYLE type="text/css"> H1 { color: blue }
H1.yellow { color: yellow } </STYLE>
```

In this example, first-level headings (H1) appear in blue letters, and headings of the new class called H1.yellow appear in yellow letters.

A style sheet can be linked to a page yet stored in a file by itself. When a text file contains all the information that would be included in an embedded style sheet and when the <LINK> tag is used, the file (named style.css, for example) will behave as though it were embedded. The page can reference this style sheet if the following line is placed at the head of the document:

```
<LINK rel="stylesheet" href="style.css"
type="text/css">
```

The cascading function arises from a hierarchy in which the browser follows directions. Browser defaults are the most general style rules, which are overruled by definitions in a style sheet. Inline rules stated at the tag level take precedence, followed by an embedded style sheet, followed by a linked style sheet. A class definition overrules the default presentation for a tag, and inline style definitions overrule everything else. The level of control is really what cascades.

**Cascading Style Sheet Properties** (n.) CSS properties specify individual characteristics of HTML elements. Styles dictate features of formatting and behaviors, such as the font size, the color of an object, and the distance from surrounding elements. A list of CSS properties is shown below, followed by a detailed description of each.

## Color and Background Properties

Color and background style properties control the color of text in an element and the background color or image displayed behind the element. Additional properties may be specified to control the position and appearance of a background image.

- color
- background-color
- background-image
- background-repeat
- background-attachment
- background-position
- background

### Color, Background-Color
*Values*: red, #FF0000, FF0000, rgb(255,0,0), rgb(75%,0,50%)

The name of the color, the hexadecimal value of the color, the RGB (red, green, blue) values, or the RGB percentages may be used to specify a color. The value *transparent* is the default background-color value. Recognized color names are black, silver, gray, white, maroon, red, purple, fuchsia, green, lime, olive, yellow, navy, blue, teal, and aqua.

### Background-Image
*Values*: url(images/graphic.gif)
The filename is used to identify the background image, along with the path to its location. If no background-image is desired, use the word *none*.

### Background-Repeat
*Values*: repeat, no-repeat, repeat-x, repeat-y
The repeat instruction tiles the image behind the element being defined. Repeat-X tiles the image across the element horizontally. Repeat-Y tiles the image down the element vertically. No-Repeat displays the image once behind the element.

### Background-Attachment
*Values*: fixed, scroll
Fixed keeps the background-image fixed in place as text scrolls through it. Scroll moves the image along with the text. The default is scroll.

### Background-Position
*Values*: x, y, top, left, right, bottom, center
The position is always relative to the top-left corner of the element in which an image is positioned. The "x" is the horizontal position, and "y" is the vertical position of an image. Either value may be a percentage relative to the size of the element; a fixed amount such as "1in" (one inch); or one of the keywords that indicate a relative position.

### Background
This property allows you to specify all the background properties in a single string. The following order must be used when specifying background properties:
background-color, background-image, background-repeat, background-attachment, back-

ground-position

*Examples*:

    H1 {background: url(images/picture.gif)
    no-repeat fixed left bottom}
    H2 {background: red}

## Font Properties

Font properties control the font face, size, weight, and other variations of typeface.

- font-family
- font-size
- font-weight
- font
- font-style
- font-variant

### Font-Family

*Generic:* serif, sans serif, monospace, fantasy, cursive

*Specific:* Palatino, Arial, Courier, Dingbats, Zapf Chancery. Any commonly available font may be specified by name.

### Font-Size

*Specific:* pt (points), in (inches), cm (centimeter), px (pixels)

*Relative:* 150%, small, medium, large

Relative font sizes may be further qualified as follows:

| | |
|---|---|
| xx-small | 50% smaller than the x-small font |
| x-small | 50% smaller than the small font |
| small | 50% smaller than the medium font |
| medium | A medium-sized font, typically 10 point |
| large | 50% larger than the medium font |
| x-large | 50% larger than the large font |
| xx-large | 50% larger than the x-large font |
| larger | 50% larger than the parent element's font |
| smaller | 50% smaller than the parent element's font |

### Font-Weight

*Specific:* normal, bold

*Relative:* bolder, lighter

The values of 100, 200, 300, 400, 500, 600, 700, 800, and 900 are used to indicate individual font weights, where 400 is "normal," and 700 is "bold." Additional weights, if available, will be displayed in the weight closest to the specified number.

### Font

This property sets the font-weight, font-size, and font-family properties in a single string.

*Examples*:

    TD {font: bold 16pt Times}
    H1 {font: normal 20pt Arial}
    <H2 style="font: 16pt Palatino">Sample
    of Palatino Font</H2>

### Font-Style

*Values:* normal, italic

If an italic variant of the current font is available, specifying "italic" will apply this property. If an italic variant is not available, the current font may appear in "oblique" or slanted style, rather than true italic.

### Font-Variant

*Values:* normal, small-caps

If a small-caps variant of the current font is available, specifying "small-caps" will apply this property. If a small caps variant is not available, the current font will typically appear in upper case at the height of lower case letters.

## Text Properties

These properties are used to control both text-level elements and block-level elements. Features affected are the relative horizontal and vertical position of block level elements; spacing between lines of text, between words, and between letters; text decoration; and text case.

- text-align
- vertical-align
- text-indent
- line-height
- text-decoration
- text-transform
- letter-spacing
- word-spacing

## Text-Align
*Values:* left, center, right, justify
This property controls the horizontal alignment of paragraphs and other block-level elements.

## Vertical-Align
*Values:* baseline, bottom, middle, text-bottom, text-top, top, sub, super
This property controls the position of both text and image elements related to adjoining elements.

## Text-Indent
This property controls the first line of text in a paragraph. The length of the indent may be specified in an absolute value, such as ".50in" or a relative value, such as "10%."

## Line-Height
This property controls the spacing of lines within a paragraph. It does not affect the space between paragraphs. The value may be set to an absolute number or to a percentage. Values such as "1.5" or "2" refer to multiples of the current line height. Set the line height to "2" to double space. To set the line height to 1 1/2 line spacing, use "1.5" or "150%."

## Text-Decoration
*Values:* none, underline, overline, line-through, blink
This property controls the text formatting features listed.

## Text-Transform
*Values:* capitalize, uppercase, lowercase, none
This property capitalizes the first letter of every word, dictates the case of all text, or displays text in the original capitalization.

## Letter-Spacing and Word-Spacing
These properties control the space between individual letters or between words. Any recognized unit of measurement may be used to specify desired spacing, such as 4px, 3pt, 0.25in, or 2em.

## Classification Properties
These properties control a number of behaviors, some of which are not obvious. The list-style properties have a noticeable affect.

- display
- white-space
- list-style-type
- list-style-image
- list-style-position
- list-style

## Display
*Values:* block, inline, list-item, none
The display value "none" makes an element invisible, while leaving the display value empty (" ") allows an element to appear. An element is displayed when it is referred to as a "block" element, an "inline" element, or a "list-style" element. If an inappropriate value is specified it will be ignored and replaced by an acceptable value. The most commonly used display values are "none" and " ".

## White-Space
*Values:* normal, pre, nowrap
This property controls the behavior of white space. Theoretically, the value of "normal" displays text in the normal fashion. The value "pre" allows more than one space in sequence to be displayed, rather than the normal collapsed sta-

tus. The value of nowrap disables line wrapping in an element.

### List-Style-Type
*Values:* none, disc, circle, square, decimal, lower-roman, upper-roman, lower-alpha, upper-alpha

The type of bullet is specified by this property. It controls lists that are not concurrently displaying a list image.

### List-Style-Image
This property replaces the list bullet character with an image.
*Examples:*
UL {list-style-image: url(images/
newbullet.gif)}
<UL style="list-style-image:
url(newbullet.gif)">

If a value of "none" is specified, a list is displayed in the default list style.

### List-Style-Position
*Values:* inside, outside
This property controls the relationship of a bullet to the text that follows. The value "inside" places the bullet character at the left-margin of the text, and wraps subsequent text to the same position. The value "outside" causes the bullet to appear to the left of any wrapped text.

### List-Style
This property specifies two attributes at once. It controls either the list-style-type and the list-style-position, or the list-style-position and the list-style-image.

### Box Properties
This group of properties controls block-level elements both individually and in relation to adjoining elements. Some of these properties control the entire element, such as height or width. Others control only one side of the element "box," such as margin-left or padding-bottom.

- width
- height
- float
- clear
- margin
- padding
- border
- border-width
- border-style
- border-color

### Width and Height
Any recognized unit of measurement may be used to specify the height or width of an HTML object. The object will expand automatically to show all text contained in the box if the width or height assigned is too small.

### Float
*Values:* left, right, none
Elements such as images and tables are instructed to "float" to the left or to the right of adjoining text. To wrap text on the right of an image, specify a float value of "left."

### Clear
*Values:* left, right, both, none
This property works in conjunction with the float property. To prevent an element from being positioned next to a floating object, specify a value of "left" or "right" to prohibit floating objects to the left or right. Specify both to clear objects on both sides.

### Margin
*Values:* margin-top, margin-right, margin-bottom, margin-left
This property controls the left, right, top and

bottom margins around elements. The outer margins around an object may be controlled with any recognized unit of measurement.

## Padding

*Values:* padding-top, padding-left, padding-bottom, padding-right

This property controls the distance between the element text and its box or container, in the same way that collapsing controls the space between text in a cell and the cell walls in a table. Padding refers to the inner margin. The amount of padding may be specified individually for each side of a text object in a box.

## Border

This property sets uniform values for the border-style, border-width, and border-color properties. Border takes a maximum of three values. The first value specifies the border-width of all four borders. The second value specifies the border-style of all four borders. A third value specifies the color of all four borders.

## Border-Width

*Values:* thin, medium, thick, 5px, .03in

This property controls the width of a border if one is used. One to four values may be specified. If a single value is specified it will be applied to every border. If two values are specified, the first value applies to the top and bottom border and the second value to the left and

right sides. If three values are specified, the first value applies to the top border, the second value to the left and right borders, and the third value to the bottom border. If four values are specified, the values will apply respectively to the top, right, bottom and left sides. Any border may be individually specified by using the border-width-left, border-width-top, border-width-right, or border-width-bottom properties. Any recognized unit of measurement may be used to specify the border length.

## Border-Style

*Values:* none, dotted, dashed, solid, double, groove, ridge, inset, outset

This property controls the type of border around an object, and what line style is used to draw the border. Any style other than "none" will cause a border line to appear around the element. This property applies only to block-level elements. If a single value is specified, the value affects all borders. If more than one value is specified, the values are applied to the sides in the same order as the border-width properties are applied.

## Border-Color

*Values:* red, 00A0F7, #00FF00, rgb(255,0,0), rgb(0,100%,100%)

This property controls the color of a border if one is used. If a single value is specified, the value affects all sides of the object. If more than

---

### Support for CSS1

In the following table, IE 4.0 refers to Microsoft Internet Explorer version 4.0, and NC refers to Netscape Communicator.

Yes or No indicates whether the browser supports the listed CSS1 property.

| Color/Background Properties | IE 4.0 | NC |
|---|---|---|
| color | Yes | Yes |
| background-color | Yes | Yes |
| background-image | Yes | Yes |
| background-repeat | No | Yes |
| background-attachment | No | Yes |
| background-position | No | No |
| background | Yes | Yes |

## Support for CSS1 (continued)

### Font Properties IE 4.0 NC

| | | |
|---|---|---|
| font | Yes | Yes |
| font-family | Yes | Yes |
| font-size | Yes | Yes |
| font-style | Yes | Yes |
| font-variant | Yes | No |
| font-weight | Yes | Yes |

### Text Properties IE 4.0 NC

| | | |
|---|---|---|
| letter-spacing | Yes | No |
| line-height | Yes | Yes |
| text-align | Yes | Yes |
| text-decoration | Yes | Yes |
| text-indent | Yes | Yes |
| text-transform | Yes | Yes |
| vertical-align | Yes | No |
| word-spacing | No | No |

### Classification Properties IE 4.0 NC

| | | |
|---|---|---|
| display | No | Yes |
| list-style-image | No | Yes |
| list-style-position | No | Yes |
| list-style-type | No | Yes |
| white-space | No | Yes |

### Box Properties IE 4.0 NC

| | | |
|---|---|---|
| border | No | Yes |
| border-color | No | Yes |
| border-width | No | Yes |
| border-bottom | No | No |
| border-bottom-width | No | Yes |
| border-left | No | No |
| border-left-width | No | Yes |
| border-right | No | No |
| border-right-width | No | Yes |
| border-style | No | Yes |
| border-top | No | No |
| border-top-width | No | Yes |
| clear | No | Yes |
| float | No | Yes |
| height | Yes | Yes |
| margin | Yes | Yes |
| margin-bottom | No | Yes |
| margin-left | Yes | Yes |
| margin-right | Yes | Yes |
| margin-top | No | Yes |
| padding | No | Yes |
| padding-bottom | No | Yes |
| padding-left | No | No |
| padding-right | No | Yes |
| padding-top | No | Yes |
| width | Yes | Yes |

one value is specified, the values are applied to the sides in the same order as the border-width properties are applied.

## Units in CSS1

Many style sheet properties accept a length descriptor. HTML supports two types of units: relative and absolute lengths.

*Relative Units:* em, ex, px
The height of the element's font relative to the output device is expressed in em, as in "0.5em." The height of the letter X relative to the output device is expressed in "ex," as in "0.75ex." Pixels relative to the output device are expressed in "px," as in "15px." Relative units allow web pages to scale better on different devices and clients.

Absolute units define specific distances.

*Absolute Units:* in, cm, mm, pt, pc
These represent inches, as in ".5in"; centimeters, as in "1cm"; millimeters, as in "15mm"; points (1/72 inch), as in "12pt"; and pica (1 pica = 12pt), as in "1pc."

Most lengths may also be expressed as percentages. Percentages are usually relative to the parent element. If a font size of 50% is specified, it conforms the element's font size to one half of the parent element's font size.

**case** (n.) The distinction between capital (uppercase) or small (lowercase) letters or characters.

**case-sensitive** (adj.) Describes a text-matching operation that distinguishes capital letters from lowercase ones. Neither MS-DOS file names nor Internet domain names are case sensitive. Unix file names are case sensitive, as are RFC 822 local mailbox names.

**cast** (n.) 1. The actors who appear in a production. 2. The overemphasis of one hue or tint in an image.

**CAT 3** See *Category 3.*

**CAT 4** See *Category 4.*

**CAT 5** See *Category 5.*

**Category 3** (CAT 3) (n.) A standard for wiring that must be met when connecting 10-megabit-per-second (Mbps) 10BASE-T Ethernet and a 4-Mbps token ring network.

**Category 4** (CAT 4) (n.) A standard for wiring that must be met when connecting a network with a bandwidth of 20 megabits per second (Mbps) and a 16-Mbps token ring network.

**Category 5** (CAT 5) (n.) The industry standard name for unshielded twisted pair (UTP) data grade cable, usually with 24AWG wire. CAT 5 cable runs are limited to 100 meters (328 feet) due to signal radiation and attenuation considerations. Longer runs are vulnerable to interference. CAT 5 cables support applications with data transfer rates up to 100 megabits per second (Mbps). The most common application is connecting Ethernet systems.

**cathode-ray tube** (CRT) (n.) A graphic display that produces an image by directing a beam of electrons to activate a phosphor-coated surface in a vacuum tube. The technology is used in both television and computer video monitors.

**CATNIP** See *Common Architecture for Next Generation Internet Protocol.*

**CATV** See *cable television.*

**CAV** See *constant angular velocity.*

**CB** See *Citizens Band.*

**C-band** (n.) A high-frequency spectrum between 4 GHz and 8 GHz used for Fixed Satellite Service (FSS). Uplink occurs at approximately 6 GHz; downlink occurs at a rate of 3.7 GHz to 4.2 GHz.

**CBEMA** See *Computer and Business Equipment Manufacturers Association.*

**CBI** See *computer-based instruction.*

**CBL** See *computer-based learning.*

**CBT** See *computer-based training.*

**CCD** See *charge-coupled device.*

**CCIR** See *Consultative Committee for International Radio.*

**CCIR-601** (n.) The standard for digital component video that specifies component color difference coding (Y, R-Y, B-Y) and the 4:2:2 format.

**CCIR-656** See *Consultative Committee for International Radio.*

**CCIRN** See *Coordinating Committee for Intercontinental Research Networks.*

**CCITT** See *Comité Consultatif International de Télégraphique et Téléphonique.*

**CCITT Group IV** See *Comité Consultatif International de Télégraphique et Téléphonique.*

**CCITT Group III** See *Comité Consultatif International de Télégraphique et Téléphonique.*

**CCL** See *Connection Control Language.*

**CCS** See *Centrum Call Seconds* or *Common Command Set.*

**CD** See *compact disc.*

**CD horn** See *constant directivity (CD) horn.*

**CDA** See *Communications Decency Act.*

**CD-DA** See *compact disc.*

**CDDI** See *Copper Distributed Data Interface.*

**CDEV** See *control panel device.*

**CDF** See *channel definition format.*

**CD+G** See *compact disc.*

**CD-i** See *compact disc.*

**CD-i audio levels** See *compact disc.*

**CDMA** See *Code Division Multiple Access.*

**CD+MIDI** See *compact disc.*

**CDPD** See *Cellular Digital Packet Data.*

**CD-plus** See *compact disc.*

**CD-R** See *compact disc.*

**CD-ROM** See *compact disc.*

**CD-ROM drive** (n.) Compact disc–read-only memory drive; any reader or playback device for data encoded on a CD-ROM. A CD-ROM drive performs more error correction than an audio CD player. Usually controlled by a computer to read text, graphic, video, and audio files, it also reads the Red Book audio format. The accompanying figure shows a laser beam path on a CD-ROM player.

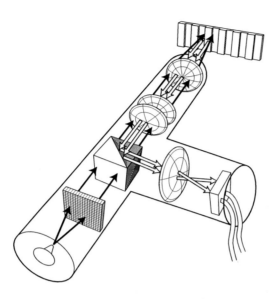

*laser beam path on a CD-ROM player*

**CD-ROM extended architecture** (CD-ROM XA) (n.) Compact disc–read-only memory extended architecture; an extension of the Yellow Book standard, generally consistent with the ISO 9660 format. It is designed to add better audio compression and to stream interleaved video with audio for multimedia applications. CD-ROM XA provides compatibility with ADPCM audio, multisession discs, Photo-CD, and CD-i. CD-ROM XA relies solely on Cross-Interleaved Reed-Solomon Code (CIRC) for error correction.

**CD-ROM extensions** (n.) Compact disc–read-only memory extensions; software routines that connect MS-DOS with specific CD-ROM drivers and compatible computers to read discs in the ISO 9660 and High Sierra formats.

**CD-ROM upgrade kit** (n.) Compact disc–read-only memory upgrade kit; a package with software, an interface card, cables, and the drive for installing a CD-ROM drive in a computer.

**CD-ROM XA** See *CD-ROM extended architecture.*

**CD-RW** See *compact disc.*

**CD-WO** See *compact disc.*

**CEA** See *Consumer Electronics Association.*

**cel** (n.) In animation, a transparent piece of film onto which images are drawn.

**cell** (n.) 1. In a spreadsheet, the point at which

71

a row and a column intersect. 2. In data transmission, a packet of information containing some bytes of address information combined with data. 3. In telecommunications, the basic geographic unit of a wireless telephone system.

**Cello** (n.) The trademark name of an outdated freeware Internet browser. Cello allows access to the World Wide Web, gopher, and file transfer protocol (FTP). It does not, however, accommodate email messages to newsgroups.

**cell relay** (n.) A high bit rate asynchronous or synchronous data multiplexing and switching technique based on Fast Packet technology. CCITT I.422 specifies a 53-byte cell with a payload of 48 bytes. The 5-byte header contains virtual channel and virtual path identifiers. Cells may be transmitted along permanent virtual circuits or mapped into SONET frames. See also *Asynchronous Transfer Mode*.

**cellular** (adj.) Describes a means of dividing an area into regions, or cells, so that each region becomes a network in which every point is located within the range of a central transmission facility.

**Cellular Digital Packet Data** (CDPD) (n.) A digital wireless transmission system based on the IBM CelluPlan II system. It enhances existing wireless networks by providing a packet overlay for the AMPS network. It moves data at 19.2 kbps over changing unused intervals in available voice channels. When all channels are in use, data is stored and forwarded when a channel becomes available. CDPD was developed as a wireless extension to an IP network, and it uses the four-octet (0.0.0.0) addressing convention. CDPD networks cover most major urban areas in the U. S., and modems are available for laptops and handheld computers.

**cellular radio** (n.) Technology that uses low-power radio transmission as an alternative to local circuits for accessing the switched telephone network; for both stationary and mobile users. Mobile calls are passed under control of a central site from one cell's transmitter to an adjoining one with minimal switching delay. See also *Advanced Mobile Phone Service*.

**Celsius** (C) (n.) A temperature scale that registers the freezing point of water as 0°C and the boiling point as 100°C under normal atmospheric pressure.

**CEMA** See *Consumer Electronics Association*.

**CE marking** (n.) The logo used in marking units certified for distribution within the European Union (EU) that meet directives as mandated by the European Commission. CE is sometimes used as an acronym for "Conformité Européenne."

*CE marking*

**center frequency** (n.) One of the parameters of a bandpass filter, the center frequency occurs at the maximum or minimum amplitude response for Butterworth filters, frequently found in audio electronics.

**centi-** (adj.) the prefix for one hundredth (10E-2), abbreviated "c."

**central office** (CO) (n.) The physical site at which a telephone company terminates customer lines and locates switching equipment that can connect those lines with other networks.

**Central Office Classes** (n.) The classes of telephone company central offices, which are as follows:

Class 1 = regional switching center
Class 2 = sectional switching center
Class 3 = primary switching center
Class 4 = toll center
Class 5 = end office or local exchange

**central processing unit** (CPU) (n.) The primary computing device, or the brain, of a computer system in which data is manipulated and in which calculations take place. It consists of a single microprocessor chip.

**centrex** (n.) Contraction of *central exchange;* business telephone service provided by a local exchange carrier (LEC) from its central office. Services include call forwarding, call transferring, call restricting, least-cost routing, intercom, and call holding. Centrex is an alternative to a private branch exchange (PBX).

**Centronics parallel** (n.) A standard 36-pin parallel interface that permits printers and other peripherals to be connected to a computer.

**Centrum Call Seconds** (CCS) (n.) In telephone traffic engineering, a unit of measurement that represents a connection where 36CCS, or one Erlang, is used. Average usage for most voice communications ranges from about 3 to 10 CCS per user station. Centrum in this case means hundred.

**CEPT** See *European Conference of Postal and Telecommunications Administrations.*

**ceramic substrate** (n.) Flat slice of ceramic, typically beryllium oxide or aluminum oxide, that holds an integrated circuit (IC).

**CERN** See *Conseil Européen pour la Recherche Nucléaire.*

**CGA** See *Color Graphics Adapter.*

**CGI** See *Common Gateway Interface.*

**CGM** See *Computer Graphics Metafile.*

**channel** (n.) 1. Either of two independent signals in a stereo audio system, designated right and left. Most audio, video, and computer playback devices provide two channels for stereo sound. 2. In an Internet Relay Chat (IRC) network, a unit of connected users. Every word each person types is read by others on the same channel. 3. A communications pathway between a host server and a client through which information (data requested by the user) is multicast. 4. In telecommunications, the smallest subdivision of a communication path on a digital, multiplexed signal over which information can be transmitted in one direction.

**channel-attached** (adj.) In telecommunications, this describes the attachment of devices directly to the input/output channels of a computer mainframe, usually an IBM. The devices are attached to a controlling unit by cables rather than by telecommunications circuits.

**channel bank** (n.) Digital Service (DS-0 to DS-1) multiplex equipment used for analog voice to pulse code modulation (PCM) conversion and multiplexing. It processes signaling information for each channel and inserts framing bits.

**channel definition format** (CDF) (n.) An application of Extensible Markup Language (XML) developed by Microsoft. It is proposed as a standard for pushing media, allowing web publishers to push content at users through a channel. Castanet technology from Marimba is an example of this technology.

**channel service unit** (CSU) (n.) An interface used to connect a computer to a digital medium in the same way that a modem is used to connect to an analog medium. A communications carrier provides a CSU to customers, who may use their own equipment to retime and regenerate the incoming signals. A digital service unit (DSU) supplies all of the transmit logic, receive logic, and timing recovery, whereas a customer must provide this information to the carrier in order to use a CSU.

**channel service unit/data service unit** (CSU/DSU) (n.) Hardware that performs the functions of both a channel service unit (CSU) and a data service unit (DSU). The CSU is used to terminate a telecommunications line for data transmission. It performs line conditioning, protection, loopback, and timing functions. The DSU terminates the data circuit to the data terminal equipment (DTE) and converts the customer's data stream into a suitable transmission format.

**chapter** (n.) Each independent segment on a videodisc.

**chapter cue** (n.) A signal in the vertical blanking interval (VBI) of a master tape identifying the first frame of a new chapter. On a videodisc pressed from this master tape, a chapter stop is encoded on the corresponding disc frame.

**chapter number** (n.) A number displayed on a screen to identify videodisc chapters.

**chapter stop** (n.) A code embedded in a videodisc to signal the break between two separate chapters, allowing access to a specific chapter.

**character** (n.) A data component that represents a single letter or symbol of input/output (I/O). Letters are normally represented by the ASCII character set, using the least significant seven bits of a byte or word.

**character-oriented** (adj.) Describes a data communications protocol that carries control information encoded as character strings. For example, typing the characters "ETX" issues an end-of-transmission command, and typing the characters "SOH" issues a start-of-header command.

**character set** (n.) A standard collection of characters, such as ASCII or Unicode. It may include letters, digits, punctuation marks, mathematical symbols, control codes, or other symbols. Every character in a set is represented by its own character code, a binary number used for storage and transmission. In the ASCII set, the letter A is represented by code 65.

**characters per second** (cps) (n.) Data transfer rate estimated by dividing the bit rate by the total character length. At 2400 bits per second (bps), eight-bit characters with start and stop bits (making 10-bit characters) are transmitted at approximately 240 cps. Advanced protocols, such as V.42bis, use longer transmission frames and data compression to increase cps.

**character user interface** (CUI) (n.) An interface in which only characters are displayed on the screen, as opposed to graphics in a graphical user interface (GUI). MS-DOS is an example.

**charge** 1. (v.) In electronics, to energize by passing current through a conducting element or battery in the direction opposite to discharge. 2. (n.) In physics, the property of matter responsible for electromagnetic interaction, designated as *negative* or *positive*. 3. (n.) A measure of this property possessed by a body or contained in a spatial region.

**charge-coupled device** (CCD) (n.) A light-detecting component used by digital cameras.

**chat** (n., adj.) An online forum for realtime, text-based discussion by participants who are logged on simultaneously. The virtual space in which such a discussion takes place is a *chat room*.

**check disc** (n.) A prototype videodisc or compact disc (CD) produced prior to mass replication to confirm the data's accuracy and integrity.

**check-password** (n.) A hacking program used to crack VMS passwords.

**checksum** (n.) A number representing the sum of a set of data bytes. The number is sent with the data set, and error correction schemes use it to determine whether the data has been accurately received.

**Chernobyl Packet** (n.) Also known as a Kamikaze Packet, a network packet that induces a broadcast storm and network meltdown. Typically, it is an IP Ethernet datagram that passes through a gateway with both source and destination Ethernet and IP address set as the respective broadcast addresses for the subnetworks that the gateway serves.

**chew** (n.) Jargon for network lag. The percentage of lost packets compared with the total number sent over a network.

**child directory** (n.) In MS-DOS, the directory that resides within a parent directory in the logical format or hierarchy.

**child record** (n.) A record that is logically lo-

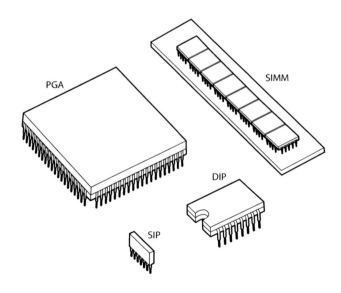

PGA

SIMM

DIP

SIP

*chip formats*

cated lower in the hierarchical tree than a parent record and that is directly linked to the parent.

**Chimera** (n.) A modular, X Window System–based web browser for Unix. It runs on SunOS 4.1.x and Linux 1.1.x. Chimera supports forms, inline images, FTP, HTTP, local file access, proxy servers, and gopher.

**chip** (n.) A silicon wafer onto which circuit paths are etched or printed photographically in layers, connecting active and passive devices within the solid structure. See figure on the previous page.

**chip set** (n.) A combination of integrated circuits (ICs) designed for a particular purpose.

**chorus** (n.) An audio effect created by the simultaneous production of tones at slightly different frequencies, resulting in a shimmering sound in the upper overtones. A violin section playing in unison creates a characteristic natural chorus effect.

**chroma** See *chrominance*.

**chroma key** (n.) A video effect created by shooting objects against a monochrome background, the color of which is "keyed" out so it can be replaced with images from another source. Foreground objects appear to be juxtaposed over the new background in the composition. This color-based video matting (overlay) technique drops all areas of a selected color (usually blue) from the foreground image and substitutes corresponding areas of the new background.

**chromatic scale** (n.) In music, refers to all 12 semitones in the octave played consecutively.

**Chrome** (n.) Multimedia technology developed by Microsoft that acts as an interface to DirectX, using a set of Extensible Markup Language (XML) tags. It can script animations through the DirectX hardware interface so that the host does more work than the server. It requires a 350-MHz Pentium II, 64 megabytes (MB) of RAM, and Accelerated Graphics Port (AGP) graphics with at least 4 MB of video memory.

**chrominance** (chroma) (n.) The color and saturation information in a video signal. Luminance must be present to make it visible. Low chroma levels appear to be washed out, whereas high levels are too vivid, causing bleeding between different colors. See also *luminance*.

**chunk** (n.) A block of a type of data used in Tagged Image File Format (TIFF) and Resource Interchange File Format (RIFF) standards.

**Chyron** (n.) 1. A manufacturer of video character generators. 2. In the computer industry, a word applied to any character generator or to lettering on the screen. Pronounced "KIE-ron."

**CIDR** See *Classless Inter-Domain Routing*.

**CIF** See *Common Image Format* or *Common Intermediate Format*.

**Cinemascope** (n.) Refers to video with a very wide (2.21:1) aspect ratio. It is one of the display resolution options in the MPEG-2 standard. When displayed on a normal television, Cinemascope material results in an extreme letterbox effect. The term was originally "CinemaScope" and was applied to film using a 2.35:1 aspect ratio.

**CinePak** (n.) A video compression algorithm that was developed by SuperMac and that was previously called *Compact Video*. Updated in 1998, CinePak is one of the most popular

CODECs for QuickTime video.

**CIRC** See *Cross-Interleaved Reed-Solomon Code.*

**circuit** (n.) Any transmission medium connecting two or more electronic devices.

**circuit-level gateway** (n.) A type of firewall that validates TCP and UDP sessions before opening a connection. It creates a handshake and then passes everything through until the session is ended.

**circuit switching** (n.) A network configuration in which a continuous connection is established between two devices, providing an uninterrupted flow of information. A telephone call is an example of circuit switching. Compare *packet switching.*

**CISC** See *complex instruction set computing.*

**Citizens Band** (CB) (n.) One of two bands used for low-power radio transmission in the United States (26.965–27.225 MHz and 462.55–469.95 MHz). CB radios are limited by the Federal Communications Commission (FCC) to 4 watts of power, limiting their range to only a few miles. CB radios became popular among truck drivers in the United States in the late 1970s.

**CIX** See *Commercial Internet Exchange.*

**cladding** (n.) A material that surrounds the core of a fiber-optic cable, providing insulation and protection.

**clapboard** (n.) A hinged slate with diagonal stripes for identification of a scene or shot. It is slapped together to cue the beginning of on-camera action. Clapboards were originally used to synchronize pictures with sound.

**class** (n.) 1. A set of objects that share a common structure and behavior. The structure is determined by the variables that represent the state of an object in the class, whereas the behavior is established by a set of methods associated with the class. Classes are related in a class hierarchy. One class could be a subclass of a superclass, or it could be composed of other classes. It may be abstract or concrete. 2. One of three types of Internet addresses, distinguished by their most significant bits.

**CLASS** See *Custom Local Area Signaling Services.*

**class hierarchy** (n.) A set of classes and their interrelationships.

**Classless Inter-Domain Routing** (CIDR) (n.) Technique supported by the Border Gateway Protocol 4 (BGP-4) that facilitates routing between multiple independent networks.

**class library** (n.) A collection of reusable classes for use with an object-oriented programming language such as Java.

**Class of Service** (COS) (n.) A designation for one of several variable network connection services available to the user of a network. The class is usually distinguished by security offered (such as encryption), transmission priority, and bandwidth. The network user designates class of service at connection establishment, typically using a symbolic name mapped to a list of potential routes, any of which may provide the requested service.

**Class X Office** (n.) A switching facility in the telephone company hierarchy. Class 5 is an end office, Class 4 is a toll center, Class 3 is a primary center, Class 2 is a sectional center, and Class 1 is a regional center. Since 1983, only Class 5 and Class 3 switches have been employed.

**clean boot** (n., v.) Bypassing the config.sys and

77

autoexec.bat files on startup.

**cleanroom** (n.) A room in which semiconductors are manufactured and CDs are pressed. It is kept virtually dust-free to reduce particle contamination. A "class 100" room has fewer than 100 particles larger than 0.5 microns in diameter per cubic foot.

**clear channel** (n.) 1. A transmission path in which the full bandwidth is available to the user because it is not shared. 2. In digital communications, the ability to provide a 64Kbps DS-0 for the customer. This implies that telephone signaling information is out of band and that a density of ones (1s) is maintained by B8ZS.

**clear to send** (CTS) (n.) A control signal used in a switched half-duplex circuit in an RS-232 modem interface to notify the computer that it has line control. In a full-duplex circuit, this is a constant signal.

**CLF** See *common log file.*

**CLI** See *Command Line Interface.*

**click** (v.) To press and release a mouse button rapidly, usually over a hot spot or icon in a graphical user interface (GUI).

**click-through rate** (n.) The percentage of viewers who click on ad banners and go to an advertiser's site. It typically ranges from 1–3% industry wide.

**client** (n.) In the client/server model, the system that initiates requests to the server, database, or processing engine. The client uses its own intelligence as it further processes the results for display. An example of a client application is a web browser, referred to as a *uni-*

*versal client.*

**client error** (n.) In relation to the Internet, a problem that occurs due to an invalid request by the client's browser. Possible errors include the following:

- 400 = Failed: Bad Request. The server could not understand the request because of incorrect syntax.

- 401 = Failed: Unauthorized. Either the request required user authorization or the authorization was refused.

- 402 = Failed: Payment Required. A successful transaction must take place before the request is fulfilled.

- 403 = Failed: Forbidden. The server understood the request but refused to fulfill it.

- 404 = Failed: Not Found. The server did not find anything matching the client's request. The URL requested may not exist.

**client/server** (adj.) A type of network architecture that distributes computing responsibility between a front-end and a back-end program. Prior to implementation of the client/server model, the burden of data processing fell on either the client (early PC environments) or the server (a typical mainframe). In the client/server model, clients share data and processing functions with the server.

**Client To Client Protocol** (CTCP) (n.) A protocol that permits structured data, such as font information, to be exchanged between Internet Relay Chat (IRC) users. A query may also be sent from one user to another using this protocol. Commands include FINGER, PING, ECHO, VERSION, DCC CHAT, DCC

SEND, TIME, and CLIENTINFO.

**clip art** (n.) Illustrations or artwork files that are made available for use in productions and projects. Catalogs of clip art categorized by subject are widely distributed, and those who purchase them are typically granted permission to use the images without concern about copyright infringement.

**Clipboard** (n.) A memory location in which data copied or cut from a document resides until it is pasted or cleared. This form of memory buffer is available in most graphical user interface (GUI) systems.

**clipper chip** (n.) An integrated circuit developed for encrypting voice communications. It conforms to the Escrow Encryption Standard (EES) and implements the Skipjack encryption algorithm.

**clipping** (n.) Operating an audio device, such as an amplifier, in an amplitude region in which signals cannot be processed linearly. Peaks of waveforms are cut off and distortion is produced. Clipped waveforms consist mostly of odd harmonics.

**clock** (n.) A timing device that generates a periodic signal used as the source for synchronizing signals in digital equipment.

**clock rate** (n.) The number of cycles per second (cps) at which a computer performs its most basic operations, such as transferring a value from one register to another, as determined by the frequency of an internal crystal-based oscillator. Common clock rates, or processor speeds, for Intel Pentium-based chips have increased steadily. Pentium 4 processors typically run at rates from 1–2 GHz.

**clock reference** (n.) A timing signal with

which audio and video devices can synchronize during recording and playback.

**clock speed** (n.) The shortest amount of time required for a central processing unit (CPU) to perform a single instruction. A computer clock generates regular timing pulses for the CPU.

**clone** (n.) Computing hardware that is based on a proprietary design and built by a third-party manufacturer.

**closed architecture** (n.) A system whose software and hardware are compatible with only one manufacturer or developer, possibly preventing the system from being freely extensible. By contrast, *open architecture* uses widely adopted standards, ensuring compatibility.

**close-up** (n.) Tightly framed video or still shot in which the subject is viewed at close range and dominates the screen. The terms *medium close-up* and *extreme close-up* define how closely the subject is framed.

**Clover key** (n.) The Macintosh Command key, also known as the *Feature key*. See figure.

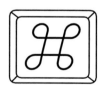

*Clover key*

**cluster** (n.) On a disk, an allocation unit consisting of at least one physical block. A file is composed of several clusters, or logical units, which may not be contiguous.

**CLUT** See *color look-up table*.

**CLV** See *constant linear velocity*.

**CMOS** See *complementary metal-oxide semiconductor*.

**CMRS** See *Commercial Mobile Radio Service*.

**CMYK** (adj.) Describes a type of color representation based on the cyan (C), magenta (M), yellow (Y), and black (K) inks used in color printing. With subtractive color mixing, one can produce all available colors from the first three inks. Black is used to add tonal range and to define edges. Cyan is a blue, and magenta is a red.

**CNA** See *computer network attack*.

**CNAME** (n.) A query that asks a domain name system (DNS) server on the Internet for a host's official hostname.

**CO** See *central office*.

**coaxial cable** (coax, pronounced "KOH-acks") (n.) A standard video cable with a single center conductor surrounded by insulation and with an outer conductor made of woven metal. If the cable is run underground or exposed to water, it is enclosed by another layer of insulation. Coaxial cable provides excellent high-frequency transmission (50–500MHz) and data rates to 45Mbps. Commonly used as CATV transmission cable, 56kbp s–45Mbps data cables, and Ethernet LAN connections. See figure.

**Cobol** See *Common Business-Oriented Language*.

**code** (n.) Any representation of information using numbers, letters, or symbols.

**CODEC** See *compression-decompression*.

**Code Division Multiple Access** (CDMA) (n.)

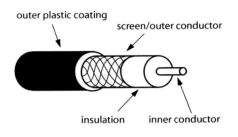

*coaxial cable construction*

A method of concurrent transmission in which a packet of data is coded to differentiate it from other packets. This is comparable to Time Division Multiple Access (TDMA), a popular but slower transmission technique. CDMA is a spread-spectrum wireless interface developed by Qualcomm. Rather than dividing the radio frequency spectrum into separate user channels by frequency slices or time slots, spread-spectrum technology separates users by assigning them digital codes within the same broad spectrum. CDMA is commonly used in Canada, the U.S., Australia, and South Korea. It differs from TDMA and GSM transmission techniques, allowing higher user capacity and immunity from interference by other signals. CDMA operates at either 800 MHz or 1900 MHz. The second generation (2G) version is referred to as CDMA One, or IS-95. Further evolved from CDMA One is the third generation (3G), referred to as CDMA2000, or 1X Multicarrier mode (1X MC).

**coded order** (n.) In video compression, the order in which frames are stored and decoded. This order is not necessarily the same as the order in which they are displayed.

**COFF** See *Common Object File Format*.

**coherent light** (n.) A light beam made up of a single frequency in which the light waves are in phase with one another. It is the type of light emitted from a laser.

**colocation** (n.) 1. Placement of one telephone operator's equipment on premises owned by another to facilitate a direct connection between networks. 2. The placement of a web server at the facility of an Internet Service Provider (ISP).

**color balance** (n.) The process of matching the strength of red, green, and blue signals in an additive color system to make an accurate shade of white and color tones from the mixture.

**color bars** (n.) A video test signal consisting of solid blocks of the three primary colors (red, green, and blue) and their combinations. The blocks are referred to as *bars*. Most frequently, the Society of Motion Picture and Television Engineers (SMPTE) version is used.

**color cycling** (n.) An animation technique in which a special effect is created by swapping colors in and out of a color look-up table (CLUT).

**Color Graphics Adapter** (CGA) (n.) One of the early IBM PC graphics standards.

**color look-up table** (CLUT) (n.) A selection of colors assigned a digital value and held in a table. A program decodes a color picture for display by matching the code stored for each pixel with the associated color value in the look-up table. This process is also called *indexed color*, and the table is referred to as a *color map*. See figure.

**color model** (n.) A means of defining the color of an image with components in three or four dimensions. The most frequently used systems include RGB (red, green, and blue light), HLS (hue, luminance, and saturation), HSV (hue,

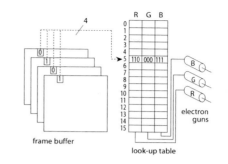

*color look-up table components*

saturation, and value) and CMYK (cyan, magenta, yellow, and black).

**color perception** (n.) The sensation of hues created by the human eye as it discerns the frequencies of electromagnetic waves. The accompanying graph illustrates the color perceived by waves in each frequency band of the spectrum, measured in nanometers. See figure.

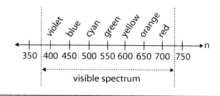

*color spectrum in nanometers*

**color space** (n.) A mathematical model that describes colors. Common models for defining color space include RGB, CMYK, HSV, and YUV.

**color subsampling** (n.) A method of reducing the size of an image by storing color data with lower resolution than luminance data. It is typically used in video with the YUV color space. The most widely used video color subsampling formats are 4:2:2, 4:1:1, and YUV9. See also *video color sampling*.

**color temperature** (n.) The relative amount of red and blue in a "white" light, measured in degrees of kelvin (K). Typical readings for video production are 5600 K outdoors and 3400 K indoors.

**colorYCC** (n.) Developed by Eastman Kodak for Photo-CD, a device-independent color-encoding process. Each color pixel is separated into two 8-bit chroma components (C) and one 8-bit luma component (Y), for a total of 24 bits. The process can also convert RGB color to YCC and vice versa. It provides image compression and high resolution for video or print graphics.

**COM** See *Component Object Model.*

**combining response** See *interpolating response.*

**Comité Consultatif International de Télégraphique et Téléphonique** (CCITT, International Telephone and Telegraph Consultative Committee) (n.) A worldwide standards organization that defines communications protocols. The recommendations enable global compatibility for voice, data, and video transmission over telecommunications devices. The CCITT has been replaced by the International Telecommunications Union (ITU). The following recommendations are among those made by the CCITT:

- **CCITT Group III** (n.) A compression standard used for facsimile transmission.

- **CCITT Group IV** (n.) A compression standard widely used for storing images on optical discs. It is based on a two-dimensional compression scheme in which every scan line is the reference line for the next scan line, and only the changes, or deltas, are stored.

**command interpreter** (n.) A resident program that reads and executes textual commands. When BIOS loads on a PC, it immediately runs the MS-DOS command interpreter command.com. The commands that it recognizes are internal, such as DIR, COPY, and PRN, unlike executables, which are external commands. Some commands may be executed within the interpreter itself, such as control constructs. Command interpreters in Unix are referred to as *shells.*

**Command key** (n.) On a Macintosh keyboard, a special key with a flower-shaped symbol that performs functions when combined with other keys. It is also known as the *Feature key* and the *Clover key.* Common functions are global menu choices:

| | |
|---|---|
| Command-A | Select all |
| Command-C | Copy selected material to Clipboard |
| Command-F | Find |
| Command-G | Find again |
| Command-I | Get information |
| Command-M | Make alias |
| Command-N | New folder or document |
| Command-O | Open |
| Command-P | Print |
| Command-Q | Quit application |
| Command-S | Save file to current folder |
| Command-V | Paste from Clipboard |
| Command-W | Close file or folder |
| Command-X | Cut to Clipboard |
| Command-Z | Undo last command or typing |

**command line** (n., adj.) In an operating system that requires keyboard characters for instructions, such as MS-DOS or Unix, a display line that prompts the user to input keyboard instructions.

**Command Line Interface** (CLI) (n.) An environment in which the user can only communicate with a program through textual input and output. Input, or keyboard commands, are interpreted and executed by the program, which provides output in the form of text or graphics on a monitor. A CLI can provide more control than a graphical user interface (GUI).

**comment out** (v.) To mark a line or section of program code with delimiters, which prevents it from being compiled or interpreted. Comments in the delimited section often give other programmers information about the program.

**Commercial Internet Exchange** (CIX) (n.) A group of Internet Service Providers who provide a backbone service free from Acceptable Use Policies (AUPs) and dedicated to commercial use.

**Commercial Mobile Radio Service** (CMRS) (n.) A regulatory classification that the Federal Communications Commission (FCC) uses to govern all commercial wireless service providers, including personal communications services (PCS), cellular, and Enhanced Specialized Mobile Radio (ESMR).

**Common Architecture for Next Generation Internet Protocol** (CATNIP) (n.) A proposed standard for IP version 6 (IPv6), also known as IP Next Generation (IPng). One of the problems addressed by this new architecture is the need for more Internet addresses. IPv6 is defined in RFC 1752.

**Common Business-Oriented Language** (Cobol, pronounced "KOE-ball") (n.) A widely used programming language developed by the Conference on Data System Languages (CODASYL) Committee between 1959 and 1961.

**common carrier** (n.) A private company that offers public telecommunications services.

**Common Command Set** (CCS) (n.) Small Computer System Interface (SCSI) commands specified in the SCSI-1 Standard X3.131–1986 Addendum 4.B, governing the communication between all SCSI devices.

**Common Gateway Interface** (CGI) (n.) A widely used set of standards designed to run external programs from a World Wide Web HTTP server. CGI defines a set of environmental variables and specifies how to pass arguments to the executing program as part of the HTTP request. It may exist as any program that accepts command line arguments. Perl is often used to write CGI scripts. A script can access information in a database, format the results as HTML, and return this information to the browser. When a server receives a CGI execution request, it creates a new process to run the external program, which can create problems if the process fails to terminate. Microsoft developed the Internet Server Application Programming Interface (ISAPI) standard, and Netscape devised NSAPI; both standards allow CGI-like tasks to run as part of the main server process, making it unnecessary to create a new process for each CGI request.

**Common Image Format** (CIF) (n.) Standard sample structure used to represent the picture information in a single frame in digital video, independent of frame rate and synchronization or blanking structure. The uncompressed bit rate for transmitting CIF at 29.97 frames per second (fps) is 36.45 megabits per second (Mbps).

**Common Intermediate Format** (CIF) (n.) A videoconferencing standard with a resolution of 352 pixels x 288 pixels. This yields an aspect ratio of 11 x 9.

**common log file** (CLF) (n.) A log file format

developed by the National Center for Supercomputing Applications (NCSA) that has become the standard logging format for the majority of web servers.

**Common Object File Format** (COFF) (n.) The executable and object file format used by Unix System V, Release 3.

**Common Object Request Broker Architecture** (CORBA, pronounced "KORE-bah") (n.) A network architecture specified by the Object Management Group (OMG), it provides the standard interface definition between OMG-compliant objects.

**Communications Decency Act** (CDA) (n.) An amendment to a federal telecommunications bill that went into effect in February 1996. The law attempted to make it criminal to post indecent language on the Internet anywhere that a minor could read it. In June 1996, a three-judge panel in Philadelphia ruled the amendment unconstitutional.

**communications port** (com port) (n.) The connector on a microcomputer for a communications interface, typically a serial port.

**Communications Satellite Corporation** (COMSAT) A private U.S. satellite carrier established by Congress in 1962 for the coordination and construction of satellite communications and facilities for international voice and data communications.

**compact disc** (CD) (n.) Originally the common term for a compact audio disc, now used freely to refer to any optical disc 4.75 inches (12 cm) in diameter containing information encoded digitally in the constant linear velocity (CLV) format. The official designation for an audio CD is compact disc–digital audio (CD-DA). The accompanying illustration shows the

evolution of compact discs and the relationship between different types of compact discs. See figure on the following page.

The following terms refer to specific types of CDs and CD formats:

- **CD-DA** (n.) Compact disc–digital audio; the format used for high-fidelity music that offers a 90+ decibel signal-to-noise ratio and 74 minutes of digital sound. The standard for this format is the Red Book. Audio files are uncompressed 16-bit, 44.1-kHz samples.

- **CD+G** (n.) Compact disc + graphics; developed by Warner New Media, this CD format is not readable by standard CD-ROM players. It includes extended graphics capabilities, as well as some limited video graphics written to the CD subcode area. The primary use is for karaoke, in which song lyrics are displayed and the music is played without vocals to accompany a person who sings the song. Pronounced "see-DEE plus GEE."

- **CD-i** (n.) Compact disc–interactive; developed in 1991 by Philips, a CD-ROM format that holds audio, digital data, still graphics, and MPEG video. These discs adhere to the Green Book standard. An infrared remote control device, a mouse, or a trackball allows users to interact with the content on the disc by clicking a cursor over hot spots on the video display.

- **CD-i audio levels** (n.) Compact disc–interactive audio levels; levels of audio encoding that are part of the Green Book specification. Level A is a method of recording audio that offers fidelity comparable to that of standard CD audio, but it compresses the data to about half as

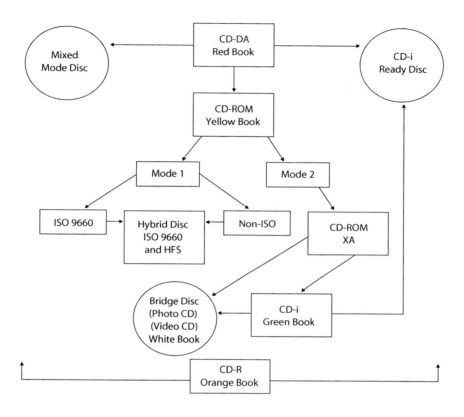

*compact disc family*

much space on a disc. Level B is used in both the CD-i and CD-ROM XA formats; this method of recording audio offers medium fidelity but is more highly compressed than level A. Used in both the CD-i and CD-ROM XA formats, level C is a method of recording audio that offers fidelity sufficient for speech. It is highly compressed.

• **CD+MIDI** (n.) Compact disc + Musical Instrument Digital Interface; developed by Warner New Media, this CD format adds

MIDI information to the digital audio data. Pronounced "see-DEE plus MID-ee." See also *Musical Instrument Digital Interface.*

• **CD-plus** (n.) A CD-ROM format from Sony and Philips that plays Red Book audio, written on the first tracks, and that includes graphics and data files readable by a microcomputer on later tracks. Windows 95 supports the CD-plus format.

• **CD-R** (n.) Compact disc–recordable; developed in 1990 by Philips and Sony, it adheres to the Orange Book standard. It permits a CD recorder to write CD-DA, CD-ROM, CD-ROM XA, and CD-i block structures to a blank CD-ROM disc. The primary applications are for prototype production discs, or *one-offs*, and for archiving data. In 1992, a second generation of CD recorders became standard. They are capable of *multisession* recording, or writing additional information to a disc without deleting existing data. To read a multisession disc, readers must be able to identify a complex table of contents (TOC), but not all readers can do this. The original ISO 9660 logical file structure does not handle multisession discs, because it was created before their invention. See figure.

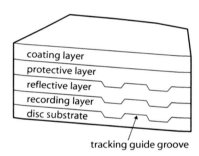

*CD-R layers*

- **CD-ROM** (n.) Compact disc–read-only memory; a 4.75-inch (12 cm) disc on which optical memory storage is encoded. CD-ROMs hold about 650 megabytes (MB) of data. The standards for this format are called the Yellow Book. The logical level standard is called ISO 9660. The Unix extension is called the *Rock Ridge Format*.

- **CD-ROM XA** (n.) Compact disc–read-only memory extended architecture; an evolution of the standard CD-ROM for-

mat that provides for ADPCM audio, multisession discs, Photo-CD, and CD-i compatibility. This format relies solely on Cross-Interleaved Reed-Solomon Code (CIRC) for error correction.

- **CD-RW** (n.) Compact disc–rewritable; a recordable CD-ROM that may be written over many times. It uses a different medium from a CD-R, which may be recorded only once.

- **CD-WO** (n.) Compact disc–write once; another name for *CD-R*.

**compact HTML** (cHTML) (n.) A subset of existing HTML 2.0, 3.2, and 4.0 specifications designed for handheld devices.

**Compact Video** (n.) Developed by SuperMac, this CODEC can compress QuickTime movies in 320 x 240 pixel resolution at high frame rates for CD-ROM playback.

**companding** (n.) The process of compressing data for transmission and expanding it on reception.

**compatibility** (n.) In relation to compact discs (CDs), the extent to which different types of discs can be read by various types of disc drives or players. For example, all CD-DA discs are fully compatible with all CD-DA players, so any such player can interpret and reproduce music from any such disc, regardless of the manufacturer.

**compatible** (adj.) Capable of running the same software, such as MS-DOS, on various hardware configurations.

**competitive access provider** (CAP) (n.) A telecommunications carrier that bypasses a local network to connect to long-distance carriers. A

CAP provides high-capacity lines to business customers and interexchange carriers and may offer switched services. Also known as *alternative access providers.*

**compiled language** (n.) Unlike an interpreted language, which is translated into machine code every time it is run, a compiled language is converted into machine language once. This code is stored and called each time the program is run. The collection of symbols used to write the program is called *source code.* The translated machine language is called *object code.* Examples of compiled languages are Pascal and C++.

**compiler** (n.) A computer program that translates higher-level language instructions into machine code that a computer can read.

**complement** (n.) The value that must be added to a number to yield a specified sum.

**complementary metal-oxide semiconductor** (CMOS) (n.) A metal-oxide semiconductor (MOS) device containing both N-channel and P-channel MOS active elements. CMOS is one of two basic processes (MOS and bipolar) used to fabricate integrated circuits (ICs).

**complex instruction set computing** (CISC) (n.) A type of microprocessing in which each instruction can perform several low-level functions, such as arithmetic operations, memory access, and address calculations. It is the predecessor of a reduced instruction set computing (RISC) processor. Common CISC processors are the Motorola 680x0 chips used in the Macintosh and in the Intel 80x86, including the 486 and Pentium.

**Component Object Model** (COM) (n.) An implementation of object linking and embedding (OLE) developed by Microsoft for interoperation of distributed objects in a network. Some of the capabilities it provides are similar to those defined in Common Object Request Broker Architecture (CORBA). In the same way that OLE provides services for a compound document, COM provides services for interface negotiation and makes networked objects available in response to an event.

**component video** (n.) A video signal in which the chrominance (color) and the luminance (brightness) components have been recorded separately. The result is better picture quality. S-VHS and Hi-8 offer two-part component, or Y/C. This format offers higher resolution than composite video (which mixes the Y and C components), because it yields increased bandwidth in the luminance portion of the signal. *Color-under,* or limited color bandwidth, is a process used in Y/C. The common betacam component system further divides color into three components (Y, R-Y, B-Y), which provide better luminance and color accuracy, and lower noise than Y/C.

**com port** See *communications port.*

**composite** 1. (v.) To build the final version of a production with layers drawn from video, graphics, and audio content, which are integrated according to the production plan. 2. (n.) In telecommunications, the output of a concentrator or multiplexer that includes the multiplexed data.

**Composite Capability/Preference Profile** (CC/PP) (n.) A general description of device capabilities and user preferences that allows a server to adapt content intended for presentation to a particular device. With an increasingly wide variety of devices connected to the Internet, there is a need to deliver content tailored to the capabilities of very different devices. Limited techniques are currently in use, such as HTML <alt> tags and HTTP "accept" headers. In order to provide increased contextualization for the interchange of information, a general-purpose profile format is required to describe the capabilities of a user agent and the preferences of its user. CC/PP is designed to meet that need. It is based on the Resource Description Framework (RDF), which was designed by the World Wide Web Consortium (W3C) as a general-purpose metadata description language. RDF provides a framework with the basic tools for both vocabulary extensibility using XML namespaces. RDF was designed to describe metadata or machine-understandable properties, and user-agent profiles are metadata intended primarily for communication between user agents and resource data providers. A CC/PP profile will contain attribute names and associated values for a server to determine the most appropriate form of a resource to deliver to a client. It will allow a client or proxy to describe its capabilities by referring to a standard profile. Conceptual work is now being done on CC/PP to enable cross-platform and device-independent data to flow freely and intelligibly among a broad range of equipment, with particular emphasis on wireless applications.

**composite video** (n.) A video signal in which all the information about color, brightness, line, field, sync, and blanking is mixed together. Cross-color artifacts are apparent in composite video, compared with component video, which has great clarity. Compare *red-green-blue*.

**composition** (n.) In video production, the visual makeup of a picture or scene. It includes such variables as balance, framing, field of view, texture, and other aesthetic considerations.

**compound document** (n.) A collection of mul-

tiple data types, each linked to the application that created it, connected by a navigable interface.

**Comprehensive Perl Archive Network** (CPAN) (n.) Internet archives with information about Perl. These archives are available at *ftp://ftp.funet.fi/pub/languages/perl/CPAN*.

**compress** (v.) To make a file significantly smaller without altering the substantive information. Compression eliminates redundant data. With analog audio files, compression limits the bandwidth and reduces the differences in amplitude between the softest and loudest sounds in a program. In most multimedia applications, digital video must be compressed in order to stream smoothly at an acceptable frame rate.

**compressed audio** (n.) In relation to digitally encoded sounds, a special processing technique that reduces the quantity of data required to define the sounds.

**Compressed SLIP** (C-SLIP) (n.) Compressed serial line Internet protocol; version of SLIP that uses Van Jacobson TCP header compression. It has no effect on the data in a packet and has nothing to do with compression by modem. It reduces a TCP header from 40 bytes to 7 bytes.

**compressed video** (n.) A video clip that is digitally encoded with computer algorithms to reduce the amount of data needed to define the video content.

**compression** (n.) The conversion of digital data, typically video and audio, into a more compact form by using complicated algorithms.

**compression-decompression** (CODEC) (n.) This may be either a software-only or a hardware-assisted scheme that is used to process digital video or audio files. The amount of data required to represent moving pictures with sound is reduced by a CODEC, which normally discards redundant data on compression. Some of the more widely used CODECs are Indeo, MPEG, CinePak, and the Sorenson Video.

**compression ratio** (n.) The size of an uncompressed data file divided by the size of the compressed version, expressing the degree to which a compression algorithm can reduce file size. The MPEG video compression algorithm typically achieves a ratio of 180:1. JPEG still-picture compression formulas achieve ratios of less than 20:1; at higher ratios, or with greater compression, they exhibit noticeable artifacts and blockiness.

**compressor** (n.) An audio signal-processing device used to reduce the dynamic range of a signal passing through it. The input dynamic range of a 100 dB signal could exit a compressor with a modified dynamic range of 60 dB. This is accomplished by using a voltage-controlled amplifier. The control voltage becomes a function of the input signal's dynamic content. The need to compress arises when sounds are recorded or broadcast. The sound of a live band may exceed 120 dB in dynamic range, while recording and broadcasting medium have a very limited dynamic range. A cassette tape and an FM broadcast both have a maximum 60 dB of dynamic range. Compressors seem to make loud sounds quieter and quiet sounds louder. Sound engineers set a threshold point below which the program is unaffected, and all audio above the threshold is compressed by the amount determined by a ratio control. In most applications, compressors are used to reduce the dynamic range of only the loudest signals.

**compromise** (n.) In network security, any intrusion into a computer system that may result in unauthorized disclosure, modification, or destruction of sensitive information.

**compulsory license** (n.) A license that permits the use of copyrighted work without the owner's specific consent, provided the user complies with legal formalities and pays a legislatively prescribed fee to the owner. Cable systems and other media distributors use copyrighted materials for a fee set by the government. There is no need for negotiation between the copyright holder and the licensee.

**CompuServe** (n.) An online Internet service provider founded in 1969 and purchased by America Online (AOL) in 1998. It is widely used internationally, with strong technical forums. The full name is CompuServe Information Service (CIS).

**computer** (n.) Programmable digital equipment that performs computations and manipulates data.

**computer-aided design/computer-aided manufacturing** (CAD/CAM) (n.) Software applications used by engineers for the graphic design of components and systems. Once components are built, they may be manipulated on screen and evaluated. CAM applications extrapolate manufacturing specifications from the CAD designs and may be used to control manufacturing processes.

**computer-aided instruction** (CAI) (n.) The use of computers to facilitate learning. Also called *computer-aided learning (CAL), computer-based instruction (CBI), computer-based learning (CBL)*, and *computer-based training (CBT)*.

**computer-aided learning** (CAL) (n.) The use of computers to facilitate learning. Also called *computer-aided instruction (CAI), computer-*

89

*based instruction (CBI), computer-based learning (CBL),* and *computer-based training (CBT).*

**computer-aided manufacturing** (CAM) (n.) Applications that use manufacturing specifications from computer-aided designs (CADs) to control the manufacturing processes. See also *computer aided design/computer-aided manufacturing.*

**Computer and Business Equipment Manufacturers Association** (CBEMA) (n.) A trade association with a rich history. Founded in Chicago as the National Association of Office Appliance Manufacturers in 1916, the organization changed its name to Office Equipment Manufacturers Institution in 1929, then to Business Equipment Manufacturers Association in 1961. In 1973 the organization became CBEMA, recognizing the importance of computers in business. In 1994 the association was reorganized and renamed the Information Technology Industry (ITI) Council. It continues to represent companies involved in the development of technology and promotes the global competitiveness of its member companies.

**computer-based instruction** (CBI) (n.) The use of computers to facilitate learning. Also called *computer-aided instruction (CAI), computer-aided learning (CAL), computer-based learning (CBL),* and *computer-based training (CBT).*

**computer-based learning** See *computer-aided learning.*

**computer-based training** See *computer-aided learning.*

**computer graphics** (n.) Any image a computer generates digitally. IBM-compatible PCs require graphics adapter cards to produce images generated by the computer on a screen. Some of the common standards for PC graphics are Color Graphics Adapter (CGA), Enhanced Graphics Adapter (EGA), Video Graphics Array (VGA), Super Video Graphics Array (SVGA), and Extended Graphics Adapter (XGA).

**Computer Graphics Metafile** (CGM) (n.) An object-oriented graphic file format used by many software applications.

**computer network attack** (CNA) (n.) Activities intended to disrupt, deny, degrade, or destroy computers and computer networks, or the information residing in them.

**Computer Oracle and Password System** (COPS) (n.) A computer network monitoring system for Unix machines. This software checks for security weaknesses on shell scripts and C programs.

**computer security** (n.) In a broad sense, this includes all procedures applied to computer systems to ensure the availability, integrity, and confidentiality of information managed by the computer system.

**Computer-Telephony Integration** (CTI) (n.) The combination of digital systems, data networks, and telecommunications infrastructure to provide communications solutions.

**COMSAT** See *Communications Satellite Corporation.*

**concatenate** (v.) In programming, to combine character strings.

**concentrator** (n.) A type of multiplexer for telecommunications signals. It allows numerous signals to be input and output simultaneously, using fewer outgoing lines than incoming lines. A concentrator may be used to connect as many as 24 individual 2400-bit-per-second (bps) lines to a host using a single

57 600-bps channel.

**concrete class** (n.) In object-oriented programming, a class that may be instantiated. Compare *abstract class.*

**condenser microphone** (n.) A microphone design in which a capacitor is created by stretching a thin diaphragm in front of a metal disc, or backplate. The diaphragm and backplate are very close together, and capacitance varies as a function of sound pressure. Changes in sound pressure cause the diaphragm to move, which changes the distance between the two surfaces. If the capacitor is first polarized with a fixed electrical charge and the movement changes the capacitance, then the backplate voltage varies proportionally to the sound pressure. To maintain a fixed charge, condenser microphones require external polarizing voltage. Some condenser mics have a battery in their circuitry, but most rely on phantom power from a microphone preamp or the mixing console.

**conditional branching** (n.) In computing, after a specified set of conditions is satisfied, the process by which previously programmed instructions take a user to a different location in the program. The destination to which the program branches is conditional, depending on the nature of a user's input. If specific conditions are not met, the computer follows the normal sequence without branching.

**conditioning** (n.) Costly treatment that may be applied to leased or dedicated voice-grade telephone company circuits used for data transmission. Once conditioned, the line should allow higher quality and faster data transmission. C-conditioning is used to improve frequency response and envelope delay distortion, available in grades C1, C2, or C4. Signal-to-noise ratio is improved by D1 conditioning.

**conduit** (n.) A pipe or tube through which cables are run. A conduit makes the installation of any type of cable much easier, and is required by many building codes.

**conference** (n.) In networked communications, an asynchronous online discussion area to which a user may post information and comments for others with access. During an audio or videoconference, all users are able to communicate in real time, or synchronously.

**confetti** (n.) Small, colored dots on a video screen caused by signal dropouts or video noise. See also *noise.*

**config.sys** (n.) A text file located in the root directory of an MS-DOS computer with system configuration commands. The operating system reads this file as the computer boots, after reading the setup file from the CMOS RAM and before running autoexec.bat. Common config.sys file commands are shown here with an explanation:

DEVICE=C:\DOS\HIMEM.SYS /testmem:off
(Load the expanded memory manager, or EMM.)

DEVICE=C:\DOS\EMM386.EXE RAM
(Load the expanded memory manager, or EMM.)

BUFFERS=10,0
(Specify memory for disk buffers.)

FILES=70
(Set the number of files that may be open simultaneously.)

DOS=UMB
(DOS is located in upper memory block, or UMB.)

LASTDRIVE=Z
(Disk drives are A: to Z:.)

FCBS=16,0
(Set the number of file control blocks, or FCBs.)

DEVICEHIGH /L:1,12048=
C:\DOS\SETVER.EXE
(Report the version of DOS to older programs.)

DOS=HIGH
(Maintain a link between DOS and UMB.)

COUNTRY=358,437 C:\DOS\COUNTRY.SYS
(Set the country code for some programs.)

STACKS=9,256
(Set dynamic stacks for hardware control.)

SHELL=C:\DOS\COMMAND.COM
C:\DOS\ /E:1024 /p
(Set the location of the command interpreter.)

**Connection Control Language** (CCL) (n.) A set of commands used to identify and manage data connections.

**connectionless** (adj.) A type of communication in which data transfer occurs between hosts without previous setup. Packets may take different routes because each is independent of the other. User Datagram Protocol (UDP) is a connectionless protocol.

**connection-oriented** (adj.) Describes communication in which data transfer moves through three phases: establishment of connection, data transfer, and release of connection. TCP is connection oriented.

**Conseil Européen pour la Recherche Nucléaire** (CERN, European Laboratory for Particle Physics) (n.) The Swiss research center at which the World Wide Web was developed.

**constant** (n.) In programming, a value that does not change. Compare *variable*.

**constant angular velocity** (CAV) (n.) The constant speed at which certain videodisc players spin a disc, regardless of the reading head's position. The tracks near the center pass under the reading head more slowly than the tracks near the perimeter. Each frame is separately addressable. The standard speed for CAV discs is 1800 rpm (NTSC) or 1500 rpm (PAL), and the disc makes one revolution for each frame. The maximum program duration is approximately 30 minutes per side on a 12-inch disc. Compare *constant linear velocity*.

**constant directivity** (CD) **horn** (n.) A high-frequency driver that exhibits constant distribution of high-frequency sound in the horizontal direction.

**constant linear velocity** (CLV) (n.) The variable rate at which certain optical disc or videodisc players spin a disc so that all data sectors pass under the reading head at the same rate. The disc rotates faster when the head is closer to the center of the disc and more slowly as the head moves away from the center of the disc. Videodiscs of this type are *extended-play discs;* they play twice as long per side as CAV discs, or up to one hour. The CLV format loses some of the control features of a CAV disc, such as freeze-frame capability. Compact discs (CDs) of all types spin at a constant linear velocity and exhibit a constant sector size. Compare *constant angular velocity*.

**constant-Q equalizer** (n.) Term for graphic and rotary equalizers describing bandwidth behavior as a function of boost/cut levels. The terms Q and *bandwidth* are interchangeable. The bandwidth remains constant for all boost/cut levels. For constant-Q designs, the area surrounding a boost/cut frequency, known as a "skirt," varies in direct proportion to the boost/cut level. Small boost/cut levels produce narrow skirts and large boost/cut levels produce wide skirts.

**constant-voltage** (adj.) In audio, a term that describes standard practices governing the interface between power amplifiers and loudspeakers used in distributed sound systems. The output voltage from a power source remains constant regardless of the load, so the output current varies, but not the voltage. The most common voltage level used in the U.S. is 70.7 volts RMS. The standard specifies that all power amplifiers put out 70.7 volts at their rated power, whatever the wattage may be.

**Consultative Committee for International Radio** (CCIR) (n.) 1. A European committee that sets radio and television standards. 2. The standard for the 625-line television system used in Western Europe, commonly referred to simply as CCIR.

The following standards are among those recommended by the committee:

- **CCIR-601** (n.) The standard for digital component video that specifies component color difference coding (Y, R-Y, B-Y) and the 4:2:2 format.

- **CCIR-656** (n.) The standard for digital component electrical interfaces that defines synchronizing signals and blanking, as well as parallel and serial interface specifications.

**Consumer Electronics Association** (CEA) (n.) Formerly the Consumer Electronics Manufacturers Association (CEMA), a group that is the primary source for information about the consumer electronics industry.

**consumer market** (n.) Also called the *domestic market,* the segment of the market in which au-

dio-video equipment is mostly used in homes and in which software consists of movies and games. The professional market uses industrial gear.

**content** (n.) The story, information, graphics, audio, and video material that is incorporated in a digital production.

**Content Scrambling System** (CSS) (n.) The method of encryption used for all DVD movies. Decryption keys vary by continent, and DVD players bought in one continent are able to decrypt only the discs sold in that continent. DVDs manufactured in Asia are not playable on DVD players sold in the U.S. because they use a different key. This is one reason for the proliferation of decryption (DeCSS) software.

**contention** (n.) In telecommunications, a method of access used by private branch exchange (PBX) or public telephone systems in which a limited number of ports serve numerous devices on a first-come, first-served basis.

**content provider** (n.) Owner or licensee of program material. Paramount and Viacom are content providers. Microsoft is both a software developer and a content provider.

**context-sensitive** (adj.) Depending on a user's actions, a context-sensitive program responds with help or prompts that are specifically related to activities in which the user is engaged.

**contiguous** (adj.) Describes a data storage file whose elements are grouped together, as opposed to being fragmented in separate locations on a disk. If a file is fragmented, it may not stream smoothly because the heads of the drive have to move around during transmission. Video files will drop frames on playback if they are not contiguous. To make all the files on a disk contiguous, one must execute the "defrag" command in

MS-DOS, the "defragment" command in Windows, or the "optimize" command with a Macintosh utility.

**continuity** (n.) 1. A condition that exists in an uninterrupted circuit or signal path. A continuity test determines whether a circuit is complete by measuring 0 ohms of resistance, whereas a broken circuit shows infinite ohms of resistance. 2. In video production, a logical succession of events that requires a video producer to position characters consistently and to place props in scenes that are meant to appear as a natural progression in time. 3. Directional consistency in camera angles from shot to shot.

**continuous branching** (n.) A feature of an interactive program that modifies the environment constantly in response to the user, rather than only at predetermined branching points or menus.

**Continuous Variable Slope Delta modulation** (CVSD) (n.) A speech digitizing and encoding technique that uses a one-bit sample to encode the difference between two successive signal levels. The sampling is usually done at 32,000 times a second, although some implementations employ lower sampling rates.

**contour control** (n.) A control found on professional DJ performance mixers that is used to change the shape or taper of the fader action. At 50 percent of travel, a fader may allow 50 percent, 10 percent, or 90 percent of the audio signal to pass depending on the taper of the control. The contour control (switched, continuous, or stepped variable) changes this amount.

**contrast** (n.) The range between the darkest and brightest components in an image. Displays often provide hardware adjustments for controlling contrast, and scanners permit software controls. Adjusting contrast in a selective manner can make relatively light or dark areas of an image visible while increasing detail.

**control channel** (n.) In wireless communications, a channel used to transmit digital control information from a base station to a cellular phone (forward), or from a cellular phone to a base station (reverse).

**control code** (n.) One of the 32 ASCII codes reserved for issuing hardware control commands, such as advancing a printer page.

**control voltage** (n.) In audio electronic circuits using voltage-controlled amplifiers, this is a DC voltage proportional to the audio input signal amplitude, sometimes frequency-dependent, which is used to set the instantaneous gain of some other device.

**Control-L** (n.) A one-way communication system in consumer model camcorders and VCRs that is used to approximately coordinate tape transport commands for automated editing.

**controller** (n.) 1. In computer hardware, a processing component that manages the flow of data between the computer and peripheral devices. 2. The input device for a video game that moves and manipulates objects on the screen. A mouse is a controller for a computer with a graphical user interface (GUI).

**control panel** (n.) In a graphical user interface (GUI), a utility program that may be used to adjust parameters for system settings, such as volume, color, and the rate of response to input devices.

**control panel device** (CDEV, pronounced "SEE-dev") (n.) A piece of system code used in the Mac OS to extend functionality.

**Control Program for Microprocessors** (CP/M) (n.) A specific microcomputer operating system (OS) developed by Digital Research Incorporated.

**Control-S** (n.) Bidirectional communication system that allows an external edit controller or compatible deck to issue tape transport commands to a slave unit VCR or camera.

**control track** (n.) 1. A track on video recorders that is imprinted with pulses to set timing and to align the tape with the recording and playback heads. 2. A rudimentary method of video positioning that counts pulses on the tape rather than reading time-stamped data to identify a frame's location.

**convergence** (n.) In a computer monitor, the alignment of the red, green, and blue light beams aimed at phosphors in a triad. The simultaneous firing of the red, green, and blue beams excites the three corresponding phosphors to generate the color white. Slight deviation of the beams due to magnetic misalignment of the electron trajectory causes colored shadows around pixels, giving the beams poor convergence. If the beams are perfectly aimed at the pixels on the screen, the monitor has good convergence.

**cookie** (n.) A handle, transaction ID, or other token of agreement between programs. The purpose of a cookie is to relate a later transaction to the current one. When a web server places a cookie on a client's hard disk, it can use that information in a subsequent connection to determine how information should be sent to that particular client. Netscape originated the concept. The decision of whether to accept a cookie offered by a web server is entirely up to the client. There is nothing inherently harmful or dangerous in accepting cookies, except that the client has no idea what information is transferred in the process. See also *HTTP cookie*.

**Coordinating Committee for Intercontinental Research Networks** (CCIRN) (n.) A committee that includes the United States Federal Networking Council (FNC) and similar agencies in Europe. The executive directors of the FNC and the European Association of Research Networks (RARE) are co-chairs of the committee. The CCIRN provides a forum for planning among North American and European research networking groups.

**copper** (n.) Network cable with a core conductor of copper or aluminum.

**Copper Distributed Data Interface** (CDDI) (n.) The implementation of Fiber Distributed Data Interface (FDDI) network protocols using twisted-pair copper wiring instead of fiber.

**coprocessor** (n.) Frequently referred to as a *math coprocessor,* a chip that was designed to execute floating-point calculations and other mathematical functions rapidly. Many spreadsheets and computer-aided design (CAD) applications are constructed to take advantage of a coprocessor's presence in a microcomputer's circuitry.

**COPS** See *Computer Oracle and Password System.*

**copyright** (n.) The ownership rights to an idea, document, graphic, sound, or other reproducible event or object. This right belongs to the creator unless creation is done under a work-for-hire contract. A copyright may be transferred to another party, or it may be licensed with limitations or contractual conditions.

### Ownership of Copyright
The act of digitizing pictures, sounds, words, and other concrete forms of expression is commonplace. The proliferation of scanners and capture cards makes the acquisition of graphics

95

and audio available to anyone with a computer. Yet multimedia producers must be especially careful about how the assets they digitize are used and distributed. A photograph is the property of the camera operator; each song belongs to its composer; text is owned by the writer; a graphic belongs to the artist; a sound is the property of the person who creates or samples it. Original work in any of these forms may not be copied and resold without express permission from the copyright holder, and it is the responsibility of the person who would digitize and use an asset to locate and secure permission from the owner.

A copyright provides ownership of intellectual property in which the author secures certain exclusive rights to an original work for a limited time. Copyright law is authorized by Article 1, Section 8 of the Constitution. The clause gives Congress the power "to promote science . . . by securing for limited times to authors . . . the exclusive right to their writings." Copyright protects the author's original expression only. It does not extend to ideas or facts presented in a copyrighted work. It does not include previously existing material that an author has incorporated into a new work.

### Recognized Copyrights in the United States

Copyright should not be confused with personality rights, such as the right of privacy, which are used to protect the name, voice, or persona of an individual. Things that are created by people are referred to as intellectual property since they are products of the mind. A work must be original to be copyrighted, and this means that it was created by the author. The work need not be different from everything preceding it, but it must embody creativity and it must be the "expression of an author." Only nonutilitarian aspects of a work are protected by copyright. If something is both a work of authorship and a useful article, copyright will not protect the useful aspects. It must exist in a fixed, tangible medium of expression. An idea is not protectable, but the expression of an idea is. In the United States, copyright includes the following rights:

1. *Reproductive Right:* The right to make copies of a work.
2. *Adaptive Right:* The right to produce derivative works based on a copyrighted work.
3. *Distribution Right:* The right to distribute copies of a work. (This includes importation right, the right to prevent unauthorized importation of a work.)
4. *Performance Right:* The right to perform a copyrighted work in public. (The performance right does not ordinarily apply to sound recordings, but a limited performance right prohibiting only digital performances of sound recordings was added in 1995.)
5. *Display Right:* The right to display a copyrighted work in public. (These rights apply to musical, dramatic, literary, choreographic, film, and video programs only. They do not apply to audio recordings or architectural designs.)

In addition to the rights that are part of copyright, United States law also provides for an author's rights in certain works of visual art such as signed and numbered limited edition paintings, photographs, or sculptures. These rights are technically not part of copyright, because they belong only to the author of the work, do not survive the author, and cannot be bought or sold (although they may be waived by contract). The two rights of an author are the rights of attribution and integrity:

• *Attribution Right:* The right of the author to claim authorship of a work, and the right to prevent being incorrectly identified as the author of a work.
• *Integrity Right:* The right to prevent inten-

tional distortion or destruction of a work and to prevent others from attributing a distorted version of the work to the author.

Not all rights last for the same period of time. Typically, a copyright endures for the life of the author plus 70 years; an author's rights, on the other hand, endure only for the life of the author. A series of restrictions on rights are found in Sections 107 through 120 of the copyright law.

## Fair Use

The "fair use" doctrine allows the courts to avoid rigid application of copyright statutes when this would inhibit creativity. Fair use originated "for criticism, comment, news reporting, teaching, . . . scholarship, or research . . . the distinction between 'fair use' and infringement may be unclear and not easily defined. There is no specific number of words, lines, or notes that may be taken safely without permission. Acknowledging the source of the copyrighted material does not substitute for obtaining permission."

The 1961 Report of the Register of Copyrights on the General Revision of the United States Copyright Law provides the following examples of fair use:

1. Reproduction by a teacher or student of a part of a work to illustrate a lesson.
2. Summary of an address or article with short quotations in a news report.
3. Quotation of short passages in a scholarly or technical work for illustration or clarification of the author's observations.
4. Quotation of excerpts in a review or criticism for purposes of illustration or comment.
5. Reproduction by a library of a portion of a work to replace a missing or damaged section.

6. Incidental reproduction in a newsreel or broadcast of a work that appears embedded in the scene of an event being reported.

Assuming that a piece of media (text, audio, graphic, or video) is the exclusive property of its creator, questions arise regarding conditions under which a portion of the piece may be used legally without specific license from the author. Permission is not required to make "fair use" of a copyrighted work. Four factors are used to determine whether a proposed use of a copyrighted work is a fair use:

1. "The purpose and character of the use." A nonprofit educational use is more likely to be deemed a fair use than a commercial use.
2. "The nature of the copyrighted work." Copying factual material is more likely to be considered a fair use than copying the same amount of artistic or fictional material.
3. "The amount and substantiality of the portion used in relation to the work as a whole." A small percentage or a limited amount is more likely to be allowable than a large part.
4. "The effect of the use upon the potential market or upon the value of a copyrighted work." No reduced earning capacity for the copyright holder should result from fair use.

The Consortium of College and University Media Centers (CCUMC) Fair Access Working Committee has made recommendations addressing the extent to which multimedia content may be used by instructors and students in an educational setting. More information may be found online at *http://www.indiana.edu/~ccumc/copyright.html*. The following guidelines are extracted from the

Working Committee's recommendations:

1. Educators may use portions of lawfully acquired copyrighted works in producing and using their own multimedia programs as teaching tools in support of an identified curriculum in face-to-face instruction. Similar use is permitted for remote instruction over an institution's electronic network, provided there are technological limitations on access to the network programs (a password or PIN) and on the total number of students enrolled.

2. Related to motion media, up to 10 percent or three minutes, whichever is less, in the aggregate of a copyrighted motion media work may be reproduced or otherwise incorporated as part of a multimedia program produced by an educator or student for educational purposes.

3. Related to text material, up to 10 percent or 1000 words may be incorporated; less than 250 words in the case of a poem, but no more than one poem by a single poet or five poems from an anthology may be used.

4. Related to music, up to 10 percent of an individual composition, or up to 10 percent of a musical recording, may be used for educational purposes. No more than 30 seconds of an individual copyrighted composition may be used in any case.

5. The reproduction of no more than five photographs and illustrations copyrighted by a single artist may be used in any one program. Not more than 10 percent or 15 images, whichever is less, may be used from a published collective work.

6. In any case where commercial reproduction and distribution will occur, licenses must be obtained.

7. Educators and students must obtain permission for all copyrighted works incorporated in programs that are distributed over uncontrolled electronic networks, for productions that are replicated beyond one copy, and in cases where institutions collaborate.

8. Citations and credit must be attributed to all sources of copyrighted works incorporated in multimedia programs, including those prepared under fair use. In the case of images used in remote instruction, the copyright notice, date, and name must appear onscreen with the image.

## Public Domain

A work in the public domain may be used by anyone for any purpose. Here are some of the ways in which a work may be deemed to be in the public domain:

1. The term of copyright has expired.

2. The work was created by the United States government and cannot be copyrighted.

3. The work is a title, a name, or a short phrase or slogan, and although it could be considered a trademark, it may not be copyrighted.

4. The copyright is forfeited. The copyright is forfeited in works published without notice prior to a change in the law that eliminated the notice requirement (March 1, 1988, the effective date of the Berne Convention Implementation Act).

5. The copyright has been abandoned. A direct statement or overt act dedicating the work to public domain is required by the copyright holder (a statement that anyone may reproduce, perform, or display the work without restrictions). Posting a work on a computer network does not constitute abandonment.

If there are any restrictions declared by the author on the use of a work, it is not public domain. It is copyrighted, and restrictions are essentially limitations. For example, the restriction that a work may only be given away for free is a limitation using the distribution right. Once a work is in the public domain, whether by expiration or dedication by the copyright holder, it cannot be restored except under certain conditions provided by the General Agreement on Tariffs and Trade (GATT) in 1994.

Failure to assert copyright against an infringer does not place a work in the public domain. At most, it might prevent the copyright owner from recovering from that infringer, if, for example, a statute of limitations has expired or if the infringer has relied on the copyright owner's failure to sue.

### Replication of Audio Recordings

The Audio Home Recording Act (AHRA) was passed in October 1992. It added 10 sections to the United States Copyright Act, one of which provided an alternative to the fair use analysis for musical recordings. It states:

> No action may be brought under this title alleging infringement of copyright based on the manufacture, importation, or distribution of a digital audio recording device, a digital audio recording medium, an analog recording device, or an analog recording medium, or based on the noncommercial use by a consumer of such a device or medium for making digital musical recordings or analog musical recordings.

This means consumers cannot be sued for making analog or digital audio copies for private noncommercial use. It applies to music only, not to recordings of spoken words. The AHRA provided that a royalty payment (the "DAT tax") be paid for each sale of digital audio tape to compensate composers for profits lost due to these copies.

The right to prevent the unauthorized fixation and trafficking in sound recordings and music videos was added to copyright law in 1994. "Rights in Unfixed Works," as they are called, resulted from GATT.

### All Rights Reserved

According to the 1911 Buenos Aires Convention on Literary and Artistic Copyrights, once copyright was obtained for a work in one signatory country, the other signatories offered protection without requiring registration, if a notice reserving rights was stated. The notice that complied with Buenos Aires was "All Rights Reserved." The "All Rights Reserved" notice no longer serves a useful purpose since the Buenos Aires Convention is not relevant today, having been superseded by other copyright treaties, such as the Universal Copyright Convention and the Berne Convention.

An official copyright notice includes the letter "C" in a circle or the word "Copyright," the year of initial publication, and the name of the copyright owner. If a copyright notice is included on a work to which the defendant in an infringement suit had access, the offender may not plead "innocent infringement." It is wise to include a notice on all published copies of a work.

### Duration of Copyright

The duration of a copyright depends on whether the work was created before or after January 1, 1978, the effective date of the Copyright Act of 1976. This act was amended by the Copyright Term Extension Act, which became law in October 1998. The amended law extends the term of most copyrights by 20 years. The Extension Act includes the following provisions:

1. Extends the duration of copyright in a work created on or after January 1, 1978, to the life of the author and 70 years (previously 50 years) after the author's death,

and applies the same extension to joint works.

2. Extends the duration of copyright in anonymous works or works made for hire on or after January 1, 1978, to 95 years (previously 75 years) from the year of the first publication, or 120 years (previously 100 years) from the year of creation, whichever expires first.
3. Prohibits the annulment or limitation of rights or remedies under state laws with respect to sound recordings fixed before February 15, 1972, until February 15, 2067 (previously 2047).
4. Extends from December 31, 2027, to December 31, 2047, the duration of copyright in works published on or before December 31, 2002.
5. Extends the duration of copyrights in their renewal term at the time of the effective date of this Act to 95 years from the date such copyrights were originally secured.

The law permits an author to terminate a transfer or a license of a renewal (executed before January 1, 1978) of a copyright (other than a work made for hire) subsisting in its renewal term on the effective date of this Act, for which the termination right has not been exercised, and has expired, by such date. Allows termination of a transfer or license grant at any time during the five years beginning at the end of 75 years from the date the copyright was originally secured. Copyrights are not renewable. Attribution and integrity rights endure only for the lifetime of the author.

During the last 20 years of any term of copyright of a published work, the law allows a library or archive to reproduce, distribute, display, or perform in digital form a copy or phonorecord of such work for purposes of preservation, scholarship, or research after deter-

mining that none of the following conditions apply:

1. The work is subject to normal commercial exploitation.
2. A copy or phonorecord of the work can be obtained at a reasonable price.
3. The copyright owner or its agent provides notice that either of such conditions applies.

The law declares that the distribution of phonorecords before January 1, 1978, shall not constitute publication of the musical work for purposes of copyright infringement under the Copyright Act of 1909.

### Copyright and the Internet
Usenet postings and email messages are copyrighted. They are "original works fixed in a tangible medium of expression." Only a clear declaration by the author would place a work into public domain. The two doctrines that allow copying are fair use and implied license. If the use was not commercial in nature, the posting was not an artistic or dramatic work, a short quotation was made for criticism and comment, and there was no impact on any market for the posting, it would probably qualify as fair use. Quoting of private email messages that met such criteria would also qualify. However, disseminating some email messages could lead to liability unrelated to copyright if the message were defamatory, an invasion of privacy, or a trade secret.

If a clearly visible limitation on the right to copy or quote is stated in the posting or message, it would be difficult to defend against infringement. On the other hand, implied license might be assumed for email messages posted to a public mailing list without stated limitations.

Postings and email messages are not usually registered with the Copyright Office. Registration is a requirement in order for a copyright owner to recover statutory damages and attorney fees. Therefore, if a copyright owner were to sue for infringement of an email or posting, he or she would probably be limited to collecting actual damages caused by the infringement (i.e., an actual monetary loss or a profit to the infringer that resulted from the infringement). Because those damages are so negligible, it would be of little benefit to sue, even if the copying of an email or posting were an infringement.

### Digital Millennium Copyright Act

Effective October 1998, this law has numerous provisions for multimedia producers worldwide and impacts those who provide Internet services. The main provisions of this Act are:

1. Implements the terms of the World Intellectual Property Organization (WIPO) Copyright Treaties (Title I).
2. Prohibits circumvention of technological measures that control access to copyrighted works (copy protection schemes) (Title I).
3. Limits liability to online service providers (Title II).
4. Provides exemptions for use of diagnostic computer programs (Title III).
5. Makes other miscellaneous changes (Title IV).
6. Provides two years of protection for certain designs for useful articles (Title V).

The WIPO Copyright Treaties Implementation Act (Title I) grants copyright protection to:

1. Sound recordings that were first fixed in a treaty party (a country other than the United States that is a party to international copyright agreements).
2. Pictorial, graphic, or sculptural works incorporated in a building or an architectural work embodied in a building located in the United States or a treaty party.

Section 103 of the Act prohibits two things. The first is circumvention of technological protection measures that control access to protected works. The second is manufacturing or distributing technology designed to circumvent measures that control access to or protect rights of copyright owners. There are two exemptions to these prohibitions. The first is for nonprofit libraries, archives, or educational institutions that gain access to a commercially exploited copyrighted work solely to make a good faith determination of whether to acquire such work, subject to certain conditions. The second exemption is for law enforcement and intelligence activities.

The law defines "copyright management information" as the title and name of author and copyright owner conveyed in connection with copies or phonorecords of a work or performances or displays. The law recognizes digital forms of this information as valid. It prescribes criminal penalties for violations committed for commercial advantage or financial gain. It makes criminal penalties inapplicable to nonprofit libraries, archives, and educational institutions. It also imposes a statute of limitations on criminal proceedings.

The Online Copyright Infringement Liability Limitation Act (Title II) amends federal copyright law to exempt an online material provider from liability for direct infringement, based solely on the intermediate storage and transmission of material through such provider's system or network, if:

1. The transmission was initiated by another person.
2. The storage and transmission is carried out through an automatic process.
3. No copy of such material is maintained in a manner ordinarily accessible to anyone other than the intended recipients and no copy is maintained any longer than necessary.

The law exempts such a provider from liability if the provider is not aware of facts or circumstances from which infringing activity is apparent and if there is no financial benefit directly attributable to the infringing activity. It further exempts a provider from any claim based on disabling online access to material in response to knowledge or information that such material is infringing, whether or not such material is in fact an infringement. The law also makes liable for damages any person who misrepresents that online material is an infringement.

The law provides that it is not a copyright infringement for the owner or lessee of a machine to make a copy of a computer program solely by activating a machine that lawfully contains an authorized copy of the program exclusively for maintenance or repair of that machine, provided:

1. The new copy is used in no other manner and is destroyed immediately after the maintenance or repair.
2. Any program that is not necessary for machine activation is not accessed or used other than to make such new copy by activation of the machine.

### Differences Between Copyright and Patent

The primary differences between a copyright and a patent in the United States are as follows:

1. The subject matter protected: A copyright covers "works of authorship" (literary, dramatic, musical, pictorial, graphic, audio-video, sound recordings, and the like). A patent covers an invention or a useful new feature of a product or process.
2. The requirement for protection: To be copyrighted, a work must be original and fixed in a tangible medium of expression. A patented invention must be new and useful. A patent is not automatic; it must be issued by the United States Patent and Trademark Office.
3. When protection begins: Copyright protection currently begins when a work is created. Patent protection begins when a patent is issued.
4. Duration of protection: Copyright protection typically lasts for 50 years beyond the author's death. Patents filed after June 8, 1995, in the United States have a term of 20 years from the filing date. Patents in effect on that date have a term of 20 years, or 17 years from the date of issue, whichever is longer.
5. Infringement: If a person other than the copyright owner independently comes up with a similar work, there is no infringement. A patent confers a monopoly that prevents others from selling the patented invention, although a person may independently reinvent a patented invention.

Another significant difference is the cost. A copyright is free. A patent is costly and the patent application process is much more complex. A copyright protects an author's rights inherent in a work. A patent provides ownership to an inventor in exchange for publicly sharing the details and specifications of an invention.

### Copyright and Employment

The company for which an employee works may own the copyrights to his or her work by applying either the assignment or the work-made-for-hire doctrine:

*Assignment:* Many companies automatically acquire a blanket assignment of copyright for any works created on the job starting at time of hiring.

*Work made for hire:* A work qualifies as a work made for hire if it was prepared by an employee within the scope of employment or if it was specially commissioned and the parties agreed in writing that it was to be considered a work for hire.

### Infringement and Penalties

Infringement is considered a civil matter (a tort). It may also be a federal crime in certain circumstances. If it is willful and committed for commercial advantage or financial gain, it is subject to criminal prosecution. In cases of offending reproduction or distribution rights of 10 or more copies with a value of more than $2500 during any 180-day period, the offense is a felony. The statute of limitation for copyright infringement for both civil suits and criminal prosecutions is three years.

The United States government may be sued for copyright infringement. Whether a state may be sued is unclear. The Eleventh Amendment says that a state cannot be sued in federal court. The Copyright Act expressly states, however, that a state can be sued for copyright infringement. Until 1996, it was generally thought that the clause in the Copyright Act did indeed make a state liable for its infringements. However, a 1996 case involving an Indian tribe suing a state on an issue completely unrelated to copyright put some important restrictions on the ability of Congress to abrogate a state's immunity. As a result, there is considerable uncertainty today as to whether a state may be sued for copyright infringement.

Works of the United States government are generally considered to be in the public domain. For purposes of copyright law, the United States Postal Service, the District of Columbia, Puerto Rico, and organized territories of the United States are not considered to be part of the United States government.

If an independent contractor working for the government produces a work, it may be copyrighted, and nothing prevents that contractor from assigning the copyright to the government. Unlike federal government works, those credited to state governments are subject to copyright.

### Securing Copyright
### on an Original Story or Song

In the United States and most other countries, a work is automatically copyrighted when it is created. The following statement is from Section 102 of the Copyright Act:

> Copyright protection subsists . . . in original works of authorship fixed in any tangible medium of expression, now known or later developed, from which they can be perceived, reproduced, or otherwise communicated, either directly or with the aid of a machine or device.

A work is "fixed" in a tangible medium of expression when its embodiment in a copy or phonorecord, by or under the authority of the author, is sufficiently permanent or stable to permit it to be perceived, reproduced, or otherwise communicated for a period of more than transitory duration.

It is not necessary to register a work with the Copyright Office or to provide a copyright notice on the work. However, it is wise to register a work and to include a copyright notice for purposes of defending it against infringement.

### How to Register a Copyright
### with the United States Copyright Office

Forms for registering are available from the Copyright Office at its online address: *http://lcweb.loc.gov/copyright/forms.html*. They are in the Adobe Acrobat (.pdf) format. A copyright may be registered by filing the appropriate form with a $20 payment for registration and two copies of the work. A Copyright Office Information Package includes the appropriate forms and instructions for filing. For information, contact the United States Copyright Office at (202) 707–3000, or call (202) 707–6737 to order forms. Packages are available for the following types of media:

- *Computer programs:* Form TX, Package 113
- *Photographs:* Form VA, Package 107
- *Motion pictures and video recordings:* Form PA, Package 110
- *Games:* Form TX, Package 108
- *Drawings, prints, and visual artworks:* Form VA, Package 115
- *Music (sheet or lyrics):* Form PA, Package 105
- *Music (sound recordings):* Form SR, Package 121
- *Dramatic scripts, plays, and screenplays:* Form PA, Package 119
- *Books, manuscripts, and nondramatic literature:* Form TX, Package 109

---

### Copyright Information on the Internet

The 1971 Paris Text of the Berne Convention is at the Cornell site:
www.law.cornell.edu/treaties/berne/overview.html

The Multilaterals Project, which provides copies of both the Berne Convention and the Universal Copyright Convention, is available at Tufts:
http://fletcher.tufts.edu/multilaterals.html

The Coalition for Networked Information (CNI) sponsors CNI-Copyright, an Internet mailing list devoted to copyright issues. The FTP site is:
ftp://ftp.cni.org/CNI/forums/cni-copyright

Some Usenet newsgroups that address copyright issues are:
misc.legal, misc.legal.computing, misc.legal.moderated, and comp.software.licensing

---

## Protecting Rights with Specific Licenses

Creators of multimedia who have ownership in content may need to consider ways to protect their interests. A licensing contract is ambiguous if the rights granted are not specific. A licensee grants an implied negative covenant to the licensor not to use the ungranted portion of the copyright to the detriment of the licensee. There are four steps that parties may take to clarify contractual license agreements:

1. Specify the rights that are granted and those that are not. One right that many multimedia producers may wish to retain is the Right to Reuse Art, or to make a number of copies to show as portfolio samples. The wording in a contract might be as follows: . . . Nothing in this Contract deprives the Licensor of the right to copy or display the Artwork otherwise exclusively licensed hereunder to the extent (1) the Artwork is not sold, (2) it is used solely for the purposes of promoting the Licensor's work in a portfolio, and (3) the Licensee shall have continuing nonexclusive rights to the Artwork.

2. The Reservation of Rights clause may be included in a license contract to avoid granting more rights than intended. It could be stated in the following terms: . . . This Contract is a complete statement of the rights granted related to the Artwork that is licensed. All rights and licenses of any kind, including copyrights and rights that might otherwise be implied that are not expressly granted in this Contract are reserved exclusively by the Licensor.

3. Multimedia producers may wish to include a Merger clause in their licenses. Such a clause is intended to prevent a court from considering previous verbal agreements (or anything else) that may modify the terms of a contract. An ex-

ample might read as follows: . . . This contract sets forth the entire agreement of the parties relating to its subject matter and merges and supersedes all prior discussions or understandings of any kind, written or oral. The terms of this contract may not be changed, modified, canceled, or terminated except by a written document signed by all parties to this contract that explicitly refers to this contract.

4. Producers and developers may choose to specify that the publisher of their work maintain accurate records related to royalties, and that an accountant be permitted to inspect the books on which royalties are based annually. This is a Standard Audit clause.

As they apply to interactive digital media, copyright laws are being defined and tested on a case-by-case basis. Precedents are being set at a time when new forms of art, and indeed the media and forms of communication by which they are fixed and transmitted, are evolving at an accelerated pace. Still, the age-old concepts of fairness and granting credit where it is due will guide decisions as they always have.

**copy stand** (n.) A table or flat surface with a photographic or video camera stationed overhead. Lamps are mounted on the sides to illuminate an image or object placed on the stand, which is the focal point of the camera.

**CORBA** See *Common Object Request Broker Architecture.*

**core** (n.) In fiber optics, the center part of an optical waveguide through which light passes. In single-mode fiber, the core diameter is 8 to 12 microns, whereas in multimode fiber, the diameter may range up to 100 microns.

**corrupted data** (n.) Data that has lost its integrity and that is partially damaged. The loss of any data can cause an entire file to become corrupted and can render it unreadable.

**COS** See *Class of Service.*

**Cosmo Player** (n.) A special browser developed for the SGI platform that interprets virtual reality modeling language (VRML) commands.

**cost per megabyte** (n.) A measure of the price for each megabyte of usable storage. The common formula is to divide the cost of the drive or of the medium by the number of megabytes. This measure alone ignores performance, which is a more significant factor in evaluating storage devices.

**cost per thousand impressions** (CPM) (n.) In marketing, this is the metric for judging the merits of a media buy. For print collateral, CPM is calculated by dividing the total cost of a given advertisement by the total estimated viewers, then multiplying this figure by 1000. On the Web, CPM is calculated using the number of actual ads served. Marketers must guess how many times a print ad is seen, whereas a web server records the exact figure.

**courseware** (n.) The aggregate of discs, books, illustrations, tapes, and computer programs required for the delivery of an instructional module. The name implies that there is a software component.

**CPAN** See *Comprehensive Perl Archive Network.*

**CPE** See *Customer Premises Equipment.*

**CP/M** See *Control Program for Microprocessors.*

**CPM** See *cost per thousand impressions.*

cps See *characters per second* or *cycles per second*.

CPU See *central processing unit*.

CR See *carriage return*.

**Crack** (n.) A popular hacking tool used to decode encrypted passwords. System administrators use Crack to assess weak passwords in order to enhance the security of an information system.

**cracker** (n.) Jargon for a person who gains unauthorized access to a computing system with malicious intent.

**cracking** (v.) Breaking into a computer system or network.

**crash** (n., v.) Usually refers to a system crash, caused by a software malfunction and remedied by rebooting the machine. A head crash on a hard disk drive causes physical damage.

**crawl** (n., v.) The steady, controlled display of text, horizontally or vertically. Rolling credits at the end of a movie are an example of text crawl. Sometimes used as slang for thin undulating lines along the edge of a video monitor that appear to "crawl" like a snake. This may be due to the alignment of video heads or to timing errors.

**crawler** (n.) A robot, typically one that searches sites on the web.

CRC See *cyclic redundancy check*.

**crest factor** (n.) The term used to represent the ratio of the peak (crest) value to the RMS value of a waveform measured over a specified time interval. A sine wave has a crest factor of 1.4 (or 3 dB), since the peak value equals 1.414 times the RMS value. Music typically has a wide crest factor range of 4–10, which may be translated to 12–20 dB. Headroom is an important factor when recording music, because the peaks occur 12–20 dB higher than the RMS value of sound levels.

**critical band** (n.) In psychoacoustics, a range of frequencies summed together by the neural system, equivalent to a bandpass filter about $\frac{1}{3}$-octave wide. The width of the band varies with the frequency range. The ear perceives a series of overlapping critical bands, each responding to a narrow range of frequencies.

**crop** (v.) To cut off one or more sides of an image to make it smaller or to eliminate unnecessary material.

**crossbar switch** (n.) An electromechanical telephone switch that connects vertical and horizontal leads by moving electronic bars. Dating from the 1930s, this technology is still employed in some central offices.

**cross-compiler** (n.) A compiler that runs on one type of processor and that generates code for another type of processor.

**crossfade control** (n.) In audio engineering, a slider or knob that is used to smoothly replace one signal with another in the mix, reducing the level of one while amplifying the other.

**crossfader** (n.) In audio, a term frequently applied to a control on DJ mixers. It is a sliding potentiometer control that allows the DJ to transition from one stereo program source to another. The crossfader is the main remix tool for a turntablist.

**cross-hatching** (n.) Filling or shading an area

of a graphic with evenly spaced intersecting lines. See figure.

*cross-hatching*

**Cross-Interleaved Reed-Solomon Code** (CIRC) (n.) The first level of error correction that is used in every compact disc (CD), and the only one that is used for audio CDs. CIRC consists of two Reed-Solomon Codes interleaved crosswise.

**crossover** (n.) An electrical circuit, either active or passive, in which filters are used to divide the audio frequency spectrum (20 Hz–20 kHz) into segments suitable for individual loudspeaker use. The wavelengths of sounds vary from over 50 feet at the low end to less than one inch at the high end. A crossover divides the signal into frequencies appropriate for each size of driver. A loudspeaker with two drivers, a woofer and a tweeter, might be crossed over at 800 Hz, splitting the high and low frequencies. Crossover circuits are characterized by their type, such as Butterworth, Bessel, and Linkwitz–Riley.

**cross-platform** (adj.) The capacity of software to run on different operating systems and hardware. Cross-platform development means that an asset is captured or prepared on a different platform from the one on which it is delivered.

**cross-polarization** (n.) Use of two transmitters, with both operating on the same frequency. In this configuration, one transmitter-receiver pair is vertically polarized, and the other is horizontally polarized.

**cross-post** (v.) To place an article on Usenet that is copied to more than one newsgroup simultaneously.

**crosstalk** (n.) Unwanted transference of electrical energy from one transmission channel to another, usually adjacent, channel.

**CRT** See *cathode-ray tube.*

**cryptography** (n.) A branch of science that addresses principles and methods for rendering plain text unintelligible and for converting encrypted messages into intelligible form.

**cryptology** (n.) The science that deals with hidden, disguised, or encrypted communications.

**C-SLIP** See *Compressed SLIP.*

**CSMA/CD** See *carrier sense multiple access with collision detection.*

**CSS** See *Cascading Style Sheets* or *Content Scrambling System.*

**CSU** See *channel service unit.*

**CSU/DSU** See *channel service unit/data service unit.*

**CTCP** See *Client To Client Protocol.*

**CTI** See *Computer-Telephony Integration.*

**CTS** See *clear to send.*

**C2** (n.) A Cross-Interleaved Reed-Solomon

Code (CIRC) that corrects burst errors and detects other errors.

**CUA Architecture** (n.) A style of user interface developed by IBM and used in OS/2 and Microsoft Windows.

**cucalorus** (n.) Lighting accessory with random cutouts that is used to simulate shadows, known as "cookie shadows" in the jargon of video producers.

**cue** 1. (v.) In audio, to monitor, with headphones, a specific source. Sometimes this term is used interchangeably with solo, a control found on a mixing board. 2. (n.) A piece of music used in film or video, ranging from a short segment of background music to a complex score. 3. (n.) An extract from the music for another part printed, usually in smaller notes, on a performer's part as a signal to enter after a long rest. 4. (n.) A gesture by a conductor to signal the entrance of a performer. 5. (n.) Any word or action that prompts another event in a performance. It might be an actor's word, an entrance, a change in lighting, or a sound effect.

**cue inserter** (n.) A specialized device used with videodisc mastering equipment to identify the field in which to place the frame ID code when recording from video. The cue inserter places cues in the vertical blanking interval (VBI) of the master tape for transfer to disc.

**cue, still** (n.) A signal in the vertical blanking interval (VBI) of a master tape that identifies a still frame on a videodisc.

**CUI** See *character user interface.*

**current** (n.) The flow of electric charge, measured in amperes. The amount of electric charge flowing past a specified circuit point per unit of time, or the rate of flow of electrons. As electrons flow in one direction, the holes left behind appear to flow in the opposite direction. Current can be visualized as electron flow (negative current flow) or hole flow (positive current flow), called *conventional* current flow.

**current loop** (n.) A data transmission technique that is predicated on current flow rather than voltage levels. A lack of current flow is recognized as a binary zero, and the presence of current flow as a binary one. This type of system is relatively insensitive to cable impedance and requires no common ground reference. The MIDI transmission protocol is an example of a current loop connecting system.

**cursor** (n.) An image, arrow, or I-beam on a computer screen that shows where information may be entered or where a mouse or light pen are located on the screen. It may be represented by any icon.

**CU-SeeMe** (n.) Developed at Cornell University in 1992, a shareware videoconferencing application for the web. It facilitates audiovisual connections between clients and supports multiuser conferencing by using servers called *reflectors* to distribute the video and audio signals between multiple clients. It is available at *http://www.cu-seeme.net/release/.* Pronounced "SEE-you-SEE-me."

**Customer Information Control System** (CICS) (n.) An IBM product and mainframe operating environment designed to enable transactions entered at remote terminals to be processed concurrently by user-written programs. It includes facilities for building and maintaining databases and is used by central offices.

**Customer Premises Equipment** (CPE) (n.)

Computers and household telephone equipment, fax machines, or modems that interconnect with the network at the customer's premises or that are owned by someone other than the telephone company that provides services.

**Custom Local Area Signaling Services** (CLASS) (n.) Enhanced telephone services that rely on the Signaling System 7 (SS7) channel to carry data about a call. CLASS enables services such as call forwarding and caller ID.

**cut** 1. (n.) In audio and video, a segment or scene taken from a production. 2. (n.) Command from the director to stop acting and recording immediately. 3. (v.) In video editing, to change scenes abruptly without using a transition.

**cut and paste** (v.) To lift and reposition a segment of a document or an image to another location on screen, to another document, or to a file created by a different application. Clips are usually stored on the clipboard during a cut and paste.

**cutaway** (n.) In video, a shot of something that is not the principal subject or action but that is related to it in some way. The technique is often used to provide transitional footage or to avoid a jump cut.

**cutoff frequency** (n.) In an audio filter, the frequency at which the signal falls off by 3 decibels from its maximum value, which is the half-power point. Cutoff frequencies are also known as the *-3 dB points* or the *corner* frequencies.

**cuts-only editing** (n.) A method of videotape editing in which shots are connected from one scene to another directly without transitions, such as *wipes* or *dissolves*. See also *cut* or *edit*.

**CVSD** See *Continuous Variable Slope Delta modulation.*

**cyber-** Jargon used by newbies and outsiders as a prefix to refer to the world of networked computers. An example is *cyberspace,* first used by William Gibson in his book *Neuromancer.*

**cybernetics** (n.) The study of nervous system controls in the brain as a basis for developing information-processing and communications technologies.

**cyberspace** (n.) Jargon used by newbies to refer to an environment made possible by a network of computers designed for exploration and communication with both data structures and other humans. This term was introduced in *Neuromancer* by William Gibson.

**cycles per second** (cps) (n.) Number of times that a regularly repeating waveform completes its motion in the time span of one second. A complete cycle includes movement through both the peak and the trough of a wave. In the case of a square wave, a cycle includes both positive and negative states.

**cyclic redundancy check** (CRC) (n.) An error detection scheme in reading, writing, or transmitting data. The value of the CRC character in a block of data received must match the value transmitted.

**cylinder** (n.) The set of tracks that are aligned vertically on platters and that are accessible without head movement in a hard disk drive. Units of data that are related to one another are placed in cylinders so that they may be read faster and so that they require less head movement, or *seek time.*

**Cyrix 6x86** (n.) A 64-bit 80x86-compatible microprocessor designed by Cyrix and manufactured by IBM. It combines aspects of both reduced instruction set computing (RISC) and complex instruction set computing (CISC) chips.

Cyrix 6x86 has a superscalar, superpipelined core and performs register renaming as well as speculative execution. It is socket-compatible with the Pentium P54C processor.

# D

**D2 tape format** (n.) A digital videotape composite format for mastering that permits multiple generations of dubbing without an apparent loss of picture quality. It is based on an eight-bit digital version of NTSC or Phase Alternation Line (PAL) composite video. Because D2 format is composite, it does not have the pristine quality of D1 format, which is a component digital format. The tape itself is 19 mm wide and can record up to 208 minutes of programming.

**D3 format** (n.) The telecommunications digital service (DS) Level 1 format with 24 eight-bit channels, each of which has a bandwidth of 8 kHz. Its data rate of 1.544 megabits per second (Mbps) is an old Bell standard in North America, not the CCITT standard of 2.048 Mbps used elsewhere.

**DA-88** (n.) A digital multitrack recorder made by Tascam that uses 8-mm videotape for a storage medium.

**DA** See *distribution amplifier.*

**D/A** See *digital-to-analog.*

**DAB** See *digital audio broadcasting.*

**DAC** See *D/A converter.*

**D/A converter** (DAC, pronounced "DACK") (n.) Digital-to-analog converter; a microprocessor chip or circuit that converts numerical data represented by a string of discrete numbers into analog information represented in continuous form, such as a signal that speakers may render into sound.

**DACS** See *Digital Access and Cross-Connect System.*

**daemon** (n.) A program that lies dormant waiting for certain conditions to occur. Unix systems run daemons to handle requests for services from other network hosts. Examples included ftpd and nfsd (file transfer), rlogind and telnetd (remote login), cron (local timed command execution), and rshd (remote command execution). Pronounced "DEE-mun."

**daisy chain** (n.) A pattern of bus wiring in which all devices receive identical signals, unless a device in the chain modifies the signal before passing it on. The Apple LocalTalk protocol (RS-485) and Thin Ethernet (10BASE2) are examples. In a more general sense, the term refers to connecting electronic devices, such as peripherals, in a series.

**daisy-wheel printer** (n.) An impact printer that prints individual letters arranged around the edge of a disk, which serves as the print head. The disk resembles a daisy with many petals or a wheel with spokes. See figure.

*daisy wheel from a printer*

**damping factor** (n.) A measure of a power amplifier's ability to control the reflex motion (back-emf) of the loudspeaker cone after the signal disappears. The damping factor of a system is the ratio of the loudspeaker's nominal impedance to the total impedance driving it.

**DAP** See *Directory Access Protocol.*

**dark fiber** (n.) Inactivated fiber-optic line with no associated opto-electronics. The term refers to the physical cable itself, rather than a certain amount of bandwidth or transport capacity. Telephone and utility companies are deploying large quantities of dark fiber to meet anticipated future demand. The opto-electronics may be added as needed.

**DARPA** See *Defense Advanced Research Projects Agency.*

**DASH** See *digital audio stationary head.*

**DAT** See *digital audio tape.*

**data** (n.) In the digital realm, information processed or produced by computers. In general, any collection of numerals, letters, and symbols that define something, whether it be an idea, document, image, condition, situation, or event.

**data area** (n.) According to ISO 9660, the space on a CD-ROM where user data is written, immediately following the system area. The data area begins at 00:02:16 absolute time.

**database** (n.) A file of information assembled in an orderly manner by a program designed to record and manipulate data. A telephone directory is an example of output from a database.

**database management system** (DBMS) (n.) A suite of programs that are used to manage structured sets of persistent data and that offer users query facilities. Oracle and Sybase are examples. A DBMS controls the organization, storage, and retrieval of fields, records, and files in a database, in addition to controlling the security and integrity of the database. Data security prevents unauthorized users from viewing or altering information in the database. A DBMS can maintain database integrity by not allowing more than one user to update the same record at the same time and by keeping duplicate records out of the database. Query languages allow users to interrogate the database interactively and to analyze its data.

Database design is the process of deciding how

to organize data into record types and how the record types should relate to one another. An information system is made up of subjects (customers, employees, vendors) and activities (orders, payments, purchases). A DBMS mirrors an organization's data structure and processes the transaction volume efficiently. Hierarchical, network, and relational databases are common methods of organizing data. *Hierarchical databases* link records together as in an organization chart, and a record type has only one owner. In *network database* structures, a record type can have multiple owners. *Relational databases* do not link records together physically, but the design of the records provides a common field to allow for matching. A relational database is the most flexible, but it may be too slow for heavy transaction processing.

**database query language** (n.) The type of programming language employed by database users to formulate requests and generate reports. A widely used example is Structured Query Language (SQL).

**database server** (n.) In a local area network (LAN), the computer that holds and manages a database. Unlike a file server, which acts as a remote disk drive, the database server performs management tasks.

**data binding** (n.) The substitution of a real value in a program after it has been compiled. During compilation, a compiler may assign symbolic addresses to certain variables or instructions. When the program is bound, or linked, the binder replaces the symbolic addresses with real machine addresses. Data binding allows the client to retrieve content from a database using a dynamic HTML interface. Microsoft Internet Explorer supports DHTML data binding.

**data bus** (n.) Circuitry for transferring data between computer components, connecting the ports, the memory, the controllers, and the microprocessor. A *system bus* is the pathway on which data travels between components within a computer. Types of PC buses are the processor bus, the address bus, the memory bus, and the input/output (I/O) bus. Two distinct types of *I/O buses* are the serial bus and the parallel bus. A *serial bus* sends one bit of data at a time and is used to send data over longer distances than the parallel bus. Some common examples of serial buses are a local area network (LAN) using 10BASE2 Ethernet, the ACCESS.bus, and the Universal Serial Bus (USB). A *parallel bus* is more limited in the distance it covers because it sends data in synchronized chunks over multiple lines, rather than bit by bit. A parallel bus can send 8, 16, 32, or 64 bits at once, along with control and address signals. The SCSI bus and IEEE 488 graphics bus are common examples of parallel buses that move data over cables and connectors to and from external components. Several internal parallel buses exist on the motherboard of a PC. The internal parallel bus as a whole moves data within a computer with a combination of connectors, voltages, and timing signals.

**data capture** (n.) A process by which analog material is read, often by an optical sensor, and converted to digital data that a computer can process. The original captured content comes from a graphic, video, or text source. In audio applications, the capture device is a sampler. To capture data is to digitize it.

**data channel** (n.) The path through which data travels between the input/output (I/O) devices and computer memory. More than one I/O operation may be performed concurrently, and the flow of information is bidirectional. On an

ISDN line, whether Basic Rate Interface (BRI) or Primary Rate Interface (PRI), the data channel carries control information and sets up connections on associated bearer channels.

**data communications equipment** (DCE) (n.) An intermediary device in a serial RS-232C communication system that receives, modulates, and parses a signal.

**data converter bits** (n.) The number of bits used to define an analog signal as it is converted to data. This number determines the precision of a data converter. Using more bits to define an analog signal results in more precise conversion. Conversion using 16 bits yields 65 536 possible identifiers, while conversion using 24 bits yields 16 777 216 possible identifiers.

**data-driven attack** (n.) In network security, a form of attack encoded in seemingly innocuous data that is triggered by a user. A data-driven attack may get through a firewall and launch an attack against a system behind the firewall.

**data encryption key** (DEK) (n.) Private information used to encode message text securely and to verify signatures.

**Data Encryption Standard** (DES) (n.) A security scheme for data communications specified by Federal Information Processing Standard (FIPS) publication 46 and approved by the National Bureau of Standards (NBS).

**Data Exchange Format** (DEF) (n.) A format for computer-aided design (CAD) programming files developed by Autodesk for its AutoCAD program. It is platform-independent and is also called *Drawing Interchange Format (DXF)*.

**data fork** (n.) The portion of a Macintosh file that contains pure data, exclusive of proprietary system data. Compare *resource fork*. See also *Macintosh file system*.

**data glove** (n.) A specialized input device that senses the position of a user's hand and then manipulates objects in a virtual reality scenario in a manner that corresponds to the hand movements.

**datagram** (n.) A self-contained block of data with sufficient information to be routed from the source to the destination computer without needing a previous exchange to have established a context for the data.

**data jack** (n.) A connector mounted in the wall for data cables, usually accepting a wide telephone-style eight-pin RJ-45 plug.

**Datakit** (n.) A circuit-switched digital network, such as X.25. It supports host-to-host and RS-232 connections for terminals and printers. Email functions (Unix-to-Unix CoPy, or UUCP) and remote login functions are performed on Datakit transport service. The version of Datakit supported by AT&T Information Systems is ISN (Information System Network).

**data link control** (DLC) (n., adj.) Characters that perform various transmission functions in data communications, including connection, initiation, termination, and error checking.

**data link layer** (n.) The second-lowest layer in the OSI model responsible for assembling and disassembling data packets sent over a network.

**data processing** (n.) Performing a systematic sequence of operations on data for future use, output, storage, or analysis.

**data rate** (n.) The speed at which data flows.

This is often a critical measurement when dealing with streams of audio or video information that require high bandwidth and that must not be interrupted. In practical application, this is the amount of information per second required to represent a streamed audio or video file. It is either expressed in kilobytes per second (KBps) or megabits per second (mbps). Video that will be read from a single-speed CD-ROM is usually encoded at a data rate of around 100 KBps; video for a double-speed CD-ROM is usually encoded at around 200 KBps. Over a network, audio encoded at a data rate of about 16 Kbps will usually play without interruption over a 56K link. The data rate of uncompressed NTSC video is approximately 27 Mbps. See Data Rate Conversion Table.

**data rate spike** (n.) A brief segment of a streaming media file that is encoded at a sig-

nificantly higher data rate than the rest of the movie. If not properly managed, spikes may cause dropped frames or other problems when they are decoded.

**data service unit** (DSU) (n.) A converter that translates digital data from an RS-232 interface or a V.35 interface on a router into an encoded format that may be transmitted over a T1 line connecting a wide area network. It allows connection of data terminal equipment (DTE) to digital services.

**data set** (n.) 1. Synonym for *modem.* 2. Another term for *file.*

**data stream** (n.) A flow of digital information that is time-stamped. An audio sample becomes a data stream when it is played back in real time. Streaming media types include ani-

---

### Data Rate Conversion Table

The following table shows the conversion of data rates between Kilobytes per second (KBps) and Megabits per second (Mbps).
To compute the Mbps, multiply KBps times 0.008192.

| Kilobytes/sec | Megabits/sec | Kilobytes/sec | Megabits/sec |
|---|---|---|---|
| 30 KB/sec | .2458 Mb/sec | 220 KB/sec | 1.802 Mb/sec |
| 40 KB/sec | .3277 Mb/sec | 230 KB/sec | 1.884 Mb/sec |
| 50 KB/sec | .4096 Mb/sec | 240 KB/sec | 1.967 Mb/sec |
| 60 KB/sec | .4915 Mb/sec | 250 KB/sec | 2.048 Mb/sec |
| 70 KB/sec | .5734 Mb/sec | 275 KB/sec | 2.253 Mb/sec |
| 80 KB/sec | .6554 Mb/sec | 300 KB/sec | 2.458 Mb/sec |
| 90 KB/sec | .7373 Mb/sec | 325 KB/sec | 2.662 Mb/sec |
| 100 KB/sec | .8192 Mb/sec | 350 KB/sec | 2.867 Mb/sec |
| 110 KB/sec | .9011 Mb/sec | 375 KB/sec | 3.072 Mb/sec |
| 120 KB/sec | .9830 Mb/sec | 400 KB/sec | 3.277 Mb/sec |
| 130 KB/sec | 1.065 Mb/sec | 450 KB/sec | 3.686 Mb/sec |
| 140 KB/sec | 1.147 Mb/sec | 500 KB/sec | 4.096 Mb/sec |
| 150 KB/sec | 1.229 Mb/sec | 600 KB/sec | 4.915 Mb/sec |
| 160 KB/sec | 1.311 Mb/sec | 700 KB/sec | 5.734 Mb/sec |
| 170 KB/sec | 1.393 Mb/sec | 800 KB/sec | 6.554 Mb/sec |
| 180 KB/sec | 1.475 Mb/sec | 900 KB/sec | 7.373 Mb/sec |
| 190 KB/sec | 1.556 Mb/sec | 1000 KB/sec | 8.192 Mb/sec |
| 200 KB/sec | 1.638 Mb/sec | 1200 KB/sec | 9.830 Mb/sec |
| 210 KB/sec | 1.720 Mb/sec | 1500 KB/sec | 12.288 Mb/sec |

mations and video clips.

**data striping** (n., v.) Segmenting logically sequential data so that it may be written to multiple disk drives in a round-robin fashion. If a processor is capable of reading or writing data faster than a single disk can supply or accept it, data striping speeds up data transfer. While data is moved from the first disk, the second disk locates the next segment. Data striping is used in redundant arrays of independent disks (RAID).

**data suit** (n.) A body suit with electrodes that a user wears when exploring a virtual world. This is an extension of the data glove idea.

**data terminal equipment** (DTE) (n.) Any computer or device that sends and receives data and that is connected to a modem or to some other data communications equipment (DCE). The designation as either DTE or DCE determines the role of the device on the network.

**data warehouse** (n.) A system that stores, retrieves, and manages large quantities of data. In business applications, this often refers to a vast accumulation of information that may be used to project or assess business activities comprehensively.

**daughterboard** (n.) An auxiliary circuit board that plugs into a connector on a motherboard or adapter card, adding functionality.

**DAVIC** See *Digital Audio Visual Council.*

**DAW** See *digital audio workstation.*

**dB** See *decibel.*

**DB connector** (n.) Data bus connector; a data bus hardware link that is available in a variety of configurations. The initials *DB* are followed by a number that indicates how many pins, or wires, may be connected. Common types of connectors are DB-9, DB-15, DB-19, DB-25, DB-37, and DB-50. Standards have been established that define pin assignments to ensure compatibility among hardware manufacturers. See figure on following page.

**DBMS** See *database management system.*

**DB-9 plug** (n.) A nine-pin RS-232C serial port, such as the one found on an IBM-compatible computer or a Sony videotape deck.

**DBS** See *Direct Broadcast Satellite.*

**DC** See *direct current.*

**DCC** See *Direct Client-to-Client.*

**DC-continuous** (adj.) Describes metallic circuits provided by a telephone company with direct current continuity. The Bell 43401 publication defines requirements for transmission over this type of circuit.

**DCE** See *data communications equipment* or *distributed computing environment.*

**D-channel** (n.) The channel that carries control signals and call data in a packet-switched mode via an ISDN interface. It typically operates at 16 kilobits per second (Kbps) over a Basic Rate Interface (BRI), with 9600 bits per second (bps) available for a voice link.

**DCI** See *Display Control Interface.*

**DCT** See *discrete cosine transform.*

**DCT coefficient** (n.) Discrete cosine transform

coefficient; output amplitude of an input signal in video capture. An eight-block-by-eight-block sample is translated into 64 two-dimensional spatial frequencies that define the spectrum of the input signal. The value of each coefficient is defined by the 64-point input signal and can be regarded as the relative amount of the two-dimensional spatial frequencies contained in the signal.

**DDC** See *Display Data Channel.*

**DDE** See *dynamic data exchange.*

**DDP** See *distributed data processing.*

**DDR** See *digital disk recorder.*

**DDS** See *Digital Dataphone Service.*

**dead tree edition** (n.) Jargon for the paper version of a publication available in an electronic format.

**debug** (v.) To isolate and correct errors or malfunctions in computer software or hardware.

**DEC** See *Digital Equipment Corporation.*

**DEC Alpha** (n.) Digital Equipment Corporation Alpha; a reduced instruction set computing (RISC) microprocessor made by DEC with a minimum clock speed of 200 MHz used in workstations.

**decibel** (dB) (n.) 1. In acoustics, a unit used to measure the amplitude of sound. 2. A measuring system first used in telephony, where signal loss is a logarithmic function of the cable length. 3. The preferred method and term for representing the ratio of different audio levels. It is mathematical shorthand that uses logarithms (powers of 10 representing numbers) to more conveniently express numbers. A dynamic range of 32,000 to 1 would be expressed as 90 dB. The equation $20 \log x/y$ is used to

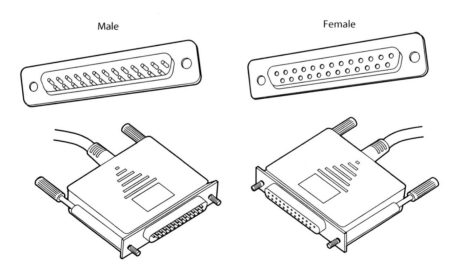

Male          Female

*DB-25 connectors*

determine decibels, where x and y are the different signal levels. Being a ratio, decibels have no units, but they are relative to a 0 dB reference point. To distinguish between reference points, a suffix letter is added as follows:

· **0 dBu** An abbreviation for the official dB (0.775 volts), a voltage reference point equal to 0.775 volts rms. This reference was first labeled dBv, but was often confused with dBV. It was changed to dBu; the "u" stands for *unterminated*.

· **+4 dBu** The standard professional audio voltage reference level, equal to 1.23 volts rms.

· **0 dBV** A unit of voltage measurement relative to 1.0 volts, not .775 volts. It is a voltage reference point equal to 1.0 volts rms.

· **-10 dBV** The standard voltage reference level for consumer and some professional audio gear, equal to 0.316 volts rms. The presence of RCA connectors is a good indicator that a piece of gear operates at -10 dBV levels.

· **0 dBm** An abbreviation for the official dB (1 milliwatt). To convert a dBm value into an equivalent voltage level, you must specify the impedance. For example, converting 0 dBm into a 600-ohm load yields an equivalent voltage level of 0.775 volts, the reference point 0 dBu. When the resistance is changed, as in the conversion of 0 dBm into a 50-ohm load, an equivalent voltage of 0.224 volts is yielded. The reference levels of +4 dBu or -10 dBV are the preferred units, because most engineers are concerned with voltage levels rather than power levels. The convention of using a reference level of 0 dBm is obsolete.

· **0 dBFS** A digital audio reference level where FS refers to "full scale." It is used in specifying A/D and D/A audio data converters. "Full scale" refers to the maximum peak voltage level possible before digital clipping, or overload of the data converter. The full scale value is fixed internally by the data converter and varies between models.

**decimal digit** (n.) Any number in the base-10 system, 0–9.

**decimate** (v.) To discard portions of a signal in order to reduce the amount of information to be encoded or compressed. Lossy compression algorithms ordinarily decimate while subsampling.

**decoder** (n.) Any hardware or software system that translates data streams into video or audio information.

**decompression** (n.) The process of restoring compressed data to its original condition.

**decrement** (v.) To decrease one step at a time.

**Decrypt CSS** (DeCSS) (n.) A program released in 1999 that decrypts a CSS-encrypted DVD movie, so that the movie may be played on any DVD player. DeCSS renders lower quality in the audio and video tracks and eliminates interactive controls. DeCSS is a controversial program, because it allows piracy of copyright-protected content.

**decryption** (n.) A procedure used in cryptography to translate encrypted data into readable text.

**DeCSS** See *Decrypt CSS*.

**dedicated** (adj.) Describes any computing system that performs one function exclusively.

**dedicated line** (n.) A telephone line leased to connect two users permanently. The line could be a voice-grade connection over ordinary public switched circuits, or it could be specified for encoded digital signals at faster rates. It is different from a dialup connection, which is only opened when either end requests service.

**de-emphasis** See *pre-emphasis.*

**de-esser** (n.) An audio signal compressor that operates at frequencies above 3 kHz to reduce the effect of sibilant vocal noises with high frequencies, such as the that produced by "s."

**DEF** See *Data Exchange Format.*

**default** (n.) The standard setting of an optional parameter. Factory defaults are the original settings for most equipment.

**Defense Advanced Research Projects Agency** (DARPA) (n.) A U.S. government agency that funded research for the ARPANET and the Internet.

**De Forest, Lee** (1873–1961) Regarded as the father of radio, he was an American electrical engineer who patented the triode electron tube in 1907, making possible the amplification and detection of radio waves. He was one of the first people to broadcast radio news.

**defragment** (defrag) (v.) To place all data on a hard disk in contiguous sectors, avoiding gaps between parts of a file or pieces of files spread geographically on the disk. When audio or video is digitized directly to a disk, the disk must be defragmented so that a continuous stream of data may be recorded on it.

**degauss** (v.) To remove a magnetic field.

**deinterlace** (v.) To remove the interlacing artifacts found in digital video converted to a noninterlaced (progressive scan) format from

video that originally contained two fields per frame.

**DEK** See *data encryption key.*

**delete** (v.) To make a file inaccessible. Data in the file allocation table (FAT) is all that is usually removed. The file's contents still exist on the storage medium and can often be recovered.

**delimiter** (n.) Any character or symbol that marks the beginning or end of a data segment. The angle brackets that surround HTML tags (<...>) are delimiters.

**delivery system** (n.) Combined hardware and software used to present or play back media, whether they be audio, video, text, images, or a combination of data types in an interactive environment.

**delta** (n.) A small quantitative change; the difference between two states.

**delta frame** (n.) In compressed video, a frame that contains only the differences between the current frame and the previous frame. It does not contain information that fully defines the image. Delta frames are created by codecs that use temporal compression. Delta frames are also called *difference frames.*

**delta modulation** (n.) A process for converting analog audio to a digital form, similar to pulse code modulation (PCM). Delta modulation is the sampling of an audio signal at 32 Kbps at 1-bit resolution, as opposed to creating eight 8-bit samples per second in PCM at the rate of 64 Kbps.

**delta YUV** (DYUV) (n.) A digital video compression format that measures the differences between adjacent pixels, rather than differences between consecutive frames. If the contrast between adjacent pixels is high, definition is lost. CD-i employs DYUV compression. Because normal vision is less sensitive to color than to intensity, DYUV encodes luminance (Y) information at full bandwidth and encodes chrominance (UV) information at half bandwidth, then stores the difference, or delta, between adjacent values.

**demarcation point** (n.) Point of interconnection between telephone company communications facilities and terminal equipment or wiring on the customer's premises. Carrier-installed facilities at the demarcation point consist of a wire or a jack. From that point on, the wiring and equipment are the customer's responsibility.

**demodulation** (n.) Process of retrieving an original signal from a modulated carrier wave. This is the technique used in data sets to make communications signals compatible with machine signals. See also *modem.*

**demon dialer** (n.) A program that repeatedly calls the same telephone number. This is a benign and legitimate method of accessing a bulletin board system (BBS). It becomes malicious when used as a denial-of-service attack.

**demonstration right** (n.) The right to display a copyrighted work publicly. Contractors who create work for hire can preserve these rights for the purpose of showing their work to prospective clients.

**demo reel** (n.) An audio tape or videotape with samples of a performer's work.

**demultiplex** (v.) To separate two or more signals previously combined by compatible multiplexing equipment. The device that pulls the

streams of data out of a larger data stream is called a *demultiplexer,* or *DEMUX.*

**DEN** See *Directory Enabled Network.*

**denial of service** (n.) An action that prevents some portion of an information system from functioning properly.

**Dense Wave Division Multiplexing** (DWDM) (n.) A protocol for transmitting data over optical connections.

**density** (n.) In reference to storage, the degree to which data is spatially distributed on a storage medium. Higher density indicates more compact storage.

**depth cueing** (n.) In three-dimensional graphics creation, a process that creates the illusion that objects fade into the distance.

**depth of field** (n.) A range in which all objects located at different distances from the camera appear in focus in the viewfinder. This range varies with the distance between camera and subject, the focal length of the camera lens, and the aperture setting.

**dequantization** (n.) A process that reverses quantization, in which many points are mapped to one point. Information lost in that mapping cannot be completely recovered in dequantization.

**derf** (v.) Security jargon for exploiting a terminal that someone else has inadvertently left logged on, providing unauthorized access to a system.

**derivative product** (n.) A work that adapts material from a previous creation. The original creator owns and may license the rights to derivative products.

**DES** See *Data Encryption Standard.*

**desktop** (n.) In a graphical user interface (GUI), the background screen on which icons and menus appear.

**desktop computer** (n.) A microcomputer that fits on top of a desk. Desktop systems have become popular for publishing and for audio or video production because of the miniaturization and proliferation of peripherals.

**Desktop Management Task Force** (DMTF) (n.) Industry consortium that sets standards for defining and controlling components on a network.

**desktop publishing** (DTP) (n.) A broad term for the use of a microcomputer with software to create text and graphics for print. Desktop publishing implies the use of page-layout programs.

**desktop video** (n.) Video that is created, edited, produced, or viewed on a microcomputer system.

**destructor** (n.) A function provided by a class in the C++ programming language that is used to delete an object.

**Deutsche Industrie Norm** (DIN, pronounced "DIHN") (n.) A type of connecting plug and mating socket with numerous pins that enables a single connector to handle more than one function or channel. A MIDI cable has a five-pin DIN plug on each end. See figure.

**developer** (n.) A person or company that creates an entertaining, educational, or informational product, such as a game, a web site, or a reference CD-ROM.

**device** (n.) A generic term for any piece of elec-

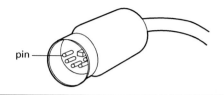

*five-pin DIN plug*

tronic equipment. In desktop computing, a printer, scanner, or CD-ROM drive is considered a device. In wireless communications, a device is any handheld subscriber unit such as a PDA, Pocket PC, mobile phone, or pager.

**device control character** (n.) Typically refers to one of four ASCII characters: DC1, DC2, DC3, or DC4. The characters are usually paired, such as DC1/DC3 to switch a device off and on (quit/start).

**device driver** (n.) A software program that controls data transfer between a computer and a peripheral device, such as a printer, CD-ROM, or cartridge drive. It may control internal system features, such as digital video or audio playback.

**device-independent bitmap** (DIB) (n.) An image format with universal transportability. In this format, the sequence in which pixels appear and their bit depth are not specifically related to their layout in a specific device. A device-dependent bitmap (DDB) image may be converted to the DIB format without loss of information.

**DFT** See *Discrete Fourier Transform.*

**DHCP** See *Dynamic Host Configuration Protocol.*

**Dhrystone** (n.) Benchmarking program that evaluates all aspects of a computer system's performance except for floating-point math performance. The program is used for measuring the processor's performance, and because it makes no operating system calls, measurements of hardware performance are not influenced by system configuration.

**diagnostic** (n.) 1. A procedure for evaluating software and hardware performance in order to troubleshoot computer systems. 2. An application that automates the scheduled maintenance and repair of complex systems.

**dialog** (n.) A question-and-answer session between an operator and a computer program that occurs in a *dialog box* in which the user chooses an option or enters data. Interaction between an operator and technology is called a *dialog*.

**dialup** (adj.) Describes the connection made between computers via phone lines and modems. In general usage, the term refers to the kind of connection made when using a terminal emulator and a regular modem (switched character-oriented asynchronous communication). The term also describes a port that accepts dialup connections. A dialup connection is referred to as a *dialup line*. Likewise, an online service or Internet Service Provider that offers dialup connectivity is said to offer *dialup service*. Any line or connection that can be addressed by modem and that is established by a switched-circuit connection using the telephone system fits this description.

**DIB** See *device-independent bitmap*.

**die** (n.) 1. A rectangular piece of semiconductor material onto which electronic circuits have been fabricated. 2. A semiconductor that is not yet packaged.

**differential line** (n.) A two-wire electrical connection in which one wire carries the original signal (+) and the other wire carries an inverted version (-) of the signal. The receiver of a signal sent over this type of line subtracts the inverted signal from the normal signal, resulting in a signal proportional to the original. Transmission noise induced in the wires is canceled in this process. The RS-422 standard specifies differential drivers and receivers, but the RS-232 standard does not.

**differential phase shift keying** (DPSK) (n.) A modulation technique used in modems.

**digerati** (n.) Analogous to *literati,* jargon that refers to computer-savvy individuals.

**digital** (adj.) Describes anything that uses discrete numerical values to represent data or signals (as opposed to a continuously fluctuating flow of current or voltage). A computer processes digital data representing text, sound, pictures, animations, or video content. Compare *analog*.

**Digital Access and Cross-Connect System** (DACS) (n.) In telephony, a Time-Slot Interchange switch that switches DS-0 channels in DS-1 data streams. It is computer-controlled and designed for keyboard entry, as opposed to automatic switching. Some of the uses are digital circuit concentration, trunk switching, and alternate routing. The term "DACS" was intended for DS-0/ DS-1 switching, but has also been applied to DS-1/ DS-3 switching. Many large DACS units include combined switching systems that allow DS-0 switching among DS-3s, always with demultiplexing of the DS-3 data streams. Interexchange and local exchange carriers offer partitioned DACS service under customer control, which allows the customer to control a Virtual Private Network (VPN) within the carrier's network.

**digital audio** (n.) Audio program material represented by binary code rather than by an analog recording. Analog audio is converted to digital audio using sampling techniques that store a numerical definition of the signal in an ordered sequence of discrete samples. An acoustic waveform is sampled thousands of times each second when it is stored digitally. This value is the *sample rate*. Each sample represents the intensity or pressure of the wave at that instant. Another parameter is the number of bits used to sample, or the *bit rate*. Audio may be encoded in linear, logarithmic, or mu-law formats. Common file name extensions for audio are .wav or .snd (MS Windows or DOS), .au (Unix), and AIFF (Macintosh). Higher sampling rates and bit rates result in a more accurate digital representation of the signal. In order to reproduce digital audio, a digital-to-analog converter (DAC) is required.

**digital audio broadcasting** (DAB) (n.) The term used by the National Radio Systems Committee (NRSC) for the next generation of digital radio broadcasting.

**digital audio stationary head** (DASH) (n.) A family of formats intended to ensure compatibility among digital multitrack studio recorders using stationary heads, as opposed to rotary heads. The DASH standard was popularized by Sony and Studer. It specifies from 2 to 48 tracks, with tape speeds from 12 to 76 centimeters per second.

**digital audio tape** (DAT, pronounced "DAHT") (n.) Developed through a collaboration between Sony and Philips in the mid-1980s, a format for storing digital audio files on magnetic tape. The complete name is *R-DAT*, where *R* stands for rotary heads in the recorder or player. In addition to storing music, the DAT format records subcode information, such as the track number and absolute

time calculated from the beginning of the tape. Up to 120 minutes of signal may be recorded on a single tape. Recording studios use DAT tapes for masters because the signal-to-noise ratio is so high and because duplicates can be made with no degradation. The DAT specification defines the following modes and characteristics:

1. Two channel, 48-kHz or 44.1-kHz sample rate, 16-bit linear encoding, 120 minutes, frequency response 2–22 kHz (±0.5 dB), SN = 93 dB, DR = 93 dB
2. Two channel, 32-kHz sample rate, 12-bit nonlinear encoding, 240 minutes, frequency response 2–14.5 kHz (±0.5 dB), SN = 92 dB, DR = 92 dB

**Digital Audio Visual Council** (DAVIC) (n.) An international group of approximately 250 companies developing an "end-to-end" standard for interactive digital media, including interfaces and requirements for applications, systems, and networks. The group includes members of the original MPEG Joint Technical Committee (JTC).

**digital audio workstation** (DAW) (n.) A software/hardware system that uses a computer as the platform for creating, editing, storing, and playing back digital audio. The computer's hard disk is the recording medium.

**digital carrier** (n.) Any medium that transmits digital signals, similar to the physical layer of the OSI network model. Carriers may be baseband or broadband.

**digital compositing** (n.) The art of combining video frames as digital signals rather than as analog signals. This allows computer images to be applied to video frames. Most current offline systems incorporate digital video frames and animations.

**Digital Dataphone Service** (DDS) (n.) A telecommunications network that typically transmits synchronous data at 56 kilobits per second (Kbps), requiring special interface equipment at both ends.

**digital delay** (n.) An audio effects processor that samples sounds, stores them digitally, and outputs them at a user-specified duration after the input. It has an effect similar to reverb when a short delay (less than 100 milliseconds) is selected. It can be used to repeat words or entire phrases when a delay of several seconds is selected.

**digital disk recorder** (DDR) (n.) A device that postproduction studios often use to record frames of video or animation because they have hardware that is capable of capturing a large field of data at once. Abekas is a popular brand of DDR.

**Digital Equipment Corporation** (DEC, pronounced "DECK") (n.) Makers of the VAX computer and VMS operating system.

**digital linear tape** (DLT) (n.) A magnetic tape storage technology developed by Digital Equipment Corporation (DEC) and later sold to Quantum. DLT reads and writes half-inch, single-hub cartridges that hold up to 35 gigabytes (GB). Since 1995, DLT has been employed widely as a backup system for large local area networks (LANs).

**digital loop carrier** (DLC) (n.) The optical fiber component of the local telephone network. DLC systems are deployed between central offices and access nodes from which copper lines run to end users. More than 50 percent of all new lines built each year are DLCs. The capacity to integrate Asymmetric Digital Subscriber Line (ADSL) into a DLC makes this service available to a much wider range of customers.

**Digital Multiplexed Interface** (DMI) (n.) A voice and data private automatic branch exchange (PABX) standard for the use of T1 transmission with 64-kilobit-per-second (Kbps) channels, allowing a more open ISDN architecture.

**digital satellite system** (DSS) (n.) Marketed to consumers as an alternative to cable television, a satellite-receiving system with a dish about 18 inches in diameter that can be used to tune into a wide range of microwave frequencies.

**digital service** (DS) (n.) A level and framing specification for synchronous data streams sent over circuits in the North American digital transmission hierarchy. This generally refers to T1, with a transmission rate of 1.544 kilobits per second (Kbps). The transmission is bipolar with a 50 percent duty-cycle signal. Telecommunications lines for data transmission have rates of data transfer specified at predetermined levels. Examples of the common transfer rates for various levels of service are shown in the following list:

| | |
|---|---|
| DS-0 | 64 kilobits per second (Kbps), the standard speed for one channel. |
| DS-1 | 1.544 megabits per second (Mbps) in North America, 2.048 Mbps elsewhere. |
| DS-1C | 3.152 Mbps in North America over T1. |
| DS-2 | 6.312 Mbps in North America over T2. |
| DS-3 | 44.736 Mbps, equal to 28 T1 channels, over T3. |
| DS-4 | 273 Mbps over a T4 facility. |

These services are defined in the following list:

- **DS-0** (n.) A digital service (DS) level zero, the standard specification for digitizing voice at 64 kilobits per second (Kbps) using pulse code modulation (PCM). DS-0 is multiplied in DS-1 and higher levels.

- **DS-1** (n.) A digital service (DS) level and a framing specification for digital signals in the North American digital transmission hierarchy over a T1 line. A DS-1 signal carries 24 voice channels encoded at 64 kilobits per second (Kbps) at a transmission rate of 1.544 megabits per second (Mbps).

- **DS-1C** (n.) A digital service (DS) level and a framing specification for digital signals in the North American digital transmission hierarchy carried on T1. A DS-1C signal uses 48 pulse code modulation (PCM) channels and has a transmission rate of 3.152 megabits per second (Mbps), twice that of DS-1. DS-1C uses two DS-1 signals that are combined and sent on a 3.152-Mbps carrier, which allows 64 kilobits per second (Kbps) for synchronization and framing using "pulse stuffing." The channel 2 signal is logically inverted, and a framing bit is stuffed in two out of three code words, resulting in 26-bit information units. The channels are interleaved and then scrambled by the addition modulo 2 of the signal with the previous bit. Finally, the bitstream is combined with a control bit sequence that permits the demultiplexer to function by preceding every 52 bits with one DS-1C framing bit. A series of 24 such 53-bit frames forms a 1272-bit "M-frame."

- **DS-2** (n.) A digital service (DS) level and a framing specification for digital signals in the North American digital transmis-sion hierarchy. A DS-2 signal uses 96 pulse code modulation (PCM) channels and has a transmission rate of 6.312 megabits per second (Mbps), twice that of DS-1C.

- **DS-3** (n.) The third digital service (DS) level and a framing specification for digital signals in the North American digital transmission hierarchy. A DS-3 signal has a transmission rate of 44.736 megabits per second (Mbps). DS-3 is used on T3 synchronous ISDN lines, for example.

**digital service unit** (DSU) (n.) Hardware that provides digital transmission between a channel service unit (CSU) and data terminal equipment (DTE), such as a modem that connects analog devices. The DSU transmitter processes the signal into bipolar pulses suitable for transmission over a digital facility. The DSU receiver extracts timing information and data from the bipolar signal.

**digital signal processor** (DSP) (n.) An integrated circuit (IC) that performs complex operations on data. The data processed is usually an audio signal in the form of a digitized waveform. Effects processors, which are common types of DSPs, perform functions such as digital delay, reverb, filtering, equalization, and stereo chorusing. The term is not limited to audio processing; it also applies to the treatment of video and other data types.

**digital signature** (n.) Data added to a message that authenticates the sender's identity through public key encryption. The sender uses a one-way hash function to generate a hash code of about 32 bits from the message data. The sender then encrypts the hash code with a private key. The receiver recomputes the hash code from the data and decrypts the received hash code with the sender's public key. If the two hash codes are equal, the receiver can be sure that data has not been corrupted and that it came from the given sender.

**Digital Subscriber Line** (DSL) (n.) A twisted-pair copper wire connection with a special modem at either end that filters out background noise and interference and allows high-speed data transfer. It is limited to a transmission distance of approximately 15 000 feet. ISDN is a DSL application with a nominal transfer rate of 128 kilobits per second (Kbps), which exceeds the peak rate that analog modems can achieve. Typically, High-Data-Rate DSL (HDSL) is used to implement T1 connections. The Asymmetric DSL (ADSL) application is a further advance in this technology, supporting up to nine megabits per second (Mbps) throughput, compared with the maximum of 2.048 Mbps handled by ISDN.

**digital subscriber line access multiplexer** (DSLAM) (n.) A device that concentrates traffic over a digital subscriber line through a process of time-division multiplexing (TDM) at the central office or at the remote line shelf. The multiplexer is usually located in the CO for termination of multiple customer DSL devices.

**digital switching** (n.) A connection in which binary-encoded information is routed between an input and an output port by means of time division multiplexing (TDM) rather than with a dedicated circuit.

**digital-to-analog** (D/A, pronounced "DEE-to-AY") (adj.) A circuit that interprets data that represents changes in motion, pressure, or light over time and that converts such data into voltages that change over time.

**Digital Versatile Disc** See *DVD.*

digital video (DV) (n.) Video program material represented by binary data rather than by an analog source. Analog video is converted to digital video through a process of encoding in which information defining the color and light is defined by data that can be reproduced by a digital-to-analog (D/A) converter for viewing. Any video that is stored or processed using bits of data is considered digital video.

**digital videocassette** (DVC) (n.) 1. A consumer tape format that records video and audio signals digitally for high resolution and lossless dubbing to another tape. This video data may be stored on a hard drive for nonlinear editing and transferred directly over the FireWire interface. 2. A video storage medium that uses 0.25-inch metal tape with a digital format similar to that of CCIR-601, combined with an adapted form of JPEG compression.

**Digital Video Disc** See *DVD.*

**Digital Video Interactive** (DVI) (n.) Developed at RCA's David Sarnoff Research Center and subsequently purchased and marketed by Intel Corporation, a technology that allows realtime compression-decompression and display of full-motion video with audio using hardware assistance on desktop computers. The highest video quality, known as Production Level Video (PLV), is achieved by using offline, nonrealtime compression on powerful parallel processing computers. Lesser-quality Real-Time Video (RTV) compression may be achieved on a desktop computer. Although the quality of DVI is high and although it is capable of 100:1 compression ratios, the proprietary hardware decoder board is not in widespread use and is not expected to be a platform of future development.

**digitize** (v.) 1. To encode images or sound in a format that may be processed by a computer.

2. To convert analog information, such as an audio signal, into digital data.

**DIMM** See *dual in-line memory module.*

**DIN** See *Deutsche Industrie Norm.*

**DIP switch** (n.) Dual in-line package switch; a miniature two-position switch mounted on a circuit board to set parameters or control functions. Pronounced "DIP." See figure.

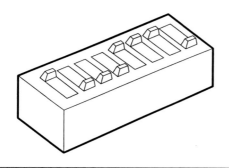

*DIP switch*

**Direct3D** (n.) The three-dimensional Application Programming Interface (API) that is part of the DirectX package for multimedia applications. Direct3D was developed by Microsoft.

**Direct Broadcast Satellite** (DBS) (n.) 1. System of transmitting digital video directly to the home via a 200-watt, high-powered satellite for reception by a small, relatively inexpensive antenna. The programming is transmitted or broadcast by satellite directly to the subscribers' premises. Ground distribution or reception equipment is only used in the uplink process to the satellite or at the subscribers' premises. Also called *Direct Satellite Service (DSS)* or *Direct-to-Home Satellite Service.* Hughes Electronics DirecTV is a well-known DBS service provider. 2. A receiver, repeater, or regenerator for microwave signals in geosynchro-nous orbit typically 22 300 miles above the surface of Earth. The footprint at this distance is approximately one-third of the globe.

**Direct Client-to-Client** (DCC) (n.) A feature of Internet Relay Chat (IRC) client software that allows users to bypass the server, sending and receiving messages and files directly. This protocol protects users from being monitored by an IRC server operator. DCC commands include DCC CHAT, DCC SEND, and DCC GET.

**direct current** (DC) (n.) A flow of electrons that moves in one direction at a relatively constant rate through a wire or a circuit. Batteries deliver DC voltage. See also *alternating current.*

**direct draw** (n.) A graphics feature of Windows 95 that permits rapid calls to the display, rather than routing the calls through the graphical device interface.

**direct inward dialing** (DID) (n.) A private branch exchange (PBX) option wherein the central office transfers the last four digits of an incoming call to the PBX and the extension is then reached directly without going through an operator.

**direct memory access** (DMA) (n.) In computing, the process of moving data to and from memory without routing it through the central processing unit (CPU).

**direct outward dialing** (DOD) (n.) A private branch exchange (PBX) feature allowing an internal caller at an extension to dial an external number without going through an operator. It is typically accessed by dialing 9 followed by the external number.

**directory** (n.) A listing of information about data files and their locations on a storage medium. In the logical format of a hard disk, a floppy disk, or a CD-ROM, this "branch" of the information tree contains other directories (subdirectories) and files.

**Directory Access Protocol** (DAP) (n.) Based on the X.500 standard, a protocol used for communication between a Directory User Agent (DUA) and a Directory System Agent (DSA).

**Directory Enabled Network** (DEN) (n.) A framework for storing information about routers, switches, and other network components within a centralized directory. It is useful for managing network equipment, controlling traffic, and setting security and usage policies. Microsoft and Cisco Systems collaborated on the DEN proposal for Windows NT 5.0.

**directory service** (n.) Networking software that has the capacity to provide information about resources available on the network, including files, printers, data sources, applications, or other users. It provides users with access to resources and information located on extended networks.

**Directory System Agent** (DSA) (n.) Software that provides directory service for a portion of an organization's directory information.

**Directory User Agent** (DUA) (n.) Software that accesses directory services for the directory user or for a search engine.

**Direct Satellite Service** (DSS) (n.) Broadcast of signals straight from a satellite source to a dish, commonly used as an alternative to cable television (CATV). DSS offers a wide variety of programming choices, as well as high-resolution video and audio.

**DirectShow** (n.) Formerly known as ActiveMovie, this is the successor to Microsoft's

Video for Windows architecture. It is built on the DirectX architecture, and supports playback of multimedia from the web, CD-ROM, and DVD-ROM.

**DirecTV** (n.) A dish and decoding system that receives television channels by satellite transmission rather than by cable. See also *Direct Broadcast Satellite.*

**DirectX** (n.) A software developers kit (SDK) for the Microsoft Windows programming interface standard. It gives programmers a standard way to access enhanced hardware features directly without using the Windows Graphics Device Interface (GDI). DirectX improves performance in graphics with DirectDraw, in audio with DirectSound, and in handling input from devices with DirectIn. It improves multimedia performance, provided that all of the hardware and software involved supports DirectX.

**disc** (n.) Any thin, round platter that stores various types of information in analog or digital formats. It is often used as the short form for CD-ROM, laser disc (analog videodisc), or compact disc–digital audio (CD-DA). The data is written in a spiral from the center to the edge. Data on a disc is read by an optical sensor that picks up reflections from a laser beam. Not to be confused with the magnetic storage medium, which is called a *disk.*

**disc geography** (n.) The relative location of files, applications, or media assets and data on discs. Closer proximity of related segments results in faster access time. See figure showing the geography of a multisession disc on the following page.

**discrete** (adj.) In digital applications, describes separate and distinct pieces of data, each of which may be part of a larger stream of information.

**discrete access** (n.) In network technology, an access method that requires each workstation to have a separate, individual connection to the host. Compare *shared access.*

**discrete cosine transform** (DCT) (n.) A video-encoding technique that uses the same approach that Fourier transform uses for audio encoding. DCT reduces the data required to represent color or grayscale levels in a video signal, applying equations that require very few pieces of information to identify the content.

**Discrete Fourier Transform** (DFT) (n.) A Fourier transform frequently used in signal processing, particularly in analyzing and compressing video and audio files. One implementation of the DFT is the Fast Fourier Transform (FFT). See also *discrete cosine transform.*

**Discrete Multi-Tone** (DMT) (n.) A digital modulation scheme that uses digital signal processors (DSPs) to transfer more than 6 megabits per second (Mbps) of data over a single copper twisted pair.

**discrete wavelet transformation** (DWT) (n.) A video compression algorithm in which spatial data is converted to frequency data and assigned to quadrants.

**disk** (n.) A circular, enclosed magnetic storage medium on which information may be accessed randomly, as opposed to sequentially. Floppy disks are small, portable storage vehicles; hard disks, or fixed disks, are capable of storing more data. Not to be confused with the optical storage medium, which is called a *disc.*

**disk cache** (n.) A segment of RAM that speeds up access to data on a disk drive. It holds a copy of recently read data from the disk, including sector information, anticipating that it will be needed again soon.

**disk mirroring** (n.) The process of writing a pair of disks simultaneously, providing a mirror-image backup if one disk fails. Both disks attach to a host controller.

**Disk Operating System** (DOS, pronounced

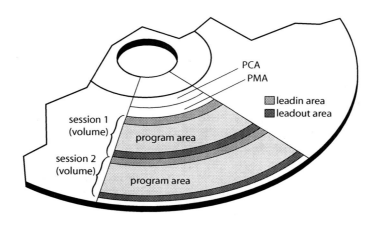

*geography of a multisession disc*

"DOSS") (n.) 1. A computing environment designed for use with a floppy or hard disk. It permits data to be transferred between a computer's memory and disk storage. 2. The Microsoft DOS (MS-DOS) designed for the IBM PC and compatibles.

**disk spanning** (n.) The method of attaching multiple drives to a single host adapter whereby all of the drives appear as a single, contiguous, logical unit.

**disk striping** (n.) The writing of data across multiple disks rather than on one drive. Data is divided into segments, each of which is written to successive drives. Disks are striped when used in an array, and this allows data to be written faster.

**dispersion** (n.) The main cause of bandwidth limitations in fiber. Dispersion causes a broadening of input pulses along the length of the fiber. Modal dispersion is caused by differential optical path lengths in a multimode fiber. Material dispersion is caused by a differential delay of various wavelengths of light in the waveguide material.

**display** (n.) A video monitor device, or cathode-ray tube (CRT), which presents numbers, characters, graphics, video, or any other visual information.

**Display Control Interface** (DCI) (n.) In an IBM-compatible computer video system, an enhancement that moves graphic data directly to the video card, bypassing the processor.

**Display Data Channel** (DDC) (n.) Standard proposed by the Video Electronics Standards Association (VESA) for bidirectional communication between computer monitors and video adapters. According to this specification, a video monitor sends an Extended Display Identification (EDID) message continuously to the video adapter. The EDID contains information about the monitor's characteristics. This information includes bandwidth, refresh rates for screen resolutions, dot pitch, support for Display Power Management Signaling (DPMS), and identifying data. This standard is intended to allow a video card to support the monitor as well as possible. Standard software utilities are implemented to control the monitor's settings. DDC uses the ACCESS.bus to communicate with the card, and some models offer an extra port on this bus for connecting other peripherals.

**display order** (n.) The order in which digital video frames should be shown. It is usually the same as the order of input to the encoder, which is typically sequential.

**dissolve** (n., v.) The gradual disintegration of a video image, or a means of transition to another frame. Fade-outs and fade-ins are examples of dissolves to and from a black screen. Dissolves between two video clips require two source VCRs in an A-B roll configuration.

**distance learning** (n.) Any learning that occurs at a site other than the classroom where an instructor is located. The term is often associated with the transmission of satellite or cable television courses for education and training. The meaning has expanded to encompass many training activities and other technologies. It is assumed that guidance and coursework are specified by an instructional program and that the activity is structured, as opposed to being a self-motivated independent study without external influence. Other terms for this type of education are *flexible learning, student-based learning,* and *student-centered learning.* The latter is particularly accurate, in that it identifies the student's location as the learning site. It is common for student-centered learning activities to occur on a campus where classroom activities are enhanced by network access and other learning technologies that students access in a library or computer lab.

**distance vector protocol** (n.) A protocol that runs on a local area network (LAN) router to minimize the number of link-level connections, or hops, a data packet must make as it travels between originating and terminating devices.

**distortion** (n.) Any alteration in an audio waveform, causing frequencies at the output of a signal-processing device that were not present at input. It typically occurs when a signal is digitally processed or amplified.

**distributed computing environment** (DCE) (n.) Standard conventions and server functionalities as established and promoted by the Open Software Foundation (OSF), a consortium led by IBM, Digital Equipment Corporation (DEC), and Hewlett-Packard. It offers an architecture of standard programming interfaces for distributing applications over heterogeneous networks.

**distributed database** (n.) A combination of multiple databases that appears to a user to be one database. The Internet domain name system (DNS) is an example.

**distributed data processing** (DDP) (n.) The use of more than one networked computer to run an application at multiple sites simultaneously.

**distributed file system** (n.) A file system that accesses data from remote locations across a network. It recognizes multiple servers, manages itself, and can be accessed from any location on the network.

**distribution amplifier** (DA) (n.) In video

postproduction, a device that delivers a signal to multiple receiving machines.

**distribution segment** (n.) A television cable that extends from a trunk to a feeder cable. Homes that are within 500 feet of a distribution segment may have a direct drop, which leads from a tap on the feeder to the home.

**dithering** (n.) A form of smart conversion from a higher bit depth to a lower bit depth used in audio and graphics files. The process attempts to improve the perceived quality of onscreen graphics when the color palette is reduced. In the conversion from 24-bit color to 8-bit color (in which millions of colors are reduced to 256 colors), dithering adds patterns of different-colored pixels to simulate the original color. The technique is also known as *error diffusion* and is applied to both audio bit rate reduction and graphics resolution. See figure.

*dithered image*

**divestiture** (n.) In telecommunications, refers to the breakup of AT&T. See *Bell operating companies*.

**DLC** See *data link control* or *digital loop carrier*.

**DLL** See *dynamic link library*.

**DLS** See *downloadable sound*.

**DLT** See *digital linear tape*.

**DMA** See *direct memory access*.

**DMA channel** (n.) Direct memory access channel; a logical pathway in a microcomputer for exchanging data between peripherals and memory or just between peripherals without passing the data through the central processing unit (CPU).

**DMI** See *Digital Multiplexed Interface.*

**DMT** See *Discrete Multi-Tone.*

**DMTF** See *Desktop Management Task Force.*

**DNS** See *domain name system.*

**DNS spoofing** (n.) Assuming the DNS name of another system. This is done by corrupting the name service cache of a victim system, or by compromising the domain name server for a valid domain.

**docking station** (n.) A base unit into which a notebook computer may be inserted, providing access to desktop peripherals and accessories.

**documentation** (n.) Materials, such as an instruction manual, that explain how to operate software or hardware. There is a trend toward putting documentation online.

**Document Type Definition** (DTD) (n.) A refinement of the Standard Generalized Markup Language (SGML) stating the official rules by which a particular type of document is to be interpreted. The HTML DTD was designed by Tim Berners-Lee and Dan Connolly to identify the unique features of HTML.

**dolby noise reduction** (n.) A process that increases the signal-to-noise ratio by raising the volume of quiet passages during recording and by lowering them to their original levels during playback. The lowering reduces noise, such

as tape hiss, that may be introduced during recording. See figure.

**Dolby noise reduction types** (n.) The Dolby A, B, C, SR, and S noise reduction (NR) systems

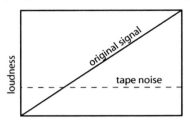

Loud sounds overpower the inherent noise and hiss on an audio tape. However, during soft passages the noise is much stronger in relation to the signal.

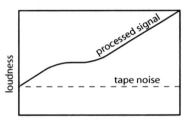

On recording, dolby processing increases the level of quiet sounds in the high-frequency range, but it does not alter loud sounds.

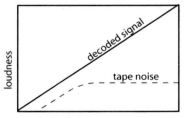

On playback the tape noise is reduced along with all the high-frequency quiet sounds that are restored to their original levels in the decoding process.

*dolby signal processing*

132

are non-linear, level-dependent *companders* (compressors/expanders). They offer various amounts of noise reduction, as shown in the accompanying table.

The Dolby A band-splitting system can reduce noise at all frequencies. The single sliding band techniques used in Dolby B and C systems are more suitable for consumer tape recording applications where the dominant noise contribution occurs at high frequencies.

The encoding process selectively boosts high frequency signals. Decoding is the exact reciprocal of this process. The amount of boost during the compansion depends on the signal level and its spectral content. For a −40 dB tone at 3 KHz, the boost applied to signals with frequencies above this would probably be the maximum 10 dB allowed. If the same tone were at a level of −20 dB, then the boost might be around 5 dB.

The Dolby B system is designed to take effect beginning at 300 Hz, and its action increases until it reaches a maximum of 10 dB above 4 kHz. Dolby C takes effect from 100 Hz and provides about 15 dB of NR at 400 Hz, increasing to a maximum of 20 dB in the critical hiss region from 2 kHz to 10 kHz. Dolby C also includes spectral skewing networks. An anti-saturation shelving network, beginning at about 2 kHz, affects the high-level signals that would cause tape saturation. A complementary network is provided in the decoding chain to provide an overall flat response.

The Dolby SR (spectral recording) and S systems provide slightly more noise reduction than Dolby C at high frequencies, 24 dB versus 20 dB. They also achieve a 10-dB NR effect at low frequencies below 200 Hz. This is obtained using a two-band approach, with a fixed-band processor handling the low frequencies and a sliding-band processor addressing high frequencies. When applying any type of Dolby noise reduction, the proper calibration of recording and playback equipment is a critical element in the effectiveness of the system.

**dolly** (n.) In video production, a camera support mounted on wheels that permits smooth movement in any direction.

**domain** (n.) In an Internet address, the part of the naming hierarchy that consists of a sequence of characters separated by dots. The five most common types of domains are .com for company, .org for nonprofit organization, .edu for educational institution, .net for network operations, and .gov for government agency. The domains are administered by Internet Network Information Center (InterNIC), and each has a primary and secondary domain name server associated with it. The primary domain name system (DNS) is located on a

### Dolby Noise Reduction Types

| Type | High-Frequency NR | Low-Frequency NR | Active Frequency Bands | Market | Year Introduced |
|------|------------------|------------------|------------------------|--------|-----------------|
| A | 10 dB | 10 dB | 4 fixed | Professional | 1967 |
| B | 10 dB | none | 1 sliding (HF) | Home | 1970 |
| C | 20 dB | none | 1 sliding (HF) | Home | 1981 |
| SR | 24 dB | 10 dB | 1 sliding (HF), 1 fixed (LF) | Professional | 1986 |
| S | 24 dB | 10 dB | 1 sliding (HF), 1 fixed (LF) | Home | 1990 |

machine in the associated network, and the server may be determined through the "nslookup" command. Country domains are common, such as uk (United Kingdom) and au (Australia). See *Internet country code* for a complete listing.

**domain name** (n.) The text name corresponding to the numeric Internet Protocol (IP) address of a computer on the Internet. For example, *www.hansenmedia.com* is a domain name.

**domain name lookup** (n.) The process of converting a numeric Internet Protocol (IP) address into a text name. For example, 192.030 .001.002 is converted to *www.thisdomain.com.*

**domain name system** (DNS) (n.) A distributed database and data query service used on the Internet to translate hostnames into Internet addresses, defined in RFC 1034, STD 13 and RFC 1035. Referred to as *resolution,* the translation enables users to keep their domain names, even though the server's Internet Protocol (IP) address could change. DNS may be configured to use a sequence of name servers in a query, predicated on domains in the name for which it is searching, until it finds a match. DNS may be queried interactively using the command "nslookup." The phrase refers to naming conventions for hosts, servers, and clients on the Internet.

**domestic market** (n.) The consumer market in a particular country or geographic area, as opposed to the industrial or professional markets.

**D1 format** (n.) Developed by the Society of Motion Picture and Television Engineers (SMPTE), a component digital videotape format that is a professional recording standard based on the CCIR-601 recommendation. The format separates the signal into one brightness channel and two color channels (Y, R-Y, B-Y). The tape is 19 mm wide and a single cassette holds up to 94 minutes of program material. Using this format, it is possible to dub multiple copies without a noticeable loss of quality in successive generations.

**dongle** (n.) 1. Jargon for *server key,* a small piece of hardware connected to the serial port that permits a secure application to run. 2. An adapter or connector that interfaces video monitors or peripherals. 3. A small DB-25 connector shell that contains EPROM and drivers. The dongle must be connected to an I/O computer port while the program that requires it is running. A dongle provides security and copy protection for commercial software.

**DOS** See *Disk Operating System.*

**DOSKey** (n.) Disk Operating System key; a utility program that permits a user to customize MS-DOS commands, create stored macros, type more than one DOS command on a line, and personalize the computing environment.

**DOS Protected Mode Interface** (DPMI) (n.) The required method by which a DOS program accesses extended memory in the Microsoft Windows environment. The service is provided by the HIMEM.SYS driver.

**dot matrix** 1. (n.) A two-dimensional pattern of dots that defines graphic elements. 2. (adj., dot-matrix) Describes a type of computer printer that uses pins to print dots on paper. The combined dots form text characters and graphic images.

**dot pitch** (n.) The smallest distance between adjacent points of color on a monitor. A small dot pitch means that the image is sharp.

**dots per inch** (dpi) (n.) A measurement of resolution that defines the output of a display or printer. A screen font usually appears at 72 dpi, whereas a laser printer usually prints at 300 dpi minimally.

**double buffering** (n.) The process of writing a graphical frame into memory at the same time that another frame is being displayed. It allows smoother transitions between frames in an animation.

**double-speed** (2X) (adj.) Describes second-generation CD-ROM drives that transfer data at twice the rate of single-speed drives. Double-speed drives should technically be capable of a data transfer rate of approximately 300 kilobytes per second (KBps), whereas single-speed drives transfer data at 150 KBps.

**downlink** 1. (n.) A transmission link from a satellite to an Earth station. 2. (v.) To receive signals from a satellite broadcast with a microwave dish.

**download** (v.) To transfer data or code from one computer to another, typically from a large host or server to a smaller client.

**downloadable sound** (DLS) (n.) A specification that enables a common playback experience on different delivery platforms when a General MIDI file is played. The DLS file, consisting of samples, is transmitted along with a MIDI sequence, so that a wavetable synthesizer can use the sample provided rather than one resident in its memory. Only sound cards and equipment with RAM available for storing samples to be played with a sequence can take advantage of this technology. Level 1 of the specification supports hardware with a wavetable engine that plays samples with loops. It provides 24 voices minimally at a sample rate of 22 kHz, with 512 kilobytes (KB) of storage reserved for samples. A full package may include up to 120 melodic instruments, eight sound effects (SFX), and 47 percussion sounds in a set on MIDI channel 10. This standard is implemented by the Yamaha XG and Roland GS formats.

**downsample** (v.) To reduce the amount of data in a stream by selecting only a percentage of the original signal, and to throw out some data to reduce the size or to meet narrow bandwidth requirements. Video signals are often downsampled during encoding.

**downstream** (adv.) The direction in which a signal travels from the transmitter, or origination point, to the receiving site.

**downward compatible** (adj.) Describes software that can be used on older computing systems and that can read files created with an earlier version of a software application.

**dpi** See *dots per inch.*

**DPMI** See *DOS Protected Mode Interface.*

**DPSK** See *differential phase shift keying.*

**drag and drop** (n.) A means of manipulating icons, text, or objects in a graphical user interface (GUI). By holding a mouse button down while moving an icon over a directory or application program and by releasing the button, a user can open a file or deposit it in the directory.

**DRAM** See *Dynamic RAM.*

**Drawing Interchange Format** (DXF) (n.) A format for computer-aided design (CAD) files developed by Autodesk for its AutoCAD program. It is platform-independent and is also called *Data Exchange Format (DEF).*

135

**drawing program** (n.) A program that produces graphical objects rather than bitmaps, which are created by painting programs. Drawing programs use mathematical formulas to define lines that can be scaled and resized without distortion.

**drift** (n.) Unwanted motion in horizontal lines of video. Drift occurs when an electronic component, such as a capacitor, becomes unstable, causing the image to scroll up slowly.

**drill-down map** (n.) A series of progressively more detailed graphics that enlarge an area of a map or of a large image. An example is an interactive city map that displays a neighborhood when the user clicks on it. A subsequent click might show a square mile in part of the neighborhood. A click on that map might bring up a square block.

**drive** (n.) Any hardware component of a computer system that spins and reads floppy disks, fixed disks, tapes, CD-ROMs, laser discs, or other media.

**drive letter** (n.) A letter of the alphabet used to identify a disk drive or peripheral connected to a microcomputer. The primary hard disk drive is generally called the *C drive*, floppy disk drives are usually *A* and *B*, and a CD-ROM drive might be *D*.

**driver** (n.) A software control program that integrates with the computer operating system to give instructions to and interface with a device such as a CD-ROM player or a video card.

**drop** (n.) Typically a copper twisted-pair or coaxial cable running from a branch of a telecommunications network to an individual customer's premises. In a cable system, a coaxial drop connects a branch of coaxial cable to a set-top box on the customer's premises or directly to a cable-ready television set.

**drop-down menu** (n.) A window that pops up below a topic selected from the menu bar, offering additional choices or functions.

**drop frame** (n.) A time code format for video that periodically skips a pulse to account for the difference between the 30 frames per second (fps) standard and the actual 29.97 fps rate found in the NTSC format. Correction for this inconsistency is accomplished by dropping two frames each minute. Any frame can be dropped except for every tenth frame.

**dropout** (n.) 1. The temporary loss of signal in data transmission. By technical telephony standards, a dropout is a period of at least 4 milliseconds during which a signal has dropped more than 12 decibels. 2. Impaired signal from an analog tape playback device caused by blank spots in the tape coating, which show up on a monitor as streaks and white specks.

**drop shadow** (n.) A graphic effect used with typefaces to create the illusion that a light source is shining on an object or a letter from above and that a shadow is cast behind and below.

**drum scanner** (n.) A data-capturing device that incorporates a cylindrical drum for mounting original images.

**DS** See *digital service.*

**DS-0** See *digital service.*

**DS-1** See *digital service.*

**DS-1C** See *digital service.*

**DS-2** See *digital service.*

DS-3 See *digital service.*

DSA See *Directory System Agent.*

DSL See *Digital Subscriber Line.*

DSLAM See *digital subscriber line access multiplexer.*

DSP See *digital signal processor.*

DSP algorithm (n.) A structured set of instructions and operations tailored to accomplish a signal processing task. For example, a Fast Fourier Transform (FFT) and a finite impulse response (FIR) filter are common digital signal processing algorithms.

DSS See *digital satellite system* or *Direct Satellite Service.*

DSU See *data service unit* or *digital service unit.*

DTD See *Document Type Definition.*

DTE See *data terminal equipment.*

DTMF See *Dual Tone Multi-Frequency.*

DTP See *desktop publishing.*

DUA See *Directory User Agent.*

dual band (adj.) In telephony, describes a wireless phone that can operate at two different frequencies using the same technology, such as a TDMA or CDMA phone that can use either the 800- or 1900-MHz band. Triple band phones in the GSM market can support transmission rates of 900 MHz, 1800 MHz, and 1900 MHz. A dual band phone provides a wider coverage area by allowing the user to access different frequencies in the same or different geographic regions.

dual-channel audio (n.) A system with two audio channels that can play them simultaneously or independently.

dual in-line memory module (DIMM) (n.) A high-density RAM package, similar to a single in-line memory module (SIMM), but with dual rather than single connections to the motherboard.

dual in-line package switch See *DIP switch.*

dual mode (adj.) In telephony, describes a mobile phone that supports more than one technology. An 800-MHz CDMA dual mode phone will also support an 800-MHz AMPS connection. A dual mode phone may also support both analog and digital technologies by picking up analog signals when digital signals are weak.

dual ported (adj.) Describes memory circuits that can be accessed simultaneously through two independent address and data buses. Such circuits are often used in video display hardware in conjunction with video RAM (VRAM). Video display hardware can read memory to display the contents on screen while the central processing unit (CPU) writes data to other areas of memory through a different port simultaneously.

Dual Tone Multi-Frequency (DTMF) (n.) The way in which a telephone system communicates what keys are pressed when a number is dialed on a touchtone device. Each key on the telephone's numeric pad generates two tones, one defining its row and the other defining its column on the pad. The exchange decodes these to identify the key pressed.

dub (v.) 1. To copy a tape, producing a second generation. 2. To insert and combine new video or audio elements on an existing tape to produce a composite master tape.

**dump** (v.) 1. To transfer digital data from one source to another. 2. To remove data or to empty a container.

**duotone** (n.) An image displayed in two colors. It is created from a grayscale image overlaid by a specified color.

**duplex** (adj.) Describes a transmission line capable of communication in two directions simultaneously.

**DV** See *digital video.*

**DVC** See *digital videocassette.*

**DVD** (Digital Video Disc, Digital Versatile Disc) (n.) Term that loosely refers to numerous configurations that define the physical structure and the data contained on a 12 cm disc. A DVD in any of several formats contains MPEG-2 video with either AC-3 (Dolby) audio or MPEG-2 audio (common in Europe). The term *Digital Versatile Disc* was originally used to indicate that the medium may contain any type of data, not just audio and video files in a proprietary format. *DVD-ROM* is the term most often used to describe a disc formatted with a larger capacity than a CD-ROM. A DVD-ROM does not necessarily contain video data, as the words would imply.

*DVD* generally refers to an optical disc with multiple data layers that exceeds the capacity of a standard CD-ROM and that may contain video, audio, or any other type of digital data. In the areas of home entertainment and computer data storage, it has the capacity to replace all existing audio tape, videotape, CD-ROM, and video game formats.

The storage capacity of a DVD is greater than

that of a CD-ROM because it has a laser beam with a shorter wavelength, smaller pits on the disc surface, a denser track pitch, and more efficient channel encoding. A visible red laser with a wavelength of 635 to 650 nanometers was chosen for DVD when the specification was unified from competing technologies developed by Toshiba, Sony, and Philips. The DVD specifies a laser beam of smaller diameter than the 780-nanometer infrared laser diode used by a CD-ROM. The smallest CD-ROM pits are 1.1 micrometers in diameter. The pits on a DVD are 0.4 micrometers in diameter on a single layer disc and about 10 percent larger when a second layer is used. Because a DVD has smaller pits and narrower laser beams, the tracks can be closer together. Track pitch is 0.74 micrometers on a DVD, compared with 1.6 micrometers on a CD-ROM. The modulation and encoding scheme was also modified in the DVD format to increase the density of data.

A single-layer DVD spins at a constant linear velocity (CLV) of 3.4 meters per second, approximately the same speed as an 8X CD-ROM. At this velocity, data may be extracted at a rate of 11.08 megabits per second (Mbps). The sustained audio-video media delivery rate is 9.8 Mbps, deducting overhead (formatting and private data).

**DVD Configurations**
- **DVD-ROM (Book A)** A high-capacity read-only optical disc capable of rapid data transfer that may be used as a general-purpose computer storage device. A DVD-ROM may hold any type of digital data and is readable by a DVD-ROM drive connected to a computer. This type of drive is basically an 8X CD-ROM drive with seven times the storage capacity. Files are stored in the Micro UDF/ISO 9660 Bridge format. DVD-ROM is an extension of the CD-ROM

specification with a maximum file size of 1 gigabyte (GB).

- **DVD-Video (Book B)** A high-capacity read-only optical disc capable of rapid data transfer that is used for the interactive playback of movies and games or of other video, audio, and graphic content using the MPEG-2 video compression format. The DVD-video Book B type is played on a DVD player and viewed on a television monitor. It has become one form of a "settop box." These discs may also be played on a computer with a special hardware decoder and supporting software.

- **DVD-Audio (Book C)** A high-capacity read-only optical disc capable of rapid data transfer that may be used for the playback of high-quality audio using 24-bit linear pulse code modulation (LPCM) sampled at 48 or 96 kilobytes per second (KBps). A widely agreed-upon audio standard among manufacturers had not yet been defined in 2001.

- **DVD-R (Book D)** A high-capacity write-once optical disc with rapid data transfer rates that can be used as a general-purpose computer storage device. It may be recorded but not erased. It is able to read and write up to 3.9 gigabytes (GB) of data.

- **DVD-RAM (Book E)** A high-capacity read-write optical disc capable of rapid data transfer that may be used as a general-purpose computer storage device. This format allows reading, writing, and erasing. Because phase change technology is used, the capacity for data is approximately half of that of a read-only device. A DVD-RAM disc will read and write 2.6 gigabytes (GB). It is questionable wheter a DVD-

RAM disc will be readable on either the DVD-R or the DVD-ROM drives built in the future.

**DVD Capacity**

A DVD disc may contain two data layers on each side, or four total, for a maximum capacity of 17.08 GB on a 12 cm disc. Two 0.6 mm thick substrates are bonded to form a 1.2 mm thick disc with data in the middle, similar in form factor to a CD-ROM. The most commonly produced are single-layer, single-sided discs with a 4.70-GB capacity.

A standard CD-ROM holds about 650 megabytes (MB), approximately 0.65 GB. The following list shows the capacity of the various DVD formats, with one or two sides and one or two layers. The DVD-R is a recordable format, the DVD-RAM a rewritable format. (SS/DS = single-sided/double-sided; SL/DL = single-layer/double-layer)

| Sides | Layers | Capacity |
|-------|--------|----------|
| 1 | 1 | 4.7 GB |
| 1 | 2 | 8.5 GB |
| 2 | 1 | 9.4 GB |
| 2 | 2 | 17.0 GB |

DVD SS/SL: 4.7 GB of data, 2+ hours of video
DVD SS/DL: 8.5 GB of data, 4 hours of video
DVD DS/SL: 9.4 GB of data, 4.5 hours of video
DVD DS/DL: 17 GB of data, 8+ hours of video

DVD-R SS/SL: 3.95 GB of data
DVD-R DS/SL: 7.9 GB of data

DVD-RAM SS/SL: 2.58 GB of data
DVD-RAM DS/SL: 5.16 GB of data

**DVD File Structure Hierarchy**

A DVD contains two separate types of information: navigation data, which controls the media, and presentation data, which consists of the objects themselves. Control data points to the audio-video object files on a DVD in the same way a file allocation table (FAT) points to files on a disk drive. Presentation and navigation data packets are separated at the track buffer in the DVD player model. Control data can be expressed as a series of nested layers, hierarchically listed below.

- **Title** Descriptor that distinguishes multiple movies or episodes on one disc. Each title is either a single program chain (One_Sequential_PGC_Title) or a collection of different program chains (Multi_PGC_Title).

- **Part of Title** (POT) A set of links to one or more program (PG) units on a disc. As with a Program Chain (PGC), this is a means of creating different camera angles, outcomes, or versions of the same PGC. POTs can also be used to mark scenes.

- **Program Chain** (PGC) A collection of programs with integrated or related content.

- **Program** (PG) Usually a scene consisting of multiple cells.

- **Cell** Preceded by a navigation packet and alternating video and audio packets, typically all the audio-video data associated with several Groups of Pictures (GOPs).

- **Video Object Unit** (VOBU) A related Group of Pictures (GOP).

- **Group of Pictures** (GOP) 1. The smallest unit of random access on a disc (a GOP includes a coded intraframe). 2. The largest interframe-dependent coding unit. Interframe compression is bounded within a GOP, minimally 15 frames of data (0.5

seconds in duration) in the NTSC video format (525 frames per 60 fields).

- **Packet** A block of data containing 2048 bytes, which is the sector payload size. A packet contains data from a single MPEG program stream.

- **NAV Packet** Block of data defining the playback behavior of the current cell, containing the optional Button Command.

**Logical Structure of Video Manager and Video Title Set**

A disc volume may contain up to 99 different titles, each with a navigation menu that allows the user to select a version of the title. The root menu that branches to all titles on the disc is coded within the Video Manager (VM). Each title is organized as a Video Title Set (VTS).

- **Video Manager** (VM) An object that sets up menus for a series of titles.

- **Video Manager Information** (VMGI) A menu that includes Attributes for Menu, Title Search Pointers, and PGCI for Menu.

- **Video Title Set** (VTS) A collection of video objects (VOBs). The control data (VTSI, or Video Title Set Information) for the title (VTS) includes Attributes for Menu, Attributes for Title, Part of Title Search Pointer, Time Map Table, PGCI for Menu, and PGCI for Title.

- **Program Chain Information** (PGCI) Defines the playback order of Program Chains (PGCs).

- **Video Object** (VOB) Objects that contain the actual Program Chains (PGCs), Parts of Titles (POTs), Programs (PGs), and any other program material.

**DVI** See *Digital Video Interactive.*

**Dvorak keyboard** (n.) A keyboard layout designed for speed. The most commonly used letters in the English language are positioned on the center row of keys. It was designed in the 1930s by August Dvorak and William Dealy as an alternative to the QWERTY keyboard layout. Pronounced "da-VOR-ack." See figure.

*Dvorak keyboard*

**DWDM** See *Dense Wave Division Multiplexing.*

**DWT** See *discrete wavelet transformation.*

**DXF** See *Drawing Interchange Format.*

**dye polymer** (n., adj.) A compound made of similar molecules that are linked together. A dye polymer layer that can be altered by exposure to lasers is used in optical disc recording systems.

**dynamic binding** (n.) The arrangement in which code executed to perform a given operation is determined at run time by an object-oriented programming (OOP) language. Several different classes of objects may receive a particular message.

**dynamic data exchange** (DDE) (n.) An exchange format that allows two or more programs running simultaneously in Microsoft Windows or OS/2 to communicate with one another. Multitasking is enhanced by the use of programs that can take advantage of this access to data

across applications.

**dynamic execution** (n.) Several processes that work together in the Intel Pentium Pro central processing unit (CPU), including multiple branch prediction, data flow analysis, and speculative execution.

**dynamic filtering** (n.) A process that eliminates the electronic emissions of a computing system, which are picked up by sensitive circuitry and can appear as noise in the sound board output.

**Dynamic Host Configuration Protocol** (DHCP) (n.) A MS Windows NT server protocol that provides a means of dynamically allocating Internet Protocol (IP) addresses to IBM PCs running on a local area network (LAN). A range of IP addresses are assigned to DHCP, and each client on the LAN has its TCP/IP software configured to request an IP address from the DHCP server.

**dynamic link library** (DLL) (n.) A library of programming code linked to application programs at the time that they are run rather than as a phase of their compilation. One block of library code can be shared between multiple tasks rather than duplicated. The version of a DLL must be compatible with its executable program. Dynamic linking is used in the Sun and the Microsoft Windows operating systems.

**dynamic microphone** (n.) A type of transducer and circuit that converts an acoustical signal into an electrical signal by using a coil moving in a magnetic field. This type of microphone is generally less sensitive than a condenser microphone and has a narrower frequency response.

**Dynamic RAM** (DRAM, pronounced "DEE-ram") (n.) Dynamic random access memory; a type of memory component in which the memory cells require periodic recharging. Information stored in the memory cells as positive or negative charges may be accessed randomly. DRAM consists of an integrated circuit (IC) that uses a charged capacitor.

**dynamic range** (n.) In an audio program, the difference between the lowest and the highest levels of amplitude, or loudness, expressed in decibels.

**dynamic storage allocation** (n.) While a program that uses storage space is running, a process that reserves space for data that the program may generate. The data will be stored in allocated blocks.

**DYUV** See *delta YUV.*

# E

**Earth station** (n.) Antenna and related equipment that receive or transmit satellite signals.

**Easter egg** (n.) An often humorous message buried in an application by its programmers with no documented access for the user.

**EBCDIC** See *Extended Binary-Coded Decimal Interchange Code.*

**EBU** See *European Broadcast Union.*

**EBU time code** (n.) European Broadcast Union time code; standard for time-stamping data on audio tape or videotape. Similar to Society of Motion Picture and Television Engineers (SMPTE) time code.

**ECC** See *error correction code.*

**echo** (n.) In telecommunications, the reflection of a signal back to the sending station.

**echo cancellation** (n.) A process that filters unwanted signals caused by echoes from the main audio source. Echoes occur in voice and in data communications. Two types of cancellers encountered are *acoustic* and *line.* Acoustic echo cancellers are used in teleconferencing and wireless applications to suppress the acoustic echoes caused by the microphone/loudspeaker combination at one end picking up the signal

from the other end and returning it. This is like feedback with time delay. Line echo cancellers are used to suppress electrical echoes caused by the transmission link itself. Imperfect hybrid systems and satellite round-trip delays of about 600 ms contribute to disruptive line echoes.

**EDAC** See *error detection and correction.*

**EDC** See *error detect code.*

**EDFA** See *Erbium-Doped Fiber Amplifier.*

**EDGE** See *enhanced data GSM environment.*

**edge blanking** (n.) The black part of the video signal that normally falls outside the area that is visible on a TV screen. A video capture card will often grab some of the edge surrounding the image as it encodes. This is sometimes referred to as edge noise. When viewing video on a monitor in "overscan" mode, edge blanking is visible.

**EDI** See *Electronic Data Interchange.*

**Edison effect** (n.) Also known as thermionic emission, the Edison effect describes an observation made by Thomas Edison in 1883 when he noted the emission of free electrons, or negative electricity, from a metal wire connected to an incandescent lamp's positive circuit when heated by a filament in a vacuum. This discovery led to the development of the vacuum tube by Sir John Ambrose Fleming in 1904.

**edit** (v.) 1. To combine and integrate audio or video segments from multiple media sources, creating a composite master tape. 2. To remove undesirable content from a recorded program or file.

**edit controller** (n.) A complex system that controls video and audio recording or playback machines, positioning them at appropriate points and changing modes as needed in order to assemble an edited production.

**edit decision list** (EDL) (n.) a record of the edits made in the offline, nonlinear, video editing process. The list identifies beginning and ending frames in SMPTE code. It consists of a series of entry and exit points in tapes that will be combined. Those points allow the user to recreate or modify a video program. The EDL includes the time code where cuts are to be made and where special effects are to be introduced. The list can be logged from a window dub, an offline editing system, or a computer.

**editor** (n.) 1. Any program on any operating system used to create or modify pure text files. In the Mac OS, SimpleText is the default editor, and in Microsoft Windows it is Notepad. Common editors in Unix are vi, ee, and pico. 2. A person who refines an audio or video program or text file by cutting and modifying existing data and integrating new content.

**EDL** See *edit decision list.*

**EDO DRAM** See *Extended Data Out Dynamic Random Access Memory.*

**EDO RAM** See *EDO DRAM.*

**edutainment** (n.) Entertaining and educational digital media products.

**EEPROM** See *electrically erasable programmable read-only memory.*

**effects loop** (n.) The location on an audio mixing board where an external outboard signal processor is connected. The loop consists of an output Send jack connecting to the effects box input, and an input Return jack that comes from the effects box output. Typically, two separate 1/4" connectors are provided to patch in an outboard processor using separate cables for send and receive. These jacks are usually unbalanced.

**effects processor** (n.) An audio production tool that performs operations such as reverb, delay, equalization, compression, and filtering. It may take the form of an outboard unit through which signals are routed, or it may exist as a software plug-in to an editing program.

**EFM** See *8-to-14 modulation.*

**EGA** See *Enhanced Graphics Adapter.*

**EGP** See *Exterior Gateway Protocol.*

**EHF** See *extremely high frequency.*

**EIA** See *Electronics Industries Association.*

**EIAJ** See *Electronics Industries Association of Japan.*

**EIDE** See *Extended Integrated Drive Electronics.*

**EIDS** See *Electronic Information Delivery System.*

**EISA** See *Extended Industry Standard Architecture.*

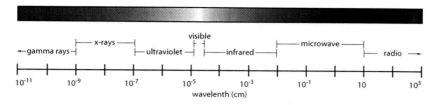

*electromagnetic spectrum*

**EJB** See *Enterprise Java Beans.*

**Elco plug** (n.) The company Elco manufactures various connectors used to connect multiple audio channels at once, most often found in recording studios on analog and digital audio-tape machines. One of these plugs, a 90-pin version (Varicon Series 8016), carries 28 shielded pairs of audio channels, allowing 3-wires per channel (positive, negative, and shield) for true balanced-line system connection. Also known as an *Elco connector.*

**electret microphone** (n.) Similar to a condenser microphone, an electret mic employs a permanent electrical charge, eliminating the need for an external polarizing voltage. The electret (acronym for *electr*icity + magn*et*) material is similar to a permanent magnet that exhibits persistent dielectric polarization. Electret elements exhibit very high output impedance, so their circuits usually employ an integral impedance converter that requires external power to operate. This low voltage power may be supplied single-ended over an unbalanced connection, or it may operate from standard phantom power.

**electrically erasable programmable read-only memory** (EEPROM) (n.) A special type of programmable read-only memory (PROM) that can be erased with an electric current before being reloaded. Pronounced "ee-EE-prom." See also *programmable read-only memory.*

**electroluminescence** (n.) The process of subjecting solid phosphor to an alternating current field, causing it to emit light. This technology is implemented in flat-panel displays for notebook computers because it is energy-efficient.

**electromagnetic interference** (EMI) (n.) Emissions from electronic devices and lighting that interfere with the performance of other devices, often introducing noise or distortion.

**electromagnetic spectrum** (n.) The distribution of electromagnetic radiation over a range of frequencies. See table and figure.

| Spectrum of Electromagnetic Radiation | | |
|---|---|---|
| **Region** | **Frequency (Hz)** | **Wavelength (cm)** |
| Radio | $< 3 \times 10^9$ | $> 10$ |
| Microwave | $3 \times 10^9 – 3 \times 10^{12}$ | $10 – 0.01$ |
| Infrared | $3 \times 10^{12} – 4.3 \times 10^{14}$ | $0.01 – 7 \times 10^5$ |
| Visible | $4.3 \times 10^{14} – 7.5 \times 10^{14}$ | $7 \times 10^5 – 4 \times 10^5$ |
| Ultraviolet | $7.5 \times 10^{14} – 3 \times 10^{17}$ | $4 \times 10^5 – 10^{-7}$ |
| X-Rays | $3 \times 10^{17} – 3 \times 10^{19}$ | $10^{-7} – 10^{-9}$ |
| Gamma Rays | $> 3 \times 10^{19}$ | $< 10^{-9}$ |

**Electronic Data Interchange** (EDI) (n.) A networking protocol that allows encrypted data to be sent between two parties over the Internet securely.

**Electronic Information Delivery System** (EIDS) (n.) A microcomputer- and videodisc-based audio-video training system contracted by the United States Army in November 1986 as the designated, standard, stand-alone, computer-based training (CBT) system. EIDS refers to both the hardware configuration, provided by Matrox Electronics under the initial contract, and the standard for courseware (i.e., it must be EIDS-compatible). With 14 000 units installed, EIDS is the largest videodisc implementation.

**electronic mail** (email) (n., adj., v.) Messages transmitted between computer users through networks or via modems and telephone lines. A mail user agent (MUA) is used to compose a message, which is then sent to a message transfer agent (MTA) program, which delivers it locally or passes it to another MTA on a network typically using Simple Mail Transfer Protocol (SMTP). Email messages adhere to the RFC 822 standard. They begin with the appropriate headers, which identify the name and email address of the sender and recipient(s), the time sent, the date sent, and a subject field. Headers are followed by a blank line and the body of the message. Most email systems support standard multipurpose Internet mail extensions (MIME), which allow the sender to attach various file types in addition to ASCII text. A signature is usually placed at the end of the body.

**electronic news gathering mixer** (ENG mixer) (n.) A portable battery-powered mixer that will accept two or three microphone inputs. It is used in the field to record speech and sound effects. Some models have built-in telephone line interfacing.

**electronic publishing** (n.) The creation and distribution of computer-generated media. Electronic publishing is similar to traditional print publishing, but the product is in the form of digital data. Content is distributed on storage devices or over networks for computer-based delivery.

**Electronic Serial Number** (ESN) (n.) A unique number belonging to an individual cellular phone that is automatically transmitted to the base station every time a call is placed by the phone. The ESN, typically stored in the subscriber identity module (SIM) card, is validated on each call. Airtime charges are made to a cellular phone account based on the activity attributed to the ESN.

**Electronics Industries Association** (EIA) (n.) A professional organization whose recommendations are identified by the prefix *RS-*, as in RS-232 and RS-422.

**Electronics Industries Association of Japan** (EIAJ) (n.) The EIAJ was founded in 1948 as a nonprofit national trade organization to develop Japan's electronics industry and represent its views. The mission of the EIAJ is to represent the Japanese electronics industry in working on the challenges it faces. The industry is being called upon to further its social commitment in areas such as the environment, safety, and product liability. Other important issues include advancing international technical standardization, supporting the creation of emerging markets, fostering technological development, and enhancing international industrial cooperation. The EIAJ offers programs with the cooperation of related organizations and associations worldwide. The EIAJ has approximately 560 full and associate members, including manufacturers in the consumer electronics, industrial electronics, and electronic components and devices sectors.

**electronic whiteboard** (n.) A device that allows users to share data, text, and images simultaneously over a telephone connection. Typically, PCs with special hardware and software are connected by an ISDN line, and a session similar to a video conference is conducted with a whiteboard. Users may draw or write on their whiteboard with markers, and a living document may be updated simultaneously by multiple users who share access to it. Some systems also allow voice messages to be sent among those connected.

**electrostatic discharge** (ESD) (n.) A sudden burst of electrical flow that occurs when static electricity is grounded, or the rapid transfer of voltage between any two objects with different electrical potentials. It is a common cause of damage to integrated circuits.

**ELF emission** (n.) Extremely low frequency emission; generated by monitors and other common appliances, a magnetic field that may be hazardous to frequent computer users.

**Emacs** (n.) Editing macros or extensible macro system; a screen editor written in C and widely used on Unix and VMS systems. Originally written at MIT, Emacs is distributed by the Free Software Foundation. Emacs offers online help and features a WYSIWYG display. A version exists for most operating systems, and modes are available for editing text in many programming languages. Pronounced "EE-maks."

**email** See *electronic mail.*

**email address** (n.) Electronic mail address; the source or destination of an email message identified by a string of characters, such as *johndoe@corporation.com.* The RFC 822 standard for email addresses is used for the majority of Internet communications. *johndoe* is the local portion, or mailbox, on the destination computer. It is the only address name required on a local area network (LAN). *corporation.com* is the host portion or domain name, and it must be included after the symbol @. Mail is stored on a server and is read whenever the user logs on.

**embedded media** (n.) Audio, video, graphic, or animation files included in an HTML page, such as RealAudio files or GIF animations. Current browser versions interpret this non-ASCII information by identifying the MIME type and using the correct application to decode it.

**EMI** See *electromagnetic interference.*

**emitter** (n.) Laser or light-emitting diode (LED) used to convert an electrical signal into an optical signal for transmission by an optical waveguide.

**EMM** See *expanded memory manager.*

**emoticon** (n.) A face made with keyboard characters. Also called a *smiley* :-)

**emphasis** (n.) In imaging, a midrange control that can cause tones to be exaggerated or minimized. It is the equivalent of a loudness control in an audio amplifier. If parts of an image are too dark and too bright, the middle tones become subdued. The detail of an image becomes clearer as the middle tones are enhanced.

**EMS** See *Expanded Memory Specification.*

**EMU8000** (n.) A hardware and software subsystem providing music synthesis sound effects to 32-voice MIDI playback. It is widely distributed as the Advanced WavEffect MIDI synthesizer chip used on the Sound Blaster AWE32 (SB AWE32) card.

**emulator** (n.) A computer system used to test programs under development and simulate their performance.

**Encapsulated PostScript** (EPS) (n.) The graphic format designed by Aldus to describe an image in Adobe's PostScript Page Description Language

(PDL). A bitmapped thumbnail version of the image is generally placed in the header of the file in TIFF format for indexing and previewing.

**encapsulation** (n.) 1. The addition of layers containing header information to a protocol data unit (PDU) from the layer above. The headers may be combined from the physical layer, the network layer (IP), and the transport layer (TCP). 2. In object-oriented programming (OOP), the way in which data structures and their methods, or procedures, are kept together.

**encode** (v.) 1. To translate images or sound into a digital format. Encoding is the final step in converting an analog signal into a data representation. Other steps are sampling and quantizing. 2. To combine three-color signals into one composite video signal.

**encoder** (n.) 1. A microprocessor-based hardware system that converts analog video signals into a series of binary numbers that define the signal content. 2. A device that transforms original RGB video signals into a luminance signal (Y) and a chrominance signal for NTSC transmission.

**encryption** (n.) A process used to encode data. Encryption makes it difficult to decode without proprietary software, thus protecting data from unauthorized access. Encrypted data is usually created by applying an algorithm that must be reapplied to translate it.

**end of file** (EOF) (n.) 1. The out-of-band value returned by sequential character-input functions in the C programming language when the end of a file has been reached. 2. The keyboard character (usually Ctrl-D, which is the ASCII end-of-transmission character) that a Unix terminal driver maps into an end-of-file condition. 3. A character placed at the conclusion of a

data set or data stream informing the reader or receiver that it has ended.

**end of message** (n.) A control character that identifies the last bit of data in a message.

**Energy Star** (n.) An energy-efficiency guideline established by the Environmental Protection Agency (EPA) to identify an upper limit for wattage that an inactive computing device may draw. Compliance is voluntary, and manufacturers whose equipment meets the guidelines may display the Energy Star logo. See figure.

*Energy Star Logo*

**engine** (n.) In software, a program (such as a database engine or search engine) that performs a function. It is usually transparent to the user. An interface is provided that allows the user to interact with the data or media.

**ENG mixer** See *electronic news gathering mixer*.

**enhanced data GSM environment** (EDGE) (n.) An improved, faster version of the second generation global system for mobile communications (GSM) that transmits data over broadband networks at 384 kbps. It is considered a "2.5G" technology, between second- and third-generation wireless service, also called GSM384.

**Enhanced Graphics Adapter** (EGA) (n.) An IBM PC display adapter that supports 16 colors from a palette of 64 colors at 640 x 350 pixels, as well as several other resolutions. See the Graphics Adapter Resolutions table on page 173. Pronounced "ee-jee-AY."

**Enhanced Small Device Interface** (ESDI, pronounced "EHZ-dee") (n.) An interface for transferring data between a mass storage device (or some other peripheral) and a microcomputer. An ESDI board has a buffer and can transfer data at 10 to 24 megabits per second (Mbps).

**Enhanced Specialized Mobile Radio** (ESMR) (n.) Developed by Nextel and Geotek Communications, an advanced two-way radio service that competes with wireless telephone service in some areas.

**enhancer** See *exciter.*

**ENQ** (n.) Enquire; an online convention for querying a user's availability. It is also the ASCII character 5.

**Enterprise Java Beans** (EJB) (n.) Customized Java components typically used on the Internet to solve problems across a wide area network (WAN).

**entropy** (n.) The degree of disorder or randomness in a system. The entropy of a system is related to the amount of information it contains and the ways in which the information can be structured. An ordered system can be defined with fewer bits of information than a disordered one.

**entropy encoder/decoder** (n.) A type of encoder/decoder that compresses and decompresses quantized DCT coefficients compactly based on spatial characteristics.

**envelope** (n.) In audio engineering, a curve created by connecting the amplitude parameters

of a sound over time. A simple envelope might consist of the attack, decay, sustain, and release levels, or ADSR. Changing the ADSR settings alters the shape of a tone but not its basic pitch. An *envelope generator* is a device used to shape these four elements.

**environment** (n.) In programming, a list of variable bindings. To evaluate a variable is to look up its value in the environment. The environment is extended with new bindings when new variables are declared or when a function's parameters are bound to its actual arguments. In most block-structured procedural languages, the environment consists of a linked list of activation records.

**EOF** See *end of file.*

**EPROM** See *erasable programmable read-only memory.*

**EPS** See *Encapsulated PostScript.*

**EQ** See *equalizer.*

**equalization** (n.) In audio recording and processing, the use of filters or attenuators to adjust output levels in specified frequency ranges. See figure.

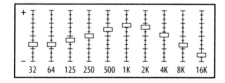

*graphic equalizer*

**equalizer** (EQ) (n.) An electronic device that modifies the frequency response of any audio signal passing through it. Equalizers are designed to change the amplitude versus the frequency characteristics of an audio signal in electronic or acoustic systems by applying filters. They are classified as fixed or adjustable, active or passive.

**erasable programmable read-only memory** (EPROM) (n.) A storage device that uses electrical charges stored in an isolated (floating) metal-oxide semiconductor (MOS) transistor gate to simulate data. Because of the isolation, an EPROM can retain a charge for more than 10 years without an external power supply. An EPROM is programmed when a charge is injected into the floating gate. The floating gate can be discharged when ultraviolet (UV) light is applied through a window in the package. This procedure erases the stored data and prepares the device to be reprogrammed. Pronounced "EE-prom."

**erase** (v.) To delete previously recorded data from a storage medium, such as a floppy disk. Data is not actually removed from the medium, but rather the pointers to it are rendered invisible. Most data can be recovered after being erased, unless the medium has been reformatted.

**Erbium-Doped Fiber Amplifier** (EDFA) (n.) The first optical amplifier that uses a portion of fiber-optic cable doped with the rare-earth element erbium and that is optically pumped with a laser diode. It can amplify a range of different wavelengths simultaneously. Erbium-Doped Amplifiers are being deployed in submarine cables.

**erlang** (n.) Named after Danish telephone engineer A. K. Erlang, a unit of measurement for traffic on telecommunications systems. One erlang equals one full hour of continuous use on one phone line.

**error control** (n.) The application of procedures to check the reliability of characters or blocks of data. Some error-control protocols, such as V.42, Microcom Networking Protocol (MNP), and U.S. Robotics High Speed Technology (HST), employ cyclic redundancy check (CRC) and automatic request for retransmission (ARQ).

**error correction code** (ECC) (n.) In CD-ROM writing, a system of scrambling data and recording redundant data onto a disc as it is premastered. During playback, this redundant data helps detect and correct errors that arise in data transmission. See also *block error correct*.

**error detect code** (EDC) (n.) On a CD-ROM, a code that consists of 32 bits of information per sector. The code is used to detect errors in the data of a sector.

**error detection and correction** (EDAC, pronounced "EE-dak.") (n.) An encoding technique that detects and corrects bit errors in digital data.

**escape sequence** (n.) A series of keystrokes that performs a function, such as moving a cursor on the screen.

**ESD** See *electrostatic discharge*.

**ESDI** See *Enhanced Small Device Interface*.

**ESF** See *Extended Super Frame*.

**ESMR** See *Enhanced Specialized Mobile Radio*.

**ESN** See *Electronic Serial Number*.

**establishing shot** (n.) A scene used in video to acquaint the viewer with the environment.

**etch** (v.) In semiconductor manufacturing, to remove specific portions of a layer through a chemical reaction.

**Ethernet** (n.) Developed at Xerox PARC in 1976, this coaxial cable local area network (LAN) standard (IEEE 802.3) was specified by Digital Equipment Corporation, Intel, and Xerox and is widely implemented throughout the industry. Packets of data are transmitted over 50-ohm coaxial cable with multiple shielding using the carrier sense multiple access with collision detection (CSMA/CD) algorithm until they arrive at the destination without colliding with other packets. The first contention slot following transmission is reserved for an acknowledge packet. A node on Ethernet is either transmitting or receiving data at any point in time. The bandwidth of 10BASE-T is about 10 megabits per second (Mbps), and 100BASE-T is capable of moving data at 100 Mbps. The gigabit (Gb) Ethernet standard allows much faster data rates. The typical disk-Ethernet-disk transfer rate with TCP/IP is 30 kilobytes per second (KBps). Version 2 specifies that the collision detection of the transceiver must be activated during the interpacket gap. In addition, it requires that when transmission finishes, the differential transmit lines are driven to zero volts. Version 2 also specifies certain network management functions, such as reporting collisions, retries, and deferrals.

**Ethernet address** (n.) The identifying hexadecimal number for an individual Ethernet controller board. It is a 48-bit number (aabbccddeeff) in which the first 24 bits (aabbcc) identify the manufacturer of the controller. Most addresses may be changed with software commands, although some are hard-wired on the controller or stored in ROM. The six hexadecimal numbers are normally written in pairs with a colon between each pair, as in 06:00:20:05:44:DC. Also known as a *MAC address*.

**Ethernet sniffing** (n.) Using software to monitor the Ethernet interface and identity packets on a local network. When the software detects a packet that fits certain criteria, it logs the packet to a file. The presence of a password is a common criterion for logging a packet.

**EtherTalk** (n.) The Ethernet protocol used by Apple computers.

**ETSI** See *European Telecommunications Standards Institute.*

**Eudora** (n.) A popular electronic mail software package developed by QUALCOMM for communicating over TCP/IP with microcomputers. Both commercial and shareware versions are available.

**Euroblock** (n.) Shortened form of European style terminal block, a specialized pluggable terminal block that consists of two pieces. The receptacle is permanently mounted on the equipment and the plug is used to terminate both balanced and unbalanced audio connections with screw terminals. This type of connection allows removal of the equipment by disconnecting the plug section rather than unscrewing each wire terminal. Also known as a *Phoenix-block.*

**European Association of Research Networks** (n.) Reseaux Associés pour la Recherche Européenne (RARE); a body of researchers representing companies that are engaged in the study of Internet-related topics.

**European Broadcast Union** (EBU) (n.) A group of organizations that work together to coordinate joint technical interests and to advise on the establishment of standards. Pronounced "ee-bee-YOU."

**European Conference of Postal and Telecommunications Administrations** (CEPT, abbreviation for *Conference Européenne des Administration des postes et des télécommunications*).

(n.) A standards group that represents most international telephone companies outside of North America and Japan.

**European Laboratory for Particle Physics** See *Conseil Européen pour la Recherche Nucléaire.*

**European Telecommunications Standards Institute** (ETSI) (n.) A not for profit organization created by the European Community (EC) and the European Post, Telephone, and Telegraphs (PTTs) charged with proposing telecommunications standards for Europe to facilitate telecommunications integration in the EC. Based in France, ETSI represents administrations, network operators, manufacturers, service providers, and users in 54 countries.

**event** (n.) In an interactive mode, an event is usually some input by the user that triggers an action. An event could be a keystroke, mouse click, or the position of the pointer.

**event-driven** (adj.) Describes a program or user interface with a main loop that waits for events to occur. An *event handler* passes details of an event to the operating system. A typical event might be a mouse click over a certain screen location.

**exception** (n.) A condition that arises because of error checking and that alters the normal behavior of a program. An exception could be generated by either hardware or software. A reset, an interrupt, or a signal from a memory management unit (MMU) are examples of hardware exceptions.

**exchange** (n.) In telecommunications, a coordination point established by a common carrier in a geographical area. The central office support and the equipment for communications services are provided at the exchange.

**exchange access** (n.) The use of telephone exchange services or facilities for the origination or termination of telephone toll services. One telephone company gives exchange access to another.

**exciter** (n.) A signal processor used primarily in music recording and performance that adds a kind of harmonic distortion found pleasing by most listeners. Even-numbered harmonics tend to make sounds soft, warm, and full. Odd-numbered harmonics tend to make sounds metallic, hollow, and bright. Lower-order harmonics control basic timbre, while higher-order harmonics control the "edge" or "bite" of the sound. Harmonic distortion can change the original sound dramatically. Exciters are sometimes known as *enhancers.*

**executable program** (n.) A type of computer program that performs a function or carries out a series of commands. It is identified by the file extension .exe in MS-DOS.

**execute** (v.) To carry out software commands.

**exit strategy** (n.) The means by which capital investors may receive a return on their investment. Acquisition by another company and the sale of shares in a public offering are two common strategies.

**expanded memory manager** (EMM) (n.) In MS-DOS, the emm386.exe program that converts extended memory into expanded memory.

**Expanded Memory Specification** (EMS) (n.) Bank switching in early IBM-compatible systems that permits 8088 chips to use more than 1 megabyte (MB) of physical memory. It has been replaced by extended memory.

**expansion bus** (n.) A circuit or pathway that

allows components to interact with a computer's CPU. Types of buses are identified in the Expansion Bus Types table, along with the width of the data path and the clock speed. See also *I/O bus*.

**expansion slot** (n.) A socket on a microcomputer motherboard into which an expansion board may be inserted. Half-sized circuit boards fit into an eight-bit ISA slot, whereas full-sized boards use a 16-bit slot. PCI boards pass 64 bits of data simultaneously and require a special type of socket for their edge connector. Examples of expansion boards that fit into slots include sound cards, video adapters, internal modems, and host controllers. The slots in multimedia computers are often filled with cards that perform special digitizing functions.

**expert system** (n.) A program that calls on information stored in a knowledge base to make decisions using an inference engine. Data is processed in a manner similar to human reasoning, and problems are solved by accessing "if-then" statements in the knowledge base.

**exponent** (n.) In mathematics, a function that raises a given constant, or base, to the power of its argument. A number that is increased by orders of magnitude has grown exponentially.

**expander** (n.) In audio, a signal processing device used to increase the dynamic range of the signal passing through it. Expanders complement compressors by restoring the peaks removed by compression. An expander seems to make the quiet sounds quieter and the loud sounds louder.

**expression** (n.) In a programming language, such as JavaScript, an expression is a phrase that an interpreter can evaluate. Expressions include operators, constants, functions, operands, variables, and parenthesis, and they are used in language programming, spreadsheet applications, and database systems. For example, $x + 10$ is an expression, because it can be evaluated, while $x = 10$ is simply a statement. $x$ and 10 are operands, and + is an operator. Every expression will have at least one operand and one or more operators.

**extended architecture** (XA) (n.) An evolution of the standard CD-ROM format that provides for adaptive differential pulse code modulation (ADPCM) audio, multiple session discs, Photo-CD, and CD-i compatibility. This CD format relies solely on Cross-Interleaved Reed-Solomon Code (CIRC) for error correction.

**extended attribute** (n.) Data that identifies a file in Windows NT and OS/2 with more infor-

**Expansion Bus Types**

| Bus | Processor | Data Path | Clock Speed |
|---|---|---|---|
| ISA | (PC/XT) | 8-bit | 8.33 MHz |
| | (PC/AT) | 16-bit | 8.33 MHz |
| EISA | (PC/80486) | 32-bit | 8.33 MHz |
| MCA | (IBM PS/2) | 32-bit | 10 MHz |
| NuBus | (Mac) | 32-bit | 10 or 20 MHz |
| VESA | (PC/80486) | 32-bit | 40 or 66 MHz |
| PCI | (PowerPC/Pentium) | 32/64-bit | 131 MHz |

## EBCDIC

| Decimal | Hex | Acronym | Function | Decimal | Hex | Acronym | Function |
|---|---|---|---|---|---|---|---|
| 0 | 0 | NUL | Null | 53 | 35 | TRN | Transparent |
| 1 | 1 | SOH | Start of Heading | 54 | 36 | NBS | Numeric Backspace |
| 2 | 2 | STX | Start of Text | 55 | 37 | EOT | End of Transmission |
| 3 | 3 | ETX | End of Text | 56 | 38 | SBS | Subscript |
| 4 | 4 | SEL | Select | 57 | 39 | IT | Indent Tab |
| 5 | 5 | HT | Horizontal Tab | 58 | 3A | RFF | Required Form Feed |
| 6 | 6 | RNL | Required New Line | 59 | 3B | CU3 | Customer Use 3 |
| 7 | 7 | DEL | Delete | 60 | 3C | DC4 | Device Control 4 |
| 8 | 8 | GE | Graphic Escape | 61 | 3D | NAK | Negative Acknowledge |
| 9 | 9 | SPS | Superscript | 62 | 3E | | (Not Assigned) |
| 10 | A | RPT | Repeat | 63 | 3F | SUB | Substitute |
| 11 | B | VT | Vertical Tab | 64 | 40 | SP | Space |
| 12 | C | FF | Form Feed | 65 | 41 | RSP | Required Space |
| 13 | D | CR | Carriage Return | 66 | 42 | | (Not Assigned) |
| 14 | E | SO | Shift Out | 67 | 43 | | (Not Assigned) |
| 15 | F | SI | Shift In | 68 | 44 | | (Not Assigned) |
| 16 | 10 | DLE | Data Length Escape | 69 | 45 | | (Not Assigned) |
| 17 | 11 | DC1 | Device Control 1 | 70 | 46 | | (Not Assigned) |
| 18 | 12 | DC2 | Device Control 2 | 71 | 47 | | (Not Assigned) |
| 19 | 13 | DC3 | Device Control 3 | 72 | 48 | | (Not Assigned) |
| 20 | 14 | RES/ENP | Restore/Enable Presentation | 73 | 49 | | (Not Assigned) |
| 21 | 15 | NL | New Line | 74 | 4A | ¢ | Cent Sign |
| 22 | 16 | BS | Backspace | 75 | 4B | . | Period |
| 23 | 17 | POC | Program-Operator Communication | 76 | 4C | < | Less-than Sign |
| 24 | 18 | CAN | Cancel | 77 | 4D | ( | Open Parenthesis |
| 25 | 19 | EM | End of Medium | 78 | 4E | + | Plus Sign |
| 26 | 1A | UBS | Unit Backspace | 79 | 4F | \| | Logical OR |
| 27 | 1B | CU1 | Customer Use 1 | 80 | 50 | & | Ampersand |
| 28 | 1C | IFS | Interchange File Separator | 81 | 51 | | (Not Assigned) |
| 29 | 1D | IGS | Interchange Group Separator | 82 | 52 | | (Not Assigned) |
| 30 | 1E | IRS | Interchange Record Separator | 83 | 53 | | (Not Assigned) |
| 31 | 1F | IUS | Interchange Unit Separator | 84 | 54 | | (Not Assigned) |
| 32 | 20 | DS | Digit Select | 85 | 55 | | (Not Assigned) |
| 33 | 21 | SOS | Start of Significance | 86 | 56 | | (Not Assigned) |
| 34 | 22 | FS | Field Separator | 87 | 57 | | (Not Assigned) |
| 35 | 23 | WUS | Word Underscore | 88 | 58 | | (Not Assigned) |
| 36 | 24 | BYP/INP | Bypass/Inhibit Presentation | 89 | 59 | | (Not Assigned) |
| 37 | 25 | LF | Line Feed | 90 | 5A | ! | Exclamation Point |
| 38 | 26 | ETB | End of Transmission Block | 91 | 5B | $ | Dollar Sign |
| 39 | 27 | ESC | Escape | 92 | 5C | * | Asterisk |
| 40 | 28 | SA | Set Attribute | 93 | 5D | ) | Close Parenthesis |
| 41 | 29 | SFE | Start Field Extended | 94 | 5E | ; | Semi-colon |
| 42 | 2A | SM/SW | Set Mode/Switch | 95 | 5F | | Logical NOT |
| 43 | 2B | CSP | Control Sequence Prefix | 96 | 60 | – | Minus Sign, Hyphen, Dash |
| 44 | 2C | MFA | Modify Field Attribute | 97 | 61 | / | Forward Slash |
| 45 | 2D | ENQ | Enquire | 98 | 62 | | (Not Assigned) |
| 46 | 2E | ACK | Acknowledge | 99 | 63 | | (Not Assigned) |
| 47 | 2F | BEL | Bell | 100 | 64 | | (Not Assigned) |
| 48 | 30 | | (Not Assigned) | 101 | 65 | | (Not Assigned) |
| 49 | 31 | | (Not Assigned) | 102 | 66 | | (Not Assigned) |
| 50 | 32 | SYN | Synchronous Idle | 103 | 67 | | (Not Assigned) |
| 51 | 33 | IR | Index Return | 104 | 68 | | (Not Assigned) |
| 52 | 34 | PP | Presentation Position | 105 | 69 | | (Not Assigned) |

| Decimal | Hex | Acronym | Function | | Decimal | Hex | Acronym | Function |
|---------|-----|---------|----------|---|---------|-----|---------|----------|
| 106 | 6A | ¦ | Broken Pipe | | 161 | A1 | ~ | Tilde |
| 107 | 6B | , | Comma | | 162 | A2 | s | |
| 108 | 6C | % | Percent Sign | | 163 | A3 | t | |
| 109 | 6D | _ | Underscore | | 164 | A4 | u | |
| 110 | 6E | > | Greater-than Sign | | 165 | A5 | v | |
| 111 | 6F | ? | Question Mark | | 166 | A6 | w | |
| 112 | 70 | | (Not Assigned) | | 167 | A7 | x | |
| 113 | 71 | | (Not Assigned) | | 168 | A8 | y | |
| 114 | 72 | | (Not Assigned) | | 169 | A9 | z | |
| 115 | 73 | | (Not Assigned) | | 170 | AA | | (Not Assigned) |
| 116 | 74 | | (Not Assigned) | | 171 | AB | | (Not Assigned) |
| 117 | 75 | | (Not Assigned) | | 172 | AC | | (Not Assigned) |
| 118 | 76 | | (Not Assigned) | | 173 | AD | | (Not Assigned) |
| 119 | 77 | | (Not Assigned) | | 174 | AE | | (Not Assigned) |
| 120 | 78 | | (Not Assigned) | | 175 | AF | | (Not Assigned) |
| 121 | 79 | ` | Grave Accent | | 176 | B0 | | (Not Assigned) |
| 122 | 7A | : | Colon | | 177 | B1 | | (Not Assigned) |
| 123 | 7B | # | Number Sign | | 178 | B2 | | (Not Assigned) |
| 124 | 7C | @ | At Sign | | 179 | B3 | | (Not Assigned) |
| 125 | 7D | ' | Single Quote | | 180 | B4 | | (Not Assigned) |
| 126 | 7E | = | Equals Sign | | 181 | B5 | | (Not Assigned) |
| 127 | 7F | " | Double Quote | | 182 | B6 | | (Not Assigned) |
| 128 | 80 | | (Not Assigned) | | 183 | B7 | | (Not Assigned) |
| 129 | 81 | a | | | 184 | B8 | | (Not Assigned) |
| 130 | 82 | b | | | 185 | B9 | | (Not Assigned) |
| 131 | 83 | c | | | 186 | BA | | (Not Assigned) |
| 132 | 84 | d | | | 187 | BB | | (Not Assigned) |
| 133 | 85 | e | | | 188 | BC | | (Not Assigned) |
| 134 | 86 | f | | | 189 | BD | | (Not Assigned) |
| 135 | 87 | g | | | 190 | BE | | (Not Assigned) |
| 136 | 88 | h | | | 191 | BF | | (Not Assigned) |
| 137 | 89 | i | | | 192 | C0 | { | Opening Brace |
| 138 | 8A | | (Not Assigned) | | 193 | C1 | A | |
| 139 | 8B | | (Not Assigned) | | 194 | C2 | B | |
| 140 | 8C | | (Not Assigned) | | 195 | C3 | C | |
| 141 | 8D | | (Not Assigned) | | 196 | C4 | D | |
| 142 | 8E | | (Not Assigned) | | 197 | C5 | E | |
| 143 | 8F | | (Not Assigned) | | 198 | C6 | F | |
| 144 | 90 | | (Not Assigned) | | 199 | C7 | G | |
| 145 | 91 | j | | | 200 | C8 | H | |
| 146 | 92 | k | | | 201 | C9 | I | |
| 147 | 93 | l | | | 202 | CA | SHY | Syllable Hyphen |
| 148 | 94 | m | | | 203 | CB | | (Not Assigned) |
| 149 | 95 | n | | | 204 | CC | | (Not Assigned) |
| 150 | 96 | o | | | 205 | CD | | (Not Assigned) |
| 151 | 97 | p | | | 206 | CE | | (Not Assigned) |
| 152 | 98 | q | | | 207 | CF | | (Not Assigned) |
| 153 | 99 | r | | | 208 | D0 | } | Closing Brace |
| 154 | 9A | | (Not Assigned) | | 209 | D1 | J | |
| 155 | 9B | | (Not Assigned) | | 210 | D2 | K | |
| 156 | 9C | | (Not Assigned) | | 211 | D3 | L | |
| 157 | 9D | | (Not Assigned) | | 212 | D4 | M | |
| 158 | 9E | | (Not Assigned) | | 213 | D5 | N | |
| 159 | 9F | | (Not Assigned) | | 214 | D6 | O | |
| 160 | A0 | | (Not Assigned) | | 215 | D7 | P | |

| Decimal | Hex | Acronym | Function | Decimal | Hex | Acronym | Function |
|---------|-----|---------|----------|---------|-----|---------|----------|
| 216 | D8 | Q | | 236 | EC | | (Not Assigned) |
| 217 | D9 | R | | 237 | ED | | (Not Assigned) |
| 218 | DA | | (Not Assigned) | 238 | EE | | (Not Assigned) |
| 219 | DB | | (Not Assigned) | 239 | EF | | (Not Assigned) |
| 220 | DC | | (Not Assigned) | 240 | F0 | 0 | Zero |
| 221 | DD | | (Not Assigned) | 241 | F1 | 1 | One |
| 222 | DE | | (Not Assigned) | 242 | F2 | 2 | Two |
| 223 | DF | | (Not Assigned) | 243 | F3 | 3 | Three |
| 224 | E0 | \ | Reverse Slash | 244 | F4 | 4 | Four |
| 225 | E1 | NSP | Numeric Space | 245 | F5 | 5 | Five |
| 226 | E2 | S | | 246 | F6 | 6 | Six |
| 227 | E3 | T | | 247 | F7 | 7 | Seven |
| 228 | E4 | U | | 248 | F8 | 8 | Eight |
| 229 | E5 | V | | 249 | F9 | 9 | Nine |
| 230 | E6 | W | | 250 | FA | | (Not Assigned) |
| 231 | E7 | X | | 251 | FB | | (Not Assigned) |
| 232 | E8 | Y | | 252 | FC | | (Not Assigned) |
| 233 | E9 | Z | | 253 | FD | | (Not Assigned) |
| 234 | EA | | (Not Assigned) | 254 | FE | | (Not Assigned) |
| 235 | EB | | (Not Assigned) | 255 | FF | EO | Eight Ones |

mation than a simple attribute contains. Information is added about the original application that created the file and the names of other related files.

**extended attribute record** (XAR) (n.) Adhering to ISO 9660 standards, a record that has attributes not listed in the directory record, including information about escape sequences, dates, permissions, and other private data.

**Extended Binary-Coded Decimal Interchange Code** (EBCDIC, pronounced "EHB-suh-dik") (n.) Code that can identify 256 eight-bit characters, as opposed to the 128-character set available in ASCII code. See table.

**extended curve** (X curve) (n.) In the film sound industry this is known as the *wide-range curve*, conforming to ISO Bulletin 2969. It specifies that the EQ curve of pink noise, at the listening position two-thirds of the way back in a theater, be flat to 2 kHz, rolling off 3 dB/octave after that. The *small-room X curve* is designed for rooms with less than 150 cubic meters, or 5,300 cubic feet. This standard specifies flat response to 2 kHz, and then rolling off at a 1.5 dB/octave rate. Some engineers use a modified small-room curve, starting the roll-off at 4 kHz, with a 3 dB/octave rate. Compare with *Academy curve*.

**Extended Data Out Dynamic Random-Access Memory** (EDO DRAM, pronounced "EE-dee-oh DEE-ram") (n.) A type of DRAM available since 1995 that accesses nearby memory locations faster than normal DRAM can. EDO DRAM allows the data outputs to be accessed and controlled more easily. In pipelined systems, it is useful for overlapping accesses in which subsequent cycles are begun before the data from the previous cycle is removed from the bus. EDO DRAM is used with Intel's Pentium processors. A compatible chipset, such as Triton, must be used to take advantage of EDO DRAM. Since early 1995, EDO DRAM has been available for computers. See also *burst EDO DRAM*.

**Extended Graphics Adapter** (XGA) (n.) An IBM

PS/2 graphics standard that provides a resolution of 1024 pixels x 768 pixels with eight-bit color. See the Graphics Adapter Resolutions table on page 173.

**Extended Industry Standard Architecture** (EISA, pronounced "EE-sah") (n.) An evolved version of Industry Standard Architecture (ISA). Announced in September 1988, it was developed primarily by Compaq in response to the IBM Micro Channel Architecture (MCA) bus. The EISA bus provides 32-bit slots for use with 386DX or higher systems. It supports adapter cards created for the older ISA standard but offers greater system expansion, fewer adapter conflicts, and a maximum bandwidth of 33 megabytes per second (MBps). Another advantage over ISA is an automated setup for adapter board interrupts and addressing issues. EISA setup software recognizes potential conflicts and automatically configures the system to avoid them through interrupt request (IRQ) sharing; in other words, multiple bus cards can share a single interrupt. This feature has also been implemented in peripheral component interconnect (PCI) bus cards. See also *Industry Standard Architecture* or *Micro Channel Architecture*.

**Extended Integrated Drive Electronics** (EIDE) (n.) An improved version of the ATA hard drive controller with faster data rates, 32-bit transactions, and (in some cases) direct memory access (DMA). Named by Western Digital in 1994, EIDE is also referred to as *Fast ATA-2*. An EIDE interface can simultaneously control up to four storage devices connected to a computer. See also *Advanced Technology Attachment* or *Integrated Drive Electronics*.

**extended memory specification** (XMS) (n.) The provision for memory located after the first megabyte (MB) of address space in an IBM-compatible computer with an 80286 or later processor.

It is not directly available in real mode, just through EMS, UMB, XMS, or HMA (High Memory Area, the first 64 kilobytes of memory above the 1-MB limit accessible by DOS); only applications executing in protected mode can use extended memory directly. In protected mode, the extended memory is provided by a supervising protected mode operating system such as Microsoft Windows. The processor makes this memory available through the use of global and local descriptor tables. Memory assigned to a local descriptor cannot be accessed by another program without causing a hardware trap, so it is considered protected. A protected mode OS such as Windows can also provide expanded memory to real mode programs. DOS Protected Mode Interface is Microsoft's prescribed method for having an MS-DOS program access extended memory in a multitasking environment.

**Extended Multitimbral Specification** (n.) A synthesizer subsystem standard followed by Multimedia PC audio board manufacturers. It permits 16 melodic notes and 16 percussive notes to sound at once, and provides a palette of nine different melodic tones and eight percussive tones.

**eXtended Server-Side Includes** (XSSI) (n.) This is a feature provided with the Apache Web-server, a freely distributed application used to host a majority of the web sites in the world. The XSSI module (mod_include) defines a set of commands that Apache will parse when a page is requested, and include in the content sent to the browser. XSSI is not dependent on the capabilities of a browser. It allows a greater variety of variables to pass according to set parameters than are available in basic SSI.

**Extended Super Frame** (ESF) (n.) In telecommunications, a process of combining 24 DS-1 (T-1) frames so that the repeating 24 framing bits (F-bits) may be used to carry encoded network management data as well as a CRC-6 frame check sequence. It is an improved version of the D4 format, which provides carrier conversion between voice and T-1 digital systems.

**extensible** (adj.) Describes a programming language or a system that may be modified by changing or adding features, and is capable of being extended.

**Extensible Markup Language** (XML) (n.) A subset of Standard Generalized Markup Language (SGML) ISO 8879, upon which Hypertext Markup Language (HTML) is also based. The objective of XML is to enable generic SGML to be served, received, and processed on the web in the same way that HTML is handled. Unlike HTML, it allows new tags to be defined and transmitted along with the content of a document.

The XML specification, recommended by the World Wide Web Consortium (W3C), describes a class of data objects called XML documents and describes how computer programs should process them. It is a restricted form of SGML and fully conforms to the SGML standard. Development was begun in 1996 by the XML Working Group of the W3C, and the standard was approved in 1998.

XML documents are comprised of storage units called entities, which contain either parsed or unparsed data. Parsed data consists of characters, some of which identify character data, and some of which identify markup. Markup defines a document's storage layout and logical structure, and XML provides a mechanism to control these elements. An XML processor is a software module that is required to read XML documents and to provide access to their content and structure. The XML processor works in conjunction with an application. The XML specification describes the required behavior of an XML processor, how it must read XML data, and the information it must provide to the application.

The XML Version 1.0 specification provides the information needed to create XML documents and to process them on the Internet. Associated standards referenced in the specification are Unicode and ISO/IEC 10646 for characters, Internet RFC 1766 for language identification tags, ISO 639 for language name codes, and ISO 3166 for country name codes.

**Extensible Stylesheet Language** (XSL) (n.) Originally called Extensible Style Language, this is a language for creating a style sheet that describes how data should be presented by a web browser reading Extensible Markup Language (XML). XSL extends the Document Style Semantics and Specification Language (DSSSL) and the Cascading Style Sheet, level 1 (CSS1) standards. Data in an XML page is contained in identified fields, unlike an HTML page. XSL provides tools to define which data fields in an XML file to display and how to display them. XSL may be used to create a style definition for one or for many XML documents. It is currently under development by the World Wide Web Consortium (W3C). This language for expressing style sheets consists of three parts:

1. XSL Transformations: (XSLT) a language for transforming XML documents;
2. Xpath: an expression language used by XSLT to access or reference parts of an XML document;
3. XSL Formatting Objects: an XML vocabulary that specifies formatting semantics.

Like a Cascading Style Sheet, an XSL style sheet is a file that describes how to display an XML document of a given type. XSL uses different syntax, but it shares the functionality and is compatible with CSS2. Although XSLT was originally intended to perform complex styling operations, such as the generation of tables of contents and indexes, it has become useful as a general purpose XML processing language. XSLT is widely used for generating HTML web pages from XML data. Advanced styling features are expressed by an XML document type that defines a set of elements called *Formatting Objects*, along with their attributes.

XSL is different from CSS in several ways. XSL uses XML notation, while CSS uses its own form of notation. In CSS, the formatting object tree is nearly identical to the source tree, and inheritance of formatting properties occurs on the source tree. In XSL, the formatting object tree may be completely different from the source tree, and inheritance of formatting properties occurs on the formatting object tree. Implementations of CSS1 and, to a lesser degree, CSS2 are widespread. XSL is gaining browser and content-authoring support.

**extension** (n.) 1. Any small program that plugs into a larger one and provides increased functionality. Extensions allow operating systems to control CD-ROM drives. 2. The letters that appear after the dot (.) in the name of an MS-DOS file to classify and identify the file type. Extensions for some of the frequently used multimedia file types are .avi (Video for Windows), .gif (compressed graphics), .jpg (compressed graphics), .mid (MIDI), .mov (QuickTime), .mpg (MPEG video), and .wav (Windows audio). The Macintosh file-naming system uses two hidden extensions called file attributes that are each four letters long. One is for the file type, and the other is for the creator. One online file extensions resource is

*http://extsearch.com*. See table.

**extent** (n.) A contiguous set of sectors on a disk, or blocks on a CD-ROM, that are occupied by a particular file or section of a file and that are numbered consecutively in ascending order. Multiextent files on a CD-recordable disc are recorded at different locations if the disc has been written in multiple sessions.

**Exterior Gateway Protocol** (EGP) (n.) Standard used to communicate routing information to the routers that connect autonomous network systems.

**external command** (XCMD) (n.) A program written to extend the functionality of the HyperCard authoring environment. It is created in another programming language and called from within HyperCard.

**eXternal Data Representation** (XDR) (n.) Developed by Sun Microsystems, a standard for machine-independent data structures. It is similar to Abstract Syntax Notation One (ASN/1).

**external functions** (XFCN) (n.) A program written to provide new features for the HyperCard authoring environment, similar to an external command (XCMD).

**extract** (v.) To decode a file encoded for network transmission. The term is usually used in reference to the uuencode/uudecode Unix utility.

**extranet** (n.) A wide area network (WAN) version of an intranet. An extranet supports and controls external access. It makes portions of a company's intranet available to the Internet, allowing customers, vendors, and remote workers to access the company's data with a web browser. Although such a facility requires high

## File Name Extensions

File descriptions marked with * are ASCII; all other file types are binary. VMS files are marked ** because they are variable.

| .ext | Description | File Usage | .ext | Description | File Usage |
|---|---|---|---|---|---|
| .acr | image file (medical) | image viewer | .euc | Japanese (Kanji) | Japanese reader |
| .aif(c) | sound (Apple, SGI) | sound player | .exe | executable file | type the file name to run |
| .aif(f) | sound (Apple, SGI) | sound player | .exe | self-extracting file | type the file name to run |
| .arc | compressed archive | pkunpak, WinZip, ARCE | .f | Freeze for Unix | unfreeze (freeze) |
| .arj | compressed | arj (DOS) | .fac | picture | picture viewer |
| .art | First Publisher clip art file | First Publisher | .fit(s) | image | image viewer |
|  |  |  | .flc | animated picture | picture viewer |
| .asc | image | image viewer | .fli | animated picture | picture viewer |
| .au | audio | u-law player | .flx | image | image viewer |
| .avi | video (MS Windows) | Media Player | .fssd | sound | sound player |
| .avr | sound | sound player | .gb | Chinese | Chinese viewer |
| .avs | animation | image viewer | .gds | image | image viewer |
| .bac | binary backup | restore | .gif | picture | picture viewer, browser |
| .bas | BASIC source | run in QBasic | .gl | animated picture | picture viewer |
| .bbm | image | image viewer | .gry | picture | picture viewer |
| .bck | **VMS backup | restore | .gz | compressed | decompress (gzip124) |
| .big | Chinese (old version) | Chinese viewer | .gzip | compressed | decompress (gzip124) |
| .big5 | Chinese (old version) | Chinese viewer | .h | *C/C++ header file | text editor |
| .bmf | image | image viewer | .ha | compressed | decompress |
| .bmp | picture (bitmap) | picture viewer | .ham | image | image viewer |
| .boo | image | image viewer (msbpct.exe) | .hlb | **VMS help libraries | various |
|  |  |  | .hlp | **VMS help files | various |
| .cgm | computer graphics metafile | CGM viewer | .hpk | compressed | decompress (hpack78.zip) |
| .clp | picture | picture viewer | .hqx | Macintosh compressed | decompress |
| .cmf | music | music player (Playcmf) | .hrz | image | image viewer |
| .com | compressed | decompress | .htm(l) | *HTML document | text editor, HTML editor |
| .com | MS-DOS executable file | type the file name to run | .hyp | compressed | decompress (hyper25.zip) |
| .com | **VMS DCL command file | command | .hz | Chinese | Chinese viewer (CWD) |
| .cpt | Macintosh compressed | decompress | .ibm | picture | picture viewer |
| .cur | image | image viewer | .ice | archive | decompress |
| .cut | image | image viewer | .ico | image | image viewer |
| .dat | **VMS data file | various | .ief | image | image viewer |
| .dcs | image | image viewer | .iff | binary data (various types) | image viewer |
| .des | *text | word processor |  |  |  |
| .dib | picture (bitmap) | picture viewer | .img | picture | picture viewer |
| .dig | *text | word processor | .ish | compressed | decompress (ish200.lzh) |
| .dl | animated picture | dl viewer | .jas | image | image viewer |
| .dlg | image | image viewer | .jbig | image | image viewer |
| .dms | compressed | decompress | .jfi | image | image viewer |
| .doc | *text (MS Word) | word processor | .jis | Japanese | Japanese reader |
| .dvi | *special TeX text | word processor | .jpc | picture | picture viewer |
| .dwc | archive | decompress (zzap) | .jpeg | picture | picture viewer, browser |
| .dwg | image | image viewer | .jpg | picture | picture viewer, browser |
| .dxf | *ASCII Drawing Interchange | AutoCAD | .lbm | image | image viewer |
|  |  |  | .lbr | archive | decompress (lue220) |
| .eps | Encapsulated PostScript image | PostScript viewer | .lha | compressed | decompress (lha213) |
|  |  |  | .lis | *program listing | DOS editor |
|  |  |  | .lm8 | picture | picture viewer |

## File Name Extensions (continued)

| .ext | Description | File Usage | .ext | Description | File Usage |
|---|---|---|---|---|---|
| .lzh | compressed | decompress (lha213) | .ppt | PowerPoint presentation | MS PowerPoint |
| .lzs | compressed | decompress (larc333.zip) | .ps | *laser printer file | word processor |
| .lzw | LHWarp | archive decompress | .psid | picture, text | picture viewer |
| .lzx | compressed | decompress | .ra | RealAudio | RealMedia player |
| .mac | MacPaint picture | picture viewer | .ras | picture | picture viewer |
| .mag | picture | picture viewer | .raw | animated picture | picture viewer |
| .man | *text manual | word processor | .rax | image | image viewer |
| .map | image | image viewer | .rgb | picture | picture viewer |
| .mat | sound | sound player | .rle | picture | picture viewer |
| .md | compressed | decompress (zzap) | .rmi | sound | sound player |
| .mgf | image | image viewer | .rol | sound | sound player |
| .mhg | multimedia | multimedia player | .scx | image | image viewer |
| .mid | music | MIDI player | .sdn | shell archive | decompress (zzap) |
| .mki | picture | picture viewer | .sea | self-extracting archive (Macintosh) | run to extract |
| .mod | music | mod player (MOD4WIN) | | | |
| .mov | multimedia | QuickTime player | .sf | sound | sound player |
| .mpa | audio | MPEG audio player | .sgi | picture | picture viewer |
| .mpg | multimedia | MPEG player | .shar | *shell archive | unshell (unshar) |
| .mps | multimedia | MPEG player | .shg | image | image viewer |
| .mp2 | audio | MPEG audio player | .shk | compressed (Macintosh) | decompress |
| .mp3 | audio | MPEG audio player | .sit | compressed (Macintosh) | decompress |
| .mrb | image | image viewer | .snd | music | music player |
| .msp | image | image viewer | .s3m | sound | sound player |
| .mtm | sound | sound player | .stm | sound | sound player |
| .mtv | picture | picture viewer | .tar | tape archive | untar (DOS) |
| .nff | image | image viewer | .tar.gz | compressed tar | decompress, untar |
| .nst | sound | sound player | .tar.Z | compressed tar | decompress, untar |
| .off | image | image viewer | .tdo | compressed | decompress (teled121) |
| .omf | image | image viewer | .tga | picture | picture viewer |
| .pak | compressed | decompress (zzap) | .tif(f) | image | image viewer |
| .pbm | picture | picture viewer | .txt | *text | word processor |
| .pcc | image | image viewer | .uc2 | compressed | decompress (uc2ins) |
| .pcd | Kodak Photo-CD | picture viewer | .ul | sound | sound player |
| .pcm | sound | sound player | .utl | sound | sound player |
| .pct | picture | picture viewer | .uud | uudecode | application |
| .pcx | picture (Paintbrush) | picture viewer | .uue | *uuencode | decode (uudecode) |
| .pdf | image | Acrobat Reader | .vic | picture | picture viewer |
| .pds | picture | picture viewer | .vik | picture | picture viewer |
| .pgm | picture | picture viewer | .vis | picture | picture viewer |
| .pic | picture | picture viewer | .voc | sound | sound player |
| .pict | picture (Macintosh) | picture viewer | .wav | sound | sound player |
| .pit | Macintosh compressed | decompress | .wmf | Windows Metafile | image viewer |
| .pm | picture | picture viewer | .xbm | picture (X Window System) | picture viewer |
| .png | image (Portable Network Graphics) | image viewer, browser | | | |
| | | | .xm | sound | sound player |
| .pnt | MacPaint | image viewer | .xpm | picture | picture viewer |
| .pol | music | music player | .xwd | image | image viewer |
| .pp | Amiga compressed | decompress (PPLib) | .y | compressed | decompress (yabba) |
| .ppm | portable pixelmap | picture viewer | .zip | compressed | decompress (unzip) |

security, it is a valuable means of delivering services and communicating efficiently.

**extremely high frequency** (EHF) (n.) Frequency in the 30- to 300-GHz range.

**extrude** (v.) To give two-dimensional objects a three-dimensional look by extending solid shadows from two-dimensional lines and shapes. This graphic effect may be applied to boldfaced print to attract attention.

**e-zine** (n.) Electronic magazine; online periodical.

# F

F See *Fahrenheit.*

f See *femto-.*

**face** (n.) In three-dimensional animation, a plane in a wireframe model.

**facility** (n.) 1. In telecommunications, the line and all equipment required to furnish a completed circuit. 2. A capability offered by hardware or software that provides functionality for the user.

**facsimile** (fax) (n.) Procedure for the analog transmission of images over telephone lines. The majority of fax machines adhere to the Group III standard, which allows for sending 200-dot-per-inch (dpi) black-and-white images. Group IV fax machines can send data at up to 64 kilobits per second (Kbps) over ISDN or leased lines and offer grayscale images at resolutions of up to 400 dpi.

**fade** (v.) In editing or production, to gradually reduce or increase visual or audio intensity, moving to or from blackness and silence. Commonly used phrases are *fade in, fade out,* and *fade to black.* To *fade in* is to bring the levels up gradually from blackness or silence to a normal brightness and volume, and to *fade out* is to reverse this process. In compressed video, very slow fades often create undesirable arti-

facts and "blockiness." Quick cuts are preferred for this reason.

**fader** (n.) A sliding volume control, or potentiometer, often used to control the amplitude of signals on a mixing board.

**fading** (n.) In microwave radio transmission, fading is a phenomenon in which atmospheric refraction or rain attenuation causes a drop in signal level received.

**fallback** (n.) When two modems experience data corruption, perhaps resulting from line noise, a feature of their protocol that allows them to renegotiate to a lower-speed connection.

**fall forward** (n.) When two modems have fallen back to a lower speed because of data corruption, a feature that allows them to return to a higher speed as the connection improves.

**FAQ** See *frequently asked questions.*

**farad** (n.) A unit of electrical capacity, measured across the terminals of a capacitor, when a charge of 1 coulomb at the input produces a change in the output of 1 volt.

**Fast ATA** (n.) Fast Advanced Technology Attachment; implementations by Seagate and Quantum of the ATA-2 interface. Also referred to as *Fast ATA-2*.

**Fahrenheit** (F) (n., adj.) A temperature scale that registers the freezing point of water as 32°F and the boiling point as 212°F, under normal atmospheric pressure.

**Fahrenheit, Gabriel Daniel** (1686-1736) German-born physicist who invented the mercury thermometer and devised the Fahrenheit temperature scale. He introduced both in 1714.

**false negative** (n.) A system event that allows an actual intrusive action to pass as non-intrusive behavior. An example is the failure of anti-virus software to detect a virus on a file, permitting it to pass into the system without issuing a warning.

**false positive** (n.) A system occurrence that classifies a legitimate action as anomalous, or a possible intrusion. An example is a case in which anti-virus software falsely indicates a clean file as infectious.

**far end** (n.) In teleconferencing, far end is the distant location of a transmission, or the other end of the telephone line, as opposed to the nearest end.

**far sound field** (n.) The sound field distant enough from the sound source so that the sound pressure level (SPL) decreases by 6 dB for each doubling of the distance from the source.

**Fast Ethernet** (n.) A version of Ethernet that allows transmission at 100 megabits per second (Mbps), compared with the 10-Mbps rate of standard Ethernet. It requires that wiring, hubs, and network cards be upgraded from standard Ethernet.

**Fast Fourier Transform** (FFT) (n.) An algorithm that computes the Fourier transform of a set of discrete data values. Given a finite set of data points, such as an audio sample, FFT expresses the data in terms of its component frequencies. It can reconstruct a signal from frequency data.

**fast packet switching** (n.) An effective message switching approach that seeks to minimize packet processing time at each node, utilizing high-speed data channels more efficiently. Examples of packet switching are Frame Relay, Cell Relay, and Signaling System 7 (SS7).

**Fast Start** (n.) The progressive download feature of QuickTime. It allows a viewer to begin watching a movie before the entire file has been fully downloaded.

**FAT** See *file allocation table.*

**fat binary** (n.) An executable file format for distributing software that may be used on either a PowerMac or a Macintosh with a Motorola 680x0 processor. It is termed *fat* because it contains two versions of the code, one for each type of processor. Fat refers to the excess baggage. In most cases the computer itself automatically chooses the appropriate version of the code at run time. The Mac OS supports fat binaries for both 680x0 and PowerPC native code.

**fat client** (n.) A networked computer with some processing capability of its own, independent from the host.

**fault-tolerant** (adj.) Describes a system that resists failure. An example is a RAID 1 mirrored system, which is fault tolerant because it provides disk input/output (I/O) even if one of the drives fails.

fax See *facsimile.*

faxmodem (n.) A device that performs the functions of both a fax machine and a modem.

fax on demand (n.) The process of ordering a fax document from a remote machine using the telephone, combining voice processing and fax technologies. Also referred to as *fax-back.*

FC See *Fibre Channel.*

FCB See *file control block.*

FCC See *Federal Communications Commission.*

F-connector (n.) A threaded coaxial cable connector used with video equipment. See figure.

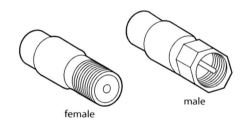

female     male

*F-connectors*

FCS See *frame check sequence.*

FDDI See *Fiber Distributed Data Interface.*

FDHD See *floppy drive high-density.*

FDI See *Feeder Distribution Interface.*

FDISK (n.) The original MS-DOS utility program used to format a hard disk to serve as a boot disk containing system files. Pronounced "EHF-disk."

FDM See *frequency-division multiplexing.*

FDMA See *Frequency Division Multiple Access.*

feature connector (n.) On a graphics adapter for a PC, a connector with 20 to 26 pins that permits access to the video signal path and that allows video signals to be mixed, or "overlayed," with computer graphics.

FEC See *Forward Error Correction.*

FED See *field emission display.*

Federal Communications Commission (FCC) (n.) The U.S. government agency that regulates telephone services, radio, and satellite communications. Regarding electronic devices, a "Class A" certification is required for equipment used in industrial applications, whereas home electronics must comply with a "Class B" certification, which specifies lower levels of radiation.

Federal Networking Council (FNC) (n.) Group of representatives from U.S. government agencies that coordinates and manages the development of communications networks, including the Internet. Among the members are representatives from the DARPA, Department of Defense, NSF, and NASA.

feed (n.) Signals received from a satellite downlink, or signals supplied to a satellite uplink terminal.

feedback (n.) 1. The electronic signal that occurs when the output of a system becomes its own input in real time. An example is the high-pitched squealing that occurs when a microphone is placed in front of a loudspeaker. 2. In an interactive instructional system, the positive or negative reinforcement of the user's responses.

165

**feeder** (n.) That part of a cable television or telecommunications network to which subscribers are connected. With cable television, the feeder is a group of wires, usually 25-pair or multiples thereof, in a single cable sheath. Feeder cable is synonymous with *backbone wiring*. Bellcore defines it as a large loop cable emanating from a central office, typically underground, with periodically placed access points.

**Feeder Distribution Interface** (FDI) (n.) An interface that distributes signals from an optical fiber trunk into multiple fiber feeders.

**femto-** (f) Prefix for one thousandth of one trillionth (10E-15).

**Ferroelectric RAM** (FRAM, pronounced "EFF-ram") (n.) Ferroelectric random-access memory; nonvolatile semiconductor memory that features fast read/write random access. A ferroelectric memory cell consists of a ferroelectric capacitor and a metal-oxide semiconductor (MOS) transistor, similar in construction to a DRAM.

**FET** See *field-effect transistor.*

**Fetch** (n.) Developed by Jim Matthews at Dartmouth College, a Macintosh program for transferring files using FTP.

**FFT** See *Fast Fourier Transform.*

**Fiber Distributed Data Interface** (FDDI) (n.) A standard for transmitting high-bandwidth traffic via fiber optics at 100 megabits per second (Mbps). A local area network (LAN) specification from ANSI, FDDI uses token ring topology. FDDI-II is an advanced, 200-Mbps version of FDDI.

**Fiber in the Loop** (FITL) (n.) In telephony, net-

works in which some fiber-optic cable is used between the central office and a customer's premises.

**fiber miles** (n.) The length in miles of actual fiber strands deployed in a network.

**fiber optics** (n.) The transmission of signals or data in the form of light pulses through a strand of glass fiber.

**Fiber to the Curb** (FTTC) (n.) Broadband architecture in which fiber-optic lines are extended past every home. Copper twisted-pair or passive coaxial drops carry signals between the fiber-optic lines and houses. An optical network unit (ONU) performs optical-to-electrical signal conversion for clusters of 8 to 12 homes.

**Fibre Channel** (FC) (n.) Defined by the ANSI X3T11 standard, a data transfer protocol capable of moving data at speeds up to 1 gigabit per second (Gbps). It was invented in 1988 by Hewlett-Packard and became an open standard in 1991 with the involvement of IBM and Sun Microsystems. In 1995 ANSI adopted the basic FC standards.

At the physical level, Fibre Channel is a serial bus that may connect 126 storage devices on a single data path. Copper twisted-pair wiring up to 30 meters long may be used between nodes, and distances of 10 kilometers may be connected with fiber-optic media. This network technology was designed for storage and server clustering. It is possible to daisy chain individual FC components, and devices are hot-swappable. The rate of data transfer is 100 megabits per second (Mbps) on a single loop and 200 Mbps over a dual loop. The dual-loop feature provides high resilience for the storage data path and overall application-processing environment. If one loop becomes unavailable, the second loop takes over. Disk storage can be safely placed more than six miles away from the host and still be online. FC maps common transport protocols, including IP and SCSI, allowing FC to merge high-speed input/output (I/O) and networking functionality in a single technology.

Fibre Channel-Arbitrated Loop (FC-AL) is the most widely accepted implementation that shares bandwidth. Designed for server clusters, a switched version of Fibre Channel gives each node a 100-Mbps dedicated channel in a "fabric" of switches and ports. A gigabit linking module (GLM) is a generic transceiver unit that integrates the key functions needed for installation of a Fibre Channel interface on a host system. The GLM provides the drivers, transmit/receive optics, serializer/deserializer, and laser safety features.

Optical Fiber Control (OFC) lasers have been specially designed for use with Fibre Channel. To protect users from eye damage, these high-powered lasers are controlled with a handshake; they turn off when unplugged. Non-OFC optics use a lower-powered laser that is safe for the eye. The industry trend is toward safer, non-OFC lasers for local area connection. Both OFC and non-OFC lasers are currently specified for use in Fibre Channel products.

Abbreviations for the ANSI X3T11 Fibre Channel standards and draft standards are as follows:

FC-PH: FC–Physical
FC-AL: FC–Arbitrated Loop
FC-GS: FC–Generic Services
FCP: FC Protocol for SCSI
FC-LE: FC Protocol for 802.2LE
FC-FP: FC Protocol for HIPPI

Two industry associations support Fibre Channel technology: the Fibre Channel Association (FCA) and its working group, the Fibre Channel Loop Community (FCLC). They may be reached at *http://www.fcloop.org*. Applications that are prime candidates for FC solutions include Internet/intranet serving, data warehousing, providing online services, streaming video, and medical imaging.

**Fidonet** (n.) Management software for a private bulletin board system (BBS) that provides procedures and data exchange standards for email, file transfer, conferencing, and other functions.

**field** (n.) 1. The horizontal lines created during one pass of an electronic beam from the top to the bottom of a screen. A field is the same as a frame in computer video because the lines are drawn sequentially. However, two interlaced fields are used to draw each frame in broadcast video formats. A single field fills only every other horizontal line of resolution. This equals one-half of a complete television scanning cycle (1/60 of a second NTSC, 1/50 of a second PAL/SECAM) per frame. 2. In a database application, the location of data within a record.

**field dominance** (n.) The order in which video fields are recorded on a videotape during edits or transfers. There are two fields per frame; field-1 dominance places a new picture in the first field of each frame, whereas field-2 dominance places it in the second.

**field-effect transistor** (FET) (n.) A board-level component in which voltage applied between the gate and the substrate controls the flow of current between the source terminal and the drain terminal. The two types are MOSFETs and Junction FETs. Both are used in circuits that require very low power consumption because a small amount of current flows through the gate of an FET.

**field emission display** (FED) (n.) A flat-panel electronic monitor that employs a matrix of cathodes, control electrodes, and phosphor elements to produce an electronic image on its screen.

**field frequency** (n.) The rate of display for each field in a video format, typically 59.94 times per second in NTSC. In general descriptions of the format, this number is rounded off to 60 fields. Two fields combine to make a frame.

**field of view** (n.) The portion of a shot, or vista, that is visible through a camera lens. The image seen in the viewfinder on many cameras does not exactly match the actual field recorded on tape or film.

**field-programmable gate array** (FPGA) (n.) A programmable logic device more versatile than traditional arrays.

FIFO See *first-in-first-out.*

**file** (n.) 1. Any collection of information that is recorded and given a unique name. It may contain text, images, sound, or an application. 2. In computing terms, a container for data.

**file allocation table** (FAT) (n.) A map of a hard disk or CD-ROM that defines the exact location of tracks, sectors, and clusters on the storage medium. Windows 98 and subsequent versions provide FAT32, an advanced 32-bit file system that allows drives with a capacity of more than two gigabytes (GB) to be formatted as a single partition. It updates the original 16-bit FAT by creating smaller disk cluster sizes, allowing more data to be stored on a hard disk. Pronounced "FAT."

**file control block** (FCB) (n.) In MS-DOS, the collected data about any file currently open.

**File Manager** (n.) In Microsoft Windows 3.1, an application program that allows the user to organize and view the files and directories on a disk. It typically resides in the "Main" program group located in the Program Manager application. In Windows 95 this function was replaced by Explorer.

**file server** (n.) A hardware and software system that provides file-handling and storage functions for multiple users on a local area network (LAN). The most common commercially available file server packages are Sun Microsystems' Network File System (NFS) for Unix and Novell Netware for IBM PC compatibles. Storing files on a file server eliminates the need to store multiple copies on individual computers.

**file transfer** (n.) Moving a file between two networked computers.

**file transfer protocol** (FTP) (n.) A client-server protocol that allows a user on one computer to transfer files to and from another computer over a TCP/IP network. It is defined in RFC 959, STD 9.

**fill** 1. (n.) A supplementary light source that softens shadows and brings out the background missed by the key light in a video shoot. 2. (n.) A color or pattern occupying a graphic region. 3. (v.) To place a color or pattern in a graphic region.

**film chain** (n.) Referred to as *telecine,* a collection of equipment used to transfer frames of film to electronic frames or videotape, including projectors, multiplexers, and cameras.

FILO See *first-in-last-out.*

**filter** 1. (n.) In a visual context, a partially transparent material that passes or blocks light of a particular color or orientation. 2. (n.) In an audio context, an electronic circuit that passes or blocks signals of a specified frequency. 3. (n.) Any device that shapes or conditions a signal, including anti-aliasing, diffusing, equalizing, and sharpening filters applied in the process of editing digital images. 4. (v.) To narrow the scope of a search by specifying ranges or types of data to exclude.

**Finder** (n.) In the Mac OS, the application that manages the graphical user interface (GUI). It is used to open, copy, delete, and move files, which are represented by icons.

**Finite Impulse Response filter** (FIR filter) (n.) A digital signal processor used in audio applications that can implement any type of response to an impulse, as long as the response is finite in length. It is a stable type of filter that calculates specific, definable output based on a computationally intensive formula that does not take into account any feedback coeffients.

**finger** (n.) A software program that may be used to detect information about a user on a Unix network, including information about patterns of usage.

**firewall** (n.) On a local area network (LAN) connected to a larger network, the security system that prevents outside intrusion and that keeps internal information from getting out. Typically, all traffic must pass through the machine on which the firewall is implemented.

**FireWire** (IEEE 1394) (n.) An interface standard that specifies a transmission method, medium, and protocol. This high-performance serial bus defines a point-to-point cable-connected virtual bus and a backplane physical layer. The cable version supports data rates of 100, 200, and 400 megabits per second (Mbps) over a cable medium supported by the standard. The backplane version operates at 12.5, 25, or 50 Mbps. Both versions are fully compatible at the link layer and above. Features include multimaster capabilities, live connection and disconnection (hot plugging), and transmission speed scalable from 100 to 400 Mbps.

The technology was developed by Texas Instruments to address the need for mass information transfer. Ordinary networks do not provide connection capabilities and bandwidth that can meet future demands. Parallel high-speed communications, such as SCSI, are not suited to long-distance transmission and do not support live connection and disconnection of peripherals, such as digital video cameras, scanners, or printers. This capability is provided by the 1394 standard. The cable version integrates I/O connectivity in personal computers using a scalable, high-speed serial interface.

The standard is a transaction-based packet technology for both chassis and peripheral devices. The serial bus behaves as though it were memory space interconnected between devices or as if devices resided in slots on the main backplane. Device addressing is 64 bits wide, allocating 10 bits for network IDs, 6 bits for node IDs, and 48 bits for memory addresses. It is capable of addressing 1023 networks with 63 nodes on each. The memory capacity for each device on the chain is 256 terabytes (TB).

Memory-based addressing views resources as registers or as memory that can be accessed with processor-to-memory transactions. A bus entity is referred to as a *node,* which may be individually identified, addressed, and reset.

169

Multiple nodes may be in a single module, and multiple ports may be in a single node.

The distance between each node should not exceed 4.5 meters, and the maximum number in a chain is 16, for a total maximum end-to-end distance of 72 meters. Cable distance between each node is limited primarily by signal attenuation. A cable with 28-gauge signal pairs may be up to 4.5 meters long, whereas a cable with 24-gauge signal pairs may be 14 meters long. A maximum of 16 cable hops is allowed between the most widely separated nodes. The end-to-end distance may vary from 72 to 224 meters, depending on the configuration.

Signals transmitted on cable and backplane environments are non-return-to-zero (NRZ) with Data-Strobe (DS) encoding. DS encoding allows only one of the two signal lines to change each data bit period, doubling the tolerance jitter. DS encoding is licensed from SGS-Thompson/INMOS.

The FireWire IEEE 1394 standard supports asynchronous and isochronous data transfers. The asynchronous format transfers data and transaction layer information to a specific address, whereas the isochronous format broadcasts data based on channel numbers rather than on specific addressing. Both nonrealtime critical applications (such as scanners and printers) and realtime critical applications (such as video and audio) can operate on the same bus because the interface provides both formats.

The serial bus 1394 could replace other peripheral connection communication methods in use today, such as the Centronics parallel, RS-232, SCSI, and Apple Desktop Bus (ADB). It would enable a single high-performance serial bus. New interfaces, such as direct connect video I/O, will employ this technology because

of its advantages. Memory space addressing is a good solution for "slotless" systems, such as personal digital assistants (PDAs). Communications at different speeds between 100 and 400 Mbps may occur simultaneously on one medium. The "hot-plugging" and dynamic reconfiguration abilities make it a user-friendly environment. This standard will allow a user to connect an expansion system with communications on demand without having to shut down and reconfigure whenever devices are added or removed.

A revision called IEEE 1394b is in progress, which will boost the data transfer rate to 3.2 Gbps, an eight-fold increase over the original 400 Mbps. It will remain a peer-to-peer topology that connects any device directly to another compatible one. The 1394b standards extend the maximum cable length from 4.5 meters to 100 meters. New cabling options will include Category 5 twisted-pair, as well as multimode fiber-optic cable for the fastest transfer rates.

**FIR Filter** See *Finite Impulse Response filter.*

**firmware** (n.) A device or machine component with a microprocessor on board. It is characterized by data in ROM that controls hardware components.

**first-in-first-out** (FIFO, pronounced "FIE-foe") (n.) A queue, or hardware buffer, from which data is taken out in the same sequence in which it was inserted. A FIFO can buffer a stream of data that is transmitted at different rates between an unsynchronized sender and receiver. The opposite of a FIFO is a *last-in-first-out (LIFO),* also known as a *stack.*

**first-in-last-out** (FILO, pronounced "FIE-low") (n.) A queue, or hardware buffer, from which data is taken out in the opposite order in which it was inserted.

**fishbowl** (v.) To isolate and monitor an unauthorized user within a system to gain information about that user.

**FITL** See *Fiber in the Loop*.

**fixed disk** (n.) A circular, enclosed magnetic storage medium on which information may be accessed randomly, as opposed to sequentially. Floppy disks are small, portable storage vehicles; hard disks, or fixed disks, can store more data by using multiple rigid platters.

**fixed repetition** (n.) An instructional design feature that repeats a lesson or module without alteration.

**Fixed Satellite Service** (FSS) (n.) Radio communications between Earth stations located at specified fixed points using one or more satellites. This service may include links between satellites. Compare *Mobile Satellite Service*.

**flag** (n.) A bit of data set to 0 or 1 that represents a particular piece of information, position, or status.

**flame** (v.) To criticize or heap indignities on an individual in a public email message, often resulting from an inappropriate or uninformed remark made by the individual who is flamed.

**flanging** (n.) Creating an audio special effect using two synchronized reel-to-reel tape recorders playing the same program simultaneously. Pressing against the flanges of the tape reels causes phase cancellations. The audible effect is like a sweeping comb filter. Digital flanging can be accomplished using delay lines and mixing techniques.

**flare** (n.) The result of excessive light beaming

into a camera lens and reflecting off of internal glass elements. A picture with flare may either show bright flashes or spots of extreme contrast reduction.

**flash memory** (n.) An EPROM module that is nonvolatile, has a fast access rate, and can be erased with ultraviolet light. The term also refers to EEPROMs, which are electronically erased. They provide data to equipment that can accept and read a small EPROM card.

**Flash ROM** (n.) An integrated circuit (IC) that contains nonvolatile, erasable, rewritable memory.

**flat** (adj.) 1. Describes an image of low contrast. 2. Describes an image with objects shaded in uniform color and brightness for each small polygon, rather than with varied shading at edges or across the polygon.

**flat-file database** (n.) A type of database that holds records in a single file. These databases are not as fast or as powerful as relational databases.

**flatten** (v.) To remove proprietary or structural information from a data file or to filter system-related data. Mapping to a "flat" ASCII file, rather than to formatted text, is an example. In multimedia the term is frequently applied to the removal of the Macintosh data fork from a QuickTime movie to prepare it for playback in Windows. After being flattened, the file must be renamed to conform to MS-DOS conventions, with up to eight legal characters followed by the .mov extension.

**flat field noise** (n.) Subtle differences in areas that should be identical between video frames. An example is pixelation in the background behind a title. This type of video noise degrades the quality of a compressed image, and could

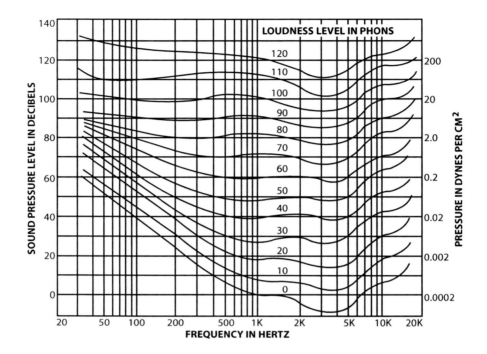

*Fletcher-Munson equal-loudness contours*

be removed with an adaptive noise reduction filter.

**FLC** (n.) A sophisticated version of the Autodesk Animator FLI animation file format that supports 640-by-480-pixel images in up to 8-bit color. Viewers for FLC files are available for most computers. Pronounced "FLICK."

**Fletcher-Munson equal-loudness contours** (n.) A graph that indicates the sensitivity of the average ear to different frequencies at different loudness levels. The X-axis shows frequency and the Y-axis shows sound pressure levels. The horizontal contours indicate the sound-pressure levels required to produce the same perceived loudness at different frequencies. See figure.

**FLI** (n.) The acronym for the original Autodesk Animator animation file format. This file format supports 320-by-240-pixel images in up to eight-bit color. FLI viewers are available for most computers. Pronounced "FLEE."

**flicker** (n.) An "interfield" flicker, also known as *jitter*, which is caused when two fields that comprise a single video frame are not identical. Two different pictures will alternate 60 times per second when viewed in a still-frame mode. A flicker is also introduced by low vertical refresh rates in a TV screen, which prevent the eye from retaining a continuous perception of successive images.

**floating-point arithmetic** (n.) The way in which a computer keeps track of the decimal point when performing calculations. Floating-point notation is used to express a quantity with a reduced number of digits. Typically, a *mantissa* consisting of several digits is qualified by a two-digit *exponent*. Example: the number 0.0057 is represented in scientific notation by $5.7 \times 10^{-3}$, and in floating-point notation by .57E - 3.

**floating-point operations per second** (FLOPS) (n.) A measurement of the speed of a scientific computer, often rated in millions (MFLOPS).

**floating-point unit** (FPU) (n.) A math coprocessor chip that performs floating-point arithmetic and by doing so offloads this computationally intensive function from the CPU. Programs that are optimized to take advantage of a math coprocessor run much faster when an FPU is present.

**floppy disk** (n.) Short for floppy diskette, a storage medium commonly used in all types of microcomputers. Physically, it consists of a paper-thin flexible disk coated with magnetic material and mounted in a plastic enclosure 3.5 or 5.25 inches in diameter. The 3.5-inch

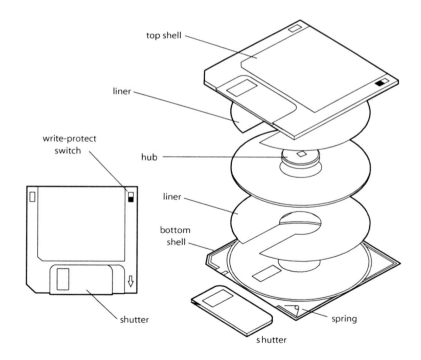

*3.5-inch floppy disk*

disks have replaced the larger size, and they hold up to 1.44 megabytes (MB) of uncompressed data. The capacity of the diskette is determined by whether the medium is single-sided (SS), double-sided (DS), double-density (DD), or high-density (HD). See figure.

**floppy drive high-density** (FDHD) (n.) A disk drive used in Macintosh computers that can read from and write to 3.5-inch disks in both double-density and high-density formats and that can accept DOS-formatted disks for cross-platform applications.

FLOPS See *floating-point operations per second.*

**flowchart** (n.) In an interactive design, a map of the user's options and corresponding responses to input. It outlines branching and shows program segments and decision points. See figure

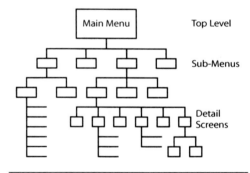

Main Menu     Top Level

Sub-Menus

Detail Screens

*flowchart*

**flow control** (n.) Processes applied in serial communications that stop the sender from sending more data until the receiving unit is prepared to receive it. The sender continues with transmission when the receiver signals to resume. It may be accomplished in either software or hardware.

**flower key** (n.) The Macintosh Command key, or the Feature key.

**fluid head** (n.) Camera tripod mount that moves smoothly, filled with a viscous fluid that dampens friction and lubricates.

**flush** (v.) 1. To delete data or to abort an output operation. 2. To force buffered data to be written to permanent memory.

**fly-by** (n.) In a 3-D virtual reality scene, the act of navigating over a map, a building, or terrain as though the user were flying an aircraft. The user assumes the role of a pilot and controls the perspective and motion with a mouse or other controls. It is useful as a tool for experiencing architecture from different viewpoints before it is constructed.

**flying erase head** (n.) In a helical scan video recorder, an erase head that rotates along with the recording heads so that it can erase a single line of video. With this technology, new segments can be added seamlessly to existing footage.

FM See *frequency modulation.*

FMV See *full-motion video.*

FNC See *Federal Networking Council.*

**focal length** (n.) With a camera lens set to infinity, the distance between the focal point (optical center) of a lens and its focal plane, the place where the image falls on the imaging chip or film. Short focal lengths result in a wide-angle view, whereas long focal lengths offer a narrow field of view. Zoom lenses provide variable focal lengths.

FOH See *Front of House.*

**fold case** (v.) To treat uppercase and lowercase text exactly the same. Case in file names should be preserved, because some operating systems, such as Unix, are case sensitive. Most text editors permit the user to specify whether a text search should be case sensitive or whether the editor should fold case.

**folder** (n.) Equivalent to a directory in a graphical user interface (GUI), an image that represents a container for documents or applications.

**Foley** (n.) Named after Jack Foley, a Hollywood director and sound engineer active in the 1940s, the process of generating sound effects by duplicating the movements of an actor onscreen. Foley artists in a sound studio watch a scene, then recreate and synchronize a new sound track with the picture.

**folio** (n.) A page number in a printed and bound document.

**font** (n.) A typeface or family of alphanumeric characters and symbols in a single style, such as Times Roman or Helvetica. The concept was originally used to define print and has been applied to computer-generated characters.

**foo** (n.) Word used by programmers to name many things, especially scratch files. Most commonly, it serves as a metasyntactic variable used in examples of syntax. It is akin to *qux, baz, garply, corge,* and *plugh* in the language of hackers.

**foobar** (n.) A metasyntactic variable that hackers use, just as they use *foo*. It is not related to the military expression *fubar*.

**footprint** (n.) 1. The amount of space on a desktop or table required for the base of a computer or peripheral. 2. In satellite communications, the territory covered by the transmitting beam of the satellite.

**Foreign Exchange** (FX) (n.) In telephony, FX

is an exchange switch outside the local access and transport area (LATA). It frequently refers to a dedicated leased line from a PBX to the FX, usually between a central office (CO) and its remote bureau, so that the PBX answers a call placed to the FX number.

**fork** (n.) One of two parts in a Macintosh file. The *resource* fork contains executable code and items used by the system, whereas the *data* fork contains user data.

**fork bomb** (n.) A single line of code that may be written on a Unix system that replicates itself when it is triggered, usually by a specific date or time. It then locks up the system by consuming all the process table entries. Also known as a *logic bomb*.

**format** 1. (v.) To prepare a storage medium by defining tracks and sectors where data will be placed in compliance with a specific operating system's requirements. Disks formatted for the Macintosh are not readable in Microsoft DOS or Windows without a cross-platform utility that translates data. 2. (n.) The specifications of a particular software-hardware platform, or a unique means of configuring data for that platform. 3. (n.) The physical and technical design feature that differentiates between types of video and audio equipment, such as 8 mm, Hi-8, S-VHS, and VHS.

**formatted capacity** (n.) Maximum amount of data that a formatted disk may contain. It is equivalent to the unformatted capacity minus the defined boundaries between sectors.

**form factor** (n.) Physical attributes of a hardware device, particularly regarding shape and size.

**Formula Translator** (FORTRAN) (n.) Developed by IBM, a computer compiling language that was originally invented to solve scientific problems but that is also used for commercial applications. The syntax consists of algebraic expressions and arithmetic statements.

**FORTRAN** See *Formula Translator.*

**forum** (n.) The generic term for a discussion group on a bulletin board system (BBS), on a mailing list, or in a Usenet newsgroup. Users submit postings for everyone with access to the forum to read whenever they log on. The forum often revolves around a thread, or topic. It differs from point-to-point personal email or a realtime chat in these ways.

**FOURCC** (n.) A four-character string created by Microsoft that uniquely identifies the data stream format used in an audio/video interleaved (AVI) file. The FOURCC assigns a value to every compression format and pixel layout so video frames transmitted between file and codec are identical. Pronounced "for-see-SEE." Visit the site *www.moviecodec.com* for more information.

**Fourier** (n.) In mathematics, typically refers to the approximation of a function through the application of a Fourier series to periodic data, although it is not restricted to periodic data. The Fourier series applies to periodic data only. The Fourier integral transform converts an infinite continuous time function into an infinite continuous frequency function, a process that is usually reversible. Discrete Fourier Transform (DFT) and Fast Fourier Transform (FFT) are examples of the Fourier series.

**Fourier, Baron Jean Baptiste Joseph** (1768–1830) French mathematician and physicist who formulated a method for analyzing periodic functions. His work led to a new branch of mathematical analysis, the theory of harmonic analysis.

**Fourier series** (n.) This is an application of the *Fourier theorem* to a periodic function, resulting in sine and cosine terms that are harmonics of the periodic frequency.

**Fourier theorem** (n.) A mathematical theorem stating that any function may be resolved into sine and cosine terms with known amplitudes and phases.

**Fourier transform** (n.) Named after J. B. Joseph Fourier, a mathematical process capable of expressing a waveform as a weighted sum of sines and cosines. Discrete Fourier Transform is generally the type used in multimedia.

**Forward Error Correction** (FEC) (n.) In telecommunications, a technique for correcting errors incurred in data transmission by the receiving data communications equipment (DCE). It is a complex process that involves a convolution of the transmitted bits, the appending of extra bits, and the use of an algorithm common to both the receiver and transmitter. It is accomplished within OSI layer 1 independent of higher layers.

**fps** See *frames per second.*

**FPGA** See *field-programmable gate array.*

**FPU** See *floating-point unit.*

**FQDN** See *Fully Qualified Domain Name.*

**fractal** (n.) A set of points, or coordinates, with a fractional dimension. In digital compression, a fractal model may be applied to an image to preserve its original shape. The model can later be used to generate repetitive features found in the image.

**fractional T1** (n.) A telecommunications service that offers customers the use of one or more channels in a T1 connection, as opposed to all 24 channels. Customers are billed according to the number of channels used.

**FRAD** See *Frame Relay Access Device*.

**fragment** (n.) 1. A portion of a packet. When a router forwards an Internet Protocol (IP) packet to a network with packet size limitations, it may break up a packet into fragments that the IP layer reassembles at the destination host. 2. A portion of a file stored on a hard disk drive that is separated from other parts of the same file. The "defragment" function eliminates fragmented files and places whole files in contiguous disk space.

**fragmented file** (n.) A file that has been written to a disk in discontiguous sectors.

**FRAM** See *Ferroelectric RAM*.

**frame** 1. (n.) A single video image that belongs to a stream of moving pictures. In an interlaced system, such as NTSC, it consists of two interlaced fields. A video frame in NTSC consists of 525 lines, whereas a frame in SECAM or PAL consists of 625 lines. In multimedia applications, a frame may refer to a still image on the screen that is not part of a video stream. 2. (n.) In telecommunications, a transmission block or encapsulated packet in the data link layer. 3. (n.) A feature of the HTML specification that allows a browser to display different HTML documents, or frames, in a single window called a frameset. An example is a list of terms in a frame on one side of the active window and a graphic image or a paragraph defining the term on the other side of the window in

a frame. 4. (v.) To compose a video shot with desired content, angle, and field of view.

**frame-accurate** (adj.) Describes professional video-editing equipment that can locate and process a specific individual image or frame. Consumer products generally can locate only approximate locations.

**frame address code** (n.) Time-stamped data that identifies a frame of video by its location. The code is placed in the vertical blanking interval (VBI) prior to the frame.

**frame buffer** (n.) 1. A RAM allocation dedicated to storing a frame of digital video and used to refresh a raster image. The buffer may include some processing ability. As with all digital video descriptors, the number of bits per pixel determines picture quality. 2. A component that records and stores the lines of a video frame and functions as a time base corrector.

**frame check sequence** (FCS) (n.) A 16-bit field containing error-checking information that appears at the end of a frame in a bit-oriented protocol.

**frame dropping** (n.) A condition caused by the inability of a decompression system to play all the encoded frames in a stream of digital video. Because playback algorithms preserve the integrity of the audio track at the expense of video frames, some frames may not be displayed on playback in order to sustain the audio track.

**frame grabber** (n.) A device that captures and stores a single video frame to be edited or printed later.

**frame rate** (n.) The number of times per second a video image is redrawn, scanned, or displayed on a monitor. The rate for NTSC format is 29.97(nearly 30) frames per second (fps). For PAL/SECAM format it is 25 fps. Film runs at 24 fps.

**Frame Relay** (n.) A data terminal equipment–data communications equipment (DTE-DCE) interface specification based on Link Access Procedure–D (LAPD, defined in Q.921), the ISDN version of Link Access Procedure–Balanced (LAPB) (X.25 data link layer). It is a form of packet switching with small packets and comparatively little error checking. A consortium of companies including StrataCom, Cisco Systems, Digital Equipment Corporation (DEC), and Northern Telecom jointly developed the specification. Frame Relay can connect dedicated lines and X.25 to Asynchronous Transfer Mode (ATM), switched multimegabit data service (SMDS), Broadband ISDN, and other "fast-packet" technologies. Frame Relay is compatible with current X.25 hardware, but it adds addressing and some control bits. Any network layer protocol may be used over the data link layer frames.

**Frame Relay Access Device** (FRAD) (n.) A telecommunications unit with hardware and software that turns packets from TCP or Systems Network Architecture (SNA) sources into frames that can be sent over a Frame Relay wide area network (WAN).

**frames per second** (fps) (n.) In video or animation, the number of times each second a new picture appears on the screen.

**framework** (n.) In object-oriented programming, a set of classes that embodies an abstract design for solutions to several related problems.

**framing** (n.) An error-control procedure in which bits are inserted into packets so that a

receiver can identify the time slot allocated to each channel in a multiplexed digital transmission line, such as T1.

**framing bit** (n.) A bit added to byte-interleaved time-multiplexed data streams to mark the beginning of each sequence of repetitive bytes. Multiple framing bit patterns provide data stream synchronization.

**framing specification** (n.) The standard that prescribes protocol bits surrounding the data bits on a communications channel in order to allow the data to be framed into chunks, such as start and stop bits in RS-232. It allows a receiver to lock in and synchronize at points along the data stream while data is being transmitted.

**Free Software Foundation** (FSF) (n.) Founded by Richard Stallman, an organization committed to the creation and dissemination of software that is free from licensing fees or restrictions. It supports the GNU project, which developed the GNU Emacs editor and a C compiler.

**freewheel** (n.) 1. An action that an audio-video synchronizing device takes when it continues to generate time code after encountering dropouts in the time code source. 2. A situation in which an audio device continues to generate audio without responding to a time code input or controls.

**freeze-frame** (n., adj.) 1. The motionless display of a single frame or image selected from video or film footage. 2. An image drawn from a longer motion sequence.

**free sound field** (n.) A sound field without an acoustic boundary or obstruction that is free from reflecting sound waves. Within a sound-absorbed boundary, a virtual free field is created. Sometimes called free field.

**free space loss** (n.) The radio signal loss between the transmitter and the receiver. It is calculated by the formula: Loss = 36.6 +20logD +20logF, where D is the distance and F is the frequency in MHz.

**frequency** (n.) 1. The property or condition of occurring at periodic intervals. 2. In physics, the number of times a specified phenomenon occurs within a given time interval. One example is the number of repetitions of a complete waveform during a unit of time. In music, higher frequencies sound as higher pitches.

**Frequency Division Multiple Access** (FDMA) (n.) In telecommunications, FDMA is an access technique that assigns several users of a radio channel to a specific frequency slot. It is the same as Frequency Division Multiplexing (FDM), except FDMA has a control channel that dynamically reassigns frequency channels among the users. It is used as a multiple access technique for satellite and cellular telephone receivers.

**frequency-division multiplexing** (FDM) (n.) A process in which the available bandwidth of a circuit is divided by frequency into narrower bands, each of which is used for a separate voice or data transmission channel. FDM was once the most common method of multiplexing long-haul connections transmitted by analog microwave signals. Modern fiber-optic trunks employ time-division multiplexing (TDM).

**frequency modulation** (FM) (n.) Change in the frequency of a carrier signal that expresses information based on the rate and degree of change. FM has been a common technique for sound synthesis since it was proposed by John Chowning in 1971. The Yamaha DX-7 family

of synthesizers used FM synthesis exclusively to generate sounds. See figures.

**frequency response** (n.) The range of frequencies, from low to high, that can be processed or reproduced by an audio system.

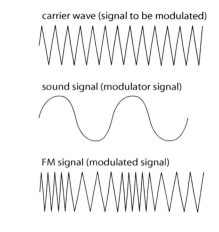

*FM broadcast signal*

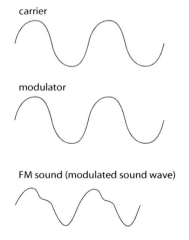

*FM-generated waveforms*

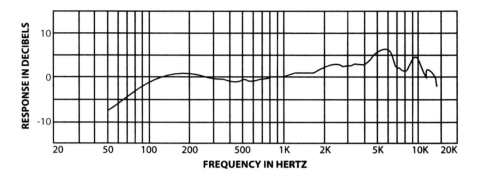

*frequency-response curve*

**frequency-response curve** (n.) The output amplitude in relation to the frequency of the input signal produced by a microphone, an amplifier, or any audio processing device. Flat response indicates that the output is the same at all input frequencies, and the curve is a straight line. See figure.

**frequency shift keying** (FSK) (n.) In telecommunications, the assignment of different audio frequencies to binary digits. Transmission of tones that change in pitch, each tone represented by a 0 or a 1, provides a receiving unit a means of identifying and keying in on information carried by the changing tones.

**frequently asked questions** (FAQ, pronounced "FACK") (n.) On the Internet, a list of commonly asked questions and answers about specific topics.

**front end** (n., adj.) Software that provides an interface to another program. An example is the visual interface used to access information in a database or in a menu-driven multimedia program. Ideally, a front-end application is user friendly.

**Front of House** (FOH) (adj.) Describes the main mixer located in the audience for sound reinforcement system in a concert hall, as opposed to the monitor mixer usually located to the side of the stage.

**FSF** See *Free Software Foundation.*

**FSK** See *frequency shift keying.*

**FSN** See *Full-Service Network.*

**FSS** See *Fixed Satellite Service.*

**f-stop** (n.) In photography, a number that represents a logarithmic value for the intensity of light in a given lens. It is a factor of the ratio between the focal distance and the diameter of the iris, or lens opening. A lens with a focal distance of 70 mm and a diaphragm diameter of 20 mm has an f-stop value of 7:2, which may be reduced to 3.5:1. This is expressed as an f-stop of f3.5. Lower ratios indicate larger lens openings and shorter focus depths. The f-stop is initially set for the depth of field. Each increasing stop doubles the amount of light emitted.

**FTP** See *file transfer protocol.*

**FTTC** See *Fiber to the Curb.*

**fulfillment** (n.) Services that include warehousing, order processing, and shipping of products, such as CD-ROMs. Fulfillment is typically performed by a duplicator or manufacturer.

**full-duplex** (adj.) Describes bidirectional, simultaneous, two-way communication over telephone lines, preferably on a four-wire circuit.

**full-frame ID** (n.) Full-frame identification; a code placed in a video stream to identify the first video field of a new film frame. Also referred to as a *white flag*.

**full-frame time code** (n.) Society of Motion Picture and Television Engineers (SMPTE) code on videotape that accounts for all frame numbers chronologically. Also known as *non-drop-frame time code*.

**full-motion video** (FMV) (n.) Moving pictures that play back at the full resolution and frame rate in which they were encoded, resulting in a smooth, continuous display. According to broadcast video standards, this is usually considered 30 frames per second (fps) in the NTSC format and 25 fps in the PAL format.

**Full-Service Network** (FSN) (n.) A broadband network that supports a range of interactive services, including switched video-on-demand (VOD). The phrase was first used by Time Warner to define the high-profile advanced hybrid fiber-coax (HFC) network trial in Orlando, Florida. Numerous FSN applications are available on the Internet.

**Fully Qualified Domain Name** (FQDN) (n.) The complete name of an address in the domain name system, as opposed to only a hostname. The hostname is just the first part of an FQDN.

**function** (n.) In programming, an equation that yields a value when it is executed or when it is invoked. This value may be used as an operand in an expression. For example, the function *square* yields the value of $X$ squared when it is invoked as the expression *square(X)*.

**fundamental** (n.) In a compound waveform, the lowest frequency of regular vibration. It is on this pitch that all harmonics in an overtone series are based; the first partial in the series.

**fuzzy logic** (n.) A set of principles introduced by Dr. Lotfi Zadeh in the 1960s. Fuzzy logic provides a means to model the uncertainty of natural language. It employs a superset of Boolean logic with references to partial truth, or values that lie between absolute true and false statements. Fuzzy logic supplements Boolean truth values with degrees of truth that are similar to probabilities.

**FX** See *Foreign Exchange*.

# G

GaAs See *gallium arsenide.*

**gaffer** (n.) A stagehand who constructs and dismantles sets for film or video productions.

**gain** (n.) In audio, the increase in signal provided by an amplifier between input level and output level. It may be positive, negative, or null (unity gain).

**gallium arsenide** (GaAs) (n.) Semiconductive material used to build circuits that are three to ten times faster than those made of silicon and that use as little as one-tenth of the power. GaAs can detect, emit, and convert light into electrical signals, facilitating the creation of integrated opto-electronic chips.

**game port** (n.) A serial connection on a computer that is used for interfacing input devices such as joysticks.

**gamma** (n.) A value that identifies the degree of contrast in a photograph or electronic image according to a gradation curve. A steep curve indicates a high gamma value and high contrast. Gamma may be adjusted by components, colors, halftones, or highlights, or it may be adjusted across an entire image. *Gamma correction* is the adjustment of contrast in an image.

**gamma correction** (n.) A procedure employed by graphics display systems to compensate for decay in the phosphor of a monitor. As the gamma value varies, some display adapters adjust the video signal accordingly. Gamma correction is used along with other techniques to achieve color matching.

**gamma ratio** (n.) Graphic displays, scanners, and most electronic cameras have nonlinear characteristics in their signal-to-light intensity. Using a mathematical power function, most of these devices transfer image data with the equation $output = input \wedge gamma$. In this equation, $\wedge$ represents the exponent *gamma* (the Greek letter), the exponent of the power function. The power function is described by a number showing the ratio between the input and output, which is the exponent *gamma.* Input and output are both scaled to a range between 0 and 1, with 0 representing black and 1 representing maximum white or a color. If a power function is applied to this measured transfer function and if the exponent is extracted, it is referred to as *gamma.*

The output of a device can be measured as a function of its input. This function is the *gamma ratio.* The output of a device with a gamma of 2.5 is two and one-half times greater than the intensity of its input. A gamma factor can also be applied to the output of a look-up table in a frame buffer, as long as the input and output are related by the same power-law expression. If all the components in an imaging system have transfer characteristics that are power functions, then the transfer function of the entire system is also a power function. The exponent, or gamma, of a system's transfer function is the product of all of the individual exponents (gammas) of the separate stages in the system. If the overall gamma of an imaging system is 1.0, its output is linearly proportional to its input. This means that the ratio between the intensities of any two areas in the reproduced image will be the same as in the original scene. Characteristics of the human eye and the differences in how devices capture and display light dictate that gamma be a variable function in systems that reproduce images.

**gamut** (n.) The range of colors that can be displayed on a video monitor.

**garbage collection** (n.) A process that reclaims storage space during the evaluation of an expression in a memory system. In systems that use dynamic storage allocation and in which expressions are represented as graphs containing pointers to data structures, garbage collection reclaims space used by subexpressions that do not point to a meaningful destination. The Java language is noted for its automatic garbage collection.

**garbage-in-garbage-out** (GIGO) (n.) Jargon used by programmers to indicate that feeding incorrect information into a system generally results in retrieving incorrect information from it.

**GAS** See *GNU assembler.*

**gate** (n.) In electronic circuitry, a pathway that may be open or closed, depending on the source

of the input, the strength of a signal, or the conductivity of chemicals used in semiconductors. Logic gates are programmed to correspond to related "if-then" statements. The state of an open or closed gate is analogous to the binary state of a 0 or a 1. The application of this analogy allows computing machinery with millions of gates to respond conditionally and to perform logical functions.

**gated** (n.) Short form of gatedaemon, pronounced "GATE-dee"; used for network routing, a program that supports multiple protocols and protocol families. It is free and available by anonymous FTP from *www.gated.cornell.edu.*

**gateway** (n.) A dedicated computer that connects to two or more networks and that routes information between them. Networks connected to a gateway may be running different protocols, such as TCP/IP and SNMP, and the gateway converts between protocols operating in the top three layers of the Open Systems Interconnection (OSI) model. The term *gateway* has generally been replaced by the word *router.*

**gauge** (n.) The diameter of a cable or a wire. Even numbers are used to identify thickness in the American Wire Gauge (AWG) scale, which rates nonferrous conductors. Smaller numbers reflect thicker wires. Greater diameter results in better conductivity and less resistance, making it possible to run thicker cables over longer distances without signal degradation. Telephone wires are thin, usually #22, #24, or #26. Standard appliance cables are #16 or #18, and house wiring is usually #12 or #14. Heavy industrial applications use #2 wiring.

**Gaussian blur** (n.) In general, a blur filter locates significant color transitions in an image and creates intermediary colors to soften the edges. A Gaussian blur is a kind of blur filter that uses a mathematical formula to create the effect of looking through a lens that is out of focus. The term is named for the German astronomer and mathematician, Karl Friedrich Gauss.

**gawk** (n.) GNU awk; a superset of standard awk that includes Plan 9 features. It has been ported to Unix, MS-DOS, and the Mac OS.

**Gb** See *gigabit.*

**GB** See *gigabyte.*

**Gbps** See *gigabits per second.*

**GBps** See *gigabytes per second.*

**GCC** See *GNU C compiler.*

**GDI** See *Graphical Device Interface.*

**General MIDI** (n.) General Musical Instrument Digital Interface; a standard configuration for MIDI systems. It refers to the assignment of particular sounds to specified preset locations. General MIDI sequencer files should sound roughly equivalent when executed by a variety of sound cards or synthesizers. This is not always the case, given the extreme differences between the sound of FM synthesizers and wavetable sample players.

Specifically, MIDI is a mapping structure that assigns instrument sounds, or voices, to each of the 128 different presets, programs, or patch locations. In a multitimbral MIDI sequence, each musical part or voice is sent to a different preset according to a "patch map." General MIDI defines the type of sound that resides at each patch location. There are 16 groups of eight instrument types. MIDI programs may be assigned to MIDI channels, and a sequence of note-on

and note-off events may be sent to each discrete channel. The determination of which voice responds to which channel is controlled by a system message that sets up the receiver.

General MIDI specification sets the first 9 channels for instruments and the 10th for percussion. The remaining channels, 11 through 16, are left open for user configuration. Because early generations of sound cards were unable to support all 16 channels, Microsoft devised a proprietary system for assigning MIDI voices in Windows. In this scheme, *Basic MIDI* devices use MIDI channels 13 through 16. In a more evolved system called *Extended MIDI,* devices use channels 1 through 9 for instruments and channel 10 for percussion; no assignments are possible for channels 11 through 16.

The first of two accompanying tables shows the General MIDI instrument program map. In addition to the 128 instruments listed in this table, the General MIDI specification assigns 47 drum sounds to a "key map." The second table shows the General MIDI percussion key map. The percussion instrument assigned to each note number is named. For your reference, middle C is note number 60. See tables in the appendix.

**General MIDI mode** (n.) General Musical Instrument Digital Interface mode; the mode in which a Microsoft Windows audio system operates if its MIDI Mapper matrix sets patches and channels to default MIDI Manufacturers Association (MMA) standards.

**General Packet Radio Service** (GPRS) (n.) A wireless, digital technology designed to work with GSM that sends packets of data across a network at high speeds. Wireless devices with GPRS are able to connect to a mobile network when Internet access is desired, and to send and receive information without dialing a number.

With circuit-switched services, wireless users must dial in to a network to connect.

**general protection fault** (GPF) (n.) An error message that occurs when software tries to read from or write to memory that it does not own or to which it has no access.

**generation** (n.) 1. In storage media, particularly magnetic tape, the number of times a dub is removed from the master. A copy of the first copy is second-generation. The quality of each successive generation on magnetic tape declines. With digital formats, there is no difference between generations. 2. In hardware, a stratification reference to major evolutionary stages in development. Successive generations incorporate significant improvements and changes.

**generational loss** (n.) Reduced quality in audio or video clarity as a result of successive duplication. See also *generation*.

**generic courseware** (n.) Educational material that appeals to a broad market, rather than custom courseware for a specific audience.

**genlock** (n.) Abbreviation for synchronization generator lock; a machine that aligns the data rate of a video image with that of a digital device to ensure accurate timing in the digital copy.

**Geographic Information System** (GIS, pronounced "jee-eye-ESS") (n.) A computer system for capturing, storing, integrating, manipulating, analyzing, and displaying maps and other data related to positions on the surface of Earth. Uses for GIS include planning, marketing, managing resources, and engineering.

**geosynchronous satellite** (n.) A satellite that orbits at the same rate as Earth rotates, so that the satellite remains stationary in relation to a given point on Earth.

**GFLOP** See *gigaflop*.

**GHz** See *gigahertz*.

**Gi** See *gibi-*.

**giant magnetoresistive** (GMR) (adj.) Describes a type of hard disk head developed by IBM. Traditional hard disks read the electrical pulse induced in a coil as a magnetized region on the disk rotates under the head. A magnetoresistive (MR) head reads the change in resistance in a special magnetic material as the magnetized region passes under the head. The giant MR head employs quantum tunneling of electrons to produce a more sensitive head that reads from and writes to smaller regions on the disk, allowing up to 10 gigabytes (GB) per square inch of storage.

**gibi-** (Gi) A prefix standardized by the International Electrotechnical Commission (IEC) to signify binary multiples. It is intended to distinguish between exact binary and decimal quantities, i.e., 1 073 741 824 as opposed to 1 000 000 000. The preferred terminology is 20 gibibits, abbreviated 20Gib, not 20 gigabits or 20Gb. See also *SI unit prefix revision*.

**GIF** See *Graphic Interchange Format*.

**giga-** Prefix meaning one billion. In the decimal system, 1 000 000 000 is expressed as 10 to the 9th power. In the binary system, it is expressed as 2 to the 30th power, or 1 073 741 824.

**gigabit** (Gb) (n.) One billion bits.

**gigabits per second** (Gbps) (n.) A measurement of data transfer in billions of bits per second.

185

**gigabyte** (GB) (n.) One billion 8-bit bytes, or 1 073 741 824 bytes.

**gigabytes per second** (GBps) (n.) A measurement of data transfer in billions of bytes per second.

**gigaflop** (GFLOP) (n.) One billion floating-point operations per second, or one million megaflops.

**gigahertz** (GHz) (n.) One billion cycles per second.

**GIGO** See *garbage-in-garbage-out.*

**GIMP** See *GNU Image Manipulation Program.*

**GIS** See *Geographic Information System.*

**GKS** (n.) A standard that specifies a system for generating and storing computer graphics. It primarily addresses object-oriented graphics, but also supports bitmaps. GKS works on the program-interface level, rather than on the user level. It is defined in the ANSI X3.124–1985 specification.

**glark** (v.) Jargon meaning to understand a term from its context.

**glass** (n.) Jargon referring to glass fiber optic connections, or fiber optics.

**glass master** (n.) The mold from which optical discs, such as CD-ROMs, are stamped. It is made of glass, and the data is stored as pits in the mold.

**glitch** (n.) Jargon for either a momentary disturbance in a signal or corrupted data.

**global file specification** (n.) A special character that matches any character or group of characters in a string comparison. In the Unix system, "?" matches any single character, and "*" matches any string of characters.

**global index** (n.) The file name extension (.gid) of a Windows file. A .gid file is created by the help browser in Windows 95 and later versions for Winhelp files (.hlp), and it stores user preferences.

**global key** (n.) A keyboard character that performs a specific global function, regardless of program context. The Escape key (Esc) is an example.

**Global Positioning System** (GPS) (n.) A U.S. government satellite system targeted to include 21 satellites orbiting at 10 900 miles from Earth. With data from GPS satellites, inexpensive receivers can provide accurate positioning information anywhere in the world.

**Global Security Service** (GSS) (n.) A network protection protocol that provides features such as a single login to multiple services.

**Global System for Mobile communications** (GSM) (n.) The most widely used digital cellular phone system in the world, prevalent throughout Europe. The interface is based on narrowband time division multiple access (TDMA) technology in which available frequency bands are divided into time slots. Each connected user has access to one time slot at regular intervals. Narrow band TDMA provides 8 channels of 13 kbps voice on a 200 kHz carrier channel. The standard also calls for half rate service using 6.5 kbps voice to provide 16 channels within 200 kHz. GSM offers incoming and outgoing data services, such as email and Internet access, and uses short messaging services (SMS). A SIM card with its own memory may be placed in any GSM compatible phone. GSM is an alternative to CDMA, but has a maximum data transfer rate of only 9.6 kbps.

**GMR** See *giant magnetoresistive.*

**GND** See *ground.*

**GNU** (n.) GNU's not Unix; a project managed by the Free Software Foundation to provide a free replacement for Unix. Emacs and the GNU C compiler (GCC) are software tools designed for this project. Pronounced "guh-NOO."

**GNU assembler** (GAS) (n.) A program offered by the GNU Project of the Free Software Foundation that translates assembly language code into machine language that a computer can run.

**GNU C compiler** (GCC) (n.) GNU's not Unix C compiler; a portable compiler for C and C++ created by Richard Stallman. It supports multiple front ends and back ends by translating instructions first into Register Transfer Language and then into assembly code for the target architecture.

**GNU Image Manipulation Program** (GIMP) (n.) A free software program for creating and editing images. GIMP's features include layered editing, a gradient editor, channel operations, alpha blending, and a scripting interface that can be expanded with plug-ins and extensions. The program was designed for Unix-platforms.

**gold disc** (n.) Jargon for a CD-recordable (CD-R). The blank disc has a lower layer of polycarbonate with a preformed track spiral, which the recording laser beam follows and inscribes. A translucent layer of green recordable material adheres to the polycarbonate, and

there is a reflective layer of gold on top. These resilient discs are coated with lacquer.

**gopher** (n.) A distributed document retrieval system defined in RFC 1436. It has been replaced by the World Wide Web, which is itself a document retrieval system that provides access to gopher documents. Gopher originated at the University of Minnesota, where the mascot is a gopher.

**GOSIP** See *Government OSI Profile.*

**GOTO** (n.) A command or keyword used in FORTRAN, Cobol, BASIC, and C to cause an unconditional jump or transfer of control from one point in the program to another.

**Gouraud shading** (n.) An efficient three-dimensional rendering algorithm that averages the luma and chroma values at each corner of a polygon.

**Government OSI Profile** (GOSIP) (n.) Government Open Systems Interconnection Profile; a refined subset of OSI standards used by U.S. government procurements to increase the efficiency of the original OSI standards. Pronounced "GAH-sup."

**GPF** See *general protection fault.*

**GPRS** See *General Packet Radio Service.*

**GPS** See *Global Positioning System.*

**graded-index** (n.) A type of optical fiber in which the refractive index of the core varies smoothly with the radius. Graded-index cores are used in multi-mode fibers utilized in LAN applications.

**gradient** (n.) A method of filling or shading an

object that blends different shades, patterns, or intensities across the surface of the object.

**grammar** (n.) In programming, a formal definition of the syntactic structure of a computer language. It is usually stated in terms of production rules, which specify the order of elements in a properly formed string. A grammar can be used to parse a sentence or to generate one. Parsing assigns a terminal syntactic category to each input token and a nonterminal category to each appropriate group of tokens. Parsing is generally preceded by lexical analysis.

**granulation noise** (n.) Audible distortion that is caused by quantization error in a digital audio system.

**Graphical Device Interface** (GDI) (n.) A software interface between a video adapter or printer and the MS Windows operating system. It provides hundreds of functions for drawing geometric shapes and rendering fonts in Windows. This set of Application Programming Interfaces (APIs) provides instructions to a generic video driver and does not support proprietary adapters and accelerators. The Display Control Interface (DCI) superceded GDI, providing direct access to the video adapter. It has been superceded by *DirectDraw*, a component of *DirectX*.

**graphical user interface** (GUI, pronounced "GOO-ey") (n.) An environment in which icons represent objects that an operator can manipulate with a pointing device. Initially designed by Xerox, a GUI serves as the basis for the Mac OS and has been used in a similar context by Microsoft Windows. See also *user interface*.

**graphic equalizer** (n.) A multi-band variable equalizer that employs sliding controls to adjust amplitudes for each band. The position of the sliders "graphs" the resulting frequency response of the equalizer. Center frequency and

bandwidth are fixed for each band.

**Graphic Interchange Format** (GIF) (n.) Defined in 1987 by CompuServe Information Service (CIS), a standard for digitized images compressed with the Lempel-Ziv-Welch (LZW) algorithm. *Graphic Interchange Format* and *GIF* are service marks of CIS, as a result of a 1994 legal action by Unisys Corporation against CIS for violating Unisys's LZW software patent. GIF 89A is an open, fully supported, nonproprietary specification available to the entire online community and used primarily on the World Wide Web. The file name extension for any GIF format is .gif. It was originally pronounced "JIFF" by its developers, but many new users who have begun working with web graphics in recent years pronounce it "GIFF" with a hard G. Both are commonly used.

**graphics** (n.) The visual content prepared for a production. Computer-generated letters, symbols, drawings, photographs, scans, slides, and all other still visuals belong to this broad category.

**graphics accelerator** (n.) A specialized circuit board containing a coprocessor that enhances the graphical performance of a computer by relieving the central processing unit (CPU) from graphics processing. A graphics accelerator is inserted in an expansion slot.

**graphics adapter** (n.) A specialized circuit board that provides a monitor with all the information it needs to display graphics. Some graphics adapters are built into the computer circuitry, but a third-party graphics card is more commonly inserted in an expansion slot. The peripheral component interconnect (PCI) bus is frequently used for this type of adapter. An advanced type of adapter for IBM compatibles is the Accelerated Graphics Port (AGP). The graphics adapter determines the resolution and refresh rate, or frequency, of the signal sent to the monitor. See Graphics Adapter Resolutions table.

## Graphics Adapter Resolutions

| Adapter | Resolution | Simultaneous Colors/Mode |
|---|---|---|
| EGA | 640 x 350 | 16/text |
| | 720 x 350 | 4/text |
| | 320 x 200 | 16/graphics |
| | 640 x 200 | 16/graphics |
| | 640 x 350 | 16/graphics |
| VGA | 720 x 400 | 16/text |
| | 360 x 400 | 16/text |
| | 640 x 480 | 16/graphics |
| | 320 x 200 | 256/text |
| Super VGA | 800 x 600 | 16 777 216/graphics |
| (Macintosh) | 832 x 624 | 16 777 216/graphics |
| XGA | 1024 x 768 | 16 777 216/graphics |
| (IBM 8514/A) | 1024 x 768 | 256/graphics |
| | 1152 x 864 | 16 777 216/graphics |
| Super XGA | 1280 x 1024 | 16 777 216/graphics |
| Ultra XGA | 1600 x 1200 | 16 777 216/graphics |
| | 1800 x 1440 | 16 777 216/graphics |
| | 1920 x 1200 | 16 777 216/graphics |
| | 2040 x 1664 | 16 777 216/graphics |

**graphics input** (n.) The use of a peripheral, such as a drawing tablet, mouse, touch screen, or light pen, to create or alter a graphics display.

**graphics input device** (n.) Any digitizer that feeds a computer x- and y-coordinates and in some cases color data.

**graphics output device** (n.) Any device that displays or records an image. Monitors and printers are examples.

**graphics tablet** (n.) A type of drawing surface, often with pressure sensitivity, that feeds a computer data defining x- and y-coordinates from a handheld input device, such as a light pen.

**gray code** (n.) A sequence of binary values where only one bit is allowed to change between successive values. This method is generally "quieter" (producing less audible interference) than straight binary coding for execution of com-

mands in audio systems.

**grayscale** (n.) In a computer graphic, the number of levels of gray that exist between black and white. With a minimum of 256 levels, resolution comparable to that of a black-and-white photograph can be achieved.

**Green Book standard** (n.) The specification for CD-i developed in 1991 by Philips. Discs that adhere to this CD-ROM format contain audio files, digital data, still graphics, and MPEG video. An infrared remote control device, a mouse, or a trackball allows users to interact with the content on the disc by clicking a cursor over hot spots on the video display.

**grep** (n.) A Unix command that searches files for lines matching a given regular expression. It is named for the subcommand "g/re/p," which means Global Regular Expression Print.

**grip** (n.) In a film or video production, the person who mounts or positions the camera according to the director's instructions. The camera itself may be mounted on a dolly, a crane, or on any other surface that provides a desirable camera angle.

**grok** (v.) Jargon meaning to understand, pronounced "GRAWK."

**ground** (GND) (n.) An electrical connection between equipment and a zero voltage point. A ground loop occurs when equipment is grounded at more than one point.

**ground start** (n.) In telephony, a signaling method where one station detects that a circuit is grounded at the other end. This is opposed to a *loop start* circuit, which signals using both tip and ring. Ground start offers supervision, as well as the ability to transfer calls back to the Central Office (CO).

**ground station** (n.) A site with a collection of electronic equipment, including a signal generator, transmitter, receiver, antenna, and communications control computers that transmit and receive signals to and from a satellite. Also known as an earth station.

**group** (n.) In audio applications, this is a combination of two or more signal channels combined and treated as a set that can be varied in overall level from a single control. Mixing consoles often provide a group function mode, where a group fader may be used to adjust the level of a group of individual channels. A group may also be referred to as a *subgroup* or *submix*.

**GSM** See *Global System for Mobile communications*.

**GSS** See *Global Security Service*.

**guard band** (n.) A narrow band of dead space between two adjacent channels. A guard band is space inserted between tracks of recorded material on audio tapes or videotapes to prevent crosstalk between tracks.

**GUI** See *graphical user interface*.

**gyrator filters** (n.) A class of active filters that use gyrator networks, which are resistor-capacitor (RC) networks that mimic inductors. A gyrator is a form of artificial inductor where a RC filter synthesizes inductive characteristics. Gyrator filters are used to replace real inductors in filter design.

**gzip** (n.) A GNU utility that reduces the size of a file using Lempel-Ziv LZ77 compression. The original file is replaced by one with the file name extension ".gz" or ".z." Compressed files may be restored by using gunzip, a companion applet that uncompresses. Gzip works on Unix systems, and versions exist for VMS and MS-DOS. Pronounced "JEE-zip."

# H

H See *henry.*

**H.261** (n.) A video compression standard developed by the International Telecommunications Union (ITU) for ISDN transmission. Data is compressed at 64*P* kilobits per second (Kbps), where *P* ranges from 1 to 30, depending on the number of ISDN channels used. Developed primarily to support videoconferencing, H.261 is referred to as P x 64, pronounced "P-TIMES-64."

**H.320** (n.) Standard for conferencing over network or telephone lines integrating voice, digital video, and control messages into an interleaved signal over one or more 64-kilobit-per-second (Kbps) channels. Video formats specified are Common Intermediate Format (CIF) at a resolution of 352 x 288 pixels and Quarter CIF (QCIF) at a resolution of 176 x 144 pixels. Both resolutions are specified at 30 frames per second (fps) with interleaved audio. Any type of circuit may be used, including ISDN, Switched 56, or fractional T1.

**Haas effect** (n.) The psychoacoustic phenomena of correctly identifying the direction of a sound source that is heard in both ears, but which arrives at each ear at a different point in time. Direct sound from any source first enters the ear closest to the source, then the ear farthest away. According to German physicist Helmut Haas in the late 1940s, humans localize a sound source based upon the first arriving sound if the subsequent arrivals are within 25-35 milliseconds. If the interlude between sounds is longer than this, then two distinct sounds are heard. The Haas effect is true even when the second arrival is louder than the first (even by as much as 10 dB). In essence we do not "hear" the delayed sound. This is the hearing example of human sensory inhibition that applies to all our senses. Sensory inhibition describes the phenomena where the response to a first stimulus causes the response to a second stimulus to be inhibited, i.e., sound first entering one ear causes us to "not hear" the delayed sound entering into the other ear (within the 35 milliseconds time window). Sound arriving at both ears simultaneously is heard as coming from straight ahead, or behind, or within the head. The Haas effect describes how full stereophonic reproduction from only two loudspeakers is possible. It is also known as the *precedence effect.*

**hacker** (n.) A person with sophisticated programming skills who can break codes and access restricted data without access privileges.

**hacking** (n.) Attempts to illegally circumvent or bypass the security mechanisms of an information system or network.

**HAL** See *Hardware Abstraction Layer.*

**half-duplex** (HD) (adj.) Describes a telecommunications circuit that provides data transmission in two directions but that can transmit in only one direction at a time.

**half-height** (adj.) Describes a floppy disk drive, CD-ROM drive, or other peripheral that is 1.625 inches tall and that may be mounted in a short drive bay. It may be either 4 or 5.75 inches wide and either 4 or 8 inches deep.

**half horizontal resolution** (HHR) (n.) An MPEG-2 file may be stored at half normal horizontal resolution (352 pixels) to create a smaller file that requires a lower data rate to stream. When displayed, the full horizontal resolution (704 pixels) is restored by the MPEG decoder.

**half-inch** (n.) Jargon for the 0.5-inch videotape used in betacam, S-VHS, and VHS video formats.

**halftone** (n.) With regard to a graphical display or a printed document, a color value created with dots. The degree of color intensity is determined by the density and diameter of the dots. Printers, scanners, and monitors use halftone graphic techniques. This method of depicting color is different from grayscale, which defines actual shades of gray. See figure.

*halftone image*

**Hamster switch** (n.) On professional DJ performance mixers, a Hamster switch reverses fader action. If a fader normally is *off* at the bottom and *on* at the top, activating the hamster switch reverses this or, alternately, swaps left for right in horizontally mounted faders. It is used to create the most comfortable and fastest fader access with either turntable, and to accommodate left-handed and right-handed performers. It is named after one of the original scratch-style crews, *The BulletProof Scratch Hamsters.*

**Handheld Device Markup Language** (HDML) (n.) A language that uses HTTP, the underlying protocol for the web, to display text versions of web pages on wireless devices. Unlike wireless markup language (WML), HDML is not based on Extensible Markup Language (XML). HDML also does not allow developers to use scripts, while WML employs its own version of JavaScript. Phone.com, now part of Openwave Systems, developed HDML and it is distributed freely. HDML can be used to recode HTML documents to fit the small screen of a handheld device.

**handle** (n.) In a graphical environment, the corner or edge of an object onto which the user may click and drag to reposition or resize an image.

**hand off** (n.) In wireless communication, the process by which a cellular phone connection on one radio frequency in one cell is passed seamlessly to another radio frequency in another cell.

**handshake** (n.) As part of the communications protocol, the exchange of signals between two devices to establish a connection.

**handwriting recognition** (n.) A hardware-software system that converts handwritten letters into text files. It can be implemented on the touch screen of a personal digital assistant (PDA), with a light pen on a graphics tablet, or by using a scanner with optical character recognition (OCR) software.

**hang** (v.) Jargon that means to wait for an event that will not occur. A system that is hung may also be referred to as *wedged* or *frozen*.

**HARC-C** See *Houston Advanced Research Center–C.*

**hard copy** (n.) Documents and images in printed, concrete form, such as pages of text, slides, prints, transparencies, graphs, and plots.

**hard disk** (n.) A fixed magnetic disk drive that stores large amounts of data. Winchester is a common type. A hard disk consists of a stack of rigid platters with multiple read/write heads. See figure.

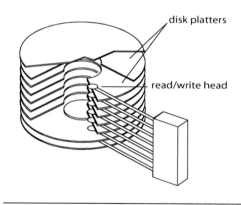

*hard disk mechanism*

**Hard-Disk Recorder** (HDR) (n.) A computer hard disk used to store digitized audio and video files. The system is configured like an analog recorder with multiple tracks and utilizes high bit-rate data converters with various interfaces.

**hard effect** (n.) A production sound that is difficult to produce live. Hard effects are typi-

cally pulled from an effects library or created for a particular project. Also known as a *spot effect.*

**hardware** (n.) The electromechanical portion of a data processing system. Computer machinery, circuit boards, monitors, peripheral devices, cables, and connectors are all hardware components.

**Hardware Abstraction Layer** (HAL) (n.) In the Microsoft Windows NT operating system, the place where the assembly language code is isolated.

**hardware key** (n.) A small connector that plugs into the parallel port of a computer. It typically contains code that the computer needs in order to perform a certain function, such as running proprietary software. Sometimes referred to as a *dongle.*

**hard wired** (adj.) A circuit or a communications link that is not switched and is dedicated to a single configuration or set of users.

**harmonic** (n.) A tone whose frequency is a multiple of the lowest tone in the harmonic series, the fundamental. Musical sounds consist of a fundamental and a number of harmonic overtones. The exception to this is the sine wave, which is devoid of harmonics. See figure on the following page.

**harmonic distortion** (n.) Signal distortion, normally analog, caused by harmonic frequencies generated from the interference between the primary signal frequencies on a channel. The power of the harmonic frequencies causing the distortion is measured in decibels as compared to the power of the input signal.

**harmonic overtone series** (n.) The pitches that naturally occur at intervals above a given fun-

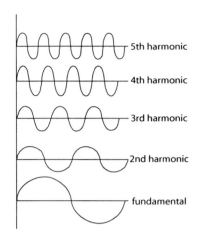

*harmonics*

damental frequency, also known as partials. Each pitch is a multiple of the fundamental frequency. When the frequency of a pitch is doubled, it sounds an octave higher. These pitches are the basis of musical chords and tonal harmony. See figure.

**hash** (n.) A collection of data in which each piece has two components, a key and a value. It is also known as an associative array. In JavaScript a hash is unordered, not indexed by numbers, as is a normal array. To assign a different graphic to each month in a calendar, all the graphics could be placed into a hash associ-

ated with each month as a key. A reference to the key month would invoke the graphic for that month. In a normal array, a number would be used as the index for the month:

```
picture[0] = "Snow";
picture[1] = "Valentine";
picture[3] = "Clover";
picture[4] = "Showers";
```

In a hash, a string with the name of the month is used as the index:

```
picture["January"] = "Snow";
picture["February"] = "Valentine";
picture["March"] = "Clover";
picture["April"] = "Showers";
```

**HAVI** See *Home Audio/Video Interoperability.*

**Hayes AT command set** (n.) A standard developed by Hayes Corporation to control intelligent modem parameters. This set of commands has become the de facto standard in the industry.

**HBI** See *horizontal blanking interval.*

**HD** See *half-duplex.*

**HDCD** See *High Definition Compatible Digital.*

**HDLC** See *High-Level Data Link Control.*

**HDML** See *Handheld Device Markup Language.*

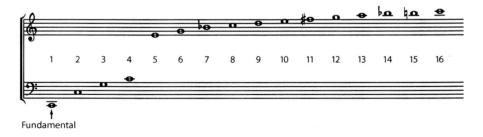

*harmonic overtone series*

**HDR** See *Hard-Disk Recorder.*

**HDSL** See *High-Data-Rate Digital Subscriber Line.*

**HDSL-2** (n.) Next generation high-speed digital subscriber line (HDSL), HDSL-2 provides symmetrical transmission of 24 DS0 at 1.544 Mbps on a single-wire pair, as opposed to the two wire pairs required by HDSL. HDSL-2 was developed for compatibility with asymmetrical digital subscriber line (ADSL), which moves data at various rates. The line coding used for HDSL-2 is Trellis-coded pulse amplitude modulation (TC-PAM).

**HDT** See *Host Digital Terminal.*

**HDTV** See *high-definition television.*

**head** (n.) An electromagnetic assembly that reads and writes data to any type of medium, such as magnetic tape, an optical disc, or the platter in a hard disk drive. See figure.

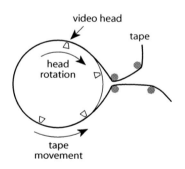

*read and write head in a VCR*

**headend** (n.) The site in a cable system or broadband coaxial network where the programming originates and the distribution network starts. Signals are usually received off the air from satellites, microwave relays, or fiber-optic cables at the headend for distribution.

**header** (n.) 1. In telecommunications and computing, information recorded at the beginning of a packet of transmitted data to identify what follows. On a CD-ROM it is recorded at the beginning of a sector, containing the address of the sector (the logical block number) and the mode in which the sector is recorded. 2. With reference to hardware, a row of pins on a circuit board that will accept a connector.

**header field** (n.) In CD-ROM terms, the address of a sector (the logical block number). It consists of four bytes recorded at the beginning of each sector that identify the address of the sector and the mode in which the sector is recorded.

**head parking** (n.) Automatic repositioning of the heads in a hard drive to move them to an unused track when a computer system is shut down, so that they will not damage data in the event of a failure.

**headroom** (n.) Related to audio dynamic range, headroom is used to express in decibels the amount of forgiveness between the normal operating level and the maximum operating level, before distortion or clipping occurs. A nominal +4 dBu system that clips at +20 dBu has 16 dB of headroom. Headroom expressed in dB accurately refers to both voltage and power.

**head slot** (n.) A small aperture in the jacket, or casing, of a floppy disk that exposes the medium to read/write heads.

**heap** (n.) In programming, the dynamic memory allocation space where blocks of memory are allocated and freed in an arbitrary order and where the pattern of allocation and the size of blocks are unknown until run time. A heap is required by languages in which functions can return arbitrary data structures.

**heartbeat** (n.) 1. In network terms, the signal emitted by a Level 2 Ethernet transceiver at the end of each packet to show that the collision-detection circuit remains connected. 2. Used by software or hardware, a regular synchronization signal that may take the form of a bus clock or a periodic interrupt.

**heat sink** (n.) A piece of metal connected to an electronic device. The heat sink dissipates heat and radiates it to the environment to prevent the device from overheating. A heat sink often has fins to increase its surface area. A gelatinous compound is frequently applied between the device and the heat sink to improve thermal conduction.

**Heidi** (n.) An Application Program Interface (API) developed by Autodesk that supports the rendering and output of three-dimensional images.

**helical scan** (n.) A tape playback system with two video heads mounted on opposite sides of a revolving drum. The head drum spins at a single frame per revolution, so each head scans one field, or half a frame, per revolution. The system achieves high tape speeds by moving the tape and the heads. The tape moves in a spiral path as it winds around the video head drum.

**Helmholtz, Hermann** (1821–1894) German physicist and acoustician, best known for his 1862 book, *On the Sensations of Tone as a Physiological Basis for a Theory of Music*. Helmholtz studied the function of the inner ear and how it distinguishes pitch, various frequencies, tones, timbres, and overtones.

**helper application** (n.) A program that enables a web browser to play multimedia file types, such as audio, video, or animation. This is analogous to an application that reads a file attached to an email message if the correct MIME type is specified and if it is available on the system.

## Hexadecimal Equivalents

| Hexadecimal | Decimal | Binary | Hexadecimal | Decimal | Binary |
|---|---|---|---|---|---|
| 01 | 1 | 00000001 | 15 | 21 | 00010101 |
| 02 | 2 | 00000010 | 16 | 22 | 00010110 |
| 03 | 3 | 00000011 | 17 | 23 | 00010111 |
| 04 | 4 | 00000100 | 18 | 24 | 00011000 |
| 05 | 5 | 00000101 | 19 | 25 | 00011001 |
| 06 | 6 | 00000110 | 1A | 26 | 00011010 |
| 07 | 7 | 00000111 | 1B | 27 | 00011011 |
| 08 | 8 | 00001000 | 1C | 28 | 00011100 |
| 09 | 9 | 00001001 | 1D | 29 | 00011101 |
| 0A | 10 | 00001010 | 1E | 30 | 00011110 |
| 0B | 11 | 00001011 | 1F | 31 | 00011111 |
| 0C | 12 | 00001100 | 20 | 32 | 00100000 |
| 0D | 13 | 00001101 | 21 | 33 | 00100001 |
| 0E | 14 | 00001110 | 22 | 34 | 00100010 |
| 0F | 15 | 00001111 | 23 | 35 | 00100011 |
| 10 | 16 | 00010000 | 24 | 36 | 00100100 |
| 11 | 17 | 00010001 | 25 | 37 | 00100101 |
| 12 | 18 | 00010010 | 26 | 38 | 00100110 |
| 13 | 19 | 00010011 | 27 | 39 | 00100111 |
| 14 | 20 | 00010100 | 28 | 40 | 00101000 |

**henry** (H) (n.) A unit of inductance named for American physicist Joseph Henry (1797–1878). A single henry is the inductance of a closed loop in which the induced voltage is 1 volt if the current flowing through it changes at the rate of 1 ampere per second.

**Hertz, Heinrich Rudolf** (1857–1894) German physicist credited with being the first to produce and receive radio waves. Hertz proved that light can be transmitted in electromagnetic waves. His experiments in the late 1880s led to his developments in wireless communications.

**hertz** (Hz) (n.) A unit of frequency measurement named for German physicist Heinrich Rudolf Hertz (1857–1894); 1 Hz equals 1 cycle per second (cps), 1 kilohertz (kHz) equals 1000 cps, and 1 megahertz (MHz) equals 1 000 000 cps.

**heuristic** (adj.) Describes a trial-and-error method of solving problems by evaluating the progress made at various steps in a process.

**heuristic routine** (n.) A software methodology that solves problems by trial and error rather than by an algorithmic procedure. A computer may be said to engage in learning during this process.

**Hewlett-Packard Graphics Language** (HPGL) (n.) A bitmapped graphic file format used by IBM-compatible graphics programs.

**hexadecimal** (n.) A numbering system with numbers 0 through 9 and letters *A* through *F*, which together are called *hex digits*. See table.

**HFC** See *hybrid fiber-coax.*

**HFS** See *Hierarchical File System.*

**HHR** See *half horizontal resolution.*

**hidden attribute** (n.) A feature that prevents files from being displayed in the directory list while MS-DOS or Windows is running.

**hidden file** (n.) A file whose attributes are set so that it is not normally shown in a directory listing. Hiding system files in MS-DOS prevents the user from accidentally deleting them.

**Hi-8 video** (n.) An improved version of the Sony 8 mm format. Hi-8 video yields higher luminance levels and better quality than standard 8 mm and provides Y/C component S-video connections.

**Hierarchical File System** (HFS) (n.) The directory structure used in the Mac OS that defines a pattern of nested folders and determines how they are stored on formatted media.

**hierarchical link** (n.) In object-oriented programming, a "parent-child" relationship between two objects. Changes made to the parent are automatically inherited by the child, but changes made to the child will not necessarily be reflected in the parent.

**hierarchical routing** (n.) Division of a network into a hierarchy of smaller networks in which each level is responsible for its own routing. The three levels of hierarchy in the Internet are backbones, midlevel networks, and stub networks.

**hierarchical structure** (n.) A system of tree-structured directories that is built in layers and based on pathways between root directories and subdirectories.

**High-Data-Rate Digital Subscriber Line** (HDSL) (n.) Telecommunications transmission

197

technology developed by Bellcore that uses a special DSL modem in T1 applications to filter out background interference in twisted-pair copper wires. A send-receive unit is required at each end of the connecting wire, and the transmission distance is limited.

**High Definition Compatible Digital** (HDCD) (n.) An enhanced audio CD technology. Developed by Keith Johnson and Pflash Pflaumer, HDCD is a 20-bit, 88.2 kHz digital audio encoding process, exhibiting higher definition than the standard CD format of 16-bits, 44.1 kHz sample rate. An HDCD decoder chip must be installed in a CD player to make it compatible with this format.

**high-definition television** (HDTV) (n.) A video format with higher resolution than the NTSC, PAL, and SECAM broadcast standards it will replace. HDTV formats range from 655 to 2125 scanning lines and display in a 16:9 aspect ratio. The HDTV format has a video bandwidth of 30 to 50 MHz, which is more than five times greater than that of standard NTSC. The most typical implementation of HDTV provides 1080 lines of horizontal resolution rather than 525 in NTSC, partially because of the wider aspect ratio. HDTV is also equipped with dolby AC-3 surround-sound and CD-quality audio. HDTV is an evolving specification that has taken many forms and shapes. Any scan line count above 480 might be considered high-definition. The Advanced Television Systems Committee (ATSC) has formulated a table of formats accepted as digital television. The ATSC Table 3 is a transmission specification, not a videotape or mastering format. It provides guidelines for how a digital television signal will be broadcast. MPEG-2 is the compression format for all signals. The ATSC Table 3 shown below defines requirements for interlaced (I) and progressively scanned (P) images, along with the various sizes, aspect ratios, and frame rates.

**High-Level Data Link Control** (HDLC) (n.) Standard ISO protocol for communications devices and software applications operating in synchronous environments. HDLC defines how data frames should be formatted for exchange between modems.

**high-level language** (HLL) (n.) Any programming language in which a single statement may be translated into numerous assembly language or machine code instructions. High-level languages are designed to be machine-independent, in contrast to an assembly language. C++, BASIC, Pascal, and FORTRAN are examples of high-level languages.

**high-pass filter** (n.) A filter that passes frequencies from a specified finite dB setting upward toward infinity. Also called a *low cut filter*.

**High-Performance Parallel Interface** (HIPPI)

| ATSC Table 3: Formats for Digital Television Transmission | | | | |
|---|---|---|---|---|
| **Vertical Lines** | **Pixel Width** | **I/P** | **Aspect Ratio** | **Frame Rate** |
| 480 | 640 | I | 4:3 | 30 |
| 480 | 640 | P | 4:3 | 24, 30, 60 |
| 480 | 704 | I | 16:9 | 30 |
| 480 | 704 | P | 16:9 | 24, 30, 60 |
| 720 | 1280 | P | 16:9 | 24, 30, 60 |
| 1080 | 1920 | I | 16:9 | 30 |
| 1080 | 1920 | p | 16:9 | 24, 30 |

(n.) ANSI standard X3T9.3 that increases the speed of a computer bus between routers, peripherals, and other computers at speeds of 800 megabits per second (Mbps) over 32 twisted pairs of copper wiring, and 1600 Mbps over 64 twisted pairs. Cable lengths are limited to 25 meters over copper wire and 300 meters over multimode optical fiber. HIPPI is a common interface for supercomputers.

**high-performance serial bus** (IEEE 1394) (n.) A serial bus interface standard that provides high-speed communication and isochronous realtime data services. It can transmit data at 100 megabits per second (Mbps), 200 Mbps, or 400 Mbps. As many as 16 cables up to 4.5 meters long may be connected in a daisy chain to a single computer. IEEE 1394 allows peer-to-peer device communication without taxing the processor or using system memory. It supports plug and play (PnP) and can supply up to 60 watts of power over a standard inexpensive six-wire cable. See also *FireWire*.

**High Sierra format** (n.) A standard CD-ROM format for file and directory placement. It was developed by computer vendors, software developers, and CD-ROM system integrators. Twelve companies began work on the format proposal in 1985 at the High Sierra Hotel in Lake Tahoe, Nevada. The ISO 9660 format is a revised version of the High Sierra format adopted by the ISO.

**High-Speed Serial Interface** (HSSI, pronounced "HISS-ee") (n.) A data communications protocol that can support serial transfer of data at a rate of 52 megabits per second (Mbps). The most common connections are wide area network (WAN) routers and leased lines, such as DS-3, which transmits at up to 44.736 Mbps.

**High Speed Technology** (HST) (n.) A high-speed modem protocol with error control, developed by U.S. Robotics.

**High Split** (n.) Broadband cable system in which the upstream signaling bandwidth is about 6 MHz to 180 MHz and the downstream bandwidth is about 220 MHz to 400 MHz. A guard band between upstream and downstream signals prevents interference between the two.

**HIPPI** See *High-Performance Parallel Interface*.

**hit** (n.) Any action or event that takes place on a web server, such as when a user views a page or downloads a file.

**HLL** See *high-level language*.

**HLS** See *hue, luminance, and saturation*.

**hologram** (n.) An image with a layered, three-dimensional appearance that is produced by a laser-based system rather than by lenses.

**Home Audio/Video Interoperability** (HAVI) (n.) Industry standard designed to link consumer electronics products using the IEEE 1394 (Firewire) interface. It was developed by a collaboration of Grundig, Hitachi, Panasonic, Philips, Sharp, Sony, Thomson Multimedia, and Toshiba. The goal of this protocol is implementation of the Firewire interface to connect digital TVs, set-top boxes, DVD players and other digital products.

**home page** (n.) A document that is accessed via the World Wide Web by using a browser, or universal client. A home page, or web page, is typically written in HTML, which provides the capacity to link "hot" words to other words, graphics, or pages. The home page is usually the point of entry for a web site, with hyperlinks

199

to the other pages.

**hop** (n.) In relation to routing, each step in a path through routers from origin to destination on a network.

**horizontal blanking interval** (HBI) (n.) The length of time required for the beam of a cathode-ray tube (CRT) to return from the right side of a line of pixels to the left side of the next line while scanning. The interval is included in the signal for each of the 525 lines in an NTSC picture. See also *vertical blanking interval.*

**horizontal resolution** (n.) The number of lines measurable across the width of a video monitor or screen. This number determines the degree of discernible detail. More lines of resolution result in better picture quality.

**host adapter** (n.) A controller card, such as a SCSI adapter, that routes data between the CPU and peripherals, such as CD-ROM drives, printers, or disk drives.

**host computer** (n.) Any computer that provides the processing power for the terminals and for the peripherals connected to it.

**Host Digital Terminal** (HDT) (n.) Interface point for information transmitted to and from an optical network unit (ONU). The HDT manages signal traffic and provides the interconnection point for local switching.

**hostname** (n.) A unique name that identifies a computer on a network. An Internet hostname is an ASCII string, such as *hansenmedia .com.* The hostname is translated, or resolved, into an Internet address by the domain name system (DNS). A single computer may have several hostnames (aliases), but only one is designated as its canonical name, in which each facet

of the complete address is defined.

**hot** (adj.) 1. Describes a defined region on the monitor that responds to a mouse click or to pressure in the case of a touch screen when an interactive program is running. Activating the defined area initiates an action or causes a process to be performed. 2. In audio terms, describes a tape recorded at the maximum possible signal level. 3. In video production, describes a camera that is in use, or "on air."

**hot fix** (n.) The replacement of a failed disk drive in a multiple drive system with a "hot spare" while the remaining drives are online. Also called a *hot swap.*

**HotJava** (n.) The Sun Microsystems web browser that can execute programs written in Java. Java applets can be included in HTML pages. Applets run on any platform that supports HotJava, including Solaris 2, and Windows.

**hot link** (n.) 1. A connecting point manifested as text, buttons, or icons that are specially tagged in an interactive program, making it possible to connect instantly to information in another location or to execute instructions simply by clicking on them or by otherwise activating the links. 2. A connection between two or more programs that updates data in linked programs automatically when it is changed in one of the associated programs. For example, making a change in a database file linked to a graph representing the data will cause a corresponding change in the graph.

**hotlist** (n.) A term that the NCSA Mosaic web browser uses to describe the list of URLs that a user has visited and chosen to add to the list. The hotlist is equivalent to *Bookmarks* in

Netscape Navigator or *Favorites* in MS Internet Explorer.

**hot spot** (n.) An area or region on the computer screen that responds to mouse clicks. An image map on a page of HTML is an example of a hot spot that provides a link to another location.

**hot swap** (n.) The replacement of a failed disk drive in a multiple drive system with a "hot spare" while the remaining drives are online. Also called a *hot fix*.

**house sync** (n.) The timing signal, typically SMPTE code, that is supplied to all audio and video recording and playback equipment in a postproduction house. A common timing source ensures rock-solid tracking between different machines.

**Houston Advanced Research Center–C** (HARC-C, pronounced "hark-SEE") (n.) A video compression algorithm based on wavelet theory and programmed in C.

**hover** (v.) In an interactive program, such as a web browser, positioning the cursor over a link or a hotspot. An action may be initiated after a predetermined period of hovering over a link.

**HPGL** See *Hewlett-Packard Graphics Language.*

**HQX** (n.) A Macintosh program that converts binary files into the seven-bit BinHex format so they can be transferred to another user as text. The file name extension for a BinHex format file is .hqx.

**HSSI** See *High-Speed Serial Interface.*

**HST** See *High Speed Technology.*

**HSV** See *hue, saturation, and value.*

**HTML** See *Hypertext Markup Language.*

**HTML 4.0** (n.) Hypertext Markup Language version 4.0; a Document Type Definition (DTD) that is a subset of Standard Generalized Markup Language (SGML) and that extends HTML version 3.2 with additional commands and features. The 4.0 version of popular browsers is unable to interpret some of the features in HTML 4.0, but most features are implemented in later versions. New elements in HTML 4.0 include the OBJECT element, the BUTTON element, and the INS and DEL elements for marking edited text.

### HTML 4.0 vs HTML 3.2

Version 4.0 of the Hypertext Markup Language (HTML) has a number of major improvements over the previous version 3.2. Version 4.0 includes the capacity to use Cascading Style Sheets (CSS) for precise formatting. The World Wide Web Consortium (W3C) recommends that developers move formatting information out of HTML text and use CSS whenever possible. Other new features are improvements to tables and forms, making them more flexible and more easily controlled. There are also new printing and multimedia features.

HTML 4.0 makes frames an official part of the specification, approving the <FRAME>, <FRAMESET>, and <IFRAME> elements. Supported by popular browsers since Netscape Navigator 2.0 and Internet Explorer 3.0, the HTML specification never defined them until version 4.0.

New characters previously not available in HTML have been included, making it a truly international language. In all previous versions of HTML, the basic character set implemented was Latin-1 (ISO 8859-1). Latin-1 is an 8-bit, single-byte-coded graphic character set capable of representing up to 256 characters. It contains letters for English, German, French, Spanish, and most Scandinavian languages. However, characters in the Greek, Hebrew, Arabic, and Cyrillic languages are not supported. Very little support is provided for scientific or mathematical symbols in Latin-1.

HTML 4.0 addresses these limitations by using the Universal Character Set (UCS). UCS is a character-by-character equivalent to Unicode 2.0, a character-encoding standard that uses a 16-bit set, thereby increasing the number of available characters to more than 65,000.

**HTML Coded Characters** (n.) Also known as "escape sequences," these codes are used in HTML to indicate a special symbol. See table.

**HTML Color Code** (n.) The use of a six-digit hexadecimal triplet, with two digits each for red, green, and blue, that identifies the exact color to be displayed. See table.

**HTTP** See *Hypertext Transfer Protocol.*

**HTTP 1.1** (n.) Hypertext Transfer Protocol version 1.1; a revision of the original HTTP that improves performance. Under HTTP 1.0, a new connection via TCP is required for each piece of data transferred from a web page. This means that an individual connection is made for each graphical object, then thrown away. The revised version employs "persistent connections," maintaining a single connection through multiple downloads and taking advantage of TCP algorithms to avoid congestion. Another important new feature is "pipelining," which allows an ordered series of HTTP requests to be made at one time and received in order. The updated HTTP 1.1 must be running on both the server and the client. New versions of Netscape and Microsoft client software include the upgrade, and it is being built into server software. Traffic on the Internet will be reduced substantially, because the number of packets sent (such as TCP "open/close" packets) will be controlled.

**HTTP cookie** (n.) Hypertext Transfer Protocol cookie; a packet of data that is sent by an HTTP server to a web browser, is stored on the client computer, and is returned by the browser each time it accesses the server that sent the cookie. Cookies may contain any kind of data that the server chooses to send, but they are primarily used to inform the server of the state of the browser and the configuration of the client. A cookie can be used by a server to identify a registered user of a site in order to avoid asking for a password on each visit.

**HTTPd** (n.) Hypertext Transfer Protocol daemon; developed by Rob McCool at the National Center for Supercomputing Applications (NCSA), HTTP 1.0 server software that makes HTML and other document types available to web browsers. It is compact and fast, and it works with most browsers. It allows a server to handle HTML forms and to execute searches.

**HTTPS** See *Hypertext Transfer Protocol, Secure.*

**hub** (n.) A network repeater that does not provide retiming functions.

**hue** (n.) A color, such as cyan, yellow, magenta, or green.

**hue, luminance, and saturation** (HLS) (n.) Three parameters of a computer graphic. *Hue* refers to the specific color. Rose, crimson, and burgundy are all red hues. *Luminance* defines the brightness, or amount of light. *Saturation* refers to the strength of a color, compared with neutral gray. Saturation is also called *intensity, depth,* or *chroma.*

**HTML 4.0 Modifications: Obsolete, Deprecated, and New Elements**

**Obsolete Elements**
The three tags removed from the HTML specification are as follows:

    <XMP>
    <PLAINTEXT>
    <LISTING>

These tags are to be replaced with `<PRE>` in all instances. Some browsers may continue to support these tags.

**Deprecated Elements**
These tags and attributes have been replaced by new HTML constructs. The W3C recommendation strongly urges that deprecated tags not be used, because they will eventually become obsolete in future browsers.

`<APPLET>...</APPLET>` — This tag allowed a Java applet to run. It should be replaced by the `<OBJECT>...</OBJECT>` tag.

`<ISINDEX>...</ISINDEX>` — This tag allowed a form to contain a basic string search. It should be replaced by the `<INPUT>` form element.

`<DIR>...</DIR>` — This tag was used to describe a directory list, which is identical to an unordered list. It should be replaced by a `<UL>...</UL>` list tag.

`<MENU>...</MENU>` — This tag was used to define a single-column menu list, which is identical to an unordered list. It should be replaced by a `<UL>...</UL>` list tag.

`<CENTER>...</CENTER>` — This tag was used to center either text or graphics. It should be replaced by a <DIV> tag, and the align attribute should be set to "center."

`<FONT>...</FONT>` — This tag was used to specify font face, size, and colors. Style sheets should be used for character formatting rather than HTML code.

`<BASEFONT>...</BASEFONT>` — This tag was used to set a base font size as a reference point for making the font larger or smaller. Style sheets should be used to set and reference relative font sizes.

`<STRIKE>...</STRIKE>` or `<S>...</S>` — These tags were used to create strikethrough characters. Style sheets should be used for all such character formatting.

`<U>...</U>` — These tags were used to underline characters. Style sheets should be used to create underlined text.

**New Elements**
The following is a brief description of new tags.

`<ABBR>...</ABBR>` — This tag identifies the abbreviated form of a term or phrase. Both a start tag and an end tag are required.

`<ACRONYM>...</ACRONYM>` — This tag identifies an acronym in a phrase of text. <ACRONYM> is similar in behavior to <EM> and <CODE>. Both a start tag and an end tag are required. Here is an example:

    This document is about <ACRONYM>HTML</ACRONYM>, which
    stands for Hypertext Markup Language. Version 4.0 should
    be used to create documents for the
    <ACRONYM>WWW</ACRONYM>.

`<BUTTON>...</BUTTON>` — This tag is used to create push buttons on forms that are similar to push buttons in most Windows applications. In its behavior, the <BUTTON> tag is like the "submit" and "reset" <INPUT> elements. The representation of a <BUTTON> has a 3-dimensional look, with beveled edges, and it appears to be depressed when a user clicks on it. Both a start tag and an end tag for <BUTTON> are required by HTML 4.0.

HTML 4.0 Modifications: Obsolete, Deprecated, and New Elements (continued)

**New Elements (continued)**

`<BUTTON>...</BUTTON>`
(continued)

Here is an example:

```
<FORM action="http://hansenmedia.com/prog/newuser"
method="post">
Would you prefer to read these documents in German or English?
<P>
 <INPUT type="radio" name="preference" value="Yes"> Yes<BR>
  <INPUT type="radio" name="preference" value="No"> No<BR>
<P>
  <BUTTON name="submit" value="submit" type="submit">
   Send</BUTTON>
   <BUTTON name="reset" type="reset">
Reset</BUTTON>
</FORM>
```

`<COLGROUP>`
`...</COLGROUP>`

This tag allow tables to be formatted with groups of columns that share width and alignment properties, which are set by one or more of the new <COL> elements. If a <COLGROUP> is not specified and defined, HTML 4.0 formats a table with a single column group that contains all the columns. Both a start tag and an end tag are required by HTML 4.0 for <COLGROUP>. Here is an example of a table with one wide column and check box at the right side of each row.

```
<TABLE>
<COLGROUP span="8" width="20">
<COLGROUP span="1" width="0*">
<THEAD>
<TR>...
</TABLE>
```

`<FIELDSET>`
`...</FIELDSET>`

This tag allows related form fields to be grouped, providing a way for information to be classified. When a group of form elements are enclosed in <FIELDSET> tags the browser groups the elements together. Both a start tag and an end tag are required by HTML 4.0. Here is an example of code with both the <FIELDSET> and <LEGEND> tags.

```
<HEAD>
<TITLE>Size of Research Report you would like</TITLE>
</HEAD>
<BODY>
Select below for the length of the report you desire.
<FORM action="..." method="post">
    <FIELDSET>
        <LEGEND align="top">Length of Report</LEGEND>
        Number of pages in the report:
        <SELECT NAME="Pages" SIZE="5">
        <OPTION VALUE="2 pages">2
        <OPTION VALUE="3 pages">3
        <OPTION VALUE="8 pages">8</SELECT>
        Number of words per page:
        <SELECT NAME="Words per Page" SIZE="5">
        <OPTION VALUE="150 words">150
        <OPTION VALUE="200 words">200
        <OPTION VALUE="250 words">250</SELECT>
    </FIELDSET>
</FORM>
</BODY>
```

**HTML 4.0 Modifications: Obsolete, Deprecated, and New Elements** (continued)

**New Elements** (continued)

| | |
|---|---|
| `<DEL>...</DEL>` and `<INS>...</INS>` | These tags are used to identify portions of a document that have been edited since the previous version. `<DEL>...</DEL>` marks text that has been deleted. `<INS>...</INS>` is used to mark text that has been inserted. Both a start tag and an end tag are required by HTML 4.0 for <DEL> and <INS>. |
| Here is an example: | ```
This is the new and improved online tutorial on
HTML. <INS>You have three options. You may begin
the test, practice, or exit.</INS> <DEL>You have
two options. You may begin the test or exit.</DEL>
``` |
| `<LABEL>...</LABEL>` | This tag is used to specify the label text for a form field, and to identify parameters of form elements. Both a start tag and an end tag are required by HTML 4.0. |
| `<LEGEND>...</LEGEND>` | This tag is used in conjunction with <FIELDSET> to attach a label to a form grouping. Both a start tag and an end tag are required by HTML 4.0. See the <FIELDSET> example for usage. |
| `<NOFRAMES>...</NOFRAMES>` | This tag is used to specify alternate text if the browser is not able to display frames. Both a start tag and an end tag are required by HTML 4.0. Here is an example: |
| | ```
<NOFRAMES>This text is displayed by browsers unable
to render frames.</NOFRAMES>
``` |
| `<NOSCRIPT>...</NOSCRIPT>` | This new tag is used to specify alternate text if the browser is not able to execute JavaScript. No text is rendered by the browser if JavaScript is supported. It should be placed within the HEAD tags. Both a start tag and an end tag are required by HTML 4.0. Here is an example: |
| | ```
<NOSCRIPT> This text is displayed by browsers
unable to process JavaScript.</NOSCRIPT>
``` |
| `<OBJECT>...</OBJECT>` | This tag embeds an object on a page. The object could be an image, a document, a control, or an applet. Both a start tag and an end tag are required by HTML 4.0. |
| `<OPTGROUP>...</OPTGROUP>` | This tag groups menu options together in a SELECT, which is particularly useful for form accessibility. Both a start tag and an end tag are required by HTML 4.0. |
| `<PARAM>...</PARAM>` | This tag is used to pass additional parameters to a Java applet. A start tag is required, but an end tag is optional in HTML 4.0. |
| `<SPAN>...</SPAN>` | This tag is used to define a text container and apply style information to it, according to the conventions of Cascading Style Sheets (CSS). Both a start tag and an end tag are required by HTML 4.0. Here is an example: |
| | ```
<SPAN STYLE="color: red">This text is displayed in
red.</SPAN>
``` |
| `<Q>...</Q>` | This tag functions in a way similar to the <BLOCKQUOTE> tag, but applies to short quoted sections that do not require paragraph breaks. Both a start tag and an end tag are required by HTML 4.0. |

H

## HTML Color Codes

| Color Name | Code | Color Name | Code | Color Name | Code |
|---|---|---|---|---|---|
| AliceBlue | eff7ff | Cornsilk2 | ece5c6 | DimGray | 463e41 |
| AntiqueWhite | f9e8d2 | Cornsilk3 | c8c2a7 | DodgerBlue | 1589ff |
| AntiqueWhite1 | feedd6 | Cornsilk4 | 817a68 | DodgerBlue2 | 157dec |
| AntiqueWhite2 | ebdbc5 | Cyan | 00ffff | DodgerBlue3 | 1569c7 |
| AntiqueWhite3 | c8b9a6 | Cyan1 | 57feff | DodgerBlue4 | 153e7e |
| AntiqueWhite4 | 817468 | Cyan2 | 50ebec | Firebrick | 800517 |
| Aquamarine | 43b7ba | Cyan3 | 46c7c7 | Firebrick1 | f62817 |
| Aquamarine1 | 87fdce | Cyan4 | 307d7e | Firebrick2 | e42217 |
| Aquamarine2 | 7deabe | DarkGoldenrod | af7817 | Firebrick3 | c11b17 |
| Aquamarine3 | 69c69f | DarkGoldenrod1 | fbb117 | FloralWhite | fff9ee |
| Aquamarine4 | 417c64 | DarkGoldenrod2 | e8a317 | ForestGreen | 4e9258 |
| Azure | effffff | DarkGoldenrod3 | c58917 | Gainsboro | d8d9d7 |
| Azure2 | deecec | DarkGoldenrod4 | 7f5217 | GhostWhite | f7f7ff |
| Azure3 | bcc7c7 | DarkGreen | 254117 | Gold | d4a017 |
| Azure4 | 7a7d7d | DarkKhaki | b7ad59 | Gold1 | fdd017 |
| Beige | f5f3d7 | DarkOliveGreen | 4a4117 | Gold2 | eac117 |
| Bisque | fde0bc | DarkOliveGreen1 | ccfb5d | Gold3 | c7a317 |
| Bisque2 | ead0ae | DarkOliveGreen2 | bce954 | Gold4 | 806517 |
| Bisque3 | c7af92 | DarkOliveGreen3 | a0c544 | Goldenrod | edda74 |
| Bisque4 | 816e59 | DarkOliveGreen4 | 667c26 | Goldenrod1 | fbb917 |
| Black | 000000 | DarkOrange | f88017 | Goldenrod2 | e9ab17 |
| BlanchedAlmond | fee8c6 | DarkOrange1 | f87217 | Goldenrod3 | c68e17 |
| Blue | 0000ff | DarkOrange2 | e56717 | Goldenrod4 | 805817 |
| Blue1 | 1535ff | DarkOrange3 | c35617 | Gray | 736f6e |
| Blue2 | 1531ec | DarkOrange4 | 7e3117 | Gray0 | 150517 |
| Blue3 | 1528c7 | DarkOrchid | 7d1b7e | Gray18 | 250517 |
| Blue4 | 151b7e | DarkOrchid1 | b041ff | Gray21 | 2b1b17 |
| BlueViolet | 7931df | DarkOrchid2 | a23bec | Gray23 | 302217 |
| Brown | 980517 | DarkOrchid3 | 8b31c7 | Gray24 | 302226 |
| Brown1 | f63526 | DarkOrchid4 | 571b7e | Gray25 | 342826 |
| Brown2 | e42d17 | DarkSalmon | e18b6b | Gray26 | 34282c |
| Brown3 | c22217 | DarkSeaGreen | 8bb381 | Gray27 | 382d2c |
| Burlywood1 | fcce8e | DarkSeaGreen1 | c3fdb8 | Gray28 | 3b3131 |
| Burlywood2 | eabe83 | DarkSeaGreen2 | b5eaaa | Gray29 | 3e3535 |
| Burlywood3 | c6a06d | DarkSeaGreen3 | 99c68e | Gray30 | 413839 |
| Burlywood4 | 806341 | DarkSeaGreen4 | 617c58 | Gray31 | 41383c |
| CadetBlue | 578693 | DarkSlateBlue | 2b3856 | Gray32 | 463e3f |
| CadetBlue1 | 99f3ff | DarkSlateGray | 25383c | Gray34 | 4a4344 |
| CadetBlue2 | 8ee2ec | DarkSlateGray1 | 9afeff | Gray35 | 4c4646 |
| CadetBlue3 | 77bfc7 | DarkSlateGray2 | 8eebec | Gray36 | 4e4848 |
| CadetBlue4 | 4c787e | DarkSlateGray3 | 78c7c7 | Gray37 | 504a4b |
| Chartreuse | 8afb17 | DarkSlateGray4 | 4c7d7e | Gray38 | 544e4f |
| Chartreuse2 | 7fe817 | DarkTurquoise | 3b9c9c | Gray39 | 565051 |
| Chartreuse3 | 6cc417 | DarkViolet | 842dce | Gray40 | 595454 |
| Chartreuse4 | 437c17 | DeepPink | f52887 | Gray41 | 5c5858 |
| Chocolate | c85a17 | DeepPink2 | e4287c | Gray42 | 5f5a59 |
| Coral | f76541 | DeepPink3 | c12267 | Gray43 | 625d5d |
| Coral2 | e55b3c | DeepPink4 | 7d053f | Gray44 | 646060 |
| Coral3 | c34a2c | DeepSkyBlue | 3bb9ff | Gray45 | 666362 |
| Coral4 | 7e2817 | DeepSkyBlue2 | 38acec | Gray46 | 696565 |
| CornflowerBlue | 151b8d | DeepSkyBlue3 | 3090c7 | Gray47 | 6d6968 |
| Cornsilk | fff7d7 | DeepSkyBlue4 | 25587e | Gray48 | 6e6a6b |

| Color Name | Code | Color Name | Code | Color Name | Code |
|---|---|---|---|---|---|
| Gray49 | 726e6d | Green3 | 4cc417 | LightPink3 | c48189 |
| Gray50 | 747170 | Green4 | 347c17 | LightPink4 | 7f4e52 |
| Gray51 | 787473 | GreenYellow | b1fb17 | LightSalmon | f9966b |
| Gray52 | 7a7777 | Honeydew | f0feee | LightSalmon2 | e78a61 |
| Gray53 | 7c7979 | Honeydew2 | deebdc | LightSalmon3 | c47451 |
| Gray54 | 807d7c | Honeydew3 | bcc7b9 | LightSalmon4 | 7f462c |
| Gray55 | 82807e | Honeydew4 | 7a7d74 | LightSeaGreen | 3ea99f |
| Gray56 | 858381 | HotPink | f660ab | LightSkyBlue | 82cafa |
| Gray57 | 878583 | HotPink1 | f665ab | LightSkyBlue2 | a0cfec |
| Gray58 | 8b8987 | HotPink2 | e45e9d | LightSkyBlue3 | 87afc7 |
| Gray59 | 8d8b89 | HotPink3 | c25283 | LightSkyBlue4 | 566d7e |
| Gray60 | 8f8e8d | HotPink4 | 7d2252 | LightSlateBlue | 736aff |
| Gray61 | 939190 | IndianRed | 5e2217 | LightSlateGray | 6d7b8d |
| Gray62 | 959492 | IndianRed1 | f75d59 | LightSteelBlue | 728fce |
| Gray63 | 999795 | IndianRed2 | e55451 | LightSteelBlue1 | c6deff |
| Gray64 | 9a9998 | IndianRed3 | c24641 | LightSteelBlue2 | b7ceec |
| Gray65 | 9e9c9b | IndianRed4 | 7e2217 | LightSteelBlue3 | 9aadc7 |
| Gray66 | a09f9d | Ivory | ffffee | LightSteelBlue4 | 646d7e |
| Gray67 | a3a2a0 | Ivory2 | ececdc | LightYellow | fffedc |
| Gray68 | a5a4a3 | Ivory3 | c9c7b9 | LightYellow2 | edebcb |
| Gray69 | a9a8a6 | Ivory4 | 817d74 | LightYellow3 | c9c7aa |
| Gray70 | acaba9 | Khaki | ada96e | LightYellow4 | 827d6b |
| Gray71 | aeadac | Khaki1 | fff380 | LimeGreen | 41a317 |
| Gray72 | b1b1af | Khaki2 | ede275 | Linen | f9eee2 |
| Gray73 | b3b3b1 | Khaki3 | c9be62 | Magenta | ff00ff |
| Gray74 | b7b6b4 | Khaki4 | 827839 | Magenta1 | f43eff |
| Gray75 | b9b8b6 | Lavender | e3e4fa | Magenta2 | e238ec |
| Gray76 | bcbbba | LavenderBlush | fdeef4 | Magenta3 | c031c7 |
| Gray77 | bebebc | LavenderBlush2 | ebdde2 | Maroon | 810541 |
| Gray78 | c1c1bf | LavenderBlush3 | c8bbbe | Maroon1 | f535aa |
| Gray79 | c3c4c2 | LavenderBlush4 | 817679 | Maroon2 | e3319d |
| Gray80 | c7c7c5 | LawnGreen | 87f717 | Maroon3 | c12283 |
| Gray81 | cacac9 | LemonChiffon | fff8c6 | Maroon4 | 7d0552 |
| Gray82 | cccccb | LemonChiffon2 | ece5b6 | MediumAquamarine | 348781 |
| Gray83 | d0cfcf | LemonChiffon3 | c9c299 | MediumBlue | 152dc6 |
| Gray84 | d2d2d1 | LemonChiffon4 | 827b60 | MediumForestGreen | 347235 |
| Gray85 | d5d5d4 | LightBlue | addfff | MediumGoldenrod | ccb954 |
| Gray86 | d7d7d7 | LightBlue1 | bdedff | MediumOrchid | b048b5 |
| Gray87 | dbdbd9 | LightBlue2 | afdcec | MediumOrchid1 | d462ff |
| Gray88 | dddddc | LightBlue3 | 95b9c7 | MediumOrchid2 | c45aec |
| Gray89 | e0e0e0 | LightBlue4 | 5e767e | MediumOrchid3 | a74ac7 |
| Gray90 | e2e3e1 | LightCoral | e77471 | MediumOrchid4 | 6a287e |
| Gray91 | e5e6e4 | LightCyan | e0ffff | MediumPurple | 8467d7 |
| Gray92 | e8e9e8 | LightCyan2 | cfecec | MediumPurple1 | 9e7bff |
| Gray93 | ebebea | LightCyan3 | afc7c7 | MediumPurple2 | 9172ec |
| Gray94 | eeeeee | LightCyan4 | 717d7d | MediumPurple3 | 7a5dc7 |
| Gray95 | f0f1f0 | LightGoldenrod | ecd872 | MediumPurple4 | 4e387e |
| Gray96 | f4f4f3 | LightGoldenrod1 | ffe87c | MediumSeaGreen | 306754 |
| Gray97 | f6f6f5 | LightGoldenrod2 | ecd672 | MediumSlateBlue | 5e5a80 |
| Gray98 | f9f9fa | LightGoldenrod3 | c8b560 | MediumSpringGreen | 348017 |
| Gray99 | fbfbfb | LightGoldenrod4 | 817339 | MediumTurquoise | 48cccd |
| Gray100 | ffffff | LightGoldenrodYellow | faf8cc | MediumVioletRed | ca226b |
| Green | 00ff00 | LightPink | faafba | MidnightBlue | 151b54 |
| Green1 | 5ffb17 | LightPink1 | f9a7b0 | MintCream | f5fff9 |
| Green2 | 59e817 | LightPink2 | e799a3 | MistyRose | fde1dd |

207

## HTML Color Codes (continued)

| Color Name | Code | Color Name | Code | Color Name | Code |
|---|---|---|---|---|---|
| MistyRose2 | ead0cc | Pink3 | c48793 | SlateBlue2 | 6960ec |
| MistyRose3 | c6afac | Pink4 | 7f525d | SlateBlue3 | 574ec7 |
| MistyRose4 | 806f6c | Plum | b93b8f | SlateBlue4 | 342d7e |
| Moccasin | fde0ac | Plum1 | f9b7ff | SlateGray | 657383 |
| NavajoWhite | fddaa3 | Plum2 | e6a9ec | SlateGray1 | c2dfff |
| NavajoWhite2 | eac995 | Plum3 | c38ec7 | SlateGray2 | b4cfec |
| NavajoWhite3 | c7aa7d | Plum4 | 7e587e | SlateGray3 | 98afc7 |
| NavajoWhite4 | 806a4b | PowderBlue | addce3 | SlateGray4 | 616d7e |
| Navy | 150567 | Purple | 8e35efr | Snow | fff9fa |
| OldLace | fcf3e2 | Purple1 | 893bff | Snow2 | ece7e6 |
| OliveDrab | 658017 | Purple2 | 7f38ec | Snow3 | c8c4c2 |
| OliveDrab1 | c3fb17 | Purple3 | 6c2dc7 | Snow4 | 817c7b |
| OliveDrab2 | b5e917 | Purple4 | 461b7e | SpringGreen | 4aa02c |
| OliveDrab3 | 99c517 | Red | ff0000 | SpringGreen1 | 5efb6e |
| OliveDrab4 | 617c17 | Red1 | f62217 | SpringGreen2 | 57e964 |
| Orange | f87a17 | Red2 | e41b17 | SpringGreen3 | 4cc552 |
| Orange1 | fa9b17 | RosyBrown | b38481 | SpringGreen4 | 347c2c |
| Orange2 | e78e17 | RosyBrown1 | fbbbb9 | SteelBlue | 4863a0 |
| Orange3 | c57717 | RosyBrown2 | e8adaa | SteelBlue1 | 5cb3ff |
| Orange4 | 7f4817 | RosyBrown3 | c5908e | SteelBlue2 | 56a5ec |
| OrangeRed | f63817 | RosyBrown4 | 7f5a58 | SteelBlue3 | 488ac7 |
| OrangeRed2 | e43117 | RoyalBlue | 2b60de | SteelBlue4 | 2b547e |
| OrangeRed3 | c22817 | RoyalBlue1 | 306eff | Tan | d8af79 |
| OrangeRed4 | 7e0517 | RoyalBlue2 | 2b65ec | Tan1 | fa9b3c |
| Orchid | e57ded | RoyalBlue3 | 2554c7 | Tan2 | e78e35 |
| Orchid1 | f67dfa | RoyalBlue4 | 15317e | Thistle | d2b9d3 |
| Orchid2 | e473e7 | Salmon1 | f88158 | Thistle1 | fcdfff |
| Orchid3 | c160c3 | Salmon2 | e67451 | Thistle2 | e9cfec |
| Orchid4 | 7d387c | Salmon3 | c36241 | Thistle3 | c6aec7 |
| PaleGoldenrod | ede49e | Salmon4 | 7e3817 | Thistle4 | 806d7e |
| PaleGreen | 79d867 | SandyBrown | ee9a4d | Tomato | f75431 |
| PaleGreen1 | a0fc8d | SeaGreen | 4e8975 | Tomato2 | e54c2c |
| PaleGreen2 | 94e981 | SeaGreen1 | 6afb92 | Tomato3 | c23e17 |
| PaleGreen3 | 7dc56c | SeaGreen2 | 64e986 | Turquoise | 43c6db |
| PaleGreen4 | 4e7c41 | SeaGreen3 | 54c571 | Turquoise1 | 52f3ff |
| PaleTurquoise | aeebec | SeaGreen4 | 387c44 | Turquoise2 | 4ee2ec |
| PaleTurquoise1 | bcfeff | Seashell | fef3eb | Turquoise3 | 43bfc7 |
| PaleTurquoise2 | adebec | Seashell2 | ebe2d9 | Turquoise4 | 30787e |
| PaleTurquoise3 | 92c7c7 | Seashell3 | c8bfb6 | Violet | 8d38c9 |
| PaleTurquoise4 | 5e7d7e | Seashell4 | 817873 | VioletRed | e9358a |
| PaleVioletRed | d16587 | Sienna | 8a4117 | VioletRed1 | f6358a |
| PaleVioletRed1 | f778a1 | Sienna1 | f87431 | VioletRed2 | e4317f |
| PaleVioletRed2 | e56e94 | Sienna2 | e66c2c | VioletRed3 | c12869 |
| PaleVioletRed3 | c25a7c | Sienna3 | c35817 | VioletRed4 | 7d0541 |
| PaleVioletRed4 | 7e354d | Sienna4 | 7e3517 | Wheat | f3daa9 |
| PapayaWhip | feeccf | SkyBlue | 6698ff | Wheat1 | fee4b1 |
| PeachPuff | fcd5b0 | SkyBlue1 | 82caff | Wheat2 | ebd3a3 |
| PeachPuff2 | eac5a3 | SkyBlue2 | 79baec | Wheat3 | c8b189 |
| PeachPuff3 | c6a688 | SkyBlue3 | 659ec7 | Wheat4 | 816f54 |
| PeachPuff4 | 806752 | SkyBlue4 | 41627e | Yellow | ffff00 |
| Peru | c57726 | SlateBlue | 737ca1 | Yellow1 | fffc17 |
| Pink | faafbe | SlateBlue1 | 7369ff | YellowGreen | 52d017 |
| Pink2 | e7a1b0 | | | | |

## HTML 4.0 Tags and Attributes

This table lists alphabetically the HTML 4.0 tags approved by the World Wide Web Consortium (W3C). Most tags require an end tag to delimit the content between the start and end tag. If an end tag is optional, it is marked (O) in the following table. If an end tag is forbidden, it is marked (F). Some tags in version 4.0 are deprecated. This means that they may not be supported in future browser versions. Deprecated tags are marked (D) in the table, and they should be avoided.

Attributes that may be defined within the delimiters of a tag are listed under each tag. A tag may have any number of attributes in any order, providing they do not conflict with one another. If a variable is followed by ",—" in the table, multiple values may be used as long as they are separated by a comma. Some of the attributes that accept standard variables are listed here.

### URL
URL stands for uniform resource locator. This may take several forms, as listed below:

**directory**
(http://www.hansenmedia.com/knowledgebase)
**file**
(http://www.hansenmedia.com/knowledgebase/definitions.htm)
**specific location within a file**
(http://www.hansenmedia.com/knowledgebase/definitions.htm#html4)
This URL refers to a local position within the current page without requiring a full path name.

### Pixels
A measurement that defines the size of an area on the screen. It is expressed as a decimal number.

### Color
Either a proper color name or a code that identifies the exact color to be used to define the background color, text color, and link colors. It consists of the # symbol followed by a six-digit hexadecimal triplet, with two digits for red, two for green, and two for blue. For example, magenta is #ff00ff, cyan is #00ffff, and gold is #d4a017. Colors are designated as shown below, where "#code" represents a hexadecimal triplet.

&lt;body bgcolor="*#code*"&gt; for background color
&lt;body text="*#code*"&gt; for color of text (all non-hyperlinked items)
&lt;body link="*#code*"&gt; for color of unvisited links
&lt;body vlink="*#code*"&gt; for color of visited links
&lt;body alink="*#code*"&gt; for color of active links (while being selected)

An example in HTML: &lt;body bgcolor="#FFFF33" text="#000000" link="#FF00FF" vlink="#7F0000" alink="#7E587E"&gt;

### Frame size
The size of a frame, which may be expressed in several ways. A number represents a measurement in pixels. A percentage is used to define a portion of the width of a page.

### Alignment
Used to indicate the positioning of an image relative to surrounding text. It may also be used for positioning text on a page. Common options are left, right, center, and justified.

| HTML Tag/Attributes | Usage | Function |
|---|---|---|
| &lt;!&gt; | (F) | Indicates a comment that will not be rendered on a page |
| &lt;!DOCTYPE&gt; | (F) | Header info that defines the file format |
| HTML | | Contents are an HTML document |
| PUBLIC | | Contents are a readable document |
| *"standard"* | | Specifies the version of HTML used |
| | | Usage: &lt;!DOCTYPE HTML PUBLIC "-W3C HTML 4//EN"&gt; |
| &lt;/tag&gt; | | Ends the effect of the current tag (end tag) |

| HTML Tag/Attributes | Usage | Function |
|---|---|---|
| <A > | | Indicates an anchor (hypertext link) |
|   HREF="*URL*"> | | Marks the beginning of a link to a document |
|   NAME="*#name*"> | | Names the location on a page that becomes a target |
|   REL="*value,—*" | | The relationship of a link (jump to next target) |
|   REV="*value,—*" | | Reverses the relationship of a link (jump to previous link) |
|   TARGET="*value*" | | Displays contents of a URL in the named window |
| | | Values: NAME, _BLANK, _PARENT, _SELF, _TOP |
|   TITLE="*text*" | | Provides a name for the page that is linked |
| <ABBR> | | The abbreviated form of a term or phrase |
| <ACRONYM> | | Identifies the content as an acronym |
|   TITLE="*text*" | | Displays text rather than the acronym |
| <ADDRESS> | | Tightly formats text as a mailing address |
| <APPLET> | | Instructs browser to execute a Java applet |
|   ALIGN="*alignment*" | | Aligns horizontally and vertically (LEFT, CENTER, RIGHT) |
|   ALT="*text*" | | Text that is displayed if that applet cannot be loaded |
|   ARCHIVE="*value*" | | File name of an archive of multiple applets (extension .ZIP) |
|   CODE="*value,—*" | | Java class code file that executes the applet |
|   CODEBASE="*value*" | | Specifies the directory URL of the applet code |
|   DOWNLOAD="*value*" | | Specifies order in which images will be downloaded |
|   HEIGHT="*pixels*" | | Specifies the height of the display area in pixels |
|   HSPACE="*pixels*" | | Number of pixels spaced beside the applet displayed |
|   MAYSCRIPT | | Permits the browser to execute a JavaScript script |
|   NAME="*text*" | | Specifies a proper name for the applet |
|   STYLE="*text*" | | Specifies information about a style sheet (CSS) |
|   TITLE="*text*" | | Text to be displayed while applet is executing |
|   VSPACE="*pixels*" | | Number of pixels in the border above applet |
|   WSPACE="*pixels*" or ="%" | | Width of the display area |
| <AREA> | (F) | Describes the shape of a link on an image map |
|   ALT="*text*" | | Text displayed if image map cannot be rendered |
|   COORDS="*values*" | | The left, top, right, and bottom of the link area (required) |
|   HREF="*URL*" | | Location that is linked (required) |
|   ID="*text*" | | Refers to another location on the same page |
|   NOHREF | | This area is not a link |
|   SHAPE="*value*" | | Arranges image map values according to COORDS |
|   Values: RECT, CIRC, and POLY | | |
|   TARGET="*text*" | | Specifies window for display of named URL |
| | | Values: _BLANK, _PARENT, _SELF, _TOP |
| <B> | | Indicates that text is to be bold |
| <BASE> | (F) | Specifies defaults for all URLs in a document |
|   HREF="*URL*" | | Absolute URL of home page (base for relative URLs) |
|   TARGET="*text*" | | Defines name or type of window for BASE HREF value |
| | | Values: _BLANK, _PARENT, _SELF, _TOP |
| <BASEFONT> | | Changes default for fonts in document |
|   COLOR="*text*" | | Specifies the default font COLOR |
|   NAME="*text*" | | Specifies the default font NAME |
|   SIZE="*number*" | | Sets the default font SIZE between 0 and 7 |
| <BIG> | | Increases current font size by one |
| <BLOCKQUOTE> | | Indents specified text on both sides |

| HTML Tag/Attributes | Usage | Function |
|---|---|---|
| <BODY> | (O) | Indicates the beginning of page content |
| ALINK="*color*" | | Sets the color of all active links |
| BACKGROUND="*URL*" | | Sets an image as the page background (JPG, GIF, or PNG) |
| BGCOLOR="*color*" | | Sets a color for the background of a page |
| LINK="*color*" | | Sets the color of an unvisited link |
| TEXT="*color*" | | Sets the default color of all text |
| VLINK="*color*" | | Sets the visited link color |
| <BR> (F) | | Inserts a line break to start a new line of text |
| CLEAR=ALL | | Instructs browser to clear text around a graphic or table |
| CLEAR=LEFT | | Starts a new line below and left of image |
| CLEAR=NONE | | Clears text without respect to margins |
| CLEAR=RIGHT | | Starts a new line below and right of image |
| <CAPTION> | | Sets placement for a caption above or below a table |
| ALIGN=BOTTOM | | Places the caption below a table |
| ALIGN=TOP | | Places the caption above a table (default) |
| <CENTER> | (D) | Centers text or an image across a page |
| (Replaced by DIV align=center) | | |
| <CITE> | | Italicizes text for all citations |
| <CODE> | | Text is rendered in a mono-spaced font (program code) |
| | | (Note: Does not override BASEFONT NAME) |
| <COL> | (F) | Specifies properties of columns in a table |
| ALIGN="*alignment*" | | Specifies CENTER, LEFT, or RIGHT |
| SPAN="*number*" | | Specifies number of columns defined by COL |
| <COLGROUP> | | Specifies columns within a table cell |
| SPAN="*number*" | | Specifies the number of consecutive columns in group |
| WIDTH="*pixels*" or "% " | | Specifies width of columns inside a table cell |
| <DD> | (O) | Formats text as the definition of a term |
| <DFN> | | "Defining instance," the first usage of a term or acronym |
| <DIR> | | Formats text in a directory list, like a table of contents |
| <DIV> | | Generic container, divides paragraphs of text |
| ALIGN="*alignment*" | | Aligns text LEFT, RIGHT, or CENTER |
| <DL> | | Formats a definition list |
| COMPACT | | Reduces inter-item spacing in the list |
| <DT> | | Defined term from a definition list, aligned left |
| <EM> | | Emphasizes text (italic, usually) |
| <FIELDSET> | | Groups elements together, facilitating form processing |
| | | (LEGEND tag is used to create a caption for the FIELDSET) |
| CLASS="*text*" | | Indicates the class attribute of the element |
| STYLE="*text*" | | Specifies style sheet (CSS) information |
| TITLE="*text*" | | The title of the FIELDSET container |
| <FONT> | (D) | Specifies font attributes |
| COLOR="*color*" | | Changes the font color |
| SIZE="*number*" | | Changes the font to size (0-7) |
| SIZE=+"*number*" | | Increases font size (up to +6) |
| SIZE=-"*number*" | | Decreases font size (down to -6) |

| HTML Tag/Attributes | Usage | Function |
|---|---|---|
| <FORM> | | Structures a data input form |
| ACTION="*URL*" | | Location to which data is directed (cgi-bin) |
| ENCTYPE="*URL*" | | Specifies MIME encoding type |
| METHOD="*protocol*" | | Selects transfer protocol for submit (GET or POST) |
| ONRESET="*text*" | | Specifies event when RESET button is clicked |
| ONSUBMIT="*text*" | | Specifies event when SUBMIT button is clicked |
| TARGET="*text*" | | Displays a window with the FORM results returned |
| | | Values: _blank, _parent, _ self, _ top |
| <FRAME> | (F) | Sets the attributes for a frame, part of a FRAMESET |
| FRAMEBORDER="*value*" | | Sets visible or invisible property of frame border |
| | | Values: IE4 (1, 0); Navigator 4 (YES, NO) |
| MARGINHEIGHT="*pixels*" | | Sets the space above and below an object in a frame |
| MARGINWIDTH="*pixels*" | | Sets the space between an object and the sides of a frame |
| NAME="*frame*" | | Assigns a name to the frame |
| NORESIZE | | Prevents frame borders from being moved |
| SCROLLING="*value*" | | Allows scroll bars within a frame (YES or NO) |
| SRC="*URL*" | | Identifies contents to be places in the frame |
| <FRAMESET> | | Specifies the region of the screen to display frames |
| BORDER="*pixels*" | | Sets the width of frameset borders (default is 5) |
| COLS="*pixels*" or "*%*" | | Sets the height of the frame columns |
| ROWS="*pixels*" or "*%*" | | Sets the width of the frame rows |
| <H"*number*"> | | Sets the heading level for text (number 1-6) |
| ALIGN="*alignment*" | | Controls the headline alignment |
| | | Value: LEFT, CENTER, RIGHT |
| <HEAD> | (O) | The page header that defines document content |
| | | Usage: <HEAD > |
| | |     <META CONTENT="MOZILLA"> |
| | |     <TITLE> "This Home Page"</TITLE> |
| | |     </HEAD> |
| <HR> | (F) | Creates a horizontal rule line |
| ALIGN="*alignment*" | | Positions the rule line on the page |
| NOSHADE | | Solid line, not shaded (default is 3D shading) |
| SIZE="*pixels*" | | Sets thickness (height) of the line in pixels |
| WIDTH="*pixels*" or "*%*" | | Sets width of line in pixels or as a percentage of space |
| <HTML> | | Identifies an HTML formatted document (required) |
| | | Usage: <HTML > |
| | |     <BODY> |
| | |     <H2>This is a second level heading.</H2> |
| | |     <BODY> |
| | |     </HTML> |
| <I> | | Renders text in italic font |

| HTML Tag/Attributes | Usage | Function |
|---|---|---|
| <IFRAME> | | Specifies an inline subwindow, or floating frame (IE4) |
| ALIGN="*alignment*" | | Specifies the alignment of the IFRAME object |
| | | Values: LEFT, CENTER, RIGHT, TOP, MIDDLE, BOTTOM |
| FRAMEBORDER="*value*" | | Displays a 3D border around the IFRAME (default shows 3D) |
| | | Values: 0 (show no 3D), 1 (show 3D border) |
| HEIGHT="*pixels*" | | Specifies height of an IFRAME |
| MARGINHEIGHT="*pixels*" | | Determines vertical space between an object and edge of the frame |
| MARGINWIDTH="*pixels*" | | Determines horizontal space between text and the edge of the frame |
| SCROLLING="*value*" | | Controls whether content may scroll (default is AUTO) |
| | | Values: YES, NO, AUTO |
| SRC="*URL*" | | Displays contents of the URL named |
| WIDTH="*pixels*" | | Determines vertical dimensions of an IFRAME |
| <IMG> | (F) | Displays a graphical image |
| | | Usage: <IMG SRC="THISFILE.GIF " > |
| | | File types: GIF, JPG, PNG, XPM, XBM |
| ALIGN="*alignment*" | | Positions the image in relation to text |
| | | Values: BOTTOM, MIDDLE, LEFT, RIGHT, TOP |
| ALT="*text*" | | Text that replaces a graphic that cannot be displayed |
| BORDER="*pixels*" | | Identifies the thickness of a border around a graphic |
| | | Default shows border; set to "0" to make invisible |
| HEIGHT="*pixels*" | | Sets the vertical size of an image on a page |
| HSPACE="*pixels*" | | Sets the horizontal space cleared around an image |
| ISMAP | | The MAP is located on the server, or is server-side |
| SRC="*URL*" | | Source location of URL or file to be displayed (required) |
| USEMAP="*URL*" | | Specifies a client-side MAP, a file with the "#" prefix |
| VSPACE="*pixels*" | | Clears vertical space above and below image |
| WIDTH="*pixels*" or "*%*" | | Sets the width of an image horizontally |
| <INPUT> | (F) | Creates a form field, or input object (default is text) |
| ALIGN="*alignment*" | | Positions an input field on a page (default is TOP) |
| | | Values: BOTTOM, MIDDLE, LEFT, RIGHT, TOP |
| CHECKED | | Sets a check box or radio button to TRUE |
| MAXLENGTH="*number*" | | Sets maximum number of characters user may enter |
| NAME="*text*" | | Gives the form field a name |
| ONBLUR="*text*" | | When focus is removed from an object, JavaScript is executed |
| ONCHANGE="*text*" | | When contents of a box are changed, JavaScript is executed |
| ONFOCUS="*text*" | | When the form object receives focus, JavaScript is executed |
| ONSELECT="*text*" | | When user selects contents of a text box, JavaScript is executed |
| SIZE="*number*" | | Sets the size of a text box in characters |
| SRC="*URL*" | | Identifies an image file for a button on a form |
| TYPE=CHECKBOX | | A basic checkbox (yes/no) in the field |
| TYPE=FILE | | Directs browser to upload the specified file |
| TYPE=HIDDEN | | Field is not visible to the user |
| TYPE=IMAGE | | A graphical form submission button |
| TYPE=PASSWORD | | Text entry field in which text is not displayed |
| TYPE=RADIO | | An option select field (radio button) |
| TYPE=RESET | | A button that clears all fields |
| TYPE=SUBMIT | | A form submission button |
| TYPE=TEXT | | A standard text field with one line |
| | | (Note: Although not part of the HTML 4.0 specification, TEXTAREA creates a standard text field with multiple lines in both Navigator 4.0 and IE 4.0) |
| VALUE="*text*" | | Default value for a field (required by radio and checkboxes) |
| <INS> | | Text that has been inserted (used for revisions) |

213

| HTML Tag/Attributes | Usage | Function |
|---|---|---|
| <ISINDEX> | (F) (D) | Indicates that the document is a searchable index |
|   ACTION=*"text"* | | Sends text to specified CGI program, followed by a question mark |
|   PROMPT=*"text"* | | Substitutes specified text for the default prompt |
| <KBD> | | Text appears in a bold mono-spaced font (keyboard style) |
| <LABEL> | | Specifies label text for a form field |
| | | Usage: <FORM action="name" method="post"> |
| | |         <LABEL for="uname">Your User Name: </LABEL> |
| | |         <INPUT type="text" id="username"> |
| | |         </FORM> |
|   ACCESSKEY=*"text"* | | Accelerator key that puts the insertion point in the labeled text box |
|   CLASS=*"text"* | | Indicates that the subclass style sheet is used to render the LABEL |
|   FOR=*"text"* | | Specifies a name for the control object |
|   ID=*"text"* | | Specifies a unique value for the control element |
|   LANG=*"text"* | | Indicates the language to be rendered by the browser (fr=French) |
|   LANGUAGE=*"text"* | | Specifies scripting language used (default is JavaScript) |
| <LEGEND> | | Prescribes a fieldset legend |
|   ACCESSKEY=*"text"* | | Accelerator key that places focus on labeled control object |
|   CLASS=*"text"* | | Indicates that the sub-class style sheet is used to render the LEGEND |
|   ALIGN=*"alignment"* | | Positions specified LEGEND related to fieldset (default is LEFT) |
|   CLASS=*"text"* | | Indicates that the sub-class style sheet is used to render the LEGEND |
|   ID=*"text"* | | Specifies a unique value for the LEGEND |
|   LANG=*"text"* | | Indicates the language to be rendered by the browser (fr=French) |
|   LANGUAGE=*"text"* | | Specifies scripting language used (default is JavaScript) |
|   STYLE=*"text"* | | Specifies the way a Cascading Style Sheet (CSS) is to be used |
|   TITLE=*"text"* | | Indicates the title of the LEGEND |
|   VALIGN=*"alignment"* | | Places LEGEND above or below fieldset (TOP or BOTTOM) |
| <LI> | | The start of a new item on a list |
|   TYPE=1 | | Arabic numbers (1, 2, 3) (Default) |
|   TYPE=a | | Lowercase letters (a, b, c) |
|   TYPE=A | | Uppercase letters (A, B, C) |
|   TYPE=i | | Lowercase Roman numerals (i, ii, iii, iv) |
|   TYPE=I | | Uppercase Roman numerals (I, II, III, IV) |
|   TYPE=*"value"* | | Values: DISC, CIRCLE, SQUARE (shape of bullet symbol) |
|   VALUE=*"number"* | | Sets the first number to be used in a sequence |
| <LINK> | (F) | Specifies a location in a document or a different document |
| | | Must be used inside HEAD tags |
|   HREF=*"URL"* | | Displays specified HTML document when user clicks on LINK |
| | | (Required attribute; case sensitive to a browser) |
|   REL=*"value,—"* | | Defines relationship of the link, or location of style sheet (CSS) |
| | | Values: HOME, TOC, INDEX, GLOSSARY, COPYRIGHT, UP, NEXT, PREVIOUS, HELP |
| | | (required attribute) |
|   REV=*"URL"* | | Reverses relationship of a link; may be used to indicate author |
|   TITLE=*"URL"* | | The title of the document named in the LINK |
| <MAP> | | Defines the areas of a client-side image map that are links |
| | | (AREA tag is required to specify hot spots on the map) |
| | | NAME="name" The name of the map (required) |
| <MENU> | (D) | Identifies the beginning of a menu list |
|   COMPACT | | Forces tighter lines in a MENU |

| HTML Tag/Attributes | Usage | Function |
|---|---|---|
| <META> | | Contains information defining a page |
|   CONTENT=*"text"* | | The information contained (required) |
|   HTTP-EQUIV=*"value"* | | Relates information with an HTTPd response field to the server |
| | | Value: REFRESH (required attribute) |
|   NAME=*"text"* | | The type of information contained in the CONTENT attribute |
| <NOFRAMES> | | Specifies alternate text if browser cannot display frames |
| <NOSCRIPT> | | Specifies alternate text if JavaScript cannot be executed |
| <OBJECT> | | Embeds an object on a page |
| | | OBJECT could be an image, control, applet, or document |
|   ALIGN=*"alignment"* | | Positions the OBJECT in relation to text |
| | | Values: BASELINE, TEXTBOTTOM, MIDDLE, TEXTMIDDLE, LEFT, RIGHT, CENTER, TEXTTOP |
|   BORDER=*"pixels"* | | Identifies the thickness of invisible border around OBJECT |
| | | Default shows border; set to "0" to make invisible |
|   CODEBASE=*"URL"* | | Specifies the URL in the programming code to reference (required) |
|   DATA=*"URL"* | | Specifies the URL in the data to be accessed by OBJECT |
|   DECLARE | | Declares the OBJECT without instantiating it |
|   HEIGHT=*"pixels"* | | Sets the vertical size of an OBJECT on a page (required) |
|   HSPACE=*"pixels"* | | Sets the horizontal space cleared to the right or left of OBJECT |
|   ID | | Specifies a unique value that can be referenced elsewhere |
|   SHAPES | | Specifies that the OBJECT uses shaped hyperlinks |
|   STANDBY=*"text"* | | Text to be displayed while OBJECT is loading |
|   TYPE | | Specifies MIME type to be used by OBJECT |
|   USEMAP=*"URL"* | | Specifies a server-side MAP (filename and location) |
|   VSPACE=*"pixels"* | | Clears vertical space above and below OBJECT |
|   WIDTH=*"pixels"* or *"%"* | | Sets the width of the OBJECT horizontally |
| <OL> | | An ordered list by number or letter |
|   COMPACT | | Reduces inter-item spacing in the list |
|   START=*"number"* | | Specifies the first value to be used on the list |
|   TYPE=1 | | Arabic numbers (1, 2, 3) (default) |
|   TYPE=a | | Lowercase letters (a, b, c) |
|   TYPE=A | | Uppercase letters (A, B, C) |
|   TYPE=i | | Lowercase Roman numerals (i, ii, iii, iv) |
|   TYPE=I | | Uppercase Roman numerals (I, II, III, IV) |
| <OPTGROUP> | | Defines a group of options |
|   DISABLED | | Unavailable in this context |
|   LABEL=*"text"* | | Specifies LABEL for hierarchical group |
| <OPTION> | | Specifies a menu choice on a form |
|   DISABLED | | This choice may not be selected |
|   SELECTED | | The default choice in a list box |
|   VALUE=*"text"* | | This text is sent to the server if option is chosen |
| <P> | | A text paragraph |
|   ALIGN=*"alignment"* | | Defines how text is aligned horizontally |
| | | Values: CENTER, LEFT, RIGHT |
| <PARAM> | (F) | Passes parameters to a Java applet |
| <PRE> | | Preformatted text with spaces and line returns |
|   WIDTH=*"number"* | | Specifies the number of characters in each line |
| <Q> | | A short inline quotation |

| HTML Tag/Attributes | Usage | Function |
|---|---|---|
| <TD> | | Defines contents of a single table cell |
| ALIGN="alignment" | | Horizontal positioning of text in cell |
| | | Values: CENTER, LEFT, RIGHT |
| COLSPAN="number" | | The number of cells spanned by a column |
| HEIGHT="number" or "%" | | Cell height in pixels or as a percentage of table |
| NOWRAP | | No line breaks allowed in the cell |
| ROWSPAN="number" | | Number of table rows covered by the cell |
| VALIGN="alignment" | | Vertical positioning of text inside a cell |
| | | Values: BASELINE, TOP, MIDDLE, BOTTOM |
| WIDTH="pixels" or "%" | | Cell width in pixels or as a percentage of the table |
| <TEXTAREA> | | A text field with multiple lines in a form |
| COLS="number" | | The width of the field, in characters (required) |
| NAME="name" | | The name of the field (required) |
| ROWS="number" | | The height of the field, in characters (required) |
| <TFOOT> | | Renders a table footer, useful when printing multiple pages |
| <TH> | | Renders a table header cell (bold text by default) |
| ALIGN="alignment" | | Horizontal positioning of text in cell |
| | | Values: CENTER, LEFT, RIGHT |
| COLSPAN="number" | | The width of the table header in characters |
| HEIGHT="pixels" or "%" | | Cell height in pixels or as a percentage of table |
| NOWRAP | | No line breaks allowed in the cell |
| ROWSPAN="number" | | Number of table rows covered by the cell |
| VALIGN="alignment" | | Vertical positioning of text inside a cell |
| | | Values: BASELINE, TOP, MIDDLE, BOTTOM |
| WIDTH="pixels" or "%" | | Cell width in pixels or as a percentage of the table |
| <THEAD> | | Renders a page header before body of table (on each printed page) |
| <TITLE> | | Defines the title of the page shown in the title bar |
| <TR> | | Defines a table row |
| ALIGN="alignment" | | Horizontal positioning of text in cell |
| | | Values: CENTER, LEFT, RIGHT |
| VALIGN="alignment" | | Vertical positioning of text inside a cell |
| | | Values: BASELINE, BOTTOM, MIDDLE, TOP |
| <TT> | | Renders text in a fixed-width font (like a teletype) |
| | | Same as SAMP or CODE designation |
| <U> | (D) | Renders text underlined |
| <UL> | | Unordered list |
| TYPE"value" | | Substitutes a symbol for the standard bullet |
| | | Values: CIRCLE, DISC, SQUARE |
| <VAR> | | Renders text in a small fixed-width font for program variables |
| CLASS="text" | | Indicates the subclass to which element belongs |
| ID="text" | | Specifies a unique value for the element |
| LANG="text" | | Indicates the language to be rendered by the browser (fr=French) |
| LANGUAGE="text" | | Specifies scripting language used (default is JavaScript) |
| STYLE="text" | | Specifies the way a Cascading Style Sheet (CSS) is to be used |
| TITLE="text" | | Title placed in the FIELDSET container |
| <WBR> | | Allows a "word break," overriding a <NOBR> instruction |

## HTML Coded Characters

| Symbol | Code | Description |
|---|---|---|
| | &#09; | Horizontal tab |
| | &#10: | Line feed |
| | &#13; | Carriage Return |
| | &#32; | Space |
| ! | &#33; | Exclamation mark |
| " | &#34; | Quotation mark |
| # | &#35; | Number sign |
| $ | &#36; | Dollar sign |
| % | &#37; | Percent sign |
| & | &#38; | Ampersand |
| ' | &#39; | Apostrophe |
| ( | &#40; | Left parenthesis |
| ) | &#41; | Right parenthesis |
| * | &#42; | Asterisk |
| + | &#43; | Plus sign |
| , | &#44; | Comma |
| - | &#45; | Hyphen |
| . | &#46; | Period (fullstop) |
| / | &#47; | Solidus (slash) |
| | &#48;–  &#57; | Digits 0–9 |
| : | &#58; | Colon |
| ; | &#59; | Semi-colon |
| < | &#60; | Less than |
| = | &#61; | Equals sign |
| > | &#62; | Greater than |
| ? | &#63; | Question mark |
| @ | &#64; | Commercial at |
| | &#65;–  &#90; | Letters A–Z (upper case) |
| [ | &#91; | Left square bracket |
| \ | &#92; | Reverse solidus (backslash) |
| ] | &#93; | Right square bracket |
| ^ | &#94; | Caret |
| _ | &#95; | Horizontal bar (underscore) |
| ` | &#96; | Grave accent |
| | &#97;–  &#122; | Letters a–z (lower case) |
| { | &#123; | Left curly brace |
| \| | &#124; | Vertical bar |
| } | &#125; | Right curly brace |
| ~ | &#126; | Tilde |
| |   | Non-breaking Space |
| ¡ | &#161; | Inverted exclamation |
| ¢ | &#162; | ; Cent sign |
| £ | &#163; | ; Pound sterling |
| ¤ | &#164; | ; General currency sign |
| ¥ | &#165; | ; Yen sign |
| ¦ | &#166; | ; Broken vertical bar |
| § | &#167; | ; Section sign |
| ¨ | &#168; | ; Umlaut (dieresis) |
| © | &#169; | ; Copyright |
| ª | &#170; | ; Feminine ordinal |
| « | &#171; | ; Left angle quote, guillemet left |

| Symbol | Code | Description |
|---|---|---|
| ¬ | &#172; | Not sign |
| | &#173; | Soft hyphen |
| ® | &#174; | Registered trademark |
| ¯ | &#175; | Macron accent |
| ° | &#176; | Degree sign |
| ± | &#177; | Plus or minus |
| ² | &#178; | Superscript two |
| ³ | &#179; | Superscript three |
| ´ | &#180; | Acute accent |
| µ | &#181; | Micro sign |
| ¶ | &#182; | Paragraph sign |
| · | &#183; | Middle dot |
| ¸ | &#184; | Cedilla |
| ¹ | &#185; | Superscript one |
| º | &#186; | Masculine ordinal |
| » | &#187; | Right angle quote, guillemet right |
| ¼ | &#188; | Fraction one-fourth |
| ½ | &#189; | Fraction one-half |
| ¾ | &#190; | Fraction three-fourths |
| ¿ | &#191; | Inverted question mark |
| À | &#192; | Capital A, grave accent |
| Á | &#193; | Capital A, acute accent |
| Â | &#194; | Capital A, circumflex accent |
| Ã | &#195; | Capital A, tilde |
| Ä | &#196; | Capital A, dieresis or umlaut mark |
| Å | &#197; | Capital A, ring |
| Æ | &#198; | Capital AE diphthong (ligature) |
| Ç | &#199; | Capital C, cedilla |
| È | &#200; | Capital E, grave accent |
| É | &#201; | Capital E, acute accent |
| Ê | &#202; | Capital E, circumflex accent |
| Ë | &#203; | Capital E, dieresis or umlaut mark |
| Ì | &#204; | Capital I, grave accent |
| Í | &#205; | Capital I, acute accent |
| Î | &#206; | Capital I, circumflex accent |
| Ï | &#207; | Capital I, dieresis or umlaut mark |
| Ð | &#208; | Capital Eth, Icelandic |
| Ñ | &#209; | Capital N, tilde |
| Ò | &#210; | Capital O, grave accent |
| Ó | &#211; | Capital O, acute accent |
| Ô | &#212; | Capital O, circumflex accent |
| Õ | &#213; | Capital O, tilde |
| Ö | &#214; | Capital O, dieresis or umlaut mark |
| × | &#215; | Multiply sign |
| Ø | &#216; | Capital O, slash |
| Ù | &#217; | Capital U, grave accent |
| Ú | &#218; | Capital U, acute accent |

| Symbol | Code | Description | Symbol | Code | Description |
|---|---|---|---|---|---|
| Û | &#219; | Capital U, circumflex accent | í | &#237; | Small i, acute accent |
| Ü | &#220; | Capital U, dieresis or umlaut mark | î | &#238; | Small i, circumflex accent |
| Ý | &#221; | Capital Y, acute accent | ï | &#239; | Small i, dieresis or umlaut mark |
| Þ | &#222; | Capital Thorn, Icelandic | ð | &#240; | Small eth, Icelandic |
| ß | &#223; | Small sharp s, German (sz ligature) | ñ | &#241; | Small n, tilde |
| à | &#224; | Small a, grave accent | ò | &#242; | Small o, grave accent |
| á | &#225; | Small a, acute accent | ó | &#243; | Small o, acute accent |
| â | &#226; | Small a, circumflex accent | ô | &#244; | Small o, circumflex accent |
| ã | &#227; | Small a, tilde | õ | &#245; | Small o, tilde |
| ä | &#228; | Small a, dieresis or umlaut mark | ö | &#246; | Small o, dieresis or umlaut mark |
| å | &#229; | Small a, ring | ÷ | &#247; | Division sign |
| æ | &#230; | Small ae diphthong (ligature) | ø | &#248; | Small o, slash |
| ç | &#231; | Small c, cedilla | ù | &#249; | Small u, grave accent |
| è | &#232; | Small e, grave accent | ú | &#250; | Small u, acute accent |
| é | &#233; | Small e, acute accent | û | &#251; | Small u, circumflex accent |
| ê | &#234; | Small e, circumflex accent | ü | &#252; | Small u, dieresis or umlaut mark |
| ë | &#235; | Small e, dieresis or umlaut mark | ý | &#253; | Small y, acute accent |
| ì | &#236; | Small i, grave accent | þ | &#254; | Small thorn, Icelandic |
| | | | ÿ | &#255; | Small y, dieresis or umlaut mark |

**HTML Coded Characters** (continued)

**hue, saturation, and value** (HSV) (n.) A system of defining colors.

**Huffman coding** (n.) A data compression technique outlined in a paper by D. A. Huffman in 1952. Huffman coding varies the length of an encoded symbol in proportion to its information content. The more frequently a symbol or token is used in a data file, the shorter the binary string must be that represents it in the compressed stream. Huffman codes can be properly decoded because they obey the prefix property, which means that no code can be a prefix of another code. Therefore the complete set of codes can be represented as a binary tree, known as a *Huffman tree*.

**hum components** (n.) The first few harmonics of the alternating current (AC) frequency. In much of the Western Hemisphere, Japan, Tai- wan, Korea and the Philippines a 60-Hz system is used, producing 2nd and 3rd harmonics at 120 Hz and 180 Hz. In most other countries using 50-Hz AC, hum components resonate at 100 Hz and 150 Hz.

**HVAC** (n.) 1. In the construction trade, HVAC is the heating, ventilating, and air conditioning system of a building. 2. In electrical engineering, HVAC refers to high-voltage alternating current.

**hybrid** (n., adj.) 1. A combination of two diverse or competing systems that are interoperable. 2. In telecommunications, an interface box that converts a data signal traveling on two pairs (one pair for each direction of the signal) into a single pair. Conversely, it may perform the reverse operation, from one pair to two pairs. All long distance circuits consist of two pairs, and most local circuits consist of one pair. It is named for a "hybrid coil" in the telephone whose function is to keep the send and receive signals separate. 3. In telephony, an induction coil and related circuitry at a central office (CO) used to interface a two-wire local loop to a four-wire circuit, allowing for the physical separation and isolation of the send and receive signals.

**hybrid disc** (n.) 1. A CD-ROM that is in the logical disc format and that contains both ISO 9660 and Hierarchical File System (HFS) data structures, so that it is readable by both Windows and the Mac OS. 2. A multisession disc. *Hybrid disc* is the term usually used for a CD-ROM in the Orange Book format. Developed by Philips and Eastman Kodak, this format allows information to be added to previously recorded data. A Kodak Photo-CD is an example.

**hybrid fiber-coax** (HFC) (n.) Network topology for cable television that consists of combined fiber-optic feeders and traditional coaxial cables with amplifiers in the branch lines. Several telecommunications companies have implemented the HFC broadband network topology because it is affordable and scalable.

**HyperCard** (n.) An interactive authoring environment developed by Apple Computer. HyperTalk is HyperCard's scripting language that consists of English language commands and that creates links between words, buttons, and diverse media. HyperCard programs (stacks) consist of frames (cards) with routines (scripts). External commands (XCMDs) and external functions (XFCNs) are used to extend functionality.

**hyperlink** (n.) Often simply called a *link,* a connection between two points in a hypertext document or between different documents. A

browser displays a hyperlink with colored or specially formatted text. When a hyperlink is activated by a mouse click, the browser immediately seeks and displays the target of the link.

**hypermedia** (n.) Another word for *multimedia, new media,* or *digital media.* It refers to a dimensional environment with text, graphics, audio, animation, and video elements that are all linked to other elements.

**HyperTalk** (n.) The scripting language used in HyperCard.

**hypertext** (n.) Indexed words that are linked to graphics, audio, or other words not located nearby. Theodore Nelson is credited with the first usage of the term in 1965. Like the strands of a spiderweb, hypertext links connect HTML pages on the World Wide Web.

**Hypertext Markup Language** (HTML) (n.) A set of commands for marking a document so that it can be read by a web browser, such as Netscape Navigator. All home pages on the World Wide Web are HTML documents. HTML is a subset of Standard Generalized Markup Language (SGML). HTML codes, or tags, specify the function of a text string (title, heading, body, etc.), but they do not instruct a parser on how to display information. As a result, various browsers format documents differently.

**Hypertext Transfer Protocol** (HTTP) (n.) The client-server TCP/IP used for exchanging HTML documents on the World Wide Web. Version 1.1, defined by RFC 2068 in May 1997, offers major improvements over the original, which was version 1.0.

**Hypertext Transfer Protocol, Secure** (HTTPS) (n.) The Netscape variation of HTTP used to process secure transactions. The Navigator browser supports HTTPS, which is a special URL access method for connecting to HTTP servers using Secure Sockets Layer (SSL). The Internet Assigned Numbers Authority (IANA) has designated the default HTTPS port number as 443.

**Hz** See *hertz.*

# I

**IAB** See *Internet Architecture Board*.

**IANA** See *Internet Assigned Numbers Authority*.

**IAP** See *Internet Access Provider*.

**I-beam** (n.) The cursor shape in a graphical user interface (GUI) that identifies the location on the screen where characters will appear in a text-entry mode.

**IBM-compatible** (adj.) Describes a personal computer that runs MS-DOS and that is often referred to as a PC, as opposed to a Macintosh.

**IBM PC** (n.) International Business Machines Personal Computer; generic term for any microcomputer based on the Intel family of microprocessors: 8086, 8088, 80286, 80386, 80486, or Pentium. The speed of the central processing unit (CPU) is the most significant factor in performance, determined by clock rate and the number of bits the CPU can process internally.

**IBM PC AT** (n.) A version of the IBM PC released in August 1984 with an Intel 80286 processor, a 16-bit bus, a 1.2-megabyte (MB) floppy disk drive, and a larger case than the original PC had.

**IBM PC XT** (n.) An IBM-compatible personal computer that was released in March 1983 with an Intel 8088 processor. The XT 286 version was released in September 1986 with an Intel 80286 processor and an eight-bit bus.

**IBM PS/2** (n.) IBM Personal System/2; an IBM-compatible personal computer that replaced the IBM PC series in 1987. It used 8088, 80286, or 80386 processors and implemented IBM's Micro Channel Bus. It ran MS-DOS and OS/2 operating systems, and was compatible with most PC programs at the time.

**IC** See *integrated circuit*.

**ICIA** See *International Communications Industries Association*.

**ICMP** See *Internet Control Message Protocol*.

**icon** (n.) Any graphic symbol that represents an object, function, or task. Most often, it represents a file or application in a graphical user interface (GUI). When the cursor appears on top of an icon, a mouse click will generally initiate an action.

**ICT** See *Integrated Computer Telephony*.

**ICW** See *interactive courseware*.

**ID** (n.) Abbreviation for identification.

I-D See *Internet-Draft.*

IDE See *Integrated Drive Electronics.*

IDEA See *International Data Encryption Algorithm.*

iDEN See *integrated Digital Enhanced Network.*

IDIOT See *Intrusion Detection In Our Time.*

IDN See *Integrated Digital Network.*

IDSL See *ISDN digital subscriber line.*

IEC See *International Electrotechnical Commission.*

IEEE See *Institute of Electrical and Electronics Engineers.*

IEEE 802 (n.) A set of standards commonly used for local area networks (LANs) and metropolitan area networks (MANs). The 802 standards divide the data link layer into two sublayers. The first of these is the medium access control (MAC) layer, defined in 802.3, 802.5, and 802.6. MAC defines specific methods by which access may be gained to a LAN, including Ethernet random access and IBM token ring. The second sublayer is the Logical Link Control (LLC) layer, defined in 802.2. LLC addresses the processes of establishing and terminating services as well as data transfer. The three types of links described in LLC are the acknowledged connectionless link, the unacknowledged connectionless link, and the connection-mode link. The 802 specifications refer to the following network features:

- IEEE 802.1: The general architecture of LANs and internets, known as the spanning tree algorithm.

- IEEE 802.11: The standard for wireless LANs and networks.

- IEEE 802.2: The standard for frames of data sent over Ethernet, token ring, and other types of LANs.

- IEEE 802.3: The standard for carrier sense multiple access with collision detection (CSMA/CD) used in 10-megabit-per-second (Mbps) Ethernet.

- IEEE 802.4: The standard for the physical layer of a LAN with token-passing access on a bus topology.

- IEEE 802.5: The standard for the physical layer of a LAN with token-passing access on a ring topology using unshielded twisted-pair wiring.

- IEEE 802.6: The standard for metropolitan area networks (MANs), also known as distributed queue dual bus (DQDB).

IEEE 802.3 (n.) The standard defining the hardware layer and transport layer of Ethernet. The maximum packet size is 1518 bytes, and the maximum segment length is 500 meters. The maximum total length is 2.5 km, and the maximum number of hosts is 1024.

IEEE 488 (n.) An eight-bit parallel bus that allows up to 15 intelligent devices to share a single bus. Used primarily for test equipment, the IEEE 488 has a maximum data rate of about 1 megabit per second (Mbps). Also known as *General Purpose Interface Bus (GPIB)* or *Hewlett-Packard Interface Bus (HP-IB).*

IEEE 1394 See *FireWire* or *high-performance serial bus.*

**IESG** See *Internet Engineering Steering Group.*

**IETF** See *Internet Engineering Task Force.*

**IFF** See *Interchange File Format.*

**I-frame** (n.) (Intraframe) A complete MPEG frame containing the entire image, equivalent to a "keyframe" in QuickTime or AVI. See *intracoded frame.*

**IGES** See *Initial Graphics Exchange Specification.*

**IGP** See *Interior Gateway Protocol.*

**IIA** See *Information Industry Association.*

**IICS** See *International Interactive Communications Society.*

**IIR filter** See *Infinite Impulse-Response filter.*

**i-Link** (n.) The name created by Sony Corporation for their implementation of the IEEE 1394 standard in their digital imaging equipment. See *Firewire.*

**illegal character** (n.) A character that may not be used in a command or statement because it is reserved for another use. For example, an MS-DOS file name may not contain a period, because the operating system uses that character to separate the file name from its extension.

**IM** See *Instant Messaging.*

**IMA** See *Interactive Multimedia Association* or *International MIDI Association.*

**IMA audio compression** (n.) A 4:1 compression audio codec that is used to reduce the size of 16-bit sound files. When this form of compression is applied to an audio file, it is simply referred to as IMA. The standard was developed by the Interactive Multimedia Association (IMA).

**image** (n.) A collection of graphical data representing a two-dimensional scene. An image is composed of pixels arranged in an array. The pixels contain information representing the brightness and color of the image at that point, most often encoded as RGB triplets. The term is generally applied to a representation of existing objects that have been photographed and scanned digitally.

**image impedance** (n.) In an audio system, this is the level that will simultaneously terminate all of a network's inputs and outputs in both directions equally, so that input and output impedances "see" their own "image."

**image map** (n.) A graphic in an HTML document. When the mouse is clicked inside active areas of the image map, they act as links to other locations in the same way that hypertext links function.

**image parameters** (n.) The basic network functions, particularly image impedance and image transfer functions that are used to design or describe a filter.

**image processing** (n.) The manipulation of data to produce a display or to alter a previously defined graphic using digital means.

**imaging** (n.) 1. The process of digitizing graphics captured by a camera. 2. The process of recording images digitally on film, tape, CD-ROM, or disk.

**IMAP** See *Internet Message Access Protocol.*

**IMD** See *intermodulation distortion.*

**i-Mode** (information mode) (n.) A packet-based information service for mobile phones developed in Japan by NTT DoCoMo and in operation February 1999. It was the first technology to provide Internet access from cellular phones. The i-Mode language is a compact version of HTML, and it does not use the standard wireless application protocol (WAP). A version of i-Mode that does support the WAP standard is under development, which will make it compatible with wireless network structure in the U.S.

**impedance** (n.) A measure of the complex resistive and reactive attributes of a component in an alternating-current (AC) circuit. Impedance restricts current flow in an AC circuit, but it is not relevant in direct current (DC) circuits. In DC circuits, resistors limit current flow. In AC circuits, inductors and capacitors similarly limit AC current flow, because of their reactance. Impedance is similar to resistance, with certain qualifications. Impedance is the sum of the resistance *and* reactance in a circuit or device. Like resistance, reactance is measured in ohms, but it is frequency-dependant. Impedance may be considered the sum total of all current limiting ohms in a circuit. In an AC circuit phase shift exists, and the voltage and current are rarely in phase due to the storage effects (charging and discharging) of capacitors and inductors. Reactance is complex, since it has a resistive component and an elusive component of phase shift. *Resistance* has no phase shift; *reactance* in an AC circuit with capacitors and inductors includes phase shift; and *impedance* is the sum of resistance and reactance.

**import** (v.) To move data into an open file from memory. The data may be any compatible file type, such as a graphic, and it may be exported from a different application. For example, an AIFF sound file may be imported into a Macromedia Director movie and either linked to the movie or combined with all the other assets in the movie file.

**IMT 2000** See *International Mobile Telecommunications 2000.*

**in-band signaling** (n.) In telecommunications, a type of signaling consisting of tones within the voice frequency band that are carried along the same circuit as the voice path. Most telephone signals, such as request for service, dialing, and disconnect, are in-band signals.

**in-betweening** (n.) A function incorporated in some computer animation programs that automatically draws images on the screen to simulate motion between two coordinates. Also called *tweening.*

**inches per second** (ips) (n.) The running speed of an audio tape player, such as 3.75, 7.5, or 15 ips.

**incremental backup** (n.) An archival procedure that copies only files that have changed since the last backup was performed. It is a common way to save recent work from a hard disk to a floppy disk without saving information that has been archived in a full backup.

**Indeo** (n.) A family of video codecs developed by Intel that apply temporal and spatial compression, as well as data rate limiting. Indeo is typically used to compress Video for Windows and QuickTime files for CD-ROM delivery.

**indexed color system** (n.) A procedure for defining color information that obtains data from a descriptive file and that points to a table of output colors called a *color look-up table (CLUT).*

**individualized instruction** (adj.) Describes software that modifies the teaching approach or content based on student feedback in order to optimize learning.

**inductance** (n.) The ability of a coil of wire, or inductor, to block high-frequency signals from flowing through it. Inductance is measured in henrys (H).

**industrial market** (n.) The segment of video and multimedia markets that addresses training, marketing, sales, and communications for businesses rather than for home consumers. Compare *consumer market* or *domestic market*.

**Industrial, Scientific and Medical band** (ISM Band) (n.) A band of frequencies in the range of 2.4 GHz allocated by the FCC. Operators are not required to hold a license to use this bandwidth, but the equipment they use must be licensed. The ISM Band is used for Bluetooth links between devices and networks, for LAN-to-LAN bridging, and for Internet services.

**Industry Standard Architecture** (ISA, pronounced "EYE-suh") (n.) The name for a common expansion bus architecture in an IBM-compatible PC, which has been replaced by the PCI bus in recent years.

**inference engine** (n.) A program that infers new information from known facts using inference rules. An expert system or a knowledge-based system usually includes such an engine.

**inference rule** (n.) A method of combining known facts to arrive at new facts. For example, if Spot is a dog, and if all dogs have four legs, we can infer that Spot has four legs. It is possible to express the rule in Boolean algebra as (A & A => B) => B. This is to say that if proposition A is true, and if A implies B, then proposition B is also true. An inference rule can also be used to imply conditional status. For example, either the sun is shining or it is dark outside. If the sun is not shining, we can infer that it is dark. This rule may be written ((A OR B) & NOT B) => A. This is to say that if either A is true or B is true (or both), and if B is false, then A must be true.

**Infinite Impulse-Response filter** (IIR filter) (n.) A widely employed digital filter that accepts the input of digitized samples of an audio signal. Each output point is computed on the basis of a weighted sum of previous output (feedback) levels, as well as previous input values.

**infinite loop** (n.) In programming, a segment of a program that is executed repeatedly without stopping. This type of program is used to control an embedded system that is intended to run continuously until it is stopped or interrupted.

**Information Industry Association** (IIA) (n.) Established in 1968, the IIA is an organization that represents more than 550 companies involved in creating, distributing, and facilitating the use of information in print and digital formats. The IIA addresses the industry's interests in government policy and regulatory matters; promotes the industry and provides advance information about new developments and emerging technologies; and provides a business development forum for interaction among top executives in the information industry.

**infotainment** (n.) Interactive CD-ROM programs that blend entertainment with informational and educational activities.

**infrared** (n.) A spectrum of electromagnetic radiation with wavelengths that are longer than

225

visible light waves but shorter than microwaves. The infrared bandwidth lies between 0.75 and 1000 microns. This spectrum is used for fiber-optic transmission and for through-the-air transmission for short distances. Remote control devices typically rely on infrared technology.

**Infrared Data Association** (IrDA) (n.) An organization dedicated to developing standards for wireless, infrared transmission systems between computers. It was founded in 1993 and is based in Walnut Creek, California. IrDA products, which require line-of-sight transmission, began to appear in 1995. IrDA operates at the Serial IR physical layer (IrDA-SIR), which allows a half-duplex connection at up to 115.2 kbps. This speed allows the use of a common UART chip. Faster non-UART extensions for 1.15 mbps and 4 mbps have been defined. IrDA uses the Infrared Link Access Protocol (IrLAP) as a data link protocol. The Infrared Link Management Protocol (IrLMP) is also used to provide a mechanism for multiplexing two or more different data streams simultaneously. Devices with an IrDA port can send and receive commands and information between each other, eliminating the need for a physical interface. For example, a laptop, a PDA, or a desktop computer can use a printer with an IrDA port without a connecting cable.

**infrasonic** (adj.) Describes waves or vibrations with frequencies below that of audible sound.

**inheritance** (n.) In object-oriented programming (OOP), the capacity to derive new classes from existing classes. A derived class (subclass) inherits the instance variables and methods of the base class (superclass), and it may add new instance variables and methods of its own. New methods may be defined with the same names as those in the base class; in that case, the new methods override the original ones.

**in-house** (adj.) Describes production or development conducted in a company or organization without external resources, facilities, or consultants. Developing media in-house is the opposite of outsourcing production.

**INI file** (n.) A file with the extension .ini that contains data specific to a certain application in Microsoft Windows, usually defining the configuration and default settings for the application. Pronounced "IH-nee FILE."

**INIT** (n.) In the Mac OS, a utility program that initializes on startup. Conflicting INITs may cause the mouse to freeze and the system to crash. To avoid this, a user can start a Macintosh while holding down the Shift key, which disables all INITs. They may be enabled one by one until the conflict is isolated. Pronounced "ih-NIT."

**Initial Graphics Exchange Specification** (IGES) (n.) A cross-platform format for computer-aided design (CAD) programming. IGES is an industry standard defined by the American National Standards Institute (ANSI).

**initialization** (n.) A set of routines run by a device or program. Blank media must be initialized for the platform on which they will be used. If media with data stored on them are initialized, the data is eliminated. Printers on a network must be initialized for access. Microcomputers set up registers and memory locations on initialization.

**injection molding** (n.) The process of forcing melted plastic (polycarbonate) into a precast form. This is the method used to create the substrate of a compact disc.

**inline image** (n.) A graphic image displayed as a component of an HTML document among lines of text. Images are compressed in the GIF, JPEG, or PNG format. The image is called by a statement in HTML text similar to the following:

<IMG SRC=Image.gif>

**inline mixer** (n.) The typical narrow vertical strip format for each input channel on medium and large audio mixing consoles. Non-inline designs are rack-mount mixers, usually 19 inches wide and designed for standard rack cases.

**in-point** (n.) The first frame of a video segment or the beginning of an audio track that is chosen for editing.

**input** 1. (v.) To send information to a computer or processor. 2. (n.) The data sent to a processor or storage device. 3. (n.) A terminal, jack, or receptacle provided for the introduction of an electrical signal into a device.

**insert editing** (n.) Postproduction technique in which new video or audio material is inserted into preexisting material on a master tape. The time code is not altered. Compare *assemble editing*.

**insertion loss** (n.) A drop in voltage or power, as measured in decibels, resulting from placing an attenuator pad between a power source and its load impedance. It is expressed as the ratio of the voltage absorbed in the load without the pad to that when the pad is inserted. For example, if the voltage across a load is 10 volts without a pad, and is reduced to 5 volts with the pad, the insertion loss may be expressed as 6 dB.

**insertion point** (n.) The position on a screen where a cursor is blinking and where charac-

ters are entered when typed.

**insert loop** (n.) On a mixing board, an insert loop is a special input/output (I/O) point utilizing a single tip-ring-sleeve (TRS) jack following the convention of *tip = send, ring = return*, and *sleeve = ground*. The insert loop is used to patch in an outboard processor using a single cable with unbalanced line wiring. A stereo insert loop requires two jacks.

**inside wiring** (n.) Connecting cables that belong to a telephone company customer, located between the demarcation point and the telephone equipment in a home or office. It typically consists of copper twisted pairs.

**instantiation** (n.) 1. In programming, the production of an object by replacing variables with new values or other variables. 2. In object-oriented programming (OOP), the production of a particular object from its class template. This means that a structure is allocated with the types specified by the template and that instance variables are initialized with either default values or those provided by the class's constructor function.

**Instant Messaging** (IM) (n.) A realtime email conversation between two or more parties while they are logged on to an Internet service at the same time. Several Internet services, including America online (AOL) and Microsoft network (MSN), provide IM at no charge.

**Institute of Electrical and Electronics Engineers** (IEEE, pronounced "eye-triple-EE") (n.) The largest technical professional society in the world. Founded in 1884 and based in the United States, it has more than 325 000 members in 147 countries. Technical conferences and symposia are sponsored around the world in electrical, electronics, and computer engineering, as well as in computer science. Disciplines include aerospace, computers, communications, biomedical technology, electric power, and consumer electronics.

**instructional design** (n.) Teaching methodology with a detailed plan for learning activities. Designers of interactive instructional programs address such issues as questioning strategy, levels of interaction, reinforcement, and branching routines.

**instructional designer** (n.) A developer of educational training programs.

**Instructional Systems Design** (ISD) (n.) The planning and pedagogy employed to develop an effective student-centered learning program. System components include computer hardware, software, and networks.

**Instructional Television Fixed Service** (ITFS) (n.) A broadcast system that operates in a specified band of microwave frequencies exclusively established by the Federal Communications Commission (FCC) for educational programs. ITFS operates when the transmitter and receiver are within the "line of sight," a radius of approximately 20 miles. A special converter is required to receive and translate the broadcast audio, video, or data into standard television signals.

**instrument-level** See *level.*

**integrated circuit** (IC, pronounced "eye-SEE") (n.) A self-contained circuit module that passes electric current along predetermined paths. The circuit is created by arranging chemicals on the surface of a semiconductor, such as crystalline silicone. ICs may contain transistors, resistors, and many other types of processing components in their circuitry. There are several levels of ICs, categorized as follows:

- small-scale integration (SSI): 2–9 circuits

- medium-scale integration (MSI): 10–99 circuits.

- large-scale integration (LSI): 100–999 circuits.

- very large-scale integration (VLSI): 1000–9999 circuits.

- ultra large-scale integration (ULSI): more than 10 000 circuits.

**Integrated Computer Telephony** (ICT) (n.) A system that combines data communications with telecommunications. It involves the convergence of technologies such as Voice over IP (VoIP), call centers, and combined voice/data/video/fax transmission over broadband networks.

**integrated Digital Enhanced Network** (iDEN) (n.) Developed by Motorola, iDEN is based on time division multiple access (TDMA). It is an enhanced digital technology that allows users to access voice calls, data, short messages, two-way radio transmissions, and pager messages using a single wireless device. Services are available in North America from Nextel, and in South America as well as parts of Asia. iDEN phones operate at 800 MHz.

**Integrated Digital Network** (IDN) (n.) In telephony, IDN is the coordination of digital transmission, digital switching, and protocols in a circuit switched data network. IDN refers to digital networks other than integrated standard digital network (ISDN).

**Integrated Drive Electronics** (IDE) (n.) An interface standard based on the IBM PC ISA 16-bit bus for fixed disks that identifies the power and data signal interfaces between the motherboard and the integrated disk controller and drive. The IDE bus supports two devices, a master and a slave. Compaq invented the IDE bus in 1986 in collaboration with Western Digital, Imprimis, and Conner Peripherals. The first draft of a codified specification appeared in March 1989, and a finished version known then as the Advanced Technology Attachment (ATA) was sent to ANSI for ratification in November 1990. In multimedia applications, SCSI is preferred over the IDE interface, because SCSI is faster and allows more devices to be connected than IDE.

**Integrated Services Digital Network** (ISDN) (n.) An international digital telecommunications standard that accommodates voice, data, and signaling and that brings high bandwidth to the microcomputer desktop. The typical Basic Rate Interface (BRI) uses two common twisted pairs, unshielded, to deliver two 64-kilobit-per-second (Kbps) bearer B-channels and one data-signaling D-channel at 16 Kbps. The two bearer channels may be used simultaneously. The telephone connection may be approximately one mile away from the central office switch, which limits access to those in proximity of a switch. The Primary Rate Interface (PRI) carries 24 bearer channels and a 64-Kbps data channel with a capacity of nearly two megabits per second (Mbps). Among European countries, a Memorandum of Understanding (MOU) has been established that defines "Priority 1" ISDN facilities and services as follows:

- CLIP    Calling line identification presentation (displays the caller's number)

- CLIR    Calling line identification restriction (prevents the caller's number from displaying)

- DDI    Direct dialing in (to an individual user on a private exchange)

- MSN    Multiple subscriber number

- TP    Terminal portability

"Priority 2" ISDN facilities and services are defined as follows:

- AOC    Advice of charge

- CCBS    Completion of calls to busy subscriber

- CD    Call deflection

- CFB    Call forwarding busy

- CFNR    Call forwarding no reply

- CFU    Call forwarding unconditional

- COLP    Connected line identification presentation

- COLR    Connected line identification restriction

- CONF    Add-on conference call

- CUG    Closed user group

- CWL    Call waiting

- ECT    Explicit call transfer

- FPH    Freephone supplementary service

- HOLD    Call hold

- MCID    Malicious call identification

- MMC   Meet me conference

- SUB   Subaddressing

- 3PTY   Three-party service

- UUS   User-to-user signaling

**intellectual property** (n.) Content or knowledge that may be protected by copyright. Protection of the owner's rights to intellectual property has become a significant concern in multimedia, given the ease with which content can be digitized and transferred.

**interactive courseware** (ICW) (n.) The term used by the U.S. military for software used with computer-based training. ICW relies on interaction with the trainee to determine the pacing and sequence of a course of instruction.

**interactive laser disc levels** (n.) Three degrees of interactivity that were proposed by the Nebraska Videodisc Design/Production Group in 1980. They are as follows:

- Level 1: A consumer-model player with freeze-frame, picture stop, chapter stop, frame address, and dual-channel audio, but with limited memory and processing power.

- Level 2: An industrial-model player with Level 1 features plus programmable memory and faster access time.

- Level 3: A Level 1 or Level 2 player interfaced with a computer or a peripheral.

**interactive media** (n.) Analog or digital programs that allow users to control the flow of program material. The media may consist of any combination of audio, graphic, video, or animated content. Media may be produced with varying degrees of interactivity.

**Interactive Multimedia Association** (IMA) (n.) A group of corporations that create products used in the multimedia industry. The home office of the IMA is in Arlington, Virginia.

**interactive services** (n.) Services that allow a subscriber to send messages to a programming source or content provider, to control the flow of information, and to engage in two-way communications such as polling, shopping, and banking.

**interactive television** (n.) A system that can send information to a broadcast television provider via some communications device, such as a telephone, keypad, or touch screen, allowing viewers to transmit messages to the televised source.

**interactive video** (n.) Digital technology that lets the viewer control the flow of video content. In interactive video, the user's choices and decisions determine how a program is presented.

**interactive voice response** (IVR) (n.) Feature of an Integrated Computer Telephony (ICT) system that enables voice to be transmitted over an Internet connection. IVR provides transaction processing, which interacts via Internet Protocol (IP) Telephony with a database. IP Telephony includes services that allow two computers to communicate or that permit voice signals and computers to communicate. Digitally synthesized voice may be used in a telephone system to interact with callers. In addition, IVR systems perform voice recognition of simple commands and can facilitate voice dialing.

**interactivity** (n.) Reciprocal communication between a user and a playback device or a digital media system.

**Intercast** (n.) Technology developed by Intel Corporation that enables a cable television signal to include digital information in the vertical blanking interval (VBI). This information is typically a web broadcast from the cable provider, which a computer can read with a standard browser while displaying a television program in the Audio-Video Interleaved (AVI) digital video format. The interactive content delivered is intended to enhance the particular television program being viewed, such as a web page with statistics on players participating in a sporting event.

In this model, a receiving unit mounted on a circuit board in a PC can access digital services inserted into a television signal's vertical blanking interval (VBI). Each interval can carry about as much data as a 9600-baud modem carries. Transmission from the cable provider is one-way and is not interactive unless a modem on a telephone line is connected simultaneously.

**Interchange File Format** (IFF) (n.) A chunk-based, hierarchical file format originally developed for the Amiga computer by Electronic Arts. File types are generally known by a four-character designation. Audio is AIFF, and animation is ANIM. Microsoft .wav and .avi file types are based on a similar scheme known as RIFF.

**interchange levels** (n.) Under the ISO 9660 standard, the three nested levels at which a CD-ROM file may be named and recorded. Many operating systems and their extensions that read discs require Level 1 restrictions to be observed. The levels may be described as follows:

- Level 1: The files consist of a single file section in one extent. They are recorded as a continuous stream and not interleaved. File and directory names must adhere to the strict ISO 9660 naming conventions.

- Level 2: The files consist of one file section in one extent with no interleaving, but no naming restrictions apply.

- Level 3: The files are not restricted.

**interconnect** (n.) In cable television, a microwave circuit, or cable, that links headends or distribution hubs so that they can exchange programs or services.

**interexchange carrier** (IXC) (n.) Long-distance telephone company that provides telephone service between Local Access and Transport Areas (LATAs), or exchanges.

**interface** 1. (n.) A device that connects two pieces of hardware, such as the link between a computer processor and a peripheral. 2. (n.) In programming, the means by which a computer user gives instructions to and receives information from a computer. 3. (v.) To transfer data or signals by means of a connector or by using a circuit that decodes or translates.

**interference** (n.) Undesirable energy that is received with a signal and that may appear as noise caused by electromagnetic fields.

**interfield frames** (n.) Frames that result from 3:2 pulldown, the film-to-tape conversion process in which a video frame contains two fields from different film frames. See figure on the following page. See also *3:2 pulldown*.

**interframe** (n.) A compressed video frame that is based on those surrounding it. Temporal

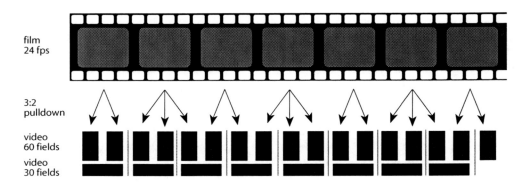

*interfield frames*

compression is applied, rather than spatial compression. It is called a "difference" or "delta" frame in QuickTime. MPEG has two types of interframes, "B-frames" and "P-frames".

**interframe coding** (n.) A method of video compression in which an encoder eliminates a portion of the data that defines a stream of images, discarding redundant data shared between consecutive frames. Compare *intraframe coding*.

**Interior Gateway Protocol** (IGP) (n.) Within an autonomous system, a protocol that distributes routing information to the routers.

**interlace** (v.) To combine two field scans to form a single video frame. In a video stream, the first field contains even-numbered scan lines, whereas the second field consists of odd-numbered lines. The two complementary fields lace together to form a single, complete frame. This practice, common to most video systems, is based on the concept of video persistence. The human eye holds the image of the first field while the second field is displayed, and it blends the two.

**interlaced GIF** (n.) Interlaced Graphic Inter-

change Format; used on the web, a type of streaming graphic in which scan lines have been rearranged. The graphic initially appears quickly in low resolution. Definition gradually improves as the complete image is loaded incrementally. Users catch a glimpse of the image before it is entirely loaded without having to wait for the entire image to be rendered to perceive it.

**interLATA** (adj.) Describes a telecommunication service that originates in one Local Access and Transport Area (LATA) and terminates in another. Regional Bell Operating Companies (RBOCs) cannot legally provide interLATA service.

**interlayer-transfer** See *print-through*.

**interleaving** (n.) Combining the video and audio data into one streaming media file. Interleaved data allows a playback device to linearly read the file while separately processing the video and audio data. For example, QuickTime's standard interleave is one second of video followed by one second of audio for the first second of the movie, then a half-second interleave is maintained. The AVI format offers several different interleave options.

232

**intermodulation distortion** (IMD) (n.) Audio distortion products produced by nonlinearities in an amplifier. The intermodulation distortion causes complex waves to produce sum and difference frequencies not harmonically related to the fundamentals of the original waves.

**International Communications Industries Association** (ICIA) (n.) A professional organization that provides its worldwide membership with education, training, and certification in communications technologies to enhance their ability to conduct business successfully, profitably, and competently. The ICIA represents individuals and organizations that derive revenue from the commercialization or utilization of communications technologies. The ICIA seeks to ensure the quality of its members' products and services by representing the communications industry to the public, to business, to education, and to the government. The ICIA engages in workforce development activities, industry technology updates, and international expositions. It offers publications, market research, and industry certification programs.

**International Data Encryption Algorithm** (IDEA) (n.) A private key encryption-decryption algorithm that uses a key twice the length of a data encryption standard (DES) key. This key typically uses 128-bits of data for encryption, and 64-bits for decryption.

**International Electrotechnical Commission** (IEC) (n.) The original international organization that set standards for electronic devices, formed in 1906 in Europe.

**International Interactive Communications Society** (IICS) (n.) A grassroots organization of multimedia developers that has supported the growth of the multimedia industry since its inception. Local chapters have been formed in many cities around the world.

**International Mobile Telecommunications 2000** (IMT 2000) (n.) An evolving standard for global wireless communications under development by the International Telecommunications Union (ITU). This technology is also referred to as third generation (3G).

**International MIDI Association** (IMA) (n.) The policy-setting group that establishes standards incorporated in the MIDI specification.

**International Telecommunications Union** (ITU) (n.) A Geneva-based organization that addresses standards used globally, such as those for video teleconferencing. The three sectors that the ITU addresses are Telecommunications Standardization (ITU-T), Radiocommunications (ITU-R), and Telecommunications Development (ITU-D).

**International Telecommunications Union–Telecommunications Standardization Sector** (ITU-T) (n.) An international body that makes technical recommendations regarding telephone and data communications systems. Prior to March 1993, ITU-T was known as Comité Consultatif International de Télégraphique et Téléphonique (CCITT). Plenary sessions are held every four years, and new standards are adopted. Having been held in 1996 and 2000, the next session is set for 2004. Study Group XVII of the ITU-T recommends standards for data communications over telephone networks, as well as V.x standards and X.n protocols.

**International Telephone and Telegraph Consultative Committee** See *Comité Consultatif International de Télégraphique et Téléphonique* or *International Telecommunications Union–Telecommunications Standardization Sector*.

233

**International Television Association** (ITVA) (n.) A professional organization of producers, technicians, engineers, and others who participate in the fields of broadcast, video, and film.

**Internet**(n.) A packet-switched network developed by the Advanced Research Projects Agency (ARPA) of the Department of Defense to give researchers access to databases and computers. The Internet dates from 1969, when the ARPANET was started. The Internet has grown into a large, diverse community of online users that is self-governing and that develops its own procedures. Physically, it is the interconnection of many small "stub" networks at campuses, research institutes, corporations, and military installations that have middle-level networks and backbones operating with multiple protocols. Nodes on the Internet share a common TCP/IP addressing interface. The Internet spans most countries, consists of several thousand networks, and has millions of users. It is expected that distributed multimedia over the Internet will rapidly increase, allowing the delivery of sounds and video over the network as bandwidth increases for more users. Internet activities include sending messages over email, conducting group discussions over Usenet, accessing databases, and browsing World Wide Web pages that are linked to one another, and conducting transactions.

**Internet Access Provider** (IAP) (n.) An organization that gives commercial and residential consumers access to the Internet. An IAP purchases an Internet link from another company with a direct link to the Internet and resells portions of that bandwidth to the general public. An IAP might buy one or more T1 links (1.544 megabits per second, or Mbps) and resell that bandwidth over ISDN lines (DSL, cable, or dialup modems). An Internet Service Provider (ISP) may also be an IAP.

**Internet address** (n.) The 32-bit host address defined by the Internet Protocol (IP) in RFC 791, STD 5. An Internet address is usually expressed in dotted-decimal notation, such as 128.121.103.76. The term should not be confused with the Fully Qualified Domain Name belonging to a host. The Internet address must be translated into an Ethernet address either by Address Resolution Protocol (ARP) or by constant mapping. The address can be split into a network address and a host number unique to each host on the network, and it can sometimes be split into a subnet address as well. Also known as an *IP address*.

**Internet address classes** (n.) A categorization of Internet address types, based on the assignment of units, or digits, to the four portions of each address that are separated by periods in dotted-decimal notation. The three types of Internet address classes are as follows:

- Class A address: The first three units are assigned by InterNIC, and the remainder are allocated by the organization to which they were assigned.

- Class B address: The first six units are assigned by InterNIC, and the remainder are allocated by the organization to which they were assigned.

- Class C address: The first nine units are assigned by InterNIC, and the remainder are allocated by the organization to which they were assigned.

**Internet Architecture Board** (IAB) (n.) Technical group that manages the Internet Engineering Task Force (IETF) and the Internet

Research Task Force (IRTF). These task forces delineate and recommend Internet protocols.

**Internet Assigned Numbers Authority** (IANA) (n.) The central registry for assigned numbers, or Internet Protocol (IP) parameters, such as port, protocol, and enterprise numbers and options, codes, and types. The currently assigned values are listed in the assigned numbers document STD 2. A number assignment may be obtained from the email address *iana@isi.edu.*

**Internet backbone** (n.) A high-capacity telecommunications network carrying a large volume of traffic. Usually SONET-based fiber-optic connections, these links form major arteries within the national public switched telephone network (PSTN). The term *Internet backbone* originally referred to NSFNET, a National Science Foundation–funded series of links operating at very high data rates.

**Internet Control Message Protocol** (ICMP) (n.) An extension of the Internet Protocol (IP) defined in RFC 792, STD 5 that permits the generation of error messages, test packets, and informational messages related to IP.

**Internet country code** (n.) A country abbreviation that identifies the top-level domain of a machine. See the accompanying table.

**Internet-Draft** (I-D) (n.) A working document of the Internet Engineering Task Force (IETF). Such a draft typically precedes an RFC and is valid for only six months.

**Internet Engineering Steering Group** (IESG) (n.) A body that consists of the Internet Engineering Task Force (IETF) area directors and the IETF chair. The IESG performs the initial technical review of Internet standards and manages the IETF.

**Internet Engineering Task Force** (IETF) (n.) An international community of network administrators, vendors, and researchers who coordinate the operation of the Internet. The U.S. government funds the IETF, and the Corporation for National Research Initiatives participates.

**Internet Explorer** (n.) A universal client, or browser, developed by Microsoft for accessing HTML documents on the World Wide Web.

**Internet Message Access Protocol** (IMAP, pronounced "EYE-map") (n.) The method by which a client can access electronic mail messages on a server. IMAP permits manipulation of remote mailboxes but does not specify a means of posting mail. This function is handled by a mail transfer protocol such as Simple Mail Transfer Protocol (SMTP).

**Internet Protocol** (IP) (n.) The network layer for the TCP/IP protocol used on Ethernet networks, defined in RFC 791, STD 5. It is a connectionless, best-effort packet-switching protocol. It provides packet routing, fragmentation, and reassembly through the data link layer.

**Internet Protocol next generation** (IPng) (n.) An Internet Engineering Task Force (IETF) proposal to update the current version of Internet Protocol. Portions of IPng address CATNIP, TUBA, and SIPP.

**Internet Registry** (IR) (n.) The place where domain names are recorded by the Defense Data Network Information Center.

**Internet Relay Chat** (IRC) (n.) A global multiuser chat system that allows people to discuss topics over "channels" on the Internet. Written in 1988 by Jarkko Oikarinen, IRC is constantly evolving as the conventions pertaining to its use change. To access an IRC, a user

# Internet Country Codes

| Country | Code | Country | Code | Country | Code |
|---|---|---|---|---|---|
| Afghanistan | af | French Southern Territories | tf | Norway | no |
| Albania | al | Gambia | gm | Oman | om |
| Algeria | dz | Georgia | ge | Pakistan | pk |
| Angola | ao | Germany | de | Palau | pw |
| Antarctica | aq | Ghana | gh | Panama | pa |
| Argentina | ar | Gibraltar | gi | Papua New Guinea | pg |
| Armenia | am | Greece | gr | Paraguay | py |
| Australia | au | Greenland | gl | Peru | pe |
| Austria | at | Grenada | gd | Philippines | ph |
| Azerbaijan | az | Guam | gu | Poland | pl |
| Bahamas | bs | Guatemala | gt | Portugal | pt |
| Bahrain | bh | Guinea | gn | Puerto Rico | pr |
| Bangladesh | bd | Guyana | gy | Qatar | qa |
| Barbados | bb | Haiti | ht | Romania | ro |
| Belarus | by | Honduras | hn | Russian Federation | ru |
| Belgium | be | Hong Kong | hk | Rwanda | rw |
| Belize | bz | Hungary | hu | Samoa | ws |
| Bermuda | bm | Iceland | is | Saudi Arabia | sa |
| Bolivia | bo | India | in | Senegal | sn |
| Bosnia | ba | Indonesia | id | Singapore | sg |
| Botswana | bw | Iran | ir | Slovakia | sk |
| Brazil | br | Iraq | iq | Slovenia | si |
| Bulgaria | bg | Ireland | ie | Solomon Islands | sb |
| Burundi | bi | Israel | il | Somalia | so |
| Cambodia | kh | Italy | it | South Africa | za |
| Cameroon | cm | Jamaica | jm | Spain | es |
| Canada | ca | Japan | jp | Sri Lanka | lk |
| Cayman Islands | ky | Jordan | jo | Sudan | sd |
| Central African Republic | cf | Kazakhstan | kz | Surinam | sr |
| Chad | td | Kenya | ke | Swaziland | sz |
| Chile | cl | Korea, Democratic | kp | Sweden | se |
| China | cn | Korea, Republic of | kr | Switzerland | ch |
| Colombia | co | Kuwait | kw | Syrian Arab Republic | sy |
| Congo | cg | Laos | la | Taiwan | tw |
| Congo, Democratic Republic | cd | Latvia | lv | Tanzania | tz |
| Costa Rica | cr | Lebanon | lb | Thailand | th |
| Croatia (Hrvatska) | hr | Liberia | lr | Trinidad & Tobago | tt |
| Cuba | cu | Lichtenstein | li | Tunisia | tn |
| Cyprus | cy | Lithuania | lt | Turkey | tr |
| Czech Republic | cz | Luxembourg | lu | Uganda | ug |
| Denmark | dk | Macau | mo | Ukraine | ua |
| Dominica | dm | Macedonia | mk | United Arab Emirates | ae |
| Dominican Republic | do | Madagascar | mg | United Kingdom | uk |
| Ecuador | ec | Malaysia | my | United States | us |
| Egypt | eg | Marshall Islands | mh | Uruguay | uy |
| El Salvador | sv | Martinique | mq | Uzbekistan | uz |
| Equatorial Guinea | gq | Micronesia | fm | Vatican City State | va |
| Estonia | ee | Monaco | mc | Venezuela | ve |
| Ethiopia | et | Mongolia | mn | Vietnam | vn |
| Falkland Islands (Malvinas) | fk | Morocco | ma | Virgin Islands (British) | vg |
| Fiji | fj | Mozambique | mz | Virgin Islands (U.S.) | vi |
| Finland | fi | Namibia | na | Western Sahara | eh |
| France | fr | Nepal | np | Yemen | ye |
| France (Metropolitan) | fx | Netherlands | nl | Yugoslavia | yu |
| French Guiana | gf | New Zealand | nz | Zambia | zm |
| French Polynesia | pf | Nicaragua | ni | Zimbabwe | zw |

must run a client program that connects to an IRC network; Telnet cannot be used. Source code for an IRC client is available by anonymous FTP to the following sites:

Windows          *cs-ftp.bu.edu:/irc/clients/pc /windows*

Unix             *ftp.funet.fi/pub/unix/irc*

Macintosh        *ftp.funet.fi/pub/unix/irc/mac*

MS-DOS           *ftp.funet.fi/pub/unix/irc/msdos*

Here are a few of the many IRC servers available for connection:

United States    *irc.bu.edupiglet.cc.utexas.edu*

Canada           *irc.mcgill.ca*

Europe           *irc.funet.ficismhp .univlyon1.frstork.doc.ic.ac.uk*

Australia        *troll.elec.uow.edu.au*

Japan            *endo.wide.ad.jp*

All IRC commands start with /, and most are one word. Typing "/help" calls for help information. Typing "/names" calls for a list of names. A user may limit the list of names by typing "/names -min 20"; only a list of channels with 20 or more people on it will be called. The output of "/names" appears as follows:

Pub: #hack      @brillo rascal mon

Pub: #Nippon   @jellyroll @molli_R

*Pub* means public (or visible) channel, # is the prefix, and *hack* is the channel name. An @ indicates the channel operator, who controls the channel.

To join a particular channel, type "/join #channelname". New users benefit from visiting the channel "#irchelp". To join a conversation, type a line of text and send it by striking the Enter key. IRC will automatically insert <nickname> before all channel messages. To leave a channel, type "/part #channelname". To access a list of channels and topics, type "/list -min 30", which will show channels with 30 or more members. Many IRC operators visit "#Twilight_Zone" frequently. Here are some widely used foreign-language channels:

## IRC Servers

| Port | Address | Country |
|------|---------|---------|
| 6667 | iapp.netscape.com | United States |
| 6667 | austin.tx.us.undernet.org | United States |
| 6667 | sanjose.ca.us.undernet.org | United States |
| 6667 | washington.dc.us.undernet.org | United States |
| 6667 | oxford.ok.eu.undernet.org | United Kingdom |
| 6667 | Montreal.qu.ca.undernet.org | Canada |
| 6667 | caen.fr.eu.undernet.org | France |
| 7000 | xgw.dal.net | Finland |
| 7000 | liberator.dal.net | United Kingdom |
| 7000 | uncc.dal.net | United States |
| 7000 | skypoint.dal.net | United States |
| 7000 | cin.dal.net | United States |

| #nippon | Japanese channel, with kanji characters |
| #espanol | Spanish channel |
| #russian | Russian channel |

An IRC users' manual is available from *cs-ftp.bu.edu:/irc/support*. It is recommended that this IRC primer be read prior to joining any list. Addresses for IRC-related mailing lists are shown here:

| "operlist" | Discusses server code, routing, and protocol. To join, send mail to *operlist-request@kei.com* with Subject: subscribe. |
| "ircd-three" | Discusses protocol revisions of the ircd (IRC server). To join, send mail to *ircd-three-request@kei.com* with Subject: subscribe. |

For more technical information, refer to the IRC RFC (RFC 1459), which is available at all RFC FTP sites, such as *cs-ftp.bu.edu:/irc/support/rfc1459.txt*. Here are other online IRC information sources:

- *cs-ftp.bu.edu:/irc/support/alt-irc-faq*

- *ftp.kei.com:/pub/irc/alt-irc-faq*

- *http://www.kei.com/irc.html*

If the Netscape Navigator 2.0 browser or a later version is used to access the Internet, the Netscape Chat plug-in, which is an IRC client, is available. A copy of this plug-in can be downloaded from *ftp://ftp20.netscape.com/pub/chat*. It should be placed in a separate directory before it is installed. More IRC servers are listed in the IRC Servers table.

238

**Internet Research Steering Group** (IRSG) (n.) The body that governs the Internet Research Task Force (IRTF).

**Internet Research Task Force** (IRTF) (n.) A group of researchers who advise the Internet Architecture Board (IAB) on issues that affect the Internet. The IRTF is chartered by the IAB to consider issues and discuss solutions.

**Internet Server Application Programming Interface** (ISAPI, pronounced "eye-SAP-ee") (n.) A programming interface between an application and the Microsoft Internet Server. Active servers created with ISAPI extensions can be complete applications themselves or can connect to other services. ISAPI is used for the same sorts of functions as Common Gateway Interface (CGI), but ISAPI uses Microsoft Windows dynamic link libraries (DLL) for greater efficiency. The server loads a DLL the first time a request is received. The DLL then stays in memory, ready to service other requests until the server decides it is no longer needed. This minimizes the overhead associated with executing such applications many times. An HTTP server can unload ISAPI application DLLs to free memory, or it can preload them to speed up the first access. Applications may be enhanced by ISAPI filters.

**Internet Service Provider** (ISP) (n.) A company that delivers Internet access to other companies and to individuals.

**Internet Society** (ISOC) (n.) A nonprofit professional organization that supports technical developments for the Internet, promotes new applications, and educates about Internet operation and use. Technical standards are developed under the auspices of the ISOC, which publishes the *Internet Society News Quarterly* and holds the annual INET conference. ISOC is supported by the U.S. government and the

Corporation for National Research Initiatives.

**Internetwork Packet eXchange** (IPX) (n.) Developed by Xerox Corporation and made popular by Novell, the basic protocol in the Novell Netware file server system. IPX is a network layer protocol. A router with IPX routing can interconnect local area networks (LANs) so that Netware clients and servers can communicate. The Sequenced Packet eXchange (SPX) transport layer protocol runs on top of IPX.

**InterNIC** (n.) Internet Network Information Center; the name of the three organizations that the National Science Foundation (NSF) selected in 1992 to receive cooperative agreements in the areas of information services, directory and database services, and registration services. General Atomics provides information services, AT&T provides directory and database services, and VeriSign, Inc., provides registration services.

**interoperability** (n.) The capacity of software and equipment from different vendors to be successfully integrated.

**interpolating response** (n.) Term adopted by Rane Corporation to describe the process of summing two adjacent bands of variable equalizers to produce a smooth response without a dip in the center. Also called *combining response*.

**interpolation** (n.) Related to graphics, the process of computing intervening values within a numerical range and applying those values to fill the spaces between given values. When a picture is enlarged, this process accomplishes higher resolution.

**interpreted language** (n.) Program code that is converted into a machine-readable format and processed simultaneously. Interpreted language is slower than a compiled language because of the translation that occurs at run time, but it is more flexible. Java is an interpreted language.

**interpreter** (n.) Any software program that executes other software programs. By contrast, a compiler does not execute its input program, or source code, but translates it into executable machine code, which is output to a file for later execution. The same source code may be run directly either by interpreting it or by compiling it and then by executing the machine code produced. It takes longer to run a program under an interpreter than to run compiled code, but it may take less time to interpret such a program than to compile and run it.

**interrupt request** (IRQ) (n.) A computer instruction that momentarily stops the normal operation of a routine. The operation can usually be resumed later from the interruption point. As the peripheral devices interface with the central processing unit (CPU), they frequently send signals to indicate that a software routine or circuit needs attention from the CPU. The term also refers to a signal line or channel used to carry the interrupt signal from hardware devices to the PC's interrupt controller chip. The original PC provided eight such lines, whereas later models provide 16. IRQ lines cannot ordinarily be shared, and each peripheral device is assigned an IRQ number. Conflicts result when two or more channels are assigned the same IRQ number on a personal computer. Installing a sound card in a PC is a situation that would require one or more interrupt channel assignments. The best choice for the sound card interrupt is usually the Sound Blaster (SB) default, IRQ 5. MS-DOS reserves this channel for a second printer port. If another device is assigned to IRQ 5, an eight-bit sound card interrupt may be moved to IRQ 7. A 16-bit sound card interrupt may be moved to any available IRQ between 8 and 15. The standard interrupt assignments are listed in the Standard Interrupt Assignments table.

### Standard Interrupt Assignments

| Number | Function |
|--------|----------|
| IRQ 0 | Timer Output 0 |
| IRQ 1 | Keyboard (buffer full) |
| IRQ 2 | Cascade from IRQ 9 |
| IRQ 3 | Serial Port 2; Serial Port 4; SDLC Communications; BSC Communications; Cluster Adapter; Network (alternate); 3278/79 (alternate) |
| IRQ 4 | Serial Port 1; Serial Port 3; SDLC Communications; BSC Communications; Voice Communications Adapter |
| IRQ 5 | Parallel Port 2, Sound Blaster Default |
| IRQ 6 | Floppy Disk Controller |
| IRQ 7 | Parallel Port 1; Cluster Adapter (alternate) |
| IRQ 8 | Realtime Clock |
| IRQ 9 | Software Redirected to INT 0A (hex); Video; Network; 3278/79 Adapter |
| IRQ 10 | Reserved |
| IRQ 11 | Reserved |
| IRQ 12 | Reserved |
| IRQ 13 | Coprocessor |
| IRQ 14 | Hard Disk Controller |
| IRQ 15 | Reserved |

**intracoded frame** (n.) In digital video, a frame with self-referential information, devoid of data that is related to previous or future frames in the sequence. Also known as an *I-frame*.

**intraframe coding** (n.) In video compression, a technique that allocates more data to the coding of highly detailed parts of a single frame at the expense of less detailed areas. Compare *interframe coding*.

**intraLATA** (adj.) Describes telecommunications services that originate and end within a single Local Access and Transport Area (LATA).

**intranet** (n.) A local area network (LAN) that uses a dedicated web server running TCP/IP to provide HTML documents and other files that clients access when using a web browser as their interface. The intranet may provide users with an external connection to the Internet, facilitating communication with both local and distant web servers. The advantages of an intranet are the speed with which streaming data can be delivered locally, the security of an internal LAN with a firewall, and the use of a single user-friendly interface for both internal and external communications.

**intrusion** (n.) In network security, this is an illegal attempt to access and compromise the integrity, privacy, and availability of an information system and its data.

**intrusion detection** (n.) Techniques for observing unauthorized activity on a computer or a network. Detection is performed through the use of security logs or audit data that track illegal activity by individuals or by anonymous software.

**Intrusion Detection In Our Time** (IDIOT) (n.) In network security, a system that uses pattern matching to detect intrusions.

**intuitive** (adj.) Describes user-friendly software that automatically gives the user options or information.

**inverse square law** (n.) A law of acoustics pertaining to the dissipation of sound waves. Sound propagates in all directions to form a spherical field, thus sound energy is inversely proportional to the square of the distance it travels. Doubling the distance it travels quarters the sound energy that remains. According to the inverse square law, the sound pressure level (SPL) is attenuated 6 dB each time the distance it travels is doubled.

**inverted tree structure** (n.) A method of providing access to a wide range of data pages, offering a series of menus until the desired page of information is reached.

**I/O bus** (n.) Input/output bus; the interface through which data or instructions are transmitted to and from a computer. Peripherals such as scanners and printers use I/O buses.

**IP** See *Internet Protocol.*

**IP address** (n.) Internet Protocol address; a unique 32-bit number that identifies a specific Internet server. It is formatted in dotted decimal notation as a series of four sets of digits separated by periods. IP addressing is defined by RFC 791, STD 5. Also known as *Internet address.*

**IP multicasting** (n.) Internet Protocol multicasting; one-to-many broadcast of data by a server using IP.

**IPng** See *Internet Protocol next generation.*

**ips** See *inches per second.*

**IPSec** See *IPSecurity.*

**IPSecurity** (IPSec) (n.) A suite of protocols that provide authentication and encryption over the Internet. IPSec works at Layer 3, rather than Layer 4, because the Secure Sockets Layer (SSL) provides services in Layer 4.

**IP splicing** (n.) An attack, which is also known as hijacking, made by an intruder who intercepts and appropriates a session. Such attacks are made after the authentication process. Deterrence against Internet Protocol (IP) splicing is dependant on encryption at the session or network layer.

**IP spoofing** (n.) In network security, an attack whereby one system impersonates another system by using an illicit IP network address.

**IP telephony** (n.) The use of networks running Internet Protocol (IP) to send and receive messages, such as voice data, to replace traditional telephone company services. The public switched telephone network (PSTN) may be used to transmit the data between modems, or a local area network (LAN) may be used.

**IPv6** (n.) Internet Protocol version 6; the next generation of IP developed by the Internet Engineering Task Force (IETF). IPv6 increases the maximum number of user addresses and provides IPSecurity, among other enhancements.

**IPX** See *Internetwork Packet eXchange.*

**IPX/SPX** (n.) The transport protocol used in most Novell Netware environments. In client-server environments in which the server engine is a network loadable module (NLM), communication between the client and the server is generally conducted over IPX/SPX.

**IR** See *Internet Registry.*

**IRC** See *Internet Relay Chat.*

**IrDA** See *Infrared Data Association.*

**IrDA port** (n.) A transmitter/receiver that processes infrared signals, typically installed on a computing device or peripheral.

**IRE units** (n.) These units are based on a linear scale for measuring the relative amplitude of a television signal with a zero reference at the blanking level. The name was derived from the Institute of Radio Engineers (IRE), founded in

1912, and merged with the IEEE in 1963.

**iris** (n.) A diaphragm in the lens of a video camera that controls the size of the aperture, regulating the amount of light that may enter the camera. The size of the iris is measured in f-stops.

**IRIX** (n.) An operating system used on Silicon Graphics systems. Pronounced "EYE-rix."

**IRQ** See *interrupt request.*

**IRSG** See *Internet Research Steering Group.*

**IRTF** See *Internet Research Task Force.*

**ISA** See *Industry Standard Architecture.*

**ISA bus** (n.) Industry Standard Architecture bus; a durable interface implemented since 1981 on PC-compatible computers. The ISA bus has been replaced by the newer, faster PCI technology. The ISA 16-bit bus replaced the eight-bit bus in 1984. The 16-bit bus has a maximum standard speed of 8.33 MHz and a maximum throughput of about eight megabytes per second (MBps). This is adequate for most common system peripherals, sound cards, and network adapters.

**ISAPI** See *Internet Server Application Programming Interface.*

**ISAPI filter** (n.) Internet Server Application Programming Interface filter; a replaceable dynamic link library (DLL) that the server calls when an HTTP request is made. Upon loading, the ISAPI filter communicates to the server what sort of notifications will be accepted. After that, whenever a selected event occurs, the filter processes the event. Examples include authentication schemes, compression, encryption, logging, and traffic analysis.

**ISD** See *Instructional Systems Design.*

**ISDN** See *Integrated Services Digital Network.*

**ISDN digital subscriber line** (IDSL) (n.) A form of digital subscriber line (DSL). It is a type of ISDN Basic Rate Interface (BRI) that delivers data. IDSL uses 2B1Q line coding, and both the B-channels and the D-channels are permanently bonded for speeds of 144 Kbps over a single wire pair.

**ISINDEX** (n.) An HTML tag that tells the browser to display a text entry box on the current page. Text that a user enters into the box is appended to the current URL as a URL-encoded query string and sent to the server by the GET method. This functionality allows simple user input to search a document. The server must map the query URL to an appropriate process and is only useful if the server has access to a search engine.

**ISMAP** (n.) An attribute of the inline image HTML tag <IMG> that specifies that if the image is selected, the browser will generate a request indicating the coordinates of the point that was clicked. This request is interpreted by a server that has mapped certain regions of the image to predetermined actions.

**ISM Band** See *Industrial, Scientific and Medical band.*

**ISO** (n.) Greek for "the same as" or "equal to." The de facto name of the International Organization for Standardization. It is not an acronym, but a play on words. This organization, founded in Geneva in 1946, is involved in the development and definition of worldwide standards. In multimedia, they have defined CD-ROM formats, compression algorithms, communications specifications, and standards for a wide range of technical software applications. They serve most fields except electrical or electronic applications, which are dealt with by the International Electrotechnical Commission (IEC). Together, the ISO and the IEC form the Joint Technical Committee (JTC), which is staffed by members from 80 countries. Pronounced "EYE-soh."

**ISOC** See *Internet Society.*

**isochronous** (adj.) Describes a type of data transmission in which characters are separated by a whole number of bit-length intervals. Timing information is embedded in the data stream. In asynchronous transmission, by contrast, characters may be separated by random-length intervals. Pronounced "Eye-SOH-kro-nus."

**ISODE** See *ISO Development Environment.*

**ISO Development Environment** (ISODE, pronounced "EYE-so-DEE-ee") (n.) Software that allows Open Systems Interconnection (OSI) services to use a TCP/IP network.

**ISO image** (n.) An exact representation of the entire set of data and programs as they will appear on a CD-ROM, including content and logical format. An ISO image is simulated on another medium, such as an optical cartridge, data tape, or CD-R. It is sent to a disc manufacturer for premastering and mastering. It is also referred to as a *CD-ROM image* or a *disc image.*

**ISO 9735** (n.) The ISO standard that defines application layer syntax. Set forth in 1988, it was amended and reprinted in 1990. Governing electronic data interchange for administration, commerce, and trade, it is known as *EDIFACT.*

**ISO 9660** (n.) An international standard that specifies the logical file format for CD-ROM files and directories. It is directly derived from the High Sierra Group Proposal. ISO 9660 discs can be read by most PC CD-ROM drives if the proper software driver has been loaded into the system.

**ISO 9000** (n.) Standards for quality management and assurance adopted by more than 90 countries. ISO 9000 standards apply to all types of organizations in many industries. A standard language for documenting quality control processes, systems to manage evidence that these practices are instituted, and third-party auditing to review and maintain certification are all parts of ISO 9000. Products are classified into generic categories: hardware, software, processed materials, and services. Documentation is central to ISO 9000 conformance.

**ISO 11172** (n.) Defined by ISO, the international standard for MPEG-1 video compression.

**ISO 13818** (n.) Defined by ISO, the international standard for MPEG-2 video compression. This is the same as ITU H.222.

**ISP** See *Internet Service Provider.*

**ITFS** See *Instructional Television Fixed Service.*

**ITU** See *International Telecommunications Union.*

**ITU-T** See *International Telecommunications Union–Telecommunications Standardization Sector.*

**ITVA** See *International Television Association.*

**IVR** See *interactive voice response.*

**IXC** See *interexchange carrier.*

# J

**jack** (n.) Related to audio, video, or computing gear, a connecting point that accepts a plug on a cable or a line. A jack is usually a female connector.

**jaggies** (n.) Jargon for undesirable artifacts that appear in a graphic display or a printout as a result of inadequate resolution. Jaggies portray lines that are not horizontal or vertical. See also *aliasing.*

**Japanese Digital Cellular** (JDC) (n.) The Japanese digital cellular telephone standard that has been renamed personal digital cellular (PDC). JDC/PDC uses time division multiple access (TDMA) to provide three channels of 8 KBps voice over a 25 kHz carrier channel providing a spectrum use improvement of 3.6 over Advanced Mobile Phone Service (AMPS). JDC/PDC operates in the upper 900 MHz and 1.5 GHz bands.

**jargon** (n.) Slang and other terms used in a particular field.

**Java** (n.) An interpreted programming language similar to C++ that is optimized for object-oriented, multithreaded, distributed computing. The interpreter—the runtime system on which Java is dependent—may either exist as a separate application or operate within another program, such as a web browser. Java allows a client computer with its own runtime environment to execute dynamic applications independently from a networked host. A Java program may be downloaded and run dynamically from a web server. The language is a secure, high-performance, portable development environment for distributing dynamic content over the Internet. Using Java eliminates the need to port an application to each different platform because the same executable runs on any computer with the proper interpreter, or "virtual machine," and with the necessary class objects. Java provides its own memory management in the form of an automatic garbage collector, which runs as a separate thread. When there are no references to an object, the garbage collector tags it for removal.

The development of Java began in 1991 by James Gosling, an employee of Sun Microsystems, who was charged with building a programming language that would operate on any platform. He began by attempting to extend the C++ compiler, but soon realized that he needed to create a new language. It eventually became known as Java, after failing a trademark search under the name of "Oak." Originally it was intended for consumer electronic devices, and prototypes were built in 1993. The World Wide Web was growing in significance, and in 1994 Sun developed a Java-capable browser called WebRunner. It later became known as HotJava.

Early in 1995 Arthur Van Hoff, who had joined the Sun team a year before, implemented the Java compiler in Java itself. Gosling's original compiler had been implemented in C. Sun Microsystems officially announced the Java Environment at SunWorld in May 1995.

Java consists of three interdependent components. The first is a programming language in which the code needed for applications is written. The second is the run-time environment, or Java Virtual Machine, which provides the architecture for applications. The third is the set of tools with which to build, compile, and run applications: the Java compiler, the Java interpreter, and the HotJava browser. The compiler lets programmers create machine-independent *bytecode,* which runs under the interpreter and browser environments.

At the heart of the Java package is a set of class libraries for the browser and the interpreter, the routines that programmers use to perform basic functions. These class libraries are a package of predeveloped and pretested code, which can be linked to create individual applications. Some of the common libraries are as follows:

- Applets: Utilities needed for interaction with any Java-enabled browser.

- AWT: Abstract Windowing Toolkit; the graphic interface tools including fonts, buttons, controls, and scrollbars.

- I/O: Standard provision for input and output, along with file utilities.

- Language Foundation: Classes for strings and arrays, part of the basic structure of Java.

- Network: Utilities for accessing network protocols like FTP, Telnet, and the web.

- Utility: Provision for stacks, vectors, encoding/decoding, and hash tables.

Although Java is similar in many ways to C++, it does not allow a procedural approach, since it is thoroughly object-oriented. In addition to the capabilities of C++, Java adds automatic boundary checking by eliminating pointers, and it performs automatic garbage collection. Due to its multithreading features, it can take care of these memory management functions in the background.

In Java the fundamental unit, or object, is referred to as a *class.* A class is a grouping of code that models the behavior of an object in software. A faucet is an example of an object in real life. All objects have a state, and the state of the faucet could be on or off, or perhaps hot or cold. The state of an object is described by *instance variables.* Variables that are controlled by a class are inaccessible to any other class, except under special conditions. The flow of water is controlled by turning a faucet on or off. In Java, a *method* is used to control a class, or object. A method is a small body of code that performs a function that can be reused. The functions of a class are limited to what is prescribed by its methods. In the plumbing of a building there are many faucets, but they are identical in function. Each faucet (class) may be either on or off (instance variable) by turning it (method). A class (faucet) must only be created once, after which it may be reused many times. Another *instance* of the faucet may be created, or reproduced, without reinventing the object. A method is all that is needed to control any number of instances of a class.

Another important aspect of an object is that

each instance *inherits* the characteristics or properties of the original object. Some aspects of a new class may be changed, while the new class retains all the properties of the old class. The new faucet could be made of brass instead of chrome. The new class becomes a *subclass* of the original *superclass*. A class is simply a template for future instances of an object.

In Java a *package* is a single compilation unit which is a collection of similar classes, and *access modifiers* control access to methods and variables. Four levels of access are defined: *Public, Private, Protected,* and *Friendly*. Public methods are freely accessible. Private methods are accessible only to the class itself. Protected variables are accessible only through methods in a given class and its subclasses. Friendly methods and variables are accessible to any classes in the same package. A program is written by creating a class, and a class is automatically a subclass of the superclass *Object*. Other superclasses are *Applet* and *Thread*.

Java is very different conceptually from C++. There are no pointers, no *goto* statements or individual functions, no multiple inheritance, and no type definitions. There are no structures or unions. Instead of header files, Java uses *interfaces*. The interface is the means by which other classes see what methods a class may implement. Java keeps track of all references to an object, and when there are no longer any references to it, Java removes it with the garbage as a low-priority thread in the background.

Java provides portability by compiling *bytecode,* which is interpreted on each platform by the run-time environment, or Java Virtual Machine (JVM). The bytecode is an executable program for the Virtual Machine, which exists only in software. The code is then interpreted and executed on the target hardware itself. All code will run on any computer for which an interpreter has been ported, including an Intel Pentium, an Apple Macintosh, or a Sun SPARCstation. Memory layout problems are solved by deferring symbolic reference to the interpreter at run time.

The robustness of Java is due in large part to its automatic memory management and strict compile-time and run-time checking. In C++, memory is addressed by the use of pointers, or variables that hold the address of the memory range used. A pointer could be misdirected to the wrong location. Java eliminates the pointer and encapsulates memory usage into classes. The syntax is strictly checked for errors upon compilation and again as it is interpreted at run time.

Multithreading is included at every level in Java, beginning at the syntactical level with synchronization modifiers in the language. Multitasking is the act of running two or more applications at once in an operating system. Multithreading is the act of executing more than one thread at once while running a single application.

Java is a secure environment for several reasons. The first stage in the interpreter is a bytecode verification to test whether code conforms to Java specification as it is received. Then the interpreter provides a distinct name space for each class that is uploaded, preventing accidental name references. Since there are no pointers when it is compiled, Java is immune to memory allocation problems. At run time it does not allow illegal processes, incorrect parameters, or violation of access restrictions.

Information about Java may be found at these web sites:

- *http://java.sun.com*

- *http://www.javasoft.com*

- *http://www.gamelan.com*

- *http://www.javaworld.com*

**JavaBeans** (n.) The trademarked component architecture of the Java programming language, developed by Sun Microsystems, IBM, and others. JavaBeans may be parts of Java programs, or it may be a group of self-contained applications. JavaBeans may be assembled to make complex applications. These applicaitons are capable of running within other component architectures, such as ActiveX and OpenDoc.

**Java Database Connectivity** (JDBC) (n.) An Application Programming Interface (API) that is a subset of the Open Database Connectivity (ODBC) API, which allows Java classes and objects to simplify programming for Structured Query Language (SQL) databases.

**Java Open Language Toolkit** (JOLT) (n.) A project aimed at providing a freely available and redistributable implementation of the Java language and tools. Related information is available at *http://www.redhat.com/linux-info/jolt*.

**JavaScript** (n.) A web scripting language developed by Netscape that was originally named LiveScript. The source code is freely available, and the language is easy to learn. The syntax is similar to that of C, yet not as complex. JavaScript is intended to enhance forms and simple database front ends on the World Wide Web. JavaScript code is embedded in an HTML document with the tag <script language= "JavaScript">. It is interpreted by recent versions of Netscape Navigator and MS Internet

Explorer. See the appendix on JavaScript for details.

**Java Virtual Machine** (JVM) (n.) The specification for a hypothetical processor that runs Java code. It is for this machine that the Java compiler creates an executable program from source code. It compiles to an intermediate stage, converting the source code to bytecode. This bytecode is more efficiently translated into native code for the processor on each particular platform. The JVM must be installed on a machine in order for any Java bytecode to run.

**Jaz drive** (n.) A removable cartridge drive from Iomega Corporation. A Jaz drive accepts disks that hold 1 gigabyte (GB) of data. An average transfer rate of 330 megabytes (MB) per minute is possible with a high-speed SCSI configuration.

**JDBC** See *Java Database Connectivity.*

**JDC** See *Japanese Digital Cellular.*

**JEDEC** See *Joint Electronic Devices Engineering Council.*

**jewel case** (n.) The plastic box in which audio CDs and CD-ROMs are packaged. The enclosed printed matter usually consists of a booklet and a tray card.

**Jigsaw** (n.) An experimental web server platform that provides a sample HTTP 1.1 implementation and other features on top of an advanced architecture implemented in Java. It is under development by the World Wide Web Consortium (W3C). Jigsaw is an Open Source Project, begun in May 1996. Jigsaw 2.2.0 was released on March 13, 2001, and included web distributing authoring and versioning (WebDAV) support. Specific configuration packages are expected to be released in future upgrades, including a proxy/cache configuration.

**JINI** (n.) A Java-based language developed by Sun Microsystems for connecting devices, like printers and disk drives, to a network.

**jitter** (n.) 1. In relation to video, a shift in the phase of pulses during transmission or playback, causing a lack of synchronization and unstable video signal reception. 2. Any slight movement of a transmission signal in time or phase that can introduce errors and loss of synchronization for high-speed synchronous communications.

**J-lead** (n.) On a chip carrier, an electrical lead curved in the shape of a *J*. This type of lead may be surface mounted on a PC board or plugged into a socket.

**jog** (v.) To move from one frame to another in a video clip, or to shuttle the clip by a single frame, or by a small number of frames, when editing.

**Joint Electronic Devices Engineering Council** (JEDEC) (n.) A group that defines standards for the electronics industry.

**Joint Photographic Expert Group** (JPEG, pronounced "JAY-peg") (n.) 1. An international consortium of hardware, software, and publishing interests. Under the auspices of the International Organization for Standardization (ISO), JPEG was defined as a universal standard for the digital compression and decompression of still images for use in computer systems. 2. The format that ISO defined. JPEG is a lossy compression scheme. It uses discrete cosine transform (DCT) and quantization to encode still images. The technique

may be used to compress images with moderate detail up to about a 15:1 ratio before visible degradation occurs. An 800-kilobyte (KB) file may be compressed to approximately 80 KB with the application of JPEG compression, and relatively little necessary data will be lost in this 10:1 ratio. When the same 800-KB file is reduced to 40 KB, which is a 20:1 ratio, artifacts may be noticeable. In the process, a single numeric chroma *descriptor* is used to identify a block of pixels that are all approximately the same color. That descriptor is multiplied by a factor that defines the area of the block. High compression ratios produce a "blocky," or pixelated, look. Simple images with little detail and few gradients lend themselves to higher compression ratios.

**Joint Technical Committee** (JTC)(n.) A working group of ISO that defines universal standards.

**JOLT** See *Java Open Language Toolkit.*

**joystick** (n.) An input device that rotates on an axis and controls the position of a cursor. A joystick may be equipped with a button that sends messages for a program to interpret. Video and arcade games are often enabled by the use of a joystick.

**JPEG** See *Joint Photographic Expert Group.*

**JTC** See *Joint Technical Committee.*

**JTC1/SC24** (n.) The ISO/IEC group responsible for creating the GKS, PHIGS, and Computer Graphics Metafile (CGM) standards. JTC1/SC24 was recently involved in standardizing multimedia presentation technologies.

**jukebox** (n.) An optical or magnetic storage unit that holds multiple discs, any of which may be selected and automatically loaded into the play station. The term usually refers to a stack of CD-ROMs.

**jump** (v.) To branch to another location in an interactive program, depending on user input.

**jump cut** (n.) An abrupt type of video edit that shows a new camera angle, a different frame size, or a notable change in the placement of the subject. This causes the subject to appear to jump. Jump cuts are generally avoided, or they are replaced with a cutaway to a related scene.

**jumper** (n.) A small clip that slips over pins on a circuit board to complete or break a circuit, thus serving as a hardware switch.

**Junction FET** (n.) A field-effect transistor without an insulated gate.

**justification** (n.) The process of allocating space in a line of text so that the left and right margins will align evenly.

**justify** (v.) To shift a numeral so that either the most significant, or the least significant digit, is placed at a specific position in a row.

**JVM** See *Java Virtual Machine.*

**J**

# K

K See *Kelvin.*

**Ka-band** (n.) Electromagnetic waves in the radio frequency spectrum between about 33 and 36 GHz. This upper portion of the microwave range is used primarily by satellites and for mobile voice transmission. Pronounced "KAY-AAY band." Compare *Ku-band.*

**Kaleida** (n.) The name adopted by collaborators from Apple Computer and IBM who sought to develop and promote new cross-platform multimedia software technologies with applications for computers, personal electronics, and communications. The Kaleida project was ended in 1995, after several years without results. See also *ScriptX.*

**karaoke** (n.) "Empty orchestra" in Japanese; the act of singing into a microphone while a laser disc or video CD plays an accompaniment track without vocals. Karaoke equipment displays the lyrics to a song as subtitles on a video monitor and mixes the input of a microphone with the recorded accompaniment. An entertainer reads the lyrics and sings into the microphone along with the recording. Karaoke is popular in homes and nightclubs in Japan. Pronounced "KAR-ah-OH-kay."

**Kb** See *kilobit.*

**KB** See *kilobyte.*

**Kbps** See *kilobits per second.*

**KBps** See *kilobytes per second.*

**Kelvin** (K) (n.) Temperature scale used to define the color of a light source. Different sources of illumination produce wavelengths of different colors. The Kelvin temperature scale is used to measure variations in color, or *color temperature*, under different types of lighting. When the white balance of a video camera is set to 3200°K, colors appear normal. This is the color of a Tungsten bulb used for photography. Daylight at early morning or dusk is also about 3200°K. Incandescent light indoors is typically about 2800°K, with a slightly red tint. A "warm" fluorescent light is about 3500°K, while a white fluorescent light is closer to 4500°K with a green tint. Daylight at midday is about 5600°K, with a blue tint. On an overcast day the color temperature may be around 7000°K. Depending on the proportion of direct and reflected light, the time of day, and cloud conditions, the exterior color temperature could be anywhere between 4200°K to over 20,000°K. Filters are used to correct for variations in color temperature when shooting video under varied lighting conditions. The British physicist William T. Kelvin constructed the scale in 1848.

**Kermit** (n.) A file transfer protocol and terminal emulation program used to download files from a host to a local computer by modem. Kermit can transfer binary files over Telnet and over other connections without corrupting data.

**kern** (v.) To control the spacing between letters in a document. Certain letter combinations require more or less space between them to become legible and pleasing to the eye. For example, the letter combination *AV* is an example of negative spacing. This allows the characters to nest without excessive white space between them.

**kernel** (n.) 1. In programming, an essential subset of a language that defines all the constructs in the language. It is also known as a *core language.* 2. A basic part of any operating system responsible for resource allocation, hardware interfaces, security, and other low-level operations.

**key** 1. (n.) A button on an input device that sends data to the computer program to which it is connected. 2. Jargon for *key frame,* an image used at the beginning or end of an animation sequence. 3. Jargon for *key light,* often the brightest light shining on the main character in a scene of a video or film production. 4. (v.) To switch between two or more video sources, based on a control signal. The control signal itself may be referred to as the key. An example is *chroma keying,* in which a color is used as a key to eliminate or to block objects of that color in a video composition. 5. (n.) A string or a value required by an algorithm that decodes encrypted data. Some encryption schemes use a private key, whereas others use a public key. 6. A value that identifies a record in a database, based on a fixed function applied to that record. The set of keys for all records forms an index.

**keyboard** (n.) 1. Any device that contains alphanumeric, symbol, and function keys that can input text or give instructions to a computer. The version that resembles a typewriter is referred to as a *QWERTY* keyboard because of the layout of the keys. 2. A piano, synthesizer, or MIDI keyboard with black and white keys used to perform music.

**keyer** (n.) In video editing, a video switcher that cuts a hole in the background and fills it with material from another source. Text and graphics are frequently "keyed" over NTSC video. The keyer superimposes two or more images by alternating among inputs during the scans across the screen that define the video image. With the aid of this technique, a weather forecaster appears to be standing in front of a map but is actually in front of a blue screen.

**key frame** (n.) 1. An image used at the beginning or end of an animation sequence or as a reference point in a video stream. 2. In compressed video, a frame that contains a complete description of itself, rather than just data about differences between it and the previous frame.

**keypad** (n.) A small keyboard that typically consists only of numeric and function keys. A keypad is found on the right side of most computer keyboards and on calculators.

**keystoning** (n.) Distortion caused when a projection angle that is not perpendicular displays graphic images or video on a flat surface. A projection that exhibits keystoning is not rectangular, because one side is longer than the opposing side. Also called *parallax.*

**key telephone system** (KTS) (n.) In telephony, key telephone system is a flexible multilane telephone system that offers outside access without a local office operator. This telephone system offers multiple access to 2 to 12 trunk lines, and 4 to 40 extensions. Sometimes considered a smaller version of a private branch exchange (PBX).

**keyword** 1. (n.) In a high-level computing language, a word that calls subroutines. 2. (adj.) Describes a type of test in some training applications that helps evaluate a learner's comprehension.

**kHz** See *kilohertz*.

**kibi-** (Ki) New prefix standardized by the International Electrotechnical Commisson (IEC) to replace "kilo" as it refers to binary numbers. See also *SI unit prefix revision*.

**kilo-** Prefix meaning one thousand. In the decimal system, 1000 is expressed as 10 to the 3rd power. In the binary system used to quantify data, this is expressed as 2 to the 10th power, or 1024.

**kilobit** (Kb) (n.) In reference to binary data, 2 to the 10th power, or 1024 bits.

**kilobits per second** (Kbps) (n.) A measurement of data transfer or movement in thousands of bits per second.

**kilobyte** (KB) (n.) 2 to the 10th eight-bit bytes, or 1024 bytes. MS-DOS can allocate a maximum of 640KB of data in RAM to conventional memory.

**kilobytes per second** (KBps) (n.) A measurement of data transfer or movement in 2 to the 10th bytes per second.

**kilohertz** (kHz) (n.) One thousand cycles per second.

**kilovoltamperes** (n.) One thousand voltamperes. See also *voltampere*.

**kiosk** (n.) A freestanding, interactive multimedia system that typically has a touch screen for input. It is often located in a public area, and it may be used to convey information or to collect data.

**kluge** (n.) Jargon for a software patch that solves a problem expediently, although not elegantly. Pronounced "KLOOJ."

**knockout** (n.) The removal of an element in a multilayered graphic so that the underlying color does not tint overlapping layers. See figure.

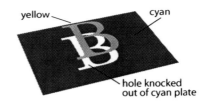

*knockout*

**knowbot** (n.) Program that scouts the web collecting information about sites, descriptive text in metatags, and URLs to be indexed by a search engine. Also known as a *spider* or a *bot*. Most of the major indexes employ knowbots, including Yahoo!, WebCrawler, Infoseek, and AltaVista.

**knowledge** (n.) The concepts and relationships assumed to exist in an artificial intelligence (AI) system. Knowledge is different from raw data, because new knowledge may be created from existing knowledge using logical inference by an AI system. Knowledge is information about a particular topic, and this information may be processed according to the rules of AI, allowing new information to be inferred.

**knowledge base** (n.) A collection of knowledge represented by a rule-based inference engine.

**Korn shell** (ksh) (n.) Written by David Korn of Bell Labs, a standard Unix shell. It is a command line interface available in a public domain version called *pdksh*.

**ksh** See *Korn shell.*

**Ku-band** (n.) A range of the electromagnetic spectrum used by satellites. Ku-band is between 12 and 14 GHz. Pronounced "KAY-YOU band." Compare *Ka-band.*

**kVA** See *kilovoltamperes.*

**K**

# L

**L2TP** See *Layer Two Tunneling Protocol.*

**lag** (n.) Delay in the transfer of data caused by a slow connection between two machines, often resulting from errors. One of the causes of lag is chew.

**Lambert shading** (n.) A method of applying a graduated shade to a surface by filling small polygons with different colors, or shades, resulting in a faceted appearance. Also called *faceted shading.* See figure.

*Lambert-shaded cylinder*

**LAN** See *local area network.*

**LANC** See *Local Application Numerical Control.*

**land** (n.) The space between pits on the surface of a compact disc.

**landing zone** (n.) The cylinder number at which the head is parked when a hard disk drive is idle or off.

**landscape** (n.) A layout in which the width of a printed page is greater than the height. In a portrait layout, the height is greater than the width. See figure.

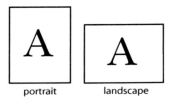

portrait          landscape

*landscape and portrait layouts*

**language** (n.) In programming, a set of instructions specified by a programmer that can be carried out by a computer. BASIC, Cobol, Pascal, FORTRAN, and C++ are common languages.

**LAPD** See *Link Access Procedure–D.*

**LAPM** See *Link Access Protocol for Modems.*

**laptop** (n.) Any portable computer. Because portables are becoming smaller and lighter, it is increasingly common to call them *notebook* computers.

**large-scale integration** (LSI) (n.) In a microprocessor, an integrated circuit (IC) that generally contains more than 100 and fewer than

1000 circuits.

**laser** (n.) Light amplification by stimulated emission of radiation; a device that generates and amplifies energy in the optical spectrum into a beam. The focused beam consists of a single wavelength of light. When it passes over an uneven surface (such as the data spiral of a compact disc), changes in the wavelength of reflections can be detected and converted into a stream of binary data.

**laser disc** (LD) (n.) A reflective optical medium, also called a *videodisc*. Laser Disc is a trademark of Pioneer, USA, and the term has been used freely to describe any thin, round platter that stores various types of information in analog or digital formats. A laser disc is an analog medium but provides a high degree of interactivity because a user can jump instantly to different points, or chapters, on a disc. The data is written in a spiral from the center to the edge. Data on a disc is read by an optical sensor that picks up reflections from a laser beam.

**laser pickup** (n.) A mechanical subsystem in an optical disc player that holds and positions the laser.

**laser printer** (n.) Any printer that uses laser optics to produce text and images on photosensitive paper. Desktop laser printers require toner cartridges and typically have a resolution ranging from 300 dots per inch (dpi) to 1200 dpi.

**laser rot** (n.) The degradation of an optical disc caused by the use of contaminated raw materials or improper process controls.

**Laservision** (LV) (n.) A trade name for the videodisc format supported by manufacturers such as Pioneer, Philips, and Sony.

**Laservision read-only memory** (LV-ROM) (n.) A laser disc format that combines analog video with digital data and audio on a 12-inch laser disc. Philips developed LV-ROM in 1986, and Pioneer reintroduced an updated version in 1990. The Pioneer version provides for digital data in the ISO 9660 (High Sierra) CD-ROM format to be encoded along with analog stereo audio and video information on a standard 12-inch videodisc. Also called *Advanced Interactive Video (AIV)*.

**last-in-first-out** (LIFO) (n.) A method of organizing data in a queue. The order in which it was received and stored is reversed, so that the last piece of data received is the first to be processed. Compare *FIFO*.

**last mile** (n.) Telecommunications jargon for the cable connection between the central office (CO) and a subscriber. Every connection between two devices over the telephone network has a "last mile" at each end. This is not a literal mile, but a generic reference to a space that might be a hundred feet or several miles. Also referred to as a local loop.

**last-on** (adj.) In teleconferencing, this describes microphone inputs on an automatic microphone mixer that stay *open* until another microphone input is activated. A last-on microphone becomes the master microphone if left open long enough.

**LATA** See *Local Access and Transport Area*.

**latency** (n.) 1. Time spent waiting for a response. 2. A component in the measurement of access time in hard disk drives and in CD-ROM drives.

**Latin-1** (n.) An eight-bit, single-byte coded graphic character set capable of representing

255

up to 256 characters. It contains letters for English, German, French, Spanish, and most Scandinavian languages, but does not support Greek, Hebrew, Arabic, or Cyrillic languages.

**layer** (n.) 1. The level in a network at which a certain protocol is in effect. Direct communication between two hardware hosts is at the bottom level. User applications make up the top level, or layer. Upper layers build on those under them. At each layer, programs use different protocols to communicate. The Open Systems Interconnection (OSI) network model has seven layers of protocols, whereas TCP/IP has five. 2. In graphics production, a page that may be placed above or below others in a stack. A layer may be transparent to varying degrees, so that those beneath it are visible. To *composite* graphics is to layer them. One example of compositing layers is the placement of titles over frames of video.

**layering** (n.) A concept applied in multimedia production to create dimensionality. In sound design, a mix may have numerous channels, or layers, with different audio tracks on each channel. A layered graphic design typically shows objects in the foreground with others in the background. When a video production is edited, materials from various sources are layered. Complex three-dimensional animations employ a high degree of layering.

**Layer Two Tunneling Protocol** (L2TP) (n.) The Internet Engineering Task Force (IETF) protocol used to create a Virtual Private Network (VPN) over the Internet. L2TP is a combination of Point-to-Point Tunneling Protocol (PPTP) from Microsoft and L2F technology from Cisco. L2TP also supports protocols other than IP, such as Internetwork Packet eXchange (IPX) and AppleTalk, as well as non-IP Security protocols.

**lay up** (v.) To transfer production sound from an edited videotape to an audio medium for sweetening. The final mix is "laid back" to the video master.

**LBA** See *Logical Block Addressing.*

**L-band** (n.) A segment of the electromagnetic spectrum that lies in the range between 390 and 1550 MHz. It is used for satellite transmission and microwave applications, such as the Global Positioning System (GPS).

**LCC** See *Leadless Chip Carrier.*

**LCD** See *liquid crystal display.*

**LD** See *laser disc.*

**LDAP** See *Lightweight Directory Access Protocol.*

**leader** (n.) In the process of storing analog recordings on magnetic tape, a clean, blank segment of tape-like material that is spliced before the first cut and between programs. Sometimes the term is used loosely to refer to a few seconds of blank tape at the head of a reel. Pronounced "LEE-der."

**lead-in** (n.) In videodisc programs, the 40 seconds of video black preceding the active program. Pronounced "LEE-din." Compare *lead-out.*

**lead-in area** (n.) A space reserved at the beginning of a recordable compact disc (CD-R) that is left blank for the disc's table of contents (TOC). The table is recorded in this space when the disc is filled or when it is permanently closed and finalized.

**leading** (n.) In electronic text or on the printed

page, the distance between the type on two lines. Leading is measured from the baseline on which type rests to the next baseline. It is therefore composed of the height of the characters plus the space between the lines. Pronounced "LED-ding."

**Leadless Chip Carrier** (LCC) (n.) An integrated circuit (IC) package with input and output pads instead of leads around the edges.

**lead-out** (n.) In videodisc programs, the 30 seconds of video black with no audio following the active program. Compare *lead-in*.

**lead-out area** (n.) A space reserved at the end of a session on a recordable compact disc (CD-R) indicating that the data has ended and that the session has been finalized.

**leapfrog attack** (n.) The use of user-ID and password information obtained from one host to compromise another host. In such an attack, a user will Telnet through one or more hosts to disguise their identity and make a trace nearly impossible.

**leased access** (n.) Local cable television system channels that the Federal Communications Commission (FCC) requires to be reserved for lease by independent video programmers.

**leased line** (n.) A dedicated telephone connection that links two or more points without passing through switching equipment. Such lines are often used to connect a local area network (LAN) with an Internet Service Provider (ISP).

**least significant bit** (LSB ) (n.) In a string of digits that store or transmit binary data, the last bit, or the bit furthest to the right, when the string is written in the usual way. The LSB is the part of a value with the slightest weighting in a mathematical calculation.

**LEC** See *local exchange carrier.*

**LED** See *light-emitting diode.*

**legacy system** (n.) A hardware-software package that remains in use because of the expense or difficulty of upgrading or replacing it with newer, more functional equipment.

**Lempel-Ziv-Welch** (LZW) (n.) Developed by Terry Welch in 1984, a lossless compression scheme used to reduce file size. A variant of Lempel-Ziv compression, LZW maintains a table that maps input strings, or recurring byte sequences, to their associated output codes. It works by identifying similarities between character codes and then recording that data in an abbreviated format. Unisys Corporation patented LZW compression and decompression in 1984.

**letterbomb** (n.) In network security, an email containing live data intended to damage or disrupt the recipient's machine or terminal.

**letterbox** (v., adj.) To crop the top and bottom of the screen while displaying video. Programs recorded in the original aspect ratio of film, which is proportionately wider than the aspect ratio of a computer or television monitor, will often appear with black bands above and below the viewing area. These bands are called the *letterbox effect*. The two formats whose framing shares a native aspect ratio of 16:9 are film and digital video. When high-definition television (HDTV) signals are viewed on a standard television tube with an approximate aspect ratio of 4:3, the letterbox effect results, unless a considerable amount of the picture is cropped from the sides. See figure.

*letterbox effect*

**level** (n.) In audio, level is the relative signal strength:

- **mic-level** The nominal signal coming directly from a microphone. It is very low, (microvolts), and requires a preamp with at least 60 dB gain before it can be used with any *line-level* equipment.
- **line-level** The normal level output from a tape player, CD player, or mixer. The standards are *+4 dBu* or *-10 dBV* audio levels.
- **instrument-level** The nominal signal from a musical instrument using an electrical pick-up, such as an electric guitar. It can vary widely, from very low *mic-levels* to high *line-levels*.

**leveler** (n.) A dynamic audio processor that maintains the strength of one audio signal at a constant level based upon the level of a second audio signal. The source of the second signal is often a microphone picking up ambient noise. The leveler monitors the background noise, dynamically increasing and decreasing the main audio signal as necessary to maintain a constant loudness differential between the two signals. The main signal might be a speaker's microphone in a noisy room.

**lexical analysis** (n.) In programming, the first stage of processing a language. Characters that comprise the source program are read one at a time and grouped into *lexemes,* which are constructs such as keywords, identifiers, literals, and punctuation. These lexemes are then passed to the parser. The process is also known as *linear analysis* or *scanning.*

**LFO** See *low-frequency oscillator.*

**library** (n.) In programming, a list of procedures or functions that can be accessed and implemented. A library is a collection of previously built code or routines.

**LIFO** See *last-in-first-out.*

**light-emitting diode** (LED, pronounced "el-ee-DEE") (n.) A semiconductor diode that emits light when current passes through it. The most common LED application is the alphanumeric display on a calculator. A laser is a type of LED that can serve as the source for optical data transmission.

**lightguide** (n.) Jargon for optical fiber, or a bundle of fibers.

**light pen** (n.) A stylus that controls the position of a cursor on a monitor. It has a light-detecting tip and is used either for graphics input on a drawing tablet or as a user interface (UI) device.

**lightwave** (n.) Synonym for fiber optics. Also refers to optical communications not transmitted by fibers.

**Lightweight Directory Access Protocol** (LDAP) (n.) A relatively simple protocol for updating and searching directories that run on TCP/IP. An LDAP directory entry is a collection of attributes with a distinguished name. Each of the entry's attributes has a type, such as "mail," and one or more values. A mail attribute might contain a value such as *brad @hansenmedia.com.* LDAP directory entries are arranged in a hierarchical structure that reflects political, geographic, or organizational boundaries. Countries reside at the top of the tree, followed by entries for states and organizations.

**limiter** (n.) In audio, a limiter is a compressor with a fixed ratio of 10:1 or greater. The signal is prevented from becoming any larger than the threshold setting. If the threshold is set at +16 dBu and the input signal increases by 10 dB to +26 dB, the output only increases by 1 dB to +17 dBu, a negligible amount. It is most useful in preventing unexpected overloads to recording equipment and to transmitters, where headroom might be exceeded unexpectedly. It is also known as a peak limiter.

**linear** (adj.) Describes a medium in which content is arranged sequentially and in which the user must move through the material by going forward or backward, as opposed to entering a data stream at any point. A videotape is linear, whereas digital media is nonlinear.

**linear audio** (n.) On a videotape, the use of a separate track dedicated to recording audio. This technique may result in low fidelity, but the audio may be edited separately from the video. It is used to replace wild sound on a field tape with narration and sound effects.

**linear PCM** (n.) A pulse code modulation (PCM) encoding system in which the signal is converted directly to a PCM word without any companding or other processing. Linear PCM distributes the value of the data evenly across the frequency spectrum. If companding is applied, a signal is compressed at input and restored to its original form on output.

**linear phase response** (n.) Any system that accurately preserves phase relationships between input and output frequencies.

**line art** (n.) Images that contain only black-and-white information with no grayscale or blended tones. This category includes halftone images that appear gray but that consist of tiny black dots on a white background.

**Linear Tape Open** (LTO) (n.) An open standard proposed by IBM, Seagate Technology, and Hewlett-Packard for increasing the areal density, access speed, and transfer rate in midrange tape storage systems. LTO competes with DLT technology, the de facto standard.

**line coding** (n.) The method used for mapping the voltage changes of a digital signal and translating them into 1 bit or 0 bits. Both transmitting and receiving devices must employ the same line coding to transfer meaningful information.

**line conditioning** (n.) Alteration of the conductive properties of wires used to transmit power or signals. Transformers, resistors, capacitors, and other components are inserted into a line, which may be a twisted pair of copper wires, to adjust and correct signal levels. Analog voice lines are typically loaded, which means that inductors are inserted at regular intervals. Dry lines, or those lacking either inductors or the DC voltage used for telephone voice transmission, are best for transmitting digital data.

**line extender** (n.) An amplifier that compensates for loss in the strength of a signal over distribution lines.

**line level** (adj.) Describes an audio signal that ranges from 100 millivolts (mV) to approximately 1 volt for full signal. A line level signal is typically the output of a preamplifier rather than the low-level signal that comes directly from a microphone.

**line noise** (n.) Electrical interference picked up

259

in a communications link, such as an RS-232 serial connection, that may cause spurious characters to appear. Line noise may be induced by poor connections, crosstalk from other circuits, electrical storms, or other electromagnetic sources.

**line printer port** (LPT) (n.) On an IBM-compatible computer, a parallel port through which a printer is often interfaced with a 25-pin connector. See also *parallel port*.

**Lingo** (n.) A scripting language used for authoring in Macromedia Director. Lingo is similar to HyperTalk, the language used in HyperCard scripting.

**link** (n.) 1. A connection between two pieces of data. An example of a link is the relationship between a hypertext anchor and the URL to which it refers. 2. A connection between network nodes.

**Link Access Procedure–D** (LAPD) (n.) A link-level protocol for the D channel in ISDN connections. LAPD has a different framing sequence from the LAP-Balanced (LAPB) protocol.

**Link Access Protocol for Modems** (LAPM) (n.) The automatic request for retransmission (ARQ) system with cyclic redundancy check (CRC) that is part of the V.42 protocol.

**link layer** (n.) Layer 2, the data link layer, in the Open Systems Interconnection (OSI) reference model.

**Link Manager Protocol** (LMP) (n.) The technology responsible for linkage, control, and security between Bluetooth radio devices.

**link rot** (n.) Jargon for the condition of links on a web page that point to locations that have

changed or no longer exist.

**Link State Routing Protocol** (n.) A routing protocol such as Open Shortest-Path First (OSPF) that allows a router to exchange information with other routers about accessing external networks. It assesses the link speeds, number of hops, traffic congestion, and other features in a network connection. Link state routers calculate the shortest path for a message and update other routers when their own routing tables change. Link state routing normally requires more processing but less transmission overhead than distance-vector routing protocols, such as RIP, which typically use a single metric and which exchange all of their table information with other routers on a regular schedule.

**Linkwitz-Riley crossover** (n.) This is the standard for professional audio active crossovers. The model L4 is a fourth-order unit with 24 dB/octave slopes, based on a combination of cascading Butterworth filters. The outputs are in phase and summed to a constant voltage response. Two Hewlett-Packard engineers, Linkwitz and Riley, designed it in 1976.

**Linux** (n.) Short for *Linus Unix;* an implementation of the Unix kernel that runs on Intel and Alpha hardware in the general release. Versions of Linux for SPARC, PowerPC, and SGI are also available. Versions that are ported to microcomputers support networking and shells. Linus Torvalds, the primary copyright holder, coordinates development of the Linux kernel. The whole kernel is available under the GNU general public license. See extensive informaiton on Linux under the Unix definition. Pronounced "LEE-nucks."

**liquid crystal display** (LCD) (n.) An array of liquid crystal cells that are turned on and off electronically, modulating light that shines from behind the display. When they are used with a projection system, large LCD panels can simulate computer graphics output. Because LCDs consume very little power, they are often used for numbers and letters on calculators, watches, and handheld games.

**LISP** (n.) Abbreviated form of <u>Lis</u>t <u>P</u>rocessor; a programming language developed by John McCarthy consisting of expressions that are lists of instructions to a computer. The lists establish relationships among themselves, and the values created by the relationships become part of the data in a LISP program. LISP is commonly used in artificial intelligence (AI) applications.

**listserv** (n.) A program that automates mailing lists on the Internet or on any large network.

**lithography** (n.) The transfer of a pattern or image from one medium to another, such as from a mask to a silicon wafer.

**little-endian** (adj.) Describes a format for storing or transmitting binary data in which the least significant byte or bit is placed at the head, or beginning of a packet. The term is adapted from the Lilliputians in *Gulliver's Travels* by Jonathan Swift; they debated whether soft-boiled eggs should be opened at the big end or the little end. Compare *big-endian*.

**live** (adj.) Describes audio/video information that is delivered in realtime, such as *live* news broadcasts. This is the opposite of *on-demand* programming. Live digital video systems must use symmetric codecs to compress and distribute content in realtime.

**LLC** See *logical link control*.

**LMDS** See *Local Multipoint Distribution Service*.

**LMP** See *Link Manager Protocol*.

**load** (v.) 1. To transfer a computer program from storage into RAM. 2. To introduce electrical current into a line or circuit.

**loading coil** (n.) An induction device employed in telephone local loops, generally those that exceed 18,000 feet in length, that compensates for the wire capacitance by adding inductance.

**Local Access and Transport Area** (LATA, pronounced "LAH-tah") (n.) A contiguous geographical area consisting of a state or metropolitan region served by a Bell Operating Company (BOC). There are 161 local telephone service areas in the United States. Calls made point to point within a single LATA are the responsibility of the local telephone company. InterLATA calls are processed by an interexchange carrier.

**Local Application Numerical Control** (LANC, pronounced "LANK") (n.) Developed by Sony, a machine control protocol for videotape recorders and players that carries Control-S data. It is implemented by a variety of camcorders in the 8 mm and S-VHS format and can transfer information in the hours:minutes:seconds:frames (hh:mm:ss:ff) format to and from digital controllers.

**local area network** (LAN) (n.) Any physical network technology that operates at high speeds over short distances, such as several thousand yards. Technologies that play roles in a LAN include Ethernet, token ring, Asynchronous Transfer Mode (ATM), Fiber Distributed Data Interface (FDDI) II, 10BASE-T, and Systems Network Architecture (SNA). The system of cables and interfaces controlled by a communications protocol that connects microcomputers for sharing resources and peripherals is all part of the LAN. Connection is also possible with an infrared or wireless link. Compare *wide area network*.

**local bus** (n.) In microcomputer architecture, a data bus with a short signal path between the main processor and input/output (I/O) processors. A local bus is frequently used for fast video functions. Popular local bus standards are the VESA and PCI buses.

**local exchange** (n.) A telecommunications provider's central office, which is where a subscriber's line is terminated.

**local exchange carrier** (LEC, pronounced "LEHK") (n.) An organization that provides intraLATA telephone service or exchange access. It may be any local telephone company in the United States, either a Bell Operating Company (BOC) or an independent, such as GTE.

**localize** (v.) To tailor the content of piece of media to fit the cultural requirements of a specific region or population.

**local loop** (n.) In telecommunications, the circuits between a telephone subscriber's residence or business site and switching equipment at the telephone company's central office.

**Local Multipoint Distribution System** (LMDS) (n.) Wireless cable service that offers multiple channels of video programming in the 27.5- to 29.5-GHz microwave spectrum. An antenna 4.5 inches in diameter is required to receive LMDS signals. Broadcast antennas serve cells that overlap in a radius of three to six miles. The first commercial LMDS operator was Cellular Vision in New York City.

**LocalTalk** (n.) The hardware used to connect Macintosh computers and peripherals for AppleTalk communications.

**location** (n.) 1. The address where data is recorded in computer memory. 2. A place where a film is shot, usually outdoors or in a "real-world" environment as opposed to in a studio with fake backgrounds.

**log** (v.) To record time code numbers that correspond to selected frames of video on tape, used by editors to identify segments for future reference.

**log file** (n.) A record created by a web server that contains all the access information, which documents activity on a web site.

**logic** (n.) 1. Philosophy that addresses the formal principles and methods of reasoning and knowledge. Logic is concerned with knowing truth. Symbols are used to formalize logical arguments and proofs representing propositions and logical connectives. Boolean algebra is applied to the basic operations of truth values using combinations of "AND," "OR," and "NOT." Predicate logic expresses the progression from premises to conclusions, or the process of deduction. 2. Formulas used to control the operation of integrated circuits (ICs) that apply relational propositions to gated circuits.

**logical** (adj.) Describes a conceptual object that serves a function or has meaning. In programming, a physical device is often referred to by a logical name. *Logical* is similar to *virtual,* because logical objects do not necessarily reside in any physical place.

**Logical Block Addressing** (LBA) (n.) A procedure that IBM-compatible microcomputers use to increase the size limit for a single Integrated Drive Electronics (IDE) hard disk from 528 megabytes (MB) to 8.4 gigabytes (GB). Addressing conversion takes place on the IDE disk controller card. Older Basic Input/Output System (BIOS) versions allow the user to select LBA mode manually.

**logical block number** (n.) A sequential address for accessing blocks of data on storage media. Blocks are numbered sequentially, beginning with 0.

**logical code** (n.) A tag that provides general directions in an HTML document. For example, the tag <EM> means "emphasis," which could be translated as either italic or bold. By contrast, a physical code indicates exactly how text should be displayed. The physical tag <B> indicates bold, and not any other general type of emphasis.

**logical device** (n.) Data in the logic of a computer that describes a peripheral or external equipment, whether or not the equipment is physically connected or even exists. It is a virtual representation of the features of a device, useful for mapping information that is passed to and from the physical device.

**logical expression** (n.) In computer logic, a comparison between two variables or values that yields a true or false answer. For example, the statement 1 > 0 is true.

**logical file format** (n.) In reference to data stored on a compact disc or on a hard drive, a structure shaped like a virtual tree of directories and files. This structure facilitates access to information. Also called *logical format.*

**logical link control** (LLC) (n.) In networking, the top portion of the data link layer in the OSI reference model. The specification is defined by IEEE 802.2. The LLC sublayer provides an interface for the data link service user with error checking. Directly below the LLC sublayer is the media access control (MAC) sublayer.

**logical unit** (LU) (n.) In IBM's Simple Network Architecture (SNA), a logical port through which a user gains access to the services of a network.

**logical unit number** (LUN, pronounced "el-yoo-EHN") (n.) Identifier for a device directly attached to a SCSI physical unit and not directly attached to the SCSI bus. A logical unit typically references a single physical unit, though not always. A SCSI hard drive is assigned a physical unit number (SCSI ID), and its controller is assigned an LUN.

**logic bomb** (n.) A computer program that activates an unauthorized act when certain conditions exist in a system. Also known as a fork bomb.

**logic gate** (n.) An integrated circuit (IC) with inputs and outputs that represent binary values as voltages. The standard amount of voltage that transistor-transistor logic (TTL) uses is 0 volts for 0 (false) compared with 5 volts for 1 (true). Gates implement Boolean functions, such as AND, OR, NAND, NOR, NOT, and XOR. Gates with *state* can hold a temporary condition or status. A *flip-flop* gate holds state, and is capable of feeding certain outputs back to certain inputs.

**login** (n., adj.) The identification and authentication process performed by users when accessing a computer system or network. A login script is run by the host computer.

**log off** (v., adj.) To end an online session with a computer or network. This is usually accomplished by typing *logoff* or *logout.*

**log on** (v.) To enter a networked multiuser

environment, typically by submitting a user name and password to the host computer.

**longitudinal redundancy check** (LRC) (n.) A procedure that tests the completeness of networked data or information stored on a data tape. LRC is based on comparing a block check character (BCC) between sender and receiver, to see if the block of data has accumulated to the same size on both ends. If they are equal, then transmission is assumed to be complete.

**longitudinal time code** (LTC) (n.) Time code information that is recorded, or "stamped," in the form of an audio signal on an available linear track of a videotape. LTC provides a means of precisely locating any point on a tape, which enables frame-accurate machine control.

**long shot** (n.) A camera view from a distance showing a broad perspective of a subject or scene.

**loop** 1. (n.) A complete, self-contained electrical connection. 2. (n.) The uninterrupted, repeated display of a series of still frames, an audio file, a video segment, or the execution of a series of instructions. 3. (v.) To cause a segment of media to repeat.

**loopback** (n.) A diagnostic test in which a signal is returned to the transmitting device from the receiving device for comparison.

**loop start** (n.) In telephony, loop start is a local loop that signals an off-hook condition by allowing direct current (DC) to flow between the tip and ring conductors. Loop start is commonly used for single line telephones.

**loop through** (n.) A feature of an audio, video, or data circuit that provides an output connector, which sends the same signal that the unit receives as input. This enables an auxiliary unit to receive the signal at approximately the same time as the original unit receives the input signal.

**loss** (n.) A reduction in signal strength, expressed in decibels (dB). It is the product of attenuation.

**lossless compression** (n.) A compression technique that reduces the storage requirements of a file yet completely preserves the original information contained in images or in other data. Compare *lossy*.

**lossless format conversion** (n.) The process of changing a file from one format to another without recompressing the data. An AVI file may be converted into a QuickTime movie without loss as long as the same codec is used under both architectures.

**lossy** (adj.) Describes encoding or compression methods that do not preserve all the original data in a file, making that data impossible to recover later. Lossy compression can greatly reduce the quantity of data required to define an object by discarding redundant and unnecessary information in images and data files while maintaining the basic content. Data lost in the quantization of high-frequency components of an image is virtually imperceptible to the human eye, however, so the discarded data may be relatively insignificant. Discrete cosine transform is a type of lossy compression. Compare *lossless compression*.

**loudness** (n.) The sound pressure level (SPL) of a sound, measured in phons (units of apparent loudness) and equal to the equivalent SPL in dB. A sound deemed as loud as a 40 dB-SPL 1 kHz tone has a loudness level of 40 phons. An increase of 10 phons, or 10 dB-SPL, is deemed *twice* as loud.

**low-frequency oscillator** (LFO) (n.) In sound synthesis, a device capable of subsonic frequency generation, used most often as a controller for other functions, such as vibrato or tremolo.

**low-level language** (n.) An assembly language that translates each statement into a single machine instruction.

**low-pass filter** (n.) In audio engineering, a filter that allows only the frequencies below a cutoff point to pass through, blocking out the higher frequencies.

**L-pad** See *attenuator*.

**LPT** See *line printer port*.

**LRC** See *longitudinal redundancy check*.

**LSI** See *large-scale integration*.

**LTC** See *longitudinal time code*.

**LTO** See *Linear Tape Open*.

**LU** See *logical unit*.

**luma** (n.) Brightness of a transmitted video signal.

**lumen** (n.) A unit of luminous flux emitted by a light source. Lumens are measured in candelas; 1 candela indicates the intensity radiated by a single candle.

**luminance** (n.) Degree of brightness or intensity. One of the three image characteristics coded in a component video signal (represented by the letter Y) and measured in lux or foot-candles. Luminance is the black-and-white portion of a video signal. The other two components of a video signal are the red and blue chroma factors.

**luminance bandwidth** (n.) The frequency range representing the degree of brightness that a video system can record or transmit. Shape detail is determined largely by this factor.

**luminance key** (n.) A signal that a switcher uses to alternate between two or more video images based on the brightness of one of the signals.

**LUN** See *logical unit number*.

**lurker** (n.) Jargon for a subscriber to a mail list or newsgroup who does not post often but who reads group postings regularly.

**lux** (n.) A unit of measurement equal to one lumen over a one-square-meter surface.

**LV** See *Laservision*.

**LV-ROM** See *Laservision read-only memory*.

**Lynx** (n.) Text-mode universal client, or browser, developed at the University of Kansas, primarily used on the Unix and MS-DOS platforms.

**LZW** See *Lempel-Ziv-Welch*.

# M

MAC See *media access control.*

**MAC address** (n.) Media access control address; a hardware address belonging to any device connected to a shared media network via the MAC protocol. A MAC address may refer to the low-level address assigned to a device on an Ethernet; such an address would be translated to an Internet Protocol (IP) address via Address Resolution Protocol (ARP). Each network interface card (NIC) is assigned a unique address when manufactured. Also known as *Ethernet address.*

**MacBinary** (n.) A representation of the data and resource forks belonging to a Macintosh file, along with relevant Finder information, expressed in eight-bit words. A Macintosh terminal emulator will recognize a MacBinary file, use file transfer protocol (FTP) to separate the file into forks, and appropriately modify the desktop to display icons and other Macintosh-compatible constructs.

**machine code** (n.) Another term for *machine language.*

**machine cycle** (n.) The four steps a processor carries out for each machine language instruction: fetch, decode, execute, and store. Performed by the control unit, the steps may be fixed in the logic of the CPU or programmed as microcode. The *fetch* cycle places the current program counter contents on the address bus and reads the word at that location into the instruction register (IR). The *decode* cycle uses the contents of the IR to determine which gates should be opened in the CPU's various functional units and buses. In the *execute* cycle, values are passed between the various functional units and buses, and the arithmetic and logic unit (ALU) is operated. During the *store* cycle, the result of the instruction is written to its destination, either a register or a memory location.

**machine-independent** (adj.) Describes software designed to perform similarly on more than one kind of computer. Java bytecode is meant to be machine-independent; the Java Virtual Machine (JVM) can be loaded on any type of computer.

**machine language** (n.) Binary code that expresses computer instructions and data in an executable form at the lowest level. No further translation is required for computer processing.

**Macintosh** (n.) Developed by Apple Computer in 1984, a popular microcomputer originally based on the Motorola 68000 series CPU. It evolved into the Power Macintosh in 1994 based on the PowerPC RISC processor. Its operating system is known as the Mac OS, a graphical user interface (GUI) originally designed by Xerox. Multimedia features such as sound generation, QuickTime video, and interactive icons have been built into the hardware and software of Macintosh computers since their inception, establishing a model in this regard for other systems designers.

**Macintosh file system** (n.) A logical construct with two parts, or forks, proprietary to the Mac OS. The *data fork* contains data that, on other operating systems, is typically stored in a file. The *resource fork* contains a collection of arbitrary attribute-value pairs, including program segments, icon bitmaps, and parametric values required by the Finder. Additional information regarding Macintosh files is stored by the Finder in a hidden file called the *Desktop Database*. It is difficult to store the different parts of a Macintosh file in other file systems that handle only consecutive data. For this reason, the data fork is often the only part sent when a file is transferred to a computer that uses another operating system. Alternatively, a Macintosh file may be converted into some other format before it is transferred.

**Macintosh Programmer's Workshop** (MPW) (n.) The environment in which applications are developed for the Macintosh system.

**Mac OS** (n.) Macintosh operating system; the proprietary operating system used by the Macintosh family of microcomputers.

**macro** (n.) A small block of code, or a series of commands, batched together and executed by a keystroke or by a combination of function keys. A macro is used to replace or automate frequently performed tasks.

**MADI** See *Multichannel Audio Digital Interface.*

**magnetic storage** (n.) Any medium used to save information encoded as variations in magnetic polarity. Common examples of magnetic storage are audio tapes, videotapes, magnetic tapes, and floppy diskettes.

**magnetic tape** (mag tape) (n.) Typically made from a mylar base, a thin, inelastic tape. It is coated with a ferromagnetic emulsion and used to record and store audio tracks, video programs, and computer data.

**magneto optical** (MO) (n.) The use of a laser beam to heat a special magnetic recording medium and to reduce its resistance to the reversal of magnetic polarity while a magnet is used to change polarity in selected spots. The medium becomes stable at normal temperatures, makes a relatively permanent record, and is housed in a protective cartridge. Most rewritable optical drives employ MO technology.

**magneto-optical disc** (n.) A high-density, read/write optical storage medium. In access speed, it is slower than a hard disk but faster than a CD-ROM. A disc is written by a laser that heats a spot on the disc surface. The spot is polarized by an electromagnet from the other side of the disc. When the disc is read, the change in polarity alters the reflection of light from the reading laser at that spot, and the difference is interpreted as a data value. A magneto-optical disc may be written and read many times, as if it were a large floppy disk.

**magnitude** (n.) A number assigned to a quantity so that it may be compared with other quantities. Properties that can be quantitatively described include volume, length, voltage, and current.

**mag tape** See *magnetic tape.*

**M**

**mailbox** (n.) A file that is the property of a user on a particular computer in which email messages are received and stored for a user to read. It may simply be an email address to which messages are sent.

**Mail Exchange** (MX) (n.) Used to define a host computer, a domain name system (DNS) record that can accept mail.

**Mail Exchange Record** (n.) A domain name system (DNS) resource record type that indicates which host can process electronic mail for a particular domain.

**mail exploder** (n.) Feature of an email delivery system that implements mailing lists. An exploder takes messages sent to a single address and delivers them to all mailboxes on a list.

**mail gateway** (n.) A connection between multiple electronic mail systems that transfers mail between them. Machines that bridge dissimilar systems on different networks use mail gateways to translate messages.

**mailing list** (n.) An alias email address that a mail exploder expands to yield other email addresses. Some mailing lists are simple reflectors that redirect mail to a list of recipients. Others are moderated, or filtered, by humans. A request to subscribe to a mailing list or to be removed from one should be sent to the administrator's address, not to the list, to prevent it from going to all recipients on the list.

**mail path** (n.) The route that a message takes through one or several mail servers from the sending point to the destination.

**mail server** (n.) Any program that distributes files or information in response to requests received through electronic mail.

**mail user agent** (MUA) (n.) A program with which a user reads and composes electronic mail messages. It provides an interface between the user and the message transfer agent (MTA). Outgoing mail is sent to an MTA for delivery, and incoming mail is picked up from the MTA. Agents running on single-user machines may pick up mail using POP. Pine is a common MUA for Unix.

**mainframe computer** (n.) The primary framework of a large computer's central processing unit (CPU).

**main loop** (n.) In an event-driven program, the top-level construct, which receives and operates on user input.

**main memory** (n.) The primary random access storage area in a computer where files and applications reside while controlled by the central processing unit (CPU).

**main processing unit** (n.) The computational core of a system. The main processing unit provides the logical, arithmetic, and control functions that access, process, and output data.

**MAN** See *metropolitan area network*.

**management information system** (MIS) (n.) Computing hardware and software designed to perform business functions, such as retrieving information, representing a database, projecting and forecasting, communicating, tracking accounts, and assisting in decision making about resource allocation.

**Manchester encoding** (n.) A digital line encoding technique in which a voltage transition occurs in the middle of each bit period. A negative-to-positive voltage transition of the bit period designates a binary "1," while a positive-to-negative transition represents a "0." The technique is primarily used on coaxial cable systems and allows for network clocking from the line frequency. Differential Manchester coding, which is used on Token Ring networks over twisted pair, is nearly identical except a relative change in phase indicates a binary "1."

**Mandelbrot set** (n.) A subset of a complex plane whose boundary is a fractal with great detail and variety. It is named for Benoit Mandelbrot, who performed the first research on the subject in the 1970s. See figure.

*Mandelbrot set*

**mapping** (n.) In graphic design, the process of specifying how a texture is applied to the surface of an object. In three-dimensional animation, the way a texture follows an object is a function of its mapping; it is also a function of the scale and orientation of the surface image.

**markup** (n.) The instructions embedded in a text document that specify general formatting features, such as headings and paragraphs. Many proprietary versions exist, but Standard Generalized Markup Language (SGML) is the universal standard.

**martian** (n.) Jargon referring to a packet that appears unexpectedly on the wrong network because of incorrect routing data.

**mask** (n.) 1. The area on a graphic screen on which nothing may be displayed. 2. In the photolithography process, a pattern of chrome and glass used to etch a layer of silicon in chip manufacturing.

**masking pattern adapted universal sub-band integrated coding and multiplexing (MUSICAM)** (n.) A flexible bit rate reduction standard for high quality audio. It was developed for digital audio broadcast by a collaboration of Centre Commun d'Etudes de Télédiffusion et Teleécommunications (CCETT) in France, Institut für Rundfunktechnik (IRT) in Germany and Philips in The Netherlands. MUSICAM operates on a bandwidth of 192 KBps, 128 kbps, and 64 kbps. The sampling rates are 32 kHz, 44.1 kHz, and 48 kHz.

**master** 1. (n.) The final edited version of a program, recorded on high-quality audio tape, videotape, or film, that is intended for broadcast or as the source for duplication. 2. (v.) To produce stamper molds used for replication. 3. (v.) In CD manufacturing, to create a glass master from which copies are reproduced. A laser beam "engraves" the pits, which represent binary data, into a photo-resistant surface.

**master mic** (n.) In teleconferencing, the master mic is the microphone input on an automatic microphone mixer that is the last of a group of microphones to detect audio. The "last-on" mic becomes the master mic if it is left open long enough.

**master port** (n.) In teleconferencing, the audio input port that is the last to detect audio.

**matrix** (n.) In switching technology, the ma-

M

trix is that portion of the switch architecture where input and output are physically interconnected.

**Matrix Math eXtensions** (MMX) (n.) An advancement in the Pentium microprocessor designed and manufactured by Intel Corporation. It is best described when it is contrasted with a non-MMX Pentium processor, such as the Pentium or the Pentium Pro. The Pentium Pro and the Pentium II MMX are both 32-bit processors with 64-bit data paths. Both have 7.5 million transistors in the microprocessor (not including the cache). The original Pentium has two 64-bit register sets: the integer register and the floating-point register. The Pentium MMX adds a third 64-bit MMX register, which has 57 new instructions. The MMX central processing unit (CPU) also adds 16 kilobytes (KB) of Level 1 (L1) cache to the chip. The MMX register loads multiple data with simultaneous processing, working on the single-instruction, multiple-data (SIMD) processing principle. In the original non-MMX Pentium, color images are processed individually, first red, then green, then blue, to display an image. The MMX processes all colors at once without a video accelerator card. MMX uses a branch prediction algorithm and logic similar to that of the Pentium Pro. MMX is available only in speeds of 166 MHz and higher. Starting at 223 MHz, the Pentium II integrates MMX technology on the chip with a standard 32KB of L1 cache and 512KB of Level 2 cache. It uses dynamic execution and speculative execution of code. MMX technology enhances the quality of audio and video by processing these types of data more efficiently and rapidly. The Pentium II and later versions incorporate dynamic execution and MMX technology in a single package.

**matte** (n.) In video production, an upper layer in a composition through which layers that lie beneath are visible through a hole cut in the matting layer. This video effect is used to frame a selected portion of the underlying layer in the same way that a matte frames a mounted painting.

**Mb** See *megabit*.

**MB** See *megabyte*.

**M-bone** See *multicast backbone*.

**Mbps** See *megabits per second*.

**MBps** See *megabytes per second*.

**MCA** See *Micro Channel Architecture*.

**MCI** See *Media Control Interface*.

**MCI driver** (n.) Media Control Interface driver; a software component that directs the recording and playback of multimedia objects. The syntax requires an MCI command to "open" a device, give it instructions, and "close" it. For basic functions all MCI devices share a set of commands, such as "play" and "stop." Microsoft originally defined 11 MCI devices that drivers control, including an undefined classification. See table.

---

**MCI Drivers**

| MCI Device | Command Syntax |
| --- | --- |
| Animation player | MCI_DEVTYPE_ANIMATION |
| Audio CD player | MCI_DEVTYPE_CD_AUDIO |
| Digital audio tape | MCI_DEVTYPE_DAT |
| Video in a window | MCI_DEVTYPE_DIGITAL_VIDEO |
| Undefined | MCI_DEVTYPE_OTHER |
| Video overlay | MCI_DEVTYPE_OVERLAY |
| Image scanner | MCI_DEVTYPE_SCANNER |
| MIDI sequencer | MCI_DEVTYPE_SEQUENCER |
| Videocassette recorder | MCI_DEVTYPE_VCR |
| Videodisc player | MCI_DEVTYPE_VIDEODISC |
| Waveform player | MCI_DEVTYPE_WAVEFORM_ AUDIO |

---

**MDI** See *multiple-document interface.*

**MDS** See *Multipoint Distribution Service.*

**mean filter** (n.) In video and image processing, a filter that replaces a pixel with the average value of its surrounding pixels. Applying a mean filter has the effect of blurring an image.

**mean time between failure** (MTBF) (n.) A measure of how long a computer peripheral, such as a hard drive, can be expected to function before it fails.

**mebi-** See *SI unit prefix revision.*

**media access control** (MAC) (n., adj.) The lower sublayer of the data link layer in the Open Systems Interconnection (OSI) model. It consists of the interface between the logical link control and the physical layer of the network. Different types of MAC are employed on different physical media.

**Media Control Interface** (MCI) (n.) A platform-independent multimedia specification published in 1990 by Microsoft and others. It provides a consistent way to control devices such as CD-ROMs and video playback units. See also *Resource Interchange File Format.*

**media-independent** (adj.) Describes any software program that delivers the same content on different playback systems.

**median filter** (n.) In video and image processing, a filter that replaces a pixel with the most typical value of pixels surrounding it, while ignoring extreme values. Applying a median filter to an image removes stray or isolated bright pixels and small details.

**Media Player** (n.) A viewer for all types of au-dio and video data streams located in the *Accessories* directory of Microsoft Windows. If the drivers are loaded for a particular media type, such as Video for Windows (.avi), this applet provides a way to view and hear a stream of data. This is an easy way to access any type of multimedia on a Windows-based system. Version 8.0, released in 2001, plays a wide variety of file types, including MPEG, MIDI, and compressed video for the web.

**medium** (n.) In a digital context, a substance or an object on which information is stored or transmitted, such as a disk or a network. In telecommunications, examples of transmission media include fiber optic cable, wire, air, and water. The plural form is *media.*

**medium shot** (n.) A camera perspective somewhere between a long shot and close-up in which subjects are viewed from a midrange distance.

**mega-** Prefix meaning one million. In the decimal system, 1 000 000 is expressed as 10 to the 6th power. In the binary system, mega- is expressed as 2 to the 20th power, or 1 048 576.

**megabit** (Mb) (n.) One million bits.

**megabits per second** (Mbps) (n.) A measurement of data transfer in millions of bits each second.

**megabyte** (MB) (n.) One million 8-bit bytes, or more precisely 1 048 576 bytes.

**megabytes per second** (MBps) (n.) A measurement of data transfer in millions of bytes each second.

**megaflop** (MFLOP) (n.) One million floating-point operations per second. A megaflop is the unit used in measuring the speed of a workstation or of a mainframe. A 25-MHz 486 computer can sustain approximately 1 MFLOP.

**megahertz** (MHz) (n.) One million cycles per second.

**Memorandum of Understanding** (MOU, pronounced "em-oh-YEW") (n.) A European agreement for telephone companies that provide ISDN services. The MOU specifies the facilities required for "Priority 1" service. See also *ISDN*.

**memory** (n.) The place in which data is recorded and stored, either permanently or temporarily. Memory is usually measured in kilobytes, megabytes, or gigabytes. It is placed in tracks and sectors on formatted media. See figure.

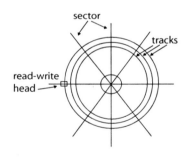

*memory configuration on a magnetic disk*

**memory bus** (n.) In a computing system, the means by which information is transferred between the central processing unit (CPU) and the main memory, or RAM. A dedicated chip set transfers information between the processor and the memory bus, so that the memory bus may be manipulated separately from the processor bus. The memory bus transfers information much more slowly than the processor bus. Slots for memory, or single in-line memory modules (SIMMs) and dual in-line

memory modules (DIMMs), are connected to the memory bus in the same way that expansion slots are connected to the input/output (I/O) bus.

**memory management unit** (MMU) (n.) Circuitry that translates virtual addresses into physical addresses to support virtual memory and paging.

**menu** (n.) A list of options from which users may choose. The options are often available through a drop-down menu bar at the top of a graphical user interface (GUI) screen.

**menu bar** (n.) A set of icons or words graphically displayed across the top of a screen or window to give the user choices. When the user clicks on an item in the menu bar, a drop-down menu appears.

**menu-driven** (adj.) Describes a type of interface that allows the user to navigate by selecting from a menu of options on the screen rather than by typing characters on a command line.

**Meridian Lossless Packing** (MLP) (n.) A lossless audio coding format developed by Meridian Audio Ltd. MLP is an optional coding scheme for use on DVD-Audio and other transmission, storage, and archiving applications. Unlike lossy data encoding, MLP does not alter the final decoded signal in any way, but reduces the size of a file for transmission or storage. It is simple to decode and requires relatively low computational power for playback.

**mesh** (n.) In three-dimensional modeling, an object defined by a series of points between which planes are defined.

**messaging** (n.) A generic term for data and

voice communications that include email, information services, and alphanumeric pager messages. Messaging usually refers to short text messages, although graphics and HTML documents may be included.

**meta-** Greek prefix denoting "with." The term indicates that new meaning or functionality is added to something. For example, the Ctrl key is a *metakey* if used in combination with another key to change the function of that other key.

**metafile** (n.) A file that contains both bitmap and vector data, providing a means of storing objects by defining their shapes mathematically in a file. An example of a metafile is the Windows graphics file type with the extension .wmf. The format is useful when moving graphics between applications, such as Microsoft PowerPoint and Macromedia Director.

**metal-oxide semiconductor** (MOS, pronounced "MOSS") (n.) A silicon wafer with channel transistors that is used to create integrated circuits (ICs) or discrete components.

**metal-oxide semiconductor field-effect transistor** (MOSFET, pronounced "MOSS-fet") (n.) A transistor with a layer of metal-oxide insulation between the current channel and the gate. MOSFETs draw very little power and are commonly used in audio amplifier circuits.

**metatag** (n.) An HTML tag that belongs in the <HEAD> portion of a document, providing information about a page that is not displayed in the browser when the page is viewed. The type of editing program used to create a page is often identified in the metatag. Information placed in the metatag of the home page of a site is used by search engines to classify the site. Capturing metatags from all the sites on the web is the work of spiders and bots.

**method** (n.) 1. In object-oriented programming (OOP), the name given to a procedure or routine associated with one or more classes. An object of a certain class knows how to perform actions, such as creating a new instance of itself. Different classes may define methods with the same name (polymorphism). 2. The code a specific class provides to perform an operation associated with one or more classes.

**metropolitan area network** (MAN) (n.) Several local area telephone networks connected over a maximum distance of 50 kilometers. They often give business customers an alternative connection to long-distance carriers and are usually high-capacity fiber-optic networks.

**MFLOP** See *megaflop.*

**MHz** See *megahertz.*

**mic-level** See *level.*

**micro-** Prefix signifying one millionth (10E-6), abbreviated "μ."

**microbrowser** (n.) A web browser designed for a smart phone or a personal digital assistant (PDA), optimized to function under the constraints of limited memory and a small screen.

**Micro Channel Architecture** (MCA) (n.) A revised bus for PC architecture that is incompatible with the original PC/AT architecture. IBM introduced MCA in its PS/2 series of microcomputers. Other vendors opposed MCA, with Compaq in the lead.

**Microcom Networking Protocol** (MNP) (n.) An asynchronous communications protocol that permits packet retransmission, data compression, and speed negotiation between two modems. The CCITT V.42 standard specifies the four classes of MNP as a backup error cor-

**M**

rection scheme for the Link Access Protocol for Modems (LAPM).

**microcomputer** (n.) A self-contained computer system with a microprocessor, input devices, display, and memory. Also called a *desktop computer* or *personal computer*.

**micron** (n.) One-millionth of a meter. Also known as a *micrometer*.

**microphone cable** (n.) A cable specifically designed for microphone connection with shielded twisted-pair wiring. It is usually designed for low current applications, with high flexibility, and low handling noise. Small gauge wire is used, surrounded by insulation most often made of rubber, neoprene, or polyvinyl chloride (PVC). Microphone cables are not intended for long runs, and are typically under 50 feet in length.

**microphone pattern** (n.) The sensitivity of a microphone to the direction of sound sources in relation to the axis of the microphone body. Sounds that originate directly in front of the microphone's diaphragm have greater intensity and fuller frequency response than sounds that emanate from the side. The cardioid microphone has excellent off-axis rejection, which is desirable in some recording situations. See figure, and note the patterns illustrated.

**microprocessor** (n.) Any integrated circuit (IC) containing the CPU of a small computer. Intel has manufactured 80286, 80386, 80486, and Pentium chips for IBM compatibles, and Motorola has made 68000, 68020, 68030, and 68040 chips for the Macintosh. These are all complex instruction set computing (CISC) chips. Apple Computer, Motorola, and IBM designed chips based on reduced instruction set computing (RISC) that are used in

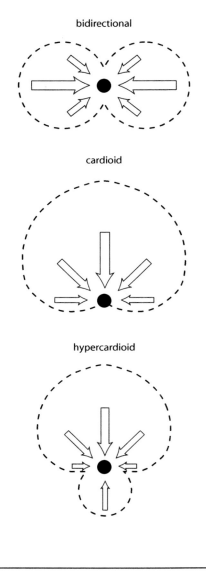

bidirectional

cardioid

hypercardioid

*microphone patterns*

PowerPC and Power Macintosh computers. Apple followed this with the G3 and G4 processors.

**microsecond** (n.) One-millionth of a second.

**Microsoft Compact Disc Extension** (MSCDEX) (n.) A driver for a CD-ROM reader connected to a computer.

**Microsoft Disk Operating System** (MS-DOS, pronounced "em-ess-DOSS") (n.) A single-user operating system that runs one program at a time and that is limited to working with one megabyte (MB) of memory, 640 kilobytes (KB) of which are usable for an application program. Special hardware permits EMS-compliant software to exceed the 1-MB limit, and some programs that run on top of DOS, such as Microsoft Windows 3.1, allow the user to load multiple applications at once and to switch between them. Features added to MS-DOS 2.0 and to subsequent versions resulted in two or more incompatible versions of many system calls, the instructions that interface an application with the operating system. MS-DOS is used on the Intel 16- and 32-bit microprocessors in IBM-compatible microcomputers.

**Microsoft Network** (MSN) (n.) A host for Internet activity. Microsoft supports MSN.

**Microsoft Windows** (MS Windows, Windows) (n.) A graphical user interface (GUI), or operating system, patented by Microsoft for use with personal computers running MS-DOS. MS Windows is loosely based on the point-and-click, icon-based interface invented by Apple Computer and deployed on all Macintosh computers. Windows 3.1 incorporates device drivers needed for multimedia functionality. Windows 95 and 98 were the next generation, leaving behind most of the dependence on MS-DOS. Windows NT was designed for networked computing applications, although the workstation version was commonly used on stand-alone computers. These versions were succeeded by Windows 2000 Professional and Windows Millennium Edition (Windows Me).

**microwave** (n.) A bandwidth of high-frequency radio waves that lies between 890 MHz and 20 GHz. Microwaves are used for line-of-sight, point-to-point, and omnidirectional transmission of audio, video, and data signals within a terrestrial range of 20 to 30 miles.

**microwave radio** (n.) A high-frequency radio transmission system that operates point-to-point. Repeaters are normally required to amplify the signal between parabolic antennas used for transmission and reception.

**mic splitter** (n.) A box fitted with female and male XLR microphone connectors allowing microphone inputs to be routed to two or more outputs. A splitter is typically passive, and either hard-wired or transformer connected. For example, it is useful to send the output of a stage microphone to a monitor mixer and a front of house (FOH) mixer simultaneously. The term has been attributed to Franklin J. Miller, founder of Sescom.

**middleware** (n.) Software that operates at the level between an application program and a network. It can mediate the interaction between separate applications across heterogeneous computing platforms on a network. Object request broker (ORB) software, which manages communication between objects, is an example.

**MIDI** See *Musical Instrument Digital Interface.*

**MIDI 1.0 specification** (n.) Musical Instrument Digital Interface 1.0 specification; the original specification for the use of MIDI com-

275

munications defined by the International MIDI Association (IMA) in collaboration with manufacturers of digital synthesizers. The specification defines a protocol for transmitting information about musical performance, not about sound itself. The five types of messages in the specification can be divided into two groups: system messages and channel messages. *System messages* send information to an entire MIDI system, whereas *channel messages* send it to selected channels. Channel messages are most common, and they follow a status byte in the data stream that identifies which of the 16 MIDI channels will receive the data. There are two kinds of channel messages: channel voice and channel mode messages. *Channel voice messages* carry information such as "note-on" or "note-off" signals for any given key number with velocity values. See the MIDI appendix for a detailed explanation of the specification.

**MIDI Manufacturers Association** (MMA) (n.) Musical Instrument Digital Interface Manufacturers Association; the organization of digital synthesis and studio equipment makers. MMA members collaborate on MIDI standards and related issues.

**MIDI mode** (n.) Musical Instrument Digital Interface mode; one of the four ways in which MIDI equipment may be configured. The modes determine which channels will be read and how many notes can be played at once. Mode 1 is OMNI ON/polyphonic, mode 2 is OMNI ON/monophonic, mode 3 is OMNI OFF/polyphonic, and mode 4 is OMNI OFF/monophonic. Channel mode messages set an instrument's mode to OMNI ON or OMNI OFF; OMNI ON means that all channels will be read, and OMNI OFF means that just one assigned channel will be read. Channel mode messages further set the equipment to respond polyphonically, playing more than one note at

a time, or monophonically, playing only one note at a time. In monophonic modes no chords are possible.

**MIDI show control** (n.) The application of musical instrument digital interface (MIDI) protocols for controlling stage and effect devices in live theater venues, multimedia, audio, visual, and similar environments. Charlie Richmond conducted a nine-month online discussion about the MIDI show control in 1990 and presented a report to the MIDI manufacturers association (MMA) in January 1991. The report was ratified by MMA's Japanese counterparts and published with industry approval in July 1991.

**MIDI system message** (n.) Musical Instrument Digital Interface system message; a message read by all devices connected to the system, unlike a channel voice or a mode message. The three types of MIDI messages—System Common, System Realtime, and System Exclusive—are defined as follows:

- System Common: Messages include *MIDI time code* (MTC) or *Quarter Frame*, *Song Position* and *Song Select* to control sequences, and *Tune Request*.

- System Realtime: Messages include the *MIDI Clock* timing pulse; *Start*, *Stop*, or *Continue* a sequence; *Active Sensing* to confirm a connection; and *System Reset* to return all devices to their default statuses.

- System Exclusive: Messages carry a manufacturer ID that only one brand of equipment recognizes. This type of message includes the *Sample Dump Standard*, which allows nonexclusive descriptions of waveforms; these can be edited and played back on different brands of sample players. It also includes MTC messages, which can be used to synchronize with SMPTE devices. The MIDI file standard allows a sequence to be read by any type of MIDI device, regardless of the platform. The file format is the Standard MIDI File (SMF).

**MIDI time code** (MTC) (n.) A regular serial voltage transmission emitted by all MIDI devices at a rate of 31 250 times per second. This allows events in a MIDI sequence to be synchronized in time.

**midlevel network** (n.) In relation to a three-level Internet hierarchy, a second-level regional network, or a transit network, that connects stub networks to the backbone.

**migration** (n.) Automatic or program-controlled movement of data between slower storage media and faster storage media. The rules of migration determine when objects are moved.

**mil** (n.) One-thousandth of an inch, or 25.4 microns.

**milli-** Prefix for one thousandth (10E-3), abbreviated "m."

**millions of instructions per second** (MIPS, pronounced "MIPPS") (n.) A measurement of computer processing speed.

**millisecond** (n.) One-thousandth of a second.

**MIME** See *multipurpose Internet mail extensions.*

**mimencode** (n.) A part of the multipurpose Internet mail extensions (MIME) protocol that replaces uuencode for use in email and news. Mimencode implements the encodings that were defined for MIME as uuencode replace-

ments and is more robust for email applications. The term is a contraction of "mime" and "encode," pronounced "MY-men-code."

**minicomputer** (n.) A parallel binary system. A minicomputer has more storage and a faster processor than a microcomputer does, but its processor is smaller and less costly than that of a mainframe computer.

**minidisc** (n.) An audio CD format developed by Sony for use with its Data Discman portable system. Invented in 1991, a minidisc holds 200 megabytes (MB) of data. The format was revised in 1992 and introduced as a rewritable magneto-optical disc format for music. The medium resembles a small floppy disk.

**minimize** (v.) In a graphical user interface (GUI), to reduce an open window to an icon or to a very small representation of the file contents.

**mip mapping** (n.) The storage of several different resolutions of a texture map to avoid recalculating texture images as a viewer zooms closer to or farther away from a textured surface.

**MIPS** See *millions of instructions per second.*

**mirror site** (n.) An FTP site on the Internet that contains the same information held by another site so that demand on the original site is distributed.

**MIS** See *management information system.*

**mission-critical** (adj.) Describes system resources that, in the event of a failure, would seriously impair the ability of an organization to function.

**mixed-mode disc** (n.) A CD including computer data and CD-DA tracks. Typically, the computer data is placed in the first track, and the audio data is placed in one or more of the following tracks.

**mixing board** (n.) Used in audio production, a device with multiple input channels that permits a user to combine signals from various sources, vary the level of each, and bus the aggregate signal to the main outputs.

**M-JPEG** See *motion-JPEG.*

**MLP** See *Meridian Lossless Packing.*

**MMA** See *MIDI Manufacturers Association.*

**MMC** See *Multimedia Marketing Council.*

**MMDS** See *Multichannel Multipoint Distribution Service.*

**MME** See *multimedia extensions.*

**MMU** See *memory management unit.*

**MMX** See *Matrix Math eXtensions.*

**MMX technology** (n.) Matrix Math eXtensions technology; a process developed by Intel for integration with their Pentium processor. The process facilitates the presentation of multimedia content, such as animation, audio, and video.

**MNP** See *Microcom Networking Protocol.*

**MO** See *magneto optical.*

**Mobile Satellite Service** (MSS) (n.) Communication by satellite connection that serves ships, aircraft, and terrestrial vehicles. MSS satellites operate in the 1.6- to 2.4-GHz fre-

quency ranges. A single MSS satellite can serve the entire United States.

**Mobile Telephone Switching Office** (MTSO) (n.) The central switch that controls the entire operation of a cellular system. Equipment in the MTSO monitors all cellular calls, tracks the location of all cellular-equipped vehicles, arranges handoffs, handles billing, and tracks usage.

**mockingbird** (n.) In network security, a process that mimics the legitimate behavior of a normal system feature but conducts damaging activities upon an unsuspecting user.

**mode** (n.) 1. With reference to CDs, the method of storing code and data. There are two basic modes. In mode 1, used with CD-ROM applications, 288 bytes of each sector are used to store error correction code, and the remaining 2048 bytes per sector store data. Mode 2, used in CD-i and CD-ROM XA, has two forms. Form 1 is similar to mode 1 in that it has Red Book error correction. Form 2 discs allow 2336 bytes per sector of non–error corrected data for information storage; this capacity is used most commonly for graphic and audio content. 2. Oscillation that may be propagated in an electromagnetic field within a waveguide. Laser-generated light exhibits modes in an optical fiber.

**model** (n.) A simplified description of the behavioral characteristics of a system. A model is often used as a basis for simulation.

**modeling** (n.) 1. In three-dimensional animation, the first step in creating a 3-D object. 2. An educational tool in which a computer system simulates a process. A user can input values and learn from the resulting changes in the process.

**modem** (n.) Contraction of modulator/demodulator; a device that converts digital data into audio signals for transmission over telephone lines and that translates the audio signals back into data on reception.

**moderator** (n.) An individual who manages an online discussion, sending submissions to a mailing list or newsgroup after determining their appropriateness.

**modular** (adj.) Composed of individual components that can stand alone or work together.

**modular code** (n.) A logic program in which each element, or object, is self-contained, stands alone, and holds all the data and instructions related to a particular task. Any element can call up any other object or element, and the recipient can perform the task for itself. The paradigm provides for object classes, methods, and inheritance. Also known as *object-oriented programming,* where the modules are independent and easily cross-linked.

**modulation** (n.) A change in the characteristics of a signal. When a carrier signal is modulated by or mixed with another signal, it is encoded with information that is analogous to information contained in another signal. The carrier transmits both signals. If the original carrier signal is of a constant level, changes in the composite signal represent the signal it is carrying. The opposite process is *demodulation,* or decoding of the data. A modem modulates a signal to transmit, and demodulates it to receive.

**Modulo-N** (n.) A programmable quantity of data that is enumerated before the numerical counter of a device resets to zero. Data communications. systems use Modulo-N to allow a certain amount of events to occur before initiating an action or permitting a response.

**moiré pattern** (n.) In a display with limited resolution, an undesirable optical effect created by overlapping grids and lines. For example, when a striped shirt is displayed on a television monitor, the scan lines may not align with the stripes, producing a moiré pattern on the screen. Pronounced "mwah-RAY."

**monitor** (n.) A picture tube or screen that can display video signals and/or computer graphics. See figure.

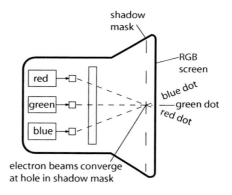

*RGB monitor*

**monitor mixer** (n.) A mixing board that generates the proper signal levels to drive on-stage loudspeaker monitors as a part of a sound-reinforcement system.

**mono 3-way** See *active crossover.*

**monochrome display** (n.) A black-and-white monitor capable of displaying shades of gray but no colors.

**monospaced font** (n.) A set of letters and symbols in which each character has the same fixed width, or pitch, as opposed to those in a proportional font.

**MOO** See *MUD Object-Oriented.*

**Moore's law** (n.) An adage credited to Gordon Moore of Intel in 1964. He stated that the speed of integrated circuits (ICs) doubled every 12 months and predicted that the pattern would continue in the future. In reality, processing power has steadily doubled about every 18 months.

**morph** (v.) To melt one image into another by smoothly moving points from their original positions to new locations in another image. Morphing is done with graphic effects software packages that create a smooth transition from one image to another.

**Morse Code** (n.) A code used in radiotelegraphy that uses long and short electromagnetic pulses to represent letters and numbers. The international code is based on the original code devised by Samuel Morse in 1844. Morse code was replaced by the Baudot code in 1870. Baudot code uses marks and spaces rather than dots and dashes to represent alphanumerical characters.

**MOS** See *metal-oxide semiconductor.*

**Mosaic** (n.) Developed at the National Center for Supercomputing Applications (NCSA), the first popular browser, or universal client, for the World Wide Web. It has evolved into Netscape Navigator.

**mosaic filter** (n.) An image-processing technique that divides an existing graphic into small squares, each of a single hue.

**MOSFET** See *metal-oxide semiconductor field-effect transistor.*

**most significant bit** (MSB) (n.) In a string of digits that store or transmit binary data, the first bit, or the bit farthest to the left, when the string is written in the usual way. If the MSB is not the first bit, it is the one with the greatest weighting.

**motherboard** (n.) The main printed circuit board in a computer, with sockets for additional boards or add-on cards. In a microcomputer the motherboard contains the bus, the microprocessor, and the chips used for interfacing with basic peripherals such as the keyboard, the display, the serial and parallel ports, and the mouse.

**Motif** (n.) Term for the standard X Window System graphical user interface (GUI) and the window manager from Open Software Foundation (OSF).

**motional feedback** See *servo loop mechanism.*

**motion blur** (n.) A blending or streaking effect added to images to simulate the appearance of moving objects. It is commonly used in animation sequences to show the path of an object.

**motion choreography** (n.) In animation and computer graphics, the process of determining the displacement, or change in position, of each object over time.

**motion compensation** (n.) A video compression scheme used in MPEG. Motion vectors are used to increase efficiency in predicting pixel values. These vectors are used to provide offsets based on the positioning of objects that move between intracoded frames (I-frames) and predictive-coded frames (P-frames). The information encoded is just the difference between the actual image and the predicted image. See also *MPEG frame type.*

**motion-JPEG** (M-JPEG, pronounced "em-

JAY-peg") (n.) Motion–Joint Photographic Expert Group; a proprietary extension of the JPEG compression standard for still images that adapts it for moving images. Used to compress a stream of moving pictures at a constant frame rate, M-JPEG provides much lower compression ratios than do video compression standards, such as MPEG, which capitalize on similarities between successive frames. M-JPEG files are editable but generally are not transportable to different hardware platforms for playback. M-JPEG is implemented differently depending on the hardware used to encode it, but QuickTime 3.0 and later versions translate M-JPEG from most proprietary formats and may be used to decode common M-JPEG files.

**motion video** (n.) 1. A video sequence with a high enough frame rate (number of pictures per second) that the sequence appears to be a continuous moving picture, not successive still images. 2. The progression of video images produced by a video camera. Motion video differs from video stills, animation, or computer graphics.

**Motorola 68000 family** (n.) A succession of 16- and 32-bit microprocessors designed and built by Motorola.

- 68000 features: 32-bit architecture internally, 16-bit architecture externally; 24-bit addressing and a linear address space; orthogonal instruction set and 16 registers that are split into data and address registers.

- 68020 features: 32-bit data and address buses; 256-byte instruction buffer.

- 68030 features: Instruction and data caches on the chip; an on-chip memory

management unit (MMU).

- 68040 features: On-chip floating-point unit (FPU); 4-kilobyte (KB) split instruction and data caches. Used in Macintosh Quadra computers.

- 68060 features: Processing speeds two to three times higher than those of the 68040; the last development from Motorola in the high-performance 68000 series.

**Motorola 680x0** (n.) Any member of the Motorola 68000 family of microprocessors. The variable $x$ stands for 0, 1, 2, 3, 4, or 6.

**MOU** See *Memorandum of Understanding.*

**mount** (v.) To make a file system available for access. Unix does this by associating a file system with a directory. The "root" file system is mounted on the root directory. This places data in a position to be manipulated.

**mouse** (n.) An input device for a computer. A mouse rolls on a smooth surface and determines the location of the cursor on the screen. A mouse has one or more buttons, which are used to "click" on icons or hot spots on the screen. The computer interprets these mouse clicks as instructions. See figure.

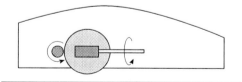

*cross-section, mechanical mouse*

**MoviePlayer** (n.) An applet used by the Macintosh to view QuickTime movies. The user interface is a standard Play Bar Controller, which allows one to start, stop, and pause a movie, adjust the volume, and watch the progress on a slider.

**Moving Picture Expert Group** (MPEG, pronounced "EM-peg") (n.) The working committee that, under the auspices of the ISO, defines standards for the digital compression and decompression of motion audio-video for use in computer systems. These standards consist of MPEG-1 (ISO/IEC 11172), MPEG-2 (ISO/IEC 13818), and later versions. The MPEG-1 standard delivers decompressed data at any rate between approximately 0.5 to 5.0 megabits per second (Mbps), allowing CD players to stream full-motion color movies at 30 frames per second (fps). MPEG-1 compression ratios as high as 200:1 are attainable. Source Image Format (SIF) is the reduced resolution obtained in MPEG-1 by decimating the 720-by-480-pixel input to 360 by 240 pixels prior to compression. The final resolution of MPEG-1 is 352 by 240 pixels. For compression bit rates lower than 3.5 Mbps, MPEG-1 SIF resolution is preferable to higher resolutions that require greater bandwidths. Captured from an NTSC source, MPEG-1 operates at 30 frames per second (fps) and 30 fields per second. MPEG-1 processes audio in 16-bit stereo at 44.1 kHz, the same rate as CD audio, or at higher rates. MPEG-2 builds on the MPEG-1 standard, extending to the higher data rates (6–15 Mbps) needed for broadcast-quality signals. MPEG-2 is designed to support a range of picture aspect ratios, including 4:3 and 16:9. It adheres to the CCIR-601 standard of 720 by 486 and 60 fields per second, as opposed to 30 fields in MPEG-1. To pass such a large amount of data, MPEG-2 needs a bit rate of at least 5 Mbps to achieve high resolution. As the compressed bit rate is reduced, output video quality declines.

**Mozilla** (n.) An open-source web browser based on an early version of Netscape Com-municator. Development is coordinated through discussion forums and Mozilla.org. Releases are periodically updated. Mozilla was first released in March, 1998.

**MP3** See *MPEG Layer-3 audio.*

**MPC** See *Multimedia Personal Computer.*

**MPC-1** See *Multimedia Personal Computer.*

**MPC-2** See *Multimedia Personal Computer.*

**MPC-3** See *Multimedia Personal Computer.*

**MPEG** See *Moving Picture Expert Group.*

**MPEG compression** (n.) Moving Picture Expert Group compression; the conversion of an analog videotape or a live video source into a stream of digits. These digits represent the original product in the MPEG digital video format. MPEG compression is a complex combination of video and audio compression techniques that reduce the size of a data file at ratios up to 200:1.

**MPEG frame type** (n.) Moving Picture Expert Group frame type; one of the three basic types of frames created by an MPEG encoder. The frame types are as follows:

1. Intracoded frame (I-frame): A picture coded using only information drawn from itself. Like a key frame, an I-frame provides an access point in the data stream.
2. Bidirectionally predictive frame (B-frame): A picture coded using motion-compensated prediction from previous and future reference frames. B-frames provide an efficient means of coding but require a memory buffer for future reference frames.
3. Predictive-coded frame (P-frame): A pic-

ture coded using motion-compensated prediction from the previous reference frame.

**MPEG layers** (n.) Moving Picture Expert Group layers; levels in an MPEG file that hold information about moving pictures. The levels are in hierarchical order and deal with a series of frames at the top level down to details about regions of a frame. From bottom to top, the different layers in an MPEG stream are as follows:

- Block: An eight-row-by-eight-column (8 x 8) block of pixels. A block is the unit to which discrete cosine transform (DCT) is applied.

- Macroblock: The four 8 x 8 blocks of luminance data and the corresponding 8 x 8 blocks of chrominance data coming from a 16 x 16 section of the luminance component of the picture. A macroblock is the basic unit for motion-compensation prediction.

- Slice: A series of macroblocks that serves as the synchronizing unit for reconstruction of the image data. Typically, a slice is all the blocks in one horizontal picture interval, as well as 16 lines of the picture.

- Picture: Source image or reconstructed data for a single frame consisting of three rectangular matrices of eight-bit numbers that represent the luminance and chrominance signals.

- Group of pictures (GOP): A self-contained sequence of pictures that starts with an I-frame and contains a variable number of P-frames and B-frames. SMPTE time code may be added to mark the first picture in a group at this layer.

- Sequence: A video sequence beginning with a "sequence header," which is followed by one or more groups of pictures, and ending with a "sequence end" code.

**MPEG-1** (n.) Moving Picture Expert Group–1; a version of the MPEG compression method. MPEG-1 is optimized for data transfer rates in the 1-to-1.5-megabit-per-second (Mbps) range, such as the transfer rate of CD-ROM drives and T1 communications links. See *Moving Picture Expert Group.*

**MPEG-2** (n.) Moving Picture Expert Group–2; a form of MPEG compression that is optimized for data transfer rates faster than five megabits per second (Mbps) and that is intended for such applications as DVD and broadcast video. See *Moving Picture Expert Group.*

**MPEG Layer-2 audio** (n.) Generally used for high bandwidth MPEG audio to achieve quality comparable to Red Book CD-Audio. It may be multiplexed with both MPEG-1 and MPEG-2 video streams. Layer 2 operates at rates from 128 kbps to 384 Kbps for stereo content.

**MPEG Layer-3 audio** (MP3) (n.) An audio format defined in the MPEG-1 specification that is widely used to distribute sound files on the Internet. This is a lower-bandwidth format than MPEG Layer-2 audio. Layer 3 operates at rates from 64 kbps to 320 Kbps.

**MPOA** See *Multiprotocol Over ATM.*

**MPW** See *Macintosh Programmer's Workshop.*

**MSAU** See *Multistation Access Unit.*

**MSB** See *most significant bit.*

**MSCDEX** See *Microsoft Compact Disc Extension.*

**MS-DOS** See *Microsoft Disk Operating System.*

**MS-DOS CD-ROM extensions** (n.) Microsoft Disk Operating System compact disc–read-only memory extensions; a set of routines that connect MS-DOS with the driver routines for specific models of CD-ROM players. The extensions allow machines running this operating system to read CD-ROM discs formatted in the ISO 9660 and High Sierra formats.

**MSN** See *Microsoft Network.*

**MSO** See *Multiple System Operator.*

**MSS** See *Mobile Satellite Service.*

**MS Windows** See *Microsoft Windows.*

**MTBF** See *mean time between failure.*

**MTC** See *MIDI time code.*

**MTSO** See *Mobile Telephone Switching Office.*

**mu** Prefix meaning one-millionth. The origin is the Greek letter $\mu$; a *u* is the ASCII character nearest in appearance. Pronounced "MY-cro."

**MUA** See *mail user agent.*

**MUD** See *multiuser dungeon.*

**MUD Object-Oriented** (MOO, pronounced "MOOH") (n.) Multiuser dungeon Object-Oriented; a visual version of a MUD.

**mu-law** (**µ-law** or **micro-law**) (Pronounced "MEW-law") (n.) Standardized in the ITU G.711 specification, a method of coding eight-bit companded audio with pulse code modulation (PCM) that yields a 72-dB dynamic range. It is used for digital voice channels over telephone lines in North America, Japan, and South Ko-

rea. It is not interchangeable with a-law coding, which is used for digital audio over telephone lines in the rest of the world. A converter must be used to translate between these two differently coded PCM voice messages. Compare *a-law.*

**multicast** (v.) To transmit the same media stream simultaneously to many recipients over a network, rather than using separate streams for each viewer. Multicast delivery results in less network traffic than unicast delivery because the signal is sent once.

**multicast backbone** (M-bone) (n.) An Internet provision for video transfer.

**Multichannel Audio Digital Interface** (MADI) (n.) An Audio Engineering Society (AES) standard that provides for 56 simultaneous digital audio channels that are conveyed point-to-point on a single coaxial cable fitted with BNC connectors, along with a separate synchronization signal. Fiber optic implementation is specified in the standard. The interface multiplexes 56 of the original AES/EBU interfaces into one sample period.

**Multichannel Multipoint Distribution Services** (MMDS) (n.) A licensed spectrum originally dedicated to "wireless cable television." In 1992 the Federal Communications Commission (FCC) re-allocated MMDS for two-way wireless Internet access. It includes the multipoint distribution services (MDS) bands from 2150-2162 MHz, as well as the band of frequencies between 2500-2690 MHz. The range of this service is more than 30 miles, and it transmits analog or digital video. As of June 1997, there are a maximum of 33 microwave channels for MMDS in each U.S. market that includes instructional television fixed service (ITFS).

**multifrequency monitor** (n.) A display unit

that can respond to a fixed number of video signal frequencies and that supports various resolutions and standards.

**multi-homed domain** (n.) The domain name, or Internet Protocol (IP) address, of one site in a multi-homed log file.

**multi-homed host** (n.) A server with numerous connections to a network. This server is capable of receiving or sending data over several links but incapable of routing traffic.

**multi-homed log file** (n.) A single log file that contains access information for multiple web sites.

**multi-homed web server** (n.) A single computer that hosts more than one web site.

**multimedia** (n., adj.) A synthesis of digital media types combining text, graphics, audio, animation, and video. Interactivity is a feature of most multimedia, which is also referred to as *digital media, new media,* or *hypermedia.*

**multimedia architecture** (n.) An integrated set of software system extensions, plug-ins, and servers that provides for the creation, storage, delivery, and playback of synchronized multiple media types. QuickTime, RealSystem, and Windows Media are examples of multimedia architectures.

**multimedia extensions** (MME) (n.) A set of software routines and specifications for running multimedia programs in Microsoft Windows 3.0. These routines and specifications were incorporated into Windows 3.1.

**Multimedia Marketing Council** (MMC) (n.) A group that owns the Multimedia Personal Computer (MPC) trademark. Composed of hardware vendors, the group collaborates with Microsoft. The MMC's specifications are marked with the MPC trademark.

**Multimedia Personal Computer** (MPC) (n.) A specification originally developed by Tandy Corporation and Microsoft as the minimum platform capable of running multimedia software. In 1993, the Multimedia Marketing Council introduced an upgraded MPC-2 standard; at that time, MPC was renamed MPC-1. MPC-2 was followed by a list of expectations for a third level, MPC-3. When these specifications were written, computers were much less powerful than current models are. Pentium MMX computers designed to deliver multimedia are many times more powerful than the MPC-3 specification requires. Specifications for these three standards are as follows:

- MPC-1 (n.) Multimedia Personal Computer–1; a specification that defines the following minimum standard requirements for a multimedia computing system:
  - a 386SX or 486 central processing unit (CPU)
  - 2 megabytes (MB) of RAM
  - a 30-MB hard disk
  - a Video Graphics Array (VGA) video display
  - an eight-bit digital audio subsystem
  - a CD-ROM drive
  - system software compatible with Windows 3.1 or higher APIs.

- MPC-2 (n.) Multimedia Personal Computer–2; a specification that defines the following minimum standard requirements for a Level 2 multimedia computing system:
  - 25-MHz 486SX with 4 megabytes (MB) of RAM
  - a 160-MB hard disk
  - a 16-bit sound card

- a 16-bit video display capable of 65 536 colors
- a double-speed CD-ROM drive
- system software compatible with Windows 3.1 or higher APIs.

- MPC-3 (n.) Multimedia Personal Computer–3; a specification that defines the following minimum system functionality for Level 3 compliance in a multimedia computing system:
  - a 75-MHz Pentium central processing unit (CPU) with 8 megabytes (MB) of RAM
  - a 520-MB hard disk
  - a 16-bit, wavetable-capable sound card with multitimbral MIDI playback
  - a 24-bit color display with MPEG-1 playback capability in hardware or software with a resolution of 352 x 240 pixels at 30 frames per second (fps)
  - a quad-speed CD-ROM drive with a 600-kilobyte-per-second (KBps) sustained transfer rate capable of playing all common CD-ROM formats, including Photo-CD and Video-CD
  - stereo speakers
  - system software compatible with Microsof Windows 3.1 and Microsoft DOS 6.0 or higher APIs.

**multimedia platform** (n.) Computing system or device used to deliver diverse media types—including text, graphics, audio, animation, and video—in an interactive environment.

**multimode fiber** (n.) An optical waveguide that permits the propagation of more than one mode. Fiber that is graded-index or step-index may be used for multimode applications.

**multiplatform** (adj.) Describes the ability of software to perform on more than one hardware platform. Such software is sometimes referred to as *cross-platform,* particularly if it has been ported to run with a different operating system and equipment than those on which it was created.

**multiple-document interface** (MDI) (n.) A feature of Microsoft Windows that permits more than one document to be open simultaneously. The borders of the application window contain all open documents. Program Manager is a typical MDI application in Windows 3.1.

**multiple inheritance** (n.) In object-oriented programming (OOP), the capacity for a subclass to be derived from multiple parents that are themselves not derived from one another.

**Multiple System Operator** (MSO) (n.) A cable company that operates more than one cable television (CATV) system. The largest MSO in the United States is Tele-Communications, Inc. (TCI).

**Multiple Virtual Line** (MVL) (n.) Developed by Paradyne Corporation, a version of Digital Subscriber Line (DSL) technology that offers many advantages over other implementations, such as Asymmetric Digital Subscriber Line (ADSL). MVL features customer installation, is compatible with existing home wiring, and operates over greater distances. It uses a lower frequency signal and requires less power. An advantage of the lower frequency is that the signal does not interfere with existing telephone service, which is a serious problem for ADSL. MVL offers 768-kilobit-per-second (Kbps) bandwidth in both directions over distances of up to 24 000 feet. The existing North American standard, based on Discrete Multi-Tone (DMT) technology, competes with MVL as a basic format for high-speed digital services.

**multiplex** (MUX, pronounced "MUCKS") (v.)
1. To combine audio and video program data along with private data in layers that provide timing information, similar to the process of interleaving. 2. To deliver two or more distinct signals combined on a single channel.

**multiplexer** (n.) In broadcast and telecommunications, a device used to divide a transmission facility into multiple subchannels. This division is accomplished by alternately allocating a common channel to several different transmitters or by splitting the total frequency bandwidth into narrower bands and transmitting different signals simultaneously.

**multipoint conference** (n.) Telecommunications term for conferencing between three or more sites.

**Multipoint Distribution Service** (MDS) (n.) A licensed spectrum in the 2.1 GHz band. MDS broadcasts microwave television signals to subscribers within line of sight at distances up to 30 miles from the antenna.

**multipoint line** (n.) A single communications channel, such as a leased telephone circuit, to which multiple stations are connected and addressed separately under a polling protocol controlled by the master station or host computer.

**multiprocessor** (n.) A computer that combines two or more similar microprocessors, providing more speed and power for complex procedures and for multitasking than a computer with a CPU does.

**Multiprotocol Over ATM** (MPOA) (n.) Multiprotocol Over Asynchronous Transfer Mode; developed by the ATM Forum, a standard that defines an architecture. This architecture will integrate packet forwarding with router-based virtual local area networks (LANs) that implement the forum's earlier LAN Emulation (LANE) standard.

**multipurpose Internet mail extensions** (MIME, pronounced "MIME") (n.) The standard method of sending and receiving attachments to email and web documents over the Internet. Most email attachments are not text (ASCII) files. They may be graphical, audio, video, or word-processed files. A binary attachment must be converted by mimencode to a type of ASCII file. Otherwise it will not be supported by Internet email. The following steps are involved in the exchange of email attachments using MIME:

1. The sender specifies the name of the file to be attached to the mail message and may choose to identify the file type (graphics, video, sounds, etc.). As a rule, the receiving mail program will automatically identify the file type if it is not specified. The file name extension indicates the format, such as .jpg, .doc, or .wav.
2. If the attachment is binary or contains something other than ASCII characters, the sending program automatically converts it to ASCII. This process increases the size of the attachment, which is then sent along with the mail message to the recipient.
3. If the recipient's mail program supports MIME, it converts the attachment back to its original binary format and pastes an icon or a line of text in the received mail message to represent the attached file. If the recipient selects that icon while in the mail program, the application program will run and will automatically display the attached file.

## MIME Types

MIME content-types supported by most web servers, identified
with file extensions, are listed in the following table.

| MIME Type | Identification | File Extension |
| --- | --- | --- |
| application/acad | AutoCAD | dwg |
| application/arj | compressed archive | arj |
| application/astound | Astound | asd, asn |
| application/clariscad | ClarisCAD | ccad |
| application/drafting | MATRA Prelude drafting | drw |
| application/dxf | DXF (AutoCAD) | dxf |
| application/i-deas | SDRC I-DEAS | unv |
| application/iges | IGES graphics format | iges, igs |
| application/java-archive | Java archive | jar |
| application/mac-binhex40 | Macintosh binary BinHex 4.0 | hqx |
| application/msaccess | Microsoft Access | mdb |
| application/msexcel | Microsoft Excel | xla, xls, xlt, xlw |
| application/mspowerpoint | Microsoft PowerPoint | pot, pps, ppt |
| application/msproject | Microsoft Project | mpp |
| application/msword | Microsoft Word | doc, word, w6w |
| application/mswrite | Microsoft Write | wri |
| application/octet-stream | uninterpreted binary | bin |
| application/oda | ODA | oda |
| application/pdf | Adobe Acrobat | pdf |
| application/postscript | PostScript | ai, eps, ps |
| application/pro_eng | PTC Pro/ENGINEER | part, prt |
| application/rtf | Rich Text Format | rtf |
| application/set | SET (French CAD) | set |
| application/sla | stereolithography | stl |
| application/solids | MATRA Prelude Solids | sol |
| application/STEP | ISO-10303 STEP data | st, step, stp |
| application/vda | VDA-FS Surface data | vda |
| application/x-bcpio | binary CPIO | bcpio |
| application/x-cpio | POSIX CPIO | cpio |
| application/x-csh | C-shell script | csh |
| application/x-director | Macromedia Director | dcr, dir, dxr |
| application/x-dvi | TeX DVI | dvi |
| application/x-dwf | AutoCAD | dwf |
| application/x-gtar | GNU tar | gtar |
| application/x-gzip | GNU ZIP | gz, gzip |
| application/x-hdf | NCSA HDF Data File | hdf |
| application/x-javascript | JavaScript | js |
| application/x-latex | LaTeX source | latex |
| application/x-macbinary | Macintosh compressed | bin |
| application/x-midi | MIDI | mid |
| application/x-mif | FrameMaker MIF | mif |
| application/x-netcdf | Unidata netCDF | cdf, nc |
| application/x-sh | Bourne shell script | sh |
| application/x-shar | shell archive | shar |
| application/x-shockwave-flash | Macromedia Shockwave | swf |
| application/x-stuffit | StuffIt archive | sit |
| application/x-sv4cpio | SVR4 CPIO | sv4cpio |
| application/x-sv4crc | SVR4 CPIO with CRC | sv4crc |
| application/x-tar | 4.3BSD tar format | tar |

| MIME Type | Identification | File Extension |
|---|---|---|
| application/x-tcl | TCL script | tcl |
| application/x-tex | TeX source | tex |
| application/x-texinfo | Texinfo (Emacs) | texi, texinfo |
| application/x-troff | Troff | roff, t, tr |
| application/x-troff-man | Troff with MAN macros | man |
| application/x-troff-me | Troff with ME macros | me |
| application/x-troff-ms | Troff with MS macros | ms |
| application/x-ustar | POSIX tar format | ustar |
| application/x-wais-source | WAIS source | src |
| application/x-winhelp | Microsoft Windows help | hlp |
| application/zip | ZIP archive | zip |
| audio/basic | BASIC audio (u-law) | au, snd |
| audio/midi | MIDI | mid, midi |
| audio/x-aiff | AIFF audio | aif, aifc, aiff |
| audio/x-mpeg | MPEG audio | mp3 |
| audio/x-pn-realaudio | RealAudio | ra, ram |
| audio/x-pn-realaudio-plugin | RealAudio plug-in | rpm |
| audio/x-voice | Voice | voc |
| audio/x-wav | Microsoft Windows WAVE audio | wav |
| image/bmp | Bitmap | bmp |
| image/gif | GIF image | gif |
| image/ief | Image Exchange Format | ief |
| image/jpeg | JPEG image | jpe, jpeg, jpg |
| image/pict | Macintosh PICT | pict |
| image/png | Portable Network Graphic | png |
| image/tiff | TIFF image | tif, tiff |
| image/x-cmu-raster | CMU raster | ras |
| image/x-portable-anymap | PBM Anymap format | pnm |
| image/x-portable-bitmap | PBM Bitmap format | pbm |
| image/x-portable-graymap | PBM Graymap format | pgm |
| image/x-portable-pixmap | PBM Pixmap format | ppm |
| image/x-rgb | RGB image | rgb |
| image/x-xbitmap | X Bitmap | xbm |
| image/x-xpixmap | X Pixmap | xpm |
| image/x-xwindowdump | X Window System dump | xwd |
| multipart/x-gzip | GNU ZIP archive | gzip |
| multipart/x-zip | PKZIP archive | zip |
| text/html | HTML | htm, html |
| text/plain | plain text | C, cc, h, txt |
| text/richtext | MIME Richtext | rtx |
| text/tab-separated-values | text with tabs | tsv |
| text/x-setext | Structurally Enhanced Text | etx |
| text/x-sgml | SGML | sgm, sgml |
| video/mpeg | MPEG video | mpe, mpeg, mpg |
| video/msvideo | Microsoft Windows video | avi |
| video/quicktime | QuickTime video | mov, qt |
| video/vdo | VDO streaming video | vdo |
| video/vivo | VIVO streaming video | viv, vivo |
| video/x-sgi-movie | SGI Movieplayer format | movie |
| x-conference/x-cooltalk | CoolTalk | ice |
| x-world/x-svr | Virtual reality | svr |
| x-world/x-vrml | VRML Worlds | wrl |
| x-world/x-vrt | Virtual reality | vrt |

**M**

MIME, an Internet format defined by the Internet Engineering Task Force (IETF), prescribes a simple standardized way to represent and encode a variety of media types for transmission via Internet mail, including textual data in non-ASCII character sets. MIME extends RFC 822 in a manner that is simple, backward-compatible, and flexible.

RFC 822, the Internet standard for message formats, is used widely beyond the boundaries of the Internet itself. Most email traffic is limited to ASCII text, which is unable to define characters found in non-English text, audio, or graphical information. To use multimedia mail on the Internet, extensions to RFC 822 are required. The RFC 822 message format and the RFC 821 Simple Mail Transfer Protocol (SMTP) transport method limit message content to seven-bit ASCII characters. RFC 822 defines a message as a structured header followed by a single, monolithic text body. This format creates problems for multipart mixed-media mail. SMTP limits the length of lines within message headers and bodies. RFC 1049 defines a mechanism for single-part nontext mail, and RFC 1154 provides a mechanism for multipart mail.

An RFC 822–compliant Internet message consists of two parts: the header and the body. The header consists of a series of field names and field bodies. A blank line marks the end of the header and the beginning of the body, which may consist exclusively of US-ASCII text.

RFC 1049 introduced a new header field, *content-type*, which marked the entire message body as containing a certain type of data. If a content-type field is not present, the body is assumed to be US-ASCII text. A problem with RFC 1049 is the lack of support for multipart mail. A message body can contain only one item other than text.

MIME defines a new content-type, *multipart*. It may be used to encapsulate multiple body parts within a single RFC 822 message body. MIME describes the set of allowable content-types, defines a subtype mechanism for content-types, and provides for standardized encoding of non-ASCII data.

The MIME format defines seven valid content-types. In this way it differs from RFC 1049, which allowed users to define new content-types freely. The seven defined content-type values are as follows:

1. Text: The default subtype is plain text, with other subtypes associated with particular rich text formats. MIME defines the subtype *richtext* for formatted email.
2. Image: Subtypes are image format names, *image/gif* and *image/jpeg*. A mail reader that does not identify an image format will at least recognize that the content is an image.
3. Audio: Subtypes are audio format names; *audio/basic* is the default. *Audio/basic* denotes single-channel 8-kHz μ-law audio data, which is the equivalent of pulse code modulation (PCM), for telephone-quality audio attached to email.
4. Video: Subtypes are video format names; *video/mpeg* is the default.
5. Message: This content-type is used to encapsulate an entire RFC 822 format message. There are two message subtypes: *message/partial* for dividing a message into several pieces for transport and *message/external-body* for passing a very large message body by reference, rather than including its entire contents within the message.
6. Multipart: This content-type is used to

pack several parts of various types and subtypes into a single RFC 822 message body.

7. Application: This content-type is used for most other kinds of data that do not fit these categories.

If Internet mail transport (SMTP, as described by RFC 821) were upgraded to permit arbitrary binary data of unlimited length in message bodies, encoding a message for transport would not be necessary. The Internet Architecture Board (IAB) RFC 1341 defining MIME has been superseded by RFC 1521.

The MIME Types table lists MIME content-types supported by most web servers and identifies their file extensions.

**multiscan monitor** (n.) A video display that accepts a range of horizontal and vertical timings, including those that correspond to VGA and RGB computer graphics. Some multiscan monitors automatically adjust to the appropriate timing based on the video source.

**multisession** (adj.) Contraction of multiple session; describes a CD-ROM format that allows information to be recorded incrementally in different recording sessions. During each session, the table of contents (TOC) is updated.

**Multistation Access Unit** (MSAU) (n.) A wiring concentration in an IBM token ring network that connects as many as eight nodes to a ring.

**MultiSync** (n.) A registered trademark of NEC Technologies, Inc., for their class of monitors designed to work with a wide range of video input frequencies and formats.

**multitask** (v.) To process more than one job at a time, typically with two or more applications running at once, and to transfer information between them. Both Microsoft Windows and the Mac OS can multitask.

**multithreading** (n.) A program execution environment that interleaves instructions from multiple independent execution messages. Multithreading differs from multitasking in that these messages, or threads, typically share more of their environment with each other than do tasks in the process of multitasking. When sharing a single address space and a set of global variables, threads may be distinguished only by the value of their program counters and stack pointers. Threads are switched very quickly, because there is so little state to save and restore.

**multitimbral** (adj.) Describes the capacity for more than one instrument, or MIDI timbre, to play simultaneously. A sequence of MIDI tracks may be created, and a different voice may be assigned to each track for multitimbral playback.

**multiuser** (adj.) Describes a networked computing environment that may be accessed by more than one person simultaneously. Unix was designed to support such an environment.

**multiuser dungeon** (MUD, pronounced "MUD") (n.) A type of multiplayer interactive game that is accessible through the Internet. A MUD is like an adventure game in a structured realtime chat forum, and it may include combat, traps, puzzles, and magic. The MUD community uses a mixture of Usenet and Internet emoticons, along with shorthand such as BBL, BRB, LOL, b4, BTW, WTF, TTFN, and WTH. Abbreviations specific to MUDs include FOAD (F*** off and die), ppl (people), TNX (thanks), UOK? (Are you OK?), and JAM (just a minute). Also called *multiuser dimension* or *multiuser domain*. See also *shorthand*.

**MUSICAM** See *masking pattern adapted universal sub-band integrated coding and multiplexing.*

**Musical Instrument Digital Interface** (MIDI, pronounced "MIH-dee") (n.) An industry-standard hardware/software system for microprocessor control of musical instruments and devices. It defines a protocol for the interchange of musical information between computers, digital musical instruments, and sound boards. MIDI is a simple serial communications bus, like a SCSI bus. The signal is a serial voltage transmission at the rate of 31,250 bits per second (bps). The messages are bytes encoded to define status (the type of message) and data (information about the preceding status byte). The cable is a shielded twisted pair of wires connected to pins 4 and 5 of a five-pin DIN plug. Pin 2 is the ground. Any device with a MIDI port can communicate with another one with similar connections. Only a MIDI interface and software are needed for a computer to control MIDI-compatible digital instruments. The file extension is .mid. See also *General MIDI.*

**mute** (v.) To silence an audio track.

**MUX** See *multiplex.*

**Muzak** (n.) The trademark name of a background music company founded in 1928 by George Owen Squier. He patented the idea of playing phonograph records through the telephone or over an intercom system. The words "music" and "Kodak" were merged to create the name.

**MVL** See *Multiple Virtual Line.*

**MX** See *Mail Exchange.*

# N

**NAB** See *National Association of Broadcasters.*

**NAK** (Negative Acknowledgment) (n.) A code returned by a receiving unit when the data sent to it is corrupt.

**NAK attack** (Negative Acknowledgment attack) (n.) In network security, an intrusion technique that takes advantage of an operating system that is temporarily in an unprotected state during asynchronous transmission interrupts.

**NAM** See *Number Assignment Module.*

**named pipe** (n.) An interprocess protocol used by OS/2 and Unix. A named pipe acts as a temporary file on disk or in memory and can be accessed by multiple processes to exchange information.

**name resolution** (n.) The process of mapping a name into its corresponding address. See also *domain name system.*

**Name Server Lookup** (NSLookup) (n.) The interactive query program originally implemented on the InterNIC domain name server that provides information about hosts in a domain.

**namespace** (n.) A qualifier added to an Extensible Markup Language (XML) tag to ensure uniqueness among XML elements. XML namespaces provide a simple method for qualifying element and attribute names used in XML documents by associating them with namespaces identified by URI references. A namespace is *declared* using a family of reserved attributes. Such an attribute's name must either be "xmlns" or have "xmlns:" as a prefix. These XML attributes may be provided directly or by default. An XML namespace is actually a collection of names, identified by a URI reference.

**NAMM** See *National Association of Music Merchants.*

**nano-** A prefix meaning one billionth (10E-9), abbreviated "n."

**nanosecond** (n.) One-billionth of a second.

**NANP** See *North American Numbering Plan.*

**NAP** See *Network Access Point.*

**NAPLPS** See *North American Presentation Level Protocol Standard.*

**narration** (n.) An audio commentary, or a voice-over, frequently used in multimedia productions to provide instructions, explain concepts, and "host" interactive programs.

**narrowband** (adj.) Describes low-bandwidth communications on frequencies under 1 GHz, typically used to transmit voice and paging messages. Most existing wireless phone services and messaging networks were narrowband in 2001.

**narrow-band filter** (n.) A passive notch filter that exhibits very high Q and an extremely narrow filter range, about 5 Hz at the -3 dB points. Patented by C. P. Boner, the narrow-band filter is particularly useful when connected in series to reduce feedback. The term applies to all filters narrower than 1/3-octave, including parametric filters and notch filters.

**narrowband PCS** (NPCS) (n.) A family of mobile or portable radio services used to provide wireless telephony, data, advanced paging, and personal communications services (PCS) to individuals and businesses that may be integrated with competing networks. This allocated spectrum in the 892-903 MHz band is intended for messages that occur in short bursts, such as two-way paging, telemetry, and computer-based messaging.

**narrowcast** 1. (v.) To direct a program toward a small, well-defined portion of the potential audience. 2. (n.) A program directed toward a specific audience.

**NAT** See *network address translation.*

**National Association of Broadcasters** (NAB) (n.) A large organization of professionals working in the fields of radio and television production and postproduction. The annual NAB conference attracts thousands of participants and vendors interested in new media technologies.

**National Association of Music Merchants** (NAMM) (n.) The organization of vendors

and suppliers of musical instruments and electronic equipment for audio applications. Their annual conference attracts a wide range of participants, both consumers and professionals, who are interested in audio and music technologies, such as MIDI.

**National Bureau of Standards** (NBS) (n.) The original name for a group that makes recommendations to the U.S. government about federal data communications specifications and other issues related to computers and electronics. This agency is now called the *National Institute of Standards and Technology (NIST).*

**National Center for Supercomputing Applications** (NCSA) (n.) Located at the University of Illinois at Champagne, Urbana, the birthplace of the universal client *Mosaic* in 1993. This program evolved into Netscape Navigator.

**National Information Infrastructure** (NII) (n.) The broad interconnection of computer, telephone, and cable networks. Often referred to as the *information superhighway.*

**National Institute of Standards and Technology** (NIST) (n.) A U.S. government body that assists in the development of standards for data communications, electronic devices, and computers. Originally known as the *National Bureau of Standards (NBS).*

**National Research and Education Network** (NREN, pronounced "EN-ren") (n.) A project that the U.S. Congress approved in 1991 to combine federal agency networks into a single high-speed network that serves as a central part of the Internet backbone.

**National Science Foundation** (NSF, pronounced "en-ess-EFF") (n.) A U.S. government agency that funds research and infrastructure development for science. The NSFNET, a backbone network that spans North America, is funded by the NSF.

**National Television Standards Committee** (NTSC) (n.) A committee of the Electronics Industries Association (EIA) that prepared the standard specifications approved by the Federal Communications Commission (FCC) in December 1953 for commercial color broadcasting in the United States. The specifications define a color television format as having 525 scan lines, a field frequency of 59.94 Hz, a broadcast bandwidth of 4 MHz, a line frequency of 15.75 kHz, a frame frequency of nearly 1/30 of a second, and a color subcarrier frequency of 3.58 MHz.

**native signal processing** (NSP) (n.) A type of computing in which a powerful microprocessor performs the work of a digital signal processor (DSP) chip in real time, allowing such activities as video decoding to be integrated with other functions in a single processing system.

**natural light** (n.) Illumination from the sun, moon, or stars, whether indoors or outdoors. Natural light has a blue tint and a higher color temperature than most artificial light.

**navigation** (n.) The means by which a user explores and controls graphic, text, audio, and video elements in a multimedia program.

**Nawk** (n.) New awk; an enhanced version of awk. Nawk is a pattern-scanning and pattern-processing language that features dynamic regular expressions, additional operators, and user-defined functions.

**NBS** See *National Bureau of Standards.*

**NC** See *network computer.*

**NC curve** See *noise criterion curve.*

**NCD** See *network computing device.*

**N-connector** (n.) A threaded coaxial cable connector named after Paul Neill.

**NCSA** See *National Center for Supercomputing Applications.*

**N curve** (normal curve) See *Academy curve.*

**NDA** See *nondisclosure agreement.*

**NDIS** See *Network Driver Interface Specification.*

**near end** (n.) In telecommunications, near end is the local connecting point, as opposed to a remote site, which is referred to as the *far end.*

**near field** (n.) The sound field in the immediate proximity of the sound source, between the source and the listener. Specifically, it is a distance of no more than one wavelength at the frequency of interest. Also known as near sound field or close field.

**near-field monitor** (n.) A loudspeaker placed at a distance of 3-4 feet (1-1½ meters) from the audio engineer in a recording studio.

**nearline** (adj.) Describes a data storage system somewhere between online, or immediately accessible, and offline, which may be very time-consuming to locate. A digital tape cartridge that stores data sequentially and provides slow access is an example of a nearline storage medium.

**Negative Acknowledgment attack** See *NAK attack.*

**negative feedback** (n.) The act of comparing a

**N**

fraction of the output signal to the input signal at the input of an audio amplifier in such a way that the amplifier will always keep this fraction of the output signal exactly the same as the input signal. It is a critical part of the design of operational amplifiers (op amps) and audio power amplifiers. Negative feedback is first attributed to the work of Bell Laboratories scientist Harold S. Black in 1934.

**nest** (v.) To embed instructions, data, or subroutines sequentially within another structure.

**Net** (n.) Common abbreviation for the Internet.

**NetBIOS** See *Network Basic Input/Output System.*

**netiquette** (n.) Contraction of network etiquette; the conventions of politeness observed on Usenet, in mailing lists, and in Internet communications in general. Guidelines include not posting to inappropriate groups and refraining from commercial advertising. Personal messages to one or two individuals should not be posted to newsgroups. When responding to an earlier posting, the minimum necessary context should be quoted. Lines should be less than 70 characters long. Before asking a question, a user should read the existing messages in the group's frequently asked questions (FAQ).

**NetMeeting** (n.) A component of Windows software that provides a videoconferencing environment. A camera, a digitizing card, a microphone, and a modem are required for audio-video communication with a limited number of other users in real time.

**Netscape Navigator** (n.) A popular universal client, or browser, used to access the World Wide Web.

**Netscape Server Application Programming Interface** (NSAPI) (n.) The application development environment for the Netscape web server.

**NetShow** (n.) Technology developed by Microsoft for streaming media. The NetShow media player plays content in most standard audio and video formats, as well as content generated by a NetShow server. The user can conveniently resize video windows on the fly. The encoder has built-in streaming capabilities. The original name for Windows Media.

**NetWare** (n.) Developed by Novell, an operating system for a local area network (LAN).

**NetWare Link State Protocol** (NLSP) (n.) Networking protocol that is a companion protocol to the Novell Internet Packet Exchange (IPX) for exchange of routing information in a Novell network. NLSP supersedes earlier Novell routing information protocols.

**NetWare loadable module** (NLM) (n.) An application program that can be dynamically loaded and unloaded on a Novell NetWare server. Examples of NLMs are Lotus Notes, Sybase's SQL Server, and Oracle Server.

**network** (n.) A group of computers, peripherals, or other equipment connected to one another for the purpose of passing information and sharing resources. Networks can be local or remote. The topology of a network is the geographic arrangement of links and nodes, which may be arranged in the shape of a star, a tree, or a ring.

**network access control** (n.) Circuits in a local area network (LAN) that determine when individual workstations may transmit messages.

**Network Access Point** (NAP) (n.) A high-speed connection to the Internet used by Internet Service Providers (ISPs). NAPs operate at the link layer of the OSI model.

**network address** (n.) 1. The network portion of an Internet Protocol (IP) address, which varies by the class of network in the following way:

- Class A network: The first byte of the IP address.

- Class B network: The first 2 bytes of the IP address.

- Class C network: The first 3 bytes of the IP address.

In all cases, the remaining portion of an IP address is the host address. Assigned Internet network addresses are globally unique. 2. In telecommunications, a binary address that is placed within the network call packet or datagram, which allows that packet or datagram to find its intended node. The number of bits required depends on the number of nodes and sub-networks interconnected. A telephone number with country and area code is a global voice network address.

**network address translation** (NAT) (n.) System that provides a single Internet Protocol (IP) address for all hosts behind a firewall. It allows an internal client to open a connection to a remote site but does not allow a translated machine to accept new connections directly from an external server.

**Network Basic Input/Output System** (NetBIOS, pronounced "NET-bye-ose") (n.) Software developed by IBM that interfaces between an individual computer's operating system and an IBM token ring network.

**network computer** (NC) (n.) On a network

node, a workstation that is similar to a scaled-down personal computer. An NC depends on the server for software applications, upgrades, and maintenance. Also known as a *thin client.*

**network computing device** (NCD) (n.) A thin client.

**Network Driver Interface Specification** (NDIS) (n.) A standard created by Microsoft for writing hardware-independent drivers.

**Network File System** (NFS) (n.) A method of sharing data files on a local area network (LAN) or on the Internet. As an extension to TCP/IP, NFS lets files on remote network nodes appear to be connected locally. Sun Microsystems' NFS is defined by RFC 1094.

**Network Information Service** (NIS) (n.) A client-server protocol developed by Sun Microsystems known as the Yellow Pages, which is licensed to most Unix vendors. It is used to distribute user names and hostnames as well as other configuration data among networked computers. The commands and functions in NIS begin with the letters "yp." Examples of NIS commands in Unix are "ypmatch" and "ypwhich."

**network interface card** (NIC, pronounced "NICK") (n.) A printed circuit board installed in an expansion slot on a computer to allow the computer to be connected to a network.

**network interface device** (NID) (n.) In telecommunications, the demarcation point on the U-loop that marks where the telephone company's service responsibility ends and the customer's responsibility begins. The NID provides U-loop circuit protection, a grounding point, and a line testing location. It allows access to the line, but it performs no other function.

**network layer** (n.) The third layer in the Open Systems Interconnection (OSI) model responsible for network routing of information packets. The network layer adds a header to define the routing addresses.

**network management** (n.) Manner of controlling the operation of a network to enhance efficiency and productivity. Network management may be divided into five categories: fault management, accounting management, configuration management, security management, and performance management.

**network security** (n.) A field of computing science that addresses the protection of networks, terminals, and systems from unauthorized disclosure or modification. Network security provides data integrity and assures that a network properly performs its critical functions without intrusion or disruption.

**Network Service Provider** (NSP) (n.) A company that provides high-speed connections to the Internet for Internet Service Providers (ISPs) and other enterprises.

**network termination type 1** (NT-1) (n.) In an integrated services digital network (ISDN), NT-1 is the principal network-to-customer interface. It is similar to a channel service unit (CSU). NT-1 terminates the digital subscriber loop and it interfaces to the customer premises equipment (CPE).

**network termination type 2** (NT-2) (n.) In an integrated services digital network (ISDN), NT-2 is a specified interface to an NT-1 from multiple user customer premises equipment (CPE). The NT-2 will normally be contained within a digital private branch exchange (PBX) or some other customer node. The NT-2 provides local address resolution and contention functions.

**network topology** (n.) The logical and physical relationship between nodes on a network, defined by the layout of links and nodes. The topology is often similar in shape to a star, a tree, or a ring. See figure on the following page.

**network user identification** (NUI, pronounced "en-you-EYE") (n.) A combination of the user's address and password on an X.25 packet-switched network.

**network weaving** (n.) Another term for *leapfrogging*.

**neural network** (n.) A processing device or a hardware-software system modeled on the design of the human brain. Most use training rules that adjust the weight of connections on the basis of presented patterns. Neural networks learn from examples and exhibit a structural capability for generalization. Neurons that make up the network may consist of simple threshold discriminators.

**newbie** (n.) Jargon for a person who is new to computing and to the Internet.

**newsgroup** (n.) A topic group or a forum on Usenet. Groups may or may not be moderated. Some moderated groups are distributed as a single large posting with an index. Examples of popular groups are *talk.politics.misc*, *comp.lang.c*, and *rec.arts.sf-lovers*.

**New Technology** (NT) (n.) The version of Microsoft Windows specified in the term *Windows NT*.

**Newton** (n.) A handheld computer manufactured by Apple Computer. Information is entered with a stylus, and handwriting recognition is built into the operating system. Known generically as a *personal digital assistant (PDA)*.

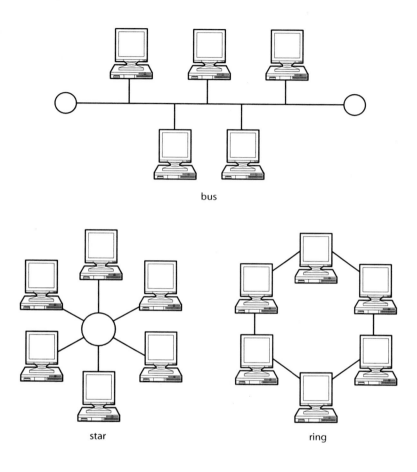

bus

star                              ring

*network topologies*

**newton** (n.) A unit of force used in physics, abbreviated N. One newton is the amount of force needed to accelerate a mass of one kilogram at the rate of one meter per second squared. This assumes that there are no other force-producing effects at work.

**NeXT computer** (n.) A desktop workstation based on the Motorola 68030 processor devel-

oped in 1985 by Steve Jobs, after he left Apple Computer. Although the computer was discontinued, the Unix-based NeXTSTEP operating system survives on other platforms.

**NeXTSTEP** (n.) A Unix-based object-oriented operating system developed for the NeXT computer and ported to the Intel Pentium family of processors.

NFS See *Network File System.*

nibble (n.) A group of four bits, or half of an 8-bit byte.

NIC See *network interface card.*

NiCad See *nickel cadmium.*

nickel cadmium (NiCad, pronounced "NYE-cad") (n.) A compound used in rechargeable batteries for notebook computers and for portable devices. This type of battery suffers from the "memory effect," wherein a battery recharged after only partial discharge will lose the capacity to hold a full charge.

NID See *network interface device.*

NII See *National Information Infrastructure.*

NIS See *Network Information Service.*

NIST See *National Institute of Standards and Technology.*

NLM See *NetWare loadable module.*

NLSP See *NetWare Link State Protocol.*

node (n.) 1. A point of connection on a network. 2. The equipment attached at a point of connection on a network.

node route processor (NRP) (n.) This unit receives asynchronous transfer mode (ATM) switch traffic from OC-3 interface ports. OC-3 is a fiber optic line that is capable of transmitting data at 155 Mbps. The NRP reassembles the ATM cells into packets, processes and segments the packets, then sends them back to the ATM switch for transmission via another OC-3 interface.

noise (n.) In a broad sense, this refers to any part of a signal that contains unwanted randomness. In audio, noise may appear as hiss or hum. In video, a noisy image appears grainy, with snow and blotchy areas. Noise generally interferes with compression, and should be minimized before encoding a signal.

noise criterion curve (NC curve) (n.) A unit of measurement for the ambient or background noise level of an occupied indoor space. The measured sound pressure levels (SPL) in octave bands are compared to a series of standard noise criteria (NC) curves to determine the "NC level" of a space. The standard NC curves take into account the equal loudness contours of normal hearing to accurately reflect the listening experience. Each NC curve is assigned a number (in 5 dB increments) corresponding to the octave band SPL measured over the octave centered at approximately 1500 Hz. A space with a background noise level of "NC-30" or lower is very quiet.

noise floor (n.) The lowest threshold of useful signal level, below which the signal is indistinguishable from ambient or system sounds.

noise gate (n.) An audio signal processor with a fixed infinite downward expansion ratio. When the incoming audio signal drops below a preset threshold point, the expander prevents any further output by reducing the gain to zero. The actual gain reduction is typically on the order of -80 dB. When the audio signal falls below the threshold, the output level becomes the residual noise of the gate. Noise gates are useful for controlling unwanted noise, such as preventing open microphones and sensitive instrument pick-ups from introducing extraneous sounds. Noise gates can be used to enhance percussion instrument sounds. Adjusting the *attack* and *release* settings for a gate can add punch to a sound. A noise gate is said to "open" and "close" as the signal passes through the threshold value.

**noise measurement filters** See *weighting filters.*

**noise reduction** (n.) The removal of unwanted components from a signal. In video, this is accomplished with blur, mean, or median filters. Uniform noise reduction applies one filter equally to each pixel. Adaptive noise reduction (ANR) applies different filters to different types of noise. In audio applications, the noise may be sampled and removed from the program material without significantly altering it.

**noise weighting** (n.) In telephony, this is the assignment of a specific numerical value to transmission impairment, which is due to the noise encountered by an average user operating a particular class of telephone subset. Noise weighting standards have been established by the agencies concerned with public telephone service.

**NOM** See *number of open mics.*

**nominal** (adj.) In audio engineering, nominal describes something insignificantly small or trifling.

**nominal span** (n.) In telephony, nominal span is the distance from a central office (CO) at which a one-milliwatt reference tone reaches an attenuation point of 35 dB.

**nondisclosure agreement** (NDA, pronounced "en-dee-AY") (n.) A common legal instrument used to keep a contractor from sharing confidential information with competitors or from making public any information discussed after a contractor signs the agreement.

**noninterlaced** (adj.) Describes a video system that draws all the horizontal lines across the screen in succession, as opposed to interlaced scanning in which even and odd lines are drawn alternately in two sweeps. A noninterlaced scan is also known as a *progressive scan.* Computer monitors are typically noninterlaced. By contrast, television video monitors are interlaced, and their signal content contains two fields for each frame.

**nonlinear** (adj.) In digital media, describes files or events that are indexed and that a user may therefore access immediately. In linear media, such as an audio tape or a videotape, the user must shuttle forward or backward to reach an event or a frame. Nonlinearity is a key distinction between digital and analog media. It is leveraged in well-conceived multimedia programs.

**nonlinear editing** (n.) A method of digital video editing that records source clips on a hard disk, allowing an editor to jump directly to any segment without shuttling through other clips.

**nonlinear quantization** (n.) In MPEG compression, the process of assigning more bits to define low-frequency data than to define high-frequency data. The human eye is more sensitive to lower frequencies. Some data is lost in the high-frequency spectrum, but the technique is extremely efficient in reducing the amount of data needed to define images. In general, this type of quantization attaches priorities to data based on its relative value during decoding and then discards less significant information.

**nonrecalibrating** (adj.) Describes a hard drive that does not pause periodically for a few milliseconds to perform a thermal recalibration,

**N**

or a cooldown. Some hard disk drives are unsuitable for capturing video files direct to disk because they have thermal sensors that interrupt the process when the drive reaches a certain temperature. Special "AV" drives designed for audio and video capture are nonrecalibrating, as are most newer drives.

**non-return-to-zero** (NRZ) (adj., n.) Describes a recording process that encodes ones and zeros as a fluctuation between two values. Each time a one occurs in a stream of digits, the value changes. The value does not change when a zero occurs. The value representing zero is not equal to the reference value, it is simply a different value than is used to represent a one. See the accompanying figure. In the top example, the magnetized value changes only on ones. In the bottom example, both ones and zeros are represented by a change in the value.

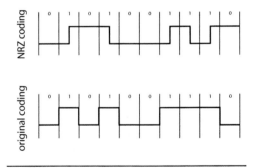

*non-return-to-zero recording*

**Non-Uniform Rational B-Spline** (NURBS, pronounced "NERBS") (n.) A basic spline function used to construct curves from a set of control points that do not share the periodic properties of a uniform B-spline.

**nonvolatile memory** (n.) A ROM whose contents are maintained by batteries when the main power is switched off. Nonvolatile memory is useful for keeping the boot sequence and the Basic Input/Output System (BIOS) instructions constantly accessible. Generally, all storage mediums other than Dynamic RAM (DRAM) are nonvolatile.

**normalize** (v.) In an audio file, to expand the highest peaks of amplitude to their greatest allowable levels, raising the amplitude of softer sounds proportionally. This expansion is a standard procedure in processing digital audio. It lends presence to a track and improves the signal-to-noise ratio.

**normaling jacks** See *patchbay.*

**normal signal path** (n.) A wiring scheme in which a signal path is established from one audio device to another without the use of a patch cord. This is known as the "normal path." Normal signal paths may be interrupted and redirected by inserting a patch cord into the front of the patchbay. The most common and easiest normal path to implement is from the upper jack to the lower jack in the patchbay.

**North American Numbering Plan** (NANP) (n.) A set of rules for the assignment of telephone area codes and the method by which calls are routed. The plan defines a three-digit area code, a three-digit exchange, and a four-digit subscriber code. The latest version was instituted in 1995, which allows the area code to be any combination of three digits. The plan previously restricted the second digit of an area code to a one or a zero. The new plan provides for 792 area code combinations and over 6 billion telephone numbers.

**North American Presentation Level Protocol Standard** (NAPLPS) (n.) A videotext protocol that permits pictures to be compressed into small blocks of data for low-bandwidth storage and transmission.

**notch filter** (n.) A particular type of cut-only equalizer used to attenuate a narrow band of frequencies. Three controls determine the notch parameters: *frequency, bandwidth,* and *depth.* Simplified units offer only a frequency control, with bandwidth and depth fixed. A notch filter may be effectively used to control feedback and to eliminate a small band of frequencies where a system resonates.

**NPCS** See *narrowband PCS.*

**NREN** See *National Research and Education Network.*

**NRP** See *node route processor.*

**NRZ** See *non-return-to-zero.*

**NSAPI** See *Netscape Server Application Programming Interface.*

**NSF** See *National Science Foundation.*

**NSFNET** (n.) National Science Foundation Network; the national backbone network funded by the NSF. The NSFNET is connected by high-speed facilities that span North America. The NSFNET is part of the Internet and is also connected to networks in Europe and in the Pacific Rim.

**NSLookup** See *Name Server Lookup.*

**NSP** See *native signal processing* or *Network Service Provider.*

**NT** See *New Technology.*

**NT-1** See *network termination type 1.*

**NT-2** See *network termination type 2.*

**NTSC** See *National Television Standards Committee.*

**NTT DoCoMo** (n.) The wireless division of Nippon Telegraph and Telephone, a primary Japanese cellular provider and developer of i-Mode technology. "Dokomo" (DoCoMo) means *everywhere* in Japanese.

**NuBus** (n.) A 32-bit bus architecture developed by Apple Computer for use in the Macintosh series of computers. It has been replaced by the PCI bus. Pronounced "NEW-bus."

**NUI** See *network user identification.*

**null modem** (n.) A cable used instead of a modem to connect serial ports on two computers directly. According to the RS-232C specification, both computers should transmit on pin 3 of their connectors and should receive on pin 2. A null modem cable has male connectors at both ends and connects pin 2 to pin 3 at opposite ends.

**Number Assignment Module** (NAM) (n.) The electronic memory in a cellular telephone that stores the electronic serial number (ESN) and compares it with the mobile identification number.

**number of open mics** (NOM) (n.) A principle that governs output levels on an automatic microphone mixer, which reduces the gain on unused microphone channels and increases the gain on active channels. The overall level remains relatively constant. NOM attenuation techniques provide the gain and stability of a single open microphone with the benefits of multiple microphones.

**NURBS** See *Non-Uniform Rational B-Spline.*

**Nyquist frequency** (n.) In digitizing audio, a sample rate equal to twice the speed of the highest-frequency component in the content being sampled, including harmonics. The rate must be at least this high to avoid aliasing, or foldover, in the sampled audio file.

# O

**object** (n.) In programming, a corporal body or an abstraction with well-defined constituents and interpretations. An object is an identifiable, encapsulated entity that provides one or more services requested by a client. In object-oriented programming (OOP), an object is an instance of a class. In general multimedia terms, an object is a stored data element, such as a video clip, an audio file, or a graphic representation of an object.

**object code** (n.) The machine language code that is output by a compiler or an assembler. Source code is converted into object code, so that a computer can read and respond to it. Object code can stand alone if a library of functions is available for linking.

**object identity** (n.) The property of an object that distinguishes it from other objects. In an object-oriented system, a property is independent of content, type, and addressability. Object identity is the only property of the object that is maintained irrespective of time or modifications.

**object linking and embedding** (OLE, pronounced "oh-LAY") (n.) Developed by Microsoft in 1990 in collaboration with other software companies, a software specification that allows developers to integrate information created by different applications. It ac-

complishes this by making simple extensions to existing graphics applications running under Microsoft Windows, Mac OS or OS/2 Presentation Manager. OLE is a standard that defines how objects interact, and it provides a software channel for passing objects. A program called *storage.dll* manages the OLE files as well as the links between originators and users. In Windows, the clipboard is a handy way to implement OLE capabilities. In any application that supports OLE, the copy-and-paste operations will transparently link objects to documents. An embedded voice annotation in a text document is a practical application of OLE that results in a crude but effective form of multimedia. Audio files must be packaged as objects because OLE does not work with raw files. The Object Packager application found in the *Accessories* directory is required to process raw files into objects for use with OLE.

**object management** (n.) The storage, retrieval, and archiving of objects in an object-oriented system.

**Object Management Group** (OMG) (n.) An organization that has developed standards and products associated with object management in a distributed networked environment. OMG has been recognized for its work on Common Object Request Broker Architecture (CORBA).

305

**object-oriented database** (OODB) (n.) A user interface that provides database management facilities in an object-oriented programming (OOP) environment. Data is stored as objects and can only be interpreted with the methods specified by its class. The relationship between similar objects is preserved, as are references between objects. Queries are extremely rapid, because the joins required by a relational database are not needed by an OODB. Without a search, a user can retrieve an object directly by following its object identifier.

**object-oriented programming** (OOP) (n.) A logic program in which each element, or object, is self-contained, stands alone, and holds all the data and instructions related to a particular task. Any element can call up any other object or element, and the recipient itself can perform the task. The paradigm provides for object classes, methods, and inheritance. OOP is also known as *modular code* because its modules are independent and easily cross-linked.

**Object Packager** (n.) A small application that is part of the Microsoft Windows system software and that is used to process raw files into objects for use with OLE. Object Packager is located in the *Accessories* directory and permanently links an object icon to the file name with which it is associated.

**object reference** (n.) An object name that reliably denotes a particular object in the Common Object Request Broker Architecture (CORBA).

**object request broker** (ORB, pronounced "ORB") (n.) An implementation of a common interface that allows multiple clients to access services provided by multiple objects. The standard, Common Object Request Broker

Architecture (CORBA), has been defined by the Object Management Group (OMG), an industry association.

**object server** (n.) An object-oriented networked database server that provides for the storage and retrieval of objects.

**OC** See *optical carrier.*

**OCLC** See *Online Computer Library Catalog.*

**OCR** See *optical character recognition.*

**octal** (n.) A number system with eight discrete values represented by the digits 0–7. It is referred to as base-8.

**octave** (n.) Acoustically, the interval between any two frequencies with a ratio of 2 to 1. In music, the higher of two tones an octave apart vibrates twice as fast and shares the same pitch name. There are 12 semitones between each musical octave, making up the chromatic scale.

**octet** (n.) Term for eight bits of data. *Octet* is used instead of *byte* to refer to data words with eight-bit bytes.

**OC-3** See *Optical Carrier Level 3.*

**OC x** (n.) Optical Carrier x; an OC whose rate of data transmission is a multiple of 51.84 megabits per second (Mbps). An OC 12 connection moves digital data at 622 Mbps.

**ODBC** See *Open Database Connectivity.*

**ODI** See *Open Data-Link Interface.*

**OEM** See *original equipment manufacturer.*

**OEM Service Release 2** (OSR-2) (n.) A collection of updates and bug fixes from Microsoft for the Windows 95 operating system. It was released in August 1996, and made available primarily to personal computer makers, or original equipment manufacturers (OEMs), to be installed on new machines.

**off-axis rejection** (n.) The pickup pattern for a microphone has a central axis that represents maximum sensitivity to sounds. When sounds are introduced from the sides of this axis, the sensitivity and frequency response of the microphone is much lower. Off-axis rejection is the term for the lower signal level the microphone produces in response to sounds that emanate from the sides rather than from the "sweet spot" in the center of the pickup pattern. See also *microphone pattern.*

**off-hook** (adj.) In telephony, the activated state of a subscriber's telephone circuit, in which the telephone or circuit is in use. Compare *on-hook.*

**offline** (adj.) 1. Describes the processing of information while disconnected from a network. The data can be distributed when the connection is made. 2. Describes an operation that occurs independently and that is not under the control of a computer. 3. In video postproduction, describes a type of editing that occurs separately from the final assembly and mastering process. 4. In video postproduction, describes a system that can make an edit decision list (EDL) or simple cuts only, rather than one that performs a full range of edits and video effects.

**offset** (n.) The difference in the time codes recorded on two videotapes. An editor might begin a program at 00:01:00:00 (in the hours:minutes:seconds:frames) format to provide room up front for color bars and a slate. If an audio engineer begins the audio program on the same tape at 00:00:45:00, the sound track has a −15 second offset. A small offset may be useful, depending on the audio equipment.

**Ogg Vorbis** (n.) An open-source digital music format for highly compressed audio files that compare favorably with MP3 files in quality and size. Ogg Vorbis encoders, decoders, and plug-ins are developed under the GNU Public License (GPL) and may be distributed freely. The extension is .ogg, and many popular media players for Windows and Macintosh platforms support this format.

**ohm** (n.) The unit used to express electrical resistance. When 1 volt of electromotive force is applied, 1 ohm of resistance allows 1 ampere of current to flow.

**OLE** See *object linking and embedding.*

**OMDR** See *Optical Memory Disc Recorder.*

**OMF** See *Open Media Framework.*

**OMG** See *Object Management Group.*

**ONA** See *Open Network Architecture.*

**on-demand** (adj.) Refers to video that is not broadcast live as it is filmed but is compressed and made available on a server for people to watch when they wish. A television broadcast is live, while watching a previously recorded performance is on-demand.

**one-bit data converter** (n.) Any data conversion scheme that uses only one binary bit, 1 or 0, to convert and store data. Examples are delta sigma modulation and adaptive delta modulation.

**one-off** (n.) A CD-recordable (CD-R) on which program data has been written.

**ones density** (n.) A condition in which the number of positive pulses (ones) in a transmission is measurable, compared to the number of negative pulses (zeroes).

**one-third octave** (n.) Frequencies spaced one-third of an octave apart. One-third of an octave represents a frequency 126 percent above a reference point, or 79.4 percent below the same point. A frequency 1/3-octave above a 1 kHz reference equals 1.26 kHz, which is usually rounded-off to 1.25 kHz for equalizers. A frequency 1/3-octave below 1 kHz equals 794 Hz, rounded off to 800 Hz. The term is most often used to express the bandwidth of equalizers and filters that are 1/3-octave wide at their -3 dB (half-power) points. This bandwidth is about the smallest region in which human hearing is able to reliably detect change.

**on-hook** (adj.) In telephony, a condition indicating the deactivated condition of a subscriber's telephone circuit. Compare *off-hook*.

**ONI** See *Optical Network Interface.*

**online** (adj.) 1. Describes the situation in which computers and peripherals have direct, interactive communication with one another on a network. 2. A traditional video-editing term that describes a comprehensive system that can edit, record, and add special effects. Online systems are expensive, so rough edits or edit decision lists (EDLs) are typically compiled using offline systems. In video postproduction, the online edit is the final editing process that integrates all the elements created and specified during the offline edit.

**Online Computer Library Catalog** (OCLC) (n.)

A nonprofit organization that provides their members, mostly libraries, with services such as reference searching, cataloging, interlibrary loan, and bibliographic verification. More than 10,000 libraries worldwide use these services.

**online service** (n.) A provider that offers dialup electronic mail, conferences, information resources, Internet access, and other communication services to users who have a computer, a modem, and a telephone line. Examples are America Online (AOL), CompuServe, Prodigy, and Microsoft Network (MSN). Each of these services has millions of users whose computers can be connected to a central file server and who can then exchange information among themselves.

**ontology** (n.) The hierarchical structuring of knowledge about things; this structure is created by categorizing things according to their essential qualities. In artificial intelligence (AI), an explicit formal specification of a way to represent the objects and the concepts that are assumed to exist in some area of knowledge and the relationships that exist among them. When the knowledge about a domain is represented in a declarative language, the set of objects that can be represented is called the *universe of discourse.* The ontology of a program may be defined by a set of representational terms.

**ONU** See *optical network unit.*

**OOB signal** See *out-of-band signal.*

**OODB** See *object-oriented database.*

**OOP** See *object-oriented programming.*

**op amp** See *operational amplifier.*

**OpenAir** (n.) A wireless LAN standard supported by the Wireless LAN Interoperability Forum (WLIF).

**open architecture** (n.) Related to microcomputers, a hardware configuration that allows circuit boards to be added in order to expand the system's functionality. The circuit boards are typically plugged into slots on a motherboard. Functionality is enhanced by connecting outboard gear or peripherals to internal expansion buses or to external ports. Software that integrates the expanded hardware with existing features is required.

**Open Database Connectivity** (ODBC) (n.) A standard for accessing diverse database systems. ODBC has interfaces for SQL, Visual Basic, and Visual C++, and it has drivers for dBASE, Access, Paradox, and other databases. ODBC 1.0 was released in September 1992. It is based on the call-level interface and was defined by the SQL Access Group.

**Open Data-Link Interface** (ODI, pronounced "oh-dee-EYE") (n.) A network card API developed by Novell that provides media and protocol independence. It allows the sharing of a single card by multiple transport layer protocols, and it resolves conflicts.

**OpenGL** (n.) Open Graphics Language; an Application Programming Interface (API) developed by Silicon Graphics as an open standard for three-dimensional computer-aided design (CAD) applications and for computer-aided visualization of images.

**Open Media Framework** (OMF) (n.) A de facto standard developed by Avid Technologies and a group of partners for specifying multimedia data types and controlling playback across different platforms for digital editing of video and audio.

**Open Network Architecture** (ONA) (n.) Telephone switches and circuits that enable unbundling, or separation of features, which facilitates interconnection with services provided by other vendors.

**OpenScript** (n.) The scripting language used by the Asymetrix ToolBook multimedia authoring program for Microsoft Windows.

**Open Shortest-Path First** (OSPF) (n.) A link state routing protocol, as opposed to a distance vector routing protocol. Defined in RFC 1247, OSPF is one of the Internet standard Interior Gateway Protocols (IGPs).

**Open Software Foundation** (OSF) (n.) An association of nine computer vendors to promote "open computing." Apollo, Digital Equipment Corporation (DEC), Hewlett-Packard, IBM, Bull, Nixdorf, Philips, Siemens, and Hitachi formed the foundation. The group plans to release common operating systems and interfaces, based on developments of Unix and the X Window System, for a wide range of hardware architectures. In 1990, the OSF announced the release of OSF/1, the industry's first open operating system.

**Open Systems Interconnection** (OSI, pronounced "oh-ess-EYE") (n.) A standard and a model for data communications. OSI has the following seven layers (see table):

1.  Physical layer (hardware, medium of connection). Specifies electrical and mechanical connections and the media access control (MAC). The physical layer is used by the data link layer directly above it. Two common physical layer protocols are CSMA/CD and token ring.

2.  Data link layer (linking protocols). Splits

## Intranet Protocols Defined by the OSI Network Reference Model

Across the top of the chart are the seven layers of the OSI Network Reference Model.
Internet and Intranet protocols are shown at each layer.

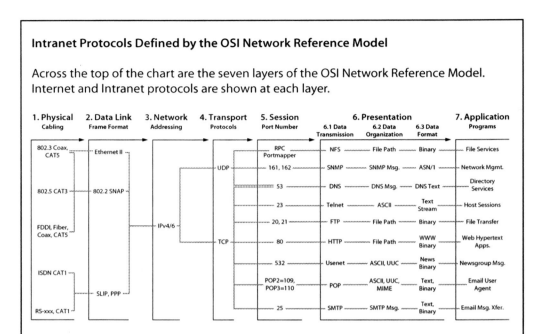

Notes:

UDP: User Datagram Protocol
TCP : Transmission Control Protocol
IPv4/6: Internet Protocol version 4 or version 6
FDDI: Fiber Distributed Data Interface
SNAP: Systems Network Architecture Protocol

data into frames, transmits the frames over the physical layer, and receives acknowledgment frames. The data link layer performs error checking and retransmits frames received incorrectly. It provides a channel to the network layer directly above it. The data link layer is divided into the upper sublayer, logical link control (LLC), and the lower sublayer, media access control (MAC).

3. Network layer (type of network). The third lowest layer, which determines routing of data packets from sender to receiver via the data link layer. The network layer is used by the transport layer directly above it. The most common network layer protocol is Internet Protocol (IP).

4. Transport layer (protocol for transfer). Determines how the network layer is used to provide point-to-point connections between hosts. It establishes and releases connections between hosts and is also referred to as the host-to-host layer. The transport layer is used by the session layer directly above it. The most common transport layer protocol is Transmission Control Protocol (TCP).

5. Session layer (means of communication). Uses the transport layer to establish a connection between processes on different hosts. It handles the creation and security of each session. The session layer is used by the presentation layer directly above it.

6. Presentation layer (adaptation of connections). Performs functions such as text compression and format conversion to facilitate communication between hosts. The presentation layer allows incompatible processes in the application layer above it to communicate using the session layer below it.

7. Application layer (specific implementation of defined facilities). Handles resource allocation and problem partitioning. The application layer delivers the user interface. The presentation layer below it provides this layer with a local representation of data independent of the format used on the network.

**Open Video System** (n.) Term used in the Telecommunications Act of 1996 to describe the setup in which a video carrier provides common carrier services. Operators of open video systems are required to make a large percentage of their channels available to other programmers. By doing so, operators are not required to obtain a local cable franchise.

**operating system** (OS) (n.) Software loaded into RAM when a computer boots up, controlling fundamental processes such as saving and retrieving files. An OS may have a command line interface, like DOS. Alternatively, it may have a graphical user interface (GUI), as do the Mac OS and OpenLook for Unix (developed by Sun Microsystems).

**operational amplifier** (op amp) (n.) An analog integrated circuit device with two opposite polarity inputs and one output, used as a basic building block in analog signal processing.

**operator** (n.) 1. Any character that represents an operation, or an action, performed on a number or a variable. Common operators include (+) addition, (-) subtraction, (*) multiplication, and (/) division. In query languages that can locate information in databases, Boolean operators (AND, OR, NOT, and NOR) are used. Another type is the relational operator, such as less than (<) and greater than (>). 2. Telecommunications term for any company that manages the operations of a network service.

**OPL** (n.) Developed by Yamaha, a type of synthesizer chip used in the Creative Labs Sound Blaster and in other popular sound boards. These chips use frequency modulation (FM) synthesis.

**optical carrier** (OC) (n.) A Synchronous Optical Network (SONET) signal.

**Optical Carrier Level 3** (OC-3) (n.) The electrical-to-optical mapping of the synchronous transport signal (STS) with frame synchronous scrambling. It consists of fiber-optic cable lines. It is used primarily with Synchronous Optical Network (SONET) networks and is capable of 155 Mbps. Other common OC levels are OC-12 (622 Mbps) and OC-48 (2.4 Gbps).

**optical character recognition** (OCR) (n.) Software used with a scanner to convert printed pages into text files.

**optical disc** (n.) A disc that stores digital data, which can be read with reflected laser light that bounces off the surface of the disc. All CDs are optical discs.

**optical disc player** (n.) Any playback device that can read data from optical media by using reflected laser light.

**optical fiber** (n.) A glass or plastic filament that is used to transmit information using infrared or visible light. An optical fiber is typically a laser-driven carrier. The beam of light is an electromagnetic signal transmitted at an extremely high frequency. Optical fiber is less expensive than copper wire, and it is less susceptible to interference than other media. The light beams do not escape from the medium because of the total internal reflection. Fiber-optic connections provide extremely high bandwidth and security.

**optical memory** (n.) Any technology incorporating storage devices that use laser light to record or read data.

**Optical Memory Disc Recorder** (OMDR) (n.) A Matsushita/Panasonic write-once analog videodisc recorder that writes to 8-inch or 12-inch blanks. The format is incompatible with laser videodisc players from Pioneer, Philips, or Sony.

**Optical Network Interface** (ONI, pronounced "oh-en-EYE") (n.) In telecommunications, a device that performs electrical-to-analog conversion. An ONI provides the interface between an optical network and telephone equipment on the customer premises if the network delivers fiber to the home.

**optical network unit** (ONU) (n.) In telecommunications, a device that converts transmitted signals onto a single band of distribution frequencies. An ONU is a type of access node that translates optical signals into electrical signals and vice versa, enabling signals to be transmitted to and from customers over coaxial and copper-twisted pairs.

**optical read-only memory** (OROM) (n.) Medium that can be read by an optical reader but that may not be written to.

**optical storage** (n.) Refers to any media that uses laser technology to store data, including CD-ROMs and magneto-optical cartridges.

**optocoupler** (n.) Any device that functions as an electrical-to-optical or optical-to-electrical transducer.

**opto-electronic device** (n.) Any equipment or component that responds to light waves in the visible, infrared, or ultraviolet spectrums. The category includes devices that emit or modify incoherent or coherent electromagnetic radiation, as well as those that use light waves for their internal operation.

**opto-electronics** (n.) All types of electrical devices that detect light, such as photodiodes, as well as those that generate, control, or amplify light, such as lasers and light-emitting diodes (LEDs).

**opto-isolator** (n.) A miniature device that converts electrical signals into light, transmits the light across a small gap, and converts it back into electrical signals. An opto-isolator makes a circuit immune to interference and ground-loop problems because no electricity flows across the gap.

**Orange Book standard** (n.) The specification for compact disc–recordable (CD-R) systems, developed by Philips and Sony. It includes specifications for the hybrid disc technology on which Eastman Kodak's Photo-CD is based.

**ORB** See *object request broker*.

**ordinate** (n.) The y-coordinate, plotted on a graph in response to the input of a function. The x-coordinate is referred to as the *abscissa*.

**original equipment manufacturer** (OEM) (n.) A manufacturer of hardware that may be modified or included in a system marketed by a value-added reseller (VAR).

**originate mode** (n.) A transmission state in

which an originating modem transmits at the low frequency defined by a communications channel and receives at the designated high frequency. The transmit and receive frequencies are the opposite of those of the called modem, which is in answer mode.

**OROM** See *optical read-only memory.*

**orthogonal** (adj.) Separate, mutually independent, and at times irrelevant. The term describes complete sets of primitives or capabilities that span the entire range of possibilities in a system and do not overlap. In logic, the set of operators NOT and OR is orthogonal. The set NAND, OR, and NOT is not orthogonal, because one of these can be expressed in terms of the others.

**orthogonal instruction set** (n.) In programming, an instruction set in which instructions all have the same format and register and can therefore be used interchangeably. The choice of register to use is orthogonal to the choice of instruction.

**orthographic projection** (n.) The visible outline of an object projected onto a surface in which the projection vector is parallel to the z-axis.

**OS** See *operating system.*

**oscillator** (n.) Any device that vibrates internally to generate a signal at a specified frequency, such as an audible tone. Usually used for test purposes, oscillators also produce musical tones.

**OSF** See *Open Software Foundation.*

**OSI** See *Open Systems Interconnection.*

**OS-9** (n.) Operating System–9; developed by Microware Corporation in 1978, a realtime operating system that has been ported to the Motorola 68000 family, Intel 80386, Intel 80486, Pentium, and the PowerPC. The kernel can exist in ROM, is modular, and has a scalable unified file system.

**OSPF** See *Open Shortest-Path First.*

**OSR-2** See *OEM Service Release 2.*

**OS/2** (n.) Operating System/2; a multitasking, higher-level operating system. OS/2 was developed by IBM and Microsoft for those microcomputers in the PS/2 series that are equipped with 80386 or later microprocessors. See also *IBM PS/2.*

**outboard** (adj.) Describes external, rack-mounted, audio signal processing equipment, such as an equalizer, a compressor, a limiter, an aural exciter, or a digital delay.

**outline font** (n.) A typeface with lines and curves defined by mathematical vectors, as opposed to a bitmap font, which is defined by individual pixels. An outline font can be scaled to any size and transformed more easily than can a bitmap font. PostScript and TrueType are both outline fonts, which are also known as *vector fonts.*

**out-of-band signal** (OOB signal) (n.) Content transmitted over a circuit that is separate from the channel carrying the voice, data, video, or other primary information. A filter is used to separate the signals. The OOB signal often contains dialing, supervisory, or other information controlling the primary signal.

**out-of-band signaling** (n.) Separation of a signal from the channel carrying information about the signal. See also *Signaling System 7.*

**out-point** (n.) The final frame of an audio or a video segment to be edited or dubbed.

313

**output** 1. (v.) To send data from a computer or processor to another device, such as a printer or disk drive. 2. (n.) The digital data sent from memory for display or transfer. 3. (n.) Any signal that is generated or passed on by any means.

**outside plant** (adj.) Describes any part of a telephone system that is exterior to a telephone company's buildings. Utility poles, access lines, load coils, and conduits are all included in this description.

**outsource** (v.) To hire specialists, consultants, or an external production company to produce segments of media types.

**outtake** (n.) Footage excluded from the final version of an audio or video production.

**overdub** (v.) To add new content or a new channel to an existing audio mix, such as a new vocal or instrumental track.

**overflow error** (n.) A buffer overrun in which data is received too fast to be captured completely and accurately. An overflow error may also occur when the memory allocation is not large enough to accept a unit of data sent to it.

**overhead** (n.) In communications, all information that is added to user-transmitted data. This includes control, routing, and error-checking information that carries network status or operational instructions, network routing information, and retransmissions of user-data messages that are received in error.

**overlay** 1. (n.) The superimposition of text or graphics onto still or motion video by digital means, such as with a character generator. 2. (v.) To show one video image positioned on top of another. If two analog video signals are to be overlaid cleanly, they must be genlocked, or synchronized to the same timing signal.

**overrun** (n.) A condition in which data is transmitted from the send unit faster than the receiving unit can accept and process it. If the buffer is overrun when recording data on a CD-R, errors will occur, and the session will fail.

**overs** (n.) Input signals that exceed the full-scale range of an A/D converter. Overs indicators may be LEDs that light up when 0 dB input is exceeded, or they may be calibrated digital meters. 0 dB full scale is the absolute highest voltage level that a converter can process. When this level is met or exceeded, the output from the converter consists of all 1s.

**oversample** (v.) To digitize audio or video data faster than normal to produce more samples, resulting in more accurate results.

**overscan** (n.) A condition in which a video signal bleeds off the edges of a monitor. When computer images are sent to a monitor in the overscan mode, up to 20 percent of the content around the edges may be lost. See figure.

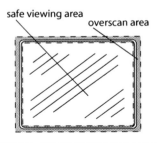

*overscan*

**overwrite** (v.) To record data on top of existing data, rendering the original data unreadable.

# P

Pa See *pascal.*

PABX See *private automatic branch exchange.*

**package** 1. (n.) Any software application or set of computer programs needed to perform a task. 2. (n.) A combination of hardware and software that constitutes a complete multimedia delivery system. 3. (v.) To combine media, printed matter, and casing for the purpose of distributing a product.

**packet** (n.) A unit of binary information organized in a block for transmission, including control data about the type of information and the length of the packet, the data itself, and error detection and correction bits.

**packet filter** (n.) A procedure that inspects each packet on a network for user-defined content, such as an IP address. It blocks any packets that attempt to reach areas that are not approved for access. A packet filter does not track the state of sessions and is one of the least secure types of firewall.

**packet filtering** (n.) A procedure performed by routers and bridges to limit the flow of information based on pre-determined criteria such as source, destination, or type of service requested. It allows a network administrator to limit protocol-specific traffic to one network segment, isolate email domains, and perform other traffic-control functions.

**Packet InterNet Groper** (Ping) 1. (n.) A program that sends an echo request to a destination on a network and waits for a reply. The request is in the Internet Control Message Protocol (ICMP) format. 2. (v.) To send an echo request to a destination on a network, as in "to ping the host computer."

**packet sniffer** (n.) A device or program that monitors packets of data traveling between computers on a network.

**packet switching** (n.) A method of transferring data by addressing blocks of information, occupying a channel only while data is being transmitted. After transmission, the channel is free to transfer other packets. The data network determines the routing during the transfer of a packet. In *circuit switching,* by contrast, the routing is determined prior to transfer. In packet switching, packets do not always arrive in the order in which they are sent. Therefore, circuit switching is used when data such as audio files must stream over a network in order.

**packet-switching data network** (PSDN) (n.) A network in which data is transmitted in packets that can be routed individually over network connections and reassembled at the destination.

**pad** See *attenuator pad.*

**PA-422** (n.) The professional audio implementation of the Electronics Industries Association's EIA-422 interconnection standard, defined and adopted as "AES Recommended Practice For Sound-Reinforcement Systems - Communications Interface (PA-422) AES 15-1991."

**page** (n.) A predetermined segment of expanded memory that can be swapped in and out of the page frame. The *page frame* is the physical location in conventional memory where expanded memory pages are stored.

**Page Description Language** (PDL) (n.) A programming language used to control the formatting and layout of a printed page. PDL sends instructions that a printer with processing capabilities can interpret. An example of a PDL is Adobe PostScript.

**Paged Memory Management Unit** (PMMU) (n.) An integrated circuit (IC) that supports virtual memory by helping the processor locate needed data, either on a hard disk or in physical memory.

**page-mode RAM** (n.) A static RAM chip that can hold information without being constantly refreshed by the central processor in a computer system. It allows faster memory performance than Dynamic RAM, which requires constant updating.

**pagination** (n.) The division of a document into pages. A word-processing program can paginate automatically or manually.

**paging** (n.) 1. A service that transmits numeric,

alphanumeric, text, or voice messages to pagers. It does not include Short Message Service, a paging feature found on mobile phones. 2. In programming, a process for increasing the available memory space by moving seldom-used parts of a program's working memory from RAM to a local disk drive. The unit of transfer is called a *page*. A memory management unit (MMU) monitors accesses to memory and splits each address into a page number and an offset within the page. Page numbers are entered in a page table for lookup. Paging permits the memory requirements of all running tasks to exceed the amount of physical memory. Swapping simply allows multiple processes to run concurrently, providing that each process on its own fits within physical memory.

**paired cable** (n.) Any cable consisting of conductors that are all twisted pairs. Paired cable is the most common communications wiring because the twist reduces the likelihood of interference between the lines.

**PAL** See *Phase Alternation Line.*

**palette** (n.) 1. In digital imagery, the number of predefined colors available for display or printing. 2. Within a software application, the onscreen selection of tools, options, or modes available to the user. A palette is most often displayed in a rectangular grid.

**palette flash** (n.) An undesirable event in which an application is instructed to change the current color palette, causing a momentary bright flash to occur. For example, if consecutive frames in a Multimedia Director movie contained different palettes, a flash would appear on the monitor between the two frames while the movie played.

**palmtop** (n.) A compact personal computer,

typically used to store contact information, telephone numbers, and meeting times and dates. Windows CE, a graphical user interface (GUI), allows the larger palmtops to use a scaled-down version of Microsoft Office applications. The Pilot, developed by PalmOS and marketed by U.S. Robotics, is a popular example.

**Palo Alto Research Center** (PARC) See *Xerox Corporation Palo Alto Research Center.*

**pan** (v.) 1. In video and film production, to rotate a camera horizontally across a panorama, changing the angle of view. 2. In computer graphics, to move in one direction along the plane of the drawing, keeping the same scale and orientation. 3. In audio production, to shift the position of a sound between the right and left stereo channels.

**pan and scan** (n.) A dynamic cropping technique used to translate between materials with different aspect ratios. Pan and scan is often used to translate movies shot on wide-screen film formats to the aspect ratio of a television display. In the pan and scan process, the image is cropped to the new aspect ratio, and the transfer operator pans within the wider original image to include important details that are near the edge. The details would be lost by a simple cropping technique. Movies that have been pan and scanned completely fill the television screen and do not exhibit the letterbox effect (black bands above and below the picture).

**panic** (v.) To malfunction, as the Unix operating system does when a critical internal consistency check fails in such a way that the system cannot continue. The kernel tries to print a message to the screen and write an image of memory into the swap area on disk for analysis later.

**Pantone Matching System** (PMS) (n.) A standard trademarked system of identifying more than 500 colors by number. PMS colors are created by an exact mixture of special base colors in specific proportions. Also known as *PMS color.*

**PAP** See *Password Authentication Protocol.*

**Paradox** (n.) Developed by Borland International, the first multi-user relational database for microcomputers with multitasking capabilities. It allows connectivity to Structured Query Language (SQL) data on a database server.

**parallel** (adj.) 1. Describes a method of transmitting data by sending a byte or a group of bits simultaneously. This contrasts with *serial data transfer,* in which bits are sent one at a time. 2. Describes the simultaneous processing of individual parts of a larger job in a computer application.

**parallel port** (n.) Interface from a computer system through which multiple bits of data are transferred in or out. This type of interface carries one bit on each wire, thereby multiplying the transfer rate obtainable over a single wire. A typical example of a parallel port is a printer port. The widely used Centronics port transfers eight bits at a time. SCSI and Integrated Drive Electronics (IDE) are special types of parallel ports.

**parallel processing** (n.) Method of using more than one computer simultaneously to process data. Flynn's taxonomy classifies both parallel and serial computers according to whether their processors execute the same instructions at the same time (single-instruction, multiple-data, or SIMD) or whether each processor executes different instructions (multiple-instruction, multiple-data, or MIMD). A *processor farm* is a group of computers cooperating on a problem or running under the control of another processor that distributes work and collects results.

**parallel processor** (n.) An integrated circuit that can perform different operations simultaneously.

**Parameter RAM** (PRAM, pronounced "PEE-ram") (n.) Parameter random-access memory; a portion of RAM used to store system configuration and startup settings on a Macintosh computer. PRAM is powered by a battery and will automatically default to factory settings if the battery is removed from the computer for a few minutes. This procedure, called *zapping* the PRAM, is a last resort when solving system problems.

**parametric equalizer** (n.) A multi-band variable equalizer that allows control of all the parameters of the internal filters, including *amplitude, center frequency,* and *bandwidth*. The user can shift the center frequency and widen or narrow the affected area. Units are available with rotary and slide controls. Some parametric equalizers are available that allow control of center frequency but not bandwidth. Units with slide controls are often called paragraphic equalizers. The frequency control may be variable (analog) or selectable in steps (digital). Cut-only parametric equalizers (with or without adjustable bandwidth) are called notch equalizers or band-reject equalizers.

**PARC** See *Xerox Corporation Palo Alto Research Center.*

**parent directory** (n.) In MS-DOS, a directory that lies one step above the child directory.

**parity** (n.) A technique used to determine whether errors were introduced in data transmission. A parity bit is appended to an array of bits to make the sum of all the bits always odd or even, and the result is checked on reception.

**parser** (n.) A computer program that determines the syntactic structure of a sentence or string of symbols in a computer language. As input, the parser takes a sequence of tokens generated by a lexical analyzer. The output from the parser might be an abstract syntax tree. Yacc is an example of a parser generator.

**particle animation** (n.) An animation technique used to depict natural forces, such as wind or gravity, as controlling the movement of small objects in a sequence.

**partition** (n.) A section of storage separately addressed by the operating system. Drives may be divided into multiple partitions.

**pascal** (Pa) (n.) A unit of pressure equal to one newton of force per square meter.

**Pascal** (n.) A programming language designed by Niklaus Wirth in 1970 and named after the French mathematician Blaise Pascal (1623–1662). The language was designed for teaching programming because it is simpler to grasp than other languages in use at that time. Pascal is based on Algorithmic Language (ALGOL) and emphasizes structured programming constructs, data structures, and strong typing. The language C has displaced Pascal from the niche it acquired in applications and systems programming.

**passband** (n.) In audio, the range of frequencies passed by a low pass, high pass, or bandpass filter. The passband is normally measured at the -3 dB point, which is the frequency point where the amplitude response is attenuated

3 dB relative to the level of the main passband. Two points are referenced in a bandpass filter: the upper and lower -3dB points. The -3dB point represents the frequency where the output power has been reduced by one-half. Mathematically, -3dB represents a multiplier of 0.707. If voltage is reduced by 0.707, the current is also reduced by 0.707 according to Ohm's law. The equation for power is voltage multiplied by current. Therefore, 0.707 times 0.707 equals 0.5, or half-power.

**passive attack** (n.) In network security, a type of intrusion that simply monitors or records data, also referred to as *eavesdropping*. A passive threat is the unauthorized interception of information, without alteration.

**passive crossover** (n.) In audio, any loudspeaker crossover that does not require power to function. This type of crossover is often built into the speaker cabinet. See *crossover*.

**passive equalizer** (n.) In audio, a variable equalizer that does not require power to function. This type of equalizer uses only passive inductors, capacitors, and resistors. They exhibit low noise, high dynamic range, reliability, and no RF interference. However, they are expensive and heavy, and they reduce signal levels.

**passive matrix display** (n.) A type of liquid crystal display (LCD) that uses one transistor for each row of pixels and one for each column. By contrast, an *active matrix display* uses a transistor for each pixel. The quality of a passive matrix display is much lower than that of an active matrix.

**password** (n.) Any string of characters or numbers that a user enters in a computing system to gain access to protected files or to receive privileges.

**Password Authentication Protocol** (PAP) (n.) An authentication scheme that Point-to-Point Protocol (PPP) servers use to validate the identity of the originator of a connection. PAP involves two-way handshaking. When a link is established, the originator sends a password pair to the server. If authentication succeeds, the server sends back an acknowledgment. If authentication fails, the server either terminates the connection or gives the originator a second chance. PAP is not a robust authentication method. Passwords are sent in the open, and there is no protection against hackers. PAP is best applied if a plain text password must be available to simulate a login at a remote host. PAP is defined in RFC 1334.

**paste** (v.) To retrieve text or a graphic from the Clipboard or memory buffer and to insert it into a document.

**patch** 1. (v.) To connect circuits with a patch cord or a cable, typically on a patch bay. 2. (n.) A last-minute instruction or command added to a software program to make it run. A patch is not part of the formal plan.

**patchbay** (n.) A rack-mounted panel with at least two rows of connectors, which are used to insert a piece of external equipment into the signal path. The top row consists of "send" jacks, and the bottom row consists of "receive" jacks. A professional quality patchbay has *tip-ring-sleeve* (TRS) jacks wired for true balanced-line interconnection (tip = positive signal, ring = negative signal, sleeve = shield ground). The two rows of jacks are tied together by shorting contacts so that the "normal" operation is to short the send and receive tip-to-tip and ring-to-ring connecting points. The sleeves are always connected. This arrangement maintains the normal signal path until something is plugged in. This interrupts the "normalled" connections. A patchbay makes it easy to route

**P**

signals between audio devices. See figure.

**path** (n.) 1. A set of descriptors in MS-DOS that identifies the location of a file. For example, the path *C:\graphics\project\filename.bmp* leads to *filename.bmp,* a specific graphics file on the C: drive. 2. Linked curves in a vector-oriented image. 3. The route that a message, an instruction, or a datagram takes as it passes through a network.

**path name** (n.) The full identifier for a file or a directory in a hierarchical file system, including the drive letter followed by a colon and the nodes from the root directory. An example might be: *C:\MyStuff\documents\Joememo.doc.* The directories are separated by a path name separator, which is the backslash symbol, \, in MS-DOS. A path name may be absolute or relative. The part of a path name that follows the last separator is called the *base name.*

**path name separator** (n.) A character that separates elements of a path name. The backslash (\) is used in MS-DOS, while the forward slash (/) is used in Unix. No directory name or file name may contain this character.

**PBX** See *private branch exchange.*

**PC** See *personal computer.*

**PCA** See *program calibration area.*

**PC/AT** See *Personal Computer/Advanced Technology.*

**PC/AT architecture** (n.) Personal Computer/ Advanced Technology architecture; architecture of the IBM 80286-based computer, which uses a 16-bit data bus. As the PC/AT architecture evolved from the 8088-based PC/XT with an eight-bit bus, it retained compatible hardware features.

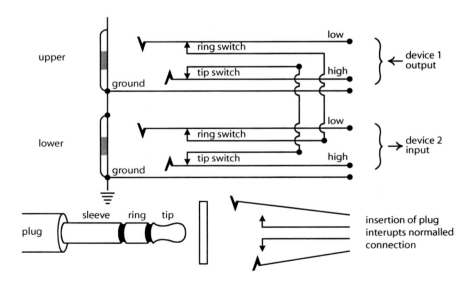

*diagram of patchbay connections*

**PCB** See *printed circuit board.*

**PCD** See *Photo–Compact Disc.*

**PC-DOS** See *Personal Computer–Disk Operating System.*

**PCI** See *peripheral component interconnect.*

**PCM** See *pulse code modulation.*

**PCMCIA** See *Personal Computer Memory Card International Association.*

**PCS** See *personal communications services.*

**PC Speaker Driver** (n.) Personal computer Speaker Driver; a Microsoft Windows program that produces sounds using software and the computer's onboard speaker. A PC Speaker Driver is not a substitute for a sound board, but it can function in that way.

**PCX** (n.) A common graphics format in Microsoft Windows. ZSoft developed PCX for the PC Paintbrush program.

**PC/XT** (n.) Early IBM personal computer based on the Intel 8088 processor with an eight-bit bus.

**PDA** See *personal digital assistant.*

**PDF** See *Portable Document Format.*

**PDL** See *Page Description Language.*

**PDS** See *Processor Direct Slot.*

**PDU** See *protocol data unit.*

**peak program meter** (PPM) (n.) A meter that accurately measures and displays peak audio signals, as opposed to average audio signals shown by a VU meter. The PPM augments the VU meter, and both are useful. The PPM is particularly valuable for digital audio recording or signal processing due to the critical monitoring required to prevent overdriving the inputs. There are two standards: IEC 60268-10 for analog meters and IEC 60268-18 for digital meters. PPMs are designed to require a finite 5 millisecond integration time so that only peaks wide enough to be audible are displayed.

**pedestal** (n.) 1. In video production, the vertical plane in which a video camera moves as it is raised or lowered, without being tilted. 2. In telecommunications, an above-ground enclosure in which buried cables are spliced and terminated.

**peer** (n.) A computer that resides on the same protocol layer of a network as another and that is connected on the lowest level.

**peer-to-peer network** (n.) A network in which each computer is independent and can serve the others or act as a workstation. Peripherals connected to any computer networked in this fashion are available to any of the other peer computers connected.

**pel** See *picture element.*

**PEM** See *Privacy Enhanced Mail.*

**penetration** (n.) In network security, successful unauthorized access to an automated information system.

**Pentium** (n.) An Intel microprocessor made with superscalar complex instruction set computing (CISC) architecture. The original Pentium had two 32-bit 486-type integer pipe-

**P**

lines and a 64-bit data bus. It offered dependency checking and branch prediction and had more than 3 million transistors and a clock rate of 66 MHz.

**Pentium Pro** (n.) Developed in 1995, an Intel microprocessor that improves on the Pentium processor. The Pentium Pro has an internal reduced instruction set computing (RISC) architecture with a CISC-RISC translator, three-way superscalar execution, and dynamic execution. It also features branch prediction and register renaming and is superpipelined. A Level 2 cache has been added, with 256 kilobytes (KB) or 512KB on a separate die. The chip has a built-in floating-point unit (FPU). The 1995 version of the Pentium Pro had a clock frequency of 133 MHz, consumed about 20 watts of power, and was about twice as fast as a 100-MHz Pentium. The Pentium Pro was optimized for 32-bit software and actually runs more slowly with 16-bit software than the original Pentium.

**Pentium II** (n.) The microprocessor that Intel introduced as the successor to the Pentium Pro. There are several versions, each intended for a different market. The standard Pentium II was designed for mainstream home and business users. The Celeron is an inexpensive version that lacks the cache of the standard Pentium II. The Xeon is intended for high performance and servers. The mobile version is used in portable computers.

Pentium II is a superscalar CPU with approximately 7.5 million transistors.

First-generation Pentium II processors, code named "Klamath," were manufactured using wafers 0.35 microns thick. They support clock rates of 233, 266, 300, and 333 MHz with an internal a bus speed of 66 MHz. Second-generation Pentium II processors, code named "Deschutes," are made using 0.25-micron wafers. They support rates of 350, 400, and 450 MHz with an internal bus speed of 100 MHz.

The Pentium II is packaged on a special daughterboard that plugs into a card-edge processor slot on the motherboard. The daughterboard is housed in a Single Edge Contact (SEC) cartridge. The standard Pentium II requires a 242-pin slot (Slot 1), while the Zeon fits in a 330-pin slot (Slot 2). Slot 1 is referred to as SEC-242, and Slot 2 is referred to as SEC-330. The daughterboard holds support chips and cache memory chips as well as the Pentium II processor.

Every type of Pentium II processor features Multimedia Extensions (MMX), integrated Level 1 and Level 2 cache controllers, Dynamic Execution and Dual Independent Bus Architecture. Each operates with a 64-bit system bus and a separate 64-bit cache bus.

**performance objective** (n.) In computer-based training (CBT), a goal that is narrowly defined and clearly stated for students in an interactive environment.

**period** (T) (n.) In a periodic function, the smallest time interval over which the function repeats itself. The period of a sine wave is the amount of time (T) it takes for the waveform to pass through 360 degrees, or to complete one cycle. It is also the reciprocal of the frequency itself: $T = 1/f$.

**peripheral** (n.) A device that is controlled by a computer but that is a separate unit interfaced with the computer, such as a printer, a scanner, or an external modem.

**peripheral component interconnect** (PCI) (n.) A local bus standard that supports up to 16 physical slots. Intel Corporation led an industry group in developing the specification, which was released in 1992 and updated in 1993. Both 32- and 64-bit implementations are defined. PCI uses bridges to insert a bus between the CPU and the native input/output (I/O) bus to address weaknesses in the Industry Standard Architecture (ISA) and Extended Industry Standard Architecture (EISA) buses. A new set of controller chips was developed to extend the processor bus rather than to tap into it directly.

The PCI bus is referred to as a *mezzanine bus,* because it adds a layer to the traditional configuration. It bypasses the standard I/O bus and uses the system bus to increase the bus clock speed, taking advantage of the CPU's data path. Most computing systems built since 1993, including the DEC Alpha and the Macintosh PowerPC, integrate the PCI bus.

The PCI bus moves data at 33 MHz, capitalizing on the full data width of the CPU. When the PCI bus is used with a 64-bit processor, data can transfer at speeds of up to 264 megabytes per second (MBps). The PCI bus operates concurrently with the processor bus, which can process data in an external cache while the PCI transfers information between other system components. PCI supports bus mastering direct memory access (DMA).

PCI adapter cards use a special type of connector. The specification identifies three different board configurations: a 5-volt specification for stationary computer systems, a 3.3-volt specification for portable machines, and a universal specification for either type of system.

PCI cards are configured through software and do not have jumpers or switches. PCI was the model for the Intel plug and play (PnP) specification, and a PnP Basic Input/Output System (BIOS) enables automatic PnP configuration of components connected through the PCI bus. In addition to automatic configuration, PCI boards support parity checking of the data and the address bus signals. The specification has been enhanced to operate at 66 MHz.

**Perl** (n.) An interpreted computer language developed by Larry Wall. Perl is a general-purpose language often used for scanning text and printing formatted reports. Many web developers use Perl. Common Gateway Interfaces (CGIs) and Perl libraries exist for several platforms. The flexibility of Perl makes it well suited for form processing. Short for Practical Extraction and Report Language or, as some would have it, Pathologically Eclectic Rubbish Lister.

**Perl5** (n.) A significant enhancement of Perl version 4. It adds real data structures, subroutine calls, and method inheritance.

**persistence** (n.) The length of time a phosphor dot on the screen of a cathode-ray tube (CRT) remains illuminated after an electron beam has energized it.

**personal communications services** (PCS) (n.) A digital cellular phone service that provides voice communications, numeric and text messaging, voice-mail, and various other functions to a single device. This device operates in the 1900 MHz band. Some providers use part of their AMPS 800 MHz allocation to offer PCS. The technology can hand off calls from transmitter to transmitter as a caller moves around in the PCS network.

**personal computer** (PC) (n.) A relatively low-cost, portable computer system for business and home use that IBM and Apple Computer

P

popularized. Strictly speaking, only an IBM-compatible model is called a *PC*.

**Personal Computer/Advanced Technology** (PC/AT) (n.) A personal computer introduced by IBM in 1984 featuring a tall case containing the Intel 80286 processor with a 16-bit bus, a 1.2-megabyte floppy disk drive, and a hard disk drive.

**Personal Computer–Disk Operating System** (PC-DOS) (n.) The IBM version of an operating system for personal computers.

**Personal Computer Memory Card International Association** (PCMCIA) (n.) Industry group that developed the specification for *PC cards,* which are credit card–sized plug-in cards for laptop computers. All types have a 68-pin connector, consisting of two rows of 34 pins. A card is 85.6 mm deep and 54 mm wide. The height of a PC card varies with its type and application.

| Type | Height | Application |
|---|---|---|
| I | 3.3 mm | Memory (RAM or Flash RAM) |
| II | 5.0 mm | Network interface card (NIC) or modem |
| III | 10.5 mm | Hard disk |
| IV | 5.5 mm | Hard disk |

A Type II slot will accept a Type I or a Type II card because a shorter card may be plugged into a slot that will accommodate a taller card. The original interface for PC cards only supported one interrupt, limiting the use of multiple-function cards.

There are several versions of the specification. The original specification defined Type I cards with no input/output (I/O) capability or software drivers because they were memory cards. Version 2.0 defined I/O but did not specify soft-

ware drivers, which the vendors provided for their cards. The interface in this version is a 16-bit data path with a 6-MHz bus speed.

Version 2.1 was a major advance in the standard, allowing the cards to work in any type of computer with a PCMCIA slot and introducing "card services," a higher-level Application Programming Interface (API). Version 2.1 also introduced plug and play (PnP), hot swapping, and Execution in Place (XIP). XIP refers to programs that can read directly from the card's own ROM. A BIOS-level interface, "socket services," gave the PC card its own standard calls, which were independent of different vendor implementations. These standard software interfaces made PC cards easier to use.

The February 1995 release of the PC card standard added specifications for 32-bit bus mastering direct memory access (DMA) support, known as *CardBus,* at speeds of up to 33 MHz. It also provided for multiple-function adapters, so an Ethernet card and a modem card could be combined in one unit. The voltage requirement was reduced from 5 volts to 3 volts, which saves battery power. The Card Information Structure (CIS) on every card specifies the manufacturer, the model number, the voltage requirements, and the input/output configuration.

**personal digital assistant** (PDA) (n.) 1. A term Apple Computer initially used to describe its Newton technology. 2. Any battery-powered handheld device that provides digital information management and communications and that is capable of calculating, scheduling, taking notes, maintaining address files, transferring data via a modem, and other similar activities.

**personal identification number** (PIN) (n.) A

number assigned to an individual user that is often used as an identifying password for access to secure data or systems.

**Personal System/2** (PS/2) (n.) The second generation of personal computers built by IBM. The PS/2 series introduced 3.5-inch 1.44 megabyte (MB) floppy disks, the VGA display standard, and Micro Channel Architecture.

**perspective correction** (n.) A technique in three-dimensional texture mapping that evaluates the appearance of a texture from different points of view and then draws and illuminates the texture automatically.

**PERT/CPM** See *project evaluation and review technique/critical path method.*

**peta-** Prefix meaning a quadrillion (10 to the 15th power), an SI unit represented by an uppercase *P*. In the binary system, it is expressed as 2 to the 50th power.

**PF** See *power factor.*

**PFC** See *power-factor-corrected.*

**PFL** See *pre-fade listen.*

**P-frame** (n.) A predictive frame in the MPEG compressed video format, one that looks at the previous frames for its makeup. It is much smaller than an I-frame since it identifies just the differences between the current and previous frames. In QuickTime or AVI it is referred to as a *delta frame.* See *MPEG frame types.*

**PGA** See *pin grid array.*

**PGP** See *Pretty Good Privacy.*

**phage** (n.) A small program that modifies other

programs or databases in unauthorized and potentially harmful ways, particularly one that propagates a virus.

**phantom power** (n.) The direct current (DC) signal sent to a condenser microphone over audio lines. Phantom power is usually between 12 volts and 48 volts.

**Phase Alternation Line** (PAL) (n.) The European standard for color television, which operates at 25 frames per second (fps) with a resolution of 768 pixels by 625 scan lines per frame. See also *National Television Standards Committee* or *Sequentiel Couleurs à Mémoire.*

**phase delay** (n.) The displacement in time between a phase-shifted sine wave and the input waveform.

**phase jitter** (n.) Deviations in the phase of an analog signal compared to the referenced phase of the main data-carrying signal, which is often caused by alternating current components in a telecommunications network.

**phase lock loop** (n.) A circuit used to synchronize a variable local oscillator with the phase of a transmitted signal. The circuit performs phase detection by comparing the frequency of a known oscillator with an incoming signal. It then feeds back the output of the detector to keep the oscillator in phase with the incoming frequency. It is used to accomplish bit-synchronization.

**phase modulation** (n.) A method of modifying the phase of a sine wave carrier signal so that it contains modulating signal information.

**phase shift** (n.) The degree to which the starting point of a waveform is early or late in relation to a reference point or to another waveform.

**P**

**phase shift keying** (PSK) (n.) A form of digital modulation in which discrete phases of the carrier signal convey a digital signal.

**PHIGS** See *Programmer's Hierarchical Interactive Graphics System.*

**Phoenix-block** (n.) A terminal block that can be unplugged or disconnected without having to remove individual wires. It is also called a *Euroblock.*

**phon** (n.) A unit of apparent loudness. It is numerically equal to the intensity in decibels of a 1,000 Hz tone at the same sound pressure level (SPL).

**phone jack** (n.) Female connector for a 0.25-inch phone plug.

**phone plug** (n.) A male audio connector with a 0.25-inch diameter. A phone plug is used to terminate the cables connecting most high-impedance and line level instruments and signal processors, such as electric guitars, synthesizers, and amplifiers. The monophonic (mono) version allows two wires to be connected to a tip and a sleeve. A stereo version permits connection of three wires that have a tip, ring, and sleeve configuration. A female receptacle for this type of plug is called a *phone jack.* On consumer audio equipment, such as portable CD players and cassette decks, this style of connector has a 0.125-inch diameter and is called a *miniature (mini) phone plug.* See figure.

*.25-inch phone plug*

**Phong shading** (n.) A method of specifying the color of each pixel in a three-dimensional model. It offers high quality but is incapable of reflection, transparency, or other advanced effects. See figure.

*Phong-shaded cone*

**phono plug** (n.) A male connector used in consumer audio gear and in composite video connections. It has a small pin in the center of a ring. Not to be confused with a phone plug, it is also called an *RCA plug.*

**Photo-CD** See *Photo–Compact Disc.*

**Photo–Compact Disc** (PCD, Photo-CD) (n.) Developed by Eastman Kodak, a compact disc format based on the hybrid disc specification and used to store scanned photographic images. Photo-CD media can be recorded in multiple sessions; in this regard the format adheres to the Orange Book specification. Film scanners are generally used to capture the graphic content for Photo-CDs. In a basic Photo-CD format, five different resolutions, or "image pacs," appear for each of the 100 images that a Photo-CD can hold. Expressed in pixels, these resolutions are 192 x 128, 384 x 256, 768 x 512, 1536 x 1024, and 3072 x 2048. Note that the aspect ratio is 3:2, as in a photograph, rather than the computer display ratio of 4:3. Images on a Photo-CD are defined in Kodak's proprietary YCC format. In

MS-DOS, the extension for this file type is .pcd.

The Portfolio version of the Photo-CD format can accommodate higher-level programming with buttons that can branch to other images or a sequence of frames. An audio clip can be attached to each frame, but it will not play continuously if different images are displayed.

**photoconductor** (n.) In fiber optics, a transducer that emits current in proportion to the amount of light it receives.

**photodiode** (n.) A component in a laser disc player that translates variations in the light reflected from the surface of a disc into the electronic signals that define the audio, video, and control tracks.

**photolithography** (n.) A process for transferring a pattern from a mask to a silicon wafer using a photosensitive emulsion and light.

**photon** (n.) In physics, a unit of light energy. Photons travel through an optical fiber the same way electrons travel through a wire cable.

**photo-realism** (n.) Computer representation or imaging that seems as faithful to detail as a photograph.

**PHP** (n.) An open-source scripting language that is embedded in HTML documents to perform interactive functions, such as accessing database information on a server. It is used primarily on Unix-based Web servers, but may also be used on Windows servers if they are properly enabled. An HTML page with a PHP script embedded usually needs the extension .php to be processed by the server.

**phracker** (n.) Jargon for a person who combines telephone network *phreaking* with computer hacking.

**phreaking** (n.) The act of cracking the telephone network.

**physical code** (n.) A tag that defines exactly how text should be displayed in an HTML document. Compare *logical code*.

**physical format** (n.) The standard for the way information is physically recorded on compact discs.

**physical layer** (n.) The lowest layer of the Open Systems Interconnection (OSI) model. The physical layer governs hardware connections, bytestream encoding for transmission, and physical transfer of information between network nodes.

**physical media** (n.) Any physical means of transferring signals between two systems. This term is typically used for media connecting the physical layer, which is the lowest layer of the Open Systems Interconnection (OSI) reference model.

**physical sector** (n.) The location in which data is placed on a compact disc or on other digital media. For example, the Yellow Book specification requires that each compact disc be divided into 270 000 physical sectors of 2336 bytes each.

**pi** (pronounced "pie") (n.) 1. In mathematics, a numerical constant, approximately 3.14159, represented by the Greek lower-case $\pi$ symbol. It expresses the ratio of the circumference to the diameter of a circle. 2. Used in reference to audio filters, it is equal to 180 degrees or integral multiples thereof.

**PIC** See *Picture file*.

**pickup** (n.) 1. An electronic transducer that sends a low-level signal corresponding to the sound produced by a musical instrument, such as an electric guitar or a bass. 2. Related to video or film production, a shot or sequence recorded after the initial shoot. The pickup is used during editing to update content. 3. Jargon for a microphone.

**pico-** A prefix meaning one-trillionth.

**PICS** (n.) A Macintosh-specific "multimedia" format developed in 1988 by Macromedia and others for exchanging animation sequences. A PICS file is a sequential assembly of several Picture format (PICT) frames.

**PICT** See *Picture format.*

**picture cue** (n.) A signal in the vertical blanking interval (VBI) of a master tape that identifies the beginning of a frame. Each cue is encoded as a frame number on a videodisc pressed from the master tape.

**picture depth** (n.) The number of bits used to store picture data, or the number of shades of color that can be represented by that number of bits. Settings can be 1-bit color (black and white), 8-bit color (256 shades), 16-bit color (65 536 shades), or 24-bit color (16.7 million shades).

**picture element** (pel, pixel) (n.) The smallest unit defined on a display. See also *pixel.*

**Picture file** (PIC, pronounced "PICK") (n.) A bitmapped graphic file format developed by Lotus Corporation for IBM-compatible programs.

**Picture format** (PICT, pronounced "PICKED") (n.) Developed by Apple Computer in 1984, a standard format for storing and exchanging black-and-white graphics files. PICT2 (1987) supports eight-bit color and grayscale. Current PICT specifications do not limit color bit depth. PICT files can contain vector images and bitmap images as well as text and an alpha channel. PICT is a ubiquitous image format on machines running the MacOS.

**picture stop** (n.) An index point on a laser disc that allows the user to stop at a particular frame. The picture stop is encoded in the vertical blanking interval (VBI).

**PIF** See *Program Information File.*

**PIN** See *personal identification number.*

**pincushion distortion** (n.) Image distortion caused when the vertical sides of a displayed image curve inward to form concave edges. Most monitors are equipped with controls that minimize this. Compare *barrel distortion.* See figure.

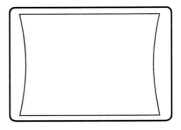

*pincushion distortion*

**PIN Diode** See *Positive Intrinsic Negative Diode.*

**Ping** See *Packet InterNet Groper.*

**Ping of Death** (n.) Using the Ping command with a packet size greater than 65 507 bits, which causes a denial of service and crashes a computer system.

**ping-pong** (v.) To mix several audio tracks on a multitrack tape recorder onto an unused track on the same tape. Ping-ponging increases the number of individual recorded layers. It is not possible to alter the mix between the tracks that are bounced onto an open track after the original tracks are erased or replaced by new program material.

**pin grid array** (PGA) (n.) A square integrated circuit (IC) with connecting pins surrounding the bottom edges on all four sides. PGA is the form factor frequently used for microprocessor chips.

**pin jack** (n.) Female connector for a phono plug. See *RCA connector*.

**pink noise** (n.) A random noise source characterized by a flat amplitude response per octave band of frequency. It has equal energy distributed throughout the spectrum. It is created by passing white noise through a filter with a 3 dB per octave rate of attenuation. Pink noise sounds less bright and richer in low frequencies than white noise. It is the preferred sound source for many acoustical measurements. The name comes from the filtering of white noise. White noise is analogous to white light in that it contains all audible frequencies distributed uniformly throughout the spectrum. Red light has longer wavelengths and lower frequencies, as does pink noise compared to white.

**pinout** (n.) A diagram that indicates how wires are terminated to pins in a connector.

**pipe** (n.) Jargon for a communications channel transporting high-speed digital signals; a connection to a network.

**pipeline** (n.) In microprocessor design, a sequence of stages, or functional units, that perform a task in several steps. Each unit takes inputs and produces outputs that are stored in its output buffer. The output buffer of one stage is the input buffer of the next stage. A pipeline works at full efficiency when it is filled and emptied at the same rate at which it processes.

**pipeline burst cache** (n.) A block of synchronous memory constructed from pipelined SRAM. In pipeline burst cache, reading from or writing to a new location takes multiple cycles, but subsequent locations are accessed in a single cycle. A Pentium microprocessor uses pipeline burst cache as a secondary cache. The first 8 bytes of data are transferred in three CPU cycles, and the next three 8-byte blocks are transferred in one cycle each.

**pit** (n.) A physical indentation in the information layer of a CD or a laser disc. Pits determine how a laser beam is reflected. In transmissive discs, pits either block the beam or allow it to pass through the disc. Pits on JVC laser discs cause a detectable change in electrical capacitance. The ones on a CD-R differ from those on a mastered disc because CD-R pits are actually mounds that the laser beam creates in the dye polymer layer. A pit may also be referred to as the space between "lands" along the data spiral of a CD.

**pixel** (pel, picture element) (n.) An abbreviation of *picture element;* the smallest raster display element represented as a screen coordinate with a specified color and intensity level. Picture resolution is measured by the number of pixels used to create an image. Common resolutions are 800 x 600 and 1024 x 768 pixels.

**pixelization** (n.) Occurs when blocks of pixels that make up an image get exaggerated or enlarged. A pixelized image looks blocky or jagged and often suffers from compression artifacts.

**PKUNZIP** (n.) A freely distributed decompression program for PKZIP.

**PKZIP** (n.) A file compression utility created by PKWare for use in MS-DOS. WinZip is a Microsoft Windows version with a graphical user interface (GUI).

**PLA** See *programmable logic array.*

**placeholder** (n.) In a multimedia production, an item used as a surrogate for the finished product until the final version is completed. The placeholder may be a graphics file or an audio file.

**plaintext** (n.) In network security, unencrypted data.

**planar** (n.) The flat capacitor between silicon and polysilicon layers in a semiconductor.

**plasma display** (n.) A flat display with a grid of electrodes in a gas-filled panel. The gas emits light when ionized by the electrodes, yielding high-quality images.

**plastic leaded chip carrier** (PLCC) (n.) A type of semiconductor package.

**platform** (n.) A particular hardware and software operating system, such as the IBM-compatible/DOS platform or the Macintosh platform.

**platter** (n.) A disk in a hard drive onto which data is written.

**playback** (n.) The realization of recorded images or sound on any kind of audio or video equipment.

**Playstation** (n.) A hardware device created by Sony Corporation for playing games.

**PLC** See *programmable logic controller.*

**PLCC** See *plastic leaded chip carrier.*

**PLD** See *programmable logic device.*

**plenum** (n.) The space between a suspended ceiling and the floor above it. It is used to circulate air in a building and often shares space with network wiring.

**plenum cable** (n.) Wiring, typically for networking, installed in the space between a ceiling and the floor above it. In some cases the cable must meet certain code requirements.

**plotter** (n.) An output device similar to a printer that draws or plots a two-dimensional image on paper. Varieties include pen plotters, electrostatic plotters, photograph plotters, ink-jet plotters, and laser plotters.

**plug** (n.) The male connector in a plug-and-jack system.

**plug and play** (PnP) 1. (n.) The ability of an operating system to identify peripherals or other interfaced components, such as speakers or a CD-ROM reader, and to configure the system transparently to incorporate them. 2. (adj., plug-and-play) Describes hardware and peripherals that an operating system automatically identifies and installs. USB features PnP peripherals.

**plug-in** (n.) A program that extends the utility of another program. Plug-ins for Netscape Navigator allow enhanced media types, such as RealMedia, to be employed.

**PLV** See *Production Level Video.*

**PMA** See *program memory area.*

**PMMA** See *polymethyl methacrylate.*

**PMMU** See *Paged Memory Management Unit.*

**PMS** See *Pantone Matching System.*

**PNG** See *Portable Network Graphics.*

**PnP** See *plug and play.*

**PNP** (n.) A bipolar transistor with an N-doped semiconductor as a base between two P-doped layers, the collector and the emitter. Doping refers to coating with a type of dopamine.

**Pocket PC** (n.) A handheld Windows-based computer that runs the Pocket PC operating system, formerly known as Windows CE. The Pocket PC OS is version 3.0 of Windows CE, with an updated interface and greater stability. It includes a suite of Pocket Office applications (Internet Explorer, Word, and Excel), handwriting recognition, an e-book reader, and wireless Internet access.

**POE** See *PowerOpen Environment.*

**point** (n.) A unit of measurement used in typography and graphic design that defines the height of text characters, the thickness of lines and borders, the size of leading, and the dimensions of other elements. Given that 1 point equals 1/72 inch, 12-point printed text is about 1/6 inch high.

**pointer** (n.) In programming, an address that identifies a location in a data structure.

**pointing device** (n.) A mouse, a pen, or a trackball that inputs spatial data to a computer. A graphical user interface (GUI) lets a user control the computer by pointing, clicking, and dragging. Movements of the pointing device are echoed on the screen by movements of the cursor.

**Point of Presence** (PoP) (n.) A collection of leased lines, routers, modems, and other telecommunications equipment located at a site. Internet Access Providers (IAPs) operate PoPs that subscribers can reach with a local telephone call. This interface connects to interLATA carriers.

**point-of-sale** (POS, pronounced "pee-oh-ESS") (adj.) Describes the place where shoppers make a buying decision. Multimedia kiosks running interactive programs that engage observers and promote or explain a product are often placed nearby to influence that decision.

**point of view** (POV, pronounced "pee-oh-VEE") (n.) In video production, a shot perspective in which the camera assumes the subject's viewpoint, giving audience members the illusion that they are looking through the subject's eyes.

**point-to-point** (adj.) Describes an uninterrupted connection between two pieces of equipment. A private telephone circuit and a satellite transmission are examples of point-to-point networks. See figure.

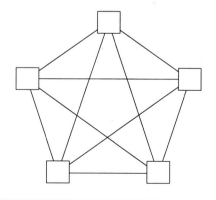

*point-to-point network*

**Point-to-Point Protocol** (PPP) (n.) Defined in RFC 1171, the Internet standard for transmitting Internet Protocol (IP) packets over serial point-to-point links. In contrast to SLIP, PPP can operate over both asynchronous connections and bit-oriented synchronous systems, dynamically configure connections with a remote network, and test that a link is usable. PPP can be configured to encapsulate AppleTalk, IP, and Internetwork Packet eXchange (IPX) protocols.

**polarity** (n.) 1. The identification of a positive or a negative charge on one side of an electrical circuit or a conductor. 2. The relationship between a stimulus input on a device and its voltage output, or vice versa. Polarity refers to a signal's reference and not to its phase shift. A signal that is 180 degrees out-of-phase with a reference source is different from a signal with inverse polarity. For a signal to be out-of-phase, a temporal reference is required, and this is not the case if it is simply inverted.

**polarization** (n.) The state in which the magnetic field of an electromagnetic wave oscillates linearly in only one direction. The direction of this magnetic field is referred to as the *polarization direction.*

**polling** (n.) 1. Connecting to a remote computer system to look for email or access information. 2. A method of controlling the sequence of transmissions with devices on a multipoint line. Polling requires each device to wait until the controlling processor clears it for transmission.

**polycarbonate** (n.) A resilient plastic used to manufacture compact discs.

**polymer** See *dye polymer.*

**polymethyl methacrylate** (PMMA) (n.) The rigid, transparent acrylic plastic used to manufacture optical media.

**polymorphism** (n.) In object-oriented programming (OOP), variables that may, at run time, refer to objects of different classes.

**PoP** See *Point of Presence.*

**POP** See *Post Office Protocol.*

**Popmail** (n.) A program that uses the Point of Presence (PoP) protocol to read email remotely across a network, usually implemented with SLIP.

**port** 1. (n.) A logical connection or channel for data flow in a communications system. Transmission Control Protocol (TCP) and User Datagram Protocol (UDP), which are transport layer protocols for Ethernet, use port numbers to demultiplex messages. 2. (v.) To translate software so that it runs on different platforms. 3. (n.) The product that results from translating software for a different platform. 4. (n.) A socket for connecting peripheral cables to a computer.

**portability** (n.) The ability to use the same software on different hardware systems or across platforms. A high degree of portability

### Values Always Contained in the First 8 Bytes of a PNG File

|  | Byte 1 | Byte 2 | Byte 3 | Byte 4 | Byte 5 | Byte 6 | Byte 7 | Byte 8 |
|---|---|---|---|---|---|---|---|---|
| decimal | 137 | 80 | 78 | 71 | 13 | 10 | 26 | 10 |
| hexadecimal | 89 | 50 | 4e | 47 | 0d | 0a | 1a | 0a |
| ASCII C Notation | \211 | P | N | G | \r | \n | \032 | \n |

reduces the need to modify programs for delivery on different hardware.

**Portable Document Format** (PDF) (n.) A document type created by Adobe Acrobat that virtually any type of computer can access. PDF Writer converts existing graphics and text files into the .pdf format. Adobe Distiller converts existing PostScript documents. PDF provides a cross-platform method to transfer information. If Acrobat Reader, a freely distributed program, has been installed on a computer, it can effectively read and manipulate this universal document type.

**Portable Network Graphics** (PNG, pronounced "PING") (n.) An extensible file format for lossless, compressed storage of images. PNG is recommended by the World Wide Web Consortium (W3C) as an Internet Media Type (image/png) to replace GIF, and it may effectively replace TIFF as well. PNG supports indexed-color, grayscale, and true color images, along with an optional alpha channel. The sample depth may vary from 1 to 16 bits. PNG may be streamed on the Internet with a progressive display option. It provides file integrity checking and simple detection of common transmission errors. PNG stores gamma and chromaticity for color matching on heterogeneous platforms.

Like GIF, PNG can index up to 256 colors, streaming progressive display, transparent layers, platform independence, and totally lossless compression. The unique features of PNG are true color (up to 48 bits per pixel), grayscale (up to 16 bits per pixel), full alpha channel (general transparency masks), image gamma information, and detection of file corruption.

GIF is copyrighted and lacks some desirable features. PNG provides a new image format in the public domain that exceeds the limitations of GIF. PNG exhibits highly flexible transparency, compression efficiency, and resistance to transmission errors. Images transferred on the Internet are sometimes processed as text by mistake, which may cause file corruption. PNG is designed so that such errors can be detected quickly and reliably.

The PNG specification exhibits some carefully calculated limitations of its own. There is neither lossy compression nor an uncompressed variant of PNG. The format does not support multiple images in one file or CMYK color space. There is not a standard chunk specified for thumbnail views. Such features could be accomplished if the basic specification were extended. PNG uses network byte order consistently, so that files may be converted on any platform that supports TCP/IP and on all PC platforms.

PNG uses a two-dimensional interlacing scheme that is more complex than the linewise interlacing of GIF. The PNG file is slightly bigger, but it draws an initial image eight times faster than GIF. Although that initial image is coarser, PNG completely renders it more quickly. Horizontal and vertical resolution never differ by more than a factor of two, and text in an interlaced PNG is readable much sooner than in an equivalent GIF image.

The variety of images and display systems used for the web creates images that are too dark or light. PNG assumes that image viewing software will compensate for image gamma whenever the image is displayed. The viewer will appropriately adjust images with no gamma or with an incorrect recorded gamma for the delivery system. PNG employs "unassociated" or "nonpremultiplied" alpha, so that images with separate transparency masks may be

333

stored without loss of data.

Filtering can reduce the compressed size of true color and grayscale images, so PNG includes a filtering capability. The filter algorithms operate on bytes rather than on pixels because filtering is usually ineffective on images with fewer than eight bits per sample. The encoder is allowed to change filters for each new scan line because adaptive filtering outperforms fixed filters and adds very little to the compressed file size. This process maximizes the quality of each scan line.

PNG allows some textual information to be stored along with the graphical data. Textual information should be stored in standard tEXt chunks with suitable keywords. Use of tEXt tells a PNG viewer that the chunk contains related text. Latin-1 is the recommended text format for these chunks because it is a direct subset of character sets commonly used on popular platforms such as Microsoft Windows and X Window System.

The values in the first 8 bytes of a PNG file are shown in the table on the previous page.

This byte order allows common file transfer problems to be detected immediately. The first 2 bytes distinguish PNG files on systems that expect the first 2 bytes to identify the file type uniquely. The first byte is a non-ASCII value, which reduces the probability that a text file may be incorrectly identified as a PNG file. The byte order also catches bad file transfers that clear bit 7. Bytes 2 through 4 name the format. The carriage return line feed (CRLF) sequence catches bad file transfers that alter new-line sequences. The Ctrl-Z character stops file display under MS-DOS. The final line feed checks for the inverse of the CRLF translation problem.

Chunk length is limited to avoid problems for

systems that cannot handle four-byte unsigned values. A separate cyclic redundancy check (CRC) is provided for each chunk in order to detect transfer errors rapidly and to validate data. If a viewer does not provide as many colors as are listed in the palette belonging to an image, a palette histogram provides the information needed to select a target palette.

Recent versions of browser software, such as Netscape Navigator and Microsoft Internet Explorer, can process and display PNG files. Numerous graphics-processing packages are capable of encoding in this highly recommended format. It is assumed that web developers will embrace PNG as superior to GIF.

**Portable Operating System Interface in Unix** (POSIX, pronounced "pah-ZICKS") (n.) An Institute of Electrical and Electronics Engineers (IEEE) standard that defines operating system services based on Unix but that other systems can implement easily.

**portmapper** (n.) A server that converts TCP/IP protocol port numbers into Remote Procedure Call (RPC) program numbers.

**portrait** (n.) A layout in which the height of a printed page is greater than the width. In a "landscape" layout, the width is greater than the height. See figure that accompanies *landscape* for portrait and landscape layouts.

**POS** See *point-of-sale.*

**positional reference** (n.) A signal that feeds a receiving device information about a location point. Audio and video equipment can use this signal to synchronize during recording or playback.

**Positive Intrinsic Negative Diode** (PIN Diode) (n.) A photodetector that converts optical signals to electrical signals in a receiver.

**POSIX** See *Portable Operating System Interface in Unix.*

**post** 1. (n.) Jargon for postproduction. 2. (v.) To send a message to a mailing list or to a group of users, as opposed to sending it to an individual recipient.

**POST** See *power-on self test.*

**posterize** (v.) To convert an image to a more elementary form by lowering all tonal values, creating a surrealistic, stark result.

**posting** (n.) A message sent to a newsgroup or a mailing list. This message is broadcast rather than sent point-to-point.

**postmaster** (n.) A contact point or address for email to be sent to an Internet site or to a UUCP network site. The Internet email standard (RFC 822) requires every machine to have a postmaster address, which is usually aliased to the system administrator.

**Post Office Protocol** (POP, pronounced "POP") (n.) The protocol that allows individual computers to retrieve electronic mail from a server.

**postproduction** (n., adj.) In the creation of video programs and multimedia productions, a phase that occurs after the original footage is shot. It includes offline and online editing, compositing, sweetening, and the final mix.

**PostScript** (n.) An interpreted, stack-based, page description language implemented by Adobe Systems in 1982. PostScript describes the appearance of text, graphical shapes, and images on printed or displayed pages in a device-independent way. PostScript has become

the language of choice for printers and for cross-platform graphical output.

**potentiometer** (n.) A component in a circuit that provides varying degrees of resistance. It may take the form of a knob, a thumbwheel, or a slider. In audio equipment, a variable potentiometer is often called a *pot,* an example of which is a fader (a sliding volume control) on a mixing board. See figure.

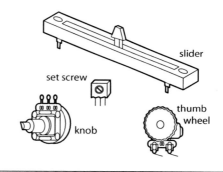

*potentiometers*

**POTS** (n.) Plain old telephone service.

**POV** See *point of view.*

**power** (n.) 1. The rate at which electrical energy is converted to another form. In a direct-current (DC) circuit, it is the product of applied voltage and current. It may also be calculated by the voltage squared divided by the resistance, or the current squared times the resistance. In an alternating-current (AC) circuit, it is the product of the effective values of the voltage and current with the cosine of the phase angle (between current and voltage). See *apparent power* and *rms power.* 2. In physics, this is the rate at which work is done, expressed as the amount of work per unit time. A common unit of measurement is the watt, defined as 1 joule per second, which is equal to the power dissipated by 1 ohm of resistance when

1 ampere of current passes through it. One unit of horsepower is equal to 745.7 watts.

**power-cycle** (v.) To turn off and turn on the power to a device with the intention of clearing an undesirable state.

**power factor** (PF) (n.) The ratio of the total power in watts under a resistive load to the total apparent power in voltamperes (VA) under a reactive load. The difference between *watts* and *VA* is due to reactive load impedance. Apparent power equals watts only for a purely resistive load with zero degrees phase shift between the applied voltage and the resultant current. Power may be considered the multiplier (ranging between 0 and 1) that is used to obtain the real power from the apparent power. To obtain the apparent power, measure the rms voltage and current of a circuit and multiply them. To obtain the real power, multiply this value by the power factor. If the load is purely resistive, then the phase difference between the voltage and current will be zero, the power factor will be one, and the apparent power will equal the true power. For any load with inductive or capacitive reactance, there will be a phase difference between the voltage and the current due to phase delay introduced by the reactive elements. Maximum voltage and current do not occur at the same instant in time, so the amount of power developed is less than the measured rms voltage and current multiplied together. Power factor is a ratio that can be expressed in several ways. It is the ratio of watts to voltamperes, of resistance to reactance, and if the phase shift in degrees is known (phase angle), it is the cosine of that angle. If the angle is zero, the PF is 1, and if the angle is 90 degrees, the PF is 0.

**power-factor-corrected** (PFC) (n.) Any system that has a power-factor-correcting device, such as a capacitor, installed to reduce the phase difference between the rms voltage and rms current.

**PowerMac** See *Power Macintosh.*

**Power Macintosh** (PowerMac) (n.) Based on the PowerPC chip, a microcomputer developed by Apple Computer and introduced in March 1994. A PowerMac system can emulate existing 680x0 code, as long as the code is provided in a fat binary version of an application along with native PowerPC code.

**power-on self test** (POST) (n.) A startup routine run by a computer. A POST scans circuits, and if the system is performing as expected, it sounds a beep.

**PowerOpen Association** (n.) An organization formed to promote the PowerOpen Environment and to support software developers. Founding members include Apple Computer, Bull Systems, Harris Computer Systems, IBM, Motorola, Tadpole Technology, and Thomson CSF. See also *PowerOpen Environment.*

**PowerOpen Environment** (POE) (n.) Specifications for PowerPC-based Application Programming Interface (API) and Application Binary Interface (ABI). The presence of the ABI specification in the POE allows it to have platform-independent binary compatibility, typically limited to particular hardware. Derived from AIX, the POE is an open standard that conforms to industry open standards.

**PowerPC** (n.) Developed by Apple Computer, IBM, and Motorola in a collaborative effort, a highly evolved microprocessor chip released in 1994 that replaced the 68000 series as the CPU for the Macintosh series. The PowerPC is based on reduced instruction set computing (RISC) processing. This family of processors from the PowerPC alliance includes the 32-bit 601, 603, and 604; and the 64-bit 620, which contains 7 million transistors. The second generation of this chip is the PowerPC 750, used in Apple G3 computers.

**PowerPC G4** (n.) Developed by Apple, Motorola and IBM, the G4 was the first microprocessor to deliver a sustained performance of over one gigaflop, with a theoretical peak performance of 5.3 gigaflops. With its "Velocity Engine," the G4 processes data in 128-bit chunks rather than traditional 32-bit or 64-bit chunks. The G4 can perform four 32-bit floating-point calculations in a single cycle. It is optimized for video, audio, and animation applications.

**PowerPoint** (n.) An application developed by Microsoft for electronic presentations, speaker support, and slide shows. Although it is capable of incorporating a variety of file types, it is not a robust multimedia authoring environment. PowerPoint has become a popular tool for creating presentations because it is bundled with the Microsoft Office suite. Files created by PowerPoint have the extension .ppt. Unfortunately, frames created in PowerPoint are not easily converted to other graphical file types, which makes it difficult to export content to other authoring environments.

**PPM** See *peak program meter.*

**PPP** See *Point-to-Point Protocol.*

**PRAM** See *Parameter RAM.*

**preamplifier** (preamp) (n.) An electrical device that increases the strength of a signal so that it is powerful enough to drive a main amplifier. A preamp is generally required to boost the signal of a microphone to an adequate level for mixing and recording.

**precedence effect** See *Haas effect.*

**predictive encoding** (n.) In MPEG compression, the storing of the difference between a prediction of the data and the actual data in subsequent frames. Encoding only these differences results in higher compression ratios.

**pre-emphasis** (n.) In audio, a high-frequency boost applied in recording. It is followed by an equal amount of de-emphasis during playback, which is intended to improve the signal-to-noise ratio.

**pre-fade listen** (PFL) (n.) On an audio mixer, a signal monitored before the main channel fader, not affected by the fader position. It is used to monitor individual input with headphones without affecting the main outputs. In broadcasting, this function is often called *cue*, and in a recording context it is called *solo*.

**pre-groove** (n.) The spiral track molded into the polycarbonate substrate for the recording laser beam to follow when writing data onto recordable compact discs.

**premastering** (n.) The process of creating a tape, a hard disk drive, or a CD-R containing data in the proper format. This data will be recorded onto a master from which compact discs will be replicated. Typically, premastering includes adding error correction and location data. The disc is reviewed and evaluated before the master disc is made.

**Premiere** (n.) A nonlinear video editing program developed by Adobe. Premiere is used in multimedia development, usually for creating and processing QuickTime movies.

**preproduction** (n., adj.) A phase that occurs before a video or multimedia program is created. Preproduction includes preparatory tasks such as flowcharting, storyboarding, scriptwriting, and designing graphics.

**preroll** (n.) In video production, the process of rewinding tape to a point that precedes the beginning of a scene or to a specific frame identified by a time code. In order to bring the tape up to speed from a dead start, it is necessary to begin rolling slightly ahead of the first frame of a segment that is to be dubbed or encoded.

**presentation layer** (n.) An Open Systems Interconnection (OSI) layer that determines how application data is encoded while it is in transit between two end systems.

**Presentation Manager** (n.) A graphical user interface supported by the IBM OS/2 operating system that can multitask between existing MS-DOS and Windows applications.

**Pretty Good Privacy** (PGP) (n.) A public key encryption application written by Philip R. Zimmermann in 1991 for MS-DOS, Unix, and other platforms. It uses an encryption algorithm claimed by U.S. patent number 4 405 829. PGP facilitates the exchange of files or messages with privacy and authentication. Secure channels are not required for the exchange of keys between users.

**pretzel key** (n.) Another name for the Macintosh Command key.

**PRI** See *Primary Rate Interface.*

**primary key** (n.) The most important data field used to identify a body of information, an object, or a record in a relational database.

**Primary Rate Interface** (PRI) (n.) An ISDN interface to primary access that operates at 1.544 megabits per second (Mbps). It consists of 23 B-channels at 64 kilobits per second (Kbps) and one D-channel at 64 Kbps. An additional eight Kbps is used for framing. Specifications for the system vary in Europe, where 30 B-channels are provided along with a 64-Kbps D-channel and where 64 Kbps is used for framing. Data and voice information may be transmitted simultaneously over all channels.

**primitive** (n.) 1. A simple graphical shape. Examples of two-dimensional primitives include squares, triangles, and circles. Examples of three-dimensional primitives include blocks, spheres, and tubes. 2. A function built into a programming language or an operating system that could not be written in the language. Primitives include arithmetic and logical operations and are implemented efficiently in machine language.

**printed circuit board** (PCB) (n.) A piece of a thin, nonconductive substance with lines for circuitry embedded and with components soldered on at connecting points. Also known as a *board* or *card.*

**printer** (n.) A common output device that prints computer-generated graphics and text on paper. A daisy-wheel printer uses a disk with characters around the outer edge. A dot matrix printer makes a pattern of small dots. A laser printer produces high-quality graphics, up to 1200 dots per inch (dpi), though commonly 300 to 600 dpi, using technology similar to that of a copy machine.

**print spooler** (n.) Software that schedules printing tasks. Rather than committing all cycles of a computer during printing whenever a print command is issued, it allows the user to be productive and perform other tasks while the printer is addressed in the background.

**print-through** (n.) A phenomena caused by winding layer upon layer of tape on a reel. This winding causes one layer to magnetize the adjacent layer, thus printing through from one layer onto another layer. It is also sometimes called *interlayer transfer* or *crosstalk*. The parts of the magnetic tape most vulnerable lie between program material where blank spots and spaces are adjacent to loud passages. Two other terms are associated with print-through. On layers played back before loud passages a "pre-echo" is heard, while on layers played back following a loud passage a "post-echo" is heard.

**Privacy Enhanced Mail** (PEM) (n.) An Internet Engineering Task Force (IETF) standard for secure electronic mail exchange.

**private automatic branch exchange** (PABX) (n.) An automatic telephone exchange that a user owns and that routes calls to and from the public telephone network.

**private branch exchange** (PBX) (n.) A phone system that internally connects lines in a business and provides a link to an outside line. Users must dial 9 to access the outside line.

**private line** (n.) A leased telephone line attached to a single user.

**private network** (n.) Any network established and operated by a private entity for users within that entity. A private network may contain circuits leased from public carriers.

**proc amp** (n.) Processing amplifier; a video image processor that alters the luminance, chroma, and sync in a signal. A proc amp is typically used to correct problems of poor color saturation, low light levels, or incorrect tint. Pronounced "PRAHK amp."

**procedural language** (n.) A programming language in which an explicit sequence of steps is specified to produce a result. Common procedural languages are BASIC, Pascal, and C.

**processing** (n.) 1. The manipulation of data from one state to another, usually at the request of an operator or a user. This is the basic function that computers perform. 2. The photographic development of a film negative.

**processor audio** (n.) Sound created and played back by computer data manipulation rather than sound digitized from an acoustical environment for playback with standard digital-to-analog (D/A) converters.

**processor bus** (n.) The routes over which data moves between the CPU and its chip set, the immediate support chips. Data moves among the CPU, the main system bus, and the external memory cache on the processor bus. Its purpose is to allow information to move to and from the CPU as fast as possible. An external cache for the CPU is usually employed in all systems with Pentium chips. The bus provides circuits for data, for addresses, and for control purposes. The processor bus in a Pentium system has 64 data lines, 32 address lines, and several associated control lines. The Pentium Pro and Pentium II have 36 address lines but are identical to the Pentium and Pentium MMX in other respects. The maximum transfer rate for the processor bus is calculated by multiplying the data width (64 bits = 8 bytes) by the clock speed of the bus, which is the same as the clock speed of the CPU.

**Processor Direct Slot** (PDS) (n.) A local bus connection in a Macintosh computer.

**production** (n.) In video terms, the activity that takes place while video or film footage is being shot. See also *postproduction* or *preproduction*.

P

339

**production audio** (n.) The sound track, including any dialog, recorded in the field while a video is shot. Production audio could be recorded on the videotape or, for better quality, on a separate field digital audio tape (DAT).

**Production Level Video** (PLV) (n.) The high-quality compression format applied to Digital Video Interactive (DVI) files.

**professional market** (n.) The segment of the population that purchases software or production equipment for use on the job, as opposed to the consumer market. See also *industrial market*.

**program** 1. (v.) To plan and define a series of computations or processes to be executed by a computer. Developing a software program includes writing code and specifying output formats. 2. (n.) Software instructions that control a computer's processes in solving problems and performing tasks. 3. (n.) Any kind of audio or video material on a tape or a disc that is prepared for an audience.

**program calibration area** (PCA) (n.) The section on a CD-R reserved so that the CD-R drive can calibrate the laser power for recording on the disc.

**Program Information File** (PIF) (n.) A file that defines how a non-Windows application program should be handled in Windows. A PIF includes such information as requirements for memory allocation and the configuration of the graphics interface. PIF has the file name extension .pif.

**programmable logic array** (PLA) (n.) A programmable logic device in which both the AND and the OR arrays are programmable.

**programmable logic controller** (PLC) (n.) A microprocessor-based device used to automate industrial machinery.

**programmable logic device** (PLD) (n.) A generic term for an integrated circuit offering a wide range of logic function building blocks, which are interconnected by a circuit designer to fit a specific application.

**programmable read-only memory** (PROM, pronounced "PEE-rom") (n.) A type of non-volatile, semiconductor ROM component that the user can program once and that can only be read thereafter.

**Program Manager** (n.) In Microsoft Windows 3.1, the primary application that controls the graphical user interface. This application displays groups of icons that represent applications and utility programs the user may select.

**program memory area** (PMA) (n.) The place on a CD-R where information about tracks and sessions is stored temporarily. Information in the PMA eventually becomes the table of contents (TOC) for a session.

**programmer** (n.) Someone who writes code for computers, defining the computational processes.

**Programmer's Hierarchical Interactive Graphics System** (PHIGS) (n.) A three-dimensional graphics and modeling support system that controls how graphical data is defined and displayed on computers.

**programmer's switch** (n.) A small push-button switch on the front or the side of a Macintosh that causes a command line prompt to appear. It supplies access to a debugger. If the computer crashes, the user can push the switch and input a code in response to the prompt, which may revive the system.

**programming language** (n.) The formal system of syntax and semantics with which computer programs are written. A language may be low-level and close to machine code, or it may be high-level if a single statement corresponds to numerous machine code instructions. A distinction is also made between *imperative languages* and *declarative languages*.

**progressive download** (n.) Online media that users may view as it downloads. Progressive download files do not adjust to match the bandwidth of a connection, as do files in a true streaming format. QuickTime's *Fast Start* feature is a progressive download technology. It is also referred to as *HTTP Streaming* because standard HTTP servers can deliver progressive download files and no special protocols are needed.

**progressive scan** (n.) A video system that creates an image by painting each successive horizontal line across the screen in a *noninterlaced* scan rather than by painting alternate sets of lines in two sweeps down the screen in an *interlaced* scan.

**progressive/sequential coding** (n.) A type of image compression used in a JPEG file in which an image coded with progressive coding may be decoded sequentially.

**project evaluation and review technique/critical path method** (PERT/CPM, pronounced "pert-see-pee-EM") (n.) A complex project management process for determining the effectiveness of a system or a program.

**PROM** See *programmable read-only memory.*

**promiscuous mode** (n.) A mode in which every network adapter reads, or sniffs, all information regardless of its destination.

**prompt** (n.) A request displayed on the computer monitor for action by the user. In MS-DOS a prompt includes a symbol for the internal hard disk or the external memory device currently being addressed.

**proof of concept** (n.) A prototype of a piece of media used to prove the viability of the project and to attract interest in a full-blown production.

**propagation** (n.) The movement of waves through or along any medium. Electromagnetic waves may propagate in a vacuum as well as in media.

**propagation delay** (n.) The length of time required for an electromagnetic signal to travel from one point to another over a transmission channel.

**proportional font** (n.) A set of characters with a variable amount of horizontal space allocated to each. Narrow letters and symbols take up less space than wide ones. Compare *monospaced font.*

**proportional Q** (n.) In an audio equalizer with this feature, the bandwidth that is affected by boosting or cutting a frequency is inversely proportional to the degree that it is altered. A small adjustment in the level is applied to a wide bandwidth. A drastic amplification or attenuation is applied to a very narrow bandwidth around the center frequency. Also known as variable Q.

**proprietary** (adj.) Describes material that is unavailable for use without permission from the owner, whether an individual or an entity. Production companies may either produce proprietary products or perform "work for hire" in which the producer is not the owner.

Proprietary software typically runs only on specific hardware platforms.

**Prospero** (n.) A distributed file system accessible over the Internet via FTP or Network File System (NFS). Clients and servers use Prospero to communicate in the Archie system. Prospero lets a user create views of a collection of files spread out over many servers on the Internet and provides a file-naming system.

**prosumer** (adj.) Describes high-tech production gear with output quality that falls between the professional and the consumer markets. The term is used in reference to camcorders and mixers that have specifications below broadcast grade but above those of equipment purchased for home use.

**protected mode** (n.) The mode in which Intel processors run, beginning with the 80286. Software written or compiled to run in protected mode may only use segment register values given to it by the operating system. Protected mode is the opposite of *real mode,* in which addresses are generated by adding an address offset to the value of a segment register shifted to the left 4 bits. The segment register and the address offset are 16 bits long, so adding the shift creates a 20-bit address. This is the origin of the 1-megabyte (MB) limit in real mode. Protected mode must be enabled by software. Compare *real mode.*

**protocol** (n.) A standard procedure or a set of rules with which software and hardware systems must comply in order to be compatible. All users must observe network protocol in order to have successful data communications. Protocols govern error handling, framing, and line control in transmitting and receiving packets. An example of a telecommunications protocol is XModem.

**protocol converter** (n.) A device for translating the data transmission code of one network or device to the corresponding code of another. A protocol converter enables pieces of equipment with different conventions to communicate with one another.

**protocol data unit** (PDU) (n.) A common term for *packet.*

**protocol stack** (n.) A layered set of protocols working together to provide network functions.

**prototype** (n.) A working model of a product used to demonstrate the product, test design ideas, or secure financing for a complete version.

**proxy gateway** (n.) A computer that passes a request for a URL from a web browser to an outside server and that returns the results. Clients on a network with a proxy gateway may be sealed off from the Internet with an agent that can access the Internet on their behalf, providing security for the users.

**proxy server** (n.) A web server that can accept URLs with a particular prefix. When it receives a URL with the special prefix, it strips off the prefix and seeks the URL in its local cache. If the document is found, it is returned immediately. If it is not found, it is fetched from a remote server, copied to the local cache, and returned to the requester.

**PSDN** See *packet-switching data network.*

**PSK** See *phase shift keying.*

**psophometer** (n.) A voltmeter with a set of weighting filters that is used to measure circuit noise in telephone systems and broadcast communications gear. The filters are said to be weighted because they give priority to certain bands of frequency, imitating how the human ear perceives sound. Pronounced "SO-fo-mee-ter."

**PSTN** See *public switched telephone network*.

**PS/2** See *Personal System/2*.

**psychoacoustics** (n.) The scientific study of the perception of sound.

**public access** 1. (n.) A block of time allocated for independent producers to air their programs on cable television. 2. (adj.) Describes multimedia kiosks used by the general public or by a wide range of visitors, often with touch screens for input.

**public domain** (n., adj.) Intellectual property that is free of a copyright or a patent and that may be duplicated or used without permission. The use of public domain software is unrestricted and free for everyone.

**public key encryption** (n.) A system devised to keep data secure. In this system, a public key is used to encrypt data, and a private key is required to translate it.

**public network** (n.) Any network that is operated by a common carrier and that provides packet-switched, circuit-switched, and leased-line circuits to the public.

**public switched telephone network** (PSTN) (n.) The global voice telephone network, including local exchanges and long distance providers.

**publish and subscribe** (n.) The ability to establish links between documents in the Macintosh 7.0 operating system or in a later one. Subscribing documents are updated automatically when changes are made to the publishing document.

**pulldown** (n.) The process that compensates for the differences in frame rates between film and video by creating new frames. For 24 fps film to be converted to 30 fps NTSC video, a 3:2 pulldown is used that creates an extra six frames per second. See *interfield frames*.

**pull down/pull up** (v.) In synchronizing audio with video tracks, to speed up or slow down the audio rate clock deliberately to correspond with speed differences in the video track. When film footage at 24 frames per second (fps) is transferred to NTSC videotape at 29.97 fps, the audio is "pulled up" to match the higher frame rate.

**pull media** (n.) In response to a user's request for content, a media file sent on the World Wide Web directly to the user via HTTP. In this sense, the user "pulls" the content. This contrasts with *push media,* which is broadcast from a server.

**pulse code** (n.) An audio signal recorded on each frame of a videotape. A pulse code allows easy access to individual frames.

**pulse code modulation** (PCM) (n.) A standard means of encoding audio information in a digital format by sampling the amplitude of the audio waveform at regular intervals and by representing that sample as a digital numerical value. Current standards are based on CCITT Recommendation G.711, which specifies more codes for low-frequency components and fewer codes for high-frequency components. Telephone systems in the United States and Japan use μ-law encoding, whereas Europe and the rest of the world use a-law encoding. See also *adaptive differential pulse code modulation*.

**pulse width modulation** (PWM) (n.) A method of representing data in which the width of a pulse in a series of pulses represents analog information.

**punch-in/punch-out** (v.) In recording audio, to engage/disengage record mode on a previously recorded track, usually for purposes of seamlessly replacing previously recorded segments.

**PureVoice codec** (n.) See *Qualcomm PureVoice codec.*

**push** 1. (v.) In programming, to place something on top of a stack or a pushdown list (pdl). 2. (n.) In terms of the web, jargon for push media.

**push media** (n.) Content sent to a user by a multicasting web server, as opposed to *pull media,* in which the user requests individual items. With push media, the user usually selects a channel that delivers a particular kind of content. Cable television is an example of push media. Pointcast and Marimba are push systems.

**PVC cable** (n.) A common type of cable sheathed with polyvinyl chloride (PVC). PVC is a tough water- and flame-retardant material, but it is not smoke-retardant. If PVC catches fire, it emits noxious gases.

**PWM** See *pulse-width modulation.*

**P x 64** (n.) A conferencing standard introduced by the CCITT for compressed motion video with audio. It was devised for transfer over copper or fiber-optic phone lines. P x 64 encodes video at 30 frames per second (fps) in real time with synchronized audio for transmission at speeds of up to four megabits per second (Mbps). Pronounced "P times sixty-four."

**Python** (n.) An interpreted, object-oriented programming language that is available for several operating systems including Unix, Windows, and Macintosh. The language is not extremely complicated and is useful for developing applications, for system administration, and for making graphical user interfaces. Python was created by Guido van Rossum, and named after Monty Python's Flying Circus. Python is copyrighted, but the source code is free and may be marketed commercially.

# Q

q In physics, the symbol for a positive or negative electrical charge.

Q (n.) In audio engineering, the quality factor of a filter. This factor is defined as the ratio of the *center frequency* (f) divided by the *bandwidth* (bw).

QA See *quality assurance.*

QAM See *quadrature amplitude modulation.*

QCIF See *Quarter CIF.*

QDesign Music codec (n.) A low-bandwidth audio codec optimized for music, available for use with QuickTime version 3 and later versions.

QI See *Query Interface.*

QIC See *Quarter-Inch Committee.*

QoS See *quality of service.*

QPSK See *quadrature phase shift keying.*

QTVR See *QuickTime VR.*

quad See *quadruplex.*

quad flat pack (n.) In surface mount technol-ogy, a commonly used package. It achieves a high lead count in a small area since the leads are brought out on all four sides of a thin square package.

quadrature amplitude modulation (QAM) (n.) A modulation process that incorporates both amplitude modulation (AM) and phase modulation to increase the number of bits per baud.

quadrature phase shift keying (QPSK) (n.) Frequency modulated transmission technique used in digital satellite transmission and in up-stream signaling in hybrid fiber-coax (HFC) networks.

quadruplex (quad) (n.) Developed by Ampex, an industrial videotape format that offers broadcast quality. It has four video heads and uses two-inch wide videotape.

quad-speed (adj.) Describes CD-ROM drives with maximum data transfer rates of approxi-mately 600 kilobytes per second (KBps), four times the rate at which first-generation CD-ROM drives operated.

Qualcomm PureVoice codec (n.) A low-band-width audio codec optimized for voice-only material, available for use with QuickTime version 3 and later versions.

**quality assurance** (QA) (n.) A discipline that addresses all business activities with the intention of improving procedures and outcomes and that submits production results to a stringent testing regimen.

**quality of service** (QoS) (n.) A measure of performance for a telecommunications system that reflects the integrity of transmission and the availability of the service.

**quantization** (n.) In video compression, a process that attempts to determine what information can be discarded safely without a significant loss in visual fidelity. Quantization uses DCT coefficients and provides many-to-one mapping. The quantization process is inherently lossy because of the many-to-one mapping process.

**quantization error** (n.) Inaccuracies in data resulting from the process of quantizing an analog waveform to a discrete level. The more data used to define a waveform, the lower the propensity for errors.

**quantize** (v.) In digitizing audio or video, to measure the amplitude of a sample at regular intervals to establish a representative numerical value to encode. Other steps in analog-to-digital (A/D) conversion are sampling and encoding.

**quantum** (n.) A small, indivisible piece of energy.

**Quarter CIF** (QCIF) (n.) Quarter Common Intermediate Format; video frame specification in the ITU-T H.261 standard that calls for a resolution of 176 x 144 pixels. This is approximately one-fourth the size of CIF, and demands a proportionally smaller bandwidth for delivery.

**Quarter-Inch Committee** (QIC) (n.) Industry association that establishes standards for 0.25-inch wide tape backup units.

**quarter-inch jack** (n.) Synonymous with 0.25-inch phone jack, a female audio connector.

**query** 1. (v.) To request information from a database. 2. ( n.) The request itself for particular information contained in a database.

**Query Interface** (QI) (n.) A database system that client programs can access in order to read or edit content.

**queue** (n.) In computing, a series of tasks or operations waiting to be performed.

**queuing** (n.) In telecommunications, a feature that allows calls or packets to be held up, or delayed, at the origination switch while waiting for a channel to become available.

**QuickDraw** (n.) A set of software routines that a Macintosh uses to display graphics.

**QuickTime** (n.) Cross-platform system-level software developed by Apple Computer in 1991 that manages the playback of all types of digital media. It is implemented as a set of extensions on the Macintosh platform and a dynamic-link library (DLL) for Windows that intergrates video, still images, animated images (sprites), vector graphics, multiple sound channels, MIDI files, 3D objects, virtual reality objects, panoramas and text across applications. QuickTime provides a method for manipulating streaming media according to time lines, maintaining synchronization between video and audio. The Movie Player is the desktop application that plays QuickTime files.

The format does not restrict the size of the

window or the frame rate, but it does depend on the processing capabilities and the speed of the machine on which it plays back. With CinePak compression, QuickTime movies can be streamed from a 2X CD-ROM reader to a 320 x 240 pixel window on most older computers. As is the case with most digital audio-video players, the audio track will command the timing, and video frames will be dropped in order to maintain continuous, smooth sound delivery.

QuickTime video files can be captured by any computer with an encoder card. The tools available for manipulating QuickTime are available from Apple Computer in the QuickTime Pro package. Adobe Premiere is the most widely used application for capturing and editing QuickTime files.

QuickTime Version 3.0, introduced in 1998, was the first to offer cross-platform development and playback. Version 5.0 handles over 70 types of files, including MIDI, MPEG, virtual reality (VR), and animations. The ISO MPEG-4 working group has identified QuickTime as the media architecture of choice. codecs from Sorenson, QDesign, Qualcomm, and many others are included for video and audio compression.

**QuickTime for Windows** (n.) A version of QuickTime from Apple Computer that has been ported over to Windows. It plays QuickTime movies that have been specially processed, or "flattened," to remove their Macintosh binary headers. QuickTime movies have different brightness and contrast characteristics when viewed on an IBM-compatible machine as op-

posed to a Macintosh, because the two systems treat the gamma component of images differently. The QuickTime for Windows runtime player is distributed for free.

**QuickTime Music** (n.) The name for the process QuickTime uses to realize a MIDI file. It allows music to be stored as instructions, rather than digitized sounds, and then played back with defined instruments within QuickTime. QuickTime Music tracks are much smaller than digitized versions of the same music.

**QuickTime Streaming** (n.) Apple's streaming media feature native to the QuickTime architecture. See *streaming*.

**QuickTime VR** (QTVR) (n.) QuickTime Virtual Reality; an extension of QuickTime version 2.0 and later versions. This extension from Apple Computer allows playback of panoramic images in a VR environment through which users may navigate. The creation of QTVR files requires some advanced resources and the capacity to digitize photographs and to connect them seamlessly into a single landscape.

**QWERTY** (adj.) Describes a standard typewriter keyboard layout. *Q, W, E, R, T,* and *Y* are the first 6 keys on the left in the top row of letters. See figure.

*QWERTY keyboard layout*

# R

RAD See *Rapid Application Development.*

radial (n.) A line drawn from the center of a disc to the edge.

radio button (n.) An interactive icon in the shape of a small circle with a dot in the center that represents a choice or a selection, usually found in a dialog box. Clicking on a radio button in a graphical user interface (GUI) selects one option and rejects all others. See figure.

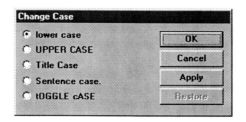

*radio buttons—lower case selected*

radio frequency (RF) (n.) Electromagnetic waves in the bandwidth between the frequencies of audio and light, from about 500 kHz to

300 GHz. These waves are propagated in the air without a guide wire or a cable. See figure.

radio frequency ID circuit (n.) A type of integrated circuit (IC) that communicates using an integrated microwave transceiver.

radio frequency identification (RFID) (n.) The recognition of a specific wavelength in the radio frequency spectrum. See figure.

radio frequency interference (RFI) (n.) In the radio frequency (RF) spectrum, noise introduced by electromagnetic radiation. This noise causes undesirable effects in nearby electronic components that may be susceptible to disturbance, such as a sound card in a computer.

radiosity (n.) A method of simulating a light source for rendering three-dimensional images. Radiosity is more computationally intensive and more accurate than *ray tracing,* an alternative method.

radix (n.) In mathematics, the base of a num-

**Radio Frequency**

| FM Radio | Cellular Phones | Pagers | PCS | Cordless Phone Wireless LAN | Satellite TV |
|---|---|---|---|---|---|
| 88–108 MHz | 806–890 MHz | 929–932 MHz | 1850–1990 MHz | 2400–2483.5 MHz | 4–16 GHz |

*uses of the radio frequency spectrum*

bering system. Binary numbers are radix 2. Decimal numbers are radix 10.

**RADSL** See *rate-adaptive digital subscriber line.*

**RAID** See *redundant arrays of independent disks.*

**rail-switcher** (n.) An audio power amplifier that has more than one power supply for the output and a method of switching between the two depending on the input signal. See *amplifier classes, Class G.*

**rainbow series** (n.) A set of technical manuals or specifications identified by the color of their covers or bindings. The names of types of CD-ROMs derive from the colors of the books containing their specifications. The series includes the Red, Yellow, Green, White, and Orange Books.

**RAM** See *random access memory.*

**RAMDAC** See *Random Access Memory Digital-to-Analog Converter.*

**RAM disk** (n.) Random access memory disk; a portion of internal dynamic memory used to emulate a virtual volume of storage space on a hard disk drive.

**RAM file** (n.) A RealVideo reference file that is placed on an HTTP server with the .ram extension. It points the RealPlayer to the location of the RealVideo file on the RealServer. See also *Real Media.*

**RAMP** See *Remote Access Maintenance Protocol.*

**random** (adj.) Describes a condition that is unpredictable, arbitrary, or not organized by a recognizable scheme. These characteristics describe the output of a random number generator, for example.

**random access** (adj.) Describes a hardware delivery system that can leap to any indexed point in data files that reside in memory. Compare *linear.*

**random access memory** (RAM, pronounced "RAM") (n.) A memory storage chip installed in a computer. RAM holds information that a microprocessor can access rapidly. Generally, the operating system and the application programs are loaded into RAM. This part of a computer's memory can read (find and display) and write (record) information, and the user can update or amend it. RAM takes the form of a volatile integrated circuit (IC) containing Static RAM (SRAM) or Dynamic RAM (DRAM). In RAM, the order in which the microprocessor accesses different locations does not affect the speed of access.

**Random Access Memory Digital-to-Analog Converter** (RAMDAC, pronounced "RAM-dack") (n.) A combination of three fast DACs for RGB values and a Static RAM (SRAM) chip. A graphics display adapter uses a RAMDAC to store the color palette and to generate the analog signals that drive a monitor. The DACs process the RGB values, and the SRAM serves as a color look-up table.

**Rapid Application Development** (RAD, pronounced "RAD") (n.) A software development tool that allows a programmer to build a user interface quickly, integrate media types, and create links between pieces of data. With the exception of Visual Basic (VB), these programs are best considered database development tools rather than multimedia design tools. Some of the common development systems are listed below:

**R**

- Delphi: A development tool from Borland based on Pascal. It compiles stand-alone machine language .exe and .dll files.

- PowerBuilder: A program developed by PowerSoft that applies its own scripting language, PowerScript, which is similar to BASIC.

- SQL Windows: A professional tool for database development from Gupta that can also handle multimedia.

- Visual Basic (VB): From Microsoft Corporation, a preferred programming tool for Windows applications. The tool makes it easy to build and reuse models with icons, buttons, and toolbars. In some cases, this program is a good choice for multimedia development in Windows because its products support OLE 2.0 and because operating system integration is automated. The program lacks a compiler, though.

**RARE** (Reseaux Associés pour la Recherche Européenne) See *European Association of Research Networks.*

**rarefaction** (n.) A region in which the density and pressure are reduced in a medium, such as air; this is caused by the passage of a sound wave.

**RARP** See *Reverse Address Resolution Protocol.*

**raster** (n., adj.) 1. The area illuminated by the scanning beam of a display grid. A raster display device stores and displays data as horizontal rows on a uniform grid. 2. Bitmap data.

**raster graphics** (n.) Images composed of pixels arranged in rows and columns, as in a bitmap. Unlike vector graphics, each pixel is defined by data that describes its color and brightness. Compare *vector graphics.*

**raster image processor** (RIP) (n.) Software that converts vector data into a bitmap, typically for printing.

**rasterize** (v.) To convert vector data into a bitmapped image.

**rate-adaptive digital subscriber line** (RADSL) (n.) A version of ASDL in which connected modems test the line at startup and adapt their operating speed to the highest rate the line can transmit without errors. In certain cases, RADSL can receive data at a downstream rate of 3 Mbps or faster.

**rave** (v.) To speak at great length with evangelical commitment about a specific subject, particularly when addressing a listserv.

**RAVE** (Renderer Acceleration Virtual Engine) (n.) Developed by Apple Computer, the Application Programming Interface (API) for QuickDraw 3D. It uses the 3DMF file format for virtual reality modeling language (VRML) files and is intended to be multiplatform-compatible.

**ray tracer** (n.) In rendering an animation, a device used in modeling that sends hypothetical light beams across a scene and that calculates visual effects and reflections from objects in the scene. See figure.

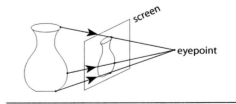

*projection in ray tracing*

**RBOC** See *Regional Bell Operating Company.*

**RCA connector** (n.) A common terminator on a cable used by most consumer audio and video equipment. The male connector is an inner pin encircled by a concentric ring. The female connector is a socket with a raised housing for the ring. A male RCA connector is also known as a *phono connector* or a *phono plug,* not to be confused with a *phone plug,* which refers to a 0.25-inch pin with no ring around it. See figure.

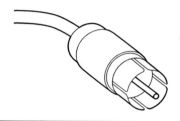

*male RCA connector, or phono plug*

**RCA phono jack** (n.) A type of RCA connector that was originally developed by The Radio Corporation of America (RCA) for internal chassis connections in radios and televisions during the 1930s. It became popular for use in cables used to connect phonograph cartridges to preamplifiers because it is inexpensive and easily fitted with the small diameter shielded cables used for the cartridge leads. It has become the standard connector used in line-level consumer and project studio sound equipment and is used for composite video signals. A phono jack is also known as a *pin jack.*

**R-DAT** See *rotating digital audio tape.*

**RDBA** See *Remote Database Access.*

**RDBMS** See *relational database management system.*

**RDF** See *Resource Description Framework.*

**reactance** (n.) Resistance that is frequency-dependant, contributed by inductors and capacitors in AC circuits.

**read** (v.) In computer terminology, to transfer information from one storage medium to another medium or device. For example, data is read from a disk and written to a computer screen. Compare *write.*

**reader** (n.) Any device that identifies and transmits data, such as a CD-ROM player.

**read-only memory** (ROM) (n.) A computer storage medium that allows the user to recall and use information (read) but not to record or amend it (write).

**real** (adj.) Not simulated. Compare *virtual.*

**RealAudio** (n.) A client-server architecture for streaming realtime sound over the web. The RealAudio encoder compresses sound into RealAudio (.ra) files, which a special server streams. On the client side, a plug-in for a browser decodes the stream of data sent from the server, decompresses it, and sends it to the sound card. A 14.4-kilobyte-per-second (KBps) modem is adequate for sound reproduction, but the speed of the connection determines the quality of the sound produced, and faster connections yield much higher quality. Files may be encoded for playback at specific rates of transfer.

**real estate** (n.) 1. The space available for data on storage media. 2. The physical space on the desktop.

**RealMedia** (n.) A proprietary audio and video file format that is compressed for delivery via the web. The company RealNetworks, formerly called Progressive Networks, provides an encoder and a decoder, or player, for RealMedia files. They also provide the RealMedia server, which is required to deliver their media files.

**real mode** (n.) An operating mode of Intel 80x86 processors. Compare *protected mode.*

**RealSystem G2** (n.) The second generation of RealVideo, simply called *RealG2.* It can be used to stream RealAudio and RealVideo over a network.

**realtime** (n., adj) The time during which a data processing event occurs. Data is received and processed so fast and the results are returned so quickly that the process seems instantaneous to the user. The term often refers to simultaneous digitization and compression of audio or video information. Compare *offline.*

**realtime counter** (n.) A unit that reads control track pulses and reports hours, minutes, seconds, and frames as a videotape machine records or plays.

**Real-Time Operating System** (RTOS) (n.) A CD-i operating system developed by Microware Corporation.

**Realtime Streaming Protocol** (RTSP) (n.) A standard for the transmission of true streaming media to one or more viewers simultaneously. It is becoming increasingly common. RTSP allows viewers to randomly access a stream and uses Realtime Transfer Protocol (RTP) rather than Hypertext Transfer Protocol (HTTP).

**Realtime Transfer Protocol** (RTP) (n.) A transport protocol designed to deliver live media to one or more viewers simultaneously. RTP is used as the transfer protocol for RTSP streaming. Defined in RFC 1889, it is part of the ITU-T H.323 specification for streaming real-time applications.

**Real-Time Video** (RTV) (n.) A low-level digital video–encoding scheme for desktop compression. RTV uses an Intel i750-based video card.

**RealVideo** (n.) A streaming media architecture developed by RealNetworks for streaming video over a network.

**reassembly** (n.) The process of reuniting a fragmented Internet Protocol (IP) packet before it is passed to the transport layer.

**reboot** (v.) To restart a computer without shutting off the power. Rebooting occurs when the Reset button is pressed or when the Restart option is chosen in software.

**receiver** (n.) 1. An electronic device designed to accept a signal that was transmitted or delivered by any means and then to decode it. Such equipment often receives and displays or reproduces broadcast audio or video signals. 2. The earpiece portion of a telephone headset that converts current into sound waves.

**recompress** (v.) To compress an already compressed video or audio file a second time. It should be avoided if at all possible because video and audio quality will be seriously degraded by multiple lossy compressions. This term is not generally used to refer to file compression processes, such as those performed with PKZIP.

**reconstruction filter** (n.) Found at the output of a digital audio processor, a low-pass filter designed to remove aliasing products, or unwanted artifacts present at multiples of the sampling frequency.

**record** 1. (n.) In a database, a group of related items, or fields, treated as a single unit of information. Pronounced "REK-erd." 2. (v.) To capture or encode an event on magnetic tape or in a digital format so that it can be preserved and reproduced later. Pronounced "ree-KORD."

**Recording Industry Association of America (RIAA)** (n.) A powerful professional trade organization that represents the recording industry in the United States. Its members manufacture and distribute 90 percent of all sound recordings produced and sold in the United States.

**rectifier** (n.) An electronic component that converts alternating current (AC) into direct current (DC).

**recursion** (n.) In programming, a case in which a procedure calls itself. A functional programming language uses recursion at times when a procedural language would use iteration.

**recursive** (adj.) A data structure or process that is in part defined or generated by itself.

**Recycle Bin** (n.) In Microsoft Windows, a receptacle represented by an icon. As with the trash can in the Mac OS, files to be deleted from a computer's storage system are placed in the Recycle Bin.

**Red Book for PostScript** (n.) 1. One of the four standard reference books about PostScript, along with the Blue Book, the Green Book, and the White Book. 2. The 1984 standards issued by the ITU-T eighth plenary assembly, including the X.400 email specification, Group 1–4 fax standards, ISDN, and the V.x recommendations. Red Book for PostScript is part of the PostScript rainbow series.

**Red Book standard** (n.) The audio CD specification that Philips and Sony developed. The specification book defining the format for audio CDs originally had a red cover. In other books defining CD standards, many parameters are based on those in the Red Book.

**red-green-blue** (RGB) 1. (n.) A type of computer color display output signal consisting of separately adjustable red, green, and blue signals or components. Compare *composite video*, in which signals are combined prior to output. RGB monitors offer higher resolution than composite monitors. Digital RGB systems are available, but most computers use analog RGB video. 2. (adj.) Describes a type of color model

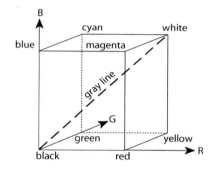

*RGB color cube*

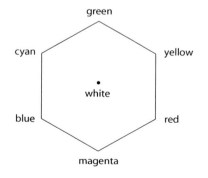

*RGB hexagon.*

**R**

in which colors are represented as the combination of red, green, and blue light. RGB color space may be represented as a square, with one corner black and the opposite corner white, or as a hexagon. See figures.

**redirector** (n.) Software that intercepts requests for resources within a computer and analyzes them for remote access requirements. A redirector may assign a local disk identification letter to a logical disk on a Netware server.

**reduced instruction set computing** (RISC, pronounced "RISK") (n., adj.) A type of microprocessor with a simplified architecture that achieves high performance by reducing the range of instruction sets and executing them faster.

**redundancy** (n.) 1. Instances in which multiple interchangeable components perform a single function to minimize the effects of failures and errors. One common form of hardware redundancy is disk mirroring. Redundancy can also be used to detect and recover from errors in software. A common example is the cyclic redundancy check (CRC), which adds redundant data to a block in order to detect corruption during storage or transmission. 2. The process of digitizing or capturing the same data or descriptive information more than once. Copies of the same data are redundant. Compression routines throw out the redundant data.

**redundant arrays of independent disks** (RAID) (n.) An integrated collection of similar hard disk drives that function together to provide greater speed and integrity of data than a single drive. Originally, the *I* stood for *inexpensive*, referring to the 3.5-inch and 5.25-inch disks used for the first RAID systems. Drives are striped so that the writing of data may be synchronized between disks, and parity refers to the bits used for error correction. The following standard RAID specifications exist:

| | |
|---|---|
| RAID 0 | Nonredundant striped array |
| RAID 1 | Mirrored arrays |
| RAID 2 | Parallel array with error correction code (ECC) |
| RAID 3 | Parallel array with parity |
| RAID 4 | Striped array with parity |
| RAID 5 | Striped array with rotating parity |

**Reed-Solomon Code** (n.) A method of error correction named for Irving Reed and Gustave Solomon, who invented it in 1960.

**reference level** (n.) An established starting point for making relative measurements, most often of signal strength or power. The most common application is in audio engineering, in which the reference is in decibels per milliwatt (dBm).

**reference noise** (n.) The level of circuit noise, or unwanted disturbance, that is inherent within a transmission medium or frequency.

**referential integrity** (n.) The consistency with which data possess properties in a relational database.

**referrer** (n.) The URL from which a web user is directed to another location.

**reflected light** (n.) In video production and photography, light that radiates or that is reflected from a surface or subject and that does not shine directly on the scene or the subject.

**reflector** (n.) 1. A lighting accessory that spreads light and fills in shadows. It is usually made of white poster board, foamcore, or reflective metal. 2. In acoustics, any object or surface that reflects the original signal. Sound waves bounce off of an efficient reflector with nominal energy loss.

**refractive index** (n.) The ratio of the velocity of light (or electromagnetic waves) in a vacuum to its velocity in a transmitting medium.

**refresh rate** (n.) The number of times per second, or the frequency, at which a displayed image is scanned or renewed on a cathode-ray tube (CRT). In NTSC video, that rate is 60 times per second. On computer monitors, rates slower than 75 Hz can cause flicker and poor picture quality.

**Regional Bell Operating Company** (RBOC, pronounced "ARE-bock") (n.) One of the seven companies created when AT&T was dissolved. These companies are Ameritech, Bell Atlantic, BellSouth, NYNEX, Pacific Telesis, SBC Communications, and US West. GTE is not among this group but is the largest local exchange carrier (LEC) in the United States.

**register** (n.) 1. A small number of high-speed memory locations in the central processing unit (CPU) of a computer. Access to data in registers is faster than access to data in RAM. 2. An addressable location in a memory-mapped peripheral device.

**regression** (n.) A mathematical method in which an empirical function is derived from a set of experimental data.

**regular expression** (n.) An object or expression that describes a pattern of characters, or a text string. The Generalized Regular Expression Parser (GREP) Unix utility searches a text file for a specific character string. In JavaScript, a regular expression is used to perform pattern matching.

**relational database** (n.) Developed by E. F. Codd, a type of database that allows data structures to be defined. The data is organized in tables, or collections of records, in which each record contains the same fields, or categories of information. The relationships between the data are defined. Certain fields are designated as keys, expediting searches. Records in different tables may be linked if they have a common field in each table. Oracle Database, FileMaker Pro, and Microsoft Access are examples.

**relational database management system** (RDBMS) (n.) Same as DBMS, since these databases are generally relational.

**relative path** (n.) A hierarchical list of directories and subdirectories that lead to a given file. It is expressed as differences from the current location. For example, "C:/media/Present2.mpg" leads to the "Present2.mpg" file, located in the directory titled "media" under the root directory C:. Relative paths are often used when files are located on the same server as the HTML page that refers to them. Graphic files are often placed in a directory named "images," and they reside on the same HTTP server as HTML pages.

**relay** (n.) A type of switch that is opened or closed electronically to connect circuitry.

**release** (n.) A version of software made public. Prerelease versions are called *alpha* or *beta* test versions.

**REM** See *remark.*

**remark** (REM, pronounced "REHM") (n.) In programming code, a comment used to describe the purpose or the temporary status of a command.

**Remote Access Maintenance Protocol** (RAMP)

355

(n.) A protocol used in Internet applications.

**remote bridge** (n.) A router that connects physically dissimilar network segments across wide area network (WAN) links.

**remote control** (n., adj.) The ability to issue a command to an interactive program with an independent, electronic device. The device is operated from a distance and often employs infrared technology.

**Remote Database Access** (RDBA) (n.) The capacity to link a computer or terminal from a distance to a database system and read or update records.

**Remote Method Invocation** (RMI) (n.) A Java Application Programming Interface (API).

**Remote Operations Service Element** (ROSE) (n.) A sub-layer program found at layer 7 of the OSI protocol.

**Remote Procedure Call** (RPC) (n.) A widely used paradigm for client-server computing. A client sends a request to a remote system to execute a designated procedure using arguments supplied, and the result is returned to the client.

**remote production unit** (n.) A van or a mobile trailer that houses audio-video equipment for production at a site other than the studio.

**removable cartridge** (n.) An enclosed optical disc that can be ejected and inserted into any similar playback device. A SyQuest reader accepts a cartridge that typically holds between 44 and 270 megabytes (MB) of data. An Iomega Zip cartridge holds 100 MB of data, whereas a Jaz cartridge holds 1000 MB.

**render** (v.) 1. To calculate attributes of an image using geometric models as a basis, thereby producing a dimensional object. 2. In animation applications, to calculate the instructions that define a complex series of images.

**repeater** (n.) An amplifier needed at regular intervals to restore the power of an analog signal. Repeaters regenerate digital signals while removing spurious noise. Regeneration and retiming ensure that the signal is clearly transmitted. In a short run, a repeater simply propagates signals from one cable to another.

**replicate** (n.) A copy of a CD or of another disc pressed from a stamper disc. Pronounced "REP-li-kat."

**replication** (n.) 1. Mass reproduction of pre-recorded discs or of media in general. Unlike duplication, the replication process periodically compares two copies of a database and updates both to reflect changes in them. 2. The ability of Lotus Notes to distribute document databases across telecommunications networks automatically. Lotus Notes supports a wide range of network protocols, including X.25 and TCP/IP.

**report** (n.) The output from a database. A report is organized according to specifications that were defined in response to a user's query.

**repurpose** (v.) To use content in a preexisting program to perform a function other than the one for which it was originally intended.

**request** (n.) In relation to the Internet, the GET (a page request) or the POST (a form submission) command placed in an HTML document. The request may instruct a Common Gateway Interface (CGI) script to access a database.

**Request For Comments** (RFC) (n.) A set of

informational documents begun in 1969. RFCs state standards to be followed by those who develop software for the Internet. The World Wide Web Consortium (W3C) approved all of the early RFCs. A comprehensive list of RFCs appears at *http://asg.web.cmu.edu/rfc/*. See the table on the next page for RFCs in common use.

**request for proposals** (RFP) (n.) A formal bidding procedure in which vendors are encouraged to respond.

**request for quotations** (RFQ) (n.) A formal procedure through which an organization invites vendors' bids for equipment or services.

**request for technology** (RFT) (n.) A procedure that standardization bodies use to request technology that meets industry requirements.

**request to send** (RTS) (n.) A standard control signal that puts a modem in the originate mode, preparing it to send data.

**Reseaux Associés pour la Recherche Européenne** See *European Association of Research Networks*.

**ResEdit** See *Resource Editor*.

**reserved memory** (n.) The address range between 640 and 1024 kilobytes (KB) on an IBM-compatible computer. MS-DOS reserves this memory for Basic Input/Output System (BIOS), video cards, and additional circuit boards.

**resistance** (n.) In an electrical circuit, the property of a conductor that inhibits the flow of current. Resistance is measured in ohms.

**resolution** (n.) 1. The number of pixels per a unit of area on a monitor screen or the dots per inch (dpi) in a printed graphic. A display with a finer grid has more pixels and a higher resolution; hence it can reproduce a more detailed image. 2. The size of a window used to display video or images, such as 640 x 480 pixels or 320 x 240 pixels. 3. The bit rate and the sample rate of a digital audio file, such as 16-bit, 44.1 KHz.

**Resource Description Framework** (RDF) (n.) Developed by the World Wide Web Consortium (W3C), a specification for a cross-platform standard for managing meta information using SML. Metadata has many uses, including cataloging, creating intelligent agents, site mapping, and managing digital signatures. RDF is designed to provide an infrastructure using Extensible Markup Language (XML) for uniform and interoperable exchange across the Web.

**Resource Editor** (ResEdit, pronounced "REZ-edit") (n.) A utility program for the Macintosh that allows a programmer to edit system resources, such as icons and dialog boxes.

**resource fork** (n.) One of the two branches in a Macintosh file. Reusable items, such as icons, fonts, dialog boxes, and menus are contained in a resource fork. Compare *data fork*. See also *Macintosh file system*.

**Resource Interchange File Format** (RIFF) (n.) Introduced by Microsoft and IBM in 1990, a cross-platform file format for images, audio, and other media types. A RIFF file can store multiple data types as distinct structures called *chunks*. See also *Media Control Interface*.

**response-based** (adj.) Describes a form of computer-based instruction that reacts to input and that causes a program to progress at a

**R**

**Requests for Comment**

This table lists sample Draft Standard RFCs. A complete listing is available at **http://asg.web.cmu.edu/rfc/**.

| Number | Designer/Creator/Date | Number | Designer/Creator/Date |
|---|---|---|---|
| 3192 | Minimal FAX address format in Internet, Mail C. Allocchio, October 2001. | 2047 | MIME Part Three: Message Header Extensions for Non-ASCII Text, K. Moore, November 1996. |
| 3191 | Minimal GSTN address format in Internet, Mail C. Allocchio, October 2001. | 2046 | MIME Part Two: Media Types, N. Freed, N. Borenstein, November 1996. |
| 2865 | Remote Authentication Dial In User Service (RADIUS), C. Rigney, S. Willens, A. Rubens, W. Simpson, June 2000. | 2045 | MIME Part One: Format of Internet Message Bodies, N. Freed, N. Borenstein, November 1996. |
| 2863 | The Interfaces Group MIB, K. McCloghrie, F. Kastenholz, June 2000. | 1994 | PPP Challenge Handshake Authentication Protocol (CHAP), W. Simpson, August 1996. |
| 2790 | Host Resources MIB, S. Waldbusser, P. Grillo, March 2000. | 1990 | The PPP Multilink Protocol (MP), K. Sklower, B. Lloyd, G. McGregor, D. Carr, T. Coradetti, August 1996. |
| 2617 | HTTP Authentication: Basic and Digest Access Authentication, J. Franks, P. Hallam-Baker, J. Hostetler, S. Lawrence, P. Leach, A. Luotonen, L. Stewart, June 1999. | 1907 | Management Information Base for Version 2 of the Simple Network Management Protocol (SNMPv2), J. Case, K. McCloghrie, M. Rose, S. Waldbusser, January 1996. |
| 2616 | Hypertext Transfer Protocol—HTTP/1.1, R. Fielding, J. Gettys, J. Mogul, H. Frystyk, L. Masinter, P. Leach, T. Berners-Lee, June 1999. | 1905 | Protocol Operations for Version 2 of the Simple Network Management Protocol (SNMPv2), J. Case, K. McCloghrie, M. Rose, S. Waldbusser, January 1996. Draft (Obsoletes RFC1448). |
| 2574 | User-based Security Model (USM) for version 3 of the Simple Network Management Protocol (SNMPv3) U. Blumenthal, B. Wijnen, April 1999 | 1850 | OSPF Version 2 Management Information Base, F. Baker, R. Coltun, November 1995. |
| 2573 | SNMP Applications, D. Levi, P. Meyer, B. Stewart, April 1999. | 1832 | XDR: External Data Representation Standard, R. Srinivasan, August 1995. |
| 2463 | Internet Control Message Protocol (ICMPv6) for the Internet Protocol Version 6 (IPv6) Specification, A. Conta, S. Deering, December 1998. | 1777 | Lightweight Directory Access Protocol, W. Yeong, T. Howes, S. Kille, March 1995. |
| 2462 | IPv6 Stateless Address Autoconfiguration, S. Thomson, T. Narten, December 1998. | 1772 | Application of the Border Gateway Protocol in the Internet, Y. Rekhter, P. Gross, March 1995. |
| 2460 | Internet Protocol, Version 6 (IPv6) Specification, S. Deering, R. Hinden, December 1998. | 1771 | A Border Gateway Protocol 4 (BGP-4), Y. Rekhter, T. Li, March 1995. |
| 2396 | Uniform Resource Identifiers (URI): Generic Syntax, T. Berners-Lee, R. Fielding, L. Masinter, August 1998. | 1757 | Remote Network Monitoring Management Information Base, S. Waldbusser, February 1995. |
| 2279 | UTF-8, a transformation format of ISO 10646, F. Yergeau, January 1998. | 1748 | IEEE 802.5 MIB using SMIv2, K. McCloghrie, E. Decker, December 1994. |
| 2131 | Dynamic Host Configuration Protocol, R. Droms, March 1997. | 1724 | RIP Version 2 MIB Extension, G. Malkin, F. Baker, November 1994. |
| 2115 | Management Information Base for Frame Relay DTEs Using SMIv2, C. Brown, F. Baker, September 1997. | 1694 | Definitions of Managed Objects for SMDS Interfaces using SMIv2, T. Brown, K. Tesink, Editors, August 1994. Draft (Obsoletes RFC1304). |
| 2067 | IP over HIPPI, J. Renwick, January 1997. | 1651 | SMTP Service Extensions, J. Klensin, N. Freed, M. Rose, E. Stefferud, D. Crocker, July 1994. |
| 2049 | MIME Part Five: Conformance Criteria and Examples, N. Freed, N. Borenstein, November 1996. | 1549 | PPP in HDLC Framing, W. Simpson, December 1993. |

**Requests for Comment** (continued)

| Number | Designer/Creator/Date | Number | Designer/Creator/Date |
|---|---|---|---|
| 1548 | The Point-to-Point Protocol (PPP), W. Simpson, December 1993. | 1305 | Network Time Protocol (Version 3) Specification, Implementation David L. Mills, March 1992. |
| 1534 | Interoperation Between DHCP and BOOTP, R. Droms, October 1993. | 1288 | The Finger User Information Protocol, D. Zimmerman, December 1991. |
| 1521 | MIME (Multipurpose Internet Mail Extensions) Part One: Mechanisms for Specifying and Describing the Format of Internet Message Bodies, N. Borenstein, N. Freed, September 1993. | 1247 | OSPF Version 2, J. Moy, Jul-01-1991. Draft. |
| | | 1225 | Post Office Protocol: Version 3, M.T. Rose, May 1991. |
| 1493 | Definitions of Managed Objects for Bridges, E. Decker, P. Langille, A. Rijsinghani, K. McCloghrie, July 1993. | 1191 | Path MTU discovery, J.C. Mogul, S.E. Deering, November 1990. Draft (Obsoletes RFC 1063). |
| 1490 | Multiprotocol Interconnect over Frame Relay, T. Bradley, C. Brown, A. Malis, July 1993. | 1188 | Proposed Standard for the Transmission of IP Datagrams over FDDI Networks, D. Katz, October 1990. |
| 1460 | Post Office Protocol—Version 3, M. Rose, June 1993. | 0954 | NICNAME/WHOIS, K. Harrenstien, M.K. Stahl, E.J. Feinler, October 1985. |
| 1356 | Multiprotocol Interconnect on X.25 and ISDN in the Packet Mode, A. Malis, D. Robinson, R. Ullmann, August 1992. | 0951 | Bootstrap Protocol, W.J. Croft, J. Gilmore, September 1985. |

learner's individual rate.

**response time** (n.) In an interactive session, the elapsed time between the end of an inquiry or user data entry and the reply from a device.

**restore** (v.) 1. To copy an archived file from backup into local storage, where it can be readily accessed. 2. To return a window in a graphical user interface (GUI) to its previous dimensions after it has been resized, minimized, or maximized.

**retide** (n.) A piece of glass with a chrome pattern for several die used in the photolithography process.

**retro-virus** (n.) A computer virus that does not engage fully until the media used to back up the system is infected, making restoration impossible.

**return code** (n.) In relation to a request made on the Internet, a message that specifies whether the transfer was successful. For a list of failed return codes, see *client error* and *server error*. Successful return codes are as follows:

200 = Success: OK.
201 = Success: Created.
202 = Success: Accepted.
203 = Success: No Response.
204 = Success: Partial Information.
300 = Success: Redirected.
301 = Success: Moved.
302 = Success: Found.
303 = Success: New Method.
304 = Success: Not Modified.

**return-to-zero** (RZ) (n.) In digital line coding, a convention that returns the signal voltage to a zero level after slightly more than one-half bit time has elapsed. See *non-return-to-zero*.

**reuse** (v.) To apply code developed for one application program in another application. Object-oriented programming (OOP) offers reusability of code through inheritance and

359

genericity. Class libraries with intelligent browsers and application generators are under development to help in this process. Polymorphic functional languages also support reusability while retaining the benefits of strong typing.

**reverb** (n.) A sound effect generated by a signal processor. When treated heavily with reverb, sounds appear to reverberate as though they were produced in a large room or concert hall. The degree of reverb applied by a processor may range from a slight amount to extreme, unrealistic proportions. Sound tracks to which effects have been applied are referred to as "wet," whereas tracks without effects are "dry."

**reverberation time** (n.) The time it takes for a sound to decay after the source stops emitting the sound. It is quantified by measuring how long it takes the sound pressure level (SPL) to decay to one-millionth of its original value, which is equal to a 60 dB reduction.

**Reverse Address Resolution Protocol** (RARP) (n.) Defined in RFC 903, a protocol that provides the reverse function of Address Resolution Protocol (ARP). RARP maps a MAC address to an Internet address. RARP is primarily used by diskless nodes attempting to initialize and locate their Internet addresses.

**reverse engineering** (n.) The process of analyzing an existing software or hardware system, identifying its components, and recreating it.

**revolutions per minute** (rpm) (n.) A measurement of the speed at which an object spins.

RF See *radio frequency.*

RFC See *Request For Comments.*

RFI See *radio frequency interference.*

RFID See *radio frequency identification.*

RFP See *request for proposals.*

RFQ See *request for quotations.*

RFT See *request for technology.*

RGB See *red-green-blue.*

**RG58** (n.) A 0.25-inch coaxial cable with low (52-ohm) impedance used for 10BASE2 Ethernet wiring. Also known as *cheapernet.*

**RG62** (n.) A specification for ARCnet coaxial cable with 93-ohm impedance.

**rheostat** (n.) An electronic component that provides variable resistance.

RIAA See *Recording Industry Association of America.*

**RIAA equalization curve** (n.) A standard proposed by the Recording Industry Association of America (RIAA), adopted by the recording industry in 1953 and reaffirmed in 1964 by both the RIAA and NAB. It was issued by the IEC as international standard IEC 60098 and remains in effect. The curve is used in cutting vinyl records, and its inverse must be applied by phonograph playback preamplifiers. The curve attenuates low frequencies and amplifies high frequencies, relative to a 1 kHz reference point, to maximize dynamic range for a lateral cut vinyl disc. The grooves in a stereo phonograph disc are cut by a chisel shaped stylus driven by two vibrating systems arranged at right angles to each other. The cutting stylus vacillates from side to side in accordance with the signal impressed on the cutter.

The movement of the groove back and forth from the center is known as "groove modulation." If the amplitude of this modulation exceeds a fixed amount, "cutover" occurs, and the cutter breaks through the wall of one groove into the wall of the previous groove. Low frequencies that cause wide undulations in the groove are attenuated to prevent overmodulation. Conversely, high frequencies are amplified to overcome the granular nature of the disc surface acting as a noise generator, thus improving the signal-to-noise ratio. See figure.

**ribbon cable** (n.) A type of cable with multiple conductors that is as flat as a ribbon.

**rib site** (n.) With an on-demand, high-speed link to a backbone site, a computer that serves as a regional distribution point for third-party traffic in electronic mail and in Usenet news. Compare *backbone site.*

**rich object** (n.) In artificial intelligence (AI),

an object that can have assertions made about it but that cannot be completely described or represented.

**Rich Text Format** (RTF) (n.) A format developed by Microsoft that defines text and that exchanges formatted text using normal alphanumeric symbols. The text includes embedded formatting information, such as italics or structural layout descriptors, along with characters. RTF is used for cross-platform applications when the characters and layout must be converted to a different word-processing application or file type.

**RIFF** See *Resource Interchange File Format.*

**ring latency** (n.) The time required for a signal to propagate once around a ring in a token ring or in an IEEE 802.5 network.

**ring signal** (n.) In telephony, a 20 Hz signal, typically at 70-75 volts, used for on-hook loop signaling. Distinctive ringing is accomplished

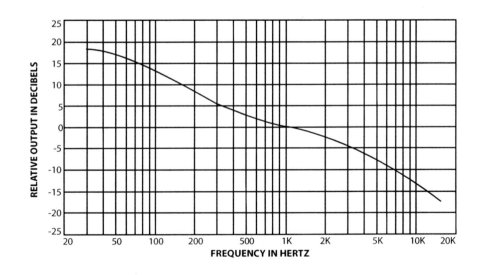

*RIAA equalization curve*

by varying the frequency of the signal within a 15 to 68 Hz range.

**ring topology** (n.) A network topology in which a series of repeaters are connected to one another with unidirectional transmission links. Connected in this way, they form a single, closed loop. Each station on the network connects to the network at a repeater.

**RIP** See *raster image processor* or *Routing Information Protocol.*

**RISC** See *reduced instruction set computing.*

**RJ-11** (n.) A telephone jack with six connecting wires that modems use when connecting to a leased line.

**RLE** See *run-length encoding.*

**RLL** See *Run-Length Limited.*

**RLV** (n.) Recordable laser videodisc developed by the Optical Disc Corporation. RLV is an outdated form of media used to record analog video and audio on a blank videodisc.

**RMI** See *Remote Method Invocation.*

**RMS** See *Root Mean Squared.*

**roaming** (n.) The use of a cellular phone outside the home service area. A roaming agreement allows users to make calls in another provider's geographic service area without operator intervention. Roaming rates are higher than home service area airtime rates.

**robot** (n.) 1. A type of program that automatically retrieves a document anywhere on the web, along with those referenced in the web. Index-building robots retrieve a significant number of the references found in search engines. Also known as a *crawler* or a *spider.* 2. A program posing as an Internet Relay Chat (IRC) or a multiuser dungeon (MUD) user and usually performing a function.

**robust** (adj.) Describes a system with the ability to recover gracefully from exceptional inputs and adverse situations. A robust system is almost bulletproof.

**Rock Ridge Format** (n.) CD-recordable specifications for Unix that permit directory structures to be updated when new files are added to the disc. The specifications include the Rock Ridge Interchange Protocol Specification (RRIPS) and the System Use Sharing Protocol (SUSP). The SUSP extension to the ISO 9660 standard allows more than one file system extension to exist on a single CD-ROM. The RRIPS specification allows POSIX files and directories to be recorded on a CD-ROM without requiring modifications to files, such as renaming. Both of these specifications are extensions of the original ISO 9660 format for CD-ROM.

**roll** (n.) Lines of text or credits that typically move up the screen, often placed at the end of a video production. A roll is produced with a titler. See also *crawl.*

**roll-off** (n.) In audio engineering, the reduction in strength of a signal over time. The rate of roll-off determines how rapidly a signal is attenuated.

**ROM** See *read-only memory.*

**root directory** (n.) In MS-DOS, the top-most directory visible on a hard disk. All subdirectories are nested under this directory.

**rootkit** (n.) A security tool used by computer hackers to obtain administrator-level access to a computer system. It does this by capturing passwords and user identifications to other machines, which then allows the hacker to access all message traffic from a computer system. Along with other functions, it can provide a backdoor into a system, collect information about other systems on the network, and mask the fact that the system has been compromised. It is an example of Trojan Horse software, and is available for several operating systems.

**Root Mean Squared** (RMS) (n.) 1. A formula used to measure the power of an audio amplifier. 2. A means of qualifying the capacity of loudspeakers.

**ROSE** See *Remote Operations Service Element.*

**rotating digital audio tape** (R-DAT, pronounced "ARE-dat") (n.) The original name of the digital audio tape (DAT) format. Some early digital audio systems used stationary heads, as do analog tape decks. Machines with rotating heads, similar to the heads in a helical scan video recorder, became the standard.

**rotational latency** (n.) The time it takes for a sector on a disk to appear below the read/write head. Rotational latency is a component of access time.

**rotational speed** (n.) The speed at which a disk spins inside a drive, measured in revolutions per minute (rpm).

**Rot-13** (n.) A form of encryption frequently used in Usenet postings. It transposes the letters *A* through *L* with the letters *M* through *Z*.

**rough cut** (n.) A working copy of an edited master tape.

**round-trip time** (RTT) (n.) The amount of delay on a network between the time a message is sent and the time the echo is returned.

**route** 1. (n.) A path taken by network traffic from the source to the destination. 2. (n.) A possible path from a particular host to another host or machine. 3. (v.) To send a message on a specific path to its destination.

**router** (n.) A protocol-dependent device that connects two or more networks at the network layer. It helps break down a large network into smaller subnetworks. Routers introduce longer delays and have lower throughput rates than bridges. Like a bridge, a router restricts local area network (LAN) traffic and passes data to a routed LAN only when it is intended for that LAN. A repeater, by contrast, indiscriminately passes along data, regardless of the intended destination. The term *router* is replacing the term *gateway.*

**routing bridge** (n.) A bridge in the media access control (MAC) layer that employs network-layer methods to determine the topology of a network.

**Routing Information Protocol** (RIP) (n.) 1. An Internet standard defined in RFC 1058, STD 34 and updated in RFC 1388. 2. A companion protocol to Internetwork Packet eXchange (IPX) for the exchange of routing information in a Novell network. RIP has been partly superseded by NetWare Link State Protocol (NLSP). This Novell protocol is not related to the Internet standard defined in RFC 1058.

**routing protocol** (n.) A method of distributing messages and data that uses a specific algorithm to define the path.

**routing table** (n.) A table stored in a router or any similar internetworking device that keeps track of routes to specific network destinations,

**R**

sometimes using metrics associated with those routes.

**routing update** (n.) The message a router sends to indicate network accessibility and host information. Most often, routing updates are sent at regular intervals, especially after a change in network topology.

**RPC** See *Remote Procedure Call.*

**rpm** See *revolutions per minute.*

**RRIPS** See *Rock Ridge Format.*

**RS** (n.) Short for recommended standard; the Electronics Industries Association (EIA) has established many RS-x standards. Among those standards are the following:

- RS-170A is a recommended standard developed by the Electronics Industries Association (EIA) that specifies the parameters of color video signals for the NTSC format used in broadcast and in most consumer video products.

- RS-232 is a set of standards that specify three kinds of interfaces: mechanical, electrical, and functional. See figure on the following page.

- RS-232C is a serial interface standard developed by the Electronics Industries Association (EIA) for use in connecting computers and peripherals. The RS-232C port is a feature on many computing devices, and most equipment with an RS-232C connector can be interfaced, as long as software drivers exist. This standard defines circuit functions and pin assignments. The physical connector comes in the traditional 25-pin version

or in the newer 9-pin model. In data communications, this specification defines the interface between data terminal equipment (DTE) and data communications equipment (DCE) using serial binary data. This is the EIA equivalent of ITU-T standard V.24. The RS-232C electrical signal is unbalanced ($\pm$ 5 volts to $\pm$ 12 volts), has polar non-return-to-zero (NRZ), and handles data transfer rates of up to 19.2 kilobits per second (Kbps).

- RS-232D is the Electronics Industries Association (EIA) equivalent of ITU-T standard V.28.

- RS-422 is the balanced version of RS-232, allowing longer runs and faster transmission. It operates in conjunction with RS-449, which specifies electrical characteristics of balanced circuits and their 37-pin connectors.

- RS-422A is a standard developed by the Electronics Industries Association (EIA) that defines the physical and functional features of a computer interface with communications equipment. A balanced line and a 40-pin connector are two of its features.

- RS-449 facilitates serial binary data interchange, usually in synchronous transmission modes. See figure on next page.

- RS-530 is a standard developed by the Electronics Industries Association (EIA) that defines a specification for the pinout of balanced interfaces, such as RS-422A with a DB-40 connector. RS-530 supersedes RS-449 and uses a 25-pin connector. It works with RS-232, but is not directly compatible.

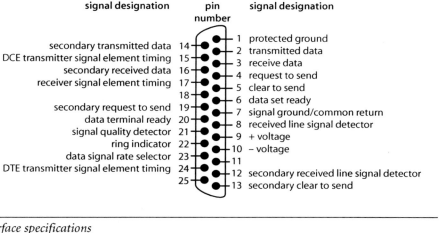

*RS-232 interface specifications*

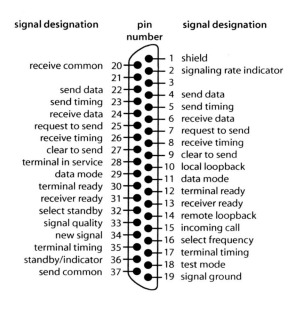

*RS-449 interface specifications*

**RTF** See *Rich Text Format.*

**RTOS** See *Real-Time Operating System.*

**RTP** See *Realtime Transfer Protocol.*

**RTS** See *request to send.*

**RTSP** See *Realtime Streaming Protocol.*

**RTT** See *round-trip time.*

**RTV** See *Real-Time Video.*

**rule of thirds** (n.) An adage used in composing a scene. The premise is that a shot is most visually appealing if important events are placed at the intersection of imaginary vertical and horizontal lines that divide the screen into thirds, as in a tic-tac-toe board.

**run-length encoding** (RLE) (n.) A compression algorithm developed by Microsoft for eight-bit video. RLE replaces sequences, or runs, of consecutive repeated data with a single character and a descriptor for the length of the run. Long, frequent sequences of the same characters yield high compression ratios. This technique is particularly useful for encoding black-and-white images in which the data units would be single-bit pixels.

**Run-Length Limited** (RLL) (adj.) Describes a means of storing data on a hard disk. RLL storage increases the density of the data, creating more compact files.

**runtime code** (n.) Program code that allows playback or delivery of a program without requiring the parent application to be present. Most multimedia authoring software tools give the developer the option of outputting a program with runtime code. In this format the program cannot be altered or reverse-engineered and requires less storage space than the parent application.

# S

**S Interface** (n.) In telecommunications, the interface between the ISDN NT-2 network adapter and the user. It allows up to eight devices to be addressed, such as a computer or a telephone. It is often combined with a "T" interface to connect the user directly to the NT-1. An RJ-45 connector is normally used for an "S" interface.

**sabin** (n.) A unit of sound absorption used in acoustical engineering. One sabin is the sound absorption of one square foot of a perfectly absorbing surface, like an open window. The sound absorption of a wall or some other surface is the area of the surface, in square feet, multiplied by a coefficient that depends on the density of the surface and on the frequency of the sound. The unit is named for Wallace Sabine, who applied it in acoustical measurements in 1911.

**safe zone** (n.) The area that is safely within a border in the video frame, so that it does not disappear when viewed on a television screen. When a video signal is displayed on a television monitor, a significant portion of the outer frame is not visible. This could be as much as 20 percent of the frame, which "bleeds" off around the edges and disappears in overscan mode. See also *overscan*.

**SALT** See *Society for Applied Learning Technology.*

**sample** (n.) The measurement of a signal level at one specific instant in time.

**sample-and-hold circuit** (S/H circuit) (n.) A circuit that digitally encodes an analog signal, such as a sound, and stores it in memory for playback at a later time. A digital delay line is an example of a S/H circuit with a user-defined duration between the original sound and its replication.

**sampled sound** (n.) A file containing data representing an event that has been digitally captured from an acoustic waveform rather than data resulting from electronic synthesis. An analog-to-digital converter is used to create an audio sample, which defines the frequency and amplitude of a sound.

**sample rate** (n.) The frequency at which bits of data are recorded in digitizing a sound. Sound is usually sampled at 44.1 kHz or 48 kHz. To reduce the amount of space required to store audio data, rates of 22.050 kHz and 11.025 kHz are used. These rates yield lower quality and are not advisable for high-fidelity music. When a sample encoded at a given bit rate is converted to a higher or a lower rate, some noise is introduced, but this is not nearly as serious as the artifacts generated in bit-rate conversion from 16-bit to 8-bit audio.

**sampling** (n.) Measuring an analog signal periodically or obtaining the values of an analog function by regularly measuring the function. Sampling is a step in the process of converting an analog signal into a digital one. The other steps are quantizing and encoding. Sampling errors can cause aliasing effects and artifacts.

**sampling frequency** (n.) The rate at which an analog signal is sampled each second as it is converted into digital data, also known as the "sample rate." For CD-Audio, the rate is 44 100 samples per second or 44.1 kHz; however, in professional audio applications, other rates are commonly used, such as 32 kHz and 48 kHz. The frequency of 44.056 kHz has also been used. On the original digital audio tape recorders (R-DAT), which used a standard helical-scan video recording mechanism for storage, there was a fixed relationship between sampling frequency and horizontal video frequency. Timing was derived from the same clock by frequency division. For NTSC systems, a sampling frequency of 44 055.94 Hz was adopted. For the PAL TV system, a frequency of 44 100 Hz was adopted. The original R-DAT plays back approximately one tenth of a percent slower. The difference in pitch between the two is imperceptible.

**SAP** See *Separate Audio Program.*

**SAPI** See *Scheduling Application Programming Interface* or *service access point identifier* or *Speech Application Programming Interface.*

**SAS** See *Statistical Analysis System.*

**SASI** See *Shugart Associates System Interface.*

**SATAN** See *Security Administrator Tool for Analyzing Networks.*

**satellite** (n.) A receiver, a repeater, or a regenerator for microwave signals that is in geosyn-

chronous orbit, typically 22,300 miles above the surface of Earth. The "footprint" at this distance is approximately one-third of the globe.

**satellite transmission delay** (n.) The time needed for a signal to travel from an Earth station to a satellite and to bounce back to a receiving station. For radio waves moving at the speed of light (186 000 miles per second) to travel 44 600 miles, the delay is approximately a quarter of a second.

**saturated color** (n.) A bright color, especially red, that does not reproduce well on a video monitor because of its strong chroma component. It tends to saturate the screen with color or to bleed around the edges, producing a blurred image.

**SB** See *Sound Blaster.*

**scalability** (n.) A feature that allows content to be delivered at a range of resolutions, from lot to high. Usually, scalable video or audio technologies allow the same data to be output over a range of quality levels, with better playback systems producing higher-quality products. A scalable font exists in a vector format and consists of a series of mathematical calculations that allow type to be resized without a loss of quality.

**Scalable Processor Architecture** (SPARC) (n.) An instruction set architecture that Sun Microsystems designed for its computers in 1985. SPARC implementations are based on RISC processors, usually contain 128 or 144 registers, and are pipelined for performance. Several different implementations of SPARC exist.

**Scalable Vector Graphics** (SVG) (n.) A language developed by the World Wide Web Consortium (W3C) for describing two-dimensional graphics in Extensible Markup Language (XML). It allows for three types of graphic objects. The first are vector graphic shapes, which may follow paths consisting of straight lines and curves. The second type is images, and the third is text. Graphical objects may be grouped or transformed and layered onto previously rendered objects. Nested transformations, clipping paths, alpha masks, filter effects, and template objects are among the features. SVG drawings may be interactive and dynamic. Animations can be defined and triggered either by embedding SVG animation elements in SVG content, or by scripting. Unlike bitmapped graphics, scalable graphics may be viewed on any type of display.

The MIME type for SVG is "image/svg+xml" according to RFC 3023. SVG files should have the extension .svg on all platforms, and gzip-compressed SVG files should have the extension .svgz on all platforms. SVG files stored on Macintosh HFS (Hierarchical File System) should be given a filetype of svg_, with a space character as the fourth letter.

The SVG Namespace is as follows:
   http://www.w3.org/2000/svg
The Public ID for SVG 1.0 is:
   PUBLIC "-//W3C//DTD SVG 1.0//EN"
System ID for SVG 1.0 is:
   http://www.w3.org/TR/2001/PR-SVG-20010719/DTD/svg10.dtd

Here is an example document type declaration for an SVG document:

<!DOCTYPE svg PUBLIC "-//W3C//DTD SVG 1.0//EN"
"http://www.w3.org/TR/2001/PR-SVG-20010719/DTD/svg10.dtd">

**scalar** 1. (n.) A single number, not a vector or a matrix of numbers. 2. (adj.) Describes a par-

allel processor that performs sequential operations that cannot be vectorized. See also *superscalar.*

**scan** 1. (v.) To convert a document or a graphic on paper or on film to a digital image format. 2. (n.) In relation to video terminology, the rapid journey of the scanning spot back and forth across the scan lines on the back side of a screen. 3. (n.) In laser disc technology, a mode of play in which the player skips over several disc tracks and displays occasional frames as it passes.

**scan area** (n.) The area to which the movement of the light source, the mirror, and the lens in a scanner is restricted.

**scan contrast** (n.) The range of values between white and black areas of a scanned image.

**scan conversion** (n.) The process of putting data into a grid format for display on a raster device. This is a necessary operation when converting from a computer's noninterlaced Video Graphics Array (VGA) format to an interlaced NTSC video source. Poor-quality scan conversion will cause annoying flicker when an NTSC monitor is used as the output from a computer video source.

**scan lines** (n.) The parallel lines on a video screen, from upper left to lower right, along which the scanner travels to pick up and lay down video information. NTSC systems use 525 scan lines to a screen; PAL systems use 625.

**scanner** (n.) 1. A hardware device that digitizes an optical image into an electronic image represented as binary data. This data can be used to create a computerized version of a photo or an illustration. A scanner can perform optical character recognition (OCR), converting printed documents to digital text

S

369

files without requiring keyboard entry. 2. A lexical analyzer.

**scanning frequency** (n.) The number of horizontal or vertical sweeps across a video screen per second.

**scanning spot** (n.) In a cathode-ray tube (CRT), the beam generated by the electron gun that travels across the screen and paints a picture with red, green, and blue dots.

**scan resolution** (n.) The detail of an image as determined by the physical limitations of a scanner as well as by the software settings. Scan resolution is the number of dots per inch (dpi) that the scanner encodes. Higher resolutions create larger files and mean that a scanner must collect more information. It is important to scan at a resolution at least as high as that at which the image will be displayed. Screen resolution is typically only 72 dpi, whereas a standard for laser printing may be 300, 600, or 1200 dpi. High-resolution film scanners can operate at levels above 2400 dpi.

**scan threshold** (n.) A user-defined setting on a scanner that instructs the detection circuitry to operate at a specified level of pixel brightness.

**scattering** (n.) The diffusion of a light beam caused by microscopic variations in the material density of the transmission medium, resulting in light-wave signal loss in optical fiber transmission.

**scene** (n.) 1. Everything visible in a camera's viewfinder. 2. In videography, a sequence of related shots taken in a single location.

**Scheduling Application Programming Interface** (SAPI) (n.) Application Programming In-

terface (API) designed to support software that aids in time management and in arranging activities. The Microsoft SAPI works with its Schedule+ application.

**SCMS** See *Serial Copy Master System.*

**score** 1. (n.) The written notation that represents a musical composition. 2. (v.) To write a musical composition. 3. (n.) In Macromedia Director, the representation of an animation sequence or a movie on a timeline, showing each frame and layer.

**screen** (n.) 1. The viewing area on a monitor, or any surface onto which images are projected. 2. A process used to produce gray levels. In the PostScript language, a screen may be defined by the shape of the spots on the screen, the size of the spots, and the screen angle. See figure.

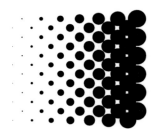

*a screen in PostScript*

**screen dump** (n.) The process of saving the image that appears on a monitor as a graphics file or sending it to a printer.

**screen saver** (n.) A program that replaces the image displayed on a monitor with a shifting pattern that prevents a monitor from being etched by a still image. This program can be set to begin after a predetermined interval of inactivity and usually remains in effect until the mouse is moved or a key is pressed. Older monochrome monitors needed this type of protection, whereas newer color monitors are not at risk.

**scrim** (n.) Translucent material used in video production to defuse the intensity of light. It is placed over a lighting source to distribute the light for a scene more evenly. A scrim is usually made of silk, gauze, or lightweight screen.

**script** (v.) 1. To author in a high-level language by using statements in English that serve as commands. The original scripting language was HyperTalk, developed by Apple Computer. 2. (n.) A document that defines all the elements of a video or a film production, including dialog, camera position, lighting, and the set itself.

**ScriptX** (n.) Developed by the Kaleida alliance, an authoring and playback software system that provides cross-platform portability of multimedia software and that is a universal development tool.

**scroll** (v.) To cause text or graphics on the computer screen to move up or down, progressively revealing more data. Most word-processing programs allow the user to scroll with an upward or a downward arrow in a scroll bar on the side of a text field.

**SCSI** See *Small Computer System Interface.*

**SCSI-1** See *Small Computer System Interface.*

**SCSI-2** See *Small Computer System Interface.*

**SCSI-3** See *Small Computer System Interface.*

**SDDS** See *Sony Dynamic Digital Sound.*

**SDH** See *Synchronous Digital Hierarchy.*

**SDIF** See *Sony digital interface format.*

**SDK** See *software developers kit.*

**SDL** See *Specification and Design Language.*

**SDLC** See *Synchronous Data Link Control.*

**SDMA** See *Space Division Multiple Access.*

**SDN** See *Software Defined Network.*

**SDRAM** See *Synchronous Dynamic RAM.*

**SDSL** See *Asymmetric Digital Subscriber Line.*

**SDV** See *Switched Digital Video.*

**SEA** See *self-extracting archive.*

**search engine** (n.) A database front end that allows a user to seek information on the Internet by keyword. Search engines may look for titles of documents, URLs, headers, or text.

**search time** (n.) The period required to locate specific data in a storage device.

**SEC** See *Single Edge Contact.*

**SECAM** See *Sequentiel Couleurs à Mémoire.*

**secondary cache** (n.) A cache between the primary cache and the main memory that is slower and larger than the primary cache. A secondary cache is typically external, accessed from the CPU.

**sector** (n.) On magnetic recording media, such as hard disks, each of the equal segments, or pie-shaped wedges, into which circular cylin-

**S**

ders are logically divided. See figure.

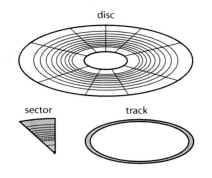

disc

sector          track

*sector layout*

**Secure Electronic Transaction** (SET) (n.) A complex protocol for ensuring the privacy and integrity of information exchanged on the Internet.

**secure network server** (n.) A machine that acts as a gateway between a protected enclave, or LAN, and the outside world.

**Secure Sockets Layer** (SSL) (n.) A protocol developed by Netscape and used by the HTTPS access method. SSL facilitates secure communication over the Internet. It is layered beneath application protocols (HTTP, SMTP, Telnet, FTP), and above the connection protocol (TCP/IP).

**Secure Transfer Protocol** (STP) (n.) A networking protocol that encrypts data.

**Security Administrator Tool for Analyzing Networks** (SATAN) (n.) A freeware program for remotely probing and identifying the vulnerabilities and security weaknesses of computer systems on a network.

**seek time** (n.) The average time required to locate specific data on a disk. It is often com-

puted as the time necessary to move the read head to the correct track and the time needed for the disk to spin one-half of a rotation, the furthest distance from any given point on the disk.

**SEG** See *special effects generator.*

**segment** (n.) 1. In system architecture, a collection of pages in a memory management system. 2. In programming, a separate section of an executable program. 3. A portion of a video or an audio program with the first and last frames or the start and stop points identified, typically by time code. 4. An excerpt from a larger piece.

**segmentation** (n.) In telecommunications, the process of dividing a user data message into smaller frames, blocks, or packets for transmission. Each packet has an integral sequence number used as a reference for reassembly of the complete message at the destination. It is also known as *fragmentation.*

**segue** (n.) A transition between two scenes, events, or musical numbers in a medley. Pronounced "SEG-way."

**self-diagnostics** (n.) Procedures that a system uses to check its own operations and to identify errors, usually performed when power is turned on.

**self-extracting archive** (SEA) (n.) An executable file that automatically decompresses itself when it is run.

**self-noise** (n.) The inherent noise level of a microphone when no signal is present. Microphone inherent self-noise is usually specified as the equivalent sound pressure level (SPL) that would give the same output voltage. Normal values are in the range of 15 to 20 dB SPL.

**self-referential** (adj.) Describes a data reduction technique based on redundancy within an encoded image. JPEG compression is self-referential. Intracoded frames, also known as *I-frames,* apply this concept in MPEG compression.

**semiconductor** (n.) 1. A material with limited conductivity. 2. An electronic component with circuitry that directs signals through gates and pathways based on the conductivity of the material. Transistors, diodes, and integrated circuits (ICs) that perform memory functions are fabricated from semiconductor materials.

**semitone** (n.) A musical interval equal to a half step. An octave is made up of 12 consecutive semitones.

**sendmail** (n.) The Berkeley Software Distribution (BSD) message transfer agent (MTA) that supports mail transport via TCP/IP using Simple Mail Transfer Protocol (SMTP). Sendmail is invoked via a mail user agent (MUA), such as the "mail" command.

**Separate Audio Program** (SAP) (n.) Audio signal that is delivered with a video program and that may be used as an alternative sound track.

**sequence** (n.) A progression of data, events, images, or sounds in a specified order. A *song* may be defined as a sequence of MIDI events.

**sequencer** (n.) 1. A computer or a controlling microprocessor that issues instructions to programmable musical instruments via MIDI. 2. The software program that enables a user to compose and edit music with a MIDI system.

**Sequentiel Couleurs à Mémoire** (SECAM, pronounced "SEE-cam") (n.) Patented by Henri de France in 1956, the French composite video standard adopted in Russia and in many Middle Eastern countries. The basis of operation is the sequential recording of primary colors in alternate lines. Specifications include a 50-Hz field frequency and 625 lines of image resolution. See also *National Television Standards Committee* or *Phase Alternation Line.*

**serial** (adj.) Describes operations pertaining to a series or describes the sequential, time-based passage of data. Serial ports on computers process data one bit at a time in an orderly fashion as they pass information to or from input and output devices, such as modems and printers. The term *serial interface* implies that each bit is sent sequentially, as opposed to having groups of bits sent simultaneously in a parallel interface.

**serial bus** (n.) Physical interface that moves bits of data individually in a series, rather than in groups as a parallel bus does.

**Serial Copy Master System** (SCMS) (n.) A function on digital audio tape (DAT) consumer decks that discourages people from making multiple copies by adding data to the program of dubs that are not first-generation.

**serializer** (n.) A converter that changes data from parallel to serial format. It is used in buses and networks.

**Serial Line Internet Protocol** (SLIP) (n.) Defined in RFC 1055, software that transforms Internet Protocol (IP), which is typically used for Ethernet, so that it can be used on a serial line, such as a modem connected to an RS-232 serial port. SLIP appends a SLIP END character to a standard Internet datagram, allowing it to be distinguished as separate. The standard port configuration is eight data bits with no

373

parity and with EIA or hardware flow control. No error detection is provided. Unlike Point-to-Point Protocol (PPP), a SLIP connection needs to have its IP address configuration set every time it is established.

**serial port** (n.) A connector on a computer in which a serial line connects peripherals that use a bitstream protocol. The usual configuration is a DB-25 connector carrying RS-232 signals. It is also known as a *comport* and is typically connected to a universal asynchronous receiver-transmitter (UART) integrated circuit (IC) that converts between serial and parallel formats.

**serial VTR control** (n.) Serial videotape recorder control; computerized remote control of the functions of a VTR via a normal RS-232 or RS-422 cable connection.

**serif** (n.) In typography, a decorative flourish or a thin line at the top or the bottom of a letter. Fonts without serifs are called *sans serif.*

**server** (n.) 1. A software program that provides a service to a client. Server and client communicate via network hardware and protocols. The server may be a daemon, which constantly awaits requests from clients. Many server types are used on the Internet, including domain name system (DNS), Network File System (NFS), FTP, and Network Information Service (NIS). 2. A networked computer that provides a service for other computers connected to it. One example is a file server with a local disk; this server accommodates requests from remote clients to read and write files on that disk.

**server error** (n.) In relation to a request made on the Internet, an error that occurs at the server. Possible errors reported by a web server include the following:

- 500 = Internal Server Error. The server encountered an unexpected condition, which prevented it from fulfilling the request.

- 501 = Not Implemented. The server is not capable of supporting the request.

- 502 = Bad Gateway. While acting as a gateway or proxy, the server received an invalid response from the upstream server it accessed in attempting to fulfill the request.

- 503 = Service Unavailable. The server was unable to handle the request because of temporary overloading.

**server-parsed HTML** (SPML) (n.) Server-parsed Hypertext Markup Language; a special type of HTML file that includes server-specific commands.

**Server-Side Include** (SSI) (n.) A standard command that allows a web server to generate data and dynamically send it to an HTML document. It is commonly used to automate tasks, such as embedding information in a document as it is requested.

An SSI command begins with an HTML comment as follows:

```
<!--This is the format for a comment-->
```

A Server-Side Include command is embedded in the comment format with the following general syntax:

```
<!--#command tag="value"-->
```

This reference is not to an HTML tag, but rather to a tag that carries information used by the server to process the command. Each SSI command begins with a pound sign (#). Each tag, or parameter of a command, is followed by an equals sign (=) and an assigned value. The following example returns the date and the time that a file was last modified:

```
<!--#echo var="LAST_MODIFIED"-->
```

The syntax and meaning of each SSI command is shown here.

## #echo

Returns the value of a variable. The six variables are:

```
LAST_MODIFIED
DOCUMENT_NAME
DOCUMENT_URI
DATE_LOCAL
DATE_GMT
QUERY_STRING_UNESCAPED
```

Example:

```
Last modified: <EM><!--#echo
var="LAST_MODIFIED"--></EM>
```

Yields the following:

```
Last modified: Tuesday, 18-Jan-02
16:41:36 EST
```

## #include

Used to embed the contents of one file in another file.
Example:

```
<!--#include file="address.txt"-->
</BODY>
</HTML>
```

This script places the text of any file identified in the HTML document that requests it. All that is needed is a reference to the appropriate file instead of retyping that file's contents in a given location.

Another tag that may be used with #include is virtual=. The file= tag requires that the file must be in the same directory as the document. The virtual= tag allows access to any document that the server can find by relative reference.

Example:

```
<!--#include virtual="/directory/
address.txt"-->
```

In this case, the address file can be placed in the site's root directory, and can be accessed from any file, even if it is located at another level in the directory tree.

## #exec

May take either of two tags:

```
cmd=
cgi=
```

The command named in the cmd= tag will be executed using /bin/sh. If the tag is cgi=, the server looks in the specified cgi-bin directory. If the result of the script is a location tag, the server constructs a link to it. Otherwise, the result of the script is merged with the HTML file.

Administrators may disable #exec to prevent it from being used to compromise the security of a site.

## #config

These tags may be used:

```
errmsg=
sizefmt=
```

S

375

```
#fsize=
timefmt=
```

errmsg= determines what message is sent back to the client if an error occurs while parsing the document.

#sizefmt= specifies the formatting to be used when the size of a file is displayed. The options are bytes= or abbrev=.

#fsize= takes either the file= or the virtual= tags, and returns the size of the specified file as formatted by #config.

timefmt= specifies the format to use when the server provides a date. The formatting string comes from Unix's strftime. The options are shown here:

| | |
|---|---|
| %a | The abbreviated weekday |
| %A | The full weekday |
| %b | The abbreviated month name |
| %B | The full month name |
| %d | The day of the month as a decimal number |
| %D | The date in mm/dd/yy format |
| %e | The day of the month in two digits |
| %H | The hour of the 24-hour clock in two digits |
| %I | The hour of the 12-hour clock in two digits |
| %j | The day of the year as a decimal number |
| %m | The month of the year in two digits |
| %M | The minutes of the hour in two digits |
| %p | The local AM or PM string |
| %r | The 12-hour clock time in local HH:MM:SS AM/PM format |
| %S | The seconds of the minute in two digits |
| %T | The 24-hour clock time in HH:MM:SS format |

| | |
|---|---|
| %U | The week of the year in two digits (Sunday first) |
| %w | The day of the week in one digit |
| %W | The week of the year in two digits (Monday first) |
| %y | The year of the century in two digits |
| %Y | Year as a decimal number |
| %Z | The time zone name |

## Variables

Six environment variables are available (exclusive of the CGI variables):

LAST_MODIFIED
Reports the last time the current file was changed.

DOCUMENT_NAME
Reports the document name.

DOCUMENT_URI
Reports the full path relative to the document root.

DATE_LOCAL
Reports the current local date and time.

DATE_GMT
Reports the current Greenwich mean time in timefmt= format.

QUERY_STRING_UNESCAPED
Reports the query string sent by the client, if any.

## Using Server-Side Includes

The SSIs must be enabled at the server level. They may be enabled for an entire site or for individual directories. They may be activated for all files or only for files with a special file extension, such as "shtml."

When the server receives a GET request from

376

a client, it checks to see if the requested file ends in shtml. If it does, the server examines the file for SSIs because of the file extension. Directives are found and processed, and the entire document is sent back with content-type set to text/html if the following line was placed in the srm.conf file:

```
AddType text/html shtml
```

The server will parse a file only if the correct file extension is used.

## Testing SSI

The following HTML document, named test.shtml, will test whether SSI is enabled on a server:

```
<HTML>
<HEAD>
<TITLE>Test for Server-Side Includes</
TITLE>
</HEAD>
<BODY>
<P>
The date last modified<BR>
<!--#echo var="LAST_MODIFIED"-->
</BODY>
</HTML>
```

When accessed, the test.shtml page should produce the following output, depending on how the time format is configured:

```
The date last modified
Fri January 18 08:15:47 2002
```

SSIs are useful for implementing standard features on a site. Most sites have the same background on all pages, a copyright notice, and a link to the webmaster. The #include SSI can automate placing this type of information on every page.

Create the following template in a text editor for pages with included body and footer

```
<HTML>
<HEAD>
<TITLE>Template</TITLE>
</HEAD>
<!--#include virtual="body.inc"-->
<H1>Header</H1>
<P>
</P>
<!--#include virtual="footer.inc"-->
</BODY>
</HTML>
```

Save this file as template.shtml, or with the appropriate file extension for your server. Note that included files are named with the extension "inc" rather than "html." The included files contain HTML, but they are not complete legal documents. This is simply a way to reference the contents of the file.

The body.inc file might contain the following:

```
<BODY BACKGROUND="wallpaper.gif">
<A HREF="AboutUs.shtml"><IMG
SRC="Images/logo.gif"
ALT="Logo" HEIGHT= 100 WIDTH=60>
```

The footer might contain copyright information and a link to the webmaster's email address. If that information changes, it only needs to be changed once in the "footer.inc" file.

Server-Side Includes are effectively used to automate a site and to provide information on the fly for visitors.

**service access point identifier** (SAPI) (n.) The logical location where data-link layer services are provided to the network layer. Used as ISDN jargon.

**service module** (SM) (n.) A term sometimes used by the telephone company to describe the equipment that terminates a channel at the service point and connects a telephone line to a customer's router or some other interface.

**service provider** (n.) An entity that buys the services of a telecommunications supplier, advertises the service, and handles the calls.

**serving area** (n.) 1. The vicinity of a broadcasting station where signal strength is at or above a stated level. 2. The geographic area handled by a telephone central office facility, most often equivalent to a LATA.

**servocontrol** (n.) A device that converts weak mechanical force into greater force, which is a particularly useful function for a controlling mechanism that positions a lever, a gear, or a drive head.

**servo-loop mechanism** (n.) A self-regulating feedback system. It consists of a sensing element, an amplifier, and a servomotor to automatically control a mechanical device. In audio, this usually refers to a class of electronic control circuits comprised of an amplifier and a feedback path from the output signal that is compared with a reference signal. This topology creates an error signal that is the difference between the reference and the output signal. The error signal causes the output to do whatever is necessary to reduce the error to zero. One example is a loudspeaker system with motional feedback. A sensor is attached to the speaker cone and provides a feedback signal that is compared against the driving signal to create more accurate control of the loudspeaker.

**session** (n.) 1. A CD-ROM recording event. If a single-session recording is closed out, no more data may be added to the disc or the index. A multisession CD-ROM XA drive will read multiple indexes, which are created when data is stored in more than one writing session on the same CD-ROM. 2. In telecommunications, a series of communications between two stations during one connection, or the logical connection between two network addressable units (NAU).

**session layer** (n.) The fifth layer in the Open Systems Interconnection (OSI) model. The session layer provides a means of communication and dialog control between end systems.

**set** (n.) A group of objects that share an identifiable characteristic. For every set, there is a predicate that is true only for those objects in the set.

**SET** See *Secure Electronic Transaction.*

**set-top box** (n.) Receiving equipment that sits on top of a television set and acts as an interface to a broadband network. It may be a simple device that translates cable television (CATV) frequencies, or it may be a complex digital device with signal processors that decode MPEG-2 satellite transmissions and demodulate them for viewing on an analog television set. It is expected that next-generation boxes will be addressable and capable of two-way communication.

**SFX** See *sound effects.*

**SGML** See *Standard Generalized Markup Language.*

**SGRAM** See *Synchronous Graphics RAM.*

**shading** (n.) In three-dimensional graphics, the gradation from light to dark, or the blending of colors on a surface. Flat shading is quickly computed but is of low quality. Gouraud shading provides better image quality but takes somewhat longer. Phong shading is of excellent quality but takes a long time to perform the necessary calculations for each pixel.

**shadow mask** (n.) A method of construction for a display or a cathode-ray tube (CRT). The shadow mask is like a panel with very small holes situated behind the screen. The holes correspond to triad locations on the screen. The shadow mask guides the electron beams to strike one of the three phosphors in a triad. See figure.

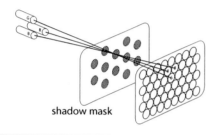
shadow mask

*shadow mask*

**shadow RAM** (n.) Shadow random-access memory; a physical memory location in IBM-compatible computers where ROM code that is frequently accessed is stored in RAM to accelerate performance. The BIOS code that is normally executed in the slower ROM is copied, or "shadowed," in RAM to improve performance.

**shallow binding** (n.) A method of storing variable bindings. In this method, one can find the current value of a variable by looking at a known location rather than by searching an environment or an association list.

**Shannon, Claude E.** (1916–) An American mathematician, known as the father of infor-

mation theory. In his master's thesis, Shannon demonstrated that Boolean algebra could be represented in electronic circuits by switches and relays.

**shared access** (n.) In network technology, an access method that permits multiple stations to use the same transmission medium. Contended and explicit access are types of shared access. Compare *discrete access,* in which each station has to have a separate connection.

**shared disc** (n.) A CD-ROM or a laser disc created through a joint production. A segment of the disc is allocated to each contributor.

**shareware** (n.) User-supported software program transferred or sold with the understanding that a fee will be paid to the program author if it meets the user's needs.

**sharpen** (v.) To enhance the distinction between darker and lighter pixels. Lines, edges, and other details in an image can be exaggerated through sharpening. Sharpening can enhance blemishes in the original, so it must be used judiciously. In the Adobe Photoshop program, the sharpen function appears as one of the filters with which a graphic selection may be processed.

**S/H circuit** See *sample-and-hold circuit.*

**shell** (n.) The user interface. A shell is an external layer of a program that provides the user with controls and access to information. Common shells in the Unix environment are Bourne, tcsh, and Korn.

**shelving response** (n.) Describes a flat (shelf-like) end-band shape when applied to program equalization. Bass and treble tone controls exhibit such a response.

379

**shielding** (n.) A metallic foil or a braid that wraps conductors in a cable to reduce interference from magnetic fields.

**Shift-click** (v., n.) To hold down the Shift key while clicking the mouse. In most Macintosh and Microsoft Windows applications, this key combination allows the user to select a range of text between the original cursor position and the spot where the Shift-click takes place. It may be used to select multiple items on the desktop, as well.

**Shockwave** (n.) A plug-in for a web browser that allows the user to view files created with Macromedia Director. "Shocked" files may contain compressed audio, animations, and a high degree of interactivity.

**short** (n.) Any video or film that lasts less than 35 minutes.

**shorthand** (n.) A system of abbreviated communication, consistently used during "talk" sessions and in chat rooms. Examples:

| | |
|---|---|
| /\/\/\ | laughter |
| AFK | Away from keyboard |
| BCNU | Be seein' you |
| BRB | Be right back |
| BTW | By the way |
| CUL8R | See you later |
| ENQ? | Are you there? |
| FOAF | Friend of a friend |
| FYI | For your information |
| \<g> | grin |
| IMHO | In my humble opinion |
| LTNS | Long time, no see |
| OIC | Oh, I see |
| OTOH | On the other hand |
| ROTFL | Rolling on the floor laughing |
| RTFM | Read the f***** manual |
| SEC | Wait a second |

| | |
|---|---|
| TIA | Thanks in advance |
| TMK | To my knowledge |
| TNX | Thanks |
| TTFN | Ta ta for now |
| WRT | With respect to |

**Short Messaging Service** (SMS) (n.) A method of delivering a brief message of fewer than about 160 characters to a digital cellular phone. Global System for Mobile Communications (GSM) phones have SMS capability. Users can send text-based messages from one device to another. Private SMS services include weather reports, news, and stock quotes.

**shot** (n.) In production work, a continuous run with a film or a videotape recorder (VTR).

**shovelware** (n.) Software of little value that is added to a CD-ROM containing a primary application to fill up space in the package.

**show control** See *MIDI Show Control.*

**Shugart Associates System Interface** (SASI, pronounced "SASS-y") (n.) The original incarnation of SCSI.

**SI** See *Système International d'Unités.*

**SI Unit prefix revision** See *Système International Unit prefix revision.*

**sibilant** (adj.) In linguistics, this describes a hissing sound like that of "s" or "sh."

**SID** See *System Identification.*

**sideband** (n.) A narrow frequency located above or below the primary frequency in a telecommunications signal.

**sidetone** (n.) In telephony, a brief line echo fed

back into the earpiece. Too much sidetone creates a perceptible echo, while too little sidetone renders the signal inaudible. Sidetones can cause acoustic feedback in teleconferencing systems if not controlled.

**SIF** See *Source Image Format.*

**SIG** See *special interest group.*

**SIGGRAPH** (Pronounced "SEE-graf") (n.) Special interest group for computer graphics; an association of computer users who share an interest in graphics. SIGGRAPH is supported by the Association for Computing Machinery (ACM) and holds an annual conference that is well attended by designers, educators, and software-hardware developers in the field of graphics.

**Signaling System 7** (SS7) (n.) Out-of-band (OOB) signaling system that uses high-speed, circuit-switched connections to process remote database interactions and provide fast call setup. SS7 makes enhanced telephony features available, such as call forwarding, caller ID, and call waiting. It plays an integral role in the deployment of ISDN. The SS7 protocol consists of the following four subprotocols:

1. Message Transfer Part (MTP), which provides functions for basic routing of signaling messages between signaling points.
2. Signaling Connection Control Part (SCCP), which provides additional routing and management functions for transfer of messages other than call setup between signaling points.
3. ISDN User Part (ISUP), which provides for transfer of call setup signaling information between signaling points.
4. Transaction Capabilities Application Part (TCAP), which provides for transfer of

non-circuit-related information between signaling points.

**signal switching point** (SSP) (n.) A telephone company switch that recognizes Intelligent Network calls and routes them according to information provided by a database.

**signal-to-noise** (S/N) (adj.) Describes the ratio between the strength of an audio or a video signal and the measurable amount of noise, or the undesirable interference, it has picked up in transfer. Higher S/N ratios mean higher-quality signals. Each generation of a tape dub has a lower S/N ratio. Digital media can achieve much higher S/N ratios than analog media can, and degradation does not occur in digital copies.

**signal transfer point** (STP) (n.) The packet switch in the Common Channel Interoffice Signaling (CCIS) system. The CCIS is a packet-switched telephone network that converts dialed digits into data, operating at 4.8 kilobits per second (Kbps).

**signature** (n.) 1. Information about the sender of an electronic mail message or a news posting appended at the end of an email message. A signature may include an ASCII logo or a memorable quote. 2. In programming, a means of separating subtyping and inheritance. The concept is similar to that of abstract base classes, but signatures have their own hierarchy and can be applied to compiled classes.

**silicon** (n.) A nonmetallic element used in the semiconductor industry as a substrate for multiple layers of material on which electrical circuits are created. Silicon begins as a crystal and grows to form a cylindrical "log," which is sliced into thin sections (typically 1/40 inch thick)

S

to create bare wafers.

**silicon-based life form** (n.) Jargon for a very intelligent machine based on silicon chips. Compare *carbon-based life form*.

**SIM** See *Subscriber Identity Module*.

**SIMD** See *single instruction, multiple data*.

**SIMM** See *single in-line memory module*.

**Simple Internet Protocol Plus** (SIPP) (n.) A proposed standard for IP version 6 (IPv6), also known as IP Next Generation (IPng). One of the problems addressed by this new architecture is the need for more Internet addresses. IPv6 is defined in RFC 1752.

**Simple Mail Transfer Protocol** (SMTP) (n.) A server-to-server protocol used to transfer email between computers. SMTP is defined in RFC 821, STD 10. It is not the same protocol used to read messages sent through email.

**Simple Management Protocol** (SMP) (n.) A popular standard for network management.

**Simple Network Management Protocol** (SNMP) (n.) The Internet standard protocol used to manage nodes on an Internet Protocol (IP) network. SNMP is defined in RFC 1157, STD 15. SNMP version 2 (SNMP v2) is a revision of SNMP that improves security, performance, confidentiality, and communication between managers. The main components are defined in RFCs 1441 through 1452.

**Simple Network Paging Protocol** (SNPP) (n.) A standard for sending one-way and two-way wireless messages to pagers. SNPP is defined in RFC 1861. It creates a link between the Internet and a Telocator Alphanumeric Pro-

tocol (TAP) paging terminal.

**simple profile** (n.) Streams of MPEG that use only intracoded frames (I-frames) and predictive-coded frames (P-frames), employing less buffer memory for decoding. Coding with a simple profile is less efficient than coding with bidirectionally predictive frames (B-frames). See also *MPEG frame type*.

**simplex** (n.) One-way transmission with the capacity either to send or to receive but not to do both at once.

**simulated annealing** (n.) A process based on successive update steps in which the length of each update step is proportional to an arbitrarily set parameter that is analogous to the role of a temperature. Simulated annealing may be applied to any minimization or learning process, and the steps may be either random or deterministic. As in the annealing of metals, the temperature is highest in the early stages of the process, which accelerates minimization or learning, and it is reduced for increased stability in later steps.

**simulation** (n.) The use of images and sound to represent a situation or an event somewhat realistically. The simulation mode is useful in training applications, enabling users to learn how to operate equipment. New techniques and technologies have evolved rapidly for simulating virtual reality (VR) with three-dimensional models, walk-throughs, and fly-bys.

**sine curve** (n.) In mathematics, the graph of the equation $y = \sin x$, also known as a sinusoid.

**sine wave** (n.) A simple, regular vibration at a single frequency, devoid of harmonic overtones. See figure.

**Sine wave**

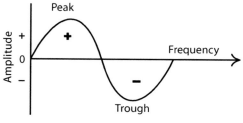

*sine wave*

**single-attached** (adj.) Connected to only one of the two rings of a Fiber Distributed Data Interface (FDDI) network. A host computer is typically connected in this fashion, whereas routers and concentrators are typically dual-attached.

**Single Edge Contact** (SEC) (n.) The housing cartridge for a Pentium II daughterboard that plugs into a card-edge processor slot on the motherboard. The standard Pentium II requires a 242-pin slot (Slot 1), while the Zeon fits in a 330-pin slot (Slot 2). Slot 1 is referred to as SEC-242, and Slot 2 is referred to as SEC-330.

**single-ended** (adj.) Describes an electrical connection with one hot wire and a second ground wire. In a *differential connection,* by contrast, a second hot wire carries an inverted version of the original signal.

**single inheritance** (n.) A way in which inheritance is resisted when a subclass may be derived from only one parent in an object-oriented language.

**single in-line memory module** (SIMM, pronounced "SIM") (n.) A high-density DRAM package with several plastic leaded chip carriers (PLCCs) connected to a single printed circuit board.

**single in-line package** (SIP) (n.) A form factor for a board-level component, such as a transistor whose connections all extend from one side.

**single-instruction, multiple-data** (SIMD) (n.) Parallel processing architecture in which one instruction operates on several pieces of data at once.

**single large expensive disk** (SLED) (n.) One high-capacity hard drive, as opposed to a redundant arrays of independent disks (RAID).

**Single-Line Digital Subscriber Line** (SDSL) (n.) See *Asymmetric Digital Subscriber Line.*

**single-mode fiber** (n.) A type of optical fiber that supports a single mode of light propagation above a cutoff wavelength. The core diameter is typically 5 to 10 mm, and transmission rates approach 100 GHz per kilometer.

**single-sideband transmission** (n.) A method of radio transmission in which one sideband of the carrier signal is transmitted and the other sideband is suppressed. The carrier wave may either be transmitted or suppressed.

**SIP** See *single in-line package.*

**SIPP** See *Simple Internet Protocol Plus.*

**SIT** See *StuffIt.*

**site** (n.) A web address or any Internet location where information can be viewed or accessed with a browser or a client application.

A home page is usually the access point to a web site.

**sitemap** (n.) A model showing the organization of a web site, often with links to the individual pages on the site. More elaborate sitemaps that provide a hierarchical description of a site may be written in the resource description format (RDF), an XML application. A browser finds an RDF sitemap by locating the <LINK rel=sitemap> tags embedded in pages on a site. These tags instruct the browser to open the sitemap and render a graphical display of the site diagram. This was one of the first implementations of RDF.

**skinny DIP** (skinny dual in-line package) (n.) Jargon for a 24- or 28-position switch with a 0.3-inch row-to-row centerline.

**skirt** (n.) Jargon for the Q-factor, or bandwidth, that is attenuated by an equalizer. See *Q*.

**skylight** (n.) In videography, a clear glass filter that absorbs ultraviolet (UV) light and reduces haze. A skylight is often used as a lens protector.

**slate** (n.) A term derived from the movie industry, in which a slate board is held up to indicate the beginning of a new "take." In a recording studio, the slate usually consists of the engineer's voice, which identifies the take number, and an accompanying log sheet with the title, duration, and other particulars about the take.

**slave** (n.) 1. In computing, a secondary unit, such as a disk drive, that is controlled by the master device or system. 2. A videotape machine whose transport system is controlled by a source deck or other master device.

**SLED** See *single large expensive disk*.

**slew rate** (n.) The maximum rate of change in an amplifier's output voltage with respect to its input voltage. It is essentially a measure of an amplifier's ability to follow its input signal rapidly and accurately.

**sliding window** (n.) A flow control technique used between two DCE devices that regulates the number of unacknowledged data packets or frames on the network. A network protocol may specify a particular technique for regulating the size of the window. TCP uses a sliding window algorithm.

**SLIP** See *Serial Line Internet Protocol*.

**slot mask** (n.) A method of guiding electron beams in a monitor. It is made of vertical wires that create the slots. The dot pitch in a slot mask is the space between the slots.

**slow motion** (n.) Display of frames in forward or in reverse at a slower-than-normal rate.

**SM** See *service module*.

**Small Computer System Interface** (SCSI, pronounced "SKUH-zee") (n.) An independent standard for a system-level interface between computers and such peripherals as hard disks, CD-ROMs, printers, and scanners. SCSI can connect a number of devices to a single controller on the computer's bus. All SCSI chains require termination at both ends, and devices on a SCSI chain must be set to different ID numbers. SCSI connections normally use single-ended drivers, as opposed to differential drivers. Single-ended SCSI can support up to six meters of cable, whereas differential SCSI can support up to 25 meters. Apple Computer established the SCSI interface in 1984 on the Macintosh computer. It was developed by Shugart Associates, which later became Seagate, so SCSI was originally called *Shugart Associates*

*System Interface (SASI)* before it became an ANSI standard in 1986. The original standard is now called *SCSI-1* to distinguish it from SCSI-2 and SCSI-3, which include specifications for wide SCSI and fast SCSI, described in the paragraphs below.

- SCSI-1: Small Computer System Interface version 1; an eight-bit-wide parallel bus used to connect disk drives and all types of peripherals to an IBM-compatible PC or to a Macintosh. The origins of SCSI are found in the selector channel architecture designed by IBM for its System/360 computers. In 1981, Shugart Associates adapted it and called it the *Shugart Associates Systems Interface (SASI)*. By 1984 Apple Computer had incorporated it in the Macintosh. In 1986, ANSI released the first version of the SCSI standard. That original version is now called *SCSI-1*.

SCSI supports hard disk drives, CD-ROM drives, optical storage units, scanners, high-speed printers, and Group 4 fax machines. Up to eight devices can share the bus, including the host controller. Each device on the bus is manually assigned a SCSI ID number between 0 and 7 by means of a switch or jumper. The number of devices supported per bus is limited by the width of the data bus. A SCSI-1 chain may include eight devices, whereas a 16-bit-wide SCSI-2 or SCSI-3 bus may support up to 16 devices.

The SCSI adapter in the host PC is normally assigned SCSI ID 7, because the highest number wins a bus arbitration. Peripherals are usually assigned IDs starting at 0. Each end of a SCSI bus must be terminated with a resistor. Other devices on the SCSI bus must not be terminated.

---

### Types of SCSI Connectors

| Connector End P=male; S=female | Description |
| --- | --- |
| RC-50 P/S | full-pitch Centronic 50-pin |
| DB-25 P/S | full-pitch D-Sub 25-pin |
| DB-50 P/S | full-pitch D-Sub 50-pin |
| RCII-50 P/S | Centronic half-pitch micro connector 50-pin |
| DBII-50 P/S | D-Sub half-pitch micro connector 50-pin |
| RC3-68 P/S | Centronic half-pitch micro connector 68-pin |
| DB3-68 P/S | D-Sub half-pitch micro connector 68-pin |

---

Macintosh computers and peripherals are connected by either DB-25 or DB-50 SCSI connectors. IBM-compatible PCs use the RJ-21 Centronics-style 50-pin connector for SCSI-1 devices. To manage peripherals on a SCSI bus, Advanced SCSI Programming Interface (ASPI) software is used in the IBM PC environment. SCSI supports multiple host adapters on each bus, so that two computers may be connected to the same SCSI bus and can control the same peripheral.

SCSI data transfers may be either asynchronous or synchronous. In the asynchronous mode there is a handshake for each transferred byte, and the maximum data transfer rate is about two megabits per second (Mbps). In the synchronous mode data flows at a preset data rate, which is commonly five Mbps for SCSI-1 devices. The initiator and the target peripheral must support synchronous transfers at the same speed.

- SCSI-2: Small Computer System Interface version 2; enhancement to the SCSI-1 specification that delivers more compatibility among devices and faster data transfer rates. *Fast SCSI* is a subset of SCSI-2 and supports transfer rates of up to 10 megabits per second (Mbps), double the five-Mbps rate of SCSI-1 on an eight-bit-wide bus. The SCSI-2 specification defines five device types not covered by SCSI-1.

The original eight-bit-wide SCSI-1 bus is called *narrow SCSI*. The connectors for the 16-bit-wide bus differs from the SCSI-1 connector. A cable with 50-pin Micro-D-type connectors is specified for 16-bit transfers. For the 32-bit bus, or *wide SCSI*, a 68-pin P-type connector is specified. The SCSI-2 bus requires an odd parity bit for every eight data bits, whereas parity was optional in SCSI-1.

A fast, wide SCSI bus can support data transfer at up to 40 Mbps, although actual transfer rates from a disk drive are typically much lower, depending on the speed of the drive. SCSI-2 controllers support different speeds of transfer to each SCSI device on the bus, so both SCSI-1 and SCSI-2 devices can coexist. An extension of SCSI-2 called *ultra SCSI* doubles the transfer speed of fast SCSI to allow transfer rates of 20 Mbps on an eight-bit connection and 40 Mbps on a 16-bit connection.

The following is a comparison of maximum theoretical data transfer rates for hard drive interfaces. Actual throughput is much slower than these maximum rates, depending on drive access times and other factors in each computer system.

| Disk Interface | Maximum Transfer Rate |
|---|---|
| SCSI-1 (asynchronous) | 2 Mbps |
| SCSI-1 (synchronous) | 5 Mbps |
| SCSI-2 fast | 10 Mbps |
| SCSI-2 16-bit-wide | 10 Mbps |
| SCSI-2 fast and 16-bit-wide | 20 Mbps |
| SCSI-2 32-bit-wide | 20 Mbps |
| SCSI-2 fast and 32-bit-wide | 40 Mbps |

When SCSI-2 and SCSI-3 devices first connect asynchronously, they handshake in eight-bit narrow mode to ensure that data will transfer properly. The initiator and target then negotiate the maximum mutual capabilities.

- SCSI-3: Small Computer System Interface version 3; enhancement to SCSI-2 that sup-

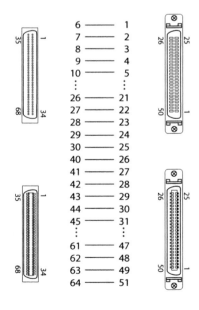

*SCSI connectors—68-pin to 50-pin conversion*

ports up to 32 devices per bus with 16-bit transfers over a P-cable (using a 68-pin Micro-D-type connector). A subset of SCSI-3 called *fast-20* supports the transfer of data at up to 20 megabits per second (Mbps) over the original eight-bit "narrow" bus and up to 40 Mbps over a 16-bit-wide P-cable. Fast-20 controllers allow both fast and slow devices on the same bus. Because of the higher transfer rate, cables should not exceed 3 meters in length for single-ended SCSI buses, about half the distance allowed in SCSI-2 connections. For a differential bus the maximum length is 25 meters, which is the same as for SCSI-2. SCSI-2 has largely replaced SCSI-1, but SCSI-3 is not as prevalent.

### SCSI-3 Standards

| Standard Number | Description |
| --- | --- |
| X3T9.2/9–10 | SCSI-3 Parallel Interface |
| X3T9.2/91–11 | SCSI-3 Interlocked Protocol |
| X3T9.2/91–13R2 | SCSI-3 Generic Packetized Protocol (GPP) |
| X3T9.2/91–189 | SCSI-3 Serial Bus Protocol (SBP) |
| X3T9.2/92–079 | SCSI-3 Architecture Model |
| X3T9.2/92–103 | SCSI-3 Fiber Channel Protocol (GPP & SBP) |
| X3T9.2/92–105 | SCSI-3 Core Commands |
| X3T9.2/92–106 | SCSI-3 Block Commands |
| X3T9.2/92–107 | SCSI-3 Stream Commands |
| X3T9.2/92–108 | SCSI-3 Graphic Commands |
| X3T9.2/92–109 | SCSI-3 Medium Changer Commands |
| X3T9.2/92–141 | SCSI-3 Queuing Model |

SCSI-3 features a serial option using a six-pin connector. *Serial SCSI* supports various types of media, including fiber and twisted pairs for distances of up to a kilometer. The serial version offers a structured protocol model, faster data transfer, longer cables, and more device classes. It increases to 32 the number of devices that may share a bus. Embedding clock information in the serial data stream eliminates signal delay problems. SCSI-3 is a combination of separate standards defined by separate groups, as listed in the SCSI-3 table.

**small-office/home-office** (soho) (adj.) Describes the market for a general level of features and sophistication in computers and peripherals.

**Smalltalk** (n.) An early object-oriented programming (OOP) system developed in 1972 by the Xerox PARC Software Concepts Group, led by Alan Kay. The system components are an interpreted language, a programming environment, and an object library. Innovations include a windowing system and a mouse. Smalltalk does not have multiple inheritance, so each class may have only one superclass.

**smart card** (n.) A device resembling a credit card with an embedded integrated circuit (IC) for storing data. Smart cards have been used to store medical and financial records, and a wide range of applications exist, including user profiles for network access worldwide.

**SmartDrive** (n.) Developed by Microsoft, a disk-caching program that speeds up disk access. A one-megabyte (MB) cache is usually adequate for most systems. At the prompt in DOS, one may type "SMARTDRV /S" to determine the size of the disk cache, to receive a report on cache hits, and to learn which drives are being cached. The hit-and-miss statistics help gauge the effectiveness of SmartDrive settings. A score in the high 80s shows that SmartDrive is well configured. A percentage below 80 indicates that the cache size should be increased. The SMARTDRV line in the autoexec.bat file may be edited to increase both the InitCacheSize and the WinCacheSize pa-

**S**

rameters. SmartDrive Monitor is an undocumented Windows program included with DOS 6.0 for managing the disk cache.

**smart hub** (n.) A concentrator for twisted-pair Ethernet or for ARCnets. Smart hub has management features that allow an administrator to configure a network and monitor performance.

**SMDS** See *switched multimegabit data service.*

**SME** See *subject matter expert.*

**SMF** See *Standard MIDI File.*

**smoothing filter** See *anti-imaging filter.*

**SMP** See *Simple Management Protocol.* May also refer to *Symbolic Manipulation Program* or *symmetrical multiprocessing.*

**SMPTE** See *Society of Motion Picture and Television Engineers.*

**SMR** See *Specialized Mobile Radio.*

**SMS** See *System Management Server* or *Short Messaging Service.*

**SMTP** See *Simple Mail Transfer Protocol.*

**smurfing** (n.) Committing a denial of service attack by spoofing the source address of an echo-request ICMP (ping) packet to the broadcast address for a network, which causes all the machines on the network to respond at once to the victim, thereby clogging the network.

**S/N** See *signal-to-noise.*

**SNA** See *Systems Network Architecture.*

**snail mail** (n.) Letters sent via the U.S. postal service.

**snarf** (v.) To appropriate a large document or a file for the purpose of using it with or without the author's permission.

**SND** (n.) A Macintosh audio file format used for system sounds, as well as for recording and playback of audio.

**sneakernet** (n.) Jargon for transferring electronic information by physically carrying media from one machine to another. Depending on the type of media and the amount of data, using sneakernet may be more efficient than using a network.

**sniffer** (n.) A program used to capture data across a computer network. Hackers use it to capture user names and passwords. A sniffer audits and identifies network traffic packets, and it is used legitimately by network administrators to troubleshoot network problems.

**SNMP** See *Simple Network Management Protocol.*

**SNPP** See *Simple Network Paging Protocol.*

**Society for Applied Learning Technology** (SALT) (n.) An association of educators and instructional designers. SALT promotes technology in education.

**Society of Motion Picture and Television Engineers** (SMPTE, pronounced "SIM-tee") 1. (n.) A professional engineering society that works to develop standards for motion picture and television equipment. 2. (adj.) Describes the SMPTE time code standard implemented in professional video-editing systems. See also *time code.*

**socket** (n.) The means of creating a virtual connection between processes in a Unix system. Sockets provide the interface with network communication facilities. They can be of two types: the bidirectional stream or the fixed-length, destination-addressed datagram. A socket has a socket address, consisting of a port number and the local host's network address.

**software** (n.) The part of a computing system that is not hardware. A distinction may be made between system software and application software, or programs. *System software* typically includes an operating system that controls other programs; user environment software, such as a command line interpreter, a window system, and a desktop; tools for building other programs, such as assemblers, compilers, linkers, libraries, interpreters, cross-reference generators, and version control; debugging, profiling, and monitoring tools; and utility programs for sorting, printing, editing, and so forth. *Application programs* perform functions, such as accounting or designing. Such software includes both source code written by humans and executable machine code produced by assemblers or compilers. It does not usually include the data processed by programs, unless this is in a format such as multimedia that depends on the use of computers for its presentation.

**Software Defined Network** (SDN) (n.) A service of the public telephone network that gives users the appearance of a private network. An IXC or LEC permits a user to have access to partitions within their DACS equipment, so that the user can reconfigure leased circuits within the public network. Network management information is also provided to the user for their circuits. AT&T introduced this service in 1985 for their largest customers using dedicated access, and refer to it as a type of Virtual Private Network (VPN).

**software developers kit** (SDK) (n.) Software that enables an application or a product to be integrated with systems, hardware, and other software.

**software handshaking** (n.) The transmission of data between two devices to establish their connection. It may involve sending Ctrl-S and Ctrl-Q characters to stop and to start transmission over an RS-232 connection.

**software interrupt** (n.) A suspension of processing caused by a machine language operation code rather than by a hardware event. It causes the processor to store the current state, store identifying information about the interrupt, and pass processor control to a first-level interrupt handler. A *trap* is similar, but it is caused by an unexpected software condition rather than by an intentional instruction.

**soho** See *small-office/home-office.*

**Solaris** (n.) Developed by Sun Microsystems, a common user environment that includes the Unix operating system and an X11-based window system. Solaris 2.x includes the SunOS 5.x version of Unix, OpenWindows 3.x, and tooltalk.

**solid-state laser** (n.) Light-emitting diode (LED) whose active medium is glass or crystal.

**solo** (v.) In recording and live-sound mixing, monitoring a single channel without affecting the main outputs. In many console designs, pressing the solo button on a channel will cause that channel to replace the main mix. This is called destructive solo.

**sone** (n.) A subjective unit of loudness, as perceived by a person with normal hearing, equal to the loudness of a pure tone having a frequency of 1,000 hertz at 40 decibels sound pressure level.

**SONET** See *Synchronous Optical Network.*

**Sony digital interface format** (SDIF) (n.) Sony's professional digital audio interface that uses a BNC-type connector for each of the two audio channels. It also uses a separate BNC-type connector for word synchronization, shared between both channels. All connections are made with unbalanced 75 ohm coaxial cables of the exact same length to preserve synchronization.

**Sony Dynamic Digital Sound** (SDDS) (n.) Sony Corporation's proprietary format for motion picture digital soundtrack systems. The signal is optically printed outside the sprocket holes along both sides of the film. Sony recently developed a single camera system that records all three digital audio formats (dolby digital, DTS, and SDDS) on a single inventory print.

**Sony 9-pin** (n.) Standard connector used for serial machine control of professional videotape and audio tape transports. The term refers to the DB-9 connector or to the port on a device.

**Sony/Philips Digital Interface Format** (s/pdif, pronounced "SPID-if") (n.) A standard for interconnecting stereo digital audio devices, similar to the Audio Engineering Society/European Broadcast Union (AES/EBU) but with lower-grade wiring. The specification is referred to as *IEC 958 Type 11.*

**SOP** See *standard operating procedures.*

**Sorenson Video codec** (n.) A high-quality, low-

bandwidth QuickTime video codec.

**sort** (v.) To arrange objects in a certain order. In a database the objects consist of one or more fields or members. One of the fields is the designated *sort key,* which means that the records will be ordered according to the values of that field.

**sound** (n.) Vibrations transmitted through a solid, a liquid, or a gas, with frequencies in the approximate range of 20 to 20,000 hertz, capable of being detected by human ears. Sound waves in the air consist of rapid variations, or disturbances in the air pressure around a steady-state value.

**Sound Blaster** (SB) 1. (n.) Developed by Creative Labs, an audio card for IBM-compatible computers that has become a de facto standard in the industry. 2. (adj.) Describes compatibility with SB software drivers, setup instructions, and configuration parameters.

**Sound Blaster AWE32** (n.) Sound Blaster Advanced WavEffect 32; common 16-bit sound card with the EMU8000 music synthesizer circuitry. The card features the Advanced Signal Processor, one megabyte (MB) of General MIDI samples, and 512 kilobytes (KB) of DRAM for additional samples. It supports CD-ROM drives by Creative Labs, Mitsumi, and Sony. It also supports General MIDI, Roland GS, and Sound Canvas MT-32 emulation.

**sound card** (n.) A circuit board added to the motherboard of a microcomputer. A sound card generates audio signals and provides output to headphones or to external speakers.

**sound effects** (SFX) (n.) Imported sounds, prerecorded and incorporated into a video sound track or an audio mix to enhance it.

**sound pressure level** (SPL) (n.) The amplitude of an audio waveform in the atmosphere.

**Sound Recorder** (n.) An applet, available in Microsoft Windows, that creates .wav audio files. The quality of the audio depends on the quality of the microphone used and the sampling circuitry on the installed sound card. To ensure the highest signal-to-noise (S/N) ratio, audio recordings should always be made by adjusting the input levels so that the meters reach, but do not exceed, peak levels. In digital recording, little headroom exists beyond the peak level, and input levels that are too hot will cause ugly distortion.

**sound track** (n.) The audio recording associated with a movie or a videotape production.

**source code** (n.) The text in which a computer program is written. It is then compiled into machine code which a processor can execute.

**Source Image Format** (SIF, pronounced "SIFF") (n.) A video parameter that specifies a resolution of 352 x 240 pixels at 30 frames per second.

**source movie** (n.) In digital video, the original movie to be compressed.

**Space Division Multiple Access** (SDMA) (n.) A wireless communications technology that allows multiple uses of a spectrum when signals are sent or received from different locations.

**Space-Division Switching** (n.) In telecommunications, the use of a circuit-switch with an actual physical path through the matrix. Such a switch may be time-shared but not time-slot interchanged. See *Time-Multiplexed Switching.*

**spam** (v.) 1. To post undesirable messages to Usenet newsgroups or mailing lists. 2. To send unsolicited email indiscriminately to promote a product or a service, similar to junk mail in the U.S. postal service.

**SPARC** See *Scalable Processor Architecture.*

**SPARCStation** (n.) Scalable Processor Architecture Station; a workstation made by Sun Microsystems based on SPARC.

**spatial compression** (n.) An image compression technique that removes redundant data within any given image. For example, a field of blue in a picture could be reduced to the coordinates of a geometric shape along with a value for the color blue, denoting an area rather than many individual blue pixels. Fine gradations between adjacent pixels are lost in spatial compression.

**spatial resolution** (n.) In graphic or video display, the number of lines or dots used to define an image. When it stands by itself, the word *resolution* usually means spatial resolution, rather than color-based or time-based resolution.

**spawn** (v.) 1. To create a child process in a multitasking operating system. 2. To open an additional browser window.

**s/pdif** See *Sony/Philips Digital Interface Format.*

**speaker cable** (n.) Lines used to connect speakers. They are usually an unshielded insulated pair, normally not twisted, characterized by heavy gauge conductors for low resistance. They are used to connect the output of a power amplifier to the input of a loudspeaker. Household "lamp cord" is often used for speaker cable.

**special effects generator** (SEG) (n.) Any video

S

signal processor that changes the way images appear on screen.

**special interest group** (SIG, pronounced "sig") (n.) A portion of the membership of a professional organization whose members have a particular interest in a certain topic or a narrow area of pursuit that is not addressed in general meetings of the organization. SIG members are self-selected, and they often meet outside of the regular program meetings of the parent organization.

**Specialized Mobile Radio** (SMR) (n.) A public telephone network service for private businesses. SMR uses mobile radiotelephones and base stations. It has been used successfully to dispatch truck and taxi fleets. Advances in digital technology make SMR a useful voice and data transmission technology because SMR signals reach approximately 25 times farther than cellular telephone signals.

**Specification and Design Language** (SDL) (n.) A specification and description of the behavior of telecommunications systems, defined by the ITU-T as Recommendation Z100. The area of application also includes process control and realtime applications. SDL provides a Graphic Representation (SDL/GR) and a textual Phrase Representation (SDL/PR), which are equivalent representations of the same semantics.

**SPECint92** (n.) A benchmark derived from the results of a set of integer benchmarks. SPECint92 is used to estimate the performance of integer code on a single-tasking computer.

**spectrum** (n.) A continuous range of frequencies.

**speculative evaluation** (n.) A process employed in parallel processing in which an evalu-ation is begun before it is needed. It can reduce overall program run time by making some results available earlier than they would be otherwise.

**speculative execution** (n.) A process that allows a superscalar processor to keep its functional units busy by executing instructions before they are needed. The Intel Pentium processor uses speculative execution. See also *branch prediction*.

**Speech Application Programming Interface** (SAPI) (n.) A standard Microsoft API for speech synthesis and speech recognition in Windows. It allows developers to test speech software.

**speech recognition** See *voice recognition*.

**speech synthesizer** (n.) A device that produces human speech sounds from data in another form, such as a text file.

**speech transmission index** (STI) (n.) On a scale of 0 to 1.0, a measurement of how well a message is understood at the receiving end of a telecommunications link. A score of 1.0 is the best possible reception and clarity.

**speed of light** (n.) A rate of $2.998 \times 10^8$ meters or 186,000 miles per second.

**spider** (n.) An automated agent or bot that searches the web for information. Search engines use a spider to locate and catalog new sites.

**spike** (n.) Abnormally high, brief voltage fluctuation that can occur on an ordinary electrical line providing power to a facility. Spikes can damage electrical circuits and components.

**spindle synchronization** (n.) A feature of some

hard disk drives in which the rotational position of their spindles is synchronized. It is implemented in the RAID 3 format.

**SPL** See *sound pressure level.*

**splice** (v.) In relation to audio and video, to cut cleanly and bind together pieces of magnetic tape from different sources in order to achieve a seamless whole. Before digital media, splicing was the only way to edit audio and video content. Modern digital editing equipment allows the user to choose segments from various sources instantly, paste them together in memory, and change the result if it is not desirable. See figure.

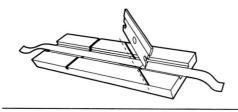

*splicing block for audio tape*

**spline** (n.) A smooth curve that interpolates multiple points and that is defined by several other curves, or polynomials. The term originally described the flexible rod used in drafting to draw a curved line.

**spline-based modeling** (n.) The use of Bezier curves in three-dimensional modeling to bend shapes more smoothly and realistically.

**split edit** (n.) In postproduction, an edit of only the audio or video portion of a program, without changing the other element in the original source.

**splitter** (n.) A device that accepts one signal and provides multiple ports through which it may be accessed.

**SPML** See *server-parsed HTML.*

**spoofing** (v.) Adopting a false identity, particularly in an attempt to gain access to a computer system or network by pretending to be an authorized user.

**spool** (n.) Simultaneous peripheral operations online; the temporary storage of data in a buffer to reduce delays in processing or printing.

**spreadsheet** (n.) A computer-generated worksheet consisting of columns and rows of numbers, letters, or other symbols. Formulas can be applied to a group of entries, and the results can be calculated automatically. Spreadsheets can be used for schedules, records of resources, accounting ledgers, balance sheets, grade books, and many other creative purposes.

**sprite** (n.) In Macromedia Director, a graphics element that can be manipulated on screen as an object.

**sprite track** (n.) A QuickTime track consisting of small graphic elements that each have position and time information associated with them. These elements are called *sprites*. A bouncing ball is an example of a sprite track, and the ball itself is an object sprite. Just the ball and its location are needed to define the frame instead of a series of bitmaps that describe each entire frame. This track may be layered over another track.

**SQL** See *Structured Query Language.*

**square-pixel digitizing** (n.) Converting an image from a television signal, whose aspect ratio differs from that of a computer monitor, and correcting for distortion that would result from squeezing and cropping rectangular pixels. NTSC signals would be distorted up to 11 percent if corrections, or square pixels, were

393

not interpolated from the rectangular pixels.

**square wave** (n.) A regular pulse with extremely fast rise and fall times. Each half of the wave cycle is either positive or negative, so it may be interpreted as a binary signal with on and off states.

**squirt the bird** (v.) Jargon meaning to direct a signal toward a telecommunications satellite.

**SRAM** See *Static RAM.*

**SSI** See *server-side include.*

**SSL** See *Secure Sockets Layer.*

**SSP** See *signal switching point.*

**SS7** See *Signaling System 7.*

**stack** (n.) 1. In programming, a data structure for storing items that are intended to be accessed in last-in-first-out (LIFO) order. Most processors include support for stacks in their instruction set architectures. Stacks are commonly used to store subroutine arguments and return addresses. 2. In the Apple HyperCard program, a set of cards, or frames, with programmed HyperScripts.

**stack overflow** (n.) In programming, an error resulting from an attempt to push more items onto a stack than the allocated space allows.

**stack pointer** (n.) A variable that points to the top of a stack. If the stack is full, the pointer indicates the most recently pushed-on item. If the stack is empty, the pointer indicates the first empty location, which is where the next item will be placed.

**stairstepping** (n.) The uneven representation of diagonal lines or curves on a computer screen because pixels form only vertical and horizontal rows on a monitor at 72 dpi. Stairstepping, which manifests itself as jagged lines, can be corrected to a degree with anti-aliasing software.

**stale pointer bug** (n.) In programming, a class of subtle programming errors resulting from code that performs dynamic allocation of memory blocks. If several pointers address a block of storage and if that storage is freed or reallocated, it may lead to intermittent lossage. The condition does not exist in higher-level languages with a garbage collector.

**stamper** (n.) A perfectly flat final mastering disc used to mold replicas.

**stand-alone** (adj.) 1. Describes a multimedia program that runs without needing the application that created it and that requires no other software support. 2. Describes equipment, such as an interactive kiosk, that is independent of a larger network.

**standard** (n.) A uniform protocol that defines communication between devices. Standards are established to reduce incompatibility between competitive technologies. They are often developed by a committee belonging to an industry association, such as ISO. The Electronics Industries Association (EIA) sets RS standards. ANSI standards for data communications usually begin with the letter *X,* as in X3.4-1967, the ASCII code standard. The ITU-T, formerly known as the CCITT, publishes recommendations, such as the V.x series, rather than standards. These recommendations refer to data transfer over telephone lines.

**Standard Generalized Markup Language** (SGML) (n.) A generic markup language for representing documents. In SGML, information is treated separately from the manner in which it is presented. SGML is an ISO standard.

**Standard MIDI File** (SMF) (n.) Standard Musical Instrument Digital Interface File; the format universally accepted by musical applications for a stream of MIDI data in a file.

**standard operating procedures** (SOP, pronounced "ess-oh-PEE") (n.) Production processes that everyone follows in developing a multimedia project. This standardization allows more than one person to contribute to the production of graphics, audio, video and code. It also may specify such things as file name conventions and settings for production equipment.

**standards organizations (n.)** As more individuals engage in creating and distributing multimedia products, the need for standardization regarding protocols, file types, compression techniques, and a host of other issues becomes increasingly critical. Much is at stake in the establishment and adoption of standards for hardware manufacturers, software developers, multimedia producers, and for end-users. This is an introduction to the organizations that make recommendations which ultimately determine how we create, deliver, and use digital media.

The International Organization for Standardization (ISO) in Geneva is the head of all national standardization bodies. "ISO" means "equal" in Greek, and is pronounced "EYE-soh." The name of the organization is a play on words rather than an acronym.

Along with the International Electrotechnical Commission (IEC), ISO coordinates national standards activities worldwide. Results of their work are published as ISO standards. Among them are standards for electrical connectors, computer protocols, file formats, and programming languages. The ISO/IEC Joint Technical Committee 1 (JTC 1) deals with information technology. An accompanying table lists ISO Technical Committees that address issues related to computing and multimedia.

The accepted procedure for developing and approving international standards is specified in the 1989 revision of the ISO/IEC directives. It is an involved process with numerous activities and critical milestones. Procedures in which committees engage include five stages of development that lead to approval and publication.

1. The Proposal Stage: Members cast ballots on the creation of a new standards project.

| ISO Technical Committees | |
| --- | --- |
| **Committee** | **Area** |
| ISO/IEC JTC 1 | Information technology. |
| ISO/IEC JTC 1/WG 3 | Open electronic data interchange. |
| ISO/IEC JTC 1/SC 1 | Vocabulary. |
| ISO/IEC JTC 1/SC 6 | Telecommunications, exchanges between systems. |
| ISO/IEC JTC 1/SC 7 | Software engineering. |
| ISO/IEC JTC 1/SC 21 | Information retrieval, transfer and management for OSI. |
| ISO/IEC JTC 1/SC 23 | Optical disc cartridges for information interchange. |
| ISO/IEC JTC 1/SC 24 | Computer graphics and image processing. |
| ISO/IEC JTC 1/SC 25 | Interconnection of information technology equipment. |
| ISO/IEC JTC 1/SC 29 | Coded representation of pictures, audio, and multimedia. |
| ISO TC 42 | Photography. |
| ISO TC 43 | Acoustics. |
| ISO TC 130 | Graphic technology. |
| ISO TC 171 | Document and image recording methods, storage, and use. |

2. The Preparatory Stage: A project leader manages the development of a working draft.

3. The Committee Stage: Consensus is achieved on a Committee Draft (CD).

4. The Approval Stage: National bodies vote on a Draft International Standard (DIS).

5. The Publication Stage: ISO publishes the International Standard (IS).

ISO standard documents are copyrighted by ISO and are not freely available as public domain documents. Other international standardization organizations (ITU and IETF) offer their documents on the Internet freely, or send out paper versions at no charge. By a liaison contribution from ISO/IEC JTC 1/SC 6 to the Internet Architecture Board (IAB), some of the OSI standards are available as PostScript files via FTP from *merit.edu* in the directory *pub/is*.

Standards documents may be obtained directly from ISO at:

ISO Sales
Case Postale 56
CH-1211 Geneve 20
Switzerland
site: www.iso.ch
email: sales@isocs.iso.ch
phone: 41 22 749 0222

The *ISO Bulletin* contains information about current standardization activities and articles about various standards. It lists all the ISO standards published or withdrawn, the DISs circulated, and the CDs registered. An annual ISO Catalogue, which lists all ISO standards in force and other ISO publications, is also available.

---

**ISO Standards Documents**

| | |
|---|---|
| ISO 646 | Seven-bit ASCII with national variants (ECMA-6). |
| ISO 2022 | ESC sequences for switching between various character sets (ECMA-35). |
| ISO 2382 | Information technology—Vocabulary. |
| ISO 3166 | Codes for the representation of names of countries. This standard defines a two-letter, a three-letter, and a numeric code for each country. US/USA/840=United States, FR/FRA/250=France, DE/DEU/276=Germany. |
| ISO 8632 | Computer Graphics Metafile (CGM). Defines file format for two-dimensional vector graphics. Part 1 defines the elements (lines, filled polygons, text, colors) that appear in a CGM, and the other parts define three encodings for these graphic elements: character encoding, binary encoding, and clear text encoding. This standard format can store resolution-independent graphics. The main difference between CGM and PostScript is that PostScript is a full programming language, while CGM is just a list of graphical elements, making CGM suitable for re-editing. |
| ISO 8879 | Standard Generalized Markup Language (SGML), a format for storing documents. |
| ISO 9127 | User documentation and cover information for software packages. |
| ISO 9541 | Font and character information interchange. |
| ISO 9592 | Programmer's Hierarchical Interactive Graphics interface (PHIGS). |
| ISO 9593 | PHIGS Language Bindings (Fortran, Pascal, Ada, C). |
| ISO 9636 | Graphical device interfaces. |
| ISO 9660 | CD-ROM volume and file structure (ECMA-119). |
| ISO 9899 | The C programming language. |
| ISO 9945 | Unix-style system calls and shell commands (POSIX). |
| ISO 10646 | A 32-bit character set called UCS containing nearly all known characters. |
| ISO 10744 | HyTime hypertext/multimedia extension to SGML. |
| ISO 10918 | Still image data compression standard (JPEG). |
| ISO 11172 | Digital video/audio compression and encoding (MPEG-1). |
| ISO 12083 | Standardized SGML document type definitions for books, tables, and formulas. |
| ISO 13818 | Digital video/audio compression and encoding (MPEG-2). |

An accompanying table gives a selected, partial listing of a few of ISO standards documents that apply to computers, telecommunications, and multimedia.

Another active organization whose work is becoming increasingly important as the need for global networks grows is the International Telecommunications Union (ITU), a United Nations agency that recommends standards for telecommunications. One of its previous bodies was the International Telephone and Telegraph Consultative Committee (CCITT), which is now called ITU-T (Telecommunications Standardization Sector). A group from the CCITT/ITU-T meets every few years and compiles a list of questions about possible improvements in international electronic communication. Experts from different countries meet in study groups to develop recommendations which are adopted and published.

Relevant to computing are the ITU-T V series of recommendations on modems (V.32 and V.42) and the X series on data networks and OSI (X.25 and X.400). In telecommunications the I and Q series define ISDN. The Z series defines specification and programming languages (SDL and CHILL). The T series relates to text communication (facsimile and video text), and the H series addresses digital sound and video encoding standards.

The names of committees have evolved in recent years. The former International Radio Consultative Committee (CCIR) and the International Frequency Registration Board (IFRB) are now together called ITU-R (Radiocommunication Sector). Previously known as the Telecommunications Development Bureau (BDT), this organization is now referred to as ITU-D.

ITU publishes many ISO computer and telecommunication-related standards under a different cover. Its recommendations and a free ITU List of Publications are available from:

International Telecommunications Union
General Secretariat—Sales Section
Place des Nations
CH-1211 Geneve 20
Switzerland
site: www.itu.int
email: helpdesk@itu.ch
phone: 41 22 7305111
fax: 41 22 73051

The following is a short list of ITU-T/CCITT recommendations that apply to multimedia and networked communications:

| | |
|---|---|
| V.34 | Duplex modem modulation up to 28 800 bps. |
| V.42 | HDLC based error correction protocol for modems. |
| V.42bis | Lempel-Ziv-based data compression algorithm for HDLC protocols. |
| V.90 | Duplex modem modulation up to 56 000 bps. |
| X.25 | An interface to a public or private packet data network. |
| X.3/ X.28/ X.29 | Specifies connection of asynchronous ASCII terminals to X.25 networks. |

The European Computer Manufacturers Association (ECMA) has been a forum for data processing experts since 1961. This group has prepared and submitted agreements for standardization to ISO, ITU, and other standards organizations. One example is the ECMA-262 standard, a version of JavaScript equivalent to Netscape's JavaScript version 1.1, using unicode characters rather than ASCII. ECMA standards are free and may be ordered from:

European Computer
Manufacturers Association
114 Rue du Rhone
CH-1204 Geneva
Switzerland
site: www.ecma.ch
e-mail: helpdesk@ecma.ch
phone: 41 22 7353634
fax: 41 22 7865231

Internet standards have been developed to promote protocol-based interoperability. There are two primary areas of responsibility under which these standards are developed. The first is strategic concerns, which are handled by the Internet Society (ISOC) and the Internet Architecture Board (IAB). The second is technical development, which is handled by the Internet Engineering Task Force (IETF) and the Internet Research Task Force (IRTF).

The ISOC is a non-profit professional society with open membership. The IAB is approved by the ISOC, as is the formal documentation of the Internet standards process. The IAB oversees the architecture and growth of the Internet and it approves members to the Internet Engineering Steering Group (IESG). Working groups belonging to the IETF define specific Internet standards by consensus. Anyone may participate in the working groups, since much work is conducted by electronic mail. The IETF meets three times per year, and the documents it produces are freely available. Internet standards are published as the online Request For Comments (RFC) series. The World Wide Web consortium maintains an up to date Internet site located at *w3c.org* with all current and historical recommendations, proposals, and drafts.

The Institute of Electrical and Electronics Engineers (IEEE) also publishes standards. The URL for the IEEE Computer Society is *www.computer.org.* Publications may be ordered by email from the IEEE Computer Society Press at *cs.books@compmail.com.*

The European Telecommunication Standards Institute (ETSI), an organization that addresses European standards for telecommunications, may be contacted at:

ETSI
F-06921 Sophia Antipolis Cedex
France
phone: 33 92 94 42 00
fax: 33 93 65 47 16

The Conference of European Posts and Telecommunications Administrations (CEPT), an agency that coordinates efforts in Europe, may be contacted at:

CEPT Liaison Office
Seilerstrasse 22
CH-3008 Bern
Switzerland
phone: 41 31 62 20 81
fax: 41 31 62 20 78

Two sources for standards in the United States are listed below:

Phillips Business Information
1201 Seven Locks Road
Potomac, MD 20854
phone: 1 301 424 3338 or 800 777 5006
fax: 1 301 309 3847

Document Center
1504 Industry Way, Unit 9
Belmont, CA 94002
phone: 1 415 591 7600
fax: 1 415 591 7617

Many standards documents are available on the Internet. An accompanying table lists some

## Standards Organizations by Country

A few standards bodies located in individual countries are listed below with street address, telephone number, and facsimile number. There are approximately 100 individual national standards bodies. Contact information is listed for the standards bodies identified by acronym, as well as for other bodies.

| Acronym | Organization |
|---|---|
| AFNOR | Association française de normalisation  France |
| ANSI | American National Standards Institute  United States |
| BIS | Bureau of Indian Standards  India |
| BSI | British Standards Institution  United Kingdom |
| DIN | Deutsches Institut fur Normung  Germany |
| DS | Dansk Standardiseringsraad  Denmark |
| NNI | Nederlands Normalisatie-instituut  Netherlands |
| NSF | Norges Standardiseringsforbund  Norway |
| SAA | Standards Association of Australia  Australia |
| SCC | Standards Council of Canada  Canada |
| UNI | Ente Nazionale Italiano di Unificazione  Italy |

**Australia**
Standards Organization of Australia
P.O. Box 1055
Strathfield-N.S.W. 2135
phone: 61 2 746 47 00
fax: 61 2 746 84 50

**Canada**
Standards Council of Canada
45 O'Connor Street, Suite 1200
Ottawa, Ontario
K1P 6N7
phone: 1 613 238 32 22
fax: 1 613 995 45 64

**Denmark**
Dansk Standardiseringsraad
Baunegaardsvej 73
DK-2900 HELLERUP
phone: 45 39 77 01 01
fax: 45 39 77 02 02
email: ds@itc.dk

**France**
Association française de
normalisation
Tour Europe
Cedex 7
F-92049 PARIS LA DÉFENSE
phone: 331 42 91 55 55
fax: 1 613 995 45 64

**Germany**
DIN, Deutsches Institut fur
Normung
Burggrafenstrasse 6
D-10787 BERLIN
phone: 49 30 26 01 0
fax: 49 30 26 01 12 31

**India**
Bureau of Indian Standards
Manak Bhavan
9 Bahadur Shah Zafar Marg
New Dehli 110002
phone: 91 11 331 79 91
fax: 91 11 331 40 62

**Italy**
Ente Nazionale Italiano di
Unificazione
Via Battistotti Sassi 11
I-20133 MILANO
phone: 39 2 70 02 41
fax: 39 2 70 10 61 06

**Japan**
Japanese Industrial Standards Committee
c/o Standards Department Agency of
  Industrial Science and Technology
Ministry of International Trade and Industry
1-3-1, Kasumigaseki, Chiyoda-ku
Tokyo 100
phone: 81 3 35 01 92 95/6
fax: 81 3 35 80 14 18

**S**

**Standards Organizations by Country** (continued)

**Netherlands**
Nederlands Normalisatie-Instituut
Kalfjeslaan 2
P.O. Box 5059
2600 GB Delft
phone: 31 15 69 03 90
fax: 31 15 69 01 90

**Norway**
Norges Standardiseringsforbund
Postboks 7020 Homansbyen
N-0306 Oslo 3
phone: 47 2 46 60 94
fax: 47 2 46 44 57

**Russian Federation**
State Committee for Standardization,
 Metrology, and Certification
Leninsky Prospekt 9
Moskva 117049
phone: 7 095 236 40 44
fax: 7 095 236 82 09

**Spain**
Asociación Española de
 Normalización y Certificación
Calle Fernández de la Hoz, 52
E-28010 Madrid
phone: 34 1 310 48 51
fax: 34 1 310 49 76

**Sweden**
SIS—Standardiseringskommissionen
 i Sverige
Box 3295
S-103 66 Stockholm
phone: 46 8 613 52 00
fax: 46 8 11 70 35

**Switzerland**
Swiss Association for
Standardization
Mülebachstr 54
CH-8008 Zurich
phone: 41 1 254 54 54
fax: 41 1 254 54 74

**United Kingdom**
British Standards Institution
2 Park Street
GB-London W1A 2BS
phone: 44 71 629 90 00
fax: 44 71 629 05 06

**United States**
American National Standards
Institute
11 West 42nd Street, 13th floor
New York 10036
phone: 1 212 642 4900
fax: 1 212 398 0023

sites that provide information on standards.

A few standards bodies located in individual countries are listed in an accompanying table.

**standard tape interconnect** (STI) (n.) A standard protocol for connecting tape formatters and controllers.

**standby time** (n.) The number of hours and minutes a fully charged cellular phone battery will remain charged without being used.

**star coupler** (n.) Passive device that distributes data from one or several input optical fibers to a greater number of output optical fibers.

**start bit** (n.) The initial bit of a transmitted character on a serial line. If the condition of a line is normally at logical 0 when no data is being transmitted, the start bit is at logical 1.

**star topology** (n.) A method of connecting devices in a local area network (LAN) that

---

**Standards Documents on the Internet**

This table lists web pages and FTP sites where information may be accessed.
Ftp addresses must be preceded by ftp://.

| Web Address | | Content |
|---|---|---|
| http://www.ietf.org | | Internet Engineering Task Force |
| http://www.edtn.com/standards/standards.htm | | Standards Watch |
| http://ncits.org | | National Committee for IT Standards |
| http://www.opengroup.org | | X/Open |

| FTP Address | Directory | Content |
|---|---|---|
| cs.ucl.ac.uk | /src | ISODE, PP, OSIMIS |
| " | /osi-ds | Internet X.500 documents |
| " | /ietf-osi-oda | Internet ODA documents |
| aun.uninett.no | /ietf/mhs-ds | X.500 based routing drafts |
| ftp.ifi.uio.no | /pub/SGML | SGML/HyTime related |
| dkuug.dk | /i18n | internationalization standards |
| ftp.ripe.net | /ietf | Internet documents |
| ftp.merit.edu | /pub/iso | some ISO standards (CLNP, etc.) |
| unicode.org | /Public | Unicode/ISO 10646 material |
| sunsite.unc.edu | /pub | Unix-Sun related |

---

routes all communications through the central hub or the controller. See also *network topology.*

**startup** (n.) The mode in which a computer begins operation when it is switched on. The operating system, drivers, and selected applications are loaded on startup.

**state** (n.) The properties of an object that characterize its current condition.

**Static RAM** (SRAM, pronounced "ESS-ram") (n.) Static random-access memory; memory that retains a static value as long as power is supplied, unlike Dynamic RAM (DRAM), which must be refreshed regularly. In contrast to ROM, SRAM will lose its contents when the power is switched off. Usually faster than DRAM, SRAM is used where speed is critical, such as in cache memory applications.

**station** (n.) Data terminal equipment (DTE), such as a user device on a network node, that sends and receives messages on a data link.

**Statistical Analysis System** (SAS, pronounced "SASS") (n.) A statistical and matrix-handling language.

**STD** See *subscriber trunk dialing.*

**STD** (n.) A standard based on a Request For Comments (RFC) that has been adopted by the Internet Architecture Board (IAB). STD citations are listed here in order, with title, date issued, and RFC number.

- STD 01: Internet official protocol standards, 1998 (RFC 2400).
- STD 02: Assigned numbers, 1994 (RFC 1700).
- STD 03: Host requirements, 1989 (RFC 1122, RFC 1123).
- STD 04: Gateway requirements, 1987 (RFC 1009).
- STD 05: Internet Protocol, 1981 (RFC 0791, RFC 792, RFC 0919, RFC 0922, RFC 0950, RFC 1112).
- STD 06: User Datagram Protocol, 1980 (RFC 0768).

**S**

- STD 07: Transmission Control Protocol, 1981 (RFC 0793).
- STD 08: Telnet Protocol, 1983 (RFC 0854, RFC 0855).
- STD 09: File transfer protocol, 1985 (RFC 0959).
- STD 10: SMTP service extensions, 1995 (RFC 1869).
- STD 11: SMTP service extension for message size declaration, 1995 (RFC 1870).
- STD 12: Network Time Protocol, 1989 (RFC 1119).
- STD 13: Domain name system, 1987 (RFC 1034, RFC 1035).
- STD 14: Mail routing and the domain system, 1986 (RFC 0974).
- STD 15: Simple Network Management Protocol (SNMP), 1990 (RFC 1157).
- STD 16: Structure of management information, 1990 (RFC 1155, RFC 1212).
- STD 17: Management information base, 1991 (RFC 1213).
- STD 18: Exterior Gateway Protocol, 1984 (RFC 0904).
- STD 19: NetBIOS Service Protocols, 1987 (RFC 1001, RFC 1002).
- STD 20: Echo Protocol, 1983 (RFC 0862).
- STD 21: Discard Protocol, 1983 (RFC 0863).
- STD 22: Character Generator Protocol, 1983 (RFC 0864).
- STD 23: Quote of the Day Protocol, 1983 (RFC 0865).
- STD 24: Active Users Protocol, 1983 (RFC 0866).
- STD 25: Daytime Protocol, 1983 (RFC 0867).
- STD 26: Time Server Protocol, 1983 (RFC 0868).
- STD 27: Binary transmission Telnet option, 1983 (RFC 0856).
- STD 28: Echo Telnet option, 1983 (RFC 0857).
- STD 29: Suppress go ahead Telnet option, 1983 (RFC 0858).
- STD 30: Status Telnet option, 1983 (RFC 0859).
- STD 31: Timing mark Telnet option, 1983 (RFC 0860).
- STD 32: Extended options list Telnet option, 1983 (RFC 0861).
- STD 33: Trivial File Transfer Protocol, 1992 (RFC 1350).
- STD 34: Routing Information Protocol, 1988 (RFC 1058).
- STD 35: ISO transport service on top of the TCP version 3, 1978 (RFC 1006).
- STD 36: Transmission of IP and ARP over FDDI Networks, 1993 (RFC 1390).
- STD 37: Ethernet Address Resolution Protocol, 1982 (RFC 0826).
- STD 38: Reverse Address Resolution Protocol, 1984 (RFC 0903).
- STD 39: Interface Message Processor (under revision), 1981.
- STD 40: Host Access Protocol specification, 1993 (RFC 1221).
- STD 41: Transmission of IP datagrams over Ethernet networks, 1984 (RFC 0894).
- STD 42: Transmission of IP datagrams over experimental Ethernet networks, 1984 (RFC 0895).
- STD 43: Transmission of IP datagrams over IEEE 802 networks, 1993 (RFC 1042).
- STD 44: DCN (disconnect frame) Local-Network Protocols, 1993 (RFC 0891).
- STD 45: Internet Protocol on network system's HYPERchannel protocol specification, 1993 (RFC 1044).
- STD 46: Transmitting IP traffic over ARCnets, 1993 (RFC 1201).
- STD 47: Transmission of IP datagrams over serial lines: SLIP, 1993 (RFC 1055).
- STD 48: Transmission of IP datagrams over NetBIOS networks, 1993 (RFC 1088).

- STD 49: Transmission of 802.2 packets over IPX networks, 1993 (RFC 1132).
- STD 50: Definitions of managed objects for the Ethernet-like interface types, 1994 (RFC 1643).
- STD 51: Point-to-Point Protocol (PPP), 1994 (RFC 1661, RFC 1662).
- STD 52: Transmission of IP datagrams over SMDS, 1991 (RFC 1209).
- STD 53: Post Office Protocol (POP) version 3, 1996 (RFC 1939).
- STD 54: OSPF version 2, 1998 (RFC 2328).
- STD 55: Multiprotocol interconnect over frame relay, 1998 (RFC 2427).
- STD 56: RIP version 2, 1998 (RFC 2453).
- STD 57: RIP Version 2 Protocol Applicability Statement, 1994 (RFC1722).
- STD 58: Conformance Statements for Structure of Management Information Version 2 (SMIv2), 1999 (RFC2580).
- STD 59: Remote Network Monitoring Management Information Base, 2000 (RFC2819).
- STD 60: SMTP Service Extension for Command Pipelining, 2000 (RFC2920).
- STD 61: A One-Time Password System, 1998 (RFC2289).

**step frame** (n.) A function in video playback equipment that permits forward or reverse movement one frame at a time.

**step index core** (n.) An optical fiber whose core exhibits a uniform refractive index. This type is used for single-mode fibers.

**step time** (n.) A method of recording discrete MIDI events one by one for later playback as a continuous stream, rather than recording in real time at a set tempo.

**stereo** (adj.) Describes sound emanating from two distinct sources, facilitating spatial placement of individual sounds in a panorama.

**stereo chorusing** See *chorus.*

**STI** See *speech transmission index* or *standard tape interconnect.*

**still frame** 1. (n.) A single frame of film or video displayed on a monitor as a static image. 2. (adj., still-frame) Describes graphical or textual information recorded on a single frame and intended to be displayed as a motionless image.

**STM** See *synchronous transfer mode.*

**stop bit** (n.) A control bit that signifies the end of an asynchronous character in data transmission. The stop bit is always the binary digit 0.

**store and forward** (n.) 1. A network process in which packets, messages, or frames are temporarily stored in a network node before being transmitted to their destination. 2. This refers to a method of delivering video content *on-demand* rather than by broadcasting it.

**storyboard** (n.) A sequence of graphic representations, often with dialog or captions, showing important scenes in a program. Used to plan a production, to visualize, and to present program ideas, a storyboard often consists of an artist's sketches in a form similar to that of a comic strip.

**STP** See *Secure Transfer Protocol* or *signal transfer point.* May also refer to *shielded twisted pair.*

**stream** (v.) To play sound or video in real time as the data is downloaded over the Internet. A plug-in to a web browser such as Netscape Navigator decompresses and plays the data as it is transferred over the World Wide Web to a computer. Streaming audio or video is an alternative to downloading an entire file, storing it on a local hard drive, and then playing it with a helper application. Streaming implies the execution of a decompression algorithm in real time. The quality of the streamed data is proportional to the speed of the Internet connection and to the power of the computer decoding the streamed file.

**streaming** (n.) Network delivery of time-based media, such as audio, video, and animation. It may refer to technologies that match the bandwidth of the media signal to the viewer's connection so that the media is always seen in realtime. It is also used to describe media that may be viewed over a network prior to being fully downloaded, while it is progressively downloaded, but not truly streamed, to the client machine.

**string** (n.) In programming, an ordered series of data values, or bytes, which are usually printable characters. Larger character sets, such as Unicode (in which each character is represented by more than eight bits), are becoming more popular. Most programming languages differentiate between strings and numeric values.

**stripe** (v.) To record time code, usually SMPTE, on a channel of a videotape prior to editing. This procedure allows accurate access to individual frames.

**structured language** (n.) A programming language in which a program may be reduced to blocks or procedures that can be written without detailed knowledge of the inner workings of other blocks, thus allowing a top-down design approach.

**Structured Query Language** (SQL) (n.) A widely used programming language for defining, modifying, and accessing information in relational databases. SQL allows queries to be made from other programs.

**STS** See *synchronous transport signal.*

**stub** (n.) In programming, a dummy procedure used to link a program with a runtime library.

**stub network** (n.) A network that carries packets to and from local hosts exclusively. Typically, it does not carry traffic for other networks, although it may have paths to other networks.

**StuffIt** (SIT) (n.) A Macintosh compressed file format. StuffIt is used to reduce the size of a file before uploading it to a network or saving it on storage media.

**stylus** (n.) An input device shaped like a pen. A stylus is used to enter text, draw lines, or point to choices on a computer screen.

**subarea** (n.) A type-4 node in the IBM System Network Architecture, defined by a computer that processes communications and its attached peripherals, all of which share a common subarea address.

**subassembly** (n.) An individually replaceable component integrated with other components to form a system.

**subchannel** (n.) In asymmetrical transmission of data, this refers to one of the component channels that are combined to constitute a main channel.

**subclass** (n.) In object-oriented programming (OOP), a class derived from a superclass by inheritance. A subclass contains all the features of the superclass, along with new features or redefined existing features.

**subcode** (n.) Control data included on a CD-ROM that defines track location and timing information. Text may also be stored in the subcode space.

**subdirectory** (n.) A data structure in the Microsoft DOS and Windows filing systems that represents a division of the root directory. A subdirectory may be further divided into numerous lower-level subdirectories to provide a means of managing data.

**subgroups** See *group.*

**subject index** (n.) An information resource in a networked computing environment with references to topics categorized by subject. Most subject indexes are arranged ontologically. Search engines differ in that they are based not on subjects but on relevance.

**subject matter expert** (SME, pronounced "SMEE") (n.) An authority on a particular subject who guides the development of content for a multimedia production or web site. It is the responsibility of the SME to ensure that technical details and facts related to the topic are accurate.

**submenu** (n.) A lower-level menu, or a series of choices, that the user reaches after selecting a main menu choice.

**submix** See *group.*

**subnet** (n.) A segment of a network that shares a network address with other portions of the network and that is identified by a subnet number.

**subnet address** (n.) The part of an Internet Protocol (IP) address that refers to a subnet. The host portion of an IP address is divided into the subnet part and the host part using an address (subnet) mask.

**subnet bit mask** (n.) A method of dividing an Internet Protocol (IP) network into smaller subnets, and identifying those subnets with some of the most significant bits from the host portion of the network address. An IP network address has 16 bits assigned as its network ID. If the complete network address is "129.4.0.0," the first 2 sets of eight bits in this dotted decimal format may be represented in binary as "10000001.00000100." The next set of eight bits is used to define the host address and the final eight bits define the station on the host. In a subnet bit mask, the alias "255," or "11111111" in binary, is used for the first 3 parts of the address, and the final eight bits may be designated locally as a number between 0 and 255. Thus, "255.255.255.0" is used to define the upper 24 bits of the address, and the last eight bits are represented by a "0" in this case. The last eight bits may be used to identify a station on the host whose address is set to a number between 0 and 255.

**subnetwork** (n.) A small network linked with other networks by a router or a bridge.

**subroutine** (n.) In programming, a sequence of instructions that perform a particular task. Most programming languages allow subroutine code to be called from multiple places, including from within itself, in which case it is *recursive.* A function is similar to a *subroutine,* except that a function is primarily called to return a value.

**subsample** (v.) When capturing data, to discard portions of a signal for the purpose of reducing the amount of data that must be com-

405

pressed. Most types of lossy compression perform this operation.

**subscribe** (v.) To request that one's address be added to a mail list or a newsgroup.

**subscriber** (n.) In telecommunications, a company or an individual that purchases communications services.

**Subscriber Identity Module** (SIM) (n.) A tiny memory card that gives a GSM or a CDMA phone its user identity and stores phone numbers and other information. A SIM can be inserted into any compatible phone, basically changing the identity of that phone.

**Subscriber Loop** (n.) Circuit connecting the central office of a telephone company to the demarcation point on a customer's premises.

**subscriber trunk dialing** (STD) (n.) European method of measuring direct long-distance calls.

**subsonic** (adj.) Describes waves moving slower than the speed of sound in a designated medium.

**Subsplit** (n.) Hybrid fiber-coax (HFC) networking term that defines an upstream channel between 5 and 50 MHz.

**substrate** (n.) In a CD-ROM or in another optical storage device, the molded plastic base on which data is encoded.

**subtractive color** (n.) Against a white background, the mixture of various intensities of the colors cyan, magenta, and yellow. Combinations of these colors can produce all visible colors.

**suffix** (n.) Also known as an extension, the last part of a filename that indicates the type of file. See *extension*.

**superscalar** (adj.) Describes a single processor that can execute two or more scalar operations in parallel, or simultaneously. Superscalar architectures, with the exception of those that are superpipelined, require multiple functional units that may or may not be identical.

**supersonic** (adj.) Describes waves moving faster than the speed of sound in a given medium, usually the air.

**supertrunk** (n.) Television cable that carries multiple video signals between the facilities of a cable television (CATV) company.

**Super-VHS** (S-VHS) (n.) Super–video home system; an advancement of the VHS videotape format, featuring higher luminance and more lines of resolution.

**Super Video Graphics Array** (SVGA) (n.) A video standard established by the Video Electronics Standards Association (VESA). Updated versions allow resolutions of up to 1280 x 1024 pixels with 24-bit color.

**supervisor mode** (n.) The mode in which an operating system usually runs. It enables execution of all instructions, including privileged instructions. It may permit access to a reserved address space, to memory management hardware, or to peripherals that may not be accessible in user mode.

**suppression** (n.) In teleconferencing, the instantaneous reduction of a sound system's overall gain to control acoustic feedback and reduce echoes.

**SureStream** (n.) A scalability feature of the RealSystem G2 server that allows multiple versions of a file to be compressed at different ratios, and delivered to users based on the speed of their connection.

**surface** (n.) A three-dimensional space defined by the relationship between three variable coordinates: $x$, $y$, and $z$.

**surface mount** (n.) With reference to PC board assembly, a technique for high-density manufacturing using a variety of semiconductor packages.

**surge protector** (n.) A device used to monitor the level of electrical current between a power source and a computer or another electronic component. When the surge protector detects a surge of voltage beyond a certain limit, the circuit is shut down or the level is automatically reduced to prevent damage to the electronics.

**surrogate travel** (n.) A virtual reality (VR) system in which point-of-view (POV) travel is simulated, allowing the user to control the path taken through the environment.

**Surround Video** (n.) A technology developed by Microsoft for transforming panoramic images into graphics files. It permits users to view their surroundings in any direction from a fixed pivot point or points. Surround Video is conceptually similar to QuickTime VR from Apple Computer.

**SUSP** See *System Use Sharing Protocol.*

**sustained transfer rate** (n.) The number of bytes per second (Bps) a CD-ROM drive or another storage medium can deliver as it reads data objects larger than its internal buffer.

**SVG** See *Scalable Vector Graphics.*

**SVGA** See *Super Video Graphics Array.*

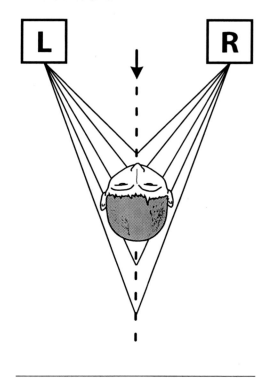

*sweet spot*

**S-VHS** See *Super-VHS.*

**S-video** See *Y/C video.*

**swap file** (n.) In Microsoft Windows 3.1, a hidden system file located on a local hard disk in contiguous space. A swap file expands apparent internal RAM and may be permanent or temporary. Also known as *virtual memory.*

**sweet spot** (n.) Identifies the location in relation to a two-loudspeaker stereo playback system where the listener is positioned equidistant from each loudspeaker. The apex of all possible isosceles (two equal sides) triangles formed by the loudspeakers and the listener.

407

The sweet spot lies anywhere on a plane extending forward from the midpoint between the speakers. See figure.

**sweetening** (n.) In video or film post-production, the development of an audio track with mixed elements, such as music, sound effects, and applause. In the process, the signal-to-noise (S/N) ratio is improved, and the general quality of the sound track is polished.

**swim** (n.) A form of drift in which a shadow image appears to move from the top to the bottom of a video screen. It is caused by noise in electronic signals or by noise generated locally in the display electronics.

**switch** (n.) 1. A device that opens or closes circuits or selects paths. In video production, a *switcher* is used to select the current signal source or the camera shot that becomes the output. 2. In MS-DOS, an argument to control the execution of a command. This argument usually involves a qualifying parameter, typically delimited by a / symbol.

**Switched Digital Video** (SDV) (n, adj.) Describes any digital video transmission received over a switched network.

**Switched 56** (n.) Switched public data transmission service at 56 kilobits per second (Kbps).

**switched line** (n.) A telecommunications link that may follow a different physical path with each use of the service, as with the public telephone system.

**switched multimegabit data service** (SMDS) (n.) A "fast-packet" service that establishes high-speed connections between local area networks (LANs) through the public telephone network.

**switched network** (n.) Any network in which switching is used to set up a continuous pathway and to transmit messages directly from the sender to the recipient. Switching is typically accomplished by disconnecting and reconnecting lines in different configurations to set up this continuous pathway.

**Switched Telephone Network** (n.) The direct dialing network of telephone lines that are generally used for dialed telephone calls. The term refers to any switching arrangement that does not require operator intervention.

**symmetrical codec** (n.) A video compression codec that encodes and decodes video in roughly the same amount of time. Live broadcast and teleconferencing systems use symmetric codecs in order to encode and distribute video in realtime as it is captured.

**symmetrical compression** (n.) In audio-video encoding, an encoding technique that can produce decoded data identical to the data that existed before encoding.

**sync** See *synchronization.*

**synchronization** (sync) (n.) A part of a video signal, or a separate signal sent with the video, that carries timing information on each frame.

**synchronized** (adj.) Describes two or more events that are coordinated exactly in time. It is especially important that audio data and video images be synchronized when combined.

**synchronous** (adj.) Occurring at the same time or in real time, rather than being temporally separated. Having a conversation or a conference in real time is synchronous communication, whereas responding to an email message two hours after it was sent is asynchronous communication. In synchronous transmission, successive bits or events all move at a constant rate. The characters are spaced by time in a synchronous transmission, rather than by start and stop bits.

**Synchronous Data Link Control** (SDLC) (n.) The protocol used in the IBM Systems Network Architecture (SNA).

**Synchronous Digital Hierarchy** (SDH) (n.) A standard defined by the ITU-T that is technically consistent with Synchronous Optical Network (SONET).

**Synchronous Dynamic RAM** (SDRAM, Synchronous DRAM) (n.) A form of DRAM chip that adds a separate clock signal to the control signals, supporting burst access modes.

**Synchronous Graphics RAM** (SGRAM) (n.) A type of Synchronous DRAM chip used in graphics hardware. SGRAM is capable of burst operation, block write, and write per bit. This type of memory provides the high throughput required for three-dimensional rendering and full-motion video (FMV).

**Synchronous Optical Network** (SONET, pronounced "SAH-net") (n.) A broadband networking standard based on point-to-point optical fiber networks. The standard provides a high-bandwidth pipe to support services based on Asynchronous Transfer Mode (ATM). SONET establishes a digital hierarchical network with a consistent transport scheme. It has been optimized for fiber, in contrast to the plain old telephone system (POTS), which was designed for copper wires. SONET carries circuit-switched data in frames at speeds up to

48 gigabits per second (Gbps) in multiples of 51.84 megabits per second (Mbps). Each SONET frame is a two-dimensional table of bytes 9 rows high and 90 columns deep. Groups of frames are called *superframes*.

Data transfer rates at different levels of SONET are shown below:

| OC Line | Rate | Capacity Level |
|---|---|---|
| OC-1 | 52 Mbps | 28 DS-1 or 1 DS-3 |
| OC-3 | 155 Mbps | 84 DS-1 or 3 DS-3 |
| OC-9 | 466 Mbps | 252 DS-1 or 9 DS-3 |
| OC-12 | 622 Mbps | 336 DS-1 or 12 DS-3 |
| OC-18 | 933 Mbps | 504 DS-1 or 18 DS-3 |
| OC-24 | 1.2 Gbps | 672 DS-1 or 24 DS-3 |
| OC-36 | 1.9 Gbps | 1008 DS-1 or 36 DS-3 |
| OC-48 | 2.5 Gbps | 1344 DS-1 or 48 DS-3 |

**synchronous transfer mode** (STM) (n.) A method of transport and switching that relies on a fixed pattern of frames. This type of time-division multiplexing is used across the network interface for broadband ISDN.

**synchronous transport signal** (STS) (n.) The equivalent of a Synchronous Optical Network (SONET) optical carrier (OC), an electrical signal that is converted to an optical signal before transmission over optical fiber. An STS frame consists of the Synchronous Payload Envelope (SPE), Section Overhead (SOH), Line Overhead (LOH), Path Overhead (POH), and Payload. The SOH and LOH combined make up the Transport Overhead (TOH).

**sync-locked** (adj.) Describes the exact alignment of two signals. This occurs when the sync pulses of a videotape recorder (VTR) are locked with those of another videotape deck or camera.

**syntax** (n.) The conventions of a programming

S

language that govern the formatting of an expression or a statement. If the expression follows a particular sequence and includes only acceptable characters, it is said to have proper syntax.

**synthesized sound** (n.) A type of sound consisting of waveforms created with mathematical formulas and produced by either analog or digital means. Such waveforms differ from ones sampled from acoustic sources.

**synthesizer** (n.) An instrument that creates sounds electronically. Controls on the instrument typically allow the user to change basic sound qualities, such as frequency, amplitude, and the envelope of each timbre. By definition, a synthesizer is not a sample player.

**SyQuest** (n.) Named after the company that manufactures it, a type of removable storage system that employs cartridges and that offers a high data transfer rate. Standard SyQuest cartridges hold 44, 88, 135, 200, or 270 megabytes (MB) of data on a 5.25-inch cartridge. A second-generation 3.5-inch cartridge holds 230 MB of data.

**sysop** See *system operator*.

**system area** (n.) The space on a CD-ROM located between the addresses 00:00:00 and 00:02:16. Data related to the operating system and error correction data are placed in the system area.

**system gain** (n.) 1. In audio, an increase in strength after a signal has passed through processing or mixing equipment. 2. In telecommunications, the gain in decibels of a microwave receiver\transmitter, mathematically calculated by adding the transmitter power output to the receiver threshold.

**System Identification** (SID) (n.) A five-digit number that indicates the service area in which a cell phone is used. Most telecommunications carriers have one SID assigned to their service area.

**system integrator** (n.) A person or company that installs, programs, and configures a variety of equipment for a service operator.

**Système International d'Unités** (SI) (n.) An international metric system introduced in France in 1960. It defines a quantity with a single unit and uses exponents to indicate powers of 10. These factors are applied to units such as Hertz, seconds, or meters. In computing and digital media, a quantity of bytes is expressed as a power of 2 rather than 10. Applying this distinction, the prefix *mega* means 1000 if it refers to Hertz, but it means 1024 if it refers to bytes. The table shows the SI prefix, the factor for each, and the decimal value. See table.

**Système International Unit prefix revision** (n.) A set of terms used to describe binary-based units. In 1998, the International Electrotechnical Commission (IEC) created these terms using names derived from the prefixes from the SI *(Système International d'Unités)*. A byte is a binary-based unit. A megabyte is not 1,000 bytes, but 1,024 bytes (2^10). The recommendation, Amendment 2 to IEC 60027-2 *Letter Symbols to be Used in Electrical Technology,* has gained little acceptance. The new recommended terms are shown in the SI Unit Prefix Revision Terms table.

For more in this topic, visit "http://physics.nist .gov/cuu/Units/binary.html".

**System Management Server** (SMS) (n.) A tool developed by Microsoft for administering a Windows NT client-server network.

## Système International d'Unités

This table shows prefixes assigned in accordance with SI (Système International d'Unités).

| Prefix | Exponent | Decimal Value |
|--------|----------|---------------|
| exa | 10 | 1 000 000 000 000 000 000 |
| peta | 10 | 1 000 000 000 000 000 |
| tera | 10 | 1 000 000 000 000 |
| giga | 10 | 1 000 000 000 |
| mega | 10 | 1 000 000 |
| kilo | 10 | 1 000 |
| hecto | 10 | 100 |
| deka | 10 | 10 |
| deci | 10 | .1 |
| centi | 10 | .01 |
| milli | 10 | .001 |
| micro | 10 | .000 001 |
| nano | 10 | .000 000 001 |
| pico | 10 | .000 000 000 001 |
| femto | 10 | .000 000 000 000 001 |

## SI Unit Prefix Revised Terms

| Factor | Name | Symbol | Origin | Derivation |
|--------|------|--------|--------|------------|
| $2^{10}$ | kibi (Ki) | kilobinary: | $(2^{10})^1$ | kilo: $(10^3)^1$ |
| $2^{20}$ | mebi (Mi) | megabinary: | $(2^{10})^2$ | mega: $(10^3)^2$ |
| $2^{30}$ | gibi (Gi) | gigabinary: | $(2^{10})^3$ | giga: $(10^3)^3$ |
| $2^{40}$ | tebi (Ti) | terabinary: | $(2^{10})^4$ | tera: $(10^3)^4$ |
| $2^{50}$ | pebi (Pi) | petabinary: | $(2^{10})^5$ | peta: $(10^3)^5$ |
| $2^{60}$ | exbi (Ei) | exabinary: | $(2^{10})^6$ | exa: $(10^3)^6$ |

**system operator** (sysop, pronounced "SIS-op") (n.) The person who takes responsibility for managing a bulletin board system (BBS) or an email service.

**System 7.5** (n.) A version of the Mac OS superseded by System 7.6 and ultimately replaced by System 8.0 in 1997.

**System 7.x** (n.) Any Mac OS later than System 7.0 and prior to System 8.

**Systems Network Architecture** (SNA) (n.) Proprietary IBM network design that preceded the OSI model. It was the first well-defined network architecture for online data processing systems, originally implemented for mainframe computing networks.

**System Use Sharing Protocol** (SUSP) (n.) An extension to the ISO 9660 standard. SUSP permits multiple file system extensions to exist on a single CD-ROM.

**S**

# T

**T carrier** (n.) An alternate term for a T-1 carrier facility.

**TA** See *Terminal Adapter.*

**table of contents** (TOC, pronounced "tee-oh-SEE") (n.) The space on a CD-ROM where information is imprinted. The information is about the tracks on the disc, their starting locations, and the total length of the data on the disc.

**Tabular Data Control** (n.) A Microsoft ActiveX control that will sort a data file, extract requested information, and deliver it to specified areas of an HTML document.

**TAC** See *Terminal Access Controller.*

**tach** (n.) The mechanical, analog equivalent of a word clock. An electronic pulse that provides information about the speed and direction of tape in a video or audio device. No location or positional information is included.

**tag** (n.) A character or a string containing identifying information and connected to a piece of data, often at the beginning and the end. In HTML, a tag is placed before and after a text string to identify features or attributes of the data.

**Tagged Image File Format** (TIFF, pronounced "TIFF") (n.) Developed in 1986 by an industry group that included Aldus, Microsoft, and others, an image format used to store and exchange graphics on IBM-compatible and Macintosh platforms.

**talk** (n.) Network protocol that allows users on two or more remote computers to carry on a realtime dialog by typing their words on the screen for the other parties to see, as in a chat room.

**talk mode** (n.) A communication style that uses shorthand to save keystrokes. Talk mode is common in electronic mail and Usenet groups. Talk mode relies on the use of shorthand that often replaces commonly used expressions with the first letter of each word. For example, "IMHO" replaces "in my humble opinion." Writing "BYE?" (Are you ready to close the conversation?) is the standard way to end a talk-mode conversation. Typographical errors are not corrected by the typist in talk mode, unless severe confusion would result. Users type "xxx" and begin from a point prior to the error instead of making corrections to their text. See also *shorthand.*

**talkback** (n.) A function on a mixing board. A microphone mounted on the console allows the engineer to speak with musicians or voice talent during a session by engaging the talkback switch. It is necessary when the console is located in a soundproof control room or amidst the audience for sound reinforcement systems.

**talk time** (n.) The number of hours and minutes a fully charged cellular phone battery will remain charged while being used.

**tally light** (n.) Indicator on the front of a camera that informs both the operator and the subject(s) that the camera is recording. The tally light is also visible in the viewfinder.

**tap** (n.) A connection to the main transmission line in a cable-based local area network (LAN).

**TAP** See *Telocator Alphanumeric Protocol.*

**tape archive** (TAR, pronounced "TAR") (n.) A Unix command with numerous options that creates a single file archive of several smaller files. The file name extension in the Unix op-

erating system is .tar.

**tape storage** (n.) A ribbon of magnetic recording media stored on a reel or a cassette. A tape can hold analog or digital data. Tape storage offers low cost per megabyte, but tape deteriorates over time. Another disadvantage is that accessing data from a tape is slow. The primary application in digital media is for archival backups, which are usually done overnight so that hard disk drives can be erased and used the next day to digitize new data.

**tape transport** (n.) The mechanical parts in a tape recorder that move the tape over the heads. See figure.

**TAPI** See *Telephony Application Programming Interface.*

**TAR** See *tape archive.*

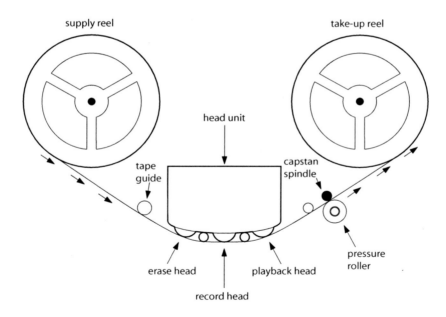

*tape transport in a reel-to-reel recorder*

**TARGA** See *Truevision Advanced Raster Graphics Adapter.*

**target machine** (n.) The platform, specifications, and configuration of hardware and software on which media is intended to perform.

**tariff** (n.) A document that establishes rates to be charged for services, equipment, or facilities offered by a regulated telephone company, filed with the state public utilities commission or the FCC. A regulated utility is required to provide services to all who request them at a fixed rate. The tariff defines both the service and the rate. A Public Utilities Commission (PUC) approves tariffs based on a formula that allows the regulated utility a certain percentage of profit.

**TB** See *terabyte.*

**TBC** See *time base corrector.*

**TBK** (n.) The file name extension for a file created by the multimedia authoring application ToolBook, developed by Asymmetrix.

**TCM** See *Trellis-coded modulation.*

**TCP** See *Transmission Control Protocol.*

**TCP and UDP with Bigger Address** (TUBA) (n.) A proposed standard for IP version 6 (IPv6), also known as IP Next Generation (IPng). One of the problems addressed by this new architecture is the need for more Internet addresses. IPv6 is defined in RFC 1752.

**TCP/IP** See *Transmission Control Protocol/ Internet Protocol.*

**TDD** See *Telecommunications Device for the Deaf.*

**TDM** See *time-division multiplexing.*

**TDMA** See *Time Division Multiple Access.*

**TDR** See *Time Domain Reflectometer.*

**tear-off menu** (n.) A small menu of frequently used tools represented by a box of icons in a graphical user interface (GUI). The menu may typically be repositioned on screen.

**technology without an interesting name** (TWAIN, pronounced "TWANE") (n.) The programming logic that allows graphics manipulation software to capture images from a scanner in a particular format that is readable by the software.

**telco** (n.) Abbreviation for *telephone company.*

**telecine** See *film chain.*

**telecommunications** (n.) The transfer of signals, sounds, and images over telephone or radio communications systems. Telecommunications includes passing information between voice systems and computer terminals over cable and wireless connections.

**Telecommunications Act of 1996** (n.) Signed into law by Bill Clinton in February 1996, the reform of U.S. cable, telecommunications, and Internet laws. This act set terms for local exchange carrier (LEC) entry into long distance, deregulated cable rates, and attempted to criminalize the distribution of pornography on the Internet.

**Telecommunications Device for the Deaf** (TDD) (n.) A terminal device that deaf people use widely for text communication over telephone lines. The standard that most TDDs use is reportedly a survivor of Baudot code implemented asynchronously at 45.5 or 50 baud: 1 start bit, 5 data bits, and 1.5 stop bits. This standard is generally incompatible with standard PC modems. A typical TDD is about the size of a small laptop computer with a QWERTY keyboard and a small screen.

**Telecommunications Industry Association** (TIA) (n.) This group was created in 1988 by the merger of the U.S. Telecommunications Suppliers Association (USTSA) and the EIA Information and Telecommunications Technologies Group (EIA/ITG). The TIA works with the EIA in developing technical standards and collecting market data for their industry.

**telecommute** (v.) While working at home, to use telecommunications equipment to maintain contact with an office.

**telecomputing** (n.) Using a combination of telephone, television, cable, and computing technologies in a single system that is typically based in the home.

**teleconference** (n.) Set up by a telecommunications provider, a telephone call that enables more than two callers to participate in an *audioconference*. The use of video in a *videoconference* further allows participants at remote sites to see each other and to share visual data.

**telemedicine** (n.) The specialized use of communications media, particularly videoconferencing, for medical purposes. It facilitates distance learning in medical education and delivers health care to patients and providers at a distance.

**telephony** (n.) With or without wiring, the transmission of electronic signals representing sounds or data to a remote location.

**Telephony Application Programming Interface** (TAPI) (n.) A Windows Application Programming Interface (API) enabling hardware-independent access to telephone-based communication. TAPI covers a rather wide area of services, from initializing a modem and placing a call to using voice mail or controlling a remote computer.

**telephoto** (n.) A camera lens with a long focal length and a narrow field of view. A telephoto is used to magnify objects that are far away.

**teletext** (n.) Computer-generated characters inserted into the vertical blanking interval (VBI) of a broadcast signal, normally during lines 18 to 21 of a one-way transmission.

**television standards** (n.) One of three standards for television signals used for both broadcast and videotape playback applications. The three formats are PAL, NTSC, and SECAM, and they have significant differences. One feature they all share is that each frame consists of two fields. PAL moves at 25 frames per second (fps) with 625 scan lines. It uses amplitude modulation (AM) at a channel bandwidth of 8 MHz. NTSC moves at 29.97 fps with 525 scan lines and uses AM at a channel bandwidth of 6 MHz. SECAM has the same frame rate and number of scan lines as PAL but uses frequency modulated (FM) subcarriers at a bandwidth of 8 MHz. In a few South American countries, hybrid formats known as *PAL-M* and *PAL-N* combine features of both NTSC and PAL. NTSC is the standard in most of Central America, whereas PAL is the standard in most western European countries. Here is a breakdown of which standards are used in various countries:

NTSC:    United States, Canada, Mexico, Japan, South Korea, the Philippines

415

PAL:      Great Britain, Germany, Spain, India, China, Australia
SECAM:    France, Hungary, Poland, Russia, Saudi Arabia, Egypt

**Telex** (n.) Short for "Teleprinter Exchange," a worldwide switched message-exchange service originally provided by Western Union in the United States. It was later sold and is now provided by AT&T. Telex uses teletypewriter stations linked to a central office for communication with other systems. The system originally used Baudot-coded data.

**Telnet** (n.) The Internet standard protocol for remote terminal connection service. Telnet allows a user at one site to interact with a system at another site as if the user's terminal were directly connected to the host computer. Telnet is defined in RFC 854, STD 8, and is extended by other RFCs. National Center for Supercomputing Applications (NCSA) Telnet is the standard on the Macintosh platform.

**Telocator Alphanumeric Protocol** (TAP) (n.) A telecommunications protocol for submitting requests to a pager service. TAP is a half-duplex, ASCII-based protocol capable of submitting alphanumeric messages.

**template** (n.) A previously designed structure or shell into which data may be placed. A template gives graphic presentations a consistent appearance.

**temporal** (adj.) Of, relating to, or limited by time.

**temporal compression** (n.) Any video compression technique that compares frames and identifies and records only the differences between them. It is also known as *interframe compression*.

**temporal redundancy** (n.) The duplication of information found at earlier points in a stream of data or in a signal.

**ter** (n.) The third version of an original CCITT standard, as in V.27ter.

**tera-** Prefix meaning a trillion. In the decimal system, 1 000 000 000 000 is expressed as 10 to the 12th power. In the binary system, tera- is expressed as 2 to the 40th power, or 1 099 511 627 776.

**terabyte** (TB) (n.) Two to the 4th power eight-bit bytes, or exactly 1 099 511 627 776 bytes.

**terminal** (n., adj.) 1. The hardware used in a computer-based information (CBI) system through which information passes. A terminal often takes the form of a remote workstation, such as a VT-100, with a visual display and keyboard connected to a central processing unit (CPU). A dumb terminal has no processing capability, whereas an intelligent terminal has its own processor. 2. Any point at which information can enter or exit a communication network.

**Terminal Access Controller** (TAC) (n.) Using the TACACS (Terminal Access Concentrator Access Control Server) protocol, which provides secure access to servers and data for LANs and telephone systems, a device that connects terminals to the Internet, typically with dialup modem connections.

**Terminal Adapter** (TA) (n.) A device that adapts ISDN Basic Rate Interface (BRI) channels to RS-232 and to other installed terminal equipment standards. The TA connects to a computer or a router, replacing a modem.

**terminal emulator** (n.) Software that allows a

networked computer to behave like a terminal, such as a VT-100. The computer presents itself as a terminal to the host computer and accepts the same escape sequences for functions.

**terminal strip** (n.) A type of wiring connector that employs screw-down posts separated by insulating barrier strips. Used for balanced and unbalanced wiring connections, where each wire is usually terminated with a crimped spade or ring connector and screwed in place. This wiring is not easily disconnected or unplugged. Contrast with *Euroblock*.

**terminate** (v.) 1. To place an electrical load at the end of a circuit. 2. To install a connector at the end of a cable.

**terminate and stay resident** (TSR) (n.) In MS-DOS, a program that remains in memory once it has been loaded from a disk.

**terminated line** (n.) A circuit with resistance at the end point equal to the characteristic impedance of the line. The resistance ensures that no standing waves or reflections will be present when a signal enters near the end of the line.

**terminator** (n.) A resistor connected to the end of a cable that matches the impedance of the line in order to prevent reflections. Network wiring schemes and SCSI chains are examples of systems that require terminators.

**tessellation** (n.) Transformation of models that exist as coordinates in space into polygons.

**texel** (n.) Abbreviation for textured pixel.

**text** (n.) A string of data that consists of standard ASCII characters and no other information. A text file contains no binary data or formatting information.

**tEXt** (n.) One of the formats by which a Portable Network Graphics (PNG) file may be extended. It is a chunk of data semantically equivalent to the Unicode character set instead of Latin-1. This chunk contains:

| | |
|---|---|
| Keyword: | 1–79 bytes (character string) |
| Null separator: | 1 byte |
| Compression flag: | 1 byte |
| Compression method: | 1 byte |
| Language tag: | 0 or more bytes (character string) |
| Null separator: | 1 byte |
| Translated keyword: | 0 or more bytes |
| Null separator: | 1 byte |
| Text: | 0 or more bytes |

The keyword is case-sensitive and it must contain only printable Latin-1 characters (33–126 and 161–255) and spaces (32), but no leading, trailing, or consecutive spaces.

**text editor** (n.) A utility program that manipulates text files, much as a word processor does. Unlike a word-processing application, a text editor does not embed control codes or escape sequences in the file for formatting. Programmers use text editors to write code or HTML documents.

**text file** (n.) A type of data file with characters that are printable letters, numbers, and symbols exclusively. The ASCII character set is most often used, and no invisible control characters are included. A text file could be created by a text editor and imported into a word processor, but it would not contain formatting information. See also *binary file* or *Rich Text Format*.

**text track** (n.) A track in a QuickTime movie that consists of text, style, positioning, and timing information, often used for subtitles.

417

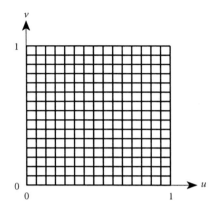

rectangular grid as a texture map

rectangular grid mapped onto a sphere

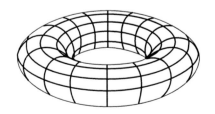

rectangular grid mapped onto a torus

**text-mode browser** (n.) Universal client incapable of displaying graphics. A text-mode browser is useful on dumb terminals and on very slow computers. It offers many of the features available in a graphical browser. Lynx is a popular browser of this type.

**texture** (n.) A surface with varied intensities. It is often used as a region descriptor in image analysis and in computer vision. Texture may be described in statistical, structural, and spectral terms. A texture can be defined by the statistical properties of its gray levels. Structural descriptors characterize a texture as consisting of primitive textural elements (texels) that are regularly arranged on the surface. The Fourier spectrum may be used to describe the global periodicity of the gray levels of a surface by identifying high-energy peaks in the spectrum.

**texture map** (n.) The shading and surface features of a two-dimensional or three-dimensional object. In addition to being an image, a texture map can be a procedure calculated from formulas. See figures.

**TFT** See *thin film transistor.*

**TFTP** See *Trivial File Transfer Protocol.*

**TGA** (n.) Captured by a Truevision video card, a TARGA format with the file name extension .tga.

**THD** See *total harmonic distortion.*

**THD+N** See *total harmonic distortion plus noise.*

**theremin** (n.) Possibly the first electronic musical instrument, invented in 1919 by the Russian Lev Sergeivitch Termen (which he later changed to Leon Theremin). It is the only musical instrument that is played without being touched. A theremin works by causing two oscillators to "beat" together. The *beat frequency* equals the difference in frequency between the two signals. Beats are a physical phenomenon occurring in the air when sounds are mixed. A theremin uses one oscillator operating well above the upper limit of human hearing as a reference tone, and another oscillator whose frequency is varied by the proximity of a human hand, for instance, to a capacitive sensing element shaped like an antenna. A typical machine has two antennas and you play it by moving your hands nearer to and farther from the antennas. One antenna controls the volume of the sound, while the other controls the frequency, or pitch, of the sound.

**thermal wax printer** (n.) A color printer that creates an image by using heated pins to melt a thin coating of wax on a ribbon, transferring the wax onto the paper.

**thin client** (n.) In a system of networked computers, a client program that relies on the server for most of its system functions. Networked personal computers operate as "fat clients," depending on the server only for file storage and printing. The benefit of thin clients over fat ones is that maintenance tasks for thin clients are centralized on the server and need to be done just once. In addition, thin clients have fewer hardware demands. Also called a *dumb terminal.*

**Thin Ethernet** (n.) A networking technology that uses thinner and cheaper coaxial cable than standard Ethernet does. Thin Ethernet adheres to the IEEE 802.3 standard. Transmission is at 10 megabits per second (Mbps) over a maximum distance of 200 meters, and cable ends are terminated with BNC connectors. Also called *cheapernet* or *10BASE2.*

**thin film transistor** (TFT) (n.) A miniature integrated circuit (IC) formed by thin layers of conductive material on an insulating substrate.

**thrash** (v.) To move about vigorously, accomplishing nothing. Overloaded paging systems waste much time thrashing, or moving data into and out of the core needlessly, as do systems with a cache conflict.

**thread** (n.) 1. A complete operation, a set of instructions, or a process executed by software that cannot be interrupted. 2. A series of interrelated messages sent over a network.

**Threaded-Neill-Concelman** (TNC) (n.) A threaded connector used with coaxial cables.

**three-finger salute** (n.) The key combination Ctrl-Alt-Delete, which causes a Windows or MS-DOS operating system to reboot. Also known as a *warm boot.*

**three-point lighting** (n.) Also known as *Rembrandt lighting,* a common setup for lights in a video production or an animation scene. From the camera perspective, the *key light* is placed to the right, behind the camera, and is elevated at a distance. The second light is placed to the left, in a symmetrical relationship to the key light. Referred to as the *fill,* this second light is an omnidirectional or a point light at about half the intensity of the key. The third light is a *back light,* placed behind the subject and directly opposed to the fill light. A spotlight is generally used for the back light and has an intensity similar to that of the key light.

**throughput** (n.) The data processing capacity of a bus, or the rate at which it can pass data. It is most often expressed in bits per second (bps).

**thumbnail** (n.) Small version of a larger graphic image. A thumbnail is typically used to index a database of graphics or to preview an

**T**

image that would take a great deal of space or time to draw at a larger resolution. An encapsulated PostScript file carries with it a TIFF thumbnail for previewing.

**THX** (n.) A term coined by Lucasfilm, Ltd. for their audio playback specification in both commercial and home cinema installations. The specification includes quality standards for the audio programs on DVDs, Laserdiscs, and VHS tapes. The first film George Lucas made was titled *THX-1138*. The acronym may be a reference to *Tomlinson Holman's eXperiment,* named for Lucasfilm's original technical director.

**TIA** See *Telecommunications Industry Association.*

**tie line** (n.) An interswitch trunk consisting of a leased or private dedicated telephone circuit that connects two PBX switches.

**TIFF** See *Tagged Image File Format.*

**Tiger** (n.) A specialized application for network security that scans a Unix computing system in an effort to uncover holes and weaknesses in its defense against intrusion.

**tilde** (n.) ASCII character 126, ~. Pronounced "TIL-deh."

**tiled windows** (n.) In a graphical user interface (GUI), an arrangement of program windows in which the windows do not overlap.

**tilt** (v.) To pivot a video camera vertically, up or down, from a stationary position and height. A tilt follows movement, contrasts the size differences of two subjects, and may give the viewer a point-of-view (POV) sense of a subject's height.

**timbre** (n.) A musical term for the color of a tone, determined primarily by its overtone structure. The difference between an oboe and a flute sounding the same note is a difference in timbre. This is not to be confused with the pitch (frequency), the loudness (amplitude), or the shape (envelope) of a tone. Pronounced "TAM-bur."

**time base corrector** (TBC) (n.) A device that resets the timing portion of a video signal to the standard values for a given video format. A TBC cleans up the output of videotape players or computer video cards prior to broadcast. It can also synchronize two independent video signals.

**time code** (n.) Address code with time-referenced information that is recorded on a spare track of videotape or that is inserted in the vertical blanking interval (VBI) of a video signal. It is expressed as an eight-digit number that displays time in hours, minutes, seconds, and video frames in the format hh:mm:ss:ff.

**time code generator** (n.) A special type of signal generator that outputs SMPTE time code in the form of a regular pulse, which is typically recorded as an audio signal on an unused track of videotape.

**time code reader** (n.) An electronic device that reads and displays SMPTE time code. It is generally integrated in a professional-quality playback or recording deck.

**Time Division Multiple Access** (TDMA) (n.) A technique for transmitting digital wireless communications. By allocating unique time slots to each user on each channel, TDMA permits many users to access a single radio frequency (RF) channel sequentially without interference.

**time-division multiplexing** (TDM) (n.) A process in which multiple channels of information are mixed and transmitted over a single telecommunications link, with the channels taking turns using the link. A periodic synchronization signal is used so the receiver can distinguish between channels. TDM is inefficient when traffic is intermittent, because a time slot is allocated even when a channel has no data to transmit. Statistical TDM overcomes this problem. The portion of the bandwidth allocated to each user varies dynamically in the statistical model.

**Time Domain Reflectometer** (TDR) (n.) An electronic device used to locate short circuits and to track impedance characteristics in a data connection cable.

**Time-Multiplexed Switching** (TMS) (n.) A circuit-switching technique in which the path through the matrix is time configured for each time-division multiplexed (TDM) code word, under computer control. It is used in nearly all digital telephone switches.

**timeout** (n.) A default action performed by a program when a predetermined period of time expires before a user enters data or offers input of any kind. This may result in initiating a screensaver or looping a sequence.

**Time-Slot Interchange** (TSI) (n.) In this switching technique, the time-division multiplexed (TDM) channels are moved in time between the input and output TDM data streams. It is used as both the initial and the final stages on large switches combined with a TMS matrix. This technology is used in Digital Access and Cross-Connect System (DACS) equipment.

**Time to Live** (TTL) (n.) A field in an Internet Protocol (IP) header that tells how many more hops a given packet will make before it is discarded or returned.

**tip-ring-sleeve** (TRS) (n.) 1. Stereo 0.25-inch connector consisting of tip (T), ring (R), and sleeve (S) sections, wired so that T = left, R = right, and S = ground/shield. 2. A balanced-line interconnect with the positive and negative signal lines tied to tip and ring respectively, and the sleeve acting as an overall shield. 3. An insert loop interconnect with T = send, R = return, and S = ground/shield, used to pass signals between a mixing board and outboard signal processors.

**tip-sleeve** (TS) (n.) Mono 0.25-inch connector consisting of a tip (T) where the signal is connected and a sleeve (S) for the ground/shield. It is used for electronic instruments and other common unbalanced connections.

**title** (n.) In electronic or digital publishing, a volume, a set of volumes, or a program on a CD-ROM.

**titler** (n.) In video post-production, a device that is used to generate characters for titles or captions that are overlaid on video frames.

**titling** (n.) The process of adding text to video to provide credits, to present captions, or to communicate printed information to the viewer.

**TMS** See *Time-Multiplexed Switching.*

**TNC** See *Threaded-Neill-Concelman.*

**TOC** See *table of contents.*

**toggle** 1. (v.) To switch between two applications or choices, such as on and off, with a single key or button. 2. (n.) Any two-position switch that may be mechanical or virtual.

**token bus** (n.) Defined by IEEE 802.4, a local network access topology in which all stations actively attached to the bus monitor it for the broadcast token, which is a supervisory frame. A station must receive the token before transmitting. Preassigned priority algorithms control bus access.

**token ring** (n., adj.) A local area network (LAN) configured in a ring, around which a token (or a special signal) is passed between terminals over a single channel. The floating message, or the token, gives each terminal permission to transmit data. A Multistation Access Unit (MSAU) controls the passage of data around the ring at speeds of up to 16 megabits per second (Mbps). IBM developed this network structure, the IEEE 802.5 standard. See figure.

T1 (n., adj.) A digital carrier facility that transmits a DS-1 formatted digital signal at 1.544 megabits per second (Mbps). Two unshielded twisted-pair telephone lines are used to transport T1 signals, one pair for each direction. Some hybrid equipment operates at half the T1 rate in full-duplex mode, separating the sent and the received signals at each end with components. The transmitted signal consists of pulses a few hundred nanoseconds wide, each inverted with respect to the preceding one. At the sending end the strength of the signal is 1 volt, and at the receiving end the strength must be greater than 0.01 volts. This requires repeaters about every 6000 feet. The information is contained in the timing of the signals, not in the polarity. A process known as *bit stuffing* is used so that the receiving apparatus will not lose track of the sending clock when a long sequence of bits of the same polarity is sent.

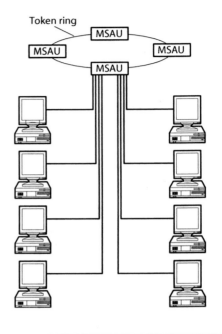

*token ring network*

Pronounced "TEE-one."

T1C (n.) A digital carrier facility that transmits a DS-1C formatted digital signal at 3.152 megabits per second (Mbps). Two twisted-pairs of copper wires are used as the transmission medium. Pronounced "TEE-one-SEE."

**tone controls** (n.) A two-band equalizer with amplitude control only over the highest and the lowest frequencies. A third control might be provided for the midband frequencies. See also *Baxandall tone controls*.

**toolbar** (n.) A collection of icons that activate program functions in a graphical user interface (GUI). In graphics programs, the tools may include a lasso selector, a text entry tool, and an eraser. Other tools determine the width and color of lines that are drawn.

**torus** (n.) A three-dimensional shape that resembles a donut and that is known as an *anchor ring*. For an example, see the bottom figure under *texture map*.

**total harmonic distortion** (THD) (n.) A measure of performance in audio gear that monitors hum and other unwanted frequencies. THD is expressed as a percentage of noise compared with the total signal. Lower percentages are better.

**total harmonic distortion plus noise** (THD+N) (n.) A common audio measurement. A single pure sine wave frequency is passed through the unit being tested, then patched back into an instrument that measures distortion. THD+N is not the most useful indicator of a unit's performance. What it tells the user about *hum, noise,* and *interference* is useful; however, that information is better conveyed by the *signal-to-noise ratio* specification.

**touch screen** (n., adj.) A display or a monitor serving as a control or input device that responds to a user's touch. Touch-screen systems employ a variety of technologies, such as plastic membranes, infrared grids, capacitance sensors, and acceleration detection devices.

**Touch-Tone** (n.) The trademark, registered by AT&T, for push-button dialing using the voice transmission path. See *DTMF*.

**T-pad** See *attenuator pad.*

**tpi** See *tracks per inch.*

**TP/IX** (n.) Internet protocol that changes TCP and User Datagram Protocol (UDP) headers into a 64-bit Internet Protocol (IP) address, a

32-bit port number, and a 64-bit sequence number. TP/IX is described in RFC 1475.

**trace packet** (n.) Useful for network troubleshooting, a unique packet in a packet-switching network that sends a report from each system element that it visits, at every stage of its progress, to a network control center.

**track** (n.) 1. On an audio tape or a videotape, the physical area that contains an individual program or some control information. It could be compared to a lane on the freeway. 2. The process through which a recorded videotape plays back. A machine that "tracks" well has its heads properly aligned. Videotape tracks are recorded diagonally. 3. One of the adjacent bands of the data spiral on a compact disc. The tracks on a hard disk exist in the form of concentric circles rather than in a spiral shape. 4. One of the separate media types that make up a movie. In addition to a video track and an audio track, some multimedia architectures such as QuickTime allow for text tracks, sprite tracks, MIDI tracks, and other types.

**trackball** (n.) An alternative input device to a mouse. A trackball functions like an upside-down mouse and requires little desktop space. Spinning the ball causes the cursor on the screen to move.

**T**

**tracking** (n.) 1. The overall amount of space between characters in a line of text. This is different from kerning, which deals with the space between certain pairs of characters. 2. In video production, lateral camera movement that is aligned with moving subjects so that the background appears to move, not the subjects. 3. The alignment of audio or video playback and record heads in relation to the tape that moves over them.

**track-relative time** (n.) A method used to determine the start and stop times of audio segments on a mixed-mode disc.

**tracks per inch** (tpi) (n.) A measurement of the density of magnetic media. A DOS-formatted, high-density, 3.5-inch floppy disk holds 135 tpi.

**traffic** (n.) Over a period of time, the number of messages transmitted on a communications circuit.

**transaction** (n.) In reference to a database system, a unit of interaction that occurs individually and coherently. 2. In data communications, a message destined for an application program. 3. In an interactive context, an exchange between a terminal or computer and another device or person.

**transactional** (adj.) Describes a retail kiosk where a customer can make a credit card purchase or conduct business.

**transceiver** (n.) A system that receives, amplifies, and retransmits a signal without altering the original content significantly.

**transcode** (v.) To convert from one video or graphic format to another, as opposed to encoding, which refers to the original capture or digitization of images.

**transducer** (n.) Any device that converts one form of energy into another, such as a microphone that converts varying sound pressure levels into an analogous varied stream of voltage.

**transfer rate** (n.) The rate at which digital information is transferred to or from a storage medium or device. For example, a single-speed compact disc reader transfers data at approximately 150 kilobytes per second (KBps).

**transistor** (n.) A semiconductor with three terminals used for amplification. It was invented in 1947 at Bell Labs and remains the fundamental component of most electronic circuits. Transistors are miniaturized and combined with other components to create complex integrated circuits (ICs), such as logic gates, microprocessors, and memory. The two types are the bipolar transistor (also called the *junction transistor*) and the field-effect transistor (FET).

**transistor-transistor logic** (TTL) (n.) Bipolar integrated circuit (IC) logic that employs transistors with multiple emitters.

**transit network** (n.) Any network with paths to at least two other networks. It passes traffic between those networks and carries traffic for its own hosts.

**transmission** (n.) The electronic transfer of a signal or data from one location or device to another.

**Transmission Control Protocol** (TCP) (n.) The transport layer protocol used for Ethernet and for the Internet, developed by the Defense Advanced Research Projects Agency (DARPA) and defined in RFC 793, STD 7. TCP is built on top of Internet Protocol (IP) and is usually combined with it. TCP adds reliable full-duplex communication, flow control, multiplexing, and process-to-process connections. Unlike the User Datagram Protocol (UDP), TCP is connection-oriented and stream-oriented.

**Transmission Control Protocol/Internet Protocol** (TCP/IP) (n.) The de facto standard Ethernet protocols for Internet communications. The Defense Advanced Research Projects Agency (DARPA) developed TCP for internetworking. It encompasses both network layer and transport layer protocols. IP is a packet-switching protocol, whereas TCP checks, tracks, and corrects transmission errors. Although TCP and IP specify two protocols at specific layers, the term *TCP/IP* is often used to refer to the entire protocol suite based on TCP and IP. That suite includes Telnet, FTP, User Datagram Protocol (UDP), and Realtime Transport Protocol (RTP).

**transmission rate** (n.) The speed at which data can be transferred across a communications medium under varying conditions.

**transparency** (n.) 1. The degree to which a computing system interferes with the process of user interaction with content. Intuitive software running on easy-to-use equipment makes technology transparent. 2. The property of a layer in a graphical composition that allows underlying layers to show through. An object with a transparent background allows lower layers to show clearly around the object in the foreground.

**transponder** (n.) A satellite communications device that can receive a signal, convert it to a new frequency, amplify it, and send it back to earth immediately. A transponder is normally contained within a retransmitting satellite.

**transport layer** (n.) The network entity responsible for end-to-end control of transmitted data in the OSI model.

**transport protocol** (n.) The protocol by which a service is delivered. Common ones are Simple Mail Transfer Protocol (SMTP), POP, and Unix-to-Unix CoPy (UUCP) for delivering Internet mail. For delivering news, Network News Transfer Protocol (NNTP) or UUCP is used.

**tree** (n.) A local area network (LAN) topology in the shape of a tree with only one route between network nodes.

**Trellis-coded modulation** (TCM) (n.) A technique employed by high-speed modems for detection and correction of data errors.

**triad** (n.) In an RGB display, a set of red, green, and blue phosphors arranged in a triangle. Three guns fire electron beams of different colors at the phosphors on the tube. The phosphors are excited by the beam, whose color matches theirs. The triad produces a single color, which is a combination of the colors of the three excited phosphors. See figure.

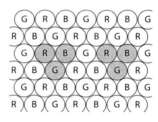

*triad-phosphor dot pattern*

**tripod** (n.) A camera mount with three legs that provides stability and aids in moving the camera smoothly.

**Trivial File Transfer Protocol** (TFTP) (n.) A weak version of FTP that lacks authentication and other basic features. TFTP can be used to boot a networked machine.

**Trojan horse** (n.) Software that secretly conveys a means of access to the system on which it runs, allowing it to invade that system with a virus and make unauthorized changes to the configuration.

**troubleshoot** (v.) To test system components for continuity and proper performance and to identify faulty connections and parts. If a visual inspection does not indicate loose con-

425

nections, voltage levels and logic circuits should be checked. If logic levels are improper, it could be the result of a malfunctioning integrated circuit (IC) or of noise caused by electromagnetic interference. Many systems are equipped with diagnostic test programs that may identify the cause of a problem. If all hardware components and connections have been tested and have passed inspection, the problem may be a bug in the software.

**TRS** See *tip-ring-sleeve.*

**true color** 1. (n.) A system in which color information belonging to an image is directly used to determine the output color, rather than serving as an index to a table of colors in a palette. 2. (adj.) Describes color systems with enough colors to create an image that looks natural to the human eye. It is typically defined as 24-bit color.

**true streaming** (n.) In serving digital video, technologies that match the bandwidth of the media signal to the client connection speed so that the media is viewed in realtime. Specialized media servers and streaming protocols such as Real-Time Streaming Protocol (RTSP) are required to enable true streaming. Compare with *progressive download.*

**TrueType** (n.) Developed by Apple Computer in 1991, a scalable font technology that is implemented in Microsoft Windows and in OS/2 operating systems, as well as in the Macintosh OS.

**Truevision Advanced Raster Graphics Adapter** (TARGA, pronounced "TAR-gah") (n.) 1. A 24-bit color image format that Truevision defined, originally for that company's line of TARGA videographics interface cards. Many other image-creation and image-editing programs have since used it as an exchange format. 2. A series of graphics cards produced by Truevision for microcomputers. The PC series was among the first to support full-color (24-bit) display.

**truncate** (v.) To eliminate without rounding off some low-order bits, often after performing an arithmetic computation.

**trunk** (n.) 1. In telecommunications, a telephone line, or a channel, between the telephone company's central office or switching center and another switching center or private branch exchange (PBX). 2. In cable television (CATV), part of a coaxial cable system that starts at the headend of a system and acts as the main distribution artery for CATV signals. The trunk cable connects with the distribution and feeder segments.

**trusted device** (n.) A device that has been authenticated, or one that is as impervious to hacking as possible.

**truth table** (n.) A simple table that identifies all possible combinations of inputs and the corresponding outputs of such Boolean functions as AND, OR, NOT, NAND, NOR, IMPLIES, and XOR.

**TS** See *tip-sleeve.*

**TSI** See *Time-Slot Interchange.*

**T-span** (n.) A telephone circuit or cable through which a T-carrier runs.

**TSR** See *terminate and stay resident.*

**T3** (n.) A combination of 28 T1 lines with an aggregate data rate of 44.736 megabits per second (Mbps).

**TTL** See *Time to Live* or *transistor-transistor logic.*

T2 (n.) A digital carrier facility that transmits a DS-2 formatted digital signal at 6.312 megabits per second (Mbps). Two twisted-pairs of copper wires are used as the transmission medium. Pronounced "TEE-two."

**TUBA** See *TCP and UDP with Bigger Address.*

**tunneling** (n.) Encapsulation of one protocol within another. By using tunneling, data can be moved between administrative domains that use a protocol unsupported by the network connecting the domains.

**turnkey system** (n.) An integrated hardware-software program that is ready to run without setup or engineering. The user simply turns a key to operate.

**turntablist** (n.) A performer who uses two or more turntables as music sources from which a mix is created by quickly cutting and combining the sounds of each source using specially designed performance mixers.

**TWAIN** See *technology without an interesting name.*

**tweak** (v.) Jargon meaning to change a value or setting slightly.

**tween** (v.) To create an interpolated image between two set images, or coordinates, in an animation or a graphics program. Tweening speeds up the creation of animated sequences by letting the user define only the key frame images and then instructing the computer to fill in the intervening pictures.

**twin-tone IMD** See *intermodulation distortion.*

**twisted pair** (n.) In telecommunications, a standard cable made up of one or more pairs of copper wire twisted around one another to reduce induction and interference between the wires. See figure.

*twisted-pair cable construction*

**two-phase commit** (n.) Physically located on independent machines, a data notation method that ensures the success or the failure of each machine. If all statements succeed, an action is committed. If any one statement fails, all statements within the transaction revert to their original condition.

**twos complement** (n.) A system that represents negative numbers with binary data. Each bit of the number is inverted. Then 1 (000...00001) is added (ignoring overflow). Using all 1s to represent −1 avoids the two representations for 0 found in ones complement. This procedure simplifies the logic required for addition and subtraction but introduces complexity for negation. The examples below show the application of this concept.

$$000...00011 = +3$$
$$000...00010 = +2$$
$$000...00001 = +1$$
$$000...00000 = 0$$
$$111...11111 = -1$$
$$111...11110 = -2$$
$$111...11101 = -3$$

**two-way messaging** (n.) In telecommunications, this occurs when a subscriber can send as well as receive a message. A cell phone conversation is an example, while paging is typically one-way messaging.

427

# U

UART See *universal asynchronous receiver-transmitter.*

UAWG Consortium (n.) Universal ADSL Working Group Consortium; a group of network operators, computer companies, and telecommunications providers that developed a standard for splitterless ADSL, or ADSL Lite, referred to as G.lite by the International Telecommunications Union–Telecommunications Standardization Sector (ITU-T). See also *Asymmetric Digital Subscriber Line.*

UCS See *Universal Character Set.*

UDMA See *Ultra DMA.*

UDP See *User Datagram Protocol.*

UDTV See *ultra-high definition television.*

UHF See *ultra-high frequency.*

UI See *user interface.*

Ultimatte (n.) A brand name for a chroma key system used to overlay multiple video images. The Ultimatte system transfers the luminance (brightness) image of the dropout color, which enables the transfer of shadows to the composite image. Pronounced "UL-ti-mat."

Ultimedia (n.) The entire line of IBM multimedia tools and technologies. The IBM PS/2 Ultimedia model M57 SLC was IBM's first PS/2 machine with built-in multimedia capabilities. The Ultimedia line, dating from 1991, complies with Multimedia Personal Computer (MPC) specifications.

Ultra DMA (UDMA) (n.) Ultra direct memory access; advanced implementation of DMA that allows commands to transfer data at 33.3 megabits per second (Mbps). This is twice the original Burst DMA transfer rate of 16.6 Mbps, using the same standard 40-pin Integrated Drive Electronics (IDE) interface cable. To employ UDMA, the drive and the Basic Input/Output System (BIOS) must be compatible with the new standard, and device drivers must be loaded in the operating system. UDMA allows a host computer to send and retrieve data faster, particularly during sequential operations. It provides enhanced data integrity capabilities to the EIDE interface. It does this through improved timing margins and through the use of cyclic redundancy check (CRC), a data transfer error detection code. UDMA is endorsed by most industry hard drive manufacturers, including Fujitsu, IBM, Maxtor, Quantum, Seagate, Toshiba, and Western Digital.

ultra-high definition television (UDTV) (n.) A proposed digital broadcast standard with higher resolution than high-definition television (HDTV). UDTV will provide approximately

3000 lines of resolution, as opposed to 1125 lines in HDTV. No standards have been established yet.

**ultra-high frequency** (UHF) (adj.) 1. Describes the radio frequency from 300 to 3000 MHz. 2. Describes the TV broadcast band occupied by UHF channels 14 through 83 in the United States, the range from 470 MHz to 890 MHz.

**ultra SCSI** (n.) A type of SCSI-2 bus that transfers data at 20 Mbps, referred to as *fast-20* by ANSI. Ultra wide SCSI transfers data at 40 Mbps. See also *Small Computer System Interface.*

**ultrasonic** (adj.) Of or relating to acoustic frequencies above the range audible to the human ear, or above approximately 20,000 hertz. Compare with *supersonic.*

**ultraviolet** (UV) (n.) Invisible electromagnetic radiation with wavelengths from 10 nanometers to 400 nanometers. Light in this spectrum is commonly used for wireless and fiber optic data transmission.

**Ultrix** (n.) A version of Unix implemented by Digital Equipment Corporation (DEC) for their RISC-based workstations.

**U-matic** (n., adj.) The trade name developed by Sony for 3/4-inch videotape recorders (VTRs) and videotape players.

**UMB** See *upper memory block.*

**UMTS** See *Universal Mobile Telecommunications System.*

**unbalanced** (adj.) In audio and telecommunications, describes channels that carry a signal on one wire and use a second wire as a ground. Unbalanced wiring is less expensive than bal-anced configurations that carry the signal as a difference between two wires, and use a third wire as the ground. Unbalanced lines are more susceptible to spurious noise than are balanced lines.

**unbalanced line** (n.) A single conductor with a ground or shield. See *balanced line.*

**underscan** (v.) To limit the electron beam in a cathode-ray tube (CRT) to scan within the boundaries of the display. This reduces the normal size of a video image by as much as 20 percent. To ensure that the complete image is always visible within a display area, it is advisable to check the boundaries of an image in underscan mode. Computer monitors usually operate in underscan mode, but the underscanning feature is available only on professional-quality NTSC video monitors.

**undo** (v.) To void the user's last action in a graphical user interface (GUI). The Edit menu in most Microsoft programs offers the Undo function, which may also be invoked with the key combination Ctrl-Z.

**unformatted capacity** (n.) The amount of data that a storage device can hold without the information that makes it readable, such as the layout of tracks and the file allocation table.

**Unicast** (n.) Point-to-point, one-to-one transmission of data. Unicasting is the standard transmission method on the Internet. *Webcasting,* by contrast, is the process of broadcasting digital information to all parties tuned in to a channel through which data is pushed, or it is the process of sending software updates on request to multiple points.

**Unicode** (n.) A character coding scheme that uses 16 bits for each character, designed to extend the capabilities of ASCII, which uses seven bits. Nearly all letters and symbols in all languages can be represented in a standard way with Unicode. The first 128 characters of Unicode are identical to those in standard ASCII.

**uniform resource locator** (URL, pronounced "you-are-EL") (n.) A means of identifying an exact location on the Internet. A URL has four parts. In *http://hansenmedia.com/html/info/default.html,* for example, there is the protocol type (*http://*), the DNS server name (*hansenmedia.com*), the subdirectory (*html/info*), and the file name (*default.html*).

**Uniform Resource Name** (URN, pronounced "you-are-EN") (n.) A naming scheme developed by the Internet Engineering Task Force (IETF) that provides for the resolution of names with greater persistence and reliability than is currently associated with URLs.

**uninterruptible power supply** (UPS) (n.) A device that can provide electrical power to a system if the normal power source fails. A UPS thereby prevents interrupted service.

**unity gain** (n.) In audio engineering, the condition in which input and output levels are equal, with no apparent amplification or attenuation.

**universal asynchronous receiver-transmitter** (UART) (n.) An integrated circuit (IC) that converts between serial and parallel data formats. For example, a UART converts the parallel data from a computer into serial data for asynchronous transmission.

**Universal Character Set** (UCS) (n.) An ISO and International Electrotechnical Commission (IEC) standard listing of symbols established in 1993. The full name is the *Universal Multiple-Octet Coded Character Set.* The first part is the Architecture and Basic Multilingual Plane (BMP), based on Unicode and on an ISO draft

for 16-bit character codes. Each plane consists of 256 x 256 locations. BMP is the initial plane, and others are supposed to follow. Java was the first programming language to define a character as 16 bits. Defined in ISO/IEC 10646, UCS includes the ASCII and Latin-1 subsets with their binary values unchanged.

**universal client** (n.) A program that runs on the client machine in a client-server network. A web browser is an example of a universal client. It is preferred by many over the term *browser.*

**Universal Mobile Telecommunications System** (UMTS) (n.) An evolving technology for rapidly moving data and multimedia over wireless devices. The European implementation of the third generation (3G) wireless phone system is referred to as UMTS. It is expected to provide service in the 2 GHz band, global roaming, and personalized features.

**universal product code** (UPC) (n.) The bar code used to identify items that are indexed in a retail store, implemented in the U.S. in 1973. It consists of a label with stripes of varied thickness that are read by an optical scanner. Information about the manufacturer and the product is encoded in the stripes. See also *bar code.*

**Universal Resource Identifier** (URI, pronounced "you-are-EYE") (n.) The term used for a short string, which is a name or address that references a file or a location on the Internet. It is used to identify a resource, such as a graphic file, that is embedded in an HTML document or the document itself. A uniform resource locator (URL) is a type of URI. A full definition of URI is contained in RFC 1630.

**Universal Serial Bus** (USB) (n.) An input/output (I/O) bus capable of data transfer at 12 megabytes per second (MBps) with up to

127 devices connected in a daisy chain. The USB specification was published in 1996 by a consortium of companies led by Intel Corporation, including Compaq, Digital Equipment Corporation, IBM, Microsoft, NEC Technologies, and Northern Telecom. In addition to a keyboard, a mouse, and a printer, a peripheral such as a CD-ROM drive or a modem may be connected to a single port on a PC. Typically, each device connected to a computer uses its own port. USB supports multiple isochronous data streams for multimedia applications. The USB specification supports self-identifying peripherals, a feature fully compatible with plug and play (PnP) systems. USB devices may be *hot plugged,* which means that power does not have to be turned off to connect or disconnect a peripheral. The operating system must support USB in order for it to function. Original versions of Windows 95 and Windows NT 4.0 do not support USB, but the OEM Service Release 2 (OSR-2) release of Windows 95 does. Windows 98, Windows NT 5.0, and all later versions of Windows fully support USB. USB has become a primary means of connection in IBM-compatible PCs. Most major hardware, software, and telecommunications providers support USB.

**Universal Serial Bus 2.0** (USB 2.0) (n.) An updated version of the USB interface that allows data transfer rates of up to 480 Mbps. Most of the original features are retained. USB devices cannot be directly connected to one another, only through a hub. Many devices have internal hubs, however, so that peripherals may be daisy-chained. Small devices, such as hubs and mice, draw their operating power from the bus, eliminating the need for additional power sources. Since 2002, most new computers are equipped with USB 2.0 as a standard bus.

**universal service access multiplexer** (USAM) (n.) A circuit board added to a digital sub-

scriber line (DSL) modem when a subscriber is connected to the central office (CO) by fiber optic cable. It converts the transmitted signals into a format compatible with fiber optic cable. A USAM cannot be used with ADSL because ADSL employs analog signals that cannot be transmitted over fiber optic cable.

**Universal Time Coordinated** (UTC) (n.) Another term for *Greenwich Mean Time.*

**Unix** (n.) Developed by Ken Thompson in 1969, the most popular general-purpose, multiuser operating system in the world. The coauthor is Dennis Ritchie, who created the C programming language. Unix became the first source-portable operating system in 1974 when it was implemented in C. Unix is the subject of an international standardization effort. It is a 32-bit system with excellent multitasking capabilities.

There are many different flavors of Unix. Linux is a popular variant that is freely distributed. The following information explains how to use most Unix systems. The availability of the commands listed here depends on the system you are using. To get online help from any Unix system, type "man programname" for local documentation on the program you specify.

Several conventions are followed in this document. Unix is case sensitive. If a capital letter is shown in a command, it is required. An empty set of angle brackets (<>) represents the <return> or <enter> key. A set of brackets with a label inside (<label>) represents the key with that label. Single quotation marks are used to indicate variable characters and file names. The single quotation marks are not to be typed in the shell window. Parentheses are used to set off instructions and are not to be included in the commands. Brackets around a [path] are not typed, but indicate that the path to a file or directory must be included in the command.

Many Unix commands are *base commands* that can be followed by a series of *switches*, or modifiers, with no space between them. Most Unix shells require a dash before the switches. The format is as follows:

```
command        -switch1switch2
```

## Networking

Networking capabilities are built into the Unix operating system. Telnet provides remote command capabilities, and FTP allows the transfer of files between machines. All networking activities require a daemon program running on the server and a client program running on the remote computer.

### Telnet
The telnet protocol allows remote computers to log in and execute standard Unix commands on a Unix server. The server may be accessed from a PC or Macintosh computer running a telnet client. From a Unix command line, type "telnet machinename" to begin using telnet.

After the client connects to the daemon on the server, the daemon will ask for a username and password. Once authenticated, the user can execute all standard Unix commands. To end a telnet session, type "exit" at the command line.

### FTP
File transfer protocol allows machines to pass files back and forth. Upon the opening of an FTP connection, the prompt is ftp>, not the standard %. If the remote machine supports anonymous FTP, you can enter the word "anonymous" in response to the request for your name and enter your email address as the password.

Other than commands for transferring files,

only three commands work under an FTP connection: ls lists directories, pwd gives the path name of the working directory, and cd allows you to change directories.

These commands function only on the host system when a user is logged in. To begin an FTP session, open the desired local directory where data will be transferred.

Individual files are transferred with the put or the get command. To transfer 'filename' from the local machine to the host, type:

```
put     'filename'
```

To retrieve 'filename' from the host and store it on the local machine, type:

```
get     'filename'
```

The FTP daemon alerts the user when a file transfer is completed.

Transferring multiple files is accomplished with the mget and mput commands. These commands will accept arguments consisting of either a list of file names or a generic name using wildcards to specify a group of files. The daemon asks before transferring each file when a group of files are sent together. Enter a "y" to send a file or an "n" to skip over a file in the group. The following command transfers the three specified files one after another from the local machine to the host:

```
mput    filename1     filename2
filename3
```

The following command retrieves all files beginning with the characters filenam and seeks confirmation before each file is transferred.

```
mget    filenam*
```

### Binary or ASCII File Transfers

The FTP program on the server must be set to binary file transfer mode to transfer compressed files. Because binary mode works for both ASCII and executable files, it is the preferred default setting. Enter "ascii" or "binary" at the FTP prompt to select the type of files to be transferred.

To terminate an FTP session and shut down the client, enter the command "bye" or "quit." Enter the command "close" to terminate the current connection and leave the client running. Initiate a new connection by typing "open machinename."

### Getting Help

The "man" pages in Unix provide an online help system. To get detailed help on any command, type "man" followed by the command. For help on chmod, enter the following at a shell prompt:

```
man    chmod
```

The online documentation for chmod will be formatted and displayed, and the more command may be used to page forward.

## More Information on Unix

Similar systems to Unix include Open Software Foundation (OSF), Version 7, Berkeley Software Distribution (BSD), Xenix, Ultrix, Linux, and GNU. *Unix* is a trademark, owned originally by AT&T, sold to Novell in 1993, and subsequently to Santa Cruz Operation, Inc. (SCO) in 1996. In 1993, Novell assigned the rights to the Unix name to X/Open Company Ltd., and they license it worldwide. For more information, go to *http://www.usenix.org*.

**Unix command** (n.) A letter or combination of letters that may be entered at the command line to perform basic functions in Unix. See the table on Unix and Linux commands.

**Unix-to-Unix CoPy** (UUCP) (n.) A store-and-forward system. Primarily used in Unix systems, UUCP is also supported on other platforms, including VMS and personal computers. The term is commonly used to refer to the international network that employs UUCP to route email and news.

---

### Passwords, Ownership, and Permissions in Unix

As a multitasking, multiuser operating system, Unix requires a security system. The three methods of security employed by Unix are individual passwords for users, file ownership by users, and permissions granted by file owners.

**Passwords**

passwd — Changes a user's password at any time. The system asks for the old password, then the new one, then a confirmation of the new password. A password should be 6–8 characters long, with at least one numeric character. Non-alphanumeric characters are acceptable.

**Ownership**

chown — The creator of a file is automatically the owner. Change ownership with the chown command, as follows: chown newowner 'fname' <>

**Permissions**

chmod — Used by a file owner to change permissions. This command uses modes to set permissions: r (read), w (write), and x (execute). Multiple permissions may be set with one chmod command by adding together modes to give o (owner), u (user group), or a (all) permissions.

## File Manipulation in Unix

File names in any of the following commands may include wildcards. The ? allows any one character, whereas * allows no character or any number of characters. All Unix switches can be combined; thus, "ls -al" would produce an expanded listing including any hidden fles.

| | |
|---|---|
| `ls` | Lists the files in the current directory; if followed by 'fname' it indicates whether that file exists.<br>-l Shows expanded listing, identifying files and directories.<br>-d Lists directories only.<br>-a Includes hidden files. |
| `cat 'fname'` | Displays the content of 'fname' on the screen, with scrolling. Multiple files can be displayed by concatenating. |
| `cat 'fname1' > > 'fname2'` | Appends (concatenates) 'fname1' at the end of 'fname2.' |
| `more 'fname'` | Displays 'fname' one screen at a time; subsequent screens are displayed by pressing <spacebar>, subsequent lines with <>. Press q to end the display. Paging backward is not possible on most systems. |
| `diff 'fname1' 'fname2'` | Compares two files and displays the differences. Lines from 1 are preceded by <, and lines from 2 are preceded by >. |

### Copying, Moving, and Deleting Files
(With both cp and mv, Unix will overwrite any existing files named 'fname2' without warning.)

| | |
|---|---|
| `cp [path]/'fname1' [path]/'fname2'` | Copies 1 to 2. If no path is specified, the current directory is used. |
| `mv [path]/'fname1' [path]/'fname2'` | Changes the name of the file from 1 to 2. |
| `rm [path]/'fname'` | Removes (deletes) 'fname.' Concatenation is possible; wildcards may be used. Unix does not allow recovery of deleted files.<br>-i Requires confirmation for each specific file deleted. |

### Compressing, Backing Up, and Restoring Files
Compressing a file in Unix typically applies the Ziv-Lempel algorithm. Related files can be combined and compressed as one file using the tar utility.

| | |
|---|---|
| `compress 'fname'` | Encodes 'fname,' reduces its size, and adds the extension .Z.<br>-v The percentage of the compression will be listed upon completion. |
| `uncompress 'fname'` | Restores 'fname.Z' to its unencoded state. |
| `gzip 'fname'` | Encodes 'fname' using a different compression algorithm and adds the extension .gz. |
| `gunzip 'fname'` | Restores 'fname.gz' to its unencoded state. |
| `tar -cvf 'fname1.tar' [path] /'fname2' 'fname3'` | Copies 'fname2' and 'fname3' to the archive 'fname1.tar.'<br>-c Specifies a new archive.<br>-v Displays a list of the files being archived (verbose mode).<br>-f Creates the archive as a file. |
| `tar -xvf [path]/ 'fname.tar'` | Restores files from an archive file and displays a list of them on the screen.<br>-x Restores files from an archive file. |

## File Manipulation in Unix (continued)

### Directory Manipulation

| | |
|---|---|
| mkdir [path] 'dirname' | Creates the directory 'dirname' in the location specified by [path]. If [path] is not given, 'dirname' is created in the current directory. |
| cd [path] 'dirname' | Changes to the directory 'dirname' at the location [path]. Type "$home" at the beginning of [path] to start at the root directory; $home as 'dirname' returns the user to the home directory. |
| cd | Returns the user to the home directory on most systems, or moves one directory up the tree. |
| pwd | Displays the path of the working directory. |
| rmdir [path] 'dirname'<br>rm -r 'dirname' | Removes the specified directory, but only if it is empty.<br>Removes the specified directory and its contents recursively through all subdirectories. (On most systems, the rm command does not ask for confirmation unless the -i switch is set.) |

### Monitoring the System and Disk Usage

The following commands allow a user to check whether a process is running in the background and to shut down a program without waiting for it to finish.

| | |
|---|---|
| ps -a | Provides a list of current processes. -ef gives more details than -a. |
| top -i # | Lists the running processes and the percentage of cpu usage by each, updating the list every # seconds. Press q to end the display. |
| kill [PID] | Kills the process with the given process identification. |
| kill -HUP [PID] | Causes the process specified to reread its configuration file, allowing it to be restarted with different parameters. |

To check the available disk space:

| | |
|---|---|
| df -k | Displays a list of directories, their sizes, and the percentage of the disk in use. The -k option displays the size in kilobytes rather than blocks. |
| du -k [path] | Provides a listing of the files in the directory specified by [path] and their sizes. |
| dtree | Displays the directory structure. |

## Using Unix Mail

This table lists commands for using Unix mail.

### Reading and Processing Received Mail in Unix

The following are command-line options for sending mail:

| | |
|---|---|
| mail | Invokes the mail client. If mail has been received, headers are displayed. |
| p | Displays the current message. To make a message current, enter its number. |
| + | Displays the next message. |
| - (dash) | Displays the previous message. |
| M | Displays the current message, page by page. |
| d | Deletes the current message. To delete a specific message, add its number. |
| u | Restores (undeletes) the most recently deleted message. |
| s 'fname' | Saves the current message as 'fname' with headers. |
| w 'fname' | Saves the current message with no headers. |

## Using Unix Mail (continued)

### Editors
The most common Unix text editor is vi. It is a line editor, meaning that its functions normally are executed line by line or word by word. It operates in either command or insert mode. Some editing functions may be carried out from command mode.

### Starting vi

| | |
|---|---|
| vi 'fname' | If 'fname' does not already exist, it will be created. A number of files may be loaded simultaneously by concatenating file names. Move to the next file by typing "n." |

### Command Mode

| | |
|---|---|
| : (colon) | Type a colon (:) to enter command mode. Then type a command and press <>. |
| :q | Leaves vi. |
| :q! | Leaves without saving the file buffer. |
| :w 'fname' | Writes the current file to a disk as 'fname'; if a file of that name already exists, it will be overwritten. |
| :lnumber1, lnumber2 w 'fname' | Writes the portion of the current file that lies between lnumber1 and lnumber2 to 'fname.' |
| :x | Saves the file and quits (:wq may also be used). |

### Sending Mail
In compose mode Mail will prompt for a subject. Type a subject and press <>; then type the message.

| | |
|---|---|
| ~v : | Switches to vi to compose the message (see the Editors section below). |
| <Ctrl>C | Aborts composition without sending the mail. |
| . (period) | Alone on a line, the . command terminates composition and sends the mail. |
| ~r 'fname' | Incorporates 'fname' in the current message, at the current cursor position. |
| r | Replies to the current message; enters compose mode. |
| q | Quits Mail (the command x may also be used). |

### Moving Around in a File
The following commands are not prefaced with a colon. They are used to move the cursor within a file for viewing or to reach the point where editing is to begin.

| | |
|---|---|
| - (dash) or <up arrow> | Move up one line. |
| <down arrow> | Move down one line. |
| <backspace> or <down arrow> | Move left one character. |
| <spacebar> or <right arrow> | Move right one character. |
| $ | Move to the end of the line. |
| ^ | Move to the beginning of the line. |
| H | Move to the top of the screen. |
| L | Move to the bottom of the screen. |
| M | Move to the middle of the screen. |
| <Ctrl>D | Move down half a page. |

## Using Unix Mail (continued)

### Moving Around in a File (continued)

| | |
|---|---|
| `<Ctrl> U` | Move up half a page. |
| `<Ctrl> F` | Move down a whole page. |
| `<Ctrl> B` | Move up a whole page. |
| `'lnumber' G` | Go to a specific line (:set nu displays line numbers). |
| `G` | Go to the end of the file. |
| `/'text'` | Search forward for 'text' in a file. |
| `?'text'` | Search backward for 'text' in a file. |
| `n` | Continue the search for the next instance of 'text' (when using /'text' and ?'text'). |
| `N` | Go back to the previous instance of 'text.' |

### Editing in Command Mode

Editing commands that can be used without entering insert mode:

| | |
|---|---|
| `x` | Delete the character under the cursor; nx (n = a number) deletes n characters. |
| `dd` | Delete the current line; ndd deletes n lines. |
| `p` | Enter the most recently deleted text after the cursor; p pastes in front of the cursor. |
| `yy` | Copy the line to the buffer (yank). |
| `O <esc>` | Insert a blank line above the cursor. |
| `o <esc>` | Insert a blank line below the cursor. |
| `r 'newchar'` | Replace the character at the cursor with 'newchar.' |
| `R 'newchars'` | Replace multiple characters. |
| `:r 'fname'` | Insert the file 'fname' in the current file at the cursor. |

*Note: All replace commands put vi in insert mode; type <esc> to return to command mode.*

| | |
|---|---|
| `u` | Undo the most recent change. |
| `. (period)` | Repeat the last command. |

### Editing in Insert Mode

In insert mode vi behaves like a standard ASCII text editor. After entering insert mode, vi remains in insert mode until <esc> is pressed; commands that belong to command mode are not executed. Typed characters are entered as text.

| | |
|---|---|
| `i :` | Enter insert mode; text fills to the left of the cursor. |
| `a :` | Enter insert mode; text fills to the right of the cursor. |
| `I :` | Insert text at the beginning of the line. |
| `A :` | Insert text at the end of the line. |
| `<Esc> :` | Exit insert mode. |

# List of Unix/Linux Commands

| Command | Function | Command | Function |
|---|---|---|---|
| addbib | Create or extend a bibliographic database. | echo | Echo arguments to the standard output. |
| alias | Create short nicknames for long commands. | ed, red | Start a basic line editor. |
| | | enscript | Print a text file in a special way. |
| apropos | Locate commands by keyword lookup. | eqn, neqn, checkeq | Typeset mathematics. |
| ar | Create library archives and add or extract files. | error | Insert compiler error messages at the responsible source-file lines. |
| at, batch | Execute a command at a specified time. | ex, edit, e | Start a line editor. |
| awk | Start a pattern scanning and processing language. | exit | Exit the current shell (may log you out). |
| | | expand, unexpand | Expand Tab characters to Space characters, and vice versa. |
| banner | Display a string in large letters. | expr | Evaluate an argument as a logical, arithmetic, or string expression. |
| basename | Display portions of path names and file names. | file | Determine the type of a file by examining its contents. |
| biff | Give notice of incoming mail messages. | find | Find files by name, or by other characteristics. |
| bin-mail, binmail | Start a mail-processing program. | | |
| cal | Display a calendar. | finger | Display information about users. |
| calendar | Start a simple reminder service. | fmt, fmt_mail | Start a simple text and mail-message formatter. |
| cat | Concatenate and display. | | |
| cb | Start a simple C program beautifier. | fold | Fold long lines for display on an output device of a given width. |
| cc | Start a C compiler. | | |
| cd, chdir | Change the working directory. | ftp | Start a file transfer program. |
| checknr | Check nroff and troff input files and report possible errors. | gcore | Get core images of the running processes. |
| | | gprof | Display call-graph profile data. |
| chgrp | Change the group ownership of a file. | grep | Search a file or files for a regular expression or a string. |
| chmod | Change the permissions mode of a file. | | |
| chown | Change the ownership of a file or directory to another user. | groups | Display a user's group memberships. |
| | | gzip | Compress a file and add the extension .gz. |
| clear | Clear the screen. | | |
| cmp | Perform a byte-by-byte comparison of two files. | gunzip | Restores a compressed file to its unencoded state. |
| colcrt | Filter nroff output for a terminal lacking overstrike capability. | hashmake, hashcheck | Report spelling errors. |
| comm | Display lines in common, and lines not in common, between two sorted lists. | head | Display the first few lines of a text file. |
| | | history | Show the name of the current host system. |
| compress | Compress files. | | |
| cp | Copy or duplicate a file. | imake | Open the C preprocessor interface to the make utility. |
| cpio | Copy file archives in and out of an archive file. | | |
| | | indent | Indent and format a C program source file. |
| cpp | Start the C language preprocessor. | install | Install files. |
| csh | Start a shell (command interpreter) with a C-like syntax and interactive features. | join | Apply this relational database operator. |
| | | kill | Terminate a process. |
| ctags | Create a tags file for use with ex and vi. | last | Show the last logins by a user or terminal. |
| date | Display or set the date. | ld, ld.so | Open the link editor, or dynamic link editor. |
| dbx | Start a source-level debugger. | leave | Remind user when to leave. |
| deroff | Remove nroff, troff, tbl, and eqn constructs. | less | Show one page at a time (opposite of more). |
| df | Report the free disk space on file systems. | ex | Start a lexical analysis program generator. |
| diff | Display line-by-line differences between pairs of text files. | lint | Start a C program verifier. |
| | | ln | Make hard or symbolic links to files. |
| dtree | Display the directory structure. | login | Log in to the system. |
| du | Display the number of disk blocks used per directory or file. | | |

# List of Unix/Linux Commands (continued)

| Command | Function | Command | Function |
|---|---|---|---|
| llook | Find words in the system dictionary or lines in a sorted list. | roffbib | Format and print a bibliographic database. |
| lookbib | Find references in a bibliographic database. | rsh | Open a remote shell. |
| lorder | Find an ordering relation for an object library. | rup, ruptime | Show the host status of local machines. |
| lp, cancel | Send/cancel requests to a printer. | rusers | Show who's logged in on local machines. |
| lpq | Display the queue of printer jobs. | rwall | Write to all users over a network. |
| lpr | Send a job to the printer. | rwho | Show who's logged in on local machines. |
| lprm | Remove jobs from the printer queue. | sccs | Open the front end for the Source Code Control System (SCCS) |
| ls | List the contents of a directory. | sccs-admin, admin | Create and administer SCCS history files. |
| mail, Mail | Read or send mail messages. | sccs-cdc, cdc | Change the delta commentary of an SCCS delta. |
| make | Maintain, update, and regenerate related programs and files. | sccs-comb, comb | Combine SCCS deltas. |
| man | Display Unix reference manual pages; get help on a command. | sccs-delta, delta | Make a delta to an SCCS file. |
| mesg | Permit or deny messages on the terminal. | sccs-get, get | Retrieve a version of an SCCS file. |
| mkdir, md | Make a directory. | sccs-help, help | Ask for help regarding SCCS error or warning messages. |
| mkstr | Create an error message file by massaging C source files. | sccs-prs, prs | Display selected portions of an SCCS history. |
| more, page | Display a text file one page at a time. | sccs-prt, prt | Display delta table information from an SCCS file. |
| mv | Move or rename files. | sccs-rmdel, rmdel | Remove a delta from an SCCS file. |
| nawk | Start the pattern scanning and processing language. | sccs-sact, sact | Show the editing-activity status of an SCCS file. |
| nice | Run a command at low priority. | sccs-sccsdiff, sccsdiff | Compare two versions of an SCCS file. |
| nm | Print a symbol name list. | | |
| nroff | Format documents for display or for a line-printer. | sccs-unget, unget | Undo a previous get of an SCCS file. |
| od | Make an octal, decimal, hexadecimal, or ascii dump. | sccs-val, val | Validate an SCCS file. |
| passwd, chfn, chsh | Change local or Network Information System (NIS) password. | script | Make a typescript of a terminal session. |
| paste | Join corresponding lines of several files or subsequent lines of one file. | sed | Start a stream editor. |
| | | sh | Open the shell, a standard Unix system command interpreter. |
| pr | Prepare file(s) for printing. | size | Display the size of an object file. |
| printenv | Display the environment variables currently set. | sleep | Suspend execution for a specified interval. |
| prof | Display profile data. | sort | Sort and collate lines. |
| ps | Display the status of current processes. | sortbib | Sort a bibliographic database. |
| ptx | Generate a permutated index. | spell, spellin | Report spelling errors. |
| pwd | Display the path name of the current working directory. | split | Split a file into pieces. |
| quota | Display a user's disk quota and usage. | strings | Find printable strings in an object file or in a binary file. |
| ranlib | Convert archives to random libraries. | strip | Remove symbols and relocation bits from an object file. |
| rcp | Copy remote files. | | |
| rcs | Change RCS (revision history) file attributes. | stty | Set or alter the options for a terminal. |
| rcsdiff | Compare RCS revisions. | su | Super-user; temporarily switch to a different user ID. |
| rev | Reverse the order of characters in each line. | symorder | Rearrange a list of symbols. |
| rlogin | Remote log in to another machine (see telnet). | tabs | Set tab stops on a terminal. |
| | | tail | Display the last part of a file. |
| rm, rmdir | Remove (unlink) a file or directory. | talk | Talk to another user. |

## List of Unix/Linux Commands (continued)

| Command | Function | Command | Function |
|---|---|---|---|
| tar | Create tape archives, and add or extract files. | uux | Perform remote system command execution. |
| tbl | Format tables for nroff or troff. | vacation | Reply to mail automatically. |
| tee | Replicate the standard output. | vgrind | Grind nice program listings. |
| telnet | Open a connection to a remote system using Telnet protocol. | vi, view, vedit | Start the visual display editor based on ex. |
| test | Return true or false according to a conditional expression. | vtroff | Troff to a raster plotter. |
| tftp | Open a trivial file transfer program. | w | Show who is logged in and what they are doing. |
| time | Time a command. | wait | Wait for a process to finish. |
| touch | Update the access and modification times of a file. | wall | Write to all users logged in. |
| troff | Typeset or format documents. | wc | Display a count of lines, words, and characters. |
| true, false | Provide truth values. | what | Extract SCCS-version information from a file. |
| tsort | Perform a topological sort. | | |
| tty | Display the name of the terminal. | whatis | Display a one-line summary of a keyword. |
| ue | Start the Full Screen Text Editor Version 3.9e. | whereis | Locate the binary, source, and manual page files for a command. |
| ul | Underline. | which | Locate a command; display its path name or alias. |
| uncompress | Expand compressed files. | | |
| unifdef | Resolve and remove ifdef lines from cpp input. | who | Show who is logged in on the system. |
| uniq | Remove or report adjacent duplicate lines. | whoami | Display the effective current user name. |
| units | Start the conversion program. | write | Write a message to another user. |
| uptime | Show how long the system has been up. | xargs | Construct the arguments list(s) and execute a command. |
| users | Display a compact list of users logged in. | xstr | Extract strings from C programs to implement shared strings. |
| uucp, uulog, uuname | Copy from system to system. | yacc | Start yet another compiler-compiler, a parsing program generator |
| uudecode | Decode the ASCII representation of a binary file. | yes | Be repetitively affirmative. |
| uuencode | Encode a binary file. | zcat | Display compressed files. |
| uusend | Send a file to a remote host. | | |

**unshielded twisted pair** (UTP) (n.) Standard networking cable under the Category 3 specification for network wiring.

**unzip** (v.) To use the PKUNZIP or WinZip program to extract files from a ZIP archive. Commonly used on MS-DOS or Windows systems, PKUNZIP is the companion to PKZIP, an archiving tool that creates ZIP archives. Both programs are from PKWare. Compare *zip.*

**UPC** See *universal product code.*

**upgrade** (n.) A recent release or version of a software program that includes more features or performs better than the previous one.

**uplink** (n.) A transmission system that sends signals to an orbiting satellite.

**upload** (v.) To send a file to a networked host or to another machine.

**upper memory** (n.) An area outside the first 640 kilobytes (KB) of conventional memory reserved for system software in MS-DOS. Programs cannot store information in upper memory. Upper memory blocks are typically used for terminate and stay resident (TSR) programs and device drivers.

**upper memory block** (UMB) (n.) In the MS-DOS operating system, 64 kilobytes (KB) of the expanded memory page frame above the first 640KB. The UMB can be used to store terminate and stay resident (TSR) programs or device drivers, leaving conventional memory free.

**UPS** See *uninterruptible power supply.*

**upstream** (adj.) In a two-way television network, describes the direction a signal travels from a receive site back to an origination site.

**URI** See *Universal Resource Identifier.*

**URL** See *uniform resource locator.*

**URN** See *Uniform Resource Name.*

**USAM** See *universal service access multiplexer.*

**USB** See *Universal Serial Bus.*

**USB 2.0** See *Universal Serial Bus 2.0.*

**Usenet** (n.) Users' Network; running primarily on Unix machines, a massive bulletin board system (BBS) where people post and read messages and documents. A user needs a news reader in order to participate. Most Internet hosts subscribe to Usenet. Network News Transfer Protocol (NNTP) is the protocol commonly used to transfer news articles between a news server and a news reader. Usenet was started at Duke University in 1979 and is now the largest decentralized information utility.

**user** (n.) 1. The operator of a computer program. 2. Any person who interacts with an agent to view, hear, or use a resource.

**user address** (n.) An individual's domain name or Internet Protocol (IP) address.

**user agent** (n.) The browser and platform used by a visitor to access a web server.

**user authentication** (n.) The act of checking for the user's name to allow access to a site or server. This is done automatically upon login by most servers.

**user bits** (n.) In terms of an 80-bit SMPTE time code word, undefined bits that are available for uses other than time code.

**User Datagram Protocol** (UDP) (n.) Connectionless protocol that adds reliability and multiplexing to Internet Protocol (IP). UDP is defined in RFC 768, STD 6 as an Internet standard transport layer protocol. The data transmission standard used by realtime transfer protocol (RTP) for broadcasting streaming media over Internet protocol (IP) networks. UDP is designed for realtime broadcast and does not engage all of the error correction features of TCP. Data may be lost and not resent in UDP transmission if there are network problems. UDP is an alternative to TCP, and in addition to being used for streaming media, it is used for wireless Internet applications.

**user-friendly** (adj.) Describes a program or system designed for ease of operation.

**user interface** (UI) (n.) Software that facilitates communication with a computer. It may consist of a single line on which commands are entered, or it may consist of icons and menu bars in a graphical user interface (GUI).

**user name** (n.) In a host system that is accessible to multiple users, a unique identifier given to each user. Identification is required for accounting, security, login, and resource management. After typing in the user name, the user enters a password to access a service. A user name might be any string of alphanumeric characters. Typically, the name contains some combination of the first name, the last name, and initials of the individual user. Either system administrators or users may choose user names. They may serve as mailbox names in electronic mail addresses as well.

**user session** (n.) A period of activity for one user of a web site. A unique user is identified by the user's Internet Protocol (IP) address or domain name. By default, a user session is generally terminated when a user stays inactive for more than 30 minutes.

**UTC** See *Universal Time Coordinated.*

**utility program** (n.) Small application designed to support the operation of software and hardware. Examples of MS-DOS utilities are CHKDSK and DEFRAG.

**UTP** See *unshielded twisted pair.*

**UUCP** See *Unix-to-Unix CoPy.*

**uuencode/uudecode** (n.) A program that converts binary files into ASCII files for transmission and that decodes them upon reception. Pronounced "you-you-en-CODE-you-you-de-CODE."

**UUNET** (n.) A company that provides high-speed communications networks that carry Internet traffic. These wide-bandwith networks are the backbones of the Internet zand meet at Network Access Points (NAPs). UUNET provides many Internet Service Providers (ISPs) with their connection to a backbone.

**UV** See *ultraviolet.*

# V

**V** See *volt.*

**VA** See *voltampere.*

**vaccine** (n.) A software application that injects itself into an executable program, performs a signature check, and warns if there have been any changes. Some vaccines proactively warn against attempts to make unauthorized alterations to a system or resident programs, and some provide recovery functions.

**vacuum tube** (n.) An electron tube in which most of the air has been removed, permitting electrons to move freely. The first tube was a two-element diode, invented and patented by Ambrose Fleming in 1904. Three years later, Lee De Forest developed the first triode (known as the "Audion") by adding a grid between the cathode emitter and the anode collector, creating the first amplifier. A change of voltage at the grid produced a corresponding greater change of voltage at the anode. Transistors in integrated circuits perform the same functions that tubes were designed to perform at a fraction of the size and power consumption.

**validation** (n.) 1. The process of assessing and refining testing procedures and other components of an instructional design. 2. A method of ensuring that the coding of a web page is in compliance with the current HTML specifications. The World Wide Web Consortium (W3C) offers online validation for HTML 4.0 at: http://validator.w3.org.

**value** (n.) In relation to color, the degree of lightness or darkness, or the intensity.

**value-added reseller** (VAR, pronounced "VAHR") (n.) A company that assembles systems, provides a package for customers, and offers service after the sale.

**valve** (n.) The term for vacuum tube among the British because the first tube was known as the "Fleming valve", named after its inventor Ambrose Fleming.

**Van Jacobson compression** (n.) Method of compressing TCP headers to decrease round-trip times with SLIP. Versions of SLIP implementing this type of compression are called *Compressed SLIP* or *C-SLIP.*

**vaporware** (n.) Software that has been announced but not released.

**VAR** See *value-added reseller.*

**variable** (n.) An object in a programming language that may assume different values, one at a time, of a prescribed data type. Compare *constant.*

443

**variable bit-rate encoding** (VBR) (n.) A two-pass process of analyzing and then compressing movies to achieve an optimal data rate for each portion of the movie. It produces movies with data rates that vary from moment to moment, rather than adhering to a uniform, flat data rate. It works by analyzing the complexity of the passage and assigning different amounts of bits accordingly (more bits for complex passages, fewer bits for simple passages). It can radically improve the quality of the compressed video and can ensure the smallest file size with the best results.

**variable frame-length movie** (n.) A digital video file with frames that are not all of equal duration. The QuickTime architecture can accommodate this type of movie.

**variable-length coding** (n.) In MPEG compression, the technique of assigning shorter identifiers, or code words, to more common events, and longer code words to less common events. Also known as *entropy coding*.

**Variable Length Subnet Mask** (VLSM) (n.) Implemented in the Open Shortest-Path First (OSPF) routing protocol, a means of dividing a single Internet Protocol (IP) block into smaller networks, or subnets, of different sizes.

**variable-Q equalizer** See *proportional Q*.

**varied repetition** (n.) A technique used by instructional designers to present a segment of a lesson several times. The lesson has the same content each time but is presented in different ways.

**VAX** See *Virtual Address Extension*.

**VAX/VMS** See *Virtual Address Extension/Virtual Memory System*.

**VB** See *Visual Basic*.

**VBI** See *vertical blanking interval*.

**VBR** See *variable bit-rate encoding*.

**VBX** (n.) The file name extension for Visual Basic (VB).

**VCA** See *voltage controlled amplifier*.

**VCL** See *Visual Component Library*.

**VCR** See *videocassette recorder*.

**VDSL** See *very-high-bit-rate digital subscriber line*.

**VDT** See *video display terminal*.

**vector** (n.) In graphics, a line or a movement defined by its end points or by a defined position and one other point.

**vector data** (n.) Information that defines the characteristics of lines in a graphic.

**vector graphics** (n.) Images represented by mathematically defined shapes, such as lines, polygons, text, and groups of objects as opposed to bitmaps of these entities. Compare *raster graphics*.

**vectorscope** (n.) An instrument that tests a video signal and displays results as displacement in a circular pattern. The location of dots on the scope indicates the timing of various components of the test signal relative to signal reference points. A vectorscope is widely used to evaluate and adjust the color component of video signals.

**Venn diagram** (n.) A graphic representation of regions that represent parameters, or sets. Logical operations may be illustrated by the intersection, inclusion, or exclusion of regions in a Venn diagram. The overlapping circles in a Venn diagram represent a logical relationship between sets. See figure.

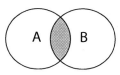

*Venn diagram*

**VERONICA** (Very Easy Rodent-Oriented Netwide Index to Computerized Archives) (n.) A search tool for the Internet.

**vertical application** (n.) An application program that provides functionality to a specific business process, such as accounting.

**vertical blanking interval** (VBI) (n.) In a video signal, the period during which picture information is suppressed and in which the scanning beam returns from the bottom of the picture to the top. Technically, the VBI consists of lines 1 through 21 of video field 1 and lines 263 through 284 of field 2 in the NTSC format. Frame numbers, flags, and closed captions are placed in this interval to maintain image stability and to provide access to a frame. A cable modem may use this space to send the equivalent of a 9600-bps signal during blanking interval. See also *horizontal blanking interval.*

**vertical edge blanking** (n.) See *edge blanking.*

**vertical interval switching** (n.) Alternating rapidly between two video signals during the vertical blanking interval (VBI) at the end of a scan, leaving no noticeable shift in the output signal.

**vertical interval time code** (VITC, pronounced

"VIT-see") (n.) The insertion of SMPTE time code into the vertical blanking interval (VBI) between the two fields of a video frame. This method eliminates errors that may occur from tape stretch, which is a problem when longitudinal time code (LTC) is used. Unlike LTC, VITC can be read when a tape is paused. VITC appears as a row of dots on top of each video field and allows an operator to locate a specific frame.

**vertical market** (n.) A special group that requires products suited to its needs. The medical profession is a vertical market with unique information needs. By contrast, the markets for office management products are not highly differentiated.

**vertical redundancy check** (VRC) (n.) A parity check that is performed on each character of an ASCII block as the block is received.

**Very Easy Rodent-Oriented Netwide Index to Computerized Archives** See *VERONICA.*

**very-high-bit-rate digital subscriber line** (VDSL) (n.) A version of DSL technology that allows asymmetrical transmission at high data transfer rates. The downstream bit rate can reach 55 Mbps, and the upstream rate is 2.3 Mbps. VDSL is only viable within close proximity of the central office (CO), typically 4500 feet or less. It is also referred to as "very high-speed DSL" or "very high data rate DSL."

**Very High-Speed Digital Subscriber Line** (VH-DSL) (n.) Variant of Asymmetric Digital Subscriber Line (ADSL) capable of delivering switched digital video over existing copper twisted pairs that are less than 3000 feet long. Also called *BDSL* (Broadband DSL) or *VDSL.*

**very large-scale integration** (VLSI) (n.) An

integrated circuit (IC) that generally incorporates between 1000 and 9999 command processes, or logic gates, on a single silicon chip.

**VESA** See *Video Electronics Standards Association.*

**VF** See *voice frequency.*

**VfW** See *Video for Windows.*

**VGA** See *Video Graphics Array.*

**VH-DSL** See *Very High-Speed Digital Subscriber Line.*

**VHS** See *video home system.*

**video** (n.) The translation of moving images into electronic signals. The term *video* implies a stream of visual images displayed at a constant frame rate, usually with an audio track. The signals can be broadcast through the air via high-frequency carrier waves or distributed via closed-circuit cable. Video applications include commercial broadcasts, corporate communications, marketing, home entertainment, arcade games, security systems, and the moving picture component of multimedia programs.

**video bandwidth** (n.) Measured in MHz, the range of frequencies at which pixels may be processed by a monitor.

**video black** (n.) A portion of videotape with no images or sound recorded on it. Video black is used as a buffer between programs and is inserted before and after tape segments.

**videocassette** (n.) The case that holds magnetic tape used for videotape applications, most often in the VHS format.

**videocassette recorder** (VCR) (n.) A home videotaping device.

**Video-CD** (n.) Video–compact disc; a full-motion digital video format on CD-ROM using MPEG-1 video compression and incorporating a program control bar with controls similar to those of a VCR. Video-CD conforms to the White Book specification.

**video clip** (n.) A section of recorded video taken from a longer video recording.

**video color sampling** (n.) A process applied in digitizing the color portion of video that compresses the chrominance to various degrees. Three numbers are used to represent ratios between sample rates and color clock rates in digital video. A:B:C: notation is used to represent the ratios as follows:

(A) The basic sample rate compared with the color clock rate.

(B) The color horizontal downsampling rate compared with the basic sampling rate.

(C) The color vertical downsampling rate plus 1.

Some of the common sub-sampling formats are shown below:

- **4:1:1 Color** (n.) A moderately compressed method of video color sub-sampling in which the luminance channel is not sub-sampled, but the chrominance channel has one fourth of the original resolution. Most of the DV formats use 4:1:1 color.

- **4:2:0 Color** (n.) A moderately compressed method of video color sub-sampling with results similar to 4:1:1. This is the standard method of encoding color for MPEG.

- **4:2:2 Color** (n.) These ratios indicate that

the sampling is done at four times the color clock rate (3.58 MHz), that two horizontal chroma samples are taken for every four luminance samples, and that there is no reduction in vertical color resolution (1+1). It is a slightly compressed method of video color sub-sampling in which the luminance channel is not sub-sampled, but the chrominance channel has half the original resolution. This is the ratio defined in the CCIR-601 standard for professional videotape equipment and the D-1 format. It is used in most professional video formats, such as BetaCam SP.

- **4:4:4 Color** (n.) This designation represents totally uncompressed video color that has no sub-sampling.

**video compression** (n.) Data reduction in digital files that represent sequences of images. The reduction applies the concept that there are usually minor changes from one frame to the next. The differences in content between frames are encoded in the *interframe* coding technique, and content that is similar between frames is discarded. Another method of reducing file size in video compression is *intraframe* coding, in which data that defines an individual frame is reduced using discrete cosine transform (DCT). MPEG is a video compression format, as is the H.261 standard.

**videoconference** (n.) A meeting between participants at remote sites who can see and hear each other and share visual data in real time. Such a conference is possible when two or more locations are linked by fast telecommunications lines.

**videodisc** (n.) An optical laser disc, 9 or 12 inches in diameter, that stores data, text, still images, and full-motion video (FMV) in an analog format. The term *videodisc* refers to any

platter from which video content can be decoded and displayed on a monitor, including a Video-CD in the White Book format. A Video-CD contains video compressed using the MPEG-1 specification.

**videodisc formats** (n.) 1. Optical videodisc or laser disc. 2. CD-ROM formatted for either CD-i or Video-CD. 3. DVD, a specification introduced in 1995, and developed through the collaboration of Philips, Sony, Toshiba, and Panasonic.

**video display** (n.) Any cathode-ray tube (CRT) in the raster format that displays information from a video source. See also *monitor*.

**video display terminal** (VDT) (n.) A networked client with a keyboard and a screen. Workstations and dumb terminals are VDTs.

**video driver** (n.) The software interface between an application program and the video card hardware.

**Video Electronics Standards Association** (VESA, pronounced "VEE-sah") (n.) An industry trade group formed to codify the software interface for advanced video cards. The acronym is used to refer to the VESA local bus interface and to describe the slot on a computer that accepts a VESA card.

**Video for Windows** (VfW) (n.) Developed by Microsoft in 1992, a scalable digital video format that decodes digital video .avi files. It runs in all implementations of Microsoft Windows. This type of video file can be compressed by several popular CODECs, including Indeo and CinePak, making the files smaller and allowing them to stream at higher data rates.

**video game** (n.) Interactive game produced for a personal computer or for an arcade console, generally distributed on a ROM cartridge or on a CD-ROM.

**Video Graphics Array** (VGA, pronounced "vee-gee-AY") (n.) A graphics display standard introduced in 1987 by IBM for PS/2 computers. The basic specification provides for 640 x 480 pixel resolution and 256 simultaneous colors. The standard has been expanded by graphics card manufacturers. See also *Super Video Graphics Array* and *Extended Graphics Adapter.*

**video head** (n.) A component in a videotape player over which the tape passes. The head reads, erases, or records the video signal.

**video home system** (VHS) (n.) A popular consumer 0.5-inch videotape format developed by Matsushita and JVC.

**video-in-a-window** (n.) The placement of a video clip on top of the background on a computer monitor. Video-in-a-window may be incorporated in the form of a quarter-screen box playing compressed digital video in one of the popular software codecs, such as QuickTime or Video for Windows (VfW). It may also be input by means of a special video adapter card that can display an NTSC or a PAL signal on a Video Graphics Array (VGA) monitor.

**video information system** (VIS) (n.) Introduced by Tandy Corporation in 1992, a consumer multimedia player designed to plug into a home TV and to provide playback of interactive titles and standard audio CDs.

**video object** (n.) A file that contains a video clip.

**video-on-demand** (VOD) (n.) A system that allows users to select video programming from

a broadband network. The system affords the user playback controls over a video.

**video overlay** (n.) The placement of computer-generated video over analog video, including letters produced by dedicated titling systems. A video overlay system requires a genlock to synchronize input signals.

**videophone** (n.) A telephone product used to transmit and receive compressed video and audio over existing telephone lines.

**video RAM** (VRAM, pronounced "VEE-ram") (n.) Video random-access memory; a special memory chip that is designed for video applications and that usually has a special port for video information. Other data travels through another port.

**video reprocessing** (n.) A common editing technique in which video from a computer source is keyed over existing video. See also *overlay.*

**video server** (n.) A networked storage device, typically a hard disk, an optical drive, or a CD-ROM jukebox, holding video data that is accessible online to delivery systems or workstations. A video server may perform decoding operations for its clients, or this may be performed at each workstation.

**videotape** (n.) Used to record moving pictures, a type of magnetic tape that can also record synchronized audio signals. See figure.

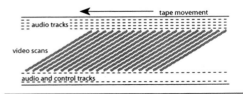

*information on a videotape*

**videotape formats** (n.) The analog tape standards used in recording video, informally differentiated by the width of the tape.

- 1-inch: Format used for professional broadcast-quality video recording and editing. This format is stored on open reels.

- 0.75-inch: Sony U-matic format. This format is stored in thick cassettes.

- 0.5-inch: Cassette-based format. VHS and Sony Betamax produce low-end consumer videotapes of this width. S-VHS and Super Beta produce higher-quality video in the 0.5-inch format.

- 8 mm: Consumer format that provides good-quality recording on small tape cassettes. This format is popular in handheld camcorders. An enhanced version called *Hi-8* has improved resolution and is comparable to S-VHS in quality. Hi-8 and S-VHS have 400 lines of resolution and S-video (Y/C video) separation, but the greater width of S-VHS tape makes it less prone to dropouts.

Many professionals prefer Sony Betacam SP for shooting and D-2 (digital composite) for editing masters. Professional studios use two digital formats: D-1 (digital component) by Sony and D-5 by Panasonic.

**videotext** (n.) A distribution system for information that uses screens of text as the primary content. Videotext services can be distributed through cable or broadcast television systems, or they can be sent over telephone lines to a computer that can construct the images on screen. The graphics are of relatively low resolution, and a proprietary decoder is required.

**video user interface** (VUI) (n.) Onscreen controls that allow a viewer to select channels or programs and control playback parameters.

**videowall** (n.) A rectangular configuration of monitors combined to form a large display. The monitors are generally controlled by a computer that distributes a single video image so that each tube contains one portion of the complete image.

**viewer** (n.) Software application that displays data in a specific format. A PowerPoint viewer displays presentations created with PowerPoint. If a viewer is installed, a file may be played without requiring the application that created the file.

**viewfinder** (n.) A small window on a camera through which the operator can see approximately what appears in the camera lens. Typically, the picture in a viewfinder is not framed exactly the way it will appear on film or video.

**virtual** (adj.) Describes an object, an entity, or a relationship that exists in software rather than in a tangible, physical condition. In computing, a virtual device could represent a hardware peripheral. The use of virtual devices helps programmers avoid hardware incompatibilities as actual configurations evolve. *Virtual* is a commonly used term for anything that exists but that has no concrete manifestation. An ensemble of samplers playing a MIDI score is called a *virtual orchestra*. Compare *real*.

**virtual address** (n.) The location of a device, such as a printer, belonging to a guest operating system. The virtual address is mapped to a physical device.

**Virtual Address Extension** (VAX, pronounced "VACKS") (n.) Released in 1978, a minicomputer design that was popular among programmers but that was replaced by powerful microcomputers 10 years later.

**Virtual Address Extension/Virtual Memory System** (VAX/VMS) (n.) A minicomputer and operating system (OS) developed by Digital Equipment Corporation (DEC). *OpenVMA*, a newer version of the OS, runs on the DEC Alpha and other types of processors.

**virtual circuit** (n.) A voice or data link that appears to the user to be a dedicated circuit, but which may be a temporary connection routed by whatever physical path is available at the time the connection is requested. A logical rather than a specific physical path over which a connection is made. A virtual circuit is a connection-oriented network service that does not rely on any particular routing pattern.

**virtual device driver** (VxD) (n.) A software agent in Microsoft Windows running as part of the kernel. A VxD has access to the memory of the kernel and of all running processes, as well as access to the hardware. VxDs written for Windows 3.x may generally be implemented in Windows 95 and later versions.

**virtual disk** (n.) A conceptual drive rather than a physical drive. The user is not concerned with how the data is physically written. A virtual drive may span multiple physical drives, but it will appear to the user as only one drive.

**Virtual Loadable Module** (VLM) (n.) A term introduced by Novell for software modules that can be dynamically loaded to extend the functionality of the VLM Netware Requester for MS-DOS, which became standard beginning with Novell Netware 4.0.

**virtual machine** (n.) An abstract computing machine for which an interpreter exists. Virtual machines are used to implement portable executors for high-level languages. Java depends on the local installation of its virtual machine to function.

**virtual memory** (n.) The address space available to a process running in a system with a memory management unit (MMU). Hard disk space is used to virtually simulate internal RAM. Virtual memory may be much larger than the amount of physical RAM installed. The virtual address space is divided into pages. Paging allows the excess to be stored on disk and copied to RAM as required. This makes it possible to run programs whose code plus data size exceeds the amount of available RAM. A page is copied from disk to RAM when an attempt is made to access it and when it is not already present. This paging is performed automatically by collaboration between the CPU, the MMU, and the operating system.

**Virtual Memory System** (VMS) (n.) The proprietary operating system developed by Digital Equipment Corporation (DEC) for its VAX minicomputer.

**Virtual Private Network** (VPN) (n.) Technology that enables secure delivery of private data over the Internet by employing protected servers and encrypting data. VPN allows economical remote access to private data by eliminating the need for remote access hardware and systems.

**virtual reality** (VR) (n.) A realistic, computer-generated world in which users may participate by using data gloves and head-mounted graphic display units.

**virtual reality modeling language** (VRML) (n.) The standard for delivering virtual worlds on the Internet. VRML 1.0 was released in May

1995 as an adaptation of the Silicon Graphics Open Inventor file format, which described static scenes. In December 1995 it was proposed that the next version of VRML incorporate programmable behaviors. The official VRML 2.0 specification was released in August 1996.

A stand-alone viewer or a plug-in for a browser is needed for viewing VRML. Netscape Navigator provides the Live3D plug-in as a standard component. The Cosmo Player from SGI is one of the more advanced tools.

A VRML file consists of text commands that a VRML viewer interprets and displays as an image. This image is called a *world* or a *scene*. Color, texture, lighting, sound, and motion are features of a virtual world. The text files that define a virtual world are similar to HTML files but have more complexity. A number of applications that render three-dimensional (3-D) models can export objects and scenes in the VRML format.

VRML files have "nodes" that define 3-D objects, such as cubes, spheres, and other shapes in a 3-D coordinate system. VRML adds dimensionality and advanced interactivity to HTML. A VRML viewer allows a user to navigate worlds, seeing 3-D objects from different perspectives. The mouse is used to provide perspective on the world and to move around in it. For example, a scene rotates around its center when the user clicks and drags the right mouse button in a circular direction.

There are several means of navigating in a VRML world. In Walk mode, the arrow keys move the cursor or an onscreen object up, down, right, or left in the scene. This can also be accomplished by clicking and dragging the mouse. In Fly mode, navigation functions are similar to those in a flight simulator. In Exam-

ine mode, the user may rotate the world around an object to change perspectives. In a VRML world, a user may visit predetermined points called *viewpoints*. It is possible to jump from one viewpoint to another in a virtual world, which is a valuable feature for a disoriented user. The user may adjust lighting and other details about the appearance of a world.

A VRML file is identifiable by its header, a necessary component of every legal file. An appropriate header would be *#VRML V2.0 utf8*. *#VRML* indicates the file type, *V2.0* indicates the version, and *utf8* identifies the character set to be used.

Utf8 allows the file to be written with non-ASCII characters, similar to Unicode, according to the ISO 10646 standard. HTML requires the use of special coded characters, or escape sequences, to represent non-ASCII characters. VRML does not require exclusively ASCII text, and the alphabet in any language can be used to create a VRML file. Comments may be inserted in a VRML file after the # character because the viewer ignores anything after that character on a line. The exception to this is the header, or the first line of the file.

Common terms have special definitions in the language of VRML. A *node* is a predefined word that describes something in a VRML scene. It is the VRML equivalent of a *tag* in HTML. A node is written with the first letter capitalized in every word. The VRML 2.0 specification defines both *Group* and *Leaf* nodes. A Group node can contain any number of Child nodes, but a Leaf node can include only specified nodes. Basic *field types* help define the characteristics of a node. Field types can be any kind of data, from integer numbers to color values.

Braces ({ }) are used to delimit the scope of the node in the same way that the angle brackets (< >) are used in HTML, but the name of a node lies outside the brackets rather than inside. Unlike HTML tags, VRML nodes may be nested inside other nodes. All the parameters of a node are contained within a set of braces.

The basic building blocks of VRML are *primitives,* such as the Sphere, the Cone, the Box, and the Cylinder. These basic shapes render faster than complex ones. All geometry nodes must exist as the child of a Shape node, which has two fields: "appearance" and "geometry." Each object must be assigned a color because the default color for all objects is black. The Material node contains the color command, along with textures. The Transform node is a grouping node, used to locate and move objects. The Anchor node is also a grouping node, sending the browser to the URL identified in the link, which may be another VRML world.

The goal of the developers of VRML 2.0 is to provide a richer and more interactive user experience than is possible within the static boundaries of HTML or VRML 1.0. Static worlds are enhanced in VRML 2.0 with interaction, animation, scripting, and prototyping.

Version 2.0 of VRML adds many new nodes that were not available in version 1.0. Some of these allow the creation of *backdrops* for scenes with distant objects, as well as the *fog* effect. Another new node provides irregular "terrain" to replace flat planes and surfaces. Following terrain allows the user to travel up and down steps or ramps. Version 2.0 offers 3-D spatial Sound nodes. It is easier to optimize and parse files in VRML 2.0 than in VRML 1.0, thanks to a simplified "scene-graph" structure.

A user can directly interact with objects and creatures. New Sensor nodes set off events in specified areas of a world in response to ob-

jects. Collision detection defines the consistent behavior of solid objects.

Version 2.0 includes a number of animation tools called *Interpolators.* They allow the user to create predefined animations involving many features of a world. Interpolators can create objects such as flying birds, automatically opening doors, and objects that change color and morph from one shape to another. Interpolators can provide guided tours that move the user along a predefined path.

**Virtual Telecommunications Access Method** (VTAM) (n.) Programs designed to control communications between nodes and applications in Systems Network Architecture (SNA).

**virus** (n.) A self-replicating, destructive program.

**VIS** See *video information system.*

**visible light** (n.) Electromagnetic radiation in the spectrum between 400 nanometers and 700 nanometers that the unaided human eye can see.

**Visual Basic** (VB) (n.) A programming environment developed by Microsoft.

**Visual Component Library** (VCL) (n.) A library of objects for the Borland Delphi rapid application development software.

**visualization** (n.) In computer graphics, a technique that allows a computer to present graphic images or representations of phenomena that normally could not be viewed. Visualization is becoming an important tool in many science and engineering fields.

**visual programming** (n.) Creating programs

in a language that supports visual interaction and allows the programmer to manipulate visual information.

**VITC** See *vertical interval time code.*

**VLM** See *Virtual Loadable Module.*

**VLSI** See *very large-scale integration.*

**VLSM** See *Variable Length Subnet Mask.*

**VMS** (n.) See *Virtual Memory System.*

**VOD** See *video-on-demand.*

**voice-activated** (adj.) Describes a program executed or controlled by the sound of a human voice.

**voice channel** (n.) In a telecommunications connection, the segment of the bandwidth allocated to transmitting voice messages.

**voice coil** (n.) An element present at both ends of a sound reinforcement system. In a microphone, the voice coil vibrates as sound waves strike it. In a loudspeaker, the wire coil connected to the cone causes the cone to vibrate.

**voice frequency** (VF) (n.) An analog signal within the frequency range of transmitted speech, normally from 300 Hz to 3.4 kHz. It is packaged within a 4 kHz channel.

**voice-grade channel** (n.) Signal path suitable for the transmission of speech, fax, analog, or digital data. A voice-grade channel has a frequency range of approximately 300 Hz to 3 kHz.

**voice mail** (n.) A system in which voice messages are recorded on a messaging system connected to a telephone private branch exchange (PBX). The addressee may access the messages after they are recorded.

**voice-over** (n., adj.) Narration for a video or movie in which the narrator does not appear on screen. A voice-over is recorded during postproduction.

**voice recognition** (n.) A system in which a computer recognizes human speech and converts it into binary code or text files. Also known as *speech recognition.*

**volatile storage** (n.) A type of storage device in which data is lost if operating power is interrupted or if battery backup is not provided. An example of volatile storage is RAM.

**volt** (V or E) (n.) A unit of electromotive force and electric potential, equal to the difference of electric potential between two points on a conducting wire carrying a constant current of one ampere when the power dissipated between the points is one watt.

**voltage** (n.) A quantity of electromotive force measured between two points in an electrical circuit. The voltage between two points may also be identified as the charge between those points (expressed in coulombs) divided by the capacitance (expressed in farads). The capacitance depends on the dielectric constant of the insulators present. Voltage is analogous to the pressure of water in a pipe, whereas current is analogous to the amount of water flowing over a unit of time.

**voltage controlled amplifier** (VCA) (n.) An electronic circuit comprised of three terminals: input, output, and control. The output voltage is a function of the input voltage and the control port. The gain of the stage is determined by the control signal, which is usually a

DC voltage, but could be a current signal or even a digital code. They are the main element in dynamic controllers, such as compressors, expanders, limiters, and noise gates.

**voltampere** (VA) (n.) The product of rms voltage and rms current in an electronic circuit. It is a unit of apparent power.

**volume** (n.) A block of memory on a disk or a tape that may consume the entire medium or that may represent just a partition.

**volume label** (n.) The name a user assigns to a disk or a block of memory when it is formatted using MS-DOS.

**voxel** (n.) A volume element that is the three-dimensional (3-D) equivalent of a pixel. In other words, a voxel is the smallest region that may be defined discretely in a 3-D imaging system.

**VPN** See *Virtual Private Network.*

**VR** See *virtual reality.*

**VRAM** See *video RAM.*

**VRC** See *vertical redundancy check.*

**VRML** See *virtual reality modeling language.*

**VTAM** See *Virtual Telecommunications Access Method.*

**VT-100** (n.) Built by Digital Equipment Corporation (DEC) in the early 1980s, a cathode-ray tube (CRT) video terminal whose control codes still form the basis of the X terminal set and of the ANSI and IBM PC standards. Most terminal emulators provide VT-100 compatibility.

**VT-200** (n.) The Digital Equipment Corpora-

tion (DEC) video terminal that superseded the VT-100 series.

**VUI** See *video user interface.*

**VU meter** (n.) Volume unit meter; a measuring device used in audio recording and broadcasting to indicate amplitude levels relative to a standard. A VU is a form of decibel (dB) reference. It equals 1 milliwatt of power that meets with a 600-ohm load. VU meters are calibrated in order to indicate 0 dB as the maximum undistorted signal level, with a red zone for levels that exceed that point. See figure.

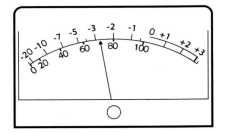

*VU meter*

**V.x** (n.) A series of ITU-T standards for error correction, data compression, and testing for modem operations. The suffix *bis* indicates a second evolution, and the suffix *ter* a third evolution. Chronological developments are listed below:

- V.21: Modem protocol for 300-bit-per-second (bps), two-wire, full-duplex communications using frequency shift keying (FSK) modulation. All modern modems support both V.21 and a similar variant, Bell 103.

- V.22: Modem protocol that allows data rates of 1200 bps. V.22bis doubled this data rate.

- V.22bis: Modem protocol that allows a data rate of 2400 bps, twice that of V.22.

  V.23: Modem protocol that allows half-duplex (unidirectional) data transmission at 1200 bps.

- V.24: Standard defining interchange circuits between data terminal equipment (DTE) and data communications equipment (DCE). V.24 is the ITU-T equivalent of EIA standard RS-232C. V.24 recommends 12 modem carrier frequencies that do not interfere with Dual Tone Multi-Frequency (DTMF) or with other telephone control tones.

  | Group A: | 920 Hz, 1000 Hz, 1080 Hz, 1160 Hz |
  | Group B: | 1320 Hz, 1400 Hz, 1480 Hz, 1560 Hz |
  | Group C: | 1720 Hz, 1800 Hz, 1880 Hz, 1960 Hz |

- V.25: Standard that allows an auto-answer modem to determine the correct modulation standard to use.

- V.27: Protocol for duplex modems transmitting at 4800 bps with manual equalization over leased lines.

- V.27bis: Protocol for duplex modems transmitting at 2400/4800 bps with automatic equalization over leased lines.

- V.27ter: Protocol for duplex modems transmitting at 4800 bps over leased lines.

- V.28: Standard for double-current, unbalanced interchange circuits used in telecommunications.

- V.29: Protocol for duplex or half-duplex modems transmitting at 9600 bps point-to-point over four-wire leased telephone lines.

- V.32: Protocol for duplex modems transmitting at 4800 or 9600 bps with echo cancellation. Bidirectional data transmission is accomplished by subtracting what is sent from what is received.

- V.32bis: Extension of the V.32 modem protocol, allowing speeds of 7200, 12,000, and 14,400 bps. The modem will select the appropriate speed according to the current line conditions.

- V.32ter: Extension of the V.32bis modem protocol, allowing speeds of 19.2 kilobits per second (Kbps). Modem manufacturers extended V.32bis while waiting for V.34 to be developed.

- V.34: Standard modem serial line protocol for data signaling rates of up to 28,800 bps for use on the general switched telephone network and on leased point-to-point, two-wire, telephone-type circuits.

- V.35: Standard for data transmission at 48 Kbps over 60- to 108-kHz group band circuits. V.35 includes the 34-pin V.34 connector specifications normally implemented on a modular RJ-45 connector.

- V.42: Standard protocol with error correction between modems. V.42 includes Microcom Networking Protocol (MNP) up to Level 4.

- V.42bis: Extension of the V.42 standard modem protocol. V.42bis includes compression levels exceeding MNP-5.

- V.54: Standard that defines methods and

devices for loop testing in modems.

- V.70: Standard modem protocol for Digital Simultaneous Voice and Data (DSVD).

- V.80: Defines the application interface for H.324 videoconferencing over modems.

- V.90: Standard modem protocol that incorporates the features of two competing formats, "X2" (3Com) and "K56flex" (Rockwell). It receives data at 56 kilobits per second (Kbps) and transmits at 33.6 Kbps.

**VxD** See *virtual device driver*.

**W** See *watt*.

**WABI** See *Windows Application Binary Interface*.

**wafer** (n.) A thin disk or a slice of silicon on which separate chips can be fabricated and cut into individual die.

**WAIS** See *Wide Area Information Servers*.

**wait state** (n.) A pause during which a processor waits one or more clock cycles until memory responds. A "zero wait state" system uses fast memory or a memory cache system to avoid wait states.

**walk-through** (n.) 1. A simulation that creates the effect of traveling through a computerized architectural model in which the viewer can interactively navigate a path. 2. In film and video production, a rehearsal without cameras.

**walla** (n.) Jargon for background crowd noises in a movie.

**WAN** See *wide area network*.

**WAP** See *Wireless Application Protocol*.

**WAP gateway** (n.) Software that compiles raw Wireless Markup Language (WML) data for a microbrowser, and vice versa.

**warez** (n.) Jargon for software that is pirated and often distributed over bulletin board systems (BBSs). Pronounced "WAIRZ."

**warm boot** (v.) To restart a computer without turning off the power. In the Mac OS this is accomplished by selecting Restart from the Special menu. On an IBM-compatible machine it is done with the key combination Ctrl-Alt-Delete, which is known as a *three-finger salute*.

**WASP** See *wireless application service provider*.

**watermarking** (v.) 1. With reference to images, the act of adding an identifying code that may be used to grant access to a user, or to maintain intellectual property rights. 2. In digital audio or video, this is embedded code within the digitized audio or video image that can be recovered but which will not affect the quality of the product. Most methods consist of very short segments a few microseconds long containing all the relevant data about the copyright owner and performance royalties.

**WATS** See *wide area telephone service*.

**watt** (W) (n.) A unit of power equal to one joule per second.

**.wav** (n.) A Microsoft DOS and Windows file name extension, or a suffix, used to indicate a sound file. This type of file consists of a set of digitized samples representing waveforms. A sound card can realize these samples.

**WAVE** (n.) The preferred standard of multimedia sound for Microsoft and IBM. It is a RIFF file containing pulse code modulation (PCM) waveform audio data, and it is identified with the .wav extension.

**waveform** (n.) The representation variations in pressure that define a wave. A waveform may exist in any spectral range, but the term typically refers to audio and video waves. The frequency, amplitude, and all other parameters of a waveform may be digitized and stored in a wavetable as a sample.

**waveform monitor** (n.) A test instrument that displays a video signal graphed over a selected interval of time, rather than displaying a video picture. A waveform monitor measures video gain and sync pulses, as well as the frequency and amplitude of waves.

**waveguide** (n.) A conducting or dielectric device that can support and propagate one or more modes. The term generally refers to fiber-optic transmission media.

**wavelength** (n.) The distance between successive peaks of a regularly repeating waveform.

**Wavelength Division Multiplexing** (WDM) (n.) The combination of more than one light source and detector that operate at different wavelengths through the same fiber and that simultaneously transmit independent optical signals.

**wavelet** (n.) A waveform defined in both the frequency and the temporal domains. A Fourier transform converts a signal into a continuous series of sine waves, each with constant frequency and amplitude and with infinite duration. Most actual waves have a finite duration, however, and their frequencies change abruptly. Wavelet transforms convert a signal into a series of smaller waves, or wavelets. Signals processed by the wavelet transform are stored more efficiently than those processed by the Fourier transform. Actual waveforms with rough edges are better approximated by wavelet transforms.

**wavetable** (n.) A collection of digitized sound waves stored as samples in computer memory. A wavetable in a sound card holds the instrument sounds that a MIDI file uses to play music.

**wavetable synthesis** (n.) Audio signals that are based on digital samples of recorded sounds rather than on sounds that are artificially synthesized by a means such as frequency modulation (FM).

**WBMP** See *Wireless bitmap.*

**WCDMA** See *wideband CDMA.*

**WDM** See *Wavelength Division Multiplexing.*

**web** See *World Wide Web.*

**web browser** (n.) A universal client application used to read HTML files found on the World Wide Web. The two most widely used browsers are Netscape Navigator and MS Internet Explorer.

**webcasting** (n.) The act of broadcasting content, typically streaming media, from a web server. Webcasting works on a one-to-many principle, rather than the usual one-to-one principle that governs most Internet connections.

**WebDAV** (Web Distributed Authoring and Versioning) (n.) A set of extensions to the HTTP protocol that allows users to collaboratively edit and manage files on remote web servers securely.

**Web Distributed Authoring and Versioning** See *WebDAV.*

**webmaster** (n.) The person who maintains a World Wide Web server and its contents.

**web page** (n.) An HTML file that is identified by a URL and that a web browser can read. A web page may contain text, hypertext links to other locations, and images in the GIF and JPEG formats. Some servers can generate pages dynamically in response to a request by a Common Gateway Interface (CGI) script.

**Web Request Broker** (WRB) (n.) A multithreaded HTTP server from Oracle Corporation that translates Oracle 7 database requests into HTML for delivery to the universal client.

**web ring** (n.) A group of websites that share a common theme.

**web server** (n.) A networked computer that responds to HTTP requests from remote clients by sending HTML documents. Multiple hostnames, known as *virtual servers,* may be mapped to the same computer. Apache and HTTPd are commonly used web servers.

**web site** (n.) A collection of HTML documents, known as *web pages,* that are delivered by a web server. The hostname portion of a URL identifies a web site.

**WELL** See *Whole Earth 'Lectronic Link.*

**wet** (n.) Refers to an audio track that has been treated with signal processing, particularly reverb. A wet track is processed with reverb, delay, or other effects, whereas a "dry" track has no effects.

**what you see is what you get** (WYSIWYG, pronounced "WIZZ-ee-wig") (n., adj.) A way of displaying graphics in some desktop publishing applications in which the screen reflects the exact way the printed page will appear.

**weighting filters** (n.) In audio, special filters used in measuring loudness levels and in noise measurements of equipment. The filter weights certain frequency bands higher than others. The objective is to obtain measurements that correlate closely with the subjective perception of noise. Weighting filters are band-limiting filters that compensate for the fact that the ear's loudness vs. frequency response is not flat. Four weighting filter designs are described below:

- **A-weighting** The A-curve is a wide bandpass filter centered at 2.5 kHz, with ~20 dB attenuation at 100 Hz and ~10 dB attenuation at 20 kHz. It heavily attenuates the low end, with a more modest effect on high frequencies. It is the inverse of the 30-phon (30 dB-SPL) equal-loudness curve of Fletcher Munson. This is the least revealing scale.

- **C-weighting** The C-curve is flat but has very limited bandwidth, with -3 dB corners at 31.5 Hz and 8 kHz, respectively.

- **ITU-R 468-weighting** This filter was designed to maximize its response to the types of impulsive noise coupled into audio cables as they pass through telephone switching facilities. It also correlates well with noise perception since modern research has shown that frequencies between 1 kHz and 9 kHz are more annoying than indicated by A-weighting curve testing. The ITU-R 468-curve peaks at 6.3 kHz, where it has 12 dB of gain (relative to 1 kHz). From that point, it gently rolls off low frequencies at a 6 dB per octave rate, but it quickly attenuates high frequencies at ~30 dB per octave (it is down -22.5 dB at 20 kHz, relative to +12 dB at 6.3 kHz).

• **ITU-R (CCIR) 2 kHz-weighting** This curve is based on the ITU-R 468 curve. Dolby Laboratories proposed using an average-response meter with the ITU-R 468-curve instead of the true quasi-peak meters used by the Europeans in specifying their equipment. They also shifted the 0 dB reference point up from 1 kHz to 2 kHz, sliding the curve down 6 dB. This became known as the ITU-R ARM (average response meter).

**Wheatstone bridge** (n.) An instrument used for measuring resistance. The circuit is a 4-arm bridge, all arms of which are resistive. The bridge is a two-port network, with two terminal pairs across opposite corners. When voltage is applied to one port, by suitable adjustment of the resistive elements in the network, zero output can be obtained at the signal output port. Under these circumstances, the bridge is termed "balanced." See *balanced circuit*.

**Whetstone** (n.) Program that simulates other arithmetic-intensive programs used in scientific computing to benchmark system performance. Whetstone tests do not perform input/output (I/O) or system calls. The units of measurement defining the speed at which a system performs floating-point operations are known as Whetstones.

**white balance** (n., adj.) An adjustment made to a camera or another video source so that a white object will produce the proper signal. Most consumer camcorders have automatic white-balance circuits. It is imperative to calibrate a video camera when light conditions change. This is often accomplished by recording a white page of paper full screen at the depth of the background. The camera then automatically corrects color as needed.

**White Book standard** (n.) 1. Developed by Philips and JVC in 1993, a specification for storing MPEG-1 video on a CD-ROM. The White Book standard is an extension of the Red Book standard for digital audio, the Yellow Book standard for CD-ROM, the Green Book standard for CD-i, and the Orange Book standard for CD-R. As with the other standards, the name of the White Book standard describes the color of its cover. 2. The fourth book in Adobe's PostScript series, describing the format of Type 1 fonts. The other three official guides are known as the Blue Book, the Green Book, and the Red Book.

**white flag** (n.) In the transfer of film to videotape, a code used to mark a new full frame. Also known as *full-frame ID*.

**white level** (n.) The level of the brightest possible white value in a video signal. In most video formats, the white level equals the minimum voltage.

**white noise** (n.) Analogous to white light containing equal amounts of all visible frequencies, white noise contains equal amounts of all audible frequencies. Technically, the bandwidth of noise is infinite, but for audio purposes it is limited to 20 Hz–20 kHz.

**white pages** (n.) Databases with basic information about Internet users, such as telephone numbers, email addresses, and street addresses. The white pages can be searched to gather information about individuals.

**white paper** (n.) A treatise defining a new technology or describing a process that is being implemented. White papers typically represent research, and they often project uses and applications of the topic under investigation.

**whois** (n.) An Internet directory service that locates information about networks and users on a remote server. Servers may respond to a TCP query or to the finger protocol. A list of whois servers appears at the FTP/gopher address *sipb.mit.edu*.

**Whole Earth 'Lectronic Link** (WELL) (n.) Popular online service based in Sausalito, California. The URL is *http://www.well.com*.

**wide-angle** (adj.) Describes a camera lens with a short focal length and a broad field of view.

**Wide Area Information Servers** (WAIS) (n.) A distributed information retrieval system that allows clients to retrieve documents by inputting keywords. A WAIS search returns a list of documents, prioritized according to the frequency with which the keyword occurs. Public domain versions are available, and a client can retrieve text or multimedia documents stored on a server. A relevance feedback mechanism allows the results of initial searches to improve future searches. The web and gopher are examples of other information retrieval systems. WAIS is supported by Apple Computer, Thinking Machines, and Dow Jones.

**wide area network** (WAN, pronounced "WAN") (n.) The integration of geographically distant or technologically incompatible local area networks (LANs). Technologies that contribute to the existence of these networks include Asynchronous Transfer Mode (ATM), ISDN, CCITT X.25, and frame relay. See also *local area network.*

**wide area telephone service** (WATS, pronounced "WAHTS") (n.) A long-distance toll service, inward or outward, offered at a discount by a telephone company.

**wideband** (n.) A data transmission system with a large bandwidth and with multiple-channel access.

**wideband CDMA** (WCDMA) (n.) A third generation (3G) wireless technology that increases data transmission rates in GSM systems by using a 5 MHz carrier rather than the 200 KHz carrier used in standard CDMA, allowing data transfer rates up to 2 Mbps.

**widescreen TV** (n.) Widescreen television; for high-definition television (HDTV) broadcast, a proposed ratio of 16:9, or 1.78:1, rather than the normal 4:3 aspect ratio for the screen. 16:9 is a ratio more similar to that of the film processors Cinemascope and Panavision, which exhibit aspect ratios in the range of 2.35:1. When the wider aspect ratio is shown on a standard screen, the result is called the *letterbox* effect.

**wide SCSI** (n.) Wide Small Computer System Interface; a form of SCSI-2 interface that allows a 16-bit bus and that supports transfer rates up to 20 megabytes per second (MBps), as does fast SCSI. The SCSI-2 version of wide SCSI that permits a 32-bit bus supports transfer rates up to 40 MBps. *Wide SCSI* generally refers to 16-bit-wide SCSI.

**widow** (n.) At the end of a paragraph, a short line of text or a partial word that is separated by a page or column break and that therefore appears on the next page or the next column.

**wild** (adj.) 1. Describes audio tracks that are recorded live in the field along with the video frames. 2. Describes audio tracks or sound effects that are not synchronized with a video track. Wild effects may be gathered and synchronized in postproduction. If an error is introduced in the sync signal during postproduction, audio tracks can become wild, or out of sync, by mistake.

**wildcard** See *global file specification.*

**WIMP** (n.) Windows, Icons, Menus, and Pointing device; a graphical user interface (GUI) invented at Xerox PARC, originally used by the Mac OS, and replicated by other systems.

**Win95** See *Windows 95.*

**Win98** See *Windows 98.*

**Winchester disk** (n.) A drive that consists of a stack of platters. The original development project for hard disk drives at IBM was called *Winchester.*

**window** (n.) 1. A defined area on a monitor designated for video or for other information. 2. The portion of a display in which a document or an application runs in a graphical user interface (GUI). An independent program will be displayed in its own window on the monitor. Several windows may be open at once in a multitasking environment. 3. A flow-control mechanism in data communications. The size of the window is equal to the number of

frames, packets, or messages that can be sent from a transmitter to a receiver before any reverse acknowledgment is required.

**window dub** (n.) A videotape with a small window superimposed on each frame. The window displays positional information in time code as the tape plays. The window is called a *time code window.*

**Windows** See *Microsoft Windows.*

**Windows 3.1** (n.) A version of Microsoft Windows with TrueType fonts and object linking and embedding (OLE). Windows 3.11 is the updated version.

**Windows 95** (Win95) (n.) Released in August 1995, the version of the Microsoft Windows operating system for IBM-compatible computers that superseded Windows 3.1. Win95 is a complete operating system, not merely a graphical user interface (GUI) running on top of MS-DOS as Windows 3.1 is. Win95 provides 32-bit application support, preemptive multitasking, and threading. Networking is available in the form of TCP/IP, Internetwork Packet eXchange (IPX), SLIP, PPP, and Windows Sockets (Winsock).

**Windows 98** (Win98) (n.) Released in 1998, the version of the Microsoft Windows operating system for IBM-compatible computers that superseded Windows 95. It is not significantly different from Win95, but incorporates numerous minor repairs and upgrades to the system. One notable advance is the FAT32 file system, which enables files on a hard disk to be stored in smaller blocks. The Internet Explorer browser is tightly integrated with this operating system.

**Windows Application Binary Interface** (WABI, pronounced "WAH-bee") (n.) A Sun

Microsystems software package that lets Microsoft Windows applications run in the X Window System. WABI 2.2 runs under Solaris on the SPARC, Intel, and PowerPC platforms. It translates USER.DLL, KERNEL.DLL, and GDI.DLL, the three core Windows libraries that redirect Windows calls to Solaris equivalents. For code other than core library calls, WABI either executes the instructions directly on the hardware, if it is Intel, or emulates them, either one instruction at a time or by translating a block of instructions and caching the result.

**Windows CE** (n.) A condensed version of the Microsoft Windows operating system for handheld PCs. Version 3.0 of Windows CE was updated and renamed Pocket PC.

**Windows for Workgroups 3.11** (n.) An upgrade to Windows 3.1. The upgrade added 32-bit file access, improved performance, and provided fax capability.

**Windows Media** (n.) The streaming media architecture implemented in the Microsoft Windows operating system. It is capable of playing many file types and decoding a wide range of codecs. The proprietary audio and video codecs for Windows Media files yield very impressive results, especially when viewed in the Windows environment.

**Windows Metafile** (WMF) (n.) A format that stores an image as a series of Windows Graphical Device Interface (GDI) functions. The files, which are scalable drawings rather than bitmaps, require little storage space, display quickly on the screen, and are transportable among applications.

**Windows NT** (n.) Windows New Technology; a 32-bit hardware-independent operating sys-

tem from Microsoft that was originally designed for IBM-compatible workstations, servers, and corporate networks. Based on a microkernel, it has 32-bit addressing for up to 4 gigabytes (GB) of RAM. Windows NT features virtual hardware access to protect applications from crashing, installable file systems, and built-in networking. It offers multiprocessor support and high security.

**Windows Sockets** (Winsock) (n.) A specification conceived in 1991 for Microsoft Windows network software. Winsock defines how applications access network services, especially TCP/IP. Winsock provides a single Application Programming Interface (API) for which application developers may program. It is supported by Windows for Workgroups, Win32s, Windows 95, and Windows NT.

**WinG** (Pronounced "win-GEE") (n.) A library of high-performance graphics routines that enhance the performance of Microsoft Windows. WinG adds halftone ability so that a system with an 8-bit palette can effectively present 24-bit color. The runtime library may be distributed without permission from Microsoft. It consists of WING.DLL for 16-bit systems and WING32.DLL for 32-bit implementations.

**Winsock** See *Windows Sockets.*

**Wintel** (n.) A contraction of the words "Windows" and "Intel." Jargon for Intel microprocessor-based systems running Windows software. It is estimated that over 80 percent of all personal computers are configured with these components.

**Win32** (n.) A 32-bit Application Programming Interface (API) that is supported by recent versions of Microsoft Windows and that

**W**

incorporates features such as multiple threads and remote control of networked computers.

**Win32s** (n.) A software layer on top of Windows 3.1 that allows 32-bit applications to run.

**WinToon** (n.) Developed by Microsoft, an animation engine that runs in Windows 95. It efficiently layers a moving image in the foreground over a static background by minimizing the updates to redundant data from screen to screen.

**WinZip** (n.) The Microsoft Windows version of PKZIP, a compression utility.

**wipe** (n., v.) In video special effects, a transitional effect that erases an image by replacing it with another one.

**wire frame model** (n.) A three-dimensional representation of an object made with line segments. A wire frame model is created before an object is rendered.

**wireless** (adj.) Describes a network without a cable or a fiber-optic link between sending and receiving units. In a wireless network, telephone or data signals are transmitted via high-frequency waves.

**Wireless Application Protocol** (WAP) (n.) A set of protocols that allows mobile phones and other digital wireless devices to access the Internet, to receive email and faxes, and to conduct other transactions securely. WAP is compatible with CDMA, GSM, and many other standards. It utilizes a light version of TCP/IP for transmitting data between devices.

**wireless application service provider** (WASP) (n.) A vendor that provides hosted wireless applications, typically by subscription.

**Wireless bitmap** (WBMP) (n.) A one-bit, black and white image format used in the Wireless Application Protocol (WAP).

**wireless Internet service provider** (WISP) (n.) A vendor that specializes in providing wireless access to the Internet.

**Wireless LAN** (n.) A local area network that uses radio frequency (RF) technology to transmit data through the air, spanning relatively short distances within a building or small campus. A wireless LAN often serves as an extension to an existing wired LAN, with base stations as nodes. An unlicensed frequency, such as the 2.4 GHz band, is commonly used. Unlike Infrared Data Association (IrDA) products, line-of-sight transmission is not required. Radio frequency is broadcast over an area of several hundred to a thousand feet and can penetrate walls and other nonmetal barriers. Roaming users are handed off from one access point to another, as in a cellular phone system. The protocol used is 802.11.

**Wireless LAN Interoperability Forum** (WLIF) (n.) An industry group with members that endorse products that are interoperable with major standards, such as OpenAir and IEEE 802.11.

**Wireless Markup Language** (WML) (n.) A specialized version of XML used to create Web pages and applications for very small, typically monochrome screens of wireless handheld devices. WML is compatible with the wireless application protocol and may be used in conjunction with *WMLScript* to create dynamic content. It is a version of Handheld Device Markup Language (HDML).

**wireless modem** (n.) Any type of modem with an antenna that transmits and receives messages through the air. Wireless modems come in many varieties and operate using a diverse range of technologies.

**wireless spectrum** (n.) A band of frequencies over which wireless signals transmit data and voice information. Wireless carriers in the U.S. bid for control of narrow frequency bands at auctions held by the Federal Communications Commission (FCC). Similar auctions have occurred in several European nations. With more bandwidth, service providers will be able to increase transmission speeds and employ third generation (3G) technologies.

**wiring closet** (n.) The termination point for customer premises wiring that allows a central point of access for servicing.

**WISP** See *wireless Internet service provider.*

**wizard** (n.) A help file with templates accessed through a dialog box. Wizards come bundled with Microsoft Windows applications.

**WLIF** See *Wireless LAN Interoperability Forum.*

**WMF** See *Windows Metafile.*

**WML** See *Wireless Markup Language.*

**WMLS** See *WMLScript.*

**WMLScript** (WMLS) (n.) Wireless Markup Language Script; a subset of JavaScript for programming mobile devices.

**WOL** (n.) Abbreviation for Wireless Online, Wake-on LAN, or Wireless Optical Link.

**word** (n.) An ordered set of bits designated as the standard unit in which information may be transmitted, stored, or operated upon within a given computer. Words might consist of 8, 16, 32, or 64 bits.

**word clock** (n.) A type of timing reference signal found in virtually all digital audio production equipment. The connector is typically a BNC type, and the signal consists of clock information running at the sample rate of the program material. This is the same as an AES/EBU null clock signal.

**word length** (adj.) The number of bits in a word.

**word wrap** (n.) The capacity of a text editor or a word processor to send characters automatically to the next line when they reach the right margin. With word wrap, no line break or carriage return character is introduced.

**workstation** (n.) A monitor and a keyboard located on a network. Other devices may be connected to the network as well. A workstation may take the form of a dumb terminal connected to a server, or it could be a powerful networked computer.

**World Wide Web** (web, WWW) (n.) A distributed information retrieval system that operates over the Internet in a client-server environment. The web was developed by Tim Berners-Lee at the CERN High-Energy Physics Laboratories in Geneva, Switzerland. Hypertext links refer to HTML documents via a URL, which may refer to local or remote resources. These resources are accessible through FTP, gopher, Telnet, or news, as well as through the HTTP protocol used to transfer hypertext documents. A client program, or a browser, follows a link or sends a query to a server. The World Wide Web Consortium (W3C) is the primary standards body for the web.

**World Wide Web Consortium** (W3C) (n.) A

group created at MIT in 1994. The W3C works with the global community to establish international standards for client and server protocols that enable Internet communications. Netscape Communications Corporation was a founding member. The director is Tim Berners-Lee, who is credited with developing HTML.

**worm** (n.) Self-propagating, self-replicating computer program that spawns in a network environment. A 1982 issue of *ACM Communications* first identified network worms.

**WORM** See *write-once-read-many*.

**WRB** See *Web Request Broker*.

**writable optical media** (n.) A catchall phrase for any optical media on which a user can record data. Magneto-optical (MO) cartridges used in write-once-read-many (WORM) drives and CD-recordables (CD-Rs), or "one-offs," both fit in this category.

**write** (v.) To move data from one physical place to another or from one medium to another.

**write-back** (adj.) Describes a type of computer cache in which data is written to main memory only when it is forced out of the cache. Compare *write-through*.

**write-once-read-many** (WORM) (n.) Optical storage in which the laser physically and permanently alters the surface of a disk by burning pits in it. A WORM drive is excellent for long-term storage of important data, but the medium can be used only once; the data cannot be erased nor the space reclaimed. See also *CD-R* under *compact disc*.

**write-through** (adj.) Describes a type of computer cache in which data is written to main memory at the same time as it is written to the cache. Compare *write-back*.

**W3C** See *World Wide Web Consortium*.

**WWW** See *World Wide Web*.

**WYSIWYG** See *what you see is what you get*.

# X–Z

X The electronic symbol for reactance.

X See *X Window System.*

X **curve** See *extended curve.*

**XA** See *extended architecture* or *CD-ROM extended architecture.*

**Xanadu** (n.) Utopian plan devised by Theodor Holm Nelson in the early 1970s. The plan was to integrate all the library collections in the world into a single system. The web embodies some of his principles, including the capacity for nonlinear exploration of textual and other information.

**XAR** See *extended attribute record.*

**X BitMap** (XBM) (n.) One of the approved graphics formats that may be used for placing images on the web.

**XBM** See *X BitMap.*

**XCMD** See *external command.*

**X curve** See *extended curve.*

**x-digital subscriber line** See *xDSL.*

**XDR** See *eXternal Data Representation.*

**xDSL** (x-digital subscriber line) (n.) A family of technologies that transmit digital information, and in some cases analog information, over existing copper-wire pairs for limited distances from the telephone company central office (CO). The "x" is used to denote any of several letters for the xDSL family members. These include asymmetric DSL (ADSL), high-bit-rate DSL (HDSL), ISDN DSL (IDSL), single-pair symmetrical services DSL (SDSL), and very-high-bit-rate digital subscriber line (VDSL). All of these services offer subscribers high-speed data transmission downstream and, typically, a lower rate of transmission upstream to the CO.

**Xenix** (n.) Developed by Microsoft in 1979, a Unix-like operating system for use on Intel processors. Santa Cruz Operation, Inc. (SCO) was contracted by Microsoft to continue to develop and market the product.

**Xerox Corporation Palo Alto Research Center** (Xerox PARC) (n.) The laboratories where many hardware and software innovations were developed from the early 1970s to the mid-1980s. Among them were the mouse, graphical user interfaces (GUIs), the laser printer, the local area network (LAN), and object-oriented programming (OOP).

**Xerox Network System** (XNS) (n.) An aging

local area network (LAN) protocol developed by Xerox Corporation. Packet size is limited to 576 bytes in this system. It serves as the basis for the third and fourth layers of the Novell and the 3Com LAN protocols currently in use.

**Xerox PARC** See *Xerox Corporation Palo Alto Research Center.*

**XFCN** See *external functions.*

**XGA** See *Extended Graphics Adapter.*

**XHTML** (n.) A markup language that is a hybrid combination of HTML 4.0 and XML. The primary goal of XHTML is to establish a means for web developers to update HTML documents so that they are compliant with the XML standard, which will be implemented in future generations of web browsers.

**XLR connector** (n.) An audio connector used for most low-impedance microphones and for balanced lines between professional signal-processing equipment. Three wires are soldered to three pins inside the barrel of the connector. The ground wire or the shield is typically connected to pin 1. Pins 2 and 3 carry the same signal in equal strength, but with a reversed phase relationship. This allows for the cancellation of unwanted noise over long cables. The microphone lines used in most recording studios are 200-ohm balanced lines with the shield grounded only at the preamp end. If the shields are grounded at more than one point, a ground loop may be created, producing a 60-cycle hum. XLR connector was originally a registered trademark of ITT-Cannon. See figure.

**XML** See *Extensible Markup Language.*

**XModem** (n.) Developed by Ward Christensen

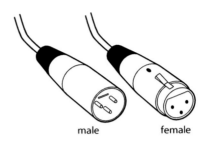

*XLR connectors*

in the late 1970s, a common protocol for file transfer over serial lines connecting modems. XModem uses 128-byte packets with error detection and lets a receiving unit request retransmission of a corrupted packet from the sending unit. Sending and receiving programs can negotiate and establish the best rate of transfer that they can both support. Standard XModem specifies a one-second timeout during the reception of characters in the data block portion of a packet. Chuck Forsberg improved on XModem by developing YModem and ZModem.

**XMS** See *extended memory specification.*

**Xn** (n.) Any network-oriented windowed system based on TCP/IP. The most popular windowed system is X11.

**XNS** See *Xerox Network System.*

**X-off/X-on** (n.) Shorthand for "transmission off/transmission on," a peripheral-device data flow control protocol used by an attached terminal for the control of modems.

**X/Open** (n.) A consortium of computer manufacturers and software developers that promotes the design of portable Unix-based applications. Formed in 1984, X/Open is dedicated to reducing incompatibility between information systems. In 1996 X/Open consolidated with the Open Software Foundation to form the Open Group. For more information visit the web sites maintained by these organizations: *http://www.osf.org* and *http://opengroup.com.*

**XOR** (n.) Acronym for *exclusive OR*, a type of logic gate where the output of 1 is based upon the presence of a signal at either the A or B input but not at both.

**X PixMap** (XPM) (n.) An approved graphics format for placing images on the web.

**XPM** See *X PixMap.*

**X Series** (n.) Referred to as X.n (pronounced "EX-dot-en"), a set of recommendations prepared by the ITU-T that defines interface features for data terminal equipment (DTE) and data communications equipment (DCE). The rules for connecting devices to the public switched telephone network (PSTN) and public data networks (PDNs) are set forth in the X Series. Some of the primary recommendations are described here:

- X.3: The ISO approved ITU-T standard specifying the basic functions and the user-selectable capabilities of a Packet Assembly/Disassembly (PAD) device in a public data network.

- X.21: A digital signal interface recommendation by the ITU-T. X.21 specifies data terminal equipment–data communications equipment (DTE-DCE) physical interface elements, data transfer up to 64 Kbps, alignment of call control characters and error-checking characters, elements of the call control phase for cir-

cuit-switched services, and test loops.

- X.25: A protocol suite for the data terminal equipment–data communications equipment (DTE-DCE) interface in a packet-switched network, recommended by the ITU-T and approved by ISO. X.25 defines three levels: the physical level, the data link level, and the packet level. These levels are similar to the lower three layers of the Open Systems Interconnection (OSI) reference model. X.25 describes how data passes through public data communications networks worldwide. The three levels are further defined as follows:

   Level 1: The physical and electrical characteristics of data terminal equipment (DTE) and data communications equipment (DCE). A duplex synchronous link is specified to provide a transmission path between terminal equipment and the network.

   Level 2: The accessing protocol for public packet-switching networks with error correction.

   Level 3: The procedures for constructing and controlling data packets that are passed between data terminals and circuit equipment.

- X.28: The ISO approved ITU-T standard that specifies how to control a Packet Assembly/Disassembly (PAD) device from character-mode DTE.

- X.29: The ISO approved ITU-T standard specifying procedures for the exchange of control information and user data between a Packet Assembly/Disassembly (PAD) device and remote packet-mode data terminal equipment (DTE). Character-mode DTEs are known as *X.29 terminals*.

- X.75: The ITU-T standard that specifies protocols for communication between two packet-switching data networks (PSDNs).

- X.400: The standard that defines how messages are exchanged between different email systems. It is a set of protocols that translate messages, but does not include the sender's name in messages sent.

- X.500: Defines the method by which different types of workstations may exchange email using a single consolidated directory.

**XSL** See *Extensible Stylesheet Language.*

**XSSI** See *eXtended Server-Side Includes.*

**X terminal** (n.) A dedicated terminal that runs X-server software. X terminal is a standard architecture for Unix machines.

**X3T10** (n.) The Advanced Technology Attachment (ATA) standards body.

**X Window System** (X) (n.) A windowed system often mistakenly called *X Windows*. A specification for device-independent windowing operations on bitmap display devices, it was originally developed by MIT's Project Athena. The server is the computer, or the X terminal, and the screen, the keyboard, the mouse, the server program, and the clients are application programs. Clients may run on the same computer as the server or on a different computer, and they communicate over Ethernet via TCP/IP protocols. X clients run on what is often con-

sidered a file server, but in X, the screen, the keyboard, and the mouse are served out to the applications. X is used on many Unix systems.

**x-y coordinates** (n.) Points on a plane divided horizontally by the x-axis and divided vertically by the y-axis. X-y coordinates are used to plot graphs and to identify locations on a two-dimensional display. Another plane may be added, providing a z-axis for three-dimensional models.

**Y** Abbreviation for luminance in a video signal.

**Yahoo!** (Yet Another Hierarchically Officious Oracle!) (n.) One of the largest hierarchical indexes of content on the World Wide Web.

**YCC format** See *colorYCC.*

**Y/C video** (n.) A type of video signal used in the Hi-8 and the S-VHS videotape formats. It transmits luminance and color as separate components, avoiding the combination used in composite video and the resulting loss of picture quality. Also known as *S-video.*

**Y-connector** (n.) A three-wire circuit that is star connected. It is also spelled "wye-connector." A Y-connector may be used to split an audio signal from an output to drive two inputs. It may not, however, be used to sum or mix two signals together to drive a single input.

**Year 2000** (Y2K, pronounced "WIE-to-kay") (n., adj.) A situation that caused problems in software systems at the turn of the century. Some programs, particularly those written many years ago, provided only the last two digits defining the year in a date. When the year *00* occurred, some of these programs did not continue to function properly.

**Yellow Book standard** (n.) The specification for standard CD-ROMs. Based on the Red Book audio standard, which preceded it, this standard defines two new modes: mode 1 and mode 2. It also establishes a third layer of error correction.

**Yet Another Hierarchically Officious Oracle!** See *Yahoo!*.

**YMCK** (n.) Abbreviation for yellow, magenta, cyan, and black. See also *CMYK*.

**YModem** (n.) A file transfer protocol used between modems. Chuck Forsberg developed it as the successor to XModem. He later developed ZModem to improve on YModem. Whereas XModem uses 128-byte packets, YModem can also use 1-kilobyte (KB) packets. YModem is a batch protocol, but YModem-G is a nonstop version with no error correction during transmission. File sizes are included in the YModem header when both binary and text files are sent. Files transferred via YModem should therefore preserve their exact length. File modification times may also be present in the YModem header. YModem can fall back to smaller packets when necessary, but there is no backward compatibility with XModem's error detection.

**YModem-G** (n.) A streaming version of YModem released in the early 1980s in which the transmitter sends packets to the receiver as rapidly as possible without waiting for acknowledgments. An error will cause the file transfer to abort completely.

**Y2K** See *Year 2000*.

**YUV color system** (n.) A method of defining video signals that separates the luminance (Y)

and the chrominance (UV) components. Human vision is much more sensitive to variations in intensity than to variations in color. The YUV encoding process takes advantage of this phenomenon and provides a wider bandwidth for luminance information than for chrominance information. Individually, the letters *YUV* signify intensity, hue, and value.

**YUV9** (n.) An image color format with significant sub-sampling, typically used with compressed video technologies, such as Indeo and Sorenson Video. For every 16 luminance (Y) samples in a 4x4 pixel block, a single hue (U) component and a single chroma value (V) is used. Such radical color sub-sampling produces relatively small files with low color fidelity. YUV9 sub-sampling may result in undesirable artifacts at the edges of highly saturated areas.

**YUV video** (n.) The coding process used in CD-I, in which the luminance signal (Y) is recorded at full bandwidth on each line and chrominance values (U and V) are recorded at half bandwidth on alternate lines.

**Z** The electronic symbol for impedance.

**zap** (v.) Jargon meaning to fry a chip with static electricity.

**z-buffer** (n.) The memory allocated to holding the depth value of pixels.

**zero insertion force** (ZIF, pronounced "ZIFF") (adj.) Describes a type of socket used on a motherboard to allow the manual replacement of one processor chip with another.

**zero level** (n.) In audio production, a relative level of intensity. *Analog zero* is a nominal decibel (dB) level near the top of a VU meter, and loud sounds are likely to exceed it during recording. *Digital zero,* which is the highest level that may be recorded without distortion, is an absolute limit. Depending on equipment settings, analog zero usually equals 18 dB below digital zero.

**zero transmission-level point** (0TLP) (n.) In telephony, the reference for measuring the signal power gain and loss of a circuit, at which a zero dB signal level is established.

ZIF See *zero insertion force.*

**zig-zag sequence** (n.) A reordering of quantized DCT coefficients designed to facilitate entropy coding by placing low-frequency coefficients before high-frequency ones.

**zip** (v.) To compress a file using PKZIP or WinZip, an archiving program. The PKZIP program is commonly used on MS-DOS or Windows systems. The companion program is PKUNZIP. Compare *unzip.*

**ZIP** (n.) A file name extension for compressed files. Such files are commonly used on IBM-compatible computers.

**Zip drive** (n.) A cartridge drive developed by Iomega Corporation that reads and writes to removable 100-megabyte (MB) hard disks.

**ZModem** (n.) A file transfer protocol developed by Chuck Forsberg with error checking and crash recovery. Its transfer rate is similar to that of YModem-G. ZModem does not wait for acknowledgment after each block is sent but sends blocks in rapid succession, as the YModem-G protocol does. A ZModem transfer may be reconstructed at a later date, and the previously transferred information need not be present if a transmission is canceled or interrupted for any reason.

**Zobel network** (n.) A Zobel network is used in an audio amplifier to dampen high frequency oscillations that might occur in the absence of loads at high frequencies. The network limits the rising impedance of a loudspeaker due to the speaker coil inductance. It is also referred to as a *Boucherot cell.* Some loudspeaker crossover designs include Zobel networks wired across the high frequency driver to compensate for the rise in impedance at high frequencies due to the inductance of the voice coil. The goal is to try to keep the load seen by the crossover circuitry as resistive as possible.

**zone** (n.) 1. A single network or domain name controlled by a specific authority. Individual zones, or domains, are delegated to individual Internet Service Providers (ISPs) by InterNIC, which controls the .com domain name system (DNS) zone. 2. In AppleTalk, a logical group of network devices.

**zoom** (v.) To enlarge or reduce the size of an image as it is displayed in a camera. This is done by changing the focal length of a zoom lens. Like optical systems, some digital systems give the user a zoom control, although digital zoom is not as high in resolution as is optical zoom.

**zoom ratio** (n.) The difference in magnification between the widest angle setting and the most extreme telephoto setting in a zoom lens. A 10:1 zoom ratio indicates that objects will appear 10 times closer at the extreme telephoto setting than they appear at the extreme wide-angle setting.

**z-sorting** (n.) In three-dimensional graphics, a method used to determine which pixels are shown. Z-sorting puts polygons in order from front to back and displays them in front. A more accurate method of sorting is z-buffering, in which the depth value of individual pixels is stored and the lowest value for each pixel is shown.

**z-transform** (n.) The mathematical process used to relate coefficients of a digital audio filter to its frequency response and to evaluate the stability of the filter.

**X Y Z**

# HTML

## Basic Tutorial on HTML

HTML documents are plain-text (also known as ASCII) files that can be created using any text editor, such as Emacs or vi on a Unix system, SimpleText on a Macintosh, or Notepad on an IBM-compatible machine. You can also use word-processing software if you save the document as "text only." In order to make HTML documents available to anyone with a web browser on the Internet, you will need to have them posted on a server. A webmaster at an educational institution, a corporation, or a commercial Internet Service Provider (ISP) will be able to assist you.

There are many WYSIWYG editors available to automate HTML development and new tools for creating and managing entire sites. You may wish to try them after you learn some of the basics of HTML tagging. It is useful to know enough HTML to code a document before you become reliant on a WYSIWYG editor.

### HTML Tags

An "element" is a fundamental component of the structure of a text document. Some examples of elements are heads, tables, paragraphs, and lists. HTML "tags" are used to mark the elements of a file for your browser. Elements may contain plain text, other elements, or both.

Tags identify the various elements in an HTML document. HTML tags consist of a left angle bracket (<), a tag name, and a right angle bracket (>). Tags are usually paired (e.g., <H1> and </H1>) to start and end the tag instruction. The end tag looks like the start tag except a slash (/) precedes the text within the brackets. Not all tags are supported by all web browsers. A browser usually ignores a tag that it does not support.

Some elements may include an "attribute," which is additional information included inside the start tag. For example, you can specify the alignment of images (top, middle, or bottom) by including the appropriate attribute with the image source HTML code. Tags that have optional attributes are noted below.

*This document is adapted from* A Beginner's Guide to HTML, *which was created by the National Center for Supercomputing. It is printed with permission from the Board of Trustees of the University of Illinois. Source URL: http://www.ncsa.uiuc.edu/General/Internet/WWW/HTMLPrimer.html*

*Note:* HTML is not case sensitive. <title> is equivalent to <TITLE> or <TiTlE>. There are a few exceptions noted in the Escape Sequences section below.

### A Minimal HTML Document

Every HTML document should contain certain standard HTML tags. Each document consists of head and body text. The head contains the title, and the body contains the actual text that is made up of paragraphs, lists, and other elements. Browsers expect specific information because they are programmed according to HTML and SGML specifications.

Required elements are shown in this sample document:

```
<html>
<head>
<TITLE>A Simple HTML Example</TITLE>
</head>
<body>
<H1>HTML is Easy To Learn</H1>
<P>Welcome to the world of HTML.
This is the first paragraph. While short, it is
still a paragraph!</P>
<P>And this is the second paragraph.</P>
</body>
</html>
```

The required elements are the <HTML>, <HEAD>, <TITLE>, and <BODY> tags, along with their corresponding end tags. Because you should include these tags in each file, you might want to create a template file with them. Some browsers will format your HTML file correctly even if these tags are not included, while other browsers will not.

To view a copy of the file that your browser reads to generate the information in your current window, select View Source (or the equivalent) from the browser menu. The file contents, along with all the HTML tags, are displayed in a new window.

This is an excellent way to discover how HTML is used and to learn tips and constructs. Of course, the HTML that you find might not be technically correct. Once you become familiar with HTML and check the many online and hard-copy references on the subject, you will learn to distinguish between "good" and "bad" HTML. You can save a source file with the HTML codes and use it as a template for one of your web pages, or you can modify the format to suit your purposes.

# Markup Tags

### HTML

This element tells your browser that the file contains HTML-coded information. The file extension .html also indicates that it is an HTML document. If you are restricted to 8.3 file names, use only .htm for your extension.

## Head

The head element identifies the first part of your HTML-coded document. It contains the title, which is shown as part of your browser's window.

## Title

The title element contains your document title and identifies its content in a global context. The title is displayed somewhere on the browser window (usually at the top), but not within the text area. The title is also displayed on someone's hot list or bookmark list, so choose something descriptive, unique, and relatively short. A title is also used during a WAIS search of a server.

For example, you might include a shortened title of a book with the chapter contents; for example, "NCSA Mosaic Guide (Windows): Installation." This tells the software name, the platform, and the chapter contents, which is more useful than calling the document Installation. Generally, titles should be restricted to 64 characters or fewer.

## Body

The second part of your HTML document is the body, which contains the content of your document (displayed within the text area of your browser window). The tags explained below are used in the body of your HTML document.

## Headings

HTML has six levels of headings, numbered 1 through 6, with 1 being the most prominent. Web browsers display headings in larger and/or bolder fonts than normal body text. The first heading in each document should be tagged <H1>.

The syntax of the heading element is <Hn>Text of heading</Hn> where $n$ is a number between 1 and 6 specifying the level of the heading.

Do not skip levels of headings in your document. For example, don't start with a level-one heading (<H1>) and follow it with a level-three (<H3>) heading.

## Paragraphs

Unlike documents in most word processors, carriage returns in HTML files aren't significant. It doesn't matter how long your lines of text are, but it is best to restrict them to fewer than 72 characters in length. Word wrapping can occur at any point in your source file, and multiple spaces are collapsed into a single space by your browser.

In the example shown in the "Minimal HTML Document" section, the first paragraph is coded as

```
<P>Welcome to the world of HTML.
This is the first paragraph.
While short, it is
still a paragraph!</P>
```

In the source file there is a line break between the sentences. A web browser ignores this line break and starts a new paragraph only when it encounters another <P> tag.

*Important:* You must indicate paragraphs with <P> elements. A browser ignores any indentations or blank lines in the source text. Without <P> elements, the document becomes one large paragraph. (One exception is text tagged as "preformatted," which is explained below.) For example, the following would produce identical output to the "Minimal HTML" example:

```
<H1>Level-one heading</H1> <P>Welcome to the world of
HTML. This is the first paragraph. While short, it is
still a paragraph! </P>

<P>And this is the second paragraph.</P>
```

To preserve readability in HTML files, put headings on separate lines, use a blank line or two where it helps identify the start of a new section, and separate paragraphs with blank lines in addition to the <P> tags. These extra spaces help you when you edit your files, but your browser will ignore the extra spaces because it has its own set of rules on spacing that do not depend on the spaces you put in your source file.

*Note:* The </P> closing tag can be omitted because browsers understand that when they encounter a <P> tag, it implies that there is an end to the previous paragraph.

Using the <P> and </P> as a paragraph container means that you can center a paragraph by including the ALIGN=alignment attribute in your source file. The formatted version is below the tagged version.

```
<P ALIGN=CENTER>
This is a centered paragraph.</P>
```

This is a centered paragraph.

# Lists

HTML supports unnumbered, numbered, and definition lists. You can nest lists, but use this feature sparingly because too many nested items can make a document difficult to follow.

## Unnumbered Lists

To make an unnumbered, bulleted list:

1. Start with an opening list <UL> (for unnumbered list) tag.
2. Enter the <LI> (list item) tag followed by the individual item; no closing </LI> tag is needed.
3. End the entire list with a closing list </UL> tag.

Below is a sample three-item list:

```
<UL>
<LI> apples
<LI> bananas
<LI> grapefruit
</UL>
```

The output is:

- apples
- bananas
- grapefruit

The <LI> items can contain multiple paragraphs. Indicate the paragraphs with the <P> paragraph tags.

## Numbered Lists

A numbered list (also called an ordered list, from which the tag name derives) is identical to an unnumbered list, except it uses <OL> instead of <UL>. The items are tagged using the same <LI> tag. The following HTML code:

```
<OL>
<LI> oranges
<LI> peaches
<LI> grapes
</OL>
```

produces this formatted output:

1. oranges
2. peaches
3. grapes

## Definition Lists

A definition list (coded as <DL>) usually consists of alternating a definition term (coded as <DT>) and a definition (coded as <DD>). Web browsers generally format the definition on a new line.

The following is an example of a definition list:

```
<DL>
<DT> NCSA
<DD> NCSA, the National Center for Supercomputing
Applications, is located on the campus of the University
```

```
of Illinois at Urbana-Champaign.
  <DT> Cornell Theory Center
  <DD> CTC is located on the campus of Cornell University
in Ithaca, New York.
  </DL>
```

The output looks like:

NCSA
  NCSA, the National Center for Supercomputing Applications, is located on the campus of
  the University of Illinois at Urbana-Champaign.
Cornell Theory Center
  CTC is located on the campus of Cornell University in Ithaca, New York.

The <DT> and <DD> entries can contain multiple paragraphs (indicated by <P> paragraph tags), lists, or other definition information.

The COMPACT attribute can be used routinely in case your definition terms are short. If, for example, you are showing some computer options, the options may fit on the same line as the start of the definition.

```
<DL COMPACT>
<DT> -i
<DD>invokes NCSA Mosaic for Microsoft Windows using the
initialization file defined in the path
<DT> -k
<DD>invokes NCSA Mosaic for Microsoft Windows in kiosk
mode
</DL>
```

The output looks like:

-i    invokes NCSA Mosaic for Microsoft Windows using the initialization file defined
      in the path
-k    invokes NCSA Mosaic for Microsoft Windows in kiosk mode

## Nested Lists

Lists can be nested. You can also have a number of paragraphs, each containing a nested list, in a single list item.
  Here is a sample nested list:

```
<UL>
<LI> A few New England states:
```

```
        <UL>
        <LI> Vermont
        <LI> New Hampshire
        <LI> Maine
        </UL>
   <LI> Two Midwestern states:
        <UL>
        <LI> Michigan
        <LI> Indiana
        </UL>
   </UL>
```

The nested list is displayed as:

- A few New England states:
  - Vermont
  - New Hampshire
  - Maine
- Two Midwestern states:
  - Michigan
  - Indiana

# Preformatted Text

Use the <PRE> tag (which stands for preformatted) to generate text in a fixed-width font. This tag also makes spaces, new lines, and tabs significant (multiple spaces are displayed as multiple spaces, and lines break in the same locations as in the source HTML file). This is useful for program listings, among other things. For example, the following lines:

```
<PRE>
  #!/bin/csh
  cd $SCR
  cfs get mysrc.f:mycfsdir/mysrc.f
  cfs get myinfile:mycfsdir/myinfile
  fc -02 -o mya.out mysrc.f
  mya.out
  cfs save myoutfile:mycfsdir/myoutfile
  rm *
</PRE>
```

display as:

```
  #!/bin/csh
  cd $SCR
```

481

```
cfs get mysrc.f:mycfsdir/mysrc.f
cfs get myinfile:mycfsdir/myinfile
fc -02 -o mya.out mysrc.f
mya.out
cfs save myoutfile:mycfsdir/myoutfile
rm *
```

The <PRE> tag can be used with an optional WIDTH attribute that specifies the maximum number of characters for a line. WIDTH also signals your browser to choose an appropriate font and indentation for the text. Hyperlinks can be used within <PRE> sections. You should avoid using other HTML tags within <PRE> sections, however.

Note that because <, >, and & have special meanings in HTML, you must use their escape sequences (&lt;, &gt;, and &amp;, respectively) to enter these characters. See the section on escape sequences for more information.

## Extended Quotations

Use the <BLOCKQUOTE> tag to include lengthy quotations in a separate block on the screen. Most browsers change the margins for the quotation to separate it from surrounding text.

In the example:

```
<BLOCKQUOTE>
<P>Omit needless words.</P>
<P>Vigorous writing is concise. A sentence should contain
no unnecessary words, a paragraph no unnecessary
sentences, for the same reason that a drawing should have
no unnecessary lines and a machine no unnecessary
parts.</P>
-William Strunk, Jr., 1918
</BLOCKQUOTE>
```

the result is:

> Omit needless words.
>
> Vigorous writing is concise. A sentence should contain no unnecessary words, a paragraph no unnecessary sentences, for the same reason that a drawing should have no unnecessary lines and a machine no unnecessary parts.
> -William Strunk, Jr., 1918

# Addresses

The <ADDRESS> tag is generally used to specify the author of a document, a way to contact the author (e.g., an email address), and a revision date. It is usually the last item in a file.

For example, the last line of the online version of this guide is:

```
<ADDRESS>
A Beginner's Guide to HTML/NCSA/pubs@ncsa.uiuc.edu/
revised April 96 </ADDRESS>
```

The result is:

*A Beginner's Guide to HTML / NCSA / pubs@ncsa.uiuc.edu / revised April 96*

*Note:* <ADDRESS> is not used for postal addresses. See "Forced Line Breaks" below to learn how to format postal addresses.

# Forced Line Breaks/Postal Addresses

The <BR> tag forces a line break with no extra (white) space between lines. Using <P> elements for short lines of text such as postal addresses results in unwanted additional white space. For example, with <BR>:

```
National Center for Supercomputing Applications<BR>
605 East Springfield Avenue<BR>
Champaign, Illinois 61820-5518<BR>
```

The output is:

National Center for Supercomputing Applications
605 East Springfield Avenue
Champaign, Illinois 61820-5518

# Horizontal Rules

The <HR> tag produces a horizontal line the width of the browser window. A horizontal rule is useful when you are separating sections of your document. For example, many people add a rule at the end of their text and before the <ADDRESS> information.

You can vary a rule size (thickness) and width (the percentage of the window covered by the rule). Experiment with the settings until you are satisfied with the presentation. For example, to create a four-pixel-thick centered line half as wide as the window, use the tag <HR SIZE=4 WIDTH="50%">.

# Character Formatting

HTML has two styles for individual words or sentences: logical and physical. Logical styles tag text according to its meaning, while physical styles indicate the specific appearance of a section. For example, in the preceding sentence, the words "logical styles" might be tagged as a "definition." The same effect (formatting those words in italics) could be achieved with a different tag that tells your browser to "put these words in italics."

*Note:* Some browsers do not attach any style to the <DFN> tag, so you cannot be assured that all users would see the tagged phrase in italics.

## Logical Versus Physical Styles

In the ideal SGML universe, content is divorced from presentation. Thus, SGML tags a level-one heading as a level-one heading, but it does not specify that the level-one heading should be, for instance, 24-point bold Times centered. The advantage of this approach (it's similar in concept to style sheets in many word processors) is that if you decide to change level-one headings to 20-point left-justified Helvetica, all you have to do is change the definition of the level-one heading in your web browser. Indeed, many browsers today let you define how you want the various HTML tags rendered onscreen.

Another advantage of logical tags is that they help enforce consistency in your documents. It's easier to tag something as <H1> than to remember that level-one headings are 24-point bold Times centered, for example. Consider the <STRONG> tag, which most browsers render in bold text. However, it is possible for a reader to prefer these sections to be displayed in red. Logical styles offer this flexibility.

Of course, if you want something to be displayed in italics, for example, and do not want a browser's setting to display it differently, use physical styles. Physical styles, therefore, offer consistency because something you tag a certain way will always be displayed that way for readers of your document.

Try to be consistent about which type of style you use. If you tag with physical styles, do so throughout a document. If you use logical styles, stick with them within a document. The version 4.0 release of HTML strongly advocates the use of Cascading Style Sheets (CSS) to apply styles in HTML documents.

## Logical Styles

<DFN> for a word being defined. Typically displayed in italics.
(*NCSA Mosaic is a World Wide Web browser.*)

<EM> for emphasis. Typically displayed in italics.
(*Consultants cannot reset your password unless you call the help line.*)

<CITE> for titles of books, films, etc. Typically displayed in italics.
(*For Whom the Bell Tolls*)

<CODE> for computer code. Displayed in a fixed-width font.
(The <stdio.h> header file)

<KBD> for user keyboard entry. Typically displayed in plain fixed-width font.
(Enter passwd to change your password.)

<SAMP> for a sequence of literal characters. Displayed in a fixed-width font.
(Segmentation fault: Core dumped.)

<STRONG> for strong emphasis. Typically displayed in bold.
**(Note: Always check your links to see how text is displayed.***)*

<VAR> for a variable, where you will replace the variable with specific information. Typically displayed in italics.
*(rm* *filename* *deletes the file.)*

## Physical Styles

<B>     bold text
<I>     italic text
<TT>    typewriter text (fixed-width font)

## Escape Sequences (a.k.a. Character Entities)

Character entities have two functions:
   1. Escaping special characters.
   2. Displaying other characters not available in the plain ASCII character set (primarily characters with diacritical marks).

Three ASCII characters—the left angle bracket (<), the right angle bracket (>), and the ampersand (&)—have special meanings in HTML and therefore cannot be used "as is" in text. (The angle brackets are used to indicate the beginning and end of HTML tags, and the ampersand is used to indicate the beginning of an escape sequence.) Double quote marks may be used as-is, but a character entity may also be used (&quot;).

To use one of the three characters in an HTML document, you must enter its escape sequence instead:

&lt;        escape sequence for <
&gt;        escape sequence for >
&amp;       escape sequence for &

Additional escape sequences support accented characters, such as:

&ouml;      escape sequence for a lowercase o with an umlaut: ö

&ntilde; escape sequence for a lowercase n with a tilde: ñ

&Egrave; escape sequence for an uppercase E with a grave accent: È

You can substitute other letters for the ö, ñ, and È shown above. Refer to the "HTML Coded Characters" table under the HTML entry for a complete list of special characters.

*Note:* Unlike the rest of HTML, the escape sequences are case sensitive. You cannot, for instance, use &LT; instead of &lt;.

# Linking

The chief power of HTML comes from its ability to link text and/or an image to another document or section of a document. A browser highlights the identified text or image with color and/or underlines to indicate that it is a hypertext link (often shortened to hyperlink or link).

HTML's single hypertext-related tag is <A>, which stands for anchor. To include an anchor in your document:

1. Start the anchor with <A (include a space after the A).
2. Specify the document you're linking to by entering the parameter HREF="filename" followed by a closing right angle bracket (>).
3. Enter the text that will serve as the hypertext link in the current document.
4. Enter the ending anchor tag </A>. (No space is needed before the end anchor tag.)

Here is a sample hypertext reference in a file called US.html:

```
<A HREF="MaineStats.html">Maine</A>
```

This entry makes the word *Maine* the hyperlink to the document *MaineStats.html*, which is in the same directory as the first document.

## Relative Path Names vs. Absolute Path Names

You can link to documents in other directories by specifying the relative path from the current document to the linked document. For example, a link to a file NYStats.html located in the subdirectory AtlanticStates would be:

```
<A HREF= "AtlanticStates/NYStats.html">New York</A>
```

These are called relative links because you specify the path to the linked file relative to the location of the current file. You can also use the absolute path name (the complete URL) of the file, but relative links are more efficient in accessing a server.

Path names use the standard Unix syntax. The Unix syntax for the parent directory (the directory that contains the current directory) is "..". (For more information consult a beginning Unix reference text.)

If you were in the NYStats.html file and were referring to the original document US.html, your link would look like this:

```
<A HREF="../US.html">United States</A>
```

Generally, relative links should be used for the following reasons:
1. It is easier to move a group of documents to another location (because the relative path names will still be valid).
2. It is more efficient connecting to the server.
3. There is less to type.

However, use absolute path names when linking to documents that are not directly related. For example, consider a group of documents that comprise a user manual. Links within this group should be relative links. Links to other documents (perhaps a reference to related software) should use full path names. This way if you move the user manual to a different directory, none of the links would have to be updated.

## URLs

The World Wide Web uses uniform resource locators (URLs) to specify the location of files on other servers. A URL includes the type of resource being accessed (e.g., web, gopher, WAIS), the address of the server, and the location of the file. The syntax is *scheme://host.domain [:port]/path/ filename* where *scheme* is one of the following types:

file
　　A file on your local system.
ftp
　　A file on an anonymous FTP server.
http
　　A file on a World Wide Web server.
gopher
　　A file on a gopher server.
WAIS
　　A file on a WAIS server.
news
　　A Usenet newsgroup.
telnet
　　A connection to a Telnet-based service.

The *port* number can generally be omitted, unless it is specifically requested. For example, to include a link in your document to the NCSA primer (upon which this appendix is based), enter:

```
<A HREF="http://www.ncsa.uiuc.edu/General/Internet/WWW/
HTMLPrimer.html">
NCSA's Beginner's Guide to HTML</A>
```

This entry makes the text *NCSA's Beginner's Guide to HTML* a hyperlink to your document.

## Links to Specific Sections

Anchors can also be used to move a reader to a particular section in a document (either the same or a different document) rather than to the top, which is the default. This type of an anchor is commonly called a "named anchor" because to create the links, you insert HTML names within the document.

Internal hyperlinks are used to create a "table of contents" at the top of a long document. These hyperlinks move you from one location to another in the same document. You can also link to a specific section in another document.

## Links Between Sections of Different Documents

Suppose you want to set a link from document A (documentA.html) to a specific section in another document (MaineStats.html).

Enter the HTML coding for a link to a named anchor:

```
documentA.html:

In addition to the many state parks, Maine is also home to
<a href="MaineStats.html#ANP">Acadia National Park</a>.
```

Think of the characters after the hash mark (#) as a tab within the MaineStats.html file. This tab tells your browser what should be displayed at the top of the window when the link is activated. In other words, the first line in your browser window should be the Acadia National Park heading.

Next, create the named anchor (in this example "ANP") in MaineStats.html:

```
<H2><A NAME="ANP">Acadia National Park</a></H2>
```

With both of these elements in place, you can bring a reader directly to the Acadia reference in MaineStats.html.

*Note:* You cannot make links to specific sections within a different document unless you have permission to edit the coded source of that document or that document already contains in-document named anchors. For example, you could include named anchors to the NCSA online HTML guide in a document you are writing because there are named anchors in this guide. But if this document did not have named anchors, you could not make a link to a specific section because you cannot edit the original file on NCSA's server.

## Links to Specific Sections Within the Current Document

The technique is the same except the file name is omitted. For example, to link to the ANP anchor from within MaineStats, enter:

```
...More information about <A HREF="#ANP">Acadia National
Park</A> is available elsewhere in this document.
```

Be sure to include the <A NAME=> tag where you want the link to jump to (<H2> <A NAME="ANP">Acadia National Park</A></H2>).

Named anchors are useful when you think readers will print an entire document or when you have a lot of short information you want to place online in one file.

## Mailto

You can make it easy for a reader to send email to a specific person or mail alias by including the mailto attribute in a hyperlink. The format is:

```
<A HREF="mailto:emailinfo@host">Name</a>
```

For example, enter:

```
<A HREF="mailto:brad@hansenmedia.com">Brad Hansen</a>
```

This creates a mail window configured to send email. You may put any valid Internet address in your mailto window.

## Inline Images

Most web browsers can display inline images (images next to text) that are in X BitMap (XBM), GIF, or JPEG format. Another image format recognized by current web browsers is the Portable Network Graphics (PNG) format. Each image takes time to process and slows down the initial display of a document. Carefully select your images and the number of images in a document.

To include an inline image, enter:

```
<IMG SRC=ImageName>
```

where *ImageName* is the URL of the image file.

The syntax for <IMG SRC> URLs is identical to that used in an anchor HREF. If the image file is a GIF file, then the file name part of *ImageName* must end with .gif. File names of X BitMap images must end with .xbm; JPEG image files must end with .jpg or .jpeg; and Portable Network Graphic files must end with .png.

## Image Size Attributes

Include two other attributes on <IMG> tags to tell your browser the size of the images it is downloading with the text. The HEIGHT and WIDTH attributes let the browser set aside the appropriate space (in pixels) for the images as it downloads the rest of the file. (Get the pixel size from your image-processing software, such as Adobe Photoshop.)

For example, to include a self-portrait image in a file along with the portrait's dimensions, enter:

```
<IMG SRC=SelfPortrait.gif HEIGHT=100 WIDTH=65>
```

*Note:* Some browsers use the HEIGHT and WIDTH attributes to stretch or shrink an image to fit into the allotted space when the image does not exactly match the attribute numbers. Not all browser developers think stretching/shrinking is a good idea. Do not assume your readers will have access to this feature. Check your dimensions and use the correct ones.

## Aligning Images

You have some flexibility when displaying images. You can have images separated from text and aligned to the left, right, or center, or you can have an image aligned with text. Try several possibilities to see how your information looks best.

## Aligning Text with an Image

By default, the bottom of an image is aligned with the baseline of the text that follows it. You can align images to the top or center of a paragraph using the ALIGN= attributes TOP and CENTER.

To align text with the top of the image, use the tag:

```
(<IMG SRC = "MyImage.gif" ALIGN=TOP>)
```

Note that the browser aligns only one line and then jumps to the bottom of the image for the rest of the text.

For text that is centered on the image, use the tag:

```
(<IMG SRC = "MyImage.gif" ALIGN=CENTER>)
```

Only one line of text is centered; the rest is below the image.

## Images Without Text

To display an image without any associated text (e.g., your organization's logo), make it a separate paragraph. Use the paragraph ALIGN= attribute to center the image or adjust it to the right side of the window as shown on the following page:

```
<p ALIGN=CENTER>
<IMG SRC = "MyImage.gif">
</p>
```

The image is centered and the paragraph starts below it, left-justified.

## Alternate Text for Images

Some World Wide Web browsers (primarily those that run on VT100 terminals) cannot display images. Some users turn off image loading if they have a slow connection, even if their software can display images. HTML provides a mechanism to tell readers what they are missing on your pages.

The ALT attribute lets you specify text to be displayed instead of an image. In the following example *UpArrow.gif* is the picture of an upward pointing arrow.

```
<IMG SRC="UpArrow.gif" ALT="Up">
```

With graphics-capable viewers that have image-loading turned on, the up arrow graphic is visible. With image-loading turned off, or with a VT100 browser, the word *Up* is shown in your window. It's a good idea to include alternate text for each image you use in your document as a courtesy for your readers.

## Background Graphics

Newer versions of web browsers can load an image and use it as a background when displaying a page. Some people like background images, and some don't. In general, if you want to include a background, make sure your text can be read easily when displayed on top of the image. Background images can be a texture or an object, such as a logo. You create the background image as you do any image.

However, you have to create only a small piece of the image. Using a tiling feature, a browser takes the image and repeats it across and down to fill your browser window. Basically, you generate one image, and the browser replicates it enough times to fill your window. This action is automatic when you use the background tag.

Below is the tag to include a background image included in the <BODY> statement as an attribute:

```
<BODY BACKGROUND="filename.gif">
```

## Background Color

By default, browsers display text in black on a gray background. However, you can change both elements if you want. Some HTML authors select a background color and coordinate it with a change in the color of the text.

Always preview changes like this to make sure your pages are readable. (For example, many people find red text on a black background difficult to read.)

You change the color of text, links, visited links, and active links using attributes of the <BODY> tag. For example, enter:

```
<BODY BGCOLOR="#000000" TEXT="#FFFFFF" LINK="#9690CC">
```

This creates a window with a black background (BGCOLOR), white text (TEXT), and silvery hyperlinks (LINK).

The six-digit number and letter combinations represent colors by giving their RGB (red, green, blue) value. The six digits are three two-digit numbers in sequence, representing the amount of red, green, or blue as a hexadecimal value in the range 00–FF. For example, 000000 is black (no color at all), FF0000 is bright red, and FFFFFF is white (fully saturated with all three colors). These number and letter combinations are cryptic. The six-digit color codes that map specific colors in HTML 3.2 and later are provided in the "HTML Color Table" under the HTML entry.

## External Images, Sounds, and Animation

You may want to have an image open as a separate document when a user activates a link on either a word or a smaller inline version of the image included in your document. This is called an external image, and it is useful if you do not wish to slow down the loading of the main document with large inline images.

To include a reference to an external image, enter:

```
<A HREF="MyImage.gif">link anchor</A>
```

You can also use a smaller image as a link to a larger image. Enter:

```
<A HREF="LargerImage.gif"><IMG SRC="SmallImage.gif"></A>
```

The reader sees the SmallImage.gif image and clicks it to open the LargerImage.gif file.

Use the same syntax for links to external animation and sounds. The only difference is the file extension of the linked file. For example, <A HREF="AdamsRib.mov">link anchor</A> specifies a link to a QuickTime movie. Some common file types and their extensions are:

| File Type | Extension |
|---|---|
| ASCII text | .txt |
| HTML document | .htm (or .html) |
| GIF image | .gif |
| TIFF image | .tif (or .tiff) |
| X BitMap image | .xbm |
| JPEG image | .jpg (or .jpeg) |
| PNG image | .png |
| PostScript file | .ps |
| AIFF sound file | .aif (or .aiff) |
| AU sound file | .au |
| WAV sound file | .wav |
| QuickTime movie | .mov |
| MPEG movie | .mpg (or .mpeg) |

Keep in mind your intended audience's access to helper applications and plug-ins. For example, most Unix workstations cannot view QuickTime movies.

## Tables

Before HTML tags for tables were finalized, authors had to format their tabular information carefully within <PRE> tags, counting spaces and previewing their output. Tables are useful for presenting tabular information, and they are a boon to creative HTML authors who use the table tags to present their regular web pages.

Think of your tabular information in light of the coding explained below. A table has heads where you explain what the columns/rows include, rows for information, and cells for each item. In the following table, the first column contains the header information, each row explains an HTML table tag, and each cell contains a paired tag or an explanation of the tag's function.

## Table Elements

| Element | Description |
|---|---|
| <TABLE> | Defines a table in HTML. If the BORDER attribute is present, your browser displays the table with a border. |
| <CAPTION> | Defines the caption for the title of the table. The default position of the title is centered at the top. The ALIGN=BOTTOM attribute can be used to position the caption below the table. *Note:* Any kind of markup tag can be used in the caption. |
| <TR> | Specifies a table row within a table. You may define default attributes for the entire row: ALIGN (LEFT, CENTER, RIGHT) and/or VALIGN (TOP, MIDDLE, BOTTOM). See "Table Attributes" at the end of this table for more information. |
| <TH> | Defines a table header cell. By default the text in this cell is bold and centered. Table header cells may contain other attributes to determine the characteristics of the cell and/or its contents. See "Table Attributes" at the end of this table for more information. |
| <TD> | Defines a table data cell. By default, the text in this cell is left-aligned and centered vertically. Table data cells may contain other attributes to determine the characteristics of the cell and/or its contents. See "Table Attributes" at the end of this table. |

## Table Attributes

*Note:* Attributes defined within <TH> ... </TH> or <TD> ... </TD> cells override the default alignment set in a <TR> ... </TR>. Attributes are listed below, along with their description.

ALIGN (LEFT, CENTER, RIGHT)
Horizontal alignment of a cell.

VALIGN (TOP, MIDDLE, BOTTOM)
Vertical alignment of a cell.

COLSPAN=n
The number (n) of columns a cell spans.

493

ROWSPAN=n
The number (n) of rows a cell spans.

NOWRAP
Turn off word wrapping within a cell.

## General Table Format

The general format of a table looks like this:

```
<TABLE>                              <== start of table definition

<CAPTION> caption </CAPTION>         <== caption definition

<TR>                                 <== start of first row definition
<TH> cell contents </TH>             <== first cell in row 1 (a head)

<TH> cell contents </TH>             <== last cell in row 1 (a head)
</TR>                                <== end of first row definition

<TR>                                 <== start of second row definition
<TD> cell contents </TD>             <== first cell in row 2

<TD> cell contents </TD>             <== last cell in row 2
</TR>                                <== end of second row definition

<TR>                                 <== start of last row definition
<TD> cell contents </TD>             <== first cell in last row

<TD> cell contents </TD>             <== last cell in last row
</TR>                                <== end of last row definition

</TABLE>                             <== end of table definition
```

The <TABLE> and </TABLE> tags must surround the entire table definition. The first item inside the table, CAPTION, is optional. Then you can have any number of rows defined by the <TR> and </TR> tags. Within a row you can have any number of cells defined by the <TD>...</TD> or <TH>...</TH> tags. Each row of a table is formatted independently of the rows above and below it. This lets you easily display tables like the one above with a single cell, such as *Table Attributes*, spanning columns of the table.

## Tables for Nontabular Information

Some HTML authors use tables to present nontabular information. For example, because links can be included in table cells, some authors use a table with no borders to create "one" image from separate images. Browsers that can display tables properly show the various images seamlessly, making the created image seem like an image map (one image with hyperlinked quadrants). Using table borders with images can create an impressive display as well.

# Fill-out Forms

Web forms let you return information to a web server for some action. For example, suppose you collect names and email addresses so you can email information to people who request it. For each person who enters his or her name and address, you need some information to be sent and the respondent's particulars added to a database. This information is usually processed by a script or program written in Perl or another language that manipulates text, files, and information.

The forms are not hard to code. They follow the same constructs as other HTML tags. What can be difficult is the program or script that takes the data submitted in a form and processes it. Because of the need for specialized scripts to handle the incoming form information, fill-out forms are not discussed in this primer.

# Troubleshooting

## Avoid Overlapping Tags

Consider this example of HTML:

```
<B>This is an example of <DFN>overlapping</B> HTML
tags.</DFN>
```

The word *overlapping* is in both the <B> and <DFN> tags. A browser might be confused by this coding and might not display it the way you intend. The only way to know is to check each popular browser (a time-consuming proposition).

In general, avoid overlapping tags. Look at your tags and try pairing them up. Tags (with the obvious exceptions of elements whose end tags may be omitted, such as paragraphs) should be paired without an intervening tag in between. Look again at the example above. You cannot pair the bold tags without another tag in the middle (the first definition tag). Try matching your coding up like this to see if you have any problem areas that should be fixed before you release your files to a server.

## Embed Only Anchors and Character Tags

HTML protocol allows you to embed links within other HTML tags:

```
<H1><A HREF="Destination.html">My heading</A></H1>
```

Do not embed HTML tags within an anchor:

```
<A HREF="Destination.html">
<H1>My heading</H1>
</A>
```

Although most browsers currently handle this second example, the official HTML specifications do not support this construct, and your file may not work with future browsers. Remember that browsers can be forgiving when displaying improperly coded files. However, that forgiveness may not continue in the next version of the software! When in doubt, code your files according to the HTML specification.

Character tags modify the appearance of the text within other elements:

```
<UL>
<LI><B>A bold list item</B>
<LI><I>An italic list item</I>
</UL>
```

Avoid embedding other types of HTML element tags. For example, you might be tempted to embed a heading within a list in order to make the font size larger:

```
<UL>
<LI><H1>A large heading</H1>
<LI><H2>Something slightly smaller</H2>
</UL>
```

Although some browsers handle this well, formatting of such coding is unpredictable because it is undefined. For compatibility with all browsers, avoid these kinds of constructs. Cascading Style Sheets (CSS) is the preferred method of defining style parameters in HTML documents.

What's the difference between embedding a <B> within a <LI> tag as opposed to embedding a <H1> within a <LI>? Within HTML the semantic meaning of <H1> is that it's the main heading of a document and that it should be followed by the content of the document. Therefore, it doesn't make sense to find a <H1> within a list.

Character formatting tags also are generally not additive. For example, you might expect that <B><I>some text</I></B> would produce bold-italic text. On some browsers it does; other browsers interpret only the innermost tag.

## Final Steps

Validate your code. When you put a document on a web server, check the formatting and each link (including named anchors). Ideally, you will have someone else read through and comment on your files before you consider a document finished.

You can run your coded files through an HTML validation service that will tell you if your code conforms to accepted HTML. If you are not sure your coding conforms to HTML specifications, this can be a useful teaching tool. Fortunately, the service lets you select the level of conformance you want for your files (i.e., strict, level 2, level 3). If you want to use some codes that are not officially part of the HTML specifications, this latitude is helpful.

## Dummy Images

When an <IMG SRC> tag points to an image that does not exist, a dummy image is substituted by your browser software. When this happens during your final review of your files, make sure that the referenced image does in fact exist, that the hyperlink has the correct information in the URL, and that the file permission is set appropriately (world-readable). Then check online again.

## Update Your Files

If the contents of a file are static (such as a biography of George Washington), no updating should be needed. Time-sensitive documents should be changed often.

Updating is important when the file contains information such as a weekly schedule or a deadline for a program funding announcement. Remove out-of-date files or note why something that seems dated is still on a server (e.g., the program requirements remain the same for the next cycle so the file is still available as an interim reference).

## Browsers Differ

Web browsers display HTML elements differently. Remember that not all codes used in HTML files are interpreted by all browsers. Any code a browser does not understand is usually ignored.

You could spend a lot of time making your file look perfect using your current browser. If you check that file using another browser, it may display quite differently. Hence, these words of advice: code your files using correct HTML. Leave the interpreting to the browsers and hope for the best.

## Commenting Your Files

You might want to include comments in your HTML files. Comments in HTML are like comments in a computer program—the text you enter is not used by the browser in any formatting and is not directly viewable by the reader, just as computer program comments are not used and are not viewable. The comments are accessible if a reader views the source file, however.

Comments such as the name of the person updating a file, the software and version used in creating a file, or the date that a minor edit was made are the norm.

To include a comment, enter:

```
<!-- your comments here -->
```

You must include the exclamation mark and the hyphens as shown.

# XHTML

## 1.    What is XHTML?

XHTML is a family of current and future document types and modules that reproduce, subset, and extend HTML 4 [HTML]. XHTML family document types are XML based, and ultimately are designed to work in conjunction with XML-based user agents. The details of this family and its evolution are discussed in more detail in the section on Future Directions.

   XHTML 1.0 (this specification) is the first document type in the XHTML family. It is a reformulation of the three HTML 4 document types as applications of XML 1.0 [XML]. It is intended to be used as a language for content that is both XML-conforming and, if some simple guidelines are followed, operates in HTML 4 conforming user agents. Developers who migrate their content to XHTML 1.0 will realize the following benefits:

*    XHTML documents are XML conforming. As such, they are readily viewed, edited, and validated with standard XML tools.
*    XHTML documents can be written to operate as well or better than they did before in existing HTML 4–conforming user agents as well as in new, XHTML 1.0–conforming user agents.
*    XHTML documents can utilize applications (e.g. scripts and applets) that rely upon either the HTML Document Object Model or the XML Document Object Model [DOM].
*    As the XHTML family evolves, documents conforming to XHTML 1.0 will be more likely to interoperate within and among various XHTML environments.

   The XHTML family is the next step in the evolution of the Internet. By migrating to XHTML today, content developers can enter the XML world with all of its attendant benefits, while still remaining confident in their content's backward and future compatibility.

### 1.1    What Is HTML 4?

HTML 4 [HTML] is an SGML (Standard Generalized Markup Language) application conforming to International Standard ISO 8879 and is widely regarded as the standard publishing language of the World Wide Web.

SGML is a language for describing markup languages, particularly those used in electronic document exchange, document management, and document publishing. HTML is an example of a language defined in SGML.

SGML has been around since the middle 1980's and has remained quite stable. Much of this stability stems from the fact that the language is both feature-rich and flexible. This flexibility, however, comes at a price, and that price is a level of complexity that has inhibited its adoption in a diversity of environments, including the World Wide Web.

HTML, as originally conceived, was to be a language for the exchange of scientific and other technical documents, suitable for use by non-document specialists. HTML addressed the problem of SGML complexity by specifying a small set of structural and semantic tags suitable for authoring relatively simple documents. In addition to simplifying the document structure, HTML added support for hypertext. Multimedia capabilities were added later.

In a remarkably short space of time, HTML became wildly popular and rapidly outgrew its original purpose. Since HTML's inception, there has been rapid invention of new elements for use within HTML (as a standard) and for adapting HTML to vertical, highly specialized markets. This plethora of new elements has led to compatibility problems for documents across different platforms.

As the heterogeneity of both software and platforms rapidly proliferate, it is clear that the suitability of "classic" HTML 4 for use on these platforms is somewhat limited.

## 1.2     What Is XML?

XML™ is the shorthand for Extensible Markup Language, and is an acronym of Extensible Markup Language [XML].

XML was conceived as a means of regaining the power and flexibility of SGML without most of its complexity. Although a restricted form of SGML, XML nonetheless preserves most of SGML's power and richness, and yet still retains all of SGML's commonly used features.

While retaining these beneficial features, XML removes many of the more complex features of SGML that make the authoring and design of suitable software both difficult and costly.

## 1.3     Why the Need for XHTML?

The benefits of migrating to XHTML 1.0 are described above. Some of the benefits of migrating to XHTML in general are:
- Document developers and user agent designers are constantly discovering new ways to express their ideas through new markup. In XML, it is relatively easy to introduce new elements or additional element attributes. The XHTML family is designed to accommodate these extensions through XHTML modules and techniques for developing new XHTML-conforming modules (described in the forthcoming XHTML Modularization specification). These modules will permit the combination of existing and new feature sets when developing content and when designing new user agents.
- Alternate ways of accessing the Internet are constantly being introduced. Some estimates indicate that by the year 2002, 75% of Internet document viewing will be carried out on these alternate platforms. The XHTML family is designed with general user agent interoperability in mind. Through a new user agent and document profiling mechanism,

servers, proxies, and user agents will be able to perform best effort content transformation. Ultimately, it will be possible to develop XHTML-conforming content that is usable by any XHTML-conforming user agent.

# 2. Definitions

## 2.1 Terminology

The following terms are used in this specification. These terms extend the definitions in [RFC2119] in ways based upon similar definitions in ISO/IEC 9945-1:1990 [POSIX.1]:

### Implementation-defined

A value or behavior is implementation-defined when it is left to the implementation to define (and document) the corresponding requirements for correct document construction.

### May

With respect to implementations, the word "may" is to be interpreted as an optional feature that is not required in this specification but can be provided. With respect to Document Conformance, the word "may" means that the optional feature must not be used. The term "optional" has the same definition as "may."

### Must

In this specification, the word "must" is to be interpreted as a mandatory requirement on the implementation or on Strictly Conforming XHTML Documents, depending upon the context. The term "shall" has the same definition as "must."

### Reserved

A value or behavior is unspecified, but it is not allowed to be used by Conforming Documents nor to be supported by a Conforming User Agent.

### Should

With respect to implementations, the word "should" is to be interpreted as an implementation recommendation, but not a requirement. With respect to documents, the word "should" is to be interpreted as recommended programming practice for documents and a requirement for Strictly Conforming XHTML Documents.

### Supported

Certain facilities in this specification are optional. If a facility is supported, it behaves as specified by this specification.

### Unspecified

When a value or behavior is unspecified, the specification defines no portability requirements for a facility on an implementation even when faced with a document that uses the facility. A

501

document that requires specific behavior in such an instance, rather than tolerating any behavior when using that facility, is not a Strictly Conforming XHTML Document.

## 2.2    General Terms

### Attribute

An attribute is a parameter to an element declared in the DTD. An attribute's type and value range, including a possible default value, are defined in the DTD.

### DTD

A DTD, or document type definition, is a collection of XML declarations that, as a collection, defines the legal structure, elements, and attributes that are available for use in a document that complies to the DTD.

### Document

A document is a stream of data that, after being combined with any other streams it references, is structured such that it holds information contained within elements that are organized as defined in the associated DTD. See Document Conformance for more information.

### Element

An element is a document structuring unit declared in the DTD. The element's content model is defined in the DTD, and additional semantics may be defined in the prose description of the element.

### Facilities

Functionality includes elements, attributes, and the semantics associated with those elements and attributes. An implementation supporting that functionality is said to provide the necessary facilities.

### Implementation

An implementation is a system that provides collection of facilities and services that supports this specification. See User Agent Conformance for more information.

### Parsing

Parsing is the act whereby a document is scanned, and the information contained within the document is filtered into the context of the elements in which the information is structured.

### Rendering

Rendering is the act whereby the information in a document is presented. This presentation is done in the form most appropriate to the environment (e.g. aurally, visually, in print).

## User Agent

A user agent is an implementation that retrieves and processes XHTML documents. See User Agent Conformance for more information.

## Validation

Validation is a process whereby documents are verified against the associated DTD, ensuring that the structure, use of elements, and use of attributes are consistent with the definitions in the DTD.

## Well-formed

A document is well-formed when it is structured according to the rules defined in Section 2.1 of the XML 1.0 Recommendation [XML]. Basically, this definition states that elements, delimited by their start and end tags, are nested properly within one another.

# 3. Normative Definition of XHTML 1.0

## 3.1 Document Conformance

This version of XHTML provides a definition of strictly conforming XHTML documents, which are restricted to tags and attributes from the XHTML namespace. See Section 3.1.2 for information on using XHTML with other namespaces, for instance, to include metadata expressed in RDF within XHTML documents.

### 3.1.1 Strictly Conforming Documents

A Strictly Conforming XHTML Document is a document that requires only the facilities described as mandatory in this specification. Such a document must meet all of the following criteria:

1. It must validate against one of the three DTDs found in Appendix A.
2. The root element of the document must be <html>.
3. The root element of the document must designate the XHTML namespace using the xmlns attribute XMLNAMES. The namespace for XHTML is defined to be *http://www.w3.org/1999/xhtml.*
4. There must be a DOCTYPE declaration in the document prior to the root element. The public identifier included in the DOCTYPE declaration must reference one of the three DTDs found in Appendix A using the respective Formal Public Identifier. The system identifier may be changed to reflect local system conventions.

```
<!DOCTYPE html
    PUBLIC "-//W3C//DTD XHTML 1.0 Strict//EN"
    "DTD/xhtml1-strict.dtd">

<!DOCTYPE html
    PUBLIC "-//W3C//DTD XHTML 1.0 Transitional//EN"
    "DTD/xhtml1-transitional.dtd">
```

```
<!DOCTYPE html
PUBLIC "-//W3C//DTD XHTML 1.0 Frameset//EN"
"DTD/xhtml1-frameset.dtd">
```

Here is an example of a minimal XHTML document:

```
<?xml version="1.0" encoding="UTF-8"?>
<!DOCTYPE html
    PUBLIC "-//W3C//DTD XHTML 1.0 Strict//EN"
    "DTD/xhtml1-strict.dtd">
<html xmlns="http://www.w3.org/1999/xhtml" xml:lang="en" lang="en">
  <head>
    <title>Virtual Library</title>
  </head>
  <body>
    <p>Moved to <a href="http://vlib.org/">vlib.org</a>.</p>
  </body>
</html>
```

Note that in this example, the XML declaration is included. An XML declaration like the one above is not required in all XML documents. XHTML document authors are strongly encouraged to use XML declarations in all their documents. Such a declaration is required when the character encoding of the document is other than the default UTF-8 or UTF-16.

### 3.1.2    Using XHTML with Other Namespaces

The XHTML namespace may be used with other XML namespaces as per [XMLNAMES], although such documents are not strictly conforming XHTML 1.0 documents as defined above. Future work by W3C will address ways to specify conformance for documents involving multiple namespaces.

The following example shows the way in which XHTML 1.0 could be used in conjunction with the MathML Recommendation:

```
<html xmlns="http://www.w3.org/1999/xhtml" xml:lang="en" lang="en">
  <head>
    <title>A Math Example</title>
  </head>
  <body>
    <p>The following is MathML markup:</p>
    <math xmlns="http://www.w3.org/1998/Math/MathML">
      <apply> <log/>
        <logbase>
          <cn> 3 </cn>
        </logbase>
```

```
          <ci> x </ci>
        </apply>
      </math>
    </body>
  </html>
```

The following example shows the way in which XHTML 1.0 markup could be incorporated into another XML namespace:

```
<?xml version="1.0" encoding="UTF-8"?>
<!-- initially, the default namespace is "books" -->
<book xmlns='urn:loc.gov:books'
      xmlns:isbn='urn:ISBN:0-395-36341-6' xml:lang="en" lang="en">
   <title>Cheaper by the Dozen</title>
   <isbn:number>1568491379</isbn:number>
   <notes>
      <!-- make HTML the default namespace for a hypertext commentary -->
      <p xmlns='http://www.w3.org/1999/xhtml'>
          This is also available <a href="http://www.w3.org/">online</a>.
      </p>
   </notes>
</book>
```

## 3.2    User Agent Conformance

A conforming user agent must meet all of the following criteria:

1.  In order to be consistent with the XML 1.0 Recommendation (XML), the user agent must parse and evaluate an XHTML document for well-formedness. If the user agent claims to be a validating user agent, it must also validate documents against their referenced DTDs according to (XML).

2.  When the user agent claims to support facilities defined within this specification or required by this specification through normative reference, it must do so in ways consistent with the facilities' definition.

3.  When a user agent processes an XHTML document as generic XML, it shall only recognize attributes of type ID (e.g. the id attribute on most XHTML elements) as fragment identifiers.

4.  If a user agent encounters an element it does not recognize, it must render the element's content.

5.  If a user agent encounters an attribute it does not recognize, it must ignore the entire attribute specification (i.e., the attribute and its value).

6.  If a user agent encounters an attribute value it doesn't recognize, it must use the default attribute value.

7.  If it encounters an entity reference (other than one of the predefined entities) for which the User Agent has processed no declaration (which could happen if the declaration is in

505

the external subset which the User Agent hasn't read), the entity reference should be rendered as the characters (starting with the ampersand and ending with the semi-colon) that make up the entity reference.

8. When rendering content, User Agents that encounter characters or character entity references that are recognized but not renderable should display the document in such a way that it is obvious to the user that normal rendering has not taken place.

9. The following characters are defined in [XML] as whitespace characters:
   - Space (&#x0020;)
   - Tab (&#x0009;)
   - Carriage return (&#x000D;)
   - Line feed (&#x000A;)

The XML processor normalizes different system's line end codes into one single line-feed character, that is passed up to the application. The XHTML user agent in addition, must treat the following characters as whitespace:
   - Form feed (&#x000C;)
   - Zero-width space (&#x200B;)

In elements where the xml:space attribute is set to preserve, the user agent must leave all whitespace characters intact (with the exception of leading and trailing whitespace characters, which should be removed). Otherwise, whitespace is handled according to the following rules:
   - All whitespace surrounding block elements should be removed.
   - Comments are removed entirely and do not affect whitespace handling. One whitespace character on either side of a comment is treated as two whitespace characters.
   - Leading and trailing whitespace inside a block element must be removed.
   - Line feed characters within a block element must be converted into a space (except when the xml:space attribute is set to preserve).
   - A sequence of whitespace characters must be reduced to a single space character (except when the xml:space attribute is set to preserve).
   - With regard to rendition, the User Agent should render the content in a manner appropriate to the language in which the content is written. In languages whose primary script is Latinate, the ASCII space character is typically used to encode both grammatical word boundaries and typographic whitespace; in languages whose script is related to Nagari (e.g., Sanskrit, Thai, etc.), grammatical boundaries may be encoded using the ZW "space" character, but will not typically be represented by typographic whitespace in rendered output; languages using Arabiform scripts may encode typographic whitespace using a space character, but may also use the ZW space character to delimit internal grammatical boundaries (what look like words in Arabic to an English eye frequently encode several words, e.g.

"kitAbuhum" = "kitAbu-hum" = "book them" == their book); and languages in the Chinese script tradition typically neither encode such delimiters nor use typographic whitespace in this way.
- Whitespace in attribute values is processed according to [XML].

# 4. Differences with HTML 4

Due to the fact that XHTML is an XML application, certain practices that were perfectly legal in SGML-based HTML 4 [HTML] must be changed.

## 4.1 Documents Must Be Well-formed

Well-formedness is a new concept introduced by [XML]. Essentially this means that all elements must either have closing tags or be written in a special form (as described below), and that all the elements must nest.

Although overlapping is illegal in SGML, it was widely tolerated in existing browsers.

CORRECT: nested elements

```
<p>here is an emphasized <em>paragraph</em>.</p>
```

INCORRECT: overlapping elements

```
<p>here is an emphasized <em>paragraph.</p></em>
```

## 4.2 Element and Attribute Names Must Be in Lower Case

XHTML documents must use lower case for all HTML element and attribute names. This difference is necessary because XML is case sensitive, e.g. <li> and <LI> are different tags.

## 4.3 For Non-empty Elements, End Tags Are Required

In SGML-based HTML 4 certain elements were permitted to omit the end tag, with the elements that followed implying closure. This omission is not permitted in XML-based XHTML. All elements other than those declared in the DTD as EMPTY must have an end tag.

CORRECT: terminated elements

```
<p>here is a paragraph.</p><p>here is another paragraph.</p>
```

INCORRECT: unterminated elements

```
<p>here is a paragraph.<p>here is another paragraph.
```

## 4.4 Attribute Values Must Always Be Quoted

All attribute values must be quoted, even those which appear to be numeric.

CORRECT: quoted attribute values
```
<table rows="3">
```

INCORRECT: unquoted attribute values
```
<table rows=3>
```

## 4.5 Attribute Minimization

XML does not support attribute minimization. Attribute-value pairs must be written in full. Attribute names such as compact and checked cannot occur in elements without their value being specified.

CORRECT: unminimized attributes
```
<dl compact="compact">
```

INCORRECT: minimized attributes
```
<dl compact>
```

## 4.6 Empty Elements

Empty elements must either have an end tag or the start tag must end with />. For instance, <br/> or <hr></hr>. See HTML Compatibility Guidelines for information on ways to ensure this is backward compatible with HTML 4 user agents.

CORRECT: terminated empty tags
```
<br/><hr/>
```

INCORRECT: unterminated empty tags
```
<br><hr>
```

## 4.7 Whitespace Handling in Attribute Values

In attribute values, user agents will strip leading and trailing whitespace from attribute values and map sequences of one or more whitespace characters (including line breaks) to a single inter-word space (an ASCII space character for western scripts). See Section 3.3.3 of [XML].

## 4.8 Script and Style Elements

In XHTML, the script and style elements are declared as having #PCDATA content. As a result, < and & will be treated as the start of markup, and entities such as &lt; and &amp; will be recognized as entity references by the XML processor to < and & respectively. Wrapping the content of the script or style element within a CDATA marked section avoids the expansion of these entities.

```
<script>
<![CDATA[
... unescaped script content ...
]]>
</script>
```

CDATA sections are recognized by the XML processor and appear as nodes in the Document Object Model, see Section 1.3 of the DOM Level 1 Recommendation [DOM].

An alternative is to use external script and style documents.

## 4.9    SGML Exclusions

SGML gives the writer of a DTD the ability to exclude specific elements from being contained within an element. Such prohibitions (called "exclusions") are not possible in XML.

For example, the HTML 4 Strict DTD forbids the nesting of an "a" element within another "a" element to any descendant depth. It is not possible to spell out such prohibitions in XML. Even though these prohibitions cannot be defined in the DTD, certain elements should not be nested.

## 4.10    The Elements with id and name Attributes

HTML 4 defined the name attribute for the elements a, applet, form, frame, iframe, img, and map. HTML 4 also introduced the id attribute. Both of these attributes are designed to be used as fragment identifiers.

In XML, fragment identifiers are of type ID, and there can only be a single attribute of type ID per element. Therefore, in XHTML 1.0 the id attribute is defined to be of type ID. In order to ensure that XHTML 1.0 documents are well-structured XML documents, XHTML 1.0 documents MUST use the id attribute when defining fragment identifiers, even on elements that historically have also had a name attribute. See the HTML Compatibility Guidelines for information on ensuring such anchors are backwards compatible when serving XHTML documents as media type text/html.

Note that in XHTML 1.0, the name attribute of these elements is formally deprecated, and will be removed in a subsequent version of XHTML.

# 5.    Compatibility Issues

Although there is no requirement for XHTML 1.0 documents to be compatible with existing user agents, in practice this is easy to accomplish.

## 5.1    Internet Media Type

As of the publication of this recommendation, the general recommended MIME labeling for XML-based applications has yet to be resolved.

However, XHTML Documents which follow the guidelines set forth in Appendix C, "HTML Compatibility Guidelines" may be labeled with the Internet Media Type text/html, as they are compatible with most HTML browsers. This document makes no recommendation about MIME labeling of other XHTML documents.

# 6.    Future Directions

XHTML 1.0 provides the basis for a family of document types that will extend and subset XHTML, in order to support a wide range of new devices and applications, by defining modules and specifying a mechanism for combining these modules. This mechanism will enable the extension and sub-setting of XHTML 1.0 in a uniform way through the definition of new modules.

## 6.1    Modularizing HTML

As the use of XHTML moves from the traditional desktop user agents to other platforms, it is clear that not all of the XHTML elements will be required on all platforms. For example a hand held device or a cell-phone may only support a subset of XHTML elements.

The process of modularization breaks XHTML up into a series of smaller element sets. These elements can then be recombined to meet the needs of different communities.

These modules will be defined in a later W3C document.

## 6.2    Subsets and Extensibility

Modularization brings with it several advantages:
- It provides a formal mechanism for sub-setting XHTML.
- It provides a formal mechanism for extending XHTML.
- It simplifies the transformation between document types.
- It promotes the reuse of modules in new document types.

## 6.3    Document Profiles

A document profile specifies the syntax and semantics of a set of documents. Conformance to a document profile provides a basis for interoperability guarantees. The document profile specifies the facilities required to process documents of that type, e.g. which image formats can be used, levels of scripting, style sheet support, and so on.

For product designers this enables various groups to define their own standard profile.

For authors this will obviate the need to write several different versions of documents for different clients.

For special groups such as chemists, medical doctors, or mathematicians this allows a special profile to be built using standard HTML elements plus a group of elements geared to the specialist's needs.

# Namespaces in XML

## Status of This Document

This document has been reviewed by W3C Members and other interested parties and has been endorsed by the Director as a W3C Recommendation. It is a stable document and may be used as reference material or cited as a normative reference from another document. W3C's role in making the Recommendation is to draw attention to the specification and to promote its widespread deployment. This enhances the functionality and interoperability of the Web.

## Abstract

XML namespaces provide a simple method for qualifying element and attribute names used in Extensible Markup Language documents by associating them with namespaces identified by URI references.

## Table of Contents

## Appendices

---

# 1.    Motivation and Summary

We envision applications of Extensible Markup Language (XML) where a single XML document may contain elements and attributes (here referred to as a "markup vocabulary") that are defined for and used by multiple software modules. One motivation for this is modularity; if such a markup vocabulary exists which is well-understood and for which there is useful software available, it is better to re-use this markup rather than re-invent it.

Such documents, containing multiple markup vocabularies, pose problems of recognition and collision. Software modules need to be able to recognize the tags and attributes which they are designed to process, even in the face of "collisions" occurring when markup intended for some other software package uses the same element type or attribute name.

These considerations require that document constructs should have universal names, whose scope extends beyond their containing document. This specification describes a mechanism, *XML namespaces*, which accomplishes this.

[Definition:] An **XML namespace** is a collection of names, identified by a URI reference [RFC2396], which are used in XML documents as element types and attribute names. XML namespaces differ from the "namespaces" conventionally used in computing disciplines in that the XML version has internal structure and is not, mathematically speaking, a set. These issues are discussed in "A. The Internal Structure of XML Namespaces."

[Definition:] URI references which identify namespaces are considered **identical** when they are exactly the same character-for-character. Note that URI references which are not identical in this sense may in fact be functionally equivalent. Examples include URI references which differ only in case, or which are in external entities which have different effective base URIs.

Names from XML namespaces may appear as qualified names, which contain a single colon, separating the name into a namespace prefix and a local part. The prefix, which is mapped to a URI reference, selects a namespace. The combination of the universally managed URI namespace and the document's own namespace produces identifiers that are universally unique. Mechanisms are provided for prefix scoping and defaulting.

URI references can contain characters not allowed in names, so cannot be used directly as namespace prefixes. Therefore, the namespace prefix serves as a proxy for a URI reference. An attribute-based syntax described below is used to declare the association of the namespace prefix with a URI reference; software that supports this namespace proposal must recognize and act on these declarations and prefixes.

## 1.1    A Note on Notation and Usage

Note that many of the nonterminals in the productions in this specification are defined not here but in the XML specification [XML]. When nonterminals defined here have the same names as nonterminals defined in the XML specification, the productions here in all cases match a subset of the strings matched by the corresponding ones there.

In this document's productions, the NSC is a "Namespace Constraint," one of the rules that documents conforming to this specification must follow. Note that all Internet domain names used in examples, with the exception of w3.org, are selected at random and should not be taken as having any import.

# 2.    Declaring Namespaces

[Definition:] A namespace is **declared** using a family of reserved attributes. Such an attribute's name must either be xmlns or have xmlns: as a prefix. These attributes, like any other XML attributes, may be provided directly or by default.

**Attribute Names for Namespace Declaration**

```
[1]   NSAttName         ::= PrefixedAttName
                         | DefaultAttName
[2]   PrefixedAttName   ::= 'xmlns:' NCName            [ NSC: Leading "XML" ]
[3]   DefaultAttName    ::= 'xmlns'
[4]   NCName            ::= (Letter | '_') (NCNameChar)    / An XML Name,
                                                       minus the ":" /
[5]   NCNameChar        ::= Letter | Digit | '.' | '-' | '_' |
                          CombiningChar | Extender
```

[Definition:] The attribute's value, a URI reference, is the **namespace name** identifying the namespace. The namespace name, to serve its intended purpose, should have the characteristics of uniqueness and persistence. It is not a goal that it be directly usable for retrieval of a schema (if any exists). An example of a syntax that is designed with these goals in mind is that for Uniform Resource Names [RFC2141]. However, it should be noted that ordinary URLs can be managed in such a way as to achieve these same goals.

[Definition:] If the attribute name matches PrefixedAttName, then the NCName gives the **namespace prefix**, used to associate element and attribute names with the namespace name in the attribute value in the scope of the element to which the declaration is attached. In such declarations, the namespace name may not be empty.

[Definition:] If the attribute name matches DefaultAttName, then the namespace name in the attribute value is that of the **default namespace** in the scope of the element to which the declaration is attached. In such a default declaration, the attribute value may be empty. Default namespaces and overriding of declarations are discussed in "5. Applying Namespaces to Elements and Attributes."

An example namespace declaration, which associates the namespace prefix edi with the namespace name http://ecommerce.org/schema:

```
<x xmlns:edi='http://ecommerce.org/schema'>
  <!-- the "edi" prefix is bound to http://ecommerce.org/schema
for the "x" element and contents -->
</x>
```

### Namespace Constraint: Leading "XML"

Prefixes beginning with the three-letter sequence x, m, l, in any case combination, are reserved for use by XML and XML-related specifications.

## 3.    Qualified Names

[Definition:] In XML documents conforming to this specification, some names (constructs corresponding to the nonterminal Name) may be given as **qualified names**, defined as follows:

**Qualified Name**

| | | | |
|---|---|---|---|
| [6] | QName | ::= | (Prefix ':')? LocalPart |
| [7] | Prefix | ::= | NCName |
| [8] | LocalPart | ::= | NCName |

The Prefix provides the namespace prefix part of the qualified name and must be associated with a namespace URI reference in a namespace declaration. [Definition:] The LocalPart provides the **local part** of the qualified name.

Note that the prefix functions *only* as a placeholder for a namespace name. Applications should use the namespace name, not the prefix, in constructing names whose scope extends beyond the containing document.

## 4.    Using Qualified Names

In XML documents conforming to this specification, element types are given as qualified names, as follows:

**Element Types**

| | | | | |
|---|---|---|---|---|
| [9] | STag | ::= | '<' QName (S Attribute)* S? '>' | [ NSC: Prefix Declared ] |
| [10] | ETag | ::= | '</' QName S? '>' | [ NSC: Prefix Declared ] |
| [11] | EmptyElemTag | ::= | '<' QName (S Attribute)* S? '/>' | [ NSC: Prefix Declared ] |

An example of a qualified name serving as an element type:

```
<x xmlns:edi='http://ecommerce.org/schema'>
  <!" the 'price' element's namespace is http://ecommerce.org/schema ">
  <edi:price units='Euro'>32.18</edi:price>
</x>
```

514

Attributes are either namespace declarations or their names are given as qualified names:

## Attribute

```
[12] Attribute ::=NSAttName Eq AttValue | QName Eq AttValue
[ NSC: Prefix Declared ]
```

An example of a qualified name serving as an attribute name:

```
<x xmlns:edi='http://ecommerce.org/schema'>
  <!" the 'taxClass' attribute's namespace is http://ecommerce.org/schema ">
  <lineItem edi:taxClass="exempt">Baby food</lineItem>
</x>
```

### Namespace Constraint: Prefix Declared

The namespace prefix, unless it is xml or xmlns, must have been declared in a namespace declaration attribute in either the start-tag of the element where the prefix is used or in an ancestor element (i.e. an element in whose content the prefixed markup occurs). The prefix xml is by definition bound to the namespace name http://www.w3.org/XML/1998/namespace. The prefix xmlns is used only for namespace bindings and is not itself bound to any namespace name.

This constraint may lead to operational difficulties in the case where the namespace declaration attribute is provided, not directly in the XML document entity, but via a default attribute declared in an external entity. Such declarations may not be read by software which is based on a non-validating XML processor. Many XML applications, presumably including namespace-sensitive ones, fail to require validating processors. For correct operation with such applications, namespace declarations must be provided either directly or via default attributes declared in the internal subset of the DTD.

Element names and attribute types are also given as qualified names when they appear in declarations in the DTD:

### Qualified Names in Declarations

```
[13] doctypedecl    ::= '<!DOCTYPE' S QName (S ExternalID)? S? ('[' (markupdecl
                        | PEReference | S)* ']' S?)? '>'
[14] elementdecl    ::= '<!ELEMENT' S QName S contentspec S? '>'
[15] cp             ::= (QName | choice | seq) ('?' | '*' | '+')?
[16] Mixed          ::= (' S? '#PCDATA' (S? '|' S? QName)* S? ')*'
                        | '(' S? '#PCDATA' S? ')'
[17] AttlistDecl    := '<!ATTLIST' S QName AttDef* S? '>'
[18] AttDef         ::= S (QName | NSAttName) S AttType S DefaultDecl
```

# 5. Applying Namespaces to Elements and Attributes

## 5.1 Namespace Scoping

The namespace declaration is considered to apply to the element where it is specified and to all elements within the content of that element, unless overridden by another namespace declaration with the same NSAttName part:

```
<?xml version="1.0"?>
<!" all elements here are explicitly in the HTML namespace ">
<html:html xmlns:html='http://www.w3.org/TR/REC-html40'>
  <html:head><html:title>Frobnostication</html:title></html:head>
  <html:body><html:p>Moved to
    <html:a href='http://frob.com'>here.</html:a></html:p></html:body>
</html:html>
```

Multiple namespace prefixes can be declared as attributes of a single element, as shown in this example:

```
<?xml version="1.0"?>
<!" both namespace prefixes are available throughout ">
<bk:book  xmlns:bk='urn:loc.gov:books'
          xmlns:isbn='urn:ISBN:0-395-36341-6'>
    <bk:title>Cheaper by the Dozen</bk:title>
    <isbn:number>1568491379</isbn:number>
</bk:book>
```

## 5.2 Namespace Defaulting

A default namespace is considered to apply to the element where it is declared (if that element has no namespace prefix), and to all elements with no prefix within the content of that element. If the URI reference in a default namespace declaration is empty, then unprefixed elements in the scope of the declaration are not considered to be in any namespace. Note that default namespaces do not apply directly to attributes.

```
<?xml version="1.0"?>
<!-- elements are in the HTML namespace, in this case by default -->
<html xmlns='http://www.w3.org/TR/REC-html40'>
  <head><title>Frobnostication</title></head>
  <body><p>Moved to
    <a href='http://frob.com'>here</a>.</p></body>
</html>

<?xml version="1.0"?>
<!-- unprefixed element types are from "books" -->
<book xmlns='urn:loc.gov:books'
      xmlns:isbn='urn:ISBN:0-395-36341-6'>
    <title>Cheaper by the Dozen</title>
```

516

```
      <isbn:number>1568491379</isbn:number>
</book>
```

A larger example of namespace scoping:

```
<?xml version="1.0"?>
<!-- initially, the default namespace is "books" -->
<book xmlns='urn:loc.gov:books'
      xmlns:isbn='urn:ISBN:0-395-36341-6'>
    <title>Cheaper by the Dozen</title>
    <isbn:number>1568491379</isbn:number>
    <notes>
        <!-- make HTML the default namespace for some commentary -->
        <p xmlns='urn:w3-org-ns:HTML'>
            This is a <i>funny</i> book!
        </p>
    </notes>
</book>
```

The default namespace can be set to the empty string. This has the same effect, within the scope of the declaration, of there being no default namespace.

```
<?xml version='1.0'?>
<Beers>
  <!-- the default namespace is now that of HTML -->
  <table xmlns='http://www.w3.org/TR/REC-html40'>
   <th><td>Name</td><td>Origin</td><td>Description</td></th>
   <tr>
    <!-- no default namespace inside table cells -->
    <td><brandName xmlns="">Huntsman</brandName></td>
    <td><origin xmlns="">Bath, UK</origin></td>
    <td>
        <details xmlns=""><class>Bitter</class><hop>Fuggles</hop>
          <pro>Wonderful hop, light alcohol, good summer beer</pro>
          <con>Fragile; excessive variance pub to pub</con>
          </details>
        </td>
      </tr>
    </table>
  </Beers>
```

## 5.3    Uniqueness of Attributes

In XML documents conforming to this specification, no tag may contain two attributes which:

1.  have identical names, or
2.  have qualified names with the same local part and with prefixes which have been bound to namespace names that are identical.

For example, each of the bad start-tags is illegal in the following:

```
<!-- http://www.w3.org is bound to n1 and n2 -->
<x xmlns:n1="http://www.w3.org"
   xmlns:n2="http://www.w3.org" >
 <bad a="1"     a="2" />
 <bad n1:a="1"  n2:a="2" />
</x>
```

However, each of the following is legal, the second because the default namespace does not apply to attribute names:

```
<!-- http://www.w3.org is bound to n1 and is the default -->
<x xmlns:n1="http://www.w3.org"
   xmlns="http://www.w3.org" >
 <good a="1"     b="2" />
 <good a="1"     n1:a="2" />
</x>
```

# 6. Conformance of Documents

In XML documents that conform to this specification, element types and attribute names must match the production for QName and must satisfy the "Namespace Constraints."

An XML document conforms to this specification if all other tokens in the document that are required, for XML conformance, to match the XML production for Name, match this specification's production for NCName.

The effect of conformance is that in such a document:

- · All element types and attribute names contain either zero or one colon.
- · No entity names, PI targets, or notation names contain any colons.

Strictly speaking, attribute values declared to be of types ID, IDREF(S), ENTITY(IES), and NOTATION are also Names, and thus should be colon-free. However, the declared type of attribute values is only available to processors which read markup declarations, for example validating processors. Thus, unless the use of a validating processor has been specified, there can be no assurance that the contents of attribute values have been checked for conformance to this specification.

# Appendices

# A. The Internal Structure of XML Namespaces (Non-Normative)

## A.1 The Insufficiency of the Traditional Namespace

In the computing disciplines, the term "namespace" conventionally refers to a *set* of names, i.e. a collection containing no duplicates. However, treating the names used in XML markup as such a namespace would greatly impair their usefulness. The primary use of such names in XML documents is to enable identification of logical structures in documents by software modules such as query processors, stylesheet-driven rendering engines, and schema-driven validators. Consider the following example:

```
<section><title>Book-Signing Event</title>
<signing>
  <author title="Mr" name="Vikram Seth" />
  <book title="A Suitable Boy" price="$22.95" /></signing>
<signing>
  <author title="Dr" name="Oliver Sacks" />
  <book title="The Island of the Color-Blind" price="$12.95" /></signing>
</section>
```

In this example, there are three occurrences of the name title within markup, and the name alone clearly provides insufficient information to allow correct processing by a software module.

Another problematic area comes from the use of "global" attributes, as illustrated by this example, a fragment of an XML document which is to be displayed using a CSS stylesheet:

```
<RESERVATION>
  <NAME HTML:CLASS="largeSansSerif">Layman, A</NAME>
  <SEAT CLASS="Y" HTML:CLASS="reallyImportant">33B</SEAT>
  <DEPARTURE>1997-05-24T07:55:00+1</DEPARTURE></RESERVATION>
```

In this case, the CLASS attribute, which describes the fare basis and takes values such as "J," "Y," and "C," is distinct at all semantic levels from the HTML:CLASS attribute, which is used to simulate syntactic richness in HTML, as a means of overcoming the limited element repertoire by subclassing.

XML 1.0 does not provide a built-in way to declare "global" attributes; items such as the HTML CLASS attribute are global only in their prose description and their interpretation by HTML applications. However, such attributes, an important distinguishing feature of which is that their names are unique, are commonly observed to occur in a variety of applications.

## A.2    XML Namespace Partitions

In order to support the goal of making both qualified and unqualified names useful in meeting their intended purpose, we identify the names appearing in an XML namespace as belonging to one of several disjoint traditional (i.e. set-structured) namespaces, called namespace partitions. The partitions are:

### The All Element Types Partition

All element types in an XML namespace appear in this partition. Each has a unique local part; the combination of the namespace name and the local part uniquely identifies the element type.

### The Global Attribute Partition

This partition contains the names of all attributes which are defined, in this namespace, to be global. The only required characteristic of a global attribute is that its name be unique in the global attribute partition. This specification makes no assertions as to the proper usage of such attributes. The combination of the namespace name and the attribute name uniquely identifies the global attribute.

### The Per-Element-Type Partitions

Each type in the All Element Types Partition has an associated namespace in which appear the names of the unqualified attributes that are provided for that element. This is a traditional namespace because the appearance of duplicate attribute names on an element is forbidden by XML 1.0. The combination of the attribute name with the element's type and namespace name uniquely identifies each unqualified attribute.

In XML documents conforming to this specification, the names of all qualified (prefixed) attributes are assigned to the global attribute partition, and the names of all unqualified attributes are assigned to the appropriate per-element-type partition.

## A.3    Expanded Element Types and Attribute Names

For convenience in specifying rules and in making comparisons, we define an expanded form, expressed here in XML element syntax, for each element type and attribute name in an XML document.

[Definition:] An **expanded element type** is expressed as an empty XML element of type ExpEType. It has a required type attribute which gives the type's LocalPart, and an optional ns attribute which, if the element is qualified, gives its namespace name.

[Definition:] An **expanded attribute name** is expressed as an empty XML element of type ExpAName. It has a required name attribute which gives the name. If the attribute is global, it has a required ns attribute which gives the namespace name; otherwise, it has a required attribute eltype which gives the type of the attached element, and an optional attribute elns which gives the namespace name, if known, of the attached element.

Slight variations on the examples given above will illustrate the working of expanded element types and attribute names. The following two fragments are each followed by a table showing the expansion of the names:

```
<!-- 1 --> <section xmlns='urn:com:books-r-us'>
<!-- 2 -->    <title>Book-Signing Event</title>
<!-- 3 -->    <signing>
<!-- 4 -->       <author title="Mr" name="Vikram Seth" />
<!-- 5 -->       <book title="A Suitable Boy" price="$22.95" />
              </signing>
           </section>
```

The names would expand as follows:

| Line | Name | Expanded |
|------|------|----------|
| 1 | section | <ExpEType type="section" ns="urn:com:books-r-us" /> |
| 2 | title | <ExpEType type="title" ns="urn:com:books-r-us" /> |
| 3 | signing | <ExpEType type="signing" ns="urn:com:books-r-us" /> |
| 4 | author | <ExpEType type="author" ns="urn:com:books-r-us" /> |
| 4 | title | <ExpAName name='title' eltype="author" elns="urn:com:books-r-us" /> |
| 4 | name | <ExpAName name='name' eltype="author" elns="urn:com:books-r-us" /> |
| 5 | book | <ExpEType type="book" ns="urn:com:books-r-us" /> |
| 5 | title | <ExpAName name='title' eltype="book" elns="urn:com:books-r-us" /> |
| 5 | price | <ExpAName name='price' eltype="book" elns="urn:com:books-r-us" /> |

```
<!-- 1 --> <RESERVATION xmlns:HTML="http://www.w3.org/TR/REC-html40">
<!-- 2 --> <NAME HTML:CLASS="largeSansSerif">Layman, A</NAME>
<!-- 3 --> <SEAT CLASS="Y" HTML:CLASS="largeMonotype">33B</SEAT>
<!-- 4 --> <HTML:A HREF='/cgi-bin/ResStatus'>Check Status</HTML:A>
<!-- 5 --> <DEPARTURE>1997-05-24T07:55:00+1</DEPARTURE></RESERVATION>
```

```
1  RESERVATION  <ExpEType type="RESERVATION" />
2  NAME  <ExpEType type="NAME" />
2  HTML:CLASS  <ExpAName name="CLASS" ns=http://www.w3.org/TR/REC-html40 />
3  SEAT  <ExpEType type="SEAT" />
3  CLASS  <ExpAName name="CLASS" eltype="SEAT">
3  HTML:CLASS  <ExpAName name="CLASS" ns="http://www.w3.org/TR/REC-html40" />
4  HTML:A  <ExpEType type="A" ns="http://www.w3.org/TR/REC-html40" />
4  HREF  <ExpAName name="HREF" eltype="A" elns="http://www.w3.org/TR/
   REC-html40" />
5  DEPARTURE  <ExpEType type="DEPARTURE" />
```

## A.4    Unique Expanded Attribute Names

The constraint expressed by "5.3 Uniqueness of Attributes" above may straightforwardly be implemented by requiring that no element have two attributes whose expanded names are equivalent, i.e. have the same attribute-value pairs.

# B.    Acknowledgments (Non-Normative)

This work reflects input from a very large number of people, including especially the members of the World Wide Web Consortium XML Working Group and Special Interest Group and the participants in the W3C Metadata Activity. The contributions of Charles Frankston of Microsoft were particularly valuable.

# C. References

RFC2141

IETF (Internet Engineering Task Force) *RFC 2141: URN Syntax*, ed. R. Moats. May 1997.

RFC2396

IETF (Internet Engineering Task Force) *RFC 2396: Uniform Resource Identifiers (URI): Generic Syntax*, eds. T. Berners-Lee, R. Fielding, L. Masinter. August 1998.

XML

*Extensible Markup Language (XML) 1.0*, eds. Tim Bray, Jean Paoli, and C. M. Sperberg-McQueen. 10 February 1998. Available at http://www.w3.org/TR/REC-xml.

## World Wide Web Consortium 14-January-1999

This version:

http://www.w3.org/TR/1999/REC-xml-names-19990114

http://www.w3.org/TR/1999/REC-xml-names-19990114/xml-names.xml

http://www.w3.org/TR/1999/REC-xml-names-19990114/Overview.html

Latest version:

http://www.w3.org/TR/REC-xml-names

Previous version:

http://www.w3.org/TR/1998/PR-xml-names-19981117

The list of known errors in this specification is available at http://www.w3.org/XML/xml-names-19990114-errata.

# Using Cascading Style Sheets

This guide will teach you how to:
· Use the style element
· Link to separate style sheets
· Set page margins
· Set left and right and first-line indents
· Set the amount of whitespace above and below
· Set the font type, style and size
· Add borders and backgrounds
· Set colors with named or numeric values
· Add style for browsers that don't understand CSS

## Getting Started

Let's start with setting the color of the text and the background. You can do this by using the STYLE element to set style properties for the document's tags:

```
<style type="text/css"> body { color: black; background: white; } </style>
```

The stuff between the <style> and </style> is written in special notation for style rules. Each rule starts with a tag name followed by a list of style properties bracketed by { and }. In this example, the rule matches the *body* tag. As you will see, the body tag provides the basis for setting the overall look and feel of your Web page.

Each style property starts with the property's name, then a colon and lastly the value for this property. When there is more than one style property in the list, you need to use a semicolon between each of them to delimit one property from the next. In this example, there are two properties—"color" which sets the color of the text, and "background" which sets the color of the page background. I recommend always adding the semicolon even after the last property.

Colors can be given as names or as numerical values, for instance rgb(255, 204, 204) which is a fleshy pink. The 3 numbers correspond to red, green and blue respectively in the range 0 to 255.

---

*This guide was written by Dave Raggett, 29th August 2000.*
© *2000 W3C* * *(MIT, INRIA, Keio ), All Rights Reserved.*

You can also use a hexadecimal notation; the same color can also be written as #FFCCCC. More details on color are given in a later section.

Note that the style element must be placed in the document's head along with the title element. It shouldn't be placed within the body.

## Linking to a Separate Style Sheet

If you are likely to want to use the same styles for several Web pages it is worth considering using a separate style sheet which you then link from each page. You can do this as follows:

```
<link rel="stylesheet" href="style.css">
```

The LINK tag should be placed in the document's head. The *rel* attribute must be set to the value "stylesheet" to allow the browser to recognize that the *href* attribute gives the Web address (URL) for your style sheet.

## Setting the Page Margins

Web pages look a lot nicer with bigger margins. You can set the left and right margins with the "margin-left" and "margin-right" properties, e.g.

```
<style type="text/css">  body { margin-left: 10%; margin-right: 10%; } </style>
```

This sets both margins to 10% of the window width, and the margins will scale when you resize the browser window.

## Setting Left and Right Indents

To make headings a little more distinctive, you can make them start within the margin set for the body, e.g.

```
<style type="text/css">   body { margin-left: 10%; margin-right: 10%; }
h1 { margin-left: -8%;}   h2,h3,h4,h5,h6 { margin-left: -4%; } </style>
```

This example has three style rules. One for the body, one for h1 (used for the most important headings) and one for the rest of the headings (h2, h3, h4, h5 and h6). The margins for the headings are additive to the margins for the body. Negative values are used to move the start of the headings to the left of the margin set for the body.

In the following sections, the examples of particular style rules will need to be placed within the style element in the document's head (if present) or in a linked style sheet.

## Controlling the White Space Above and Below

Browsers do a pretty good job for the white space above and below headings and paragraphs etc. Two reasons for taking control of this yourself are: when you want a lot of white space before a particular heading or paragraph, or when you need precise control for the general spacings.

The "margin-top" property specifies the space above and the "margin-bottom" specifies the space below. To set these for all h2 headings you can write:

```
h2 { margin-top: 8em; margin-bottom: 3em; }
```

The em is a very useful unit as it scales with the size of the font. One em is the height of the font. By using em's you can preserve the general look of the Web page independently of the font size. This is much safer than alternatives such as pixels or points, which can cause problems for users who need large fonts to read the text.

Points are commonly used in word processing packages, e.g. 10pt text. Unfortunately the same point size is rendered differently on different browsers. What works fine for one browser will be illegible on another! Sticking with em's avoids these problems.

To specify the space above a particular heading, you should create a named style for the heading. You do this with the *class* attribute in the markup, e.g.

```
<h2 class="subsection">Getting started</h2>
```

The style rule is then written as:

```
h2.subsection { margin-top: 8em; margin-bottom: 3em; }
```

The rule starts with the tag name, a dot and then the value of the class attribute. Be careful to avoid placing a space before or after the dot. If you do the rule won't work. There are other ways to set the styles for a particular element but the class attribute is the most flexible.

When a heading is followed by a paragraph, the value for margin-bottom for the heading isn't added to the value for margin-top for the paragraph. Instead, the maximum of the two values is used for the spacing between the heading and paragraph. This subtlety applies to margin-top and margin-bottom regardless of which tags are involved.

## First-line Indent

Sometimes you may want to indent the first line of each paragraph. The following style rule emulates the traditional way paragraphs are rendered in novels:

```
p { text-indent: 2em; margin-top: 0; margin-bottom: 0; }
```

It indents the first line of each paragraph by 2 em's and suppresses the inter-paragraph spacing.

# Controlling the Font

This section explains how to set the font and size, and how to add italic, bold and other styles.

## Font Styles

The most common styles are to place text in italic or bold. Most browsers render the *em* tag in italic and the *strong* tag in bold. Let's assume you instead want em to appear in *bold italic* and strong in **bold uppercase**:

```
em { font-style: italic; font-weight: bold; } strong { text-transform:
uppercase;  font-weight: bold; }
```

If you feel so inclined, you can fold headings to lower case as follows:

```
h2 { text-transform: lowercase; }
```

## Setting the Font Size

Most browsers use a larger font size for more important headings. If you override the default size, you run the risk of making the text too small to be legible, particularly if you use points. You are therefore recommended to specify font sizes in relative terms.

This example sets heading sizes in percentages relative to the size used for normal text:

```
h1 { font-size: 200%; } h2 { font-size: 150%; } h3 { font-size: 100%; }
```

## Setting the Font Family

It is likely that your favorite font won't be available on all browsers. To get around this, you are allowed to list several fonts in preference order. There is a short list of generic font names which are guaranteed to be available, so you are recommended to end your list with one of these: serif, sans-serif, cursive, fantasy, or monospace, for instance:

```
body { font-family: Verdana, sans-serif; } h1,h2 { font-family: Garamond,
"Times New Roman", serif; }
```

In this example, important headings would preferably be shown in Garamond, failing that in Times New Roman, and if that is unavailable in the browser's default serif font. Paragraph text would appear in Verdana or if that is unavailable in the browser's default sans-serif font.

The legibility of different fonts generally depends more on the height of lower case letters than on the font size itself. Fonts like Verdana are much more legible than ones like Times New Roman and are therefore recommended for paragraph text.

## Avoiding Problems with Fonts and Margins

My first rule is to avoid text at the body level that isn't wrapped in a block level element such as *p*. For instance:

```
<h2>Spring in Wiltshire</h2>  Blossom on the trees, bird song and the sound
of lambs bleating in the fields.
```

The text following the heading runs the risk on some browsers of being rendered with the wrong font and margins. You are therefore advised to enclose all such text in a paragraph, e.g.

```
<h2>Spring in Wiltshire</h2>  <p>Blossom on the trees, bird song and the
sound of lambs bleating in the fields.</p>
```

My second rule is to set the font family for *pre* elements, as some browsers forget to use a fixed pitch font when you set the font size or other properties for pre.

```
pre { font-family: monospace; }
```

My third rule is to set the font family on headings, p and ul elements if you intend to set borders or backgrounds on elements such as div. This is a work-around for a bug where the browser forgets to use the inherited font family, instead switching to the default font as set by the browser preferences.

```
h1,h2,h3,h4,h5,p,ul { font-family: sans-serif; }
```

# Adding Borders and Backgrounds

You can easily add a border around a heading, list, paragraph or a group of these enclosed with a *div* element. For instance:

```
div.box { border: solid; border-width: thin; width: 100% }
```

Note that without the "width" property some browsers will place the right margin too far to the right. This can then be used with markup such as:

```
<div class="box"> The content within this DIV element will be enclosed in a
box with a thin line around it. </div>
```

There are a limited choice of border types: dotted, dashed, solid, double, groove, ridge, inset and outset. The border-width property sets the width. Its values include thin, medium and thick as well as a specified width e.g. 0.1em. The border-color property allows you to set the color.

A nice effect is to paint the background of the box with a solid color or with a tiled image. To do this you use the background property. You can fill the box enclosing a div as follows:

```
div.color { background: rgb(204,204,255); padding: 0.5em; border: none; }
```

Without an explicit definition for border property some browsers will only paint the background color under each character. The padding property introduces some space between the edges of the colored region and the text it contains.

You can set different values for padding on the left, top, right and bottom sides with the padding-left, padding-top, padding-right and padding-bottom properties, e.g. padding-left: 1em.

Suppose you only want borders on some of the sides. You can control the border properties for each of the sides independently using the border-left, border-top, border-right and border-bottom family of properties together with the appropriate suffix: style, width or color, e.g.

```
p.changed { padding-left: 0.2em; border-left: solid; border-right: none;
border-top: none; border-bottom: none; border-left-width: thin;
border-color: red; }
```

which sets a red border down the left-hand side only of any paragraph with the class "changed."

# Setting Colors

Some examples for setting colors appeared in earlier sections. Here is a reminder:

```
body {color: black; background: white;} strong {color: red }
```

This sets the default to black text on a white background, but renders strong elements in red. There are 16 standard color names, which are explained just below. You can also use decimal values for red, green and blue, where each value appears in the range 0 to 255, e.g. *rgb(255, 0, 0)* is the same as *red*. You can also used hex color values which start with the '#' character followed by six hexadecimal digits. A two-way converter is included below which allows you to convert from RGB to hex color values.

## Setting Link Colors

You can use CSS to set the color for hypertext links, with a different color for links that you have yet to follow, ones you have followed, and the active color for when the link is being clicked. You can even set the color for when the mouse pointer is hovering over the link.

```
   :link { color: rgb(0, 0, 153) }  /* for unvisited links */ :visited
{ color: rgb(153, 0, 153) } /* for visited links */ :active { color:
rgb(255, 0, 102) } /* when link is clicked */ :hover { color: rgb(0, 96,
255) } /* when mouse is over link */
```

Sometimes you may want to show hypertext links without them being underlined. You can do this by setting the *text-decoration* property to *none*, for example:

```
   a.plain { text-decoration: none }
```

Which would suppress underlining for a link such as:

```
   This is <a class="plain" href="what.html">not underlined</a>
```

Most people when they see underlined text on a Web page, will expect it to be part of a hypertext link. As a result, you are advised to leave underlining on for hypertext links. A similar argument applies to the link colors, most people will interpret underlined blue text as hypertext links. You are advised to leave link colors alone, except when the color of the background would otherwise make the text hard to read.

## Color Blindness

When using color, remember that 5 to 10% of men have some form of color blindness. This can cause difficulties distinguishing between red and green, or between yellow and blue. In rare cases, there is an inability to perceive any colors at all. You are recommended to avoid foreground/ background color combinations that would make the text hard to read for people with color blindness.

## Named Colors

The standard set of color names is: aqua, black, blue, fuchsia, gray, green, lime, maroon, navy, olive, purple, red, silver, teal, white, and yellow. These 16 colors are defined in HTML 3.2 and 4.01 and correspond to the basic VGA set on PCs. Most browsers accept a wider set of color names but use of these is not recommended.

**Color names and sRGB values**

| | |
|---|---|
| black = "#000000" | green = "#008000" |
| silver = "#C0C0C0" | lime = "#00FF00" |
| gray = "#808080" | olive = "#808000" |
| white = "#FFFFFF" | yellow = "#FFFF00" |
| maroon = "#800000" | navy = "#000080" |
| red = "#FF0000" | blue = "#0000FF" |
| purple = "#800080" | teal = "#008080" |
| fuchsia = "#FF00FF" | aqua = "#00FFFF" |

Thus, the color value "#800080" is the same as "purple."

## Hexadecimal Color Values

Values like "#FF9999" represent colors as hexadecimal numbers for red, green and blue. The first two characters following the # give the number for red, the next two for green and the last two for blue. These numbers are always in the range 0 to 255 decimal. If you know the values in decimal, you can convert to hexadecimal using a calculator, like the one that comes as part of Microsoft Windows.

## Browser Safe Colors

New computers support thousands or millions of colors, but many older color systems can only show up to 256 colors at a time. To cope with this, these browsers make do with colors from a fixed palette. The effect of this is often visible as a speckling of colors as the browser tries to approximate the true color at any point in the image. This problem will gradually go away as older computers are replaced by newer models.

Most browsers support the same so called "browser safe" palette. This uses 6 evenly spaced gradations in red, green and blue and their combinations. If you select image colors from this palette, you can avoid the speckling effect. This is particularly useful for background areas of images.

If the browser is using the browser safe palette, the page background uses the nearest color in the palette. If you set the page background to a color which isn't in the browser safe palette, you run the risk that the background will have different colors depending on whether the computer is using indexed or true-color.

These are constructed from colors where red, green and blue are restricted to the values:

| RGB | 00 | 51 | 102 | 153 | 204 | 255 |
|---|---|---|---|---|---|---|
| Hex | 00 | 33 | 66 | 99 | CC | FF |

# What About Browsers That Don't Support CSS?

Older browsers, that is to say before Netscape 4.0 and Internet Explorer 4.0, either don't support CSS at all or do so inconsistently. For these browsers you can still control the style by using HTML itself.

## Setting the Color and Background

You can set the color using the BODY tag. The following example sets the background color to white and the text color to black:

```
<body bgcolor="white" text="black">
```

The BODY element should be placed before the visible content of the Web page, e.g. before the first heading. You can also control the color of hypertext links. There are three attributes for this:

- **link** for unvisited links
- **vlink** for visited links
- **alink** for the color used when you click the link

Here is an example that sets all three:

```
<body bgcolor="white" text="black" link="navy"vlink="maroon" alink="red">
```

You can also get the browser to tile the page background with an image using the background attribute to specify the Web address for the image, e.g.

```
<body bgcolor="white" background="texture.jpeg" text="black" link="navy"
vlink="maroon" alink="red">
```

It is a good idea to specify a background color using the bgcolor attribute in case the browser is unable to render the image. You should check that the colors you have chosen don't cause legibility problems. As an extreme case consider the following:

```
<body bgcolor="black">
```

Most browsers will render text in black by default. The end result is that the page will be shown with black text on a black background! Lots of people suffer from one form of color blindness or another, for example olive green may appear brown to some people.

A separate problem appears when you try to print the Web page. Many browsers will ignore the background color, but will obey the text color. Setting the text to white will often result in a blank page when printed, so the following is not recommended:

```
<body bgcolor="black" text="white">
```

You can also use the bgcolor attribute on table cells, e.g.

```
<table border="0" cellpadding="5"> <tr> <td bgcolor="yellow">colored table
cell</td>   </tr> </table>
```

Tables can be used for a variety of layout effects and have been widely exploited for this. In the future this role is likely to be supplanted by style sheets, which make it practical to achieve precise layout with less effort.

### Setting the Font, Its Size and Color

The FONT tag can be used to select the font, to set its size and the color. This example just sets the color:

```
This sentence has a <font color="yellow">word</font> in yellow.
```

The *face* attribute is used to set the font. It takes a list of fonts in preference order, e.g.

```
<font face="Garamond, Times New Roman">some text ...</font>
```

The *size* attribute can be used to select the font size as a number from 1 to 7. If you place a - or + sign before the number it is interpreted as a relative value. Use size="+1" when you want to use the next larger font size and size="-1" when you want to use the next smaller font size, e.g.

```
<font size="+1" color="maroon" face="Garamond, Times New Roman">some text
...</font>
```

There are a couple of things you should avoid: Don't choose color combinations that make text hard to read for people who are color blind. Don't use font to make regular text into headings, which should always be marked up using the h1 to h6 tags as appropriate to the importance of the heading.

# Getting Further Information

This is a short guide to styling your Web pages. It will show you how to use W3C's Cascading Style Sheets language (CSS) as well as alternatives using HTML itself. The route will steer you clear of most of the problems caused by differences between different brands and versions of browsers. For style sheets to work, it is important that your markup is free of errors. A convenient way to automatically fix markup errors is to use the HTML Tidy utility. This also tidies the markup making it easier to read and easier to edit. I recommend you regularly run Tidy over any markup you are editing. Tidy is very effective at cleaning up markup created by authoring tools with sloppy habits.

For further information on CSS and tools that support it, you should look at the W3C home page for CSS. This includes pointers to books on HTML and CSS, for example, *Raggett on HTML 4*, published in 1998 by Addison Wesley. See also *Beginning XHTML*, published in 2000 by Wrox Press. For a more detailed explanation of CSS, *Cascading Style Sheets* by Håkon Wium Lie and Bert Bos, published in 1999 by Addison Wesley, provides an in-depth look at CSS as seen by the architects of CSS themselves.

# JavaScript Objects
# and Operators

## Overview

Netscape began developing a scripting language called LiveScript in 1994. It was renamed JavaScript in December 1995, when Netscape and Sun Microsystems agreed to partner in its development. It provides a method of introducing interactivity to HTML documents that is widely used. It runs in the browser on a client computer that can access a local Java Virtual Machine (JVM). A client-side program can be executed in response to user events, such as mouse clicks. JavaScript may also be used to directly control objects, such as the browser status bar and the browser display window. It provides interactivity between Java applets and plug-ins. JavaScript can verify that information has been entered into a form, interpret the entered text, and alert the user with an appropriate message dialog.

JavaScript objects are defined here, along with their properties, methods, and event handlers. Event handlers are expressions that JavaScript executes when specific types of events occur. Independent functions not connected with any particular object are also listed, as well as operators.

JavaScript is a reduced and redefined version of the Java programming language. JavaScript is case sensitive, as is Java. A dot (.) is placed between an object and its properties. An identifier is a name used in JavaScript for a variable or a function. The first letter of an identifier may be an ASCII letter, an underscore (_), or a dollar sign ($). It may not be a number. Braces ({ }) are placed around function definitions, if-then constructs, and repeat loops. Square brackets ([ ]) are placed around optional items, such as parameters. Optional items are shown in italic. The syntax for defining a function is as follows:

```
function functionName([parameters]) {
    [statement 1]
    [statement 2]
}
```

Certain words are reserved in JavaScript; they may not be used as identifiers (function names, variable names, or loop labels). The following words are part of the language syntax and are reserved: break, case, continue, default, delete, do, else, export, for, function, if, import, in, new, return, switch, this, typeof, var, void, while, and with.

An additional list of words is reserved by the version of JavaScript standardized by the European Computer Manufacturers Association (ECMA), known as ECMA-262. The following words are reserved for future expansion in this version of the language: catch, class, const, debugger, enum, extends, finally, super, throw, and try.

A variable is a name associated with a data value. A variable contains an associated value. This statement assigns the value 5 to a variable named x:

```
x = 5
```

This script adds 2 to x and assigns the result to the new variable sum:

```
sum = x + 2
```

Variables in JavaScript are untyped, which means that they can hold data of any kind. Before a variable can be used, it must be declared with the var keyword. A variable may be declared and initialized in the same statement, as in the following lines:

```
var x = 5;
var message = "hello world"
```

A JavaScript expression is any letter, number, array, function, variable, or phrase that the interpreter can evaluate. The expression true is a Boolean literal, the phrase "hello world" is a string literal, and the number 5 is a numeric literal. All are different types of expressions.

A JavaScript program is a collection of statements. Examples of statements are if, else if, switch, while, for, break, return, and with. A complete list of statements and their syntax is included at the end of this appendix. Statements are followed by semicolons (;).

An object in JavaScript is a compound data type that can represent multiple data values with a single unit. It is a collection of properties, and each property has a name and a value. An object is created with the new operator, followed by the name of a constructor function that initializes the object. The following example creates an object and establishes its properties. Note that the double slash is used to distinguish comments from actual code.

```
// Create an object and store a reference to it.
var book = new Object();

// Set a property in the object.
book.title = "The Dictionary of Computing and Digital
Media"

// Set another property in the object.
book.appendix.title = "JavaScript Objects and Operators"
```

A method is a JavaScript function that is invoked through an object. Functions are simply values stored in variables; these variables are properties of objects.

A method may be defined by the following procedure:

```
object.method = function;
```

533

The method may be invoked as follows, with the function surrounded by parentheses:

```
object.method(function);
```

Within the body of a method, the keyword "this" may be used to refer to the related object.

To make JavaScript respond dynamically to user input, event handlers are used. They may be defined as attributes of HTML objects. An event handler contains a piece of code to be executed when a particular event occurs, such as a mouse click. That code might send a message to the status bar or pop up an alert box containing text.

JavaScript can control most of the parts of a browser and responds to user actions such as form input and page navigation. All of the processing commands are written in a script that is embedded in an HTML document and carried out on the client side without reference back to a server.

A script is embedded in HTML with the <SCRIPT> element:

```
<SCRIPT>..(text of script goes here)..</SCRIPT>
```

The text of a script is placed between the <SCRIPT> tag and its end element. Attributes are specified in the following way:

```
<SCRIPT LANGUAGE="JavaScript">

text of a script

</SCRIPT>
```

When specifying the language, it is advisable to indicate which version of JavaScript is being used. JavaScript 1.0 is generally compatible with Netscape Navigator 2.0; JavaScript 1.1 is generally compatible with Navigator 3.0. Only the 4.0 and later versions of Navigator will read all of the JavaScript 1.2 language. Some of the language in the first versions of JavaScript, 1.0 and 1.1, is implemented in Microsoft Internet Explorer version 3.0, but not consistently. In Internet Explorer 4.0 some, but not all, of the JavaScript 1.2 language is enabled. In 1997 the ECMA approved its expanded variation of JavaScript 1.1 (ECMA-262) which included international alphabets, and it is this version that is implemented in Internet Explorer 4.0. Version 5.0 and later of Internet Explorer handles most, but not all, of the JavaScript 1.2 language.

If the LANGUAGE attribute is not used, the SRC attribute may be used to identify a URL that will load the text of the script.

```
<SCRIPT LANGUAGE="language" SRC=url>
```

A user agent (browser) that is Java-enabled evaluates and stores the functions of each script it receives. The functions defined by the script are executed only when they are triggered by certain events within a page. Moving the cursor over an object or entering text into a text box may trigger the execution of a script.

The text of a script can be enclosed within comment elements to prevent browsers that are not capable of interpreting JavaScript from including it as text:

```
<SCRIPT LANGUAGE="JavaScript">

<!--"Hide script contents from incompatible browsers.

Complete text of JavaScript.

End hiding script contents."-->

</SCRIPT>
```

The following alphabetized list includes commonly used objects, properties, methods, and event handlers.

# Objects

*(with Properties, Methods, and Event Handlers)*

### anchor

The target of a hypertext link.

*Properties*

name: A string value containing the name of an anchor.

### applet

Represents a Java applet in a web page.

*Properties*

name: A string value containing the NAME.

### area

Represents a clickable area in an image map.

*Properties*

hash: An anchor name from a URL.

host: The host and domain name part of a URL.

hostname: The host, domain name, and port number of a URL.

href: The complete URL.

pathname: Just the path part of a URL, without host, domain, or port number.

port: The port number of a URL.

protocol: The protocol part of a URL, including the colon after it.

search: The query part of a URL, which follows a question mark.

target: The TARGET value of an AREA tag.

*Methods*

getSelection: Returns the current selection value as a string.

*Event Handlers*

onMouseOut: Specifies the script to be executed when a user moves the mouse outside the area defined.

onMouseOver: Specifies the script to be executed when a user moves the mouse over the area defined.

onDblClick: Specifies the script to be executed when a user double-clicks in the area.

## Array

A new array is created with the command

arrayName = new Array(*arrayLength*)

*Properties*

length: An integer defining the number of elements in an array.

prototype: A way to add properties to an Array object.

*Methods*

sort(): Sorts the elements of an array according to the function defined in parentheses, or alphabetically if no function is defined.

join(): Converts all elements of an array to concatenated strings.

reverse(): Reverses the order of elements in an array.

concat(): Combines the elements of two arrays into a third.

pop(): Removes an element from the end of an array.

push(): Adds an element to the end of an array.

slice(): Returns a portion of an array, called a subarray.

## button

Represents a push button in an HTML form. It is a reflection of an INPUT element with a TYPE attribute of "button."

*Properties*

Inherits properties, methods, and event handlers from Input and HTMLElement.

name: The name of the button element.

value: The value of the button element.

type: The TYPE attribute of an INPUT tag.

enabled: A Boolean value indicating a button's status.

form: Refers to the form object containing a button.

*Methods*

click(): Emulates the action of clicking on a button.

focus(): Gives a button focus.

*Event Handlers*

onClick: Specifies the script to be executed when the button is clicked.

onMouseDown: Specifies the script to be executed when a mouse button is pressed.

onMouseUp: Specifies the script to be executed when a mouse button is released.

onFocus: Specifies the script to be executed when a button is given focus.

## checkbox

Makes a checkbox in an HTML form available in JavaScript.

*Properties*

checked: A Boolean value indicating the status of a checkbox element.

defaultChecked: A Boolean value indicating that a checkbox element reflects the CHECKED attribute.

name: The name of the checkbox element.

value: The value of the checkbox element.

enabled: A Boolean value indicating whether the checkbox is enabled.

form: Refers to the form object containing the checkbox.

type: Indicates the TYPE attribute of the INPUT tag.

*Methods*

click(): Emulates the act of clicking the checkbox.

focus(): Gives the checkbox focus.

*Event Handlers*

onClick: Specifies the script to be executed when the checkbox is clicked.

onFocus: Specifies the script to be executed when focus is on the checkbox.

## combo

Represents a combo field in JavaScript.

*Properties*

listCount: The number of elements in a list.

listIndex: The index of the selected elements in a list.

multiSelect: A Boolean value that indicates whether a combo field is in multiselect mode.

name: The name of a combo field.

value: The value of a combo field.

enabled: A Boolean value indicating whether the combo box is enabled.

form: Refers to the form object containing the combo box.

*Methods*

click(): Emulates a click on the combo field.

clear(): Clears the contents of the combo field.

focus(): Gives the combo field focus.

addItem(*index*): Adds an item to the combo field just before the item at *index*.

removeItem(*index*): Removes the item at *index* from the combo field.

*Event Handlers*

onClick: Specifies the script to be executed when the mouse clicks on a combo field.

onFocus: Specifies the script to be executed when focus is given to a combo field.

## Date

Provides a way to use dates and times in JavaScript. Syntax for creating instances is as follows:

```
newObjectName = new Date(dateInfo)
```

If no *dateInfo* is specified, the new object returns the current date and time.

*dateInfo* may be used to specify a date and time in three ways:
1. *"month, day, year, hours;minutes;seconds"*
2. *"year, month, day"* (in integers)
3. *"year, month, day, hours, minutes, seconds"* (in integers)

*Properties*

prototype: Adds properties to a Date object.

*Methods*

getTime(): Returns the time of the current Date object in milliseconds, with 00:00:00:00 set at 12:00 a.m., January 1, 1970.

getDate(): Returns an integer for the day of the month of the current Date (1–31).

getMonth(): Returns an integer for the month in the current Date object (0–11, beginning with January).

getDay(): Returns an integer for the day of the week of the current Date (0–6, beginning with Sunday).

getHours(): Returns an integer for the hour in the current Date object (0–23).

getMinutes(): Returns an integer for the minutes in the current Date object (0–59).

getSeconds(): Returns an integer for the seconds in the current Date object (0–59).

getYear(): Returns a two-digit integer for the year in the current Date object (for example, 68 for 1968).

getTimezoneOffset(): Returns an integer in minutes representing the difference between local time and Greenwich mean time (GMT).

toGMTString(): Returns the value of the current Date object in GMT in the form Day, DD MON YYYY HH;MM;SS GMT.

toLocalString(): Returns the value of the current Date object in local time.

UTC(*yearValue, monthValue, dateValue, hoursValue, minutesValue, secondsValue*): Returns an integer number of milliseconds since 12:00 a.m., January 1, 1970, (00:00:00) in GMT.

parse(*dateString*): Returns an integer number of milliseconds between 12:00 a.m., January 1, 1970, (00:00:00:00) and the date specified in *dateString*.

Other scripts that may be used to set date values, similar to those using the get command, are setDate(*dateValue*), setHours(*hoursValue*), setMinutes(*minutesValue*), setMonth(*month Value*), setSeconds(*secondsValue*), setTime(*timeValue*), and setYear(*yearValue*).

## document

Represents the attributes of the currently displayed HTML document. Its properties are derived from the BODY element.

*Properties*

alinkColor: The color of active links, defined as a hexadecimal triplet or a string.

anchors: An array of the anchor objects in the order they appear in an HTML document. anchors.length returns the number of anchors in a document.

bgColor: The background color of the document.

cookie: The current document's cookie values.

fgColor: The foreground color of the document.

forms: An array of form objects in the order in which the forms appear in an HTML file. forms.length returns the number of forms in the document.

lastModified: The last date on which the document was modified.

linkColor: The color of links, defined as a hexadecimal triplet or a string.

links: An array of the link objects in the order in which the hypertext links appear in an HTML document. links.length returns the number of links in a document.

location: The URL of the current document, expressed as document.URL. This property is deprecated.

referrer: The URL of the calling document.

title: The name of the current document.

vlinkColor: The color of followed links, defined as a hexadecimal triplet or a string.

applets: An array of the applet objects in the order in which they appear in the HTML document. applets.length returns the number of applets in the document.

embeds: An array of the plugin objects in the order in which they appear in the HTML document. embeds.length returns the number of plug-ins in the document.

images: An array of image objects in the order in which they appear in the HTML document. images.length returns the number of images in the document.

URL: The URL of the current document.

*Methods*

close(): Closes the current output stream.

open(*mimeType*): Allows write() method and writeln() method to write to the document window. *mimeType* (optional) specifies a document type.

write(): Writes text and HTML to the specified document.

writeln(): Writes text and HTML to the specified document, and inserts a newline character.

clear(): Clears the document window.

captureEvents(): Specifies that a window with frames will capture all specified events.

releaseEvents(*eventType*): Forces the current window to release events which can then be passed to other objects.

routeEvent(*event*): Sends an event through the standard event hierarchy.

*Event Handlers*

onMouseDown: Specifies the script to be executed when a mouse button is pressed.

onMouseUp: Specifies the script to be executed when a mouse button is released.

onDblClick: Specifies the script to be executed when a mouse button is double-clicked in a particular area.

onKeyUp: Specifies the script to be executed when a particular key is released.

onKeyDown: Specifies the script to be executed when a particular key is pressed.

onKeyPress: Specifies the script to be executed when a particular key is held down.

## FileUpload

Represents a file upload element in an HTML form.

*Properties*

name: The name of the file upload element.

value: The field of a file upload element.

## form

Represents a single HTML form in JavaScript. It collects input from a user to send to a server.

*Properties*

action: The URL to which the form data is submitted. This is the form's ACTION attribute.

elements: An array of objects for each form element in sequential order.

encoding: The MIME encoding of the form as specified in the ENCTYPE attribute. This is the form's ENCTYPE attribute.

method: A method in which form data is submitted to a server. This is the form's METHOD attribute.

target: The name of the window that displays responses to form submissions. This is the form's TARGET attribute.

*Methods*

submit(): Submits form data to a server.

reset(): Resets a form.

*Event Handlers*

onSubmit: Specifies the script to be executed when a form is submitted. The value true must be returned to enable the form to be submitted. If a false value is returned, the form is not submitted.

onReset: Specifies the script to be executed when a form is reset.

## frame

Represents a frame window in JavaScript. Frames within a browser are instances of the Window object and do not exist separately.

*Properties*

frames: An array of objects for each frame in a window, sequentially ordered as they appear in the HTML source code.

parent: The name of the window containing the frame set.

self: An alternate name for the current window.

top: An alternate name for the topmost window.

window: An alternate name for the current window.

onBlur: Represents the onBlur event handler for a frame. The event handler may be changed by assigning new values to this property.

onFocus: The onFocus event handler for the frame. The event handler may be changed by assigning new values to this property.

*Methods*

alert(*message*): Displays *message* in a dialog box.

clearTimeout(*name*): Cancels the timeout identified by *name*.

close(): Closes the window.

confirm(*message*): Displays *message* in a dialog box with OK and Cancel buttons. The user determines the true or false status.

open(*url, name, features*): Opens *url* in the *name* window, or creates a new window with that name. *features* is a list of features for the new window. The feature list may contain name-value pairs as shown below:

```
width=pixels
height=pixels
status=[yes,no,1,0]
menubar=[yes,no,1,0]
scrollbars=[yes,no,1,0]
resizable=[yes,no,1,0]
toolbar=[yes,no,1,0]
location=[yes,no,1,0]
directories=[yes,no,1,0]
```

prompt(*message, response*): Displays *message* in a dialog box with the value of *response* in a text entry field. The user's response in the text entry field is returned.

setTimeout(*expression, time*): Evaluates *expression* after *time*.

blur(): Removes focus from the frame.

focus(): Gives focus to the frame.

clearInterval(*intervalID*): Cancels timeouts created with the setInterval method.

print(): Prints the contents of a frame or window.

setInterval(*expression, msec*): Evaluates *expression* after the duration specified by the *msec* parameter.

setInterval(*function, msec*): Calls *function* after the duration specified by the *msec* parameter.

*Event Handlers*

onFocus: Specifies the JavaScript code to execute when the frame is given focus.

onBlur: Specifies the script to be executed when focus is removed from the frame.

onMove: Specifies the script to be executed when the frame is moved.

onResize: Specifies the script to be executed when the frame is resized.

## Function

A means of indicating the JavaScript code that should be compiled as a function. *functionName* is used as a variable with a reference to the function.

*Properties*

arguments: An integer that represents the number of arguments in the function.

prototype: A means of adding properties to the Function object.

## hidden

Represents a hidden field in an HTML form. This invisible form element allows arbitrary data to be sent to a server when the form is submitted.

*Properties*

name: The name of a hidden element in the form of a string.

value: The value of a hidden text element in the form of a string.

type: The TYPE property of the INPUT tag.

## history

Allows JavaScript to access the Navigator browser's history list. The contents of the list are not reflected in JavaScript for security.

*Properties*

length: The number of items in the history list, expressed as an integer.

*Methods*

back(): Refers to the previous document in the list.

forward(): Refers to the next document in the list.

go(*location*): Goes to the document in the history list specified by *location*, which may be a string or integer value. As an integer it indicates the relative position of the document in the list.

### HTMLElement superclass

This is the superclass of all classes that represent HTML elements. Its objects, listed below, are used in various contexts in client-side JavaScript 1.2.

document.all[$i$]
document.anchors[$i$]
document.forms[$i$]
document.forms[$i$].elements[$j$]
document.images[$i$]
document.links[$i$]
document.*elementName*
document.*formName.elementName*

*Properties*

The following properties are implemented in Internet Explorer 4.0 only:

all[]: An array of all elements contained by an element.

children[]: All elements that are direct children of an element.

className: The value of the CLASS attribute.

document: Refers to the containing document object.

id: The value of the ID attribute.

innerHTML: The HTML text within an element.

innerText: The plain text within an element.

lang: The value of the LANG attribute.

offsetHeight: The height of an element.

offsetLeft: The x-coordinate of an element.

offsetParent: An element that contains offsetLeft and offsetTop.

offsetTop: The y-coordinate of an element.

offsetWidth: The width of an element.

outerHTML: The HTML text of an element, with start and end tags.

outerText: The plain text in a document, with start and end tags.

parentElement: An element that is the direct parent of this one.

sourceIndex: The index of an element in Document.all[].

style: The inline Cascading Style Sheets (CSS) attributes for an element.

tagName: The name of the HTML tag that created an element.

title: The value of the TITLE attribute.

*Methods*

contains(): Determines whether an element contains the one specified in ().

getAttribute(): Returns the value of a named attribute.

insertAdjacentHTML(): Inserts HTML text into the document nearest an element.

insertAdjacentText(): Inserts plain text into the document nearest an element.

removeAttribute(): Deletes an attribute and its value from an element.

scrollIntoView(): Scrolls the document so an element is visible in the window.

setAttribute(): Sets the value of an attribute of an element.

handleEvent(): Passes an event object to the appropriate event handler.

*Event Handlers*

onClick: Specifies the script to be executed when a mouse button is clicked.

onDblClick: Specifies the script to be executed when a mouse button is double-clicked on an element.

onHelp: Specifies the script to be executed when a user requests help.

onKeyDown: Specifies the script to be executed when a particular key is pressed.

onKeyPress: Specifies the script to be executed when a particular key is held down.

onKeyUp: Specifies the script to be executed when a particular key is released.

onMouseDown: Specifies the script to be executed when a mouse button is pressed.

onMouseMove: Specifies the script to be executed when a mouse button is moved.

onMouseOut: Specifies the script to be executed when the mouse is moved off of an element.

onMouseOver: Specifies the script to be executed when the mouse is moved over an element.

onMouseUp: Specifies the script to be executed when a mouse button is released.

## Image

Represents an image in an HTML document.

*Properties*

border: An integer representing the width of the border of an image in pixels.

complete: A Boolean value that indicates whether an image is done loading.

height: An integer representing the height of an image in pixels.

hspace: The HSPACE attribute of the IMG tag, expressed as an integer.

lowsrc: The URL of a low resolution version of an image.

name: The name of an Image object.

prototype: A means of adding properties to an Image object.

src: The URL of an image.

vspace: The VSPACE attribute of the IMG tag, expressed as an integer.

width: An integer representing the width of an image in pixels.

*Event Handlers*

onAbort: Specifies the script to be executed when an attempt to load an image is aborted.

onError: Specifies the script to be executed when an error occurs during image loading. If this handler is set to *null*, the error message is suppressed.

onLoad: Specifies the script to be executed when an image is completely loaded.

onKeyDown: Specifies the script to be executed when a specific key is pressed.

onKeyUp: Specifies the script to be executed when a specific key is released.

onKeyPress: Specifies the script to be executed when a specific key is held down.

## Layer

A means of embedding layers of content within a page. Layers allow dynamically positioned elements to be included in a dynamic HTML (DHTML) document.

*Properties*

above: Refers to a layer on top of the current layer.

background: Specifies the tiled background image of a layer.

below: Refers to a layer below the current layer.

bgColor: Sets the background color of a layer.

clip(*left, right, top, bottom, width, height*): Specifies the visible boundaries of the layer.

height: Specifies the height of a layer, expressed in pixels by an integer or by a percentage of the current layer.

ID: Names a layer for reference by other scripts (same as name).

left: Specifies the horizontal position of the top-left corner of the layer, along with the top property.

page[*X, Y*]: Specifies the horizontal (X) or vertical (Y) position of the top-left corner of the layer relative to the overall enclosing document.

parentLayer: Specifies the layer object that contains the current layer.

siblingAbove: Specifies the layer object directly on top of the present one.

siblingBelow: Specifies the layer object directly under the present one.

SRC: Specifies the source URL of a layer's contents.

top: Specifies the y-coordinate of the top-left corner of the layer, along with the left property.

visibility: Specifies the visibility of the layer. The three variables are *show* (visible), *hidden* (not visible), and *inherit* (properties inherited from the parent layer).

width: Specifies the width of a layer or a boundary inside of which contents remain confined or wrap.

z-index: Specifies, with an integer, the stacking order (z-order) of a layer. Sets a layer's position within the overall rotational order if there are multiple layers.

*Methods*

captureEvents(): Specifies that a window with frames will capture all specified events.

handleEvent(): Dispatches an event to the appropriate handler.

load(*source, width*): Replaces the source with HTML (or JavaScript) from the file specified in *source*. Also passes a width value in pixels.

moveAbove(*layer*): Places the current layer above the *layer* identified in the stack.

moveBelow(*layer*): Places the current layer below the *layer* identified in the stack.

moveBy(*x, y*): Changes the position of the current layer by the pixel values specified.

moveTo(*x, y*): Changes the position of the current layer (within the containing layer) to the coordinates specified in pixels.

moveToAbsolute(*x, y*): Changes the position of the current layer (within a page) to the coordinates specified in pixels.

resizeBy(*width, height*): Changes the size of the current layer by the values specified in pixels.

resizeTo(*width, height*): Changes the size of the current layer to the values specified for width and height in pixels.

releaseEvents(*eventType*): Specifies that the current window should release events on input of *eventType*.

*Event Handlers*

onBlur: Specifies the script to be executed when the layer no longer has focus.

onFocus: Specifies the script to be executed when the layer gains focus.

onLoad: Specifies the script to be executed when the layer is loaded.

onMouseOut: Specifies the script to be executed when the mouse moves off the current layer. Properties that may be used include type, target, layer[n], page[n], and screen[n].

onMouseOver: Specifies the script to be executed when the mouse enters the current layer. Properties that may be used include type, target, layer[n], page[n], and screen[n].

## link

Represents a hypertext link in the body of an HTML document.

*Properties*

hash: The anchor name in a URL referenced (follows the hash mark #).

host: The host name and port number from a URL referenced.

hostname: The numerical IP address, or domain name, from the URL referenced.

href: The entire URL referenced (the HREF attribute of the A element).

pathname: The path portion of a URL referenced.

port: The port number from the URL referenced (ftp=21; WWW=80; Usenet news=119).

protocol: The protocol from the URL referenced, including the colon but not the slashes.

search: All information passed to a GET CGI-BIN call.

target: The name of a window or frame specified in the TARGET attribute.

text: The plain text between the <A> and </A> tags that created the object.

*Event Handlers*

onMouseUp: Specifies the script to be executed when the mouse button is released.

onClick: Specifies the script to be executed when a user clicks on a link.

onDblClick: Specifies the script to be executed when the mouse button is double-clicked in a particular area.

moveMouse: Specifies the script to be executed when the mouse moves over a link.

onKeyUp: Specifies the script to be executed when a particular key is released.

onKeyDown: Specifies the script to be executed when a particular key is pressed.

onKeyPress: Specifies the script to be executed when a particular key is held down.

onMouseDown: Specifies the script to be executed when the mouse button is pressed.

onMouseOut: Specifies the script to be executed when the mouse cursor moves out of an object. In JavaScript 1.2, properties that may be used include type, target, layer[n], page[n], and screen[n].

onMouseOver: Specifies the script to be executed when the mouse moves over a hypertext link. In JavaScript 1.2, properties that may be used include type, target, layer[n], page[n], and screen[n].

## location

Reflects information about the current URL.

*Properties*

hash: The anchor name in the URL.

host: The host name and port number from the URL.

hostname: The numerical IP address, or domain name, from the URL.

href: The entire URL.

pathname: The path portion of the URL.

port: The port number from the URL.

protocol: The protocol from the URL with the colon but not the slashes.

search: All information passed to a GET CGI-BIN call.

*Methods*

reload(): Reloads the current document.

replace(*url*): Loads the *url* specified over the current entry in the history list; after this it is impossible to navigate back to the previous URL by using the Back button.

## Math

Provides properties and methods for mathematical calculations.

*Properties*

E: Euler's constant (approximately 2.718282), which is used as the base for natural logarithms.

LN2: The natural logarithm of two (approximately 0.693147).

LN10: The natural logarithm of 10 (approximately 2.302585).

LOG10E: The base 10 logarithm of e (approximately 0.434294).

LOG2E: The base 2 logarithm of e (approximately 1.442695).

PI: The value of pi for calculating the circumference and area of a circle (approximately 3.14159).

SQRT1_2: The square root of one-half (approximately 0.7071).

SQRT2: The square root of two (approximately 1.4142).

*Methods*

abs(*number*): Returns the absolute value of *number* without consideration of its sign. abs(8) is equal to abs(-8).

acos(*number*): Returns the arc cosine of *number* in radians.

asin(*number*): Returns the arc sine of *number* in radians.

atan(*number*): Returns the arc tangent of *number* in radians.

atan2(*number1, number2*): Returns the angle of the polar coordinate corresponding to the Cartesian coordinate (*number1, number2*).

ceil(*number*): Returns the smallest integer equal to or greater than *number*.

cos(*number*): Returns the cosine of *number*.

exp(*number*): Returns the value of e to the power of *number*.

floor(*number*): Returns the greatest integer equal to or less than *number*.

log(*number*): Returns the natural logarithm (base e) of *number*.

max(*number1, number2*): Returns the greater of *number1* and *number2*.

min(*number1, number2*): Returns the smaller of *number1* and *number2*.

pow(*number1, number2*): Returns the value of *number1* to the power of *number2*.

random(): Returns a random number between zero and one.

round(*number*): Returns the closest integer to *number*, rounded off.

sin(*number*): Returns the sine of *number*, which is an angle expressed in radians.

sqrt(*number*): Returns the square root of *number*.

tan(*number*): Returns the tangent of *number*, where *number* represents an angle in radians.

## mimeType

Represents a MIME type supported by the client browser.

*Properties*

description: A description of the MIME type.

enabledPlugin: Refers to the plugin object that supports the MIME type.

suffixes: A list of file suffixes for the MIME type, separated by commas.

type: A string that indicates the MIME type itself, as in "video/mpeg".

## navigator

Provides information about the version of Navigator used by the client.

*Properties*

appCodeName: The code name of the client ("Mozilla" is used for Netscape Navigator).

appName: The name of the client ("Netscape" is used for Navigator).

appVersion(*platform; country*): The version number of the client's browser.

mimeTypes: Returns an array of the MIME types supported by the client browser.

platform: Specifies the platform (Win32, MacPPC, Unix, etc.) for which Navigator was compiled on the client computer.

plugins: Returns an array of plug-ins in an HTML document in order of their appearance.

userAgent: The complete value of the user-agent header sent in an HTTP request. The appCodeName and appVersion are contained in this header.

*Methods*

javaEnabled(): Indicates whether Java is enabled in a browser.

preference(*preference.name, setValue*): Allows certain browser preferences to be set in signed scripts, as shown here:

autoupdate.enabled: Value (true/false) that sets whether autoinstall is enabled.

browser.enable_style_sheets: Value (true/false) that sets whether style sheets are enabled.

general.always_load_images: Value (true/false) that sets whether images are automatically loaded.

javascript.enabled: Value (true/false) that sets whether JavaScript is enabled.

network.cookie.cookieBehavior(0, 1, 2): Value that determines how cookies are handled, with three parameters. (0 accepts all cookies; 1 accepts only those forwarded to the originating server; 2 denies all cookies.)

network.cookie.warnAboutCookies: Value (true/false) that sets whether the browser will warn the user before accepting cookies.

security.enable_java: Value (true/false) that sets whether Java is enabled.

## option

Creates entries in a select list with the syntax shown here:

*optionName* = new Option(*optionText, optionValue, defaultSelected, selected*)
where
*selectName*.options[*index*] = *optionName*

*Properties*

defaultSelected: Specifies with a Boolean value whether an option is selected by default.

index: Specifies with an integer an option's index in the select list.

prototype: A means of adding properties to an Option object.

selected: Indicates with a Boolean value whether an option is currently selected.

text: The text displayed for an option.

value: The value sent to the server when a form is submitted.

## password

Represents a password text field from an HTML form in JavaScript.

*Properties*

defaultValue: The default value of the password element.

name: The name of the password element.

value: The value of the password element.

form: Refers to the form object containing the password field.

enabled: Indicates with a Boolean value if a password field is enabled.

*Methods*

focus(): Gives focus to the password field.

blur(): Removes focus from the password field.

select(): Selects the text in the password field.

551

*Event Handlers*

> onBlur: Specifies the script to be executed when focus is removed from the password field.
>
> onFocus: Specifies the script to be executed when focus is given to the password field.

## plugin

> Reflects a plug-in supported by the browser.

*Properties*

> description: The description provided by the plug-in itself.
>
> filename: The file name of the plug-in as it appears on the client's machine.
>
> length: The number of MIME types supported by the plug-in, described as array elements of the plug-in object.
>
> name: The name of the plug-in.

## radio

> Represents a set of graphical radio buttons in an HTML form in JavaScript. Individual radio buttons in the set are accessed numerically in order, beginning with zero. Example: myButton[0], myButton[1], myButton[2] for three radio buttons.

*Properties*

> checked: Indicates with a Boolean value whether a particular button is checked. Buttons may be selected or deselected with this property.
>
> name: The name of a set of radio buttons.
>
> value: The value of a specific radio button in a set.
>
> defaultChecked: Indicates with a Boolean value whether a particular button reflects the CHECKED attribute.
>
> length: Indicates with an integer the number of radio buttons in a set.
>
> enabled: Indicates with a Boolean value whether a particular button is enabled.
>
> form: Refers to the form object containing the radio button.

*Methods*

> click(): The act of clicking a radio button.
>
> focus(): Gives focus to a radio button.

*Event Handlers*

> onClick: Specifies the script to be executed when a radio button is clicked.
>
> onFocus: Specifies the script to be executed when a radio button is given focus.

## RegExp (JavaScript 1.2)

Represents a regular expression for pattern matching with strings. Its properties identify a series of values that may be accessed in a search. Its arguments are pattern and attributes, constructed as follows: new RegExp(*pattern, attributes*).

*Static Properties*

$1,$2,$3,.. $9: Identifies the last nine substrings enclosed in parentheses that were matched.

input: The string to which a regular expression is compared.

lastMatch: Identifies the last matched characters.

lastParen: Identifies the last matched string that appeared in parentheses.

leftContext: Identifies the string just before the most recently matched regular expression.

multiline [*true, false*]: Determines whether a search continues beyond line breaks.

rightContext: Identifies the part of a string that continues beyond the most recently matched regular expression.

*Flags*

i: Ignore case in the search (optional).

g: Perform a global match in the search for a regular expression (optional).

gi: Perform a global match, ignoring case (optional).

*Instance Properties*

source: The pattern's text in a read-only version.

ignoreCase [*true, false*]: Sets the i (ignore case) flag value.

global [*true, false*]: Sets the g (global) flag value.

lastIndex: Indicates with an integer the index position at which to begin the next matching procedure.

*Methods*

compile: Defines a new pattern and attributes for a RegExp object, usually invoked at script startup.

exec(str): Executes the search for a regular expression matching the specified string (str).

test(str): Searches for a regular expression and the string specified (str).

## reset

Represents a reset button from an HTML form in JavaScript.

*Properties*

name: The name of the reset element.

value: The value of the reset element.

enabled: Indicates with a Boolean value whether the reset button is enabled.

form: Refers to the form object containing the reset button.

*Methods*

click( ): The act of clicking the reset button.

focus( ): Specifies the script to be executed when the reset button is given focus.

*Event Handlers*

onClick: Specifies the script to be executed when the reset button is clicked.

onFocus: Specifies the script to be executed when the reset button is given focus.

## Screen (JavaScript 1.2)

Specifies characteristics of the current screen.

*Properties*

availHeight: Specifies the height of the screen in pixels, after deducting display constraints defined by the OS.

availTop: Specifies the first available vertical pixel, after deducting display constraints defined by the OS.

availWidth: Specifies the width of the current screen in pixels, after deducting display constraints defined by the OS.

colorDepth: Specifies the bit depth, or number of colors for the current screen.

height: Specifies the height of the current screen in pixels.

pixelDepth: Specifies the resolution in bits per pixel of the current screen.

width: Specifies the width of the current screen in pixels.

## select

Represents a selection list from an HTML form in JavaScript.

*Properties*

length: Identifies with an integer the number of choices in a selection list.

name: The name of a selection list.

selectedIndex: The index of the currently selected option in a selection list.

options: An array that represents the choices in a selection list.

*Properties of Options*

defaultSelected: Indicates with a Boolean value whether a particular option reflects the SELECTED attribute.

index: The index of an option.

length: The number of options in a selection list.

name: The name of the selection list.

selected: Indicates with a Boolean value whether a particular button is selected. Options may be selected or deselected with this property.

selectedIndex: Indicates with an integer the index of the currently selected option.

text: The text displayed in a selection list for a particular option.

value: The value for a specified option.

*Methods*

blur(): Takes focus away from a selection list.

focus(): Gives focus to a selection list.

*Event Handlers*

onBlur: The script code to be executed when focus is removed from a selection list.

onChange: The script to be executed when the selected option in a list changes.

onFocus: The script to be executed when focus is given to a selection list.

## String

Provides properties and methods for working with variables and string literals.

*Properties*

length: The number of characters in the string, expressed as an integer.

prototype: Means of adding properties to a String object.

*Methods*

anchor(*name*): Returns a copy of the *name* string in the <A NAME=> format.

big(): Returns a copy of the specified string in the <BIG> format.

blink(): Returns a copy of the specified string in the <BLINK> format.

bold(): Returns a copy of the specified string in the <B> format.

charAt(*index*): Returns the character at the location in a string specified by *index*.

charCodeAt(*index*): Returns the encoded value of a character at the *index* position in a string.

fixed(): Returns a copy of the specified string in the <TT> format.

indexOf(*substring, start*): Returns the index of the first occurrence of *substring*, starting the search at *start*. By default, the search starts at the beginning of the string.

italics(): Returns a copy of the specified string in the <I> format.

lastIndexOf(*substring, start*): Returns the index of the first occurrence of *substring*, beginning at *start* and searching in reverse order. By default, the search starts at the end of the string.

link(*href*): Returns a copy of the *href* string in the <A HREF=> format.

match(*regexp*): Matches the regular expression specified, expressed as a variable or as a literal.

replace(*regexp, replacement*): Locates and replaces a regular expression with *replacement*.

search(*regexp*): Locates a regular expression and matches it to the specified string.

slice(*start, end*): Extracts a substring and derives a new string.

small(): Returns a copy of the specified string in the <SMALL> format.

strike(): Returns a copy of the specified string in the <STRIKE> format.

sub(): Returns a copy of the specified string in the <SUB> format.

sup(): Returns a copy of the specified string in the <SUP> format.

toLowerCase(): Returns a copy of the specified string with lowercase characters.

toUpperCase(): Returns a copy of the specified string with uppercase characters.

fontColor(*color*): Returns a copy of the *color* string in the <FONT COLOR=> format.

fontSize(*size*): Returns a copy of the *size* string in the <FONT SIZE=> format.

split(*delimiter*): Divides a string at every occurrence of *delimiter*.

concat(*string2*): Combines two strings to make a new third one.

substring(*from, to*): Sets the number of characters within a string. Use *from* to specify the beginning point for the extraction process, ending at *to*.

### submit

Represents a submit button from an HTML form in JavaScript.

*Properties*

name: The name of the submit button element.

value: The value of the submit button element.

enabled: Indicates with a Boolean value whether the submit button is enabled.

form: Represents the form object containing a submit button.

type: The TYPE attribute of the INPUT tag.

*Methods*

click(): Simulates clicking the submit button.

focus(): Gives focus to the submit button.

*Event Handlers*

    onClick: Specifies the script to be executed when the submit button is clicked.

    onFocus: Specifies the script to be executed when the submit button is given focus.

## text

Represents a text field from an HTML form in JavaScript.

*Properties*

    defaultValue: The default value of the text element (VALUE attribute).

    name: The name of the text field element.

    value: The value of the text element.

    enabled: Indicates with a Boolean value whether a text field is enabled.

    form: Represents the form object containing a text field.

    type: The TYPE attribute of the INPUT tag.

*Methods*

    focus(): Gives focus to the text field.

    blur(): Removes focus from the text field.

    select(): Selects text in the text field.

*Event Handlers*

    onBlur: Specifies the script to be executed when focus is removed from a text field.

    onChange: Specifies the script to be executed when text field content is changed.

    onFocus: Specifies the script to be executed when the text field receives focus.

    onSelect: Specifies the script to be executed when any text in the field is selected.

## textarea

Represents a multiline text field from an HTML form in JavaScript.

*Properties*

    defaultValue: The default value of the textarea element (VALUE attribute).

    name: The name of the textarea element.

    value: The value of the textarea element.

    enabled: Indicates with a Boolean value whether a textarea field is enabled.

    form: Represents the form object containing a textarea field.

    type: The TYPE attribute of the textarea INPUT tag.

*Methods*

focus(): Gives focus to the textarea field.

blur(): Removes focus from the textarea field.

select(): Simulates selecting text in the textarea field.

*Event Handlers*

onBlur: Specifies the script to be executed when focus is removed from a textarea field.

onChange: Specifies the script to be executed when textarea field content is changed.

onFocus: Specifies the script to be executed when the textarea field receives focus.

onSelect: Specifies the script to be executed when any text in the textarea field is selected.

onKeyUp: Specifies the script to be executed when a specific key is released.

onKeyPress: Specifies the script to be executed when a specific key is held down by the user.

onKeyDown: Specifies the script to be executed when a specific key is pressed.

## window

The parent object for document, location, and history objects. This is the top-level object for an array of frames or a window. The window is the "global object," and all expressions are evaluated in the context of the current window object.

*Properties*

defaultStatus: The default value displayed in the status bar.

frames: An array of objects representing each frame in the window, ordered as they appear in the HTML source code.

name: The name of a window or frame.

parent: The name of the window containing a frameset.

self: Another name for the current window.

status: Displays a message, consisting of assigned values, in the status bar.

statusbar=[*true,false,1,0*]: Controls whether the status bar in the target window is visible.

toolbar=[*true,false,1,0*]: Controls whether the toolbar in the target window is visible.

top: Another name for the topmost window.

window: Another name for the current window.

length: Indicates with an integer the number of frames in a parent window.

opener: The window object that contains the open() method used to open the current window.

innerHeight(): Specifies the vertical size in pixels of the content area.

innerWidth(): Specifies the horizontal size in pixels of the content area.

pageXOffset: Specifies the current X position in pixels of the viewable window area.

pageYOffset: Specifies the current Y position in pixels of the viewable window area.

scrollbars [*visible=true,false*]: Controls whether scroll bars in the current window are visible.

*Methods*

alert(*message*): Causes a specified *message* to appear in a dialog box.

captureEvents(): Specifies that a window with frames will capture all specified events. Used with enableExternalCapture.

clearTimeout(*name*): Cancels the timeout specified by *name*.

clearTimeout(*timeoutId*): Cancels the deferred execution of the setTimeout identified.

confirm(*question*): Displays a *question* in a dialog box, to which a user may respond "OK" or "Cancel." Returns true or false, depending on the button selected by the user.

length(): Specifies the number of frames in a window.

prompt(*message, response*): Shows *message* in a dialog box, along with a text entry field containing the default value of *response*. Returns a string with data keyed into a text entry field.

setTimeout(*expression, delay*): Defers execution of *expression* until after *delay*, expressed in milliseconds.

stop(): Ends the current download. Simulates pressing the Stop button.

close(): Closes a specified window.

open(*url, name, features*): Opens the *url* specified in a window called *name*. A new window is created, if one does not exist by that name. The string argument "*features*" specifies parameters for the window that is opened. The following names and values may be specified. There are no spaces between values, but each is followed by a comma:

    alwaysLowered=[*yes,no,1,2*] (background window)
    alwaysRaised=[*yes,no,1,2*] (top-level window)
    directories=[*yes,no,1,0*]
    height=pixels
    location=[*yes,no,1,0*]
    menubar=[*yes,no,1,0*]
    resizable=[*yes,no,1,0*]
    scrollbars=[*yes,no,1,0*]
    status=[*yes,no,1,0*]
    toolbar=[*yes,no,1,0*]
    width=pixels

The following features may not be implemented in an Internet Explorer browser:
    dependent[*yes,no,1,2*] (on parent window)
    hotkeys=[*yes,no,1,2*]
    innerWidth=pixels
    innerHeight=pixels
    outerWidth=pixels

```
outerHeight=pixels
screenX=pixels
screenY=pixels
z-lock=[yes,no,1,2]
```

blur(): Removes focus from the window, in most cases sending it to the background.

focus(): Gives keyboard focus to the top window, in most cases bringing it to the front.

scrollTo(*x, y*): Scrolls the current window to the specified *x*- and *y*-coordinates.

The following methods are new in JavaScript 1.2 and may not be implemented in an Internet Explorer browser:

back(): Calls the previous URL visited, similar to activating the Back browser button.

clearInterval(*intervalID*): Eliminates timeouts created with the setInterval method.

disableExternalCapture(): Prevents a current window with frames from capturing events that occur in pages loaded from another location.

enableExternalCapture(): Allows a current window with frames to capture events that occur in pages loaded from another location.

event(): Describes the most recent event to occur in a window.

find([*string*], [*true, false*], [*true, false*]): Finds the *string* specified in the target window. The first Boolean true/false parameter specifies whether the search is case sensitive. The second true/false parameter specifies whether the search should be performed in reverse order.

forward(): Moves to the next URL listed, similar to activating the Forward browser button.

home(): Directs the browser to the user's home page.

moveBy(*x, y*): Repositions a window to the right (*x*) or down (*y*), according to the specified values.

movoTo(*x, y*): Positions the upper-left corner of a window at the specified location.

print(): Sends the contents of a frame or window to a printer. Simulates pressing the Print button.

releaseEvents(*eventType*): Rather than capturing events in the current window, allows them to be passed on to other objects.

resizeBy(*horizontal, vertical*): Beginning from the lower-right corner, resizes the window.

resizeTo(*outerWidth, outerHeight*): Applies the specified *outerWidth* and *outerHeight* properties to the window.

routeEvent(*event*): Sends an event through the normal hierarchy.

scrollBy(*horizontal, vertical*): Causes the viewing area of the current window to be scrolled by the number of pixels specified by the *horizontal* or *vertical* values.

scrollTo(*x, y*): Beginning at the upper-left corner of the current window, scrolls it to the position specified in the *x*- and *y*-coordinates.

setInterval(*expression, msec*): Evaluates the specified *expression* after the period identified by the *msec* parameter.

setInterval(*function, msec, args*): Continuously calls a *function* after the period specified by the *msec* parameter.

*Event Handlers*

onLoad: The script to be executed when the window or frame is done loading.

onUnload: The script to be executed when a user exits the document in a frame or window.

onBlur: The script to be executed when focus is removed from the window.

onError: The script to be executed when a JavaScript error is returned while a document is loading. A JavaScript error message will not be displayed to the user if this event handler is set to null.

onFocus: The script to be executed when the window receives focus.

onResize: The script to be executed when the window is resized by a user.

onMove: The script to be executed when the window is repositioned by a user.

onDragDrop: The script to be executed when an object is dropped into the window by a user.

# Symbolic Operators

## Arithmetic Operators

+        Adds the operands on the left and on the right. (When used with strings rather than integers, it combines the operands into one string.)

-        When used as a binary operator, subtracts the right operand from the left operand.

-        Performs unary negation when placed immediately before an operand; converts an operand from positive to negative, and vice versa.

*        Multiplies two operands.

/        Divides the left operand by the right operand.

%        Returns the remainder of the left operand divided by the right operand.

++      Increases an operand by one (may be applied before or after an operand).

--       Decreases an operand by one (may be applied before or after an operand).

## Assignment Operators

These operators work with both numbers and strings. For example, with numbers the operator += performs addition and assignment. For strings it performs concatenation and assignment.

= Assigns the value of the right operand to an expression. It causes the variable, element, or property a to refer to the value b.

Example: a = b is equivalent to b

+= Adds the left and right operands, then assigns the total to the left operand. (When used with strings rather than integers, concatenation of the two operands is performed.)

Example: a += b is equivalent to a = a + b

-= Subtracts the right operand from the left operand, then assigns the result to the left operand.

Example: a -= b is equivalent to a = a - b

*= Multiplies two operands, then assigns the result to the left operand.

Example: a *= b is equivalent to a = a * b

/= Divides the left operand by the right operand, then assigns the value to the left operand.

Example: a /= b is equivalent to a = a / b

%= Divides the left operand by the right operand, then assigns the remainder to the left operand.

Example: a %= b is equivalent to a = a % b

## Bitwise Operators

These operators treat their operands as binary numbers, convert them to integers with 32 bits, and return a JavaScript numerical value.

AND (&) Pairs corresponding bits, and returns 1 for each pair of 1s. Returns 0 for any other combination.

OR (|) Pairs corresponding bits, and returns 1 for each pair if either of the bits is a 1. Returns 0 if both bits are 0.

XOR (^) Pairs corresponding bits, and returns 1 for each pair where only one bit is a 1. Returns 0 for any other combination.

<< Shifts bits to the left by the number of bits indicated by the right operand. Bits shifted to the left are discarded, and zeros are shifted over from the right.

>> Shifts bits to the right by the number of bits indicated by the right operand. Bits shifted to the right are discarded. The bit furthest to the left is duplicated and shifted over from the left.

>>> Shifts bits to the right by the number of bits indicated by the right operand. Bits shifted to the right are discarded. Zeros are shifted over from the left.

## Logical Operators

These operators perform Boolean algebra. They are particularly useful in complex comparisons that involve more than one variable, combined with if, while, and for statements.

| && (logical AND) | Returns true when both operands are true, otherwise returns false. |
| || (logical OR) | Returns true if either operand is true. Returns false only when both operands are false. |
| ! (logical NOT) | Returns true if the operand is false, and returns false if the operand is true. This unary operator precedes the operand. |

## Equality and Identity Operators

| == | Returns true if operands are equal (numbers, strings, or Boolean values) or if they refer to the same object (function, array, or object). This operator compares for equality without comparing type only in Internet Explorer 4.0. |
| != | Returns true if operands are not equal or they refer to different objects. |
| === | Returns true only if operands are identical without comparing type. |
| !== | Returns true only if operands are not equal without comparing type. |

## Comparison Operators

| > | Returns true if the left operand is greater than the right operand. |
| < | Returns true if the left operand is less than the right operand. |
| >= | Returns true if the left operand is greater than or equal to the right operand. |
| <= | Returns true if the left operand is less than or equal to the right operand. |

## Conditional Operators

typeof: Returns the type of its single operand. Types that are returned are object, string, number, boolean, function, or undefined.

void: Discards its operand value or returns an undefined value. This unary operator may precede an expression with any value.

(? :): This is a ternary operator, which uses three operands. Returns value1 if the condition is true, otherwise returns value2.

Example: condition ? value1 : value2

## Independent Functions

escape(*character*): Returns a string with *character* ASCII-encoded for transmission across networks to all computer platforms. Non-ASCII characters are encoded in the format %*xx*, where *xx* is two hexadecimal digits representing the character in ISO 8859 (Latin-1) coding.

eval(*code*): Returns the result of evaluating an arithmetic expression, or executes the JavaScript statements represented by *code* and returns the value.

isNaN(*value*): Evaluates *value* to determine whether it is NaN (not a number), and returns a Boolean value.

parseFloat(*string*): Returns the value of *string* after converting it to a floating-point number. This function returns NaN (zero in MS Windows) when it encounters the first character that cannot be converted to a number.

parseInt(*string, radix*): Returns the value of *string* after converting it to an integer in base *radix*. This function returns NaN (zero in MS Windows) when it encounters the first character that cannot be converted to an integer.

unescape(*string*): Returns a character based on the ASCII encoding contained in *string*. It decodes a previously escaped string.

## Table of Operators

In this table, the first three columns on the left show the operators, types of operands, and operations performed. The associativity is shown in the next column (LTR = left to right, RTL = right to left). The order of precedence that each operator takes is shown in the last column on the right.

| Operator | Type of Operand | Operation | Associativity | Precedence |
|---|---|---|---|---|
| (,) | Any | Multiple Evaluation | LTR | 1 |
| (=) | Variable, Any | Assignment | RTL | 2 |
| (+=, -=, *=, /=, %=, <<=, >>=, >>>=, &=, ^=, \|=) | Variable, Any | Assignment with Operation | RTL | 2 |
| (? :) | Boolean, Any | Conditional (ternary) | RTL | 3 |
| (\|\|) | Boolean | Logical OR | LTR | 4 |
| (&&) | Boolean | Logical AND | LTR | 5 |
| (\|) | Integer | Bitwise OR | LTR | 6 |
| (^) | Integer | Bitwise XOR | LTR | 7 |
| (&) | Integer | Bitwise AND | LTR | 8 |
| (==, != ) | Any | Checks for Equality/Identity | LTR | 9 |
| (<, <=, >, >=) | Numbers/Strings | Relational | LTR | 10 |
| (<<, >>, >>>) | Integer | Shift | LTR | 11 |
| (+, -) | Integer String (+ only) | Addition/Subtraction, Concatenation | LTR | 12 |
| (*, /, %) | Integer | Multiply/Divide/Remainder | LTR | 13 |
| (++, --, -) | Integer | Increment/Decrement/Negate (unary) | RTL | 14 |
| ( ~) | Integer | Bitwise Complement (unary) | | |
| (!) | Boolean | Logical Complement (unary) | | |
| new | Constructor Call | Create New Object (unary) | | |
| type of | Any | Return Data Type (unary) | | |
| void | Any | Return Undefined Value (unary) | | |
| ([ ], ( ), .) | Array, Integer | Array Index | LTR | 15 |
| | Functions, Arguments | Function Calls | | |
| | Object, Property | Property Access | | |

# Statements

break: Exits from a for or a while loop and passes program control to the statement following the loop.

case: Labels a statement within a switch statement (JavaScript 1.2 only).

comment: Allows a programmer to comment on code. Comments are enclosed in a /* (start) */ (end) structure.

continue: Continues iteration of a while or a for loop after the execution of the statements within the loop.

default: Labels the default statement within a switch statement (JavaScript 1.2 only).

do/while: Sets up a continuous loop that executes statements and code until the condition evaluates to false (JavaScript 1.2 only).

export(*expression*): In secure, signed scripts, it allows all of the properties, functions, and variables to be exported to another script. Used in conjunction with an import statement, it makes the *expression* variable or function accessible in other windows or execution contexts (JavaScript 1.2 only).

for([*expression*]; [*condition*]; [*increment*];): Opens a for loop. Arguments initialize a variable (*expression*), create a condition to test for (*condition*), and specify incrementation.

for/in: Introduces a variable to all the properties of an object and executes a block of code for each one, looping through the properties.

function [name]([*arg1,... argn*]): Declares a function that event handlers or other processes may access.

if/else: Conditionally executes code. Example: If (*expression*) *statement1* [else *statement2*]. Nested statements and functions will be executed depending on whether the condition described by *expression* is true or false.

import(*variables*): In secure, signed scripts this statement allows all properties, functions, and variables to be imported from another script. Used in conjunction with the export statement, the named variables are imported (JavaScript 1.2 only).

label(*identifier: statement*): Gives *statement* the name *identifier*. Creates a pointer to code located elsewhere in the script. The script is redirected to the labeled statement (JavaScript 1.2 only).

return [*expression*]: Specifies an expression or value to be returned by a given function.

switch(*expression*): Evaluates an expression and attempts to match it to a case or default pattern or label. If the expression matches the case, statements associated with the label are executed (JavaScript 1.2 only).

this: A statement that refers to a specific object. For example, this.width = w passes a specified value to an object.

var [*name*]: Declares and initializes the variable name.

while(*expression*): A statement that constructs and begins a while loop. As long as a condition is true, the specified code is executed.

with(*object*): A statement that sets the value for the default object and adds it to the front of a chain.

# Digital Audio Production

## A Trip to the Studio

Our client wants a half-minute narration over music to play when a visitor hits his web site. Tomorrow. No problem, we just booked an hour of time at the audio studio this morning. Here's how the trip to the studio went.

8:03 A.M.

When we arrived, the receptionist immediately offered us coffee, soda, or juice. My partner and I both thought juice sounded good, so the receptionist told us to go on back and raid the fridge. The engineer met us there, poured himself a cup of coffee, and led us to a comfortable listening room. The walls were lined with CDs. "I cued up five cuts from the production music library. They all have the sort of groove you described. Here's number one." We listened to them all and picked number three. It was perfect. "That's $135 for a needle-drop," he said, grabbing the disc and dashing out. We followed him down the hall to Studio A.

8:14 A.M.

We sat behind the console, and the engineer popped the CD into the computer. He ripped the cut we selected from the disc and converted it into a WAV file. Then he opened ProTools and placed the file in the first track. The voice talent had entered the booth, and the engineer went in with a glass of water and the script my partner had given him. He seemed pleased that the script was short and printed in a 20-point font. Then he adjusted the microphone, pointing it down towards her mouth about six inches away. He told her to put on the cans (headphones), and came back into the studio to set the levels.

8:22 A.M.

She read through the script perfectly the first time. The engineer pushed the talkback button on the console, and asked her to move into the mic slightly and to speak a bit faster. He had noticed that the duration of the take would be a few seconds too long, and it had to fit in 30 seconds. The third take had the right feel, and we thanked the talent. The engineer noted that we could have been there a long time with an amateur voice, at $175 an hour for Studio A and $300 an hour for the talent.

8:34 A.M.

The next step was to drop in a few sound effects. The engineer opened a database with thousands of samples, neatly categorized and indexed. We auditioned several and chose three that would enhance the mix. He laid them into open channels of ProTools and quickly performed his magic at mixing levels. Then he compressed the dynamic range and played back the finished mix for our approval. It sounded great, so we had him burn a CD-R with the high resolution original along with compressed versions in MP3, QuickTime, and RealAudio formats.

8:55 A.M.

We left the studio smiling because we had a professional product under budget and on time. "Same billing address?" asked the receptionist. I replied, "Yes, thanks. You guys saved our lives again!"

## Audio Parameters

The engineer that did our recording had years of experience with recording gear and digital systems. He also knew a lot about sound. Anyone who undertakes an audio project needs to have a grasp of the physical properties of sound and concepts of acoustics. A sound consists of waves of varying pressure, or vibrations, in the atmosphere. Two important features of every sound are frequency and amplitude. These are factors we can measure and edit digitally.

*Frequency* is pitch. Higher pitched sound waves move faster than lower pitched sound waves. The length of a waveform determines its frequency. Frequency is measured in *hertz* (Hz) or cycles per second. A single cycle includes both the peak and the trough of the wave. The harmonic series consists of combined waves, each moving at a multiple of the fundamental lowest frequency. This series of overtones, referred to as partials, is the genesis of the tones found in musical chords. The range of human hearing is generally between 20Hz and 20KHz. As a point of reference, middle C on a keyboard is about 256Hz.

*Amplitude* is power, the volume, intensity, or loudness of a sound. The height of a waveform determines the amplitude. Sound pressure is measured in *decibels*. An electronic signal representing a sound is also measured in decibels, but in this case, the decibel is a reference voltage indicating the relative strength of the signal.

*Dynamic range* is the difference between the loudest and the softest levels in a sound track. *Stereo* sound consists of two separate channels of audio. Phase relationships exist between these two channels, and there is a possibility that sounds coming from different channels may cancel one another if they are out of phase. In this context, phase refers to the point in time that one wave begins compared to another.

*Acoustics* play a role in how we deal with sound when recording or playing it back. Hard surfaces reflect sound and create natural reverb in a room. Acoustic treatment, such as curtains and foam, is often applied to the walls of a recording studio. *Dry* sounds are devoid of reverb or other extraneous content, and *wet* sounds are heavily processed with effects.

# Production Tools

In order to define a sound digitally, we must convert it from its natural condition, which is analog. Anything that is analog, such as sound pressure, can vary over an infinite range without finite gradations or discrete levels. A knob is an analog controller and can be smoothly turned to control the volume of an amplifier. A digital control over the amplifier gives the user discrete levels to select. The sweeping second hand of a clock is an analog readout while a digital watch shows 60 discrete increments.

Pieces of analog equipment used for sound production and recording are microphones, mixers, and signal processors. If a processor is not integrated within a mixing board, it is referred to as an *outboard* processor. *Signal processing* is the term used to describe how a signal is manipulated as it moves in a path from a microphone to a mixer, through processors, and then to an amplifier and speakers. Processors include equalizers (EQ), amplifiers, filters, compressors, limiters, gates, and reverb units, to name a few.

## Cables and Connectors

Signals are moved electronically between devices by means of cables and connectors. Cables vary in several ways. There are usually two wires and a shield or ground wire in an audio cable. In stereo applications, one is for the left channel, the other is for the right channel, and the third is for grounding. Cables should be well-shielded from external noise so that they don't behave like an antenna. The diameter of the wire in the cable can vary, typically from a narrow gauge of 20 to 24 to a wider gauge of 14 to 18. Generally, larger-gauge wires offer less resistance and the current flows more freely through them. Speaker wire, which resembles lamp cord, typically has two conductors and is not shielded.

A distinction is often made in audio connections between balanced and unbalanced lines or cables. Unbalanced cables have one conductor with a shield and carry a single signal. Balanced lines have two conductors and a shield. The two conductors carry the same signal, but the polarity is reversed in one. This means that they are 180 degrees out of phase with each other, reducing the possibility of interference.

Connectors attached to the ends of a cable may be male or female in design. A male connector, with pins, is typically called a plug. A female connector is called a jack, with receptacles rather than pins, may either be attached to a cable or mounted on a piece of equipment. The common types of audio connectors are the male and female XLR, 1/4-inch phone, RCA (phono), and 1/8-inch mini plug. The phone plug or the mini plug may be stereo with a tip, sleeve, and ring (TSR) or mono with just a tip and sleeve.

## Microphones

The microphone is a critical component in the recording chain, and a high quality mic is essential for a faithful reproduction of sound. Microphones may be broadly categorized by how they function, as either *condenser* or *dynamic*.

Condenser and dynamic microphones employ different techniques to reproduce sounds. Condenser microphones have an electrically charged diaphragm that moves in response to the varying pressure of sound waves. As the diaphragm moves, the capacitance value of the diaphragm changes. The capacitance change is converted into a low impedance electrical signal that is transmitted by the microphone. The circuitry converts the signal into a form accepted by the input of standard audio equipment. Condenser microphones require external power, provided by a battery, or "phantom" power, provided by a mixing board or pre-amp.

An electrical charge must be maintained on the diaphragm for a condenser microphone to function. The diaphragm of an electret microphone is permanently charged. Other condenser microphones use external power to keep the diaphragm charged.

Dynamic microphones require no external power to operate. They operate on the same principle as a loudspeaker. A dynamic microphone has a fine wire coil attached to the back of the diaphragm. The coil is surrounded by a magnetic field created by a permanent magnet in the microphone. As the diaphragm moves, the coil moves. The movement of the coil in the magnetic field generates the electrical signal.

Dynamic microphones are durable and relatively inexpensive because their construction is less complex, but they can produce a high-quality sound. Dynamic microphones have a broad dynamic range with minimal distortion at high sound levels. They are predominantly used in sound reinforcement applications. These high impedance mics use an unbalanced cable with a ¼-inch phone connector.

Condenser microphones are more complex, and therefore usually more costly, than dynamic microphones. They typically provide higher signal levels (volume) and broader and flatter frequency response (particularly at higher frequencies) and can be made extremely small without affecting performance. Condenser microphones provide the most realistic sound quality and are used for most studio applications. They use a balanced line with XLR connectors.

High-quality mics are available from many manufacturers. Some of the best-known names in the field are Shure, AKG, AudioTechnica, Neumann, Sennheiser, and Crown.

Each microphone has a pickup pattern that determines in what direction it is most sensitive to sound. Directional mics typically exhibit "off-axis rejection," which means that sounds coming from somewhere other than the axis of sensitivity are not reproduced well. Common patterns are the cardioid, the hypercardioid, and the unidirectional. A shotgun mic is used to capture sound from a distance because it has a very narrow pattern, similar to the beam of a spotlight. A lapel mic, or lavaliere, is attached to the clothing of a presenter.

## Signal Sources

The first step in creating a digital audio file is to convert a signal that consists of a series of voltages into a series of digits that faithfully represents the original signal with an analog-to-digital (A/D) converter. The converter performs sampling, quantizing, and smoothing. An assortment of analog equipment, such as microphones, mixers, recording decks, and CD-Audio players can provide the signal source.

The two most common signal sources are a microphone and the output of a tape deck or a CD-Audio player. These two sources have different signal levels. It is important to match the output level of the source with the level that the input is designed to receive. Digital signal levels and decibels are discussed in depth later. Sounds are usually sampled by connecting the source to a sound card on the computer.

# Digital Levels

In acoustics, the decibel (dB) is used to measure variation in air pressure. In audio engineering, the decibel expresses the difference in intensity between two signals, or the ratio between the two powers. To double the power of a signal is to increase its level by 3 dB. To double the voltage of a signal increases its power four times, which results in a 6-dB increase. The reference value of a 0-dBm signal has been standardized as 1 milliwatt at 600 Hz in a 600-ohm line. This represents a level of 0.7746 volts.

When recording to magnetic tape, it is common practice to keep the level meters close to 0 dB, which fully saturates the tape. The level meters read in VU (volume units). This reading is based on the strength of the electrical current. Doing so ensures a high signal-to-noise ratio and allows some "headroom" to avoid distortion. Recording a few peaks in the "red" that rise above 0 usually doesn't cause any problems since the tape saturation point is not an absolute.

In the digital realm, where amplitudes are stored as discrete numbers instead of continuous variables, the saturation point is an absolute value. Instead of having a flexible and forgiving recording ceiling, the absolute maximum amplitudes are -32,768 and +32,767 in 16-bit audio. No signal can be stored with a value that exceeds these numbers. The input signal gets chopped down to these values and wave peaks are clipped off, resulting in audible distortion. Digital audio has absolutely no headroom. When you hit the "red" zone on the meter, the signal is clipped.

To determine the level at which a signal should be recorded digitally, the maximum possible sample amplitude is used as a reference point. This value (32,768) is referred to as 0 decibels or 0 dB. Decibels represent fractions logarithmically. The equation used to convert to decibels is $dB = 20 \log (\text{amplitude}/32{,}768)$.

Start with a sine wave with peak amplitude of 50 percent of full scale. Applying the equation, the result is 20 log (0.50) or -6.0 dB. When the amplitude of a signal is cut in half, 6 dB is subtracted from its dB value. Doubling the amplitude of a signal increases its dB value by 6 dB. The lowest peak dB possible is -90.3 dB. Decibels are used for convenience. It is easier to express a value as -90 dB than as 0.000030 (1/32,768).

A peak meter shows the maximum amplitudes reached during a recording in dB. It is a useful tool to determine whether a recorded signal has clipped. Peak meters are not as precise as RMS (root mean square) power readings when measuring loudness. The peak amplitude of a square wave is much higher than that of a sine wave using the RMS method of measurement. On an RMS meter, a maximum amplitude square wave reaches 0 dB. A maximum amplitude sine wave reaches -3 dB.

If the loudest section of an audio track can be determined in advance, recording levels can be set so that the peaks are close to 0 dB and the dynamic range of the digital medium is maximized. In most cases, the loudest level is unknown, so it is safe to allow at least 3 to 6 dB of headroom for unexpected peaks. Headroom can be defined as the amount of additional saturation a recording device will tolerate after its meters read 0 dB and before distortion occurs. A digital recording system has no headroom, so it is best to begin recording below 0 dB to allow for unexpected peaks. Some DAT recorders show a reading of -18 dB as the nominal level. This would be equivalent to 0 dB on analog tape recorders with that much headroom.

# Digital Recording

## Computer Sound Cards

There are many sound cards available for capturing audio on the personal computer. They all contain analog to digital converters, and the quality of these converters determines the quality of the sound and the signal-to-noise (S/N) ratio. An audio card typically has two inputs and two outputs. One input is for a microphone, which reads a low level, and the other is for line-level input, which is a higher voltage. Since the signal from a microphone is so low, the sound card has a built-in pre-amp that boosts it. On most sound cards, these pre-amps are not of high quality, and a cleaner signal can be achieved from an external pre-amp. Of the two outputs, one is a lower-level line output for recording from the sound card, and the other is amplified slightly for headphones. The Macintosh has traditionally had built-in sound recording and playback capabilities, but the iMac, G4, and other recent models require an external A/D converter. Most PC audio cards, such as the Sound Blaster from Creative Labs, as well as Turtle Beach cards and Yamaha cards, can all record audio files with decent quality. DigiDesign is a manufacturer of professional audio processing equipment, such as the AudioMedia III card. Most professional studios use an outboard dedicated A/D converter.

## Sampling

Digitizing sound is called sampling. Two important variables that may be controlled when sampling are the bit rate and the sample rate. Common bit rates are 8-bit, 16-bit, and 24-bit. An 8-bit sample has very poor audio quality. A 16-bit sample is the standard for CD audio and delivers high fidelity. Professional quality audio is sampled at 24 bits or higher. The sample rate determines how many times per second a wave is analyzed and recorded. The sample rate must be twice as fast as the highest frequency that appears in the sound track sampled. This principle is referred to as the "Nyquist theorem." The most common file types for digital audio are .wav for Windows, .aiff for Macintosh, and .au for Unix.

Each increase in bit rate doubles the size of the data file.
- 8-bit = 256 available integers to define a sound parameter
- 16-bit = 65,536 available integers (256 times better!)
- 24-bit = 16.7 million available integers

In converting from one bit rate to another, dithering noise may be introduced by software as it attempts to redefine the wave with less data. This noise is similar to the anomalies that occur in a dithered graphic that has been reduced from 16 bits to 8 bits.

Each increase in the sample rate also doubles the size of the file. The most common sample rates used in digital audio are 44,100; 22,050; and 11,025 samples per second. The Red Book CD-Audio specifies 16-bit, 44.1K samples. In stereo, one minute of data requires about 10 megabytes of storage space. That is why CD-Recordable blanks are defined as having "73 minutes" of storage space. Professional equipment, such as DAT recorders and high-end sampling cards, also sample at 48K and 96K. As a convenience, many DAT recorders will record in a "long play" mode at 32K.

The following table shows the amount of data in megabytes or kilobytes required for one minute of uncompressed audio at common sample rates and bit rates. The highest frequency found in a sample is half the sample rate, which means that an 11.050K sample has a maximum frequency of approximately 5.5 KHz. Because of the low quality of the 8-bit format, it is more useful for voice tracks than for music or complex mixes.

| Sample Rate | Bit Rate | One Minute Stereo | One Minute Mono |
|---|---|---|---|
| 48K | 16-bit | 11.346 MB | 5.673 MB |
| 44.1K | 16-bit | 10.350 MB | 5.175 MB |
| 32K | 16-bit | 7.564 MB | 3.782 MB |
| 22.050K | 16-bit | 5.178 MB | 2.589 MB |
| 22.050K | 8-bit | 2.592 MB | 1.296 MB |
| 11.025K | 8-bit | 1.296 MB | 648 KB |

# Processing Sound with Software

## Capturing the Sample

Several types of software packages are available for working with audio. Most of these perform both the capture and editing functions. When sampling audio, it is critical to monitor the input levels on a meter at all times. Audio capture programs provide a level meter or some way of viewing the input level in real time. If the input level is too low, the recording will be of poor quality and very noisy. If input levels are too high, the result will be distorted and peaks will be clipped off. Unacceptable distortion is introduced when input levels are too high.

Sound Forge, developed by Sonic Foundry, is a popular professional quality software package for capturing and editing audio in Windows. In addition to controlling the digitizing process, it offers the capability to perform a wide variety of processes and effects, to translate a file into a number of different formats, and to compress the file into many commonly used formats. A comparable program for the Macintosh is SoundEdit 16 from Macromedia. This application is also used to capture, edit, and manipulate sound files. For those who are on a tight budget or experimenting with audio production, there are many shareware packages available for download from the Internet for audio production. Professional audio engineers use programs such as DigiDesign ProTools for multitrack recording and mixing.

## Applications for Editing and Processing

Once a sound has been digitally recorded, the first step is to evaluate the waveform on the screen while listening to it critically. It may be best to record it again if there are major imperfections. Listen for noise in the background, for pops, and for hiss. A "60-cycle hum" may be present, caused by faulty grounding of the AC circuit. There may be detectable "RF noise" that sounds like static. Look at the levels of the waveform on the monitor. If peaks are clipped off because they exceeded the maximum input level, the track will be distorted. It may be best to re-sample in this case.

A series of "takes" is pretty common for many reasons. The producer has choices between different versions of the content, and the engineer has choices between various signal levels. Once a usable waveform has been captured with the appropriate content, the next step is to trim

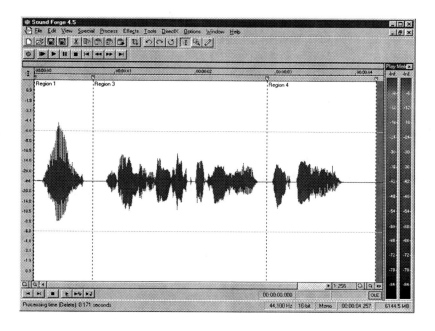

*Figure 1—Sound Forge interface*

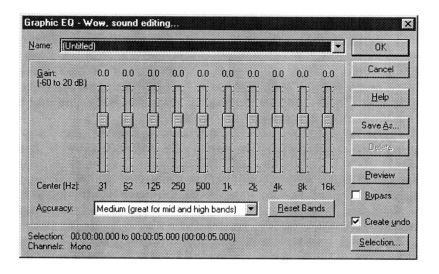

*Figure 2—Sound Forge graphic equalizer*

off dead space at the beginning and at the end. Cut as close to the program material as possible. After trimming the wave, determine which effects could be applied to improve the product, and audition them.

Most software allows the user to "undo" a process or effect that has been applied. This is referred to as "non-destructive" editing. Some editing software offers only one level of undo, which means that only the last change that was applied can be reversed. It is wise to save each version of the processed wave, if the software does not allow you to reverse a series of processes.

Undesirable pops and spikes can be eliminated by selecting the offensive portion of the waveform and reducing the level in that region. Is also possible to increase the amplitude in any region of the track.

When viewing a waveform in a software editor, the line in the center of the waveform represents silence or -90 dB. A full spectrum sound, which reaches the top of the window, is a strong waveform with a peak amplitude of 0 dB. Short waves that do not rise far above the center line are weak and may need to be boosted. The distance between the soft sounds and the loud sounds is referred to as the "dynamic range" of the track. If the track is "hot," signal levels are uniformly high. This is a very desirable condition for sound used in multimedia and the web, particularly if it will be compressed later.

## Signal Processing and Special Effects

The following are some typical processes that are performed on sounds to manipulate them or to improve their quality.

- Normalize—To normalize is to increase the loudest sound to a peak value or to a percentage of full spectrum and to proportionally increase the amplitude of all the sounds throughout the sample. Applying this effect can improve the signal level and the general presence of a track. It may be wise to select and reduce the strongest peaks in a track first so that the whole track can be increased by a greater percentage.
- Equalization (EQ)—Equalization affects the relative strength of a signal in a region of specific frequencies or "bands." A parametric equalizer allows the user to identify a narrow frequency range and amplify or attenuate just the sounds in that frequency range. The width of the band that is treated is referred to as the "Q" factor. For example, most tape hiss lies between 8 kHz and 12 kHz, so attenuating that frequency range may reduce the noise. Unfortunately, this can make the program sound dull, since all the other desirable high frequency content in that range is also reduced.
- Filters—These are applied to remove or reduce sound in a specific band of frequencies. Filters may allow sounds to pass, or they may reject sounds above or below a preset frequency.
- Compressor—This processor reduces the difference between loud and soft sounds, making the dynamic range smaller. It usually boosts soft sounds more than loud sounds.
- Limiter—A limiter prevents a signal from passing through the circuit above a specified level or limit. Limiting the level sent to a sound card when recording can eliminate clipped sounds, which result from peaks in the input level that are too high.
- Pan—To pan a sound is to move it between the left and right stereo channels. If a sound is panned equally to both channels, it sounds as if it is in the center of the aural panorama.

- **Gate**—A gate establishes a level below which quiet sounds are eliminated. It is used to remove tape hiss or quiet background noise on a track. Setting the gate level just above the "noise floor" will effectively silence the most quiet portions of a track, but aggressive application of this process can produce "pumping" and "breathing" as the gate cuts in and out.
- **Delay**—A basic delay line continuously creates a copy of the original sound then mixes it with the sound file to create an echo effect. The duration between the original sound and the echo is user-defined. A "slap-back" effect results from a setting of about half a second. Multiple echoes can be produced with a delay processor.
- **Reverb**—This effect simulates an acoustic space, such as a concert hall. Often the settings on a reverb processor are chosen by selecting the size and type of room that would dictate the reflections of sound.
- **Chorus**—This effect occurs naturally when two or more voices or instruments play the same note at the same time. Variations in pitch and intensity create a "shimmering" sound, such as that produced by a violin section playing in unison.
- **Vibrato**—This effect introduces small periodic changes, or modulations, in the pitch.

# Storage Formats

Reel-to-reel magnetic tapes have a limited shelf life. Recordings in the DAT format last longer because the information stored on them is of a different type. A CD-Recordable typically has a life expectancy of 100 years. When performing frequent recording sessions directly to hard disk, it is a good practice to back up the data on the hard drive and defragment it often. A fragmented disk can lead to problems, such as storing parts of the same file in discontiguous sectors. A CD-Recordable is a cost-effective medium for backing up data, and the same blanks can be formatted for CD-Audio players. Optical media, such as Zip or Jaz cartridges, may also be used.

Some of the more common audio storage formats are:

- **Tape**—Magnetic tape was the first widespread storage format for audio. Tape is an analog format, and works by arranging particles on the surface of the tape that are analogous to the shape of sound waves. The quality of magnetic tape recording is dependent upon the speed with which the tape moves across the heads and the width of the track that is recorded. Cassette tapes are very low quality because the tape moves slowly and the width of recording tracks is extremely narrow. Considerable loss of quality occurs in each successive generation when "dubbing," or copying, from one tape to another.
- **Digital Audio Tape (DAT)**—Sound may be digitized by a Digital Audio Tape (DAT) recorder and stored as digits (1s and 0s) on the tape. A DAT recorder performs the analog to digital conversion when recording and digital to analog conversion on playback. The digital audio file can be transferred from one DAT to another or to a computer hard drive with no loss of quality using an AES/EBU or an S/PDIF interface.
- **CD-Audio**—Digital audio may be sampled by the sound card in a computer and stored directly on a hard disk drive. It may then be formatted for CD-Audio in the Red Book format. This format allows 73 minutes of 16-bit, 44.1K audio to be burned onto a standard blank CD-Recordable disc. When properly formatted, the product will play back on any CD-Audio player.

· **MiniDisc (MD)**—Another popular format is the Sony MiniDisc. The MiniDisc records very good quality audio, but it is not quite as pristine as a professional DAT recorder. The discs are smaller in diameter than an audio CD, and the recorders are durable and portable. Blank media may be reused many times.

# Compressing Audio Files

Audio files are relatively large. The standard .wav, aiff, and .au formats are not compressed. When audio files are compressed, some quality is lost, and the degree of compression determines how much data is thrown out. When preparing an audio file for compression, there are some processing techniques that will greatly improve the quality of the result. Begin with a file that is normalized to full spectrum with a very high signal-to-noise ratio, preferably compressed within a narrow dynamic range. It may also be helpful to cut the highest and lowest frequencies before compressing since this data is usually lost.

There are several commonly used *codecs* (compression/decompression algorithms) to make a file smaller. To compress a file is to encode it into a different file type, and users need to have the application or plug-in resident on their machines to decode the file. The most widely used formats are listed below.

· **MP3**—MPEG-1, Layer Three, is the compressed audio format developed by the Moving Picture Expert Group for use with MPEG-1 video. The suffix .mpg is used to identify any type of MPEG-1 file. It has become popular as a method of sharing music on the web. Applying this codec can reduce the file size to a small fraction of its original size without significantly reducing quality. This file type has received much attention from record labels concerned with illegal piracy of copyrighted music. Among the various algorithms available for encoding MP3 files, the Fraunhoffer is a recognized standard. Many MP3 players are available as shareware, such as M-Player and Sonique. The Windows Media Player and QuickTime can both decode MP3 files.

· **RealAudio**—This codec has been used since 1994 for delivering sound files over the web at narrow bandwidths, with the extension .ra. Developed by Progressive Networks, it is among the family of audio and video codecs in the evolving RealMedia (.rm) family. The player and encoder are both freely available from prognet.com. It is necessary to have the RealMedia server installed in order to stream audio or video files to a client, but the player can be used as a stand-alone device. Several general-purpose audio players are able to decode RealAudio files.

· **QuickTime**—This venerable architecture supports all types of streaming media, and there are numerous codecs that may be applied to audio files. The extension for all types of QuickTime files is .mov. The version of the QuickTime player installed on users' machines determines whether they will be able to decode the file. Two popular QuickTime version 4.0 codecs are QDesign Music and Qualcomm PureVoice.

· **Windows Media**—These codecs are capable of high-quality compression in either audio or video formats, applying the .asf suffix to the file. Windows Media Audio V2 compression creates smaller files than the Fraunhoffer MP3 compressor, with equivalent or higher fidelity. A current version of the Windows Media Player should be installed on the client machine for best results. A full installation of Internet Explorer includes the plug-in.

- **Macromedia Shockwave and/or Flash**—Both of these compressors are similar to MP3, yet they are capable of streaming audio files embedded in a Shockwave or Flash movie. The latest plug-in for Shockwave/Flash is recommended for best results. A special server is not required to stream these audio files in real time.
- **Liquid Audio**—This proprietary codec is used to compress music. It is used by a number of independent labels and songwriters to distribute their compositions. It renders good sound quality, and the player is able to decode several other compressed file types.

## Delivery of Sound Files on the World Wide Web

The Internet is a packet-driven network, not designed for streaming media. Media that must stream, such as audio, is time sensitive. For smooth continuous playback, all the bits need to be lined up and ready for decoding when the file begins to play. Otherwise, they must be buffered on the client computer at a fast enough rate to allow continuous playback while downloading progresses. RealMedia servers address these challenges in streaming data, as do the Windows Media Server running under Windows NT and the Macintosh QuickTime server. In all cases, the browser on the client computer must have the exact same version of the codec for decoding that was used to encode the file. It is wise to make users aware of any audio codecs they will need and provide a link for them to follow to download and install the proper codec.

# Recording a Voice Session

Noise and distortion are the major concerns, and good hardware can make a dramatic difference in the resulting recording.

The first and most critical choice is the microphone. Each microphone will imprint different characteristics on a recording. Microphones supplied with sound cards are generally of very poor quality. For best results, use a condenser mic and a pre-amp connected to the line input of the sound card. Microphone pre-amplifiers built into sound cards are also of poor quality, so using the line input instead of the mic input will improve the results.

Sound cards vary widely in their quality of sound recording. Recordings made with inexpensive cards have excessive background noise, especially when the built-in microphone input is used. Professional cards are of higher quality and considerably more expensive. When evaluating a high-end sound card, make sure that it is MPC compatible. If the sound card has only DirectX compatibility, it may not work with your recording software.

## Windows Volume Control

The Volume Control program built into Microsoft Windows controls all of the features of the sound card. The Volume Control program can be started by double-clicking the speaker icon in the "system tray."

When the Volume Control program opens, it displays the default playback volume controls. This display can be modified by making selections from the menu bar Options/Properties. You have the following controls:

- **Mixer device**—Your computer can have more than one sound card. Most recording software only works with the first card installed in the system (this should be the first card displayed in this selection box). You should not normally need to change this setting.
- **Adjust volume**—You can select Playback (the default), Recording, or Other. To control the playback volume, make sure Playback is selected. To set recording sources and levels, select Recording.
- **Show volume controls**—You can display all of the controls at once or select just the controls you are interested in using.

You may need to start your recording software and the Volume Control programs together. Changes made in the recording controls for microphone and line sources will also be displayed on the corresponding controls of the recording software. Changes made in the recording software will display in the Volume Control program as well. Some sound cards are supplied with a custom volume control program that displays the controls differently from the standard Windows Volume Control program.

## Recording Techniques

Getting the best possible sound quality requires experimentation with a few recording parameters to find what works best in your situation. Voices should be recorded in a quiet room. You will need to isolate the mic from computer fans and other sources of noise. Use a "unidirectional" mic that picks up sound in a single direction instead of an "omnidirectional" microphone. Use the best microphone available and a microphone stand to eliminate the problem of handling noise added to the recording.

Position the microphone close to the person speaking, about six inches in front of his or her mouth. The exact distance will depend on how loudly the person speaks, the type of microphone, and the desired sound. Experiment with placing the microphone in different positions, such as directly in front of the mouth, above the mouth pointing down, or to one side of the mouth. Try to pick up as little environmental noise as possible.

Microphones increase low frequencies when placed closer to the mouth. Close positioning also increases detailed vocal sounds, such as wind noises from the popping of "p" sounds and the sibilance of "s" sounds. Placing the mic below the lips often tends to accentuate undesirable sounds. Changing the microphone position can help control these problems. Positioning a screen of nylon mesh between the mouth and the microphone can greatly reduce explosive sounds.

## Monitor the Levels

With analog tape recorders, recording at the highest possible level before distortion will usually provide the best results. With digital recording in general, this is not necessarily true. *Watch the level meters at all times.* Adjust the input level as needed to keep it in a medium to high range on the level meters for most of the recording. If the clipping indicators light up, this may indicate that an overload of the digital signal has occurred. This can cause undesirable distortion to be added to the recording.

Audition the loudest sections of the material to be recorded with the recording software's level monitoring enabled. Monitor the volume level display and clipping indicators before making the actual recording. Speak with the same intensity during the level-setting process that you will use in the actual recording.

## Maintain Consistent Levels

The presentation will be easier for the listener to hear if all of the words are spoken in a strong, consistent fashion, especially if the track is later compressed. The dynamic range of Internet audio and other highly compressed files is very limited. Words that are very soft in a sentence may be lost. Listen to the results of your recording session before quitting since it may be difficult to simulate the exact conditions again.

# Sound Design

There are a number of reasons for embedding sound in media production and web sites. Sound serves the following basic functions:

· Ambient Sound: Background audio establishes an environment. Examples are the sound of birds in a forest, traffic on a busy street, crowd noise, factory equipment, or waves crashing on the beach.

· Underscore: This is a type of background sound dominated by music, which sets a mood. It may include sound effects in the mix. A logo theme is a more dramatic example of music used in a consistent fashion in a production. Different music tracks may be used to distinguish different segments of a production.

· Voice: Narration is one of the most common ways of communicating with a user. The voice might be a host, offering assistance with the operation of the program. In many cases, voice tracks are a significant element of the user interface, giving instructions or feedback to the user. When synchronized with video, a story is often told that clarifies the action on the screen.

· Sound Effects (SFX): This category includes short sounds, such as button clicks and transition sounds that lend interest to a program. Often, sound effects are used with animation to emphasize movements on the screen.

# Recent Developments in Pro-audio

Dolby Digital and 5.1-channel Surround Sound are current standards for digital audio. Surround Sound provides two front channels, two surround channels, and a front center channel. The ".1" channel is for bass frequencies only, which are sent to a subwoofer. DVD sound tracks typically are encoded in the Dolby AC-3 format, which also delivers 5.1-channel audio. Expect more audio production and delivery to take advantage of these multiple channels. The specification for an audio-only DVD format to replace the audio CD has spent many years in the draft mode, due to rapid advances and different business models. It will provide higher fidelity and many hours of music on a single disc.

# Digital Video Production

Viewing video productions is a very popular activity in this day and age. It might be at the movie theater, over broadcast or cable television, on DVD or VHS tape, or from a video server on a local area network. The promise of streaming video to the majority of home desktop computers over the Internet is just around the corner, as we see broadband networks proliferate. This requires a high-bandwidth connection, a fast microprocessor, and the latest decoding software.

There is something mystical and wondrous surrounding the production of high quality video. Coupled with the complexity of production tools, a lack of knowledge helps keep the promise of distributed video to the desktop a thing of the future. Given that production equipment is now within the budget of hobbyists, and the fact that software applications are highly evolved and much easier to use, the door has been flung open to anyone with creative ideas and the incentive to learn how to produce digital video. Creating digital video involves these steps:

1. **Plan the Production:** Identify your audience and your objectives. Create a storyboard, a schedule, and a budget, and determine the methods of delivery that will be used. Test the results of the process from beginning to end on a few short clips.

2. **Shoot the Video:** Select a tape format and record your video with a high-quality camera, logging your scenes carefully as you shoot. Take care to light well, keep backgrounds still, and monitor the audio. Shoot on digital video (DV) tape if possible.

3. **Capture the Video:** Import the video over a Firewire interface from a DV tape player or camera directly to your hard disk. If the tape is analog, encode it with a capture card on a computer optimized for video capture. Compress as little as possible at this stage.

4. **Edit and Add Effects:** Use a non-linear editing program, adding transitions between scenes and special effects. Sweeten the audio track as needed. Save the edited file uncompressed and archive it. This may require a lot of storage space.

5. **Compress the Movie:** Apply your choice of codecs for distribution. The architecture selected for delivery may dictate your compression options. Adjust the contrast and picture quality, testing various bit rates, frame rates, and resolutions on the target platform.

6. **Prepare for Distribution:** For CD-ROM, build an interface with an interactive authoring tool and burn a CD-Recordable disc with the digital video files. For DVD, build the standard interface for MPEG-2 video and AC-3 audio. For the Internet, use HTML to point to the compressed files on a server in QuickTime, Windows Media, or RealMedia format.

# 1. Plan the Production

First, determine exactly what you hope to accomplish with your project. Evaluate the target audience and the requirements of delivering video to them. With a clear idea of the project goals and audience, choose the delivery methods. Then create project specifications, a storyboard, and a script. If this is a work for hire, the client should approve the project plan in writing prior to production.

## Determine Your Goals

What are you trying to communicate to the viewer? How will it be delivered? If it will be online, how many users will need to be able to access it simultaneously? Will the media be viewed in a linear fashion, or will it be part of an interactive experience?

## Determine the Minimum System Requirements for Playback

Make these decisions early in the planning process. Higher quality video requires faster machines and newer technologies. Will viewers need to have a particular codec installed? It may be wise to prepare multiple versions of the video files and deliver the most appropriate version to each viewer, depending on the system and bandwidth. The alternative is to produce more highly compressed video of poorer quality intended for the "lowest common denominator" machine, if reaching a broad audience is the goal.

## Choose the Technologies and Tools

Make sure the technology can support your goals, required media types, playback platforms, and interactivity. Select the hardware and software that will be used to create the project, including audio/video capture hardware, editing software, compression tools, codecs and encoders, authoring software, CD burners, HTML tools, and media servers.

Architectures, such as QuickTime or RealMedia, are system extensions that allow a computer to display video. Applying a codec (compressor/decompressor) makes the video and audio compact enough to play from a CD-ROM or over the web. Each codec has different characteristics and applications. A format is the file description in which files are stored and are part of an architecture. For example, the QuickTime architecture has a QuickTime movie file format (.mov), and it may be compressed with the Sorenson codec.

## Architectures

An architecture controls how dynamic media is handled by a computer, including how movies are displayed. The various architectures have some features in common, but there are differences between them. Some are intended for streaming over the Internet, while others are intended for CD-ROM delivery. Some work best on particular types of computers and operating systems. Selecting the architecture depends on the video application and the delivery platform.

QuickTime, RealMedia, and Windows Media are examples of digital A/V architectures. Each of these includes software components that provide for the creation, storage, and playback of media; each defines standard formats for storing media; and each supports certain codecs for audio and video compression.

QuickTime is a multiplatform, industry-standard, multimedia software architecture developed by Apple Computer. It is used to author and publish synchronized media types, including graphics, sound, video, text, music, VR (virtual reality), and 3D files. QuickTime 4 supports "real time" streaming.

RealMedia is exclusively intended to deliver audio and video content over the Internet. It supports both live and "on-demand" video. The RealMedia Server is required to stream videos, but the player may be used in a stand-alone context.

Windows Media is Microsoft's solution for delivery of multimedia. The Windows Media server supports both live and "on-demand" video over a TCP/IP connection. The AVI format was originally created for CD-ROM video, although it is also used on the web to some degree. It is no longer supported by Microsoft and has been incorporated into DirectShow. The extension is .asf for Windows Media files.

Emblaze is a Java-based video architecture for distributing video over the Internet. It does not require a plug-in, but it does require the latest version of Java and a fast computer. Recent versions intended for wireless devices are available.

MPEG is a family of compression algorithms, including MPEG-1, MPEG-2, and MPEG-4. MPEG Layer III Audio, commonly referred to as MP3, is a subset of the MPEG specification.

### Document Everything

Create a detailed project specification and a master plan to track your progress. Write a script for the video prior to filming. Too much improvisation wastes time and tape. Carefully prepared questions speed up an interview and improve the quality of responses. Make a master form for logging videotape footage with scenes, time code, and comments.

### Perform Tests

Apply the complete production process from start to finish on a few sample clips. You may learn something later in the process that requires a change early in the process. For example, the face of a presenter may be too small when the movie is reduced to 120 x 160 resolution. Shooting up close would solve this problem, but it is not possible to shoot all the footage again. Play back samples of compressed video on your minimum target machine, looking for dropped frames, skips in the audio track, or lack of synchronization between the audio and video tracks. Simulate the user's experience by uploading a clip to the server and accessing it at the same data rate on the same type of machine the target user will use.

## 2.    Shoot the Video

These recommendations are for creating movies that will compress well since most of the loss in quality occurs during compression. The goal of shooting for compressed video is to produce a crisp video signal with the least noise, camera movement, and fine detail as possible so that the movie will look good in a small window. Before selecting a master tape format, evaluate your options and the technical side of the process.

## Different Video Formats

It is helpful to understand how the information on analog videotape is formatted in order to understand the data that results when it is encoded digitally. Most video recorded or broadcast in the U.S. is in the NTSC format. This specification calls for a broadcast bandwidth of 4 MHz and a color subcarrier frequency of 3.58 MHz. It has 525 horizontal scan lines, 29.97 frames per second, and two fields per frame. These two fields alternate and are *interlaced*.

There are several differences between how a computer monitor displays an image and how a television screen works. One major difference is that the computer monitor displays images in one pass from top to bottom, called *progressive scan*, as opposed to the interlaced fields found in the NTSC signal. When converting material on videotape, it is necessary to compensate for these and other differences between television video and computer video.

## Spatial Resolution

The size of a video frame on a television does not conform to a 4:3 aspect ratio, as does a computer monitor. The spatial resolution of a television is typically 720 x 486 pixels, and if it is squeezed into a 4:3 computer screen set to 640 x 480, it results in pixels that are not square. Objects may look taller and thinner than they really are. The capture hardware or software may need to compensate for non-square pixels.

## Interlaced Video

A standard NTSC television set is designed to receive and display interlaced video. Each interlaced video frame consists of two *fields*. Each field is made up of either the even or the odd lines of the image, and these are alternated. When displaying video, a television screen draws alternating fields about 60 times per second. Our vision assembles these fields to create approximately 30 whole frames per second. The images appear smooth to the eye due to a phenomenon known as *persistence of vision*. On a television, the phosphors respond slowly, which helps to obscure the comb-like patterns of alternating lines. A computer monitor uses faster phosphors with sharper resolution. The effects of interlaced video are undesirable, and they should be minimized during capture and compression.

## Progressive Scan

A computer monitor scans each frame from the top to bottom, left to right, progressively drawing each line. It does not interlace fields or lines of video. This method is referred to as *non-interlaced*, or progressive scan. There are two deinterlacing techniques. One is to blend the two fields together, which preserves motion well and can produce sharp images. However, if individual frames are composed of two fields, a motion blur or double image may appear in areas of fast motion. The other way to deinterlace a video is to discard either even or odd fields. This removes the motion blur in still frames, but motion may not appear as smooth.

## Telecine

A more complex form of interlacing occurs when material originally shot on film at 24 frames per second (fps) is transferred to video that plays at 30 fps. This conversion is called the *telecine* process. In order to create six additional frames per second, new frames are made by interlacing repeated frames of the source material. Frames that are derived from two different frames of the original film are called *interfield* frames. These interfield frames result from *3:2 pulldown*, which is another name for telecine. *Inverse telecine* is the term for removing the 3:2 pulldown.

## Color, Contrast, and Noise

A computer monitor is capable of a much broader color range, or *gamut*, than a television screen. Vivid colors and pure blacks and whites are possible. Among the compromises necessary for television are the use of "NTSC safe" colors, which rules out highly saturated reds and oranges. These colors will bleed onto more neutral hues around them.

## Composite vs. Component

A *composite* signal, with color and light information combined on a single channel, contains a lot of video noise. This appears as "snow," or a dirty residue on the picture. The VHS format is composite by nature. The RCA connector used to patch the video signal carries all of the information. A *component* signal, with color and light separated, has less inherent noise. The S-video format provides for two channels, or Y/C video. Hi-8 and S-VHS tapes use this format. It is also the analog output signal from a DVCAM. The highest quality analog format is the three-part component (Y, R-Y, B-Y), which further divides the color spectrum into two channels. It is used in Betacam SP and other master formats.

## Use the Best Available Camera

A high-quality original is the first important step towards a high-quality compressed movie. In addition to lower noise, professional cameras produce a sharper image and better colors with their superior optics and multichip design. Common types of cameras are described below:

- **Betacam SP** (Professional) This format will yield higher resolution and less noise than the other formats listed here, with adequate color information for blue screen work. Betacam is an analog format, so the output will need to be encoded by a capture card for use in a digital editing system.
- **MiniDV, DVCPro, and DVCAM** (Pro-sumer) DV is a high-quality, digital format that integrates extremely well with desktop computers. The three formats of DV are miniDV, DVCPro, and DVCAM. MiniDV is the most common and is generally used in consumer cameras. DVCPro and DVCAM are professional formats and are not as widely available. DV tapes are recorded with a slight degree of compression, similar to 5:1 Motion-JPEG. The DV format is far superior to Hi-8, S-VHS, and other consumer formats. DV is digital, so it does not suffer from generation loss as copies are made. A miniDV camera is easily connected to a computer with a Firewire card (IEEE-1394 specification), which Sony calls "i-Link." Some DV cameras offer a progressive scan feature, which records each frame as a single non-interlaced image instead of two separate interlaced fields. Progressive scan source material may not look as good on a television screen as interlaced material, but it is superior for computer delivery. If you know the material will be compressed later, shoot in this format. The miniDV format uses 4:1:1 color subsampling, which is insufficient for high-quality blue screen work. The Panasonic DVCPro 50 format has higher color resolution, with 4:2:2 color subsampling. This means that the amount of color information is not reduced significantly.

- **Hi-8, S-VHS, and VHS** (Consumer) Both Hi-8 and S-VHS follow the S-video specification, with 500 lines of resolution and Y/C light and color separation, or *component* video. Both formats produce noisier signals with lower resolution than DV formats, but they are superior to VHS. VHS contains only 256 scan lines and combines light and color information in a single channel of composite video. Since these are analog formats, a capture card is required to digitize the video.

## Light for Compression

Movies that are well-lit and have a low level of contrast between images will compress better than video shot with weak lighting. Low light conditions produce a grainy image that does not compress well. Cinepak is a common codec that performs best with bright images.

## Use a Tripod and Minimize Motion

The use of a tripod often makes a dramatic impact in the quality of the final movie. Keeping the camera steady reduces subtle differences between frames, improving the temporal compression of the video. Any change in the image will cause the compressor to work harder. This applies both to camera movement and to subject movement. Use hard cuts instead of panning rapidly across a scene. Zoom slowly and only when necessary. Keep subjects as static as possible.

## Minimize Detail

Keeping the detail within a scene to a minimum will help the video compress better spatially. It will also make the video easier to see when the movie is reduced in size for desktop delivery. Ask subjects to wear clothes that don't have high contrast patterns. Plain colors are best. Stripes and checked patterns can cause moiré patterns when the video is resized and compressed. Keep the background plain for an interview. Painted backdrops are very good. Do not shoot in front of a window (to avoid reflections). You may wish to put the background out of focus to minimize detail. Bushes and trees are a particularly poor choice for the background because of the high degree of detail and motion.

## Blue Screen

Shooting with a blue curtain or painted background can improve the final results if you composite an actor into a digital still frame and "key" out the blue. The background has little video noise in it, and it compresses well. However, blue screen video is difficult to produce. One of the secrets to shooting good blue screen video is to light with slightly yellow gels (colored filters) to improve the color spectrum. If it is not necessary to composite an actor over a different background, a painted backdrop is a simple effective option.

## Record Clean Audio

The goal is to record a high-quality, noise-free audio signal with a strong level. Use remote microphones whenever possible to reduce camera noise. The internal microphone installed in a camcorder picks up excessive noise from the zoom motor. The operator who handles the camera also introduces noise. Minimize unnecessary noise in the audio signal such as wind and ambient sound. A wireless lavaliere microphone is ideal for recording a speaker's voice.

# 3.  Capture the Video

The quickest and easiest way to get digital video files into a computer for editing and compression is by transferring them from a DV camera or deck using the Firewire interface. DV cameras already store their video in a digital format, so there is no need to encode or capture from a DV source. One convenient way to digitize video is simply to dub it from an analog tape format to a DV deck or camera. The digital capture operation is performed automatically, without the hazards of dropped frames and other problems that may be introduced by a computer system with a capture card. The Sony Vaio line of computers comes with Firewire ports and software for capture, supporting the "i-Link" feature on their cameras. Macintosh G3 and G4 systems come with built-in Firewire and the "i-movie" application for capturing and editing DV formats.

A capture card is used to digitize an analog video signal and store it on the computer's hard drive. Depending on the system, the captured file may be as large as 20 megabytes for each running second. Many gigabytes of free space on the hard drive may be required for a video project. Be sure that the hard drive used for capture does not periodically pause to recalibrate. Higher capture rates yield higher image quality. The quality of a capture card will affect the quality of the final movie. More expensive systems, such as the Media 100, Avid Media Composer, Digital Origin Telecast, and Truevision Targa 2000, provide better image quality and more features than less expensive cards such as the Pinnacle DC-30 or the Truevision Bravado card.

## System Configuration

Configuring a system to capture video can be a tedious undertaking. Only minimal system software should be running, and all extensions that are not required should be unloaded. A fast drive that has been defragmented should be prepared to receive the video file in real time. All unnecessary devices, such as scanners and Zip drives, should be removed. Some compressionists place a diskette in the internal floppy drive and a CD in the player to prevent the system from checking those resources.

## Capture Applications

Most cards are shipped with an application to control the capture process. One of the more popular and robust of these is Adobe Premiere. In Premiere, if the "Warn on Dropped Frames" option is selected, the system flashes a message when frames are lost during capture.

## Avoiding Dropped Frames

The most common problem in capturing video is dropped frames. This means that some frames of the original video do not get encoded. An attempt to capture NTSC video at the original rate of 29.97 frames per second (fps) is futile if the computer system is only capable of encoding at 15 fps. Dropped frames may be sporadic, which make the digitized product appear to pause randomly. Although NTSC video plays at 29.97 frames per second, some applications attempt to capture at 30 fps. This difference in frame rates may cause a warning that you have dropped frames. Dropped frames may be a result of trying to capture video at a rate that the system cannot sustain in megabits per second. Reducing the quality setting during capture may allow the system to make its best effort without dropping frames.

## Capture Settings

Generally, it is best to capture at the largest possible resolution. A 640 x 480 capture may yield better results if the final resolution is to be a 320 x 240 movie. When a larger image is reduced to a smaller final size, several pixels are averaged to make each final image pixel. This may reduce video noise and improve the image quality. Some capture cards are optimized to encode at 320 x 240 or 640 x 480. Capture at a default size, in the 4:3 aspect ratio, to avoid dropping frames.

There are a couple of deinterlacing options when video is captured at full-screen resolution, such as blending fields to preserve the motion blur effect of interlacing. If the original source was shot on film and transferred to videotape, capturing at full-screen resolution and the original frame rate will allow the software to remove the 3:2 pulldown and return the material to its original 24 fps. This will look much better when compressed, and the file size will be smaller.

The typical capture process converts the analog video into a digital file and stores it on a hard drive. A quality capture card, a fast hard drive, and a finely tuned system are all interdependent in getting good results. The audio card may be integrated to receive a signal while capturing. Test a few sample clips, and check audio levels carefully on playback. Capture audio at 44.1 kHz, 16-bit resolution, in either mono or stereo depending on the project specification. Audio that is recorded with video in the DV format is normally sampled at 48 kHz by the camera itself.

Captured video often exhibits a black edge on the perimeter, called "overscan" or "edge blanking." If the source material was edited for television and intended for a normal receiver in the underscan mode, the black edges are part of the original content. Almost all capture cards will grab images all the way out to the edge, which includes a black stripe. Black borders are easy to crop, if the captured image is larger than the final movie dimensions. If video is captured at the final size, it will be necessary to scale it up to remove edge noise, which will degrade image quality. There may be *edge noise* around the perimeter of the captured video. Ragged edges that *crawl* on playback can also be cropped if the capture size is larger than the desired final size.

## Quality Settings

The *quality* setting on the capture system controls how much hardware compression is applied during capture. Larger files with superior image quality are captured on the higher quality settings. If the maximum rate of capture is exceeded by the demands of the quality setting, the capture card will drop frames. Capture video at the maximum quality the system can handle, usually a minimum of 4 to 6 megabits per second. A faster drive, an Ultra SCSI interface card, or a RAID system can improve capture rates.

## Capture from Master Tapes

Digitize directly from master tapes, not copies. Any second-generation tape will have more noise than the original master. Excessive playing of master tapes will degrade their quality, particularly with a fragile Hi-8 master.

## Monitor the Audio Track

Test the audio levels on a few clips before capturing your whole project. If the track is distorted, it will need to be captured again.

# 4.    Edit and Add Effects

Video editing is an enjoyable and creative process. An editor combines segments of video, assembles them in order, and adds transitions and effects. Adobe Premiere is one of the more widely used desktop editing applications.

## Basic Assembly

Many simple capture programs also include the capability to assemble selected cuts into a larger movie. This is generally done by importing the desired segments of the original clips and arranging them in order, along a timeline, to create a new movie. It may be possible to add some simple transitions between cuts, such as fades and wipes. When the assembly is complete with transitions, see that the audio track is synchronized with the video and shows strong levels. Title and save the final movie uncompressed and archive it. If using the QuickTime architecture, save it as "Self Contained." The final step will be to compress the movie.

## Complex Edits

Adobe Premiere, Avid Cinema, Strata VideoShop, U-Lead Media Studio, and other editing programs can all produce sophisticated results. These programs feature a timeline-based interface that allows a user to put clips in order and apply transitions between the clips. There are many plug-ins made by third parties for Premiere to add special effects, transitions, and filters. Avid Cinema is one of the easiest editing packages to learn, but it lacks some of the advanced features of Premiere. Adobe AfterEffects allows a user to composite various layers of video and to create special effects with plug-ins. It is a powerful and complicated tool, the video equivalent of Photoshop in the graphics world.

## Correct Video Problems Before Editing

Clips with shifts in color, gamma problems, and other problems that appear during shooting or capture should be repaired prior to editing. Ideally, all the clips that are assembled will conform to similar color and contrast levels.

## Transitions

Like using too many different fonts in a document, it is a bad practice to add too many elaborate transitions. They may be distracting to the viewer, and they pose problems in compression. Quick cuts from one scene to the next work well, as do quick cross-fades, keeping both to a minimum. It is possible to create a scene that zooms out from the center, spins, wraps around a cube, and flies away. Only in rare instances is this kind of "eye candy" appropriate to enhance or clarify the message. A simple cross-fade dissolve with a maximum one-second duration will compress well and can be used in just about any editing situation.

## Edit and Render at High Resolution

Perform all editing and effects processing on uncompressed video at the highest resolution available. Do not resize the video with the editing software. Render, which means to output the final product, at the highest quality possible. If you input DV using Firewire, render to the DV format with the same window size and audio sample rate to avoid losing quality.

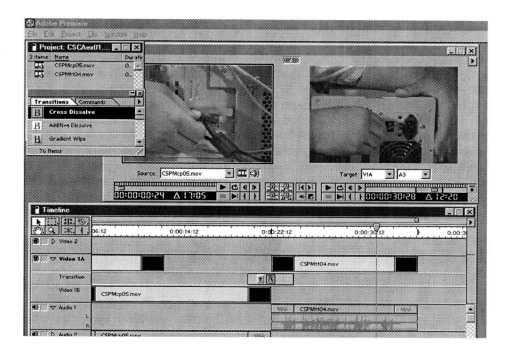

*Figure 1—Screen from Adobe Premiere editing window*

## Archive Formats

Save the edited file uncompressed or at least in the same resolution and size at which it was captured and edited. Do not save it in the capture hardware format, which is usually lossy (or degraded) and requires the exact same system to open the file. The Animation codec at 100 percent quality is a lossless software-only format. Budget lots of room for archiving this uncompressed, edited master file. If there is not enough space for the backup, a compromise is to use the Photo JPEG codec at 100 percent quality. This will compress it significantly, and some scenes may contain visible artifacts. Among the options for archiving the uncompressed, edited movie are CD, DVD, removable cartridges, and DAT tapes.

# 5. Compress the Movie

Raw video is defined by more data than can be stored or transferred easily. Uncompressed NTSC video requires about 27 megabytes of data for each running second. To arrive at this figure, multiply each frame (720 x 486) times 24 bits of color, times 30 frames per second. At this size, less than 25 seconds would fit on a CD-ROM. The data transfer rate of the fastest CD-ROM player would not be adequate to play uncompressed video without dropping frames. Another bottleneck in desktop video is the speed with which the video card can redraw the screen. Current DirectDraw routines on the Windows platform improve performance, but this is just for the video portion. The data rate of uncompressed CD-quality audio is 150 kilobytes per second (KBps), which is equal to the data transfer rate of a full T1 Internet connection before adding any video.

Compression is a process that reduces the size of files by removing redundant data. Significant reduction is accomplished if some of the less critical data is also removed, which results in degraded images and sound, or *lossy* compression. Once data is thrown out during lossy compression, it can never be restored. A codec is an algorithm that both compresses and decompresses a media file, and the same codec must be applied at each end of the process. When selecting a codec to apply, a major consideration is whether the same version of the same codec will be previously installed on the target machine, or whether the viewer will be required to download and install a new codec to see the movie.

## How Codecs Work

Video is generally compressed with both spatial (interframe) and temporal (intraframe) techniques to remove redundant data. These are very different processes.

Spatial Compression: This method removes redundant data within a given image or frame. It operates primarily on areas of flat color with very similar pixels. The codec specifies the coordinates of the area and the color without great detail. Spatial compression also occurs when the JPEG algorithm is applied to a still graphic. Removing fine details before compressing can improve the spatial compression of an image. Video noise may appear to be fine detail to the codec, and removing it will improve spatial compression. Shooting video with basic, still backgrounds leads to better compression.

Temporal Compression: In this method, the codec identifies only differences between consecutive frames and stores those differences rather than the entire image. The original reference frame from which the differences are calculated is called a *keyframe*. A keyframe in any video stream contains the complete image and may be used as an index point. Frames based on the differences between frames are *delta* frames. They define only the areas that are different from the previous frame and are smaller than keyframes. A new keyframe is placed at regular intervals to compensate for errors in delta frames.

Using a tripod when shooting reduces camera movement, providing a stable background that improves temporal compression. Avoiding complex transitions and frequent cuts that completely redraw the frame can contribute to smoother-looking compressed video.

## Applying Codecs

A codec performs many mathematical calculations that generate each compressed frame, which may take several seconds. Later, the frame must be decompressed fast enough to play in real time at the established frame rate. An *asymmetric* codec takes longer to compress, but it decompresses without delay. Codecs used for live broadcasts and video teleconferencing must be *symmetric*, meaning they both compress and decompress in the same amount of time. The H.263 specification is a symmetric codec used for teleconferencing.

## Available Codecs

There are several ways to determine the codecs currently loaded on a machine. In Windows 95 or later, open the Control Panel and check under Multimedia/Devices/Video Compression Codecs. The list of video codecs there will include the ones that the operating system installed, as well as those that are installed along with a new version of Media Player (or any other media-viewing device). That list may include such items as Cinepak, ClearVideo, Duck TrueMotion, Indeo (versions 3.2 and 5.04), Microsoft H.263, Microsoft MPEG-4, mvicod32, RLE, VDOWave, Video 1, and the Vivo H.263 codecs. When a new version of QuickTime is installed, all of the recent versions of both video and audio codecs are automatically installed on the computer.

Audio codecs are listed in the same location and may include the following: Microsoft CCITT A-Law and u_Law, Fraunhoffer MPEG Layer-3 (MP3), Indeo audio, Microsoft IMA ADPCM, TrueSpeech, Voxware, Windows Media Audio, and Microsoft PCM Converter.

## Widely Used Codecs

Some codecs are designed to work with Windows Media, and others are designed to work with QuickTime. The RealMedia codec is intended for use when media is streamed from a Real Server, but it can be viewed with the Windows Media or QuickTime player. For wide distribution, the Sorenson Video or the Cinepak codec is used in most cases for compressing QuickTime movies. Both play very well on any platform. For Windows delivery, the Windows Media codecs or the Indeo 5.04 codec are popular choices. Each codec performs best within a specific range of data rates.

The Sorenson Video codec produces high-quality video at any data rate. Because it places considerably high playback requirements on the client machine, Sorenson is a good choice when streaming at data rates of around 100 KBps or less. It is a preferred QuickTime codec for low bandwidth delivery and is widely used to compress movies on the Internet. Conversely, Cinepak has low playback requirements and looks better at data rates of 250 KBps and higher. Cinepak is installed on a wide range of machines and is most commonly used for CD-ROM titles targeting a broad audience.

The recent Windows Media ASF compression algorithms are excellent for both video and audio, whether streaming at low bandwidth or delivering on CD-ROM. The Windows server can automatically scale the transfer to best fit the client bandwidth. Indeo 5.04 is a decent general-purpose codec that uses YUV color space.

MPEG-1 is a very efficient algorithm for creating highly compressed audio/video multiplexed files and was designed for playback at bit rates between 1 to 3 megabits per second from single-speed CD-ROMs. The native screen resolution of MPEG-1 is 352 x 240, which may be interpolated smoothly to double that size or resized to any resolution. The frame rate by default is 30 frames per second. The Fraunhoffer MPEG Audio Layer-3 codec is the de facto standard for MP3 audio-only files.

MPEG-2 is the higher-speed version of MPEG-1, designed for playback at bit rates between 6 to 15 megabits per second. This is faster than many older computer systems can display smoothly without hardware assistance. It is the standard compressed video format for DVD movies, along with the Dolby AC-3 audio compression format used in the U.S. In Europe, the MPEG-2 audio compression format is more commonly used than AC-3.

## Processing to Improve Compression

Several factors contribute to the apparent quality of a digital video. Among those that are easily improved with software are the contrast, black and white levels, hue and saturation, and undesirable video noise. One of the first steps to perform before compressing is to crop the video frame to eliminate any edge noise or black borders introduced by capturing scenes intended to be viewed in the underscan mode. Sophisticated software can be used to scale the image to your target resolution. The most powerful and widely used tool for processing and compressing digital video is Media Cleaner, or simply Cleaner, from Discreet (formerly Terran). Cleaner will allow all of the following operations to be performed with excellent results.

## Color and Contrast

Most video segments can be improved for desktop delivery by increasing the contrast by 10 or 15 percent. Doing this appears to remove a thick residue from the video screen. It is also a good idea to restore black areas to true black, using the Black Restore feature. Perform a similar operation to restore white areas, improving image quality and compression. The video may be improved by carefully adjusting the brightness or gamma in small increments. After selecting settings for these adjustments, scrub through the video looking for scenes in which the changes introduced may be unnatural or too severe.

## Noise Reduction

Much better spatial compression is achieved if the granular detail in an image is reduced. Video noise appears to the compressor as though it were fine details that should be retained. A blur filter can be applied to reduce the noise and improve compression, but the final result will be less crisp. Adaptive noise reduction is a much better solution, provided by Media Cleaner. The adaptive noise reduction filter blurs areas of low contrast, but leaves edges sharp, improving the compressed result. Any live video will benefit from this filter.

## Selecting Compression Settings

When choosing the settings for a compressed video file, the most important decisions to be made are which codec to use, the size of the video window (screen resolution), the frame rate, the data rate, and the frequency of keyframes. There are limiting factors and trade-offs involved with each choice, and they are usually based on the way in which the audience will access the video files.

There are two very different types of audiences for digital video. In one case, the developer is able to specify and configure the exact system on which the video will be viewed, such as in a kiosk or on a corporate intranet. In the other case, the general public is the audience, and the minimum system requirements for viewing the video will be rather low. Within these two categories, there is the option to deliver the video locally, from a CD-ROM or other media, or to deliver it over a network. The latter choice severely limits the data rate and frame rate in most cases and negatively impacts the quality of the video experience.

## Selecting a Video Codec

The choice of codec is in some cases dependent on the architecture selected. If QuickTime is used, a broad set of options exists. For movies that may need to stream over the Internet at less than 100 kilobytes per second, Sorenson Video will probably yield the best results. Quality is improved considerably if variable bit rate encoding is used. The current Windows Media video compression formats compete favorably with Sorenson.

## Selecting an Audio Codec

When using the QuickTime architecture, there are several good options. For streaming complex audio at low bandwidth over the Internet, the QDesign Music codec is a good choice for content containing music. It is possible to select the data rate with the QDesign Music codec. Test the result by first allocating about 1 kilobit per kilohertz. At this rate, an audio file with vocals sampled at 22 kHz will stream at 22 kilobits per second (2.5 Kbps). Instrumental music may only require half of a kilobit per kilohertz. A stereo soundtrack requires a somewhat higher data rate than mono. QDesign produces better results on audio tracks with levels reduced to 70 percent of full (-3db). This can be accomplished by normalizing the track to 70 percent.

As the data rate is increased, the quality improves, but QDesign requires considerable processing power. This can rob cycles from a video track and cause dropped frames if the audio data rate is set too high. As with all audio/video architectures, the audio track will be allocated the computing cycles needed to play smoothly at the expense of dropped video frames. This is a good argument for testing combined audio/video rates and compromising to get the best mix.

The Qualcomm PureVoice codec is designed to produce clearly intelligible speech at extremely low bit rates. This is an excellent choice for video of a talking head. It is not useful for music of complex tracks, because it tries to model everything as speech. It is typically used to compress 8 kHz audio, but higher sample rates yield better results.

IMA 4:1 compression is a good choice for CD-ROM audio since it is widely installed and leaves a lot of computing cycles for video. MPEG-1 is an excellent choice for the highest quality multiplexed audio/video delivered from CD-ROM or DVD and plays on most platforms. For Windows-specific delivery over the Internet, the latest Windows Media codecs for both video and audio yield excellent quality.

## Selecting the Data Rate

The data rate, or bit rate, is the most important factor in determining the quality of compressed video. It determines the file size and must be matched to the method of delivery that is specified for the video. The factors that contribute to the data rate requirements are the media (CD-ROM or DVD) or connection speed (56K, ISDN, or T1) that is used, the amount of storage space available, and the minimum speed of the target machine.

Here are some data rate guidelines. It will be necessary to test playback on the minimum target machine to determine the optimal rate.

- **CD-ROM:** A combined (A/V) data rate of 180 to 220 kilobytes per second (KBps) is a conservative rate for cross-platform 2X-speed video. A cross-platform 4x-speed CD-ROM should be able to sustain 250 to 300 KBps. Speed ratings for CD-ROM players are misleading. A specification may be the burst speed and not sustainable for video. The ability of the video system to redraw the screen may be a more important factor than the transfer speed of the drive.

- **DVD-ROM:** Transfer speeds are usually equivalent to an 8X-speed CD-ROM, approximately 1 megabyte per second. A DVD-R holds about 4.7 gigabytes of data. Four gigabytes of data can contain several hours of high-quality video.
- **Internet:** The type of connection and the volume of traffic impact potential throughput. It may be advisable to compress a video at several different rates for different connection speeds. For a 56K modem, do not exceed about 5 KBps; for ISDN, keep it under 12 KBps; and for a T1 line, limit the rate to about 20 KBps. This accounts for all of the overhead that the Internet introduces, including error correction in the HTTP protocol.
- **Local Area Network (LAN):** A high-speed LAN should be able to transfer video at around 30 to 60 KBps.

## Modem Transfer Rates vs. Video Bit Rates

The data transfer rate of modems is expressed in kilobits per second. A 56K modem usually processes data at around 40 Kbps, due to error correction and other factors. This translates into five kilobytes per second (KBps), after dividing by eight to convert bits to bytes. Video bit rates are typically expressed in kilobytes per second (KBps), not kilobits per second (Kbps).

## Fitting Video on a Disc

A standard 74-minute CD-ROM holds about 650 megabytes (MB) of data. Components other than video, such as installers, read-me files, and a menu-driven program with graphics, might leave 600 MB for video. If a predetermined number of minutes of video must fit on the disc, divide the number of kilobytes of space on the disc by the length of the movie in seconds to determine the maximum bit rate for the movie. A 40-minute video lasts 2,400 seconds. A disc with 600,000 kilobytes of space divided by 2,400 allows a maximum bit rate of 250 kilobytes per second (KBps).

Video compressed with the Sorenson Video codec requires a fast processor to decode video at high bit rates. Video compressed at 200 KBps with the Sorenson codec may require a 300 MHz Pentium II or Macintosh G3 running at 250 MHz minimally to play smoothly. Only testing the compressed video on the minimum target machine will prove whether it can decode without dropping frames.

## Selecting the Frame Rate

The frame rate is the number of times per second the computer completely redraws the video window. A high frame rate requires considerable computing power and an extremely high-speed connection if the video is streamed over the Internet. Frame rates for desktop video typically range from 12 to 30 frames per second (fps). Motion appears relatively smooth at about 15 frames per second. For reference, film is shot at 24 fps, PAL video at 25 fps, and NTSC video at slightly under 30 fps (29.97). Choosing the frame rate that seems to suit the content is rather subjective. At a given bit rate, a low frame rate will produce sharper images but jerky motion. At the same bit rate, a high frame rate produces blurred images but smoother motion. There is always a trade-off in creating multimedia. The best way to select the frame rate is to test several for the best compromise between clarity and smoothness. A frame rate that is an even divisor of the source frame rate usually yields best results. For NTSC video, use 30, 15, 10, or 7.5 fps. For PAL video use 25 or 12.5 fps, and for film use 24 or 12 fps.

## Selecting the Size of the Video Window

A number of factors must be considered in making this decision, most importantly the nature of the content itself and the degree of detail that needs to be clearly displayed. A talking head that fills the window may be effective at a small window size, such as 240 x 180. However, a training video demonstrating the performance of a process that requires detail may need to be shown at 320 x 240 or larger. At a given bit rate, larger window sizes will be very pixilated, with poor image quality compared to smaller windows. Many video cards are able to "interpolate" a double-sized image from the original with much better results than are achieved by decoding an image that is twice as large. Avoid expanding the video window on playback to an arbitrary size that is not an exact multiple of the original.

Other factors to consider in determining the optimal window size are the data rate, the frame rate, the codec, and the target machine. Changing any one of these factors will impact the others radically. Use the smallest possible window to get the message across when streaming video over the Internet. The maximum size for a window delivered over a 56K modem is about 160 x 120, over ISDN about 192 x 144, and over a T1 line about 240 x 180. From a CD-ROM, 320 x 240 is most common, or 352 x 240 for MPEG. With a fast processor, 640 x 480 is easily decoded from CD-ROM. A DVD-ROM can play back at 640 x 480. Twice as much content can be stored at 320 x 240 and then doubled on playback with smooth interpolation.

## Selecting a Keyframe Rate

Each keyframe completely defines the image in the frame, while delta frames are approximations based on the best guesses that the compression engine can make. Much more data is required to define each keyframe than the frames between them. It is important to have enough keyframes to support changes in the video scenes and maintain the integrity of images while avoiding unnecessary keyframes that merely add bulk to the size of the video.

The content of the video and the method of compression are factors in choosing the keyframe rate. Using the Cinepak codec, it is common to place a keyframe each second. For video with fast action and rapidly shifting backgrounds, it may be better to place one every half second. In an active clip running at 12 frames per second (fps), it may be best to place a keyframe every six frames. With Indeo 5.04 and Windows Media codecs, the need for keyframes is very closely related to the pace of the action. For a talking head, every few seconds is sufficient, but for fast action this is not enough. The Sorenson Video codec works best with relatively infrequent keyframes, typically every 10 seconds. A keyframe every 150 frames for video running at 15 fps is usually adequate.

If a user will randomly access points in the video, more frequent keyframes will allow more freedom. If a delta frame is accessed, it must be calculated from the nearest keyframe, which may take time to recover. It is best to place cues in the video track at keyframes you plan to make accessible to the user.

## Using Media Cleaner to Compress Video

To begin, launch Cleaner and open a video clip in the File menu, or drag the source movie onto Media Cleaner's Process Window. A small icon of the movie appears in the Process Window. View the original movie by double-clicking on the icon of the movie in the Process Window. Click and drag over the movie to set the cropping rectangle, if the image needs to be cropped. The movie controller may be set to start and end points as desired. Return to the Process Window and open the Advanced Settings dialog box by double-clicking in the "Setting" column of the clip.

On the left column of the Settings Window, there are many presets defined for various delivery options, ranging from "QT-1X CD-ROM, Cinepak" to "RealVideo-Web Movie." A good way to learn about Cleaner is to select a preset similar to the project specifications and look closely at the Summary settings for Output, Tracks, Image, Adjust, Compress, and Audio.

The real power of Cleaner lies in the many ways the user can process a video. Under the "Adjust" tab, experiment with increasing the brightness and contrast of the clip. Windows display gamma is different from Mac OS gamma, and video looks much darker in Windows at the same gamma setting. Try setting the gamma in Cleaner 20 to 30 points lower when working in Windows. Also, vary the Hue and Saturation settings to see the results. Test variations in the Black restore and the White restore features to achieve more consistent levels.

Open the "Compress" tab and select a codec, the frame rate, keyframe frequency, and the bit rate for the video. In QuickTime, there is the option of Variable Bit Rate (VBR) encoding, which greatly improves the final product. The movie may also be constrained to a specified data rate. Next, open the "Image" tab and resize the image as needed, apply Blur or Sharpen filters, and use the Flat Field Adaptive Noise Reduction filter for good results in most situations. Under the "Audio" tab, choose a codec, the sample rate, the bit depth, and data rate. Mono is generally chosen over stereo since it consumes half the space and requires half the bandwidth. There is also a control for the volume level, where the Normalize option is found. Among the other audio processing options are High and Low Filters, Noise Removal, and Dynamic Range adjustments. It is best not to be too aggressive with any of these processes, which can significantly alter the sound quality.

It may be best to apply processes to the video clip to see the results first, before compressing. This may speed up the time it takes to perform the compression. Click on the "Start" button to apply any of the operations chosen in the settings. Cleaner will prompt for a destination for the final files before processing. While processing or compression is being applied to the clip, the results can be previewed using the Before/After slider in the output window. After a few seconds, the process can be cancelled and changes made to the settings as needed. Remember that QuickTime movies will need to be "flattened" to play in the Windows environment if they are created in the Mac OS. To flatten a movie is to remove the Macintosh headers from the data stream and apply the .mov extension.

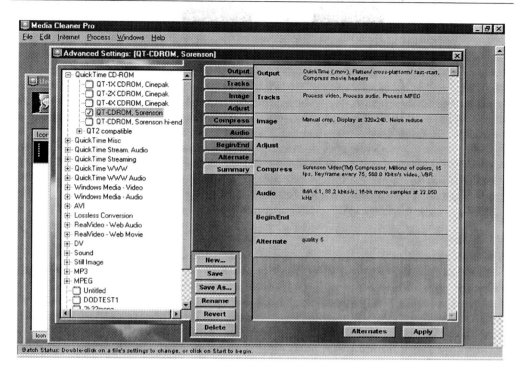

*Figure 2—Screen from Media Cleaner Pro*

# 6.    Prepare for Distribution

The two primary options for distribution are removable media and network delivery. The majority of compressed video is designed for delivery from removable media, such as CD-ROM or DVD, rather than over a network. This is because the data that defines video and audio content needs to flow uninterrupted in a fast, reliable way to the computer's processor, and then to the video and sound cards. The Internet is a packet-driven network. HTTP was never intended to stream data continuously, but rather to move small, discrete packets of data from place to place. The route through which data is passed and the transfer rate are both variables. With faster connections and the Real Time Streaming Protocol (RTSP), streaming media over the Internet is possible, but it still is not as reliable as delivery from local media. When using an RTSP server, replace the http:// with rtsp:// in the URL. A web-CD offers the best of both worlds. It is a hybrid CD-ROM that contains video files for delivery along with HTML-based programs for use while connected to the Internet.

## Authoring an Interactive Interface

Project specifications often require a context for video files. This may include background information and a navigation system that allows users to interact with the content, to select clips, and to control playback. The most widely used tool for authoring an interactive title is Macromedia

Director. QuickTime integrates especially well with Director. Movies can be linked to interactive menus, and the program provides control over text, graphics, animation, and audio media types. It is wise to test the playback of compressed video running within the Director environment to ensure that the bit rate is not too high. This can cause dropped frames, as Director manages other events happening along with the video. It is best to minimize other activity while a video is playing. It is advisable to place the video window on the stage of Director so that the top left coordinate is a multiple of four on both the X and the Y axis. Place nothing on top of the video window, and set the property of the movie to play "direct to stage." Place all of the compressed video files in a directory at the root level of the CD-ROM, and link them as cast members to the Director "projector," which is a stand-alone executable application created by Director for distribution. Another option is to create a Shockwave version of the Director movie; however, embedded links to video files on a server should be carefully tested on various playback platforms.

## Recording a CD-ROM

After testing the compressed video linked to an interactive presentation program, the next step is to record a CD-ROM for mastering or distribution. CD-Recordable (CD-R) drives, or burners, are commonplace and easy to use, and the media is inexpensive. Unless there are extreme time constraints, it is safest to record the master at a slower speed (2X or 4X). This has no effect on the playback speed, but it lets the recording process work at a more reliable pace and avoids buffer overrun. The standard length of a CD-R is 74 minutes, which holds 650 megabytes (MB). The number 74 refers to the number of minutes of stereo Red Book audio (4.1 K, 16-bit) that the disc can contain. The recommended software packages for burning CD-Rs are Easy CD Creator from Roxio for Windows and Toast from Astarte for the Mac OS.

## Web Delivery

This involves building HTML pages that contain pointers to the video files on the server and placing the files on the server using file transfer protocol (FTP). One very easy way to do both is with the Macromedia application Dreamweaver, which has built-in FTP capability. It can also synchronize new files on a hard drive with a web site. Those who use the Windows environment may also perform these functions with Microsoft FrontPage. It is important to plan and design the information architecture of the site thoroughly before creating any graphics or HTML documents.

## Embedding Movies in HTML

The <EMBED> tag is used to link a compressed video file to an HTML document. Most editors, such as Dreamweaver and FrontPage, automate this process. If Media Cleaner is used to compress the video, it creates the <EMBED> tags ready to paste into a web page. An audio file can also be embedded to provide a soundtrack for a web page.

## Linking to QuickTime Files

QuickTime allows two options: displaying the movie within the browser or calling up the player. It is necessary to use the Pro version of QuickTime, available from Apple, to create a movie link. To link to an image, open the image (JPEG, GIF, PNG, TIFF, or BMP) in QuickTime, and select Save As from the File menu. Choose Make Movie Self-Contained, and close the dialog box. This static movie has the same dimensions as the image and can be used as a "poster" on the web page to play the movie in place within the browser. When the movie plays, playback controls will appear, making it necessary to add 16 pixels to the height attribute of the movie. An embed tag for a poster movie might appear as follows:

```
<embed src="Qtvideo1.mov" height="336" width="240"
    controller="false" href="http or rtsp content"
    type="video/quicktime" target="myself"> </embed>
```

The target becomes "quicktimeplayer" if you choose to launch the player. The height and width attributes can be any size, since the player will pop up over the browser window.

Download the MakeRefMovie tool from the Apple site to create a reference movie. The reference movie provides a single link to streaming movies encoded at different bit rates. Another useful tool is the Plug-in Helper from Apple. If a movie is exported from the Plug-in Helper with the "Disallow Saving" box checked, viewers cannot copy it. Another useful tool is LiveStage Pro from Totally Hip Software. It can be used to create wired sprites for intermovie communication.

## Streaming Video on the Web

True streaming differs from downloading a file and then playing it. Progressive download is still not considered streaming, although a video or audio file can begin playing before downloading is complete. For streaming video, a special server and protocol is required. The RealMedia server was designed for this purpose, along with the RealMedia Player, recently dubbed the "G2" player. Windows Media can be streamed from a properly configured Windows server, and it is capable of sensing the connection rate and "scaling" the data transfer rate of the video to match the client. A Macintosh server can stream QuickTime, and there are several options that can be controlled in this flexible environment. QuickTime movies can be "wired" for interactivity. Wired movies can include custom controllers, hotspots to jump around in the movie, or links to another URL.

## Kiosk Presentation

Another popular method of distributing video is through free-standing kiosks, usually with a touch-screen interface. The major advantage in this type of delivery is total control over all the technology used for playback. Hours of full-screen, high-quality movies can be stored on a hard drive in a secure enclosure. Kiosks are popular at museums and nature centers, and they are used to provide point-of-sale information and product demonstration in the marketplace.

## The Future of Digital Video

With the proliferation of DV camcorders and the relative ease with which video content can be imported into the computing environment, the amount of video that shows up on computers will increase exponentially. And, as broadband Internet service is available to rapidly growing numbers of subscribers, many more individuals will be able to receive videos on their home computers. Before long, compressed video may be as commonly attached to email messages as scanned photos have become. It will be very interesting to see how the Internet community addresses the incredible demand for bandwidth and storage capacity that digital video introduces. Compressed video will continue to have a significant impact on education and training, as well as on business communications. This, in turn, will influence how we humans think about the art of communication itself.

# Musical Instrument Digital Interface (MIDI)

MIDI is a communications protocol that allows digital instruments to interact with each other and with computers. MIDI has become the primary digital production tool for musicians since its invention in 1983. A MIDI file contains no sounds, just instructions describing the notes played in a performance and related information.

A large percentage of professionals working in new media have a background in the field of music, and many of them had their first creative experience with computers using MIDI. The protocol was initially designed to control digital keyboards, but as soon as computers entered the studio, they were connected to the MIDI chain. Then software became available for recording, printing, and editing musical symbols, just as word processors and graphic design programs proliferated for working with other media types.

Keyboard synthesizer technology made major advances and became very popular in the 1980s. New methods of generating sounds were the focus of considerable research and development. The synthesizer joined the world of widely used musical instruments. One desirable method of creating sounds with synthesizers was to "layer," or combine the timbres of more than one instrument. A small group of synthesizer design technicians from different manufacturers met in 1983 to discuss a communications protocol to control a number of synthesizers from one keyboard. They developed a method of connecting two synthesizers from competing manufacturers with cables that allowed either instrument to control the other. They called it the Musical Instrument Digital Interface, or MIDI.

## The MIDI Protocol

Two synthesizers can communicate using MIDI in the same way that two computers can communicate over modems. The data exchanged between MIDI devices describes the performance of musical notes. MIDI information contains commands that instruct an instrument when to start and stop playing a specific note. Additional information translates the velocity of a keystroke into the volume of a note. MIDI information can be hardware-specific. It can tell a synthesizer to change sounds, which are referred to as instruments, programs, patches, voices, or timbres. Master volume, modulation of tones, and other types of data can be transmitted. MIDI information can start and stop a song, or sequence of events, and identify a location within a song. Computers can edit and store information that defines the sounds that reside in a synthesizer. A distinction may be made between a synthesizer that uses oscillators to electronically create a sound and a sampler that plays back a looped recording of a sound wave. Memory in samplers and sound cards holds a "wave table" of samples, containing short recordings of live instrument sounds.

The basic unit of communication used in MIDI is the byte. Each MIDI command has its own particular byte sequence. The first byte is the status byte, which tells the MIDI device what function to perform. The status byte contains the MIDI channel that is being addressed. MIDI data can flow on 16 different channels simultaneously. Depending on the mode of reception and the channel to which a MIDI unit is set to receive, it will accept or ignore a status byte. The bytes that follow the status byte address the particular channel indicated by the status byte until another status byte is received.

The status byte sends commands such as Note On, Note Off, and Patch Change. Depending on the status byte, a number of different byte patterns will follow. The Note On status byte tells the MIDI device to play a note. This status byte requires a note-number byte to identify the note and a velocity byte to define the volume. These bytes are required to complete the Note On transmission.

A separate Note Off command is sent to stop the note, which is not part of the Note On command. This command also requires the same two additional bytes as the Note On byte.

Another example of a status byte is the Patch Change byte. The additional byte required by this command is the number of the new patch or voice on the synthesizer. It is important to select the desired channel when sending a Patch Change command. Patch Change data is different on every synthesizer. The International MIDI Association (IMA) has set standards, and each manufacturer has an ID number.

The SysEx status byte, which requires at least three additional bytes, can perform a variety of functions. The first additional byte is the manufacturer's ID number, the second is a data format byte, and the third is an end of transmission (EOX) byte.

## IN, OUT, and THRU

There are three five-pin ports on a typical MIDI unit for connecting a MIDI interface: IN, OUT, and THRU. The IN port accepts MIDI data that comes to the unit from an external source. These are the MIDI commands that control the instrument. The OUT port sends MIDI data from the unit, such as Note On and Patch Change messages. The THRU port sends an exact copy of the data received at the IN port. There is no change made to the data; however, a brief delay occurs in transmission.

Only three of the five conductors in a MIDI cable are used. The cable is terminated on both ends with a Deutsche Industrie Norm (DIN) plug. Data passes through the cable on pins 1 and 3, and pin 2 is shielded and connected to a common ground. Pins 4 and 5 are not used. A MIDI cable is specially grounded and shielded for efficient data transmission. The length of the cable is limited. The IMA specification allows a maximum cable length of 50 feet. The total length of a MIDI chain is unlimited, as long as no link is longer than 50 feet. Commercially available cables usually range from five to ten feet in length.

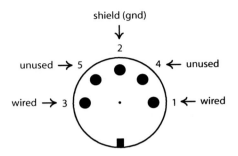

*Figure 1—MIDI cable with connectors showing pin-out*

### MIDI Chains and Loops

A MIDI chain is a series of one-way connections between MIDI equipment. The basic link is a connection between two devices. The MIDI OUT port of one device is connected to the MIDI IN port of the other. A key pressed on the first unit causes both units to sound. A key press on the second unit causes only it to sound. Several instruments may be chained together with a series of one-way links. In this type of setup, the OUT of the first unit is connected to the IN of the second, and the THRU of the second is connected to the IN of a third. If all units are set to receive on the same channel, pressing a key on the first one will cause all units to sound. Pressing a key on any of the other units will make a sound only on that device.

A MIDI loop is a MIDI chain configured for two-way transmission. A single element loop is made of two interconnecting links. The OUT port of the first unit is connected to the IN port of the second, and the OUT port of the second is connected to the IN port of the first. A key pressed on either unit will cause both units to sound, provided they are set to receive on the same channel. A feedback loop does not occur because data going into the second unit from the first is not sent from the OUT port back to the first unit. This is a configuration with two one-way links, not a multilink chain.

## MIDI Computer Interface

A special hardware interface is required to connect a computer to a MIDI device because the MIDI data transmission rate is 31.5 Kbps. This data rate is different from any other computer interface rate. Apple Computer and Commodore were the first companies to provide MIDI interface hardware. Roland Corporation later developed an interface for IBM-compatible computers, the MPU-401. Atari designed the ST series computer with MIDI ports built in. A wide range of interfaces is available for all types of systems. Some come with software to handle an entire MIDI setup and route signals on different channels to different devices in the chain. Mark of the

Unicorn and Opcode make professional quality interfaces that generate their own time code for synchronization. Interfaces are available that connect through either the parallel port or a USB port on the computer.

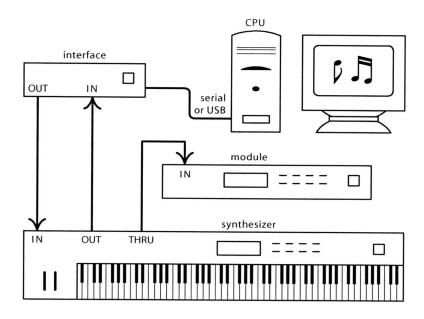

Figure 2—*Diagram of MIDI setup with synth, interface, CPU, cables, etc.*

## Software Applications

An abundance of software applications are available serving a variety of functions using the MIDI interface. One of the most widely used is the sequencer, which turns a computer into a multitrack recording studio for MIDI tracks. Sequencers allow the computer to record, store, edit, and replay MIDI data. The data can be saved in the Standard MIDI File (SMF) format as a song and realized by any sound card or synthesizer. There are thousands of MIDI files free for downloading on the World Wide Web. Most sequencers provide extensive editing capabilities as well as synchronization using MIDI Time Code (MTC) or SMPTE Time Code. In recent years, the sequencer has been endowed with multitrack audio recording functions. These programs allow the user to mix and edit live recorded tracks with MIDI tracks in a virtual studio environment. Some of the most powerful of these are ProTools from DigiDesign, Digital Performer from Mark of the Unicorn, Cubase VST from Steinberg, and Cakewalk from Twelve Tone Systems, Inc.

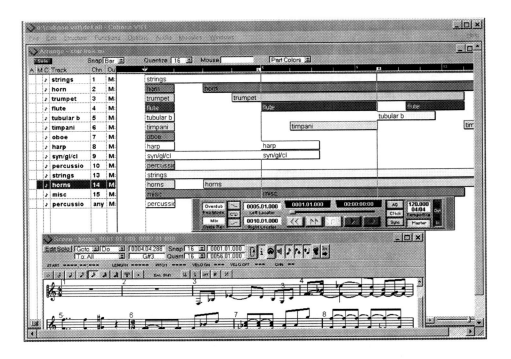

*Figure 3—Screen from Cubase VST*

Music notation programs are another popular category of MIDI applications. They display MIDI data as a musical score on the monitor, which can be edited and printed. Notes on the staff can be entered with or without a MIDI interface or keyboard. Most of the music that is composed and published today is rendered in this way. Some of the commonly used notation programs are Finale from Coda, Sibelius from Sibelius Software, Ltd., and Composer from Mark of the Unicorn.

Computer-based sample editors and librarians are often used to develop sounds that may be transferred to an instrument after they are edited. Patch librarians allow banks of sounds to be edited, stored on disk, and moved between the computer and the synthesizer via MIDI.

## Computers in MIDI Chains

A computer functions in the same way as any other unit in a MIDI chain or loop. Most interfaces have the standard three ports: IN, OUT, and THRU. A computer can serve as a MIDI data driver and supply the MIDI data for the rest of the chain. It can also receive and record MIDI data from other devices.

If the device receiving data from the computer is multitimbral, meaning that it can allocate a different sound to each MIDI channel, data sent on all 16 MIDI channels simultaneously creates an electronic orchestra. A computer-controlled MIDI chain is often used to emulate a recording studio. Scratch tracks for film scores are typically done in this environment.

# General MIDI

Compared to audio files, MIDI files are extremely small in size. This is a big advantage when transferring MIDI files over a network like the web. A music track can be embedded in a web page and begin playing after a very brief download. Sound card manufacturers have adopted a specification called "General MIDI" (GM). This standard describes a set of 128 instrument samples that appear in a specific order. The disadvantage for GM files is that the composer has little control over how the MIDI file will sound on playback because the file does not contain that actual sample that is played, just the name of the instrument on each channel.

General MIDI is really just a minor qualification to the MIDI specification that assigns a particular instrumental sound to each MIDI program number, so that an individual musical part plays back on the type of instrument for which it was intended. A well-designed MIDI file includes a Program Change message at the beginning that tells the playback device to switch to the appropriate set of instruments (programs, voices, or patches). Almost all sound cards support General MIDI, but the quality of the sound depends on the quality of the samples stored in the sound card (wave table) and on the speakers used to realize the sounds.

Program number 1 on all GM sound modules is an Acoustic Grand Piano. Patch number 25 is a Nylon String Guitar. The programs are arranged in 16 families of instruments, with each family containing eight instruments. For example, the reed family includes the Saxophone, Oboe, and Clarinet programs. The program number assigned to each instrument in General MIDI is shown in the table below.

A GM sound module that is multitimbral can play MIDI messages on all 16 channels simultaneously, with a different program sounding for each channel. All programs should sound an A440 pitch when they receive the MIDI note number 69.

The Drum Part is sent and received on MIDI channel 10. Each of the MIDI notes triggers a different drum sound on the keyboard. The assignment of drum sounds to MIDI note numbers is also shown in the table below.

The GM standard allows for Program Change messages in a MIDI song file, which applies the correct instrumentation automatically. The specification requires that a GM module be able to respond to the Pitch and Modulation controllers on a synthesizer and to play 24 notes simultaneously with dynamic voice allocation between the 16 channels. This means that the first note played is replaced by the 25th note if more than 24 notes are held at the same time.

The GM specification spells out some global settings. A module should respond to velocity data to control the volume of a note. The pitch wheel bend range should default to +/- 2 semitones. The module also should respond to Channel Pressure as well. It should respond to numbered MIDI controller messages for Modulation (1), Channel Volume (7), Pan (10), Expression (11), Sustain (64), Reset All Controllers (121), and All Notes Off (123). Channel Volume should default to 90, with all other controllers and effects off and the pitch wheel offset at 0. The module should respond to Registered Parameter Numbers that control Pitch Wheel Bend Range (0), Fine Tuning (1), and Coarse Tuning (2). Initial tuning should be the standard A440 reference. A MIDI System Exclusive message can be used to turn a module's General MIDI mode on or off.

In the accompanying tables, "Prog#" refers to the MIDI Program Change number that causes the instrument to be selected. These decimal numbers are shown on a module's display or in a sequencer's Event List. MIDI modules count the first Patch as 0, not 1. The value sent in the Program Change message is actually one less than the program number from the list. A GM module automatically adds a digit when it generates the MIDI Program Change message.

## Table of General MIDI Programs

This chart shows the names of all 128 GM instruments and the MIDI Program Change numbers used to select those instruments.

### Piano

| Prog# | Instrument |
|---|---|
| 1 | Acoustic Grand |
| 2 | Bright Acoustic |
| 3 | Electric Grand |
| 4 | Honky-Tonk |
| 5 | Electric Piano 1 |
| 6 | Electric Piano 2 |
| 7 | Harpsichord |
| 8 | Clavinet |

### Chromatic Percussion

| Prog# | Instrument |
|---|---|
| 9 | Celesta |
| 10 | Glockenspiel |
| 11 | Music Box |
| 12 | Vibraphone |
| 13 | Marimba |
| 14 | Xylophone |
| 15 | Tubular Bells |
| 16 | Dulcimer |

### Reed

| Prog# | Instrument |
|---|---|
| 65 | Soprano Sax |
| 66 | Alto Sax |
| 67 | Tenor Sax |
| 68 | Baritone Sax |
| 69 | Oboe |
| 70 | English Horn |
| 71 | Bassoon |
| 72 | Clarinet |

### Pipe

| Prog# | Instrument |
|---|---|
| 73 | Piccolo |
| 74 | Flute |
| 75 | Recorder |
| 76 | Pan Flute |
| 77 | Blown Bottle |
| 78 | Skakuhachi |
| 79 | Whistle |
| 80 | Ocarina |

### Organ

| Prog# | Instrument |
|---|---|
| 17 | Drawbar Organ |
| 18 | Percussive Organ |
| 19 | Rock Organ |
| 20 | Church Organ |
| 21 | Reed Organ |
| 22 | Accordion |
| 23 | Harmonica |
| 24 | Tango Accordion |

### Guitar

| Prog# | Instrument |
|---|---|
| 25 | Nylon String Guitar |
| 26 | Steel String Guitar |
| 27 | Electric Jazz Guitar |
| 28 | Electric Clean Guitar |
| 29 | Electric Muted Guitar |
| 30 | Overdriven Guitar |
| 31 | Distortion Guitar |
| 32 | Guitar Harmonics |

### Synth Lead

| Prog# | Instrument |
|---|---|
| 81 | Lead 1 (square) |
| 82 | Lead 2 (sawtooth) |
| 83 | Lead 3 (calliope) |
| 84 | Lead 4 (chiff) |
| 85 | Lead 5 (charang) |
| 86 | Lead 6 (voice) |
| 87 | Lead 7 (fifths) |
| 88 | Lead 8 (bass+lead) |

### Synth Pad

| Prog# | Instrument |
|---|---|
| 89 | Pad 1 (new age) |
| 90 | Pad 2 (warm) |
| 91 | Pad 3 (polysynth) |
| 92 | Pad 4 (choir) |
| 93 | Pad 5 (bowed) |
| 94 | Pad 6 (metallic) |
| 95 | Pad 7 (halo) |
| 96 | Pad 8 (sweep) |

### Bass

| Prog# | Instrument |
|---|---|
| 33 | Acoustic Bass |
| 34 | Electric Bass (finger) |
| 35 | Electric Bass (pick) |
| 36 | Fretless Bass |
| 37 | Slap Bass 1 |
| 38 | Slap Bass 2 |
| 39 | Synth Bass 1 |
| 40 | Synth Bass 2 |

### Solo Strings

| Prog# | Instrument |
|---|---|
| 41 | Violin |
| 42 | Viola |
| 43 | Cello |
| 44 | Contrabass |
| 45 | Tremolo Strings |
| 46 | Pizzicato Strings |
| 47 | Orchestral Strings |
| 48 | Timpani |

### Synth Effects

| Prog# | Instrument |
|---|---|
| 97 | FX 1 (rain) |
| 98 | FX 2 (soundtrack) |
| 99 | FX 3 (crystal) |
| 100 | FX 4 (atmosphere) |
| 101 | FX 5 (brightness) |
| 102 | FX 6 (goblins) |
| 103 | FX 7 (echoes) |
| 104 | FX 8 (sci-fi) |

### Ethnic

| Prog# | Instrument |
|---|---|
| 105 | Sitar |
| 106 | Banjo |
| 107 | Shamisen |
| 108 | Koto |
| 109 | Kalimba |
| 110 | Bagpipe |
| 111 | Fiddle |
| 112 | Shanai |

### Ensemble

| Prog# | Instrument |
|---|---|
| 49 | String Ensemble 1 |
| 50 | String Ensemble 2 |
| 51 | Synth Strings 1 |
| 52 | Synth Strings 2 |
| 53 | Choir Aahs |
| 54 | Voice Oohs |
| 55 | Synth Voice |
| 56 | Orchestra Hit |

### Brass

| Prog# | Instrument |
|---|---|
| 57 | Trumpet |
| 58 | Trombone |
| 59 | Tuba |
| 60 | Muted Trumpet |
| 61 | French Horn |
| 62 | Brass Section |
| 63 | Synth Brass 1 |
| 64 | Synth Brass 2 |

### Percussive

| Prog# | Instrument |
|---|---|
| 113 | Tinkle Bell |
| 114 | Agogo |
| 115 | Steel Drums |
| 116 | Woodblock |
| 117 | Taiko Drum |
| 118 | Melodic Tom |
| 119 | Synth Drum |
| 120 | Reverse Cymbal |

### Sound Effects

| Prog# | Instrument |
|---|---|
| 121 | Guitar Fret Noise |
| 122 | Breath Noise |
| 123 | Seashore |
| 124 | Bird Tweet |
| 125 | Telephone Ring |
| 126 | Helicopter |
| 127 | Applause |
| 128 | Gunshot |

## General MIDI Drum Sounds

This chart shows the drum sound assigned to each MIDI note number. Typically, Channel 10 is the default channel for a set of drums.

| MIDI Note# | Drum Sound | MIDI Note# | Drum Sound |
|---|---|---|---|
| 35 | Acoustic Bass Drum | 59 | Ride Cymbal 2 |
| 36 | Bass Drum 1 | 60 | Hi Bongo |
| 37 | Side Stick | 61 | Low Bongo |
| 38 | Acoustic Snare | 62 | Mute Hi Conga |
| 39 | Hand Clap | 63 | Open Hi Conga |
| 40 | Electric Snare | 64 | Low Conga |
| 41 | Low Floor Tom | 65 | High Timbale |
| 42 | Closed Hi-Hat | 66 | Low Timbale |
| 43 | High Floor Tom | 67 | High Agogo |
| 44 | Pedal Hi-Hat | 68 | Low Agogo |
| 45 | Low Tom | 69 | Cabasa |
| 46 | Open Hi-Hat | 70 | Maracas |
| 47 | Low-Mid Tom | 71 | Short Whistle |
| 48 | Hi-Mid Tom | 72 | Long Whistle |
| 49 | Crash Cymbal 1 | 73 | Short Guiro |
| 50 | High Tom | 74 | Long Guiro |
| 51 | Ride Cymbal 1 | 75 | Claves |
| 52 | Chinese Cymbal | 76 | Hi Wood Block |
| 53 | Ride Bell | 77 | Low Wood Block |
| 54 | Tambourine | 78 | Mute Cuica |
| 55 | Splash Cymbal | 79 | Open Cuica |
| 56 | Cowbell | 80 | Mute Triangle |
| 57 | Crash Cymbal 2 | 81 | Open Triangle |
| 58 | Vibraslap | | |

# MIDI Message Data Format

In the standard MIDI protocol one device is the "transmitter" and another is the "receiver." Messages include "status" bytes and "data" bytes. This arrangement is similar to common computer networking protocols. Unfortunately, there is no provision for handshaking between connected units in the MIDI protocol.

Status bytes and data bytes are easily distinguished. In all status bytes, bit 7 is a 1. All data bytes must contain a 0 in bit 7 and lie in the range between 0 and 127. MIDI applies a logical channel concept. There are 16 logical channels, encoded into bits 0 through 3 of the status bytes of messages for which a channel number is significant.

## Voice Messages

In messages with channel numbers, the status byte determines the number of data bytes for a single message. The specification divides these into "voice" and "mode" messages. The mode messages are for control of the logical channels, and the control codes are added onto the data bytes for the parameter message. The voice messages are as follows:

| Status Byte | Data Bytes |
|---|---|
| Note On | 2 each; 1 byte pitch, followed by 1 byte velocity |
| Note Off | 2 each; 1 byte pitch, followed by 1 byte velocity |
| Key Pressure | 2 each; 1 byte pitch, 1 byte pressure (after-touch) |
| Parameter | 2 each; 1 byte parameter number, 1 byte setting |
| Program | 1 byte; program selection |
| Channel Pressure | 1 byte; channel pressure (after-touch) |
| Pitch Wheel | 2 bytes; a 14-bit value, least significant 7 bits first |

For all of these messages, a convention called the "running status byte" may be used. If the transmitter wishes to send another message of the same type on the same channel under the same status byte, the status byte need not be resent.

A Note On message with a velocity of zero is synonymous with a Note Off message. Combined with the previous feature, this allows long strings of notes to be sent without repeating status bytes. The "zero velocity Note On" feature is frequently used. The pitch bytes of notes correspond to the half steps on a keyboard, with middle C = 60.

The velocity bytes for velocity sensing keyboards represent a logarithmic scale. Non-velocity sensing devices send a velocity of 64. The pitch wheel value is an absolute setting. The receiver determines the increments. The default value corresponds to a centered pitch wheel (unmodified notes).

Parameter messages are used to set controller dials, the purpose of which is left to the given device, except as noted below. The first data bytes correspond to the following controllers:

| Data Byte | Parameter Governed |
|-----------|--------------------|
| 0–31 | Continuous controllers 0–31, most significant byte |
| 32–63 | Continuous controllers 0–31, least significant byte |
| 64–95 | On/off switches |
| 96–121 | Unspecified, reserved for future |
| 122–127 | The "channel mode" messages |

The second data byte contains the seven-bit setting for the controller. The switches have data byte 0 set to OFF, 127 set to ON, with 1 through 126 undefined. If a controller only needs seven bits of resolution, it uses the most significant byte. If both are needed, the order is specified as most significant followed by least significant. With a 14-bit controller, it is legal to send only the least significant byte if the most significant doesn't need to be changed. Controller number 1 is standardized to be the modulation wheel.

## MIDI Mode Messages

These messages begin with status bytes, followed by data bytes 122 through 127. The data bytes function as further data for a group of messages that control the combination of voices and channels to be accepted by a receiver. There is an implicit "basic" channel over which a given device is to receive these messages. The receiver ignores mode messages over any other channels, no matter what mode they might be in. The basic channel for a given device may be fixed or set in some manner outside the scope of the MIDI standard.

The meaning of the values 122 through 127 is as follows:

| First Data Byte | Second Data Byte | |
|-----------------|------------------|--|
| 122 | Local control | 0 = local control off, 127 = on |
| 123 | All notes off | 0 |
| 124 | Omni mode off | 0 |
| 125 | Omni mode on | 0 |
| 126 | Mono mode | The number of monophonic channels |
| 127 | Poly mode | 0 |

Note: 124 through 127 also turn all notes off.

Local control determines whether notes played on an instrument's keyboard are sounded on the instrument or not. With local control off, the host is able to read input data if desired and to send notes to another instrument.

The mode setting messages control what channels and how many voices the receiver recognizes. There is always a basic channel. "Omni" refers to the ability to receive voice messages on all channels. "Mono" and "Poly" refer to whether multiple voices are allowed to sound at once. Unfortunately, the omni on/off state and the mono/poly state interact with each other. There are four possible settings, called "modes," with given numbers in the specification:

·   Mode 1
    Omni on/poly—Voice messages are received on all channels and assigned polyphonically. Any notes received are played, up to the maximum capacity.

·   Mode 2
    Omni on/mono—A monophonic instrument will receive single notes to play in one voice on all channels.

·   Mode 3
    Omni off/poly—A polyphonic instrument will receive voice messages on only the basic channel.

·   Mode 4
    Omni off/mono—The "mono" part is a misnomer. To operate in this mode, a receiver is supposed to receive one voice per channel. The number of channels recognized is given by the second data byte, or the maximum number of possible voices if this byte is 0. The set of channels thus defined is a sequential set, starting with the basic channel.

A receiver may ignore any mode that it cannot honor or switch to an alternate mode (typically mode 1). Receivers are supposed to default to mode 1 when they power up. The original 1.0 specification states that power-up conditions are supposed to place a receiver in a state where it will only respond to Note On/Note Off messages, requiring a setting of some sort to enable the other message types. (Current manufacturers default to "Multi" mode for startup, which is similar to Omni on/poly for multitimbral modules.)

## System Messages

In system messages, the status bytes and data bytes are used as follows:

| Message Purpose | Data Bytes |
| --- | --- |
| System Exclusive | Variable length |
| Song Position | 2 bytes; a 14-bit value, least significant byte first |
| Song Select | 1 byte; a song number |
| Tune Request | 0 |
| EOX (terminator) | 0 |

Song Position and Song Select are for controlling sequencers. The Song Position is measured in beats, which count every six MIDI clock pulses. These messages determine what is to be played on receipt of a start real-time message. The Tune Request tells analog synthesizers to tune their oscillators.

The System Exclusive message is intended for manufacturers to insert any specific messages that apply to their own product. The following data bytes lie in the range of 0 to 127. The System Exclusive is to be terminated by the EOX byte. The first data byte is to be a manufacturer's ID, assigned by the MIDI standards committee. The terminator byte is optional. A System Exclusive may also be terminated by the status byte of the next message.

## Common MIDI Manufacturer ID Numbers

"American Group"
  1  Sequential Circuits
      (originator of spec)
  4  Moog
  5  Passport Designs
  6  Lexicon
  7  Kurzweill
  8  Fender
 10  Oberheim
 11  Apple Computers
 15  JL Cooper
 18  Emu Systems
 21  Orban
 31  Voce

"European Group"
 24  Hohner
 29  PPG
 39  Soundcraft

"Japanese Group"
 40  Kawai
 41  Roland
 42  Korg
 43  Yamaha
 44  Casio

## Real-time Messages

These messages are called "real-time" messages because they may be sent anytime anywhere. This includes between data bytes of other messages. A receiver is supposed to be able to receive and process (or ignore) these messages and resume collection of the remaining data bytes for the message that was in progress. Real-time messages do not affect any running status byte in effect. All of these messages are followed by no data bytes to prevent them from being interrupted. The real-time messages are as follows:

· Timing Clock
· Start
· Continue
· Stop
· Active Sensing
· System Reset

The Timing Clock message is sent at the rate of 24 clocks per quarter note and is used to synchronize devices, particularly drum machines. Start, Continue, and Stop are for the control of sequencers and drum machines. The Continue message causes a device to pick up at the next clock mark.

The Active Sensing byte is to be sent once at least every 300 milliseconds, if it is used. Its purpose is to implement a time-out mechanism for a receiver to revert to a default state. A receiver is to operate normally until it receives one, activating the time-out mechanism from the receipt of the first Active Sensing byte.

The System Reset initializes to power-up conditions. It should be used sparingly and never sent automatically on power up.

## Who Owns a MIDI File?

As with any performance of a musical composition, the composer controls rights to the content and the performer controls rights to a particular performance of the work. Although a piece may be in the public domain, the file is still the property of the person who created it. It is legal to use a MIDI song on your web site as background music, providing the tune is in the public domain or permission has been secured from the copyright owner. Permission should also be secured from the creator of the MIDI file itself since the creation is akin to a performance. There are no restrictions on MIDI files based on public domain material other than those claimed by the creator of the file.

## The Future of MIDI

The original MIDI specification has changed very little since its creation, although some of the initial status bytes were not originally defined. The architecture of MIDI does not allow for expansion without a complete redesign of the system. Any new design would need to be backwards-compatible and operate with legacy MIDI hardware. The major enhancement to General MIDI is the capacity to send sample data along with a Standard MIDI File in downloadable sound (DLS). Not all sound cards or modules are equipped to handle this information.